Electronic Signatures in Law

Second edition

Stephen Mason

Tottel
publishing

Tottel Publishing Ltd, Maxwelton House, 41–43 Boltro Road,
Haywards Heath, West Sussex, RH16 1BJ

A CIP Catalogue record for this book is available from the British Library.

ISBN 13   978 1 84592 425 6

Typeset by Phoenix Photosetting, Chatham, Kent
Printed and bound in Great Britain by Athenæum Press Ltd,
Gateshead, Tyne and Wear

Preface to the second edition

A legal wag of my acquaintance, Louis Plowden-Wardlaw, once referred to the topic of electronic signatures as the 'burning branch of obscurity' during one of our conversations. He was indicating, indirectly, that although electronic signatures in their many forms are used daily by millions of people millions of times, nevertheless the understanding surrounding the topic was negligible. It is my sincere wish that this second edition will act to bring this topic into focus amongst members of the judiciary, lawyers, legal scholars and lay people.

In the preface to *Electronic Signatures Law and Regulation* by Lorna Brazell, published six weeks after my first edition, Graham Smith made some highly pertinent remarks about this subject. First, he commented, rightly at the time, that 'English common law has never had much truck with technological objections.' The history of how judges have responded to new technologies serves to illustrate this point. That is, until the decision in the case of *J Pereira Fernandes SA v Mehta*[1]. Should a case of a similar nature be brought before the appeal court in the future, it is to be hoped that the decision in this case will be reconsidered very carefully. Second, Graham suggested that the topic required a comparative approach, because national approaches to signatures remained in place, despite both international and regional attempts to provide for a more cohesive approach to electronic signatures across the globe. Lorna considered a number of jurisdictions in great detail in her text, an exercise that I admired, but cannot emulate: the amount of work involved would be far too much for me to undertake. I agree with Graham. A comparative approach is necessary. To this extent I have revised my original chapter on the comparison

1   [2006] 1 WLR 1543; [2006] 2 All ER 891; [2006] 1 All ER (Comm) 885; [2006] All ER (D) 264 (Apr); [2006] IP & T 546; *The Times* 16 May 2006; [2006] EWHC 813 (Ch).

of electronic signature laws, and invited lawyers from Canada, Germany and the United States of America to add commentaries to this text – I hope further commentaries covering more jurisdictions will follow in future editions. It is unquestionably the case that lawyers, when advising clients, must carefully consider the legal recognition of electronic signatures between jurisdictions. Failure to do so may cause the client unnecessary legal costs in the event of a dispute. Finally, Graham also maintained the topic should be so simple that a book on the subject ought not to be necessary. Indeed, it ought to be simple, and books on the topic ought not to be necessary. But the politicians are in thrall to the technology, so we now have the mixed bag of laws and regulations that dominate the landscape.

Although the text is primarily based on the law of England and Wales, I have tried to introduce as many examples as possible from other jurisdictions in an attempt to make the text truly comparative in nature. Chapter 1 provides an outline of the significance of signatures, and includes information about the role of notaries. Chapter 2 covers the history of the case law of signatures, primarily of England and Wales, although I have researched the United States and include cases from other jurisdictions. It is to be acknowledged that many of the cases referred to in this chapter refer to statutes that may well have been amended or appealed. However, this does not detract from the problems that lawyers and judges faced when applying legal principles to new forms of technology. As most of these cases illustrate, judges applied the underlying legal principles to the facts of the case, leaving the technology to one side, because the technology does not affect the legal principles. That judges and lawyers have had to deal with new technologies is hardly unique, and to suggest that judges are dealing with technological change for the first time in history is erroneous. Judges have always been required to apply the law, regardless of the technology used, and the development of the networked world is no different.

Chapters 3, 4, 5, 6, 7 and 8 might be considered as forming part of a group, in that the international and regional aspects of legislation are set out, and then considered in more detail for the jurisdictions covered. In many ways, this is hardly an adequate response, but it is hoped that the analysis in Chapter 9 will make up for this lacunae. Chapter 10 considers the various forms by which an electronic signature is manifest, and includes as many illustrations of the different approaches taken in various jurisdictions as was possible, given the fact that the correspondents who kindly responded to my requests were all very busy. I have decided to include the technical attributes of digital signatures, which are the subject of much hyperbole, to Chapter 15. The chapters dealing with contractual liability and non-contractual disclaimers and negligence are written with the view to the law in England and Wales, but I hope that some of the comments and analysis offered in these chapters is of relevance in other jurisdictions. Both chapters concentrate on the analysis of digital signatures, especially the way certification authorities attempt to bind the recipient of a digital signature contractually. The chapter on evidence aims to consider all forms of electronic signature, and the rules of procedure will apply to this subject respecting the burden of proof, which is an essential element for any form of evidence in digital format. Consideration is given to data protection and electronic signatures in Chapter 16.

Finally, to my knowledge, two people, both of whom I have had the good fortune to have met, are researching topics on electronic signatures for their doctorates. Aashish Srivastava is undertaking his doctorate at the Faculty of Business and Economics, Monash University, Australia, and his research topic is entitled 'Lack of acceptance of electronic signatures by Australian businesses.' His supervisors are Dr Paul von Nessen, Professor of Business Law and Taxation and Paul Sugden. Also, Minyan Wang is undertaking her doctorate at the Centre for Commercial Law Studies, Queen Mary, University of London. Her research topic is provisionally entitled 'Effective law and regulation of Information and Communications Technologies – A comparative and economic analysis of electronic signatures law and regulation.' Her supervisors are Chris Reed, Professor of Electronic Commerce Law and Ian Walden, Professor of Information and Communications Law. It will be of interest to see what their research reveals.

Stephen Mason

stephenmason@stephenmason.eu

Langford, Bedfordshire

May 2007

Author biographies

Thomas M Dunlap has been the managing partner of Dunlap, Grubb & Weaver, P.C. since 2002. Headquartered in Washington, DC, the law practice focuses on intellectual property law and litigation. Memberships include MENSA, Standard & Poor's Vista Research Panel, the American Bar Association, multiple state and Federal bars, the Federal Circuit and numerous civic organizations. He is a graduate of Washington & Lee University School of Law (Phi Delta Phi), an avid pilot and serves as a Captain (Cavalry) in the Army National Guard (29th Infantry).

Dr Martin Eßer is qualified as a German Rechtsanwalt and a member of the Technology, Media and Telecoms Team of Osborne Clarke in Cologne, Germany. He advises on all aspects of technology and intellectual property issues, but particularly on data protection and IT outsourcing. Martin has had extensive experience in the field of digital signatures and is the author of a doctoral thesis in German law on legal questions concerning digital signatures.

Valerie C Mann, a partner at Lawson Lundell LLP in Vancouver, is a corporate and commercial lawyer and chair of Lawson Lundell LLP's technology law practice group. Her practice focuses on mergers and acquisitions, corporate finance and other commercial transactions including strategic alliances, outsourcing, licensing and joint ventures for clients in the information technology, biotechnology, resource, manufacturing and service industries. She has presented papers in both Canada and the United States on venture capital financing, outsourcing, software agreements and advising early-stage companies.

Stephen Mason is Barrister and a door tenant at St Pauls Chambers, Leeds; Visiting Research Fellow and Director of the Digital Evidence Research

Programme at the British Institute of International and Comparative Law, and an Associate Senior Research Fellow at the Institute of Advanced Legal Studies. He is the general editor of *Electronic Evidence: Disclosure, Discovery & Admissibility* (LexisNexis Butterworths, 2007), author of *E-Mail, Networks and the Internet: A Concise Guide to Compliance with the Law* (xpl publishing, 6th edn, 2006) and the general editor of the *Digital Evidence Journal*.

Anila Srivastava has degrees in anthropology and law and currently practises at Lawson Lundell LLP. She intends to continue to practise as a barrister while maintaining her research and writing on subjects as diverse as Medieval animal trials, class proceedings, and electronic evidence.

Thomas S Woods, a partner at Lawson Lundell LLP in Vancouver, is a barrister whose practice focuses upon product liability and other commercial disputes, including intellectual property litigation and defamation claims. He has published articles and chapters on expert evidence, defamation, civil procedure, negligence and other legal subject matter, and has co-edited and contributed chapters to the *British Columbia Civil Trial Handbook* and *Expert Evidence in British Columbia Civil Proceedings*. In 2003 and 2006, Tom made invited presentations on the comparative law of expert evidence at symposia offered in London by the Academy of Experts.

Acknowledgments

As usual, I am indebted to the members of staff at the libraries of Middle Temple, Inner Temple, Gray's Inn and the Institute of Advanced Legal Studies. Although the American Library at Middle Temple on the third floor was closed for a good part of the time when researching for this edition because of building works, nevertheless it remains a very helpful and useful resource, and I was able to use it when the room was returned to something like normality – just as in the days when I spent hours working in the wonderful silence whilst attending the City University Diploma in Law course and the Inns of Court School of Law.

I thank the Institute of Advanced Legal Studies for renewing my Associate Research Fellowship for the academic year 2005–06, which permitted me unlimited use of the IALS Library and Information Services.

Also my thanks to Julien Hofman, Associate Professor at the Department of Commercial Law, University of Cape Town, South Africa, who very kindly sent me some of the South African cases. Also to Adrian Ailes, Research, Knowledge and Academic Services at the Public Record Office, Wendy and Alan Alstin of History Box and Dr Dianne Tillotson, each of whom kindly pointed me in the right direction with respect to seal impressions in the middle ages.

A separate note of thanks is recorded in the appendix listing the correspondents to this edition, but I wish to emphasise that many correspondents went out of their way to provide information, especially examples of case law, and without their help, this text would be even more incomplete than it is.

Finally, to my wife, Penny, for being there.

Contents

Table of statutes

Table of statutory instruments

Table of international legislation

Table of Cases

Chapter 1

The signature

This chapter aims to put the concept of the signature into a broad legal context, and to set the foundations for understanding the purpose of a signature, and why the function a signature performs remains as valid today as when the use of an impression of a seal was considered to be the best means of authentication before the advent of widespread literacy.

The purpose of a signature

1.1 Legislation providing for electronic signatures has, essentially, been directed to provide for the authenticity of the person using the signature, although various statutes provide for additional uses, such as providing for the integrity of a message or document. The major part of this text will focus on one form of electronic signature: the digital signature, although digital signatures are neither the most popular nor widely used of electronic signatures. Authentication can be the process by which a person or legal entity seeks to verify the validity or genuineness of a particular piece of information. Alternatively, it can mean the formal assertion of validity, such as the signing of a certificate: we authenticate what it certifies. In certain circumstances, there may also be a need to verify the identity of an individual or legal entity, although what is meant by 'identity' will also depend on the reason for ascertaining the identity. For instance, two commercial entities in separate jurisdictions may wish to enter into a commercial agreement. Before committing themselves to signing the agreement, both entities may require the identity of the other to be verified within their respective legal framework. It is also possible that each may require the passing of relevant board minutes to authorize the particular officers to commit their organization to the obligations set out in the contract. It may then be necessary to identify those officers that are to sign the contract, together with the authority delegated to them by the organization.

Clearly there must come a time when somebody must trust some form of authentication. A public notary can attest to most of the requirements set out in the example above, both physically and electronically, but the recipient may wish to question the identity of the public notary, and so the preoccupation with authenticating an identity could continue.

Another example relates to an entitlement. Where a person wishes to take a transfer of registered land, they will need to know that the transferor is the same person as the one named in the proprietorship register. It will not necessarily matter whether the name or address are the same. For instance, if the transferor has died, then it must be shown that the would-be transferor has the requisite authority to effect the transfer, which may be derived from the transferor in the form of instructions in a will. In this sense, the authentication of 'identity' is the relationship between individuals perceived at different times.

Authentication and identity

1.2 Documents may serve more than one function, which also means that the signature affixed to the document will also serve more than one function. Consider signatures on documents such as wills, for instance. The manuscript signature of the testator will not authenticate a will, nor is it required to. In most jurisdictions, for a will to be properly executed, it must be signed by the testator and proved by two witnesses. The function of the witnesses is to watch the person sign the will, so they can give evidence at a later date, should it be necessary, that they watched the signature of the person whose signature is affixed to the will. The manuscript signature of the testator indicates their intention to adopt the content of the will, not as an act of authentication. This is an example of the authentication of 'identity' in the form of the relationship between individuals at the time the will is signed.

Another example that reflects the reality of everyday life is in the daily transactions we enter. It is rarely necessary to establish the identity of a person or legal entity for a transaction to take place. Providing both parties to the barter are happy to buy and sell a product or service using a trusted means of exchange, both the buyer and the seller will part, comfortable that each has reached an amicable bargain. It may be that neither party to the trade will wish, or need, to meet again. However, if something goes wrong with the transaction for any reason, one party may wish to pursue the other to resolve the matter. Depending on the nature of the dispute and what action the complaining party intends to take to seek a remedy, it may be necessary to establish the identity of the party causing the problem. It will also probably be necessary to find them again, and a name and address may be helpful, although not strictly necessary or sufficient. Whether the party intending to take legal action has a name and address or not, they must still prove that whoever they have named and served, is the same person as the person who they claim owes them damages or any other remedy.

When dealing directly with other people, the need to authenticate the identity of the other party depends on a number of factors, including the nature of the goods or services sold and any legal or regulatory requirements. Where there is no requirement or need to authenticate the identity of a person or legal entity, both the buyer and the seller assess the risk involved with the transaction. For instance, a buyer may decide to purchase a CD on a Saturday market stall. If the buyer knows the trader from whom they intend to buy the item, a certain level of trust will already exist between the two. As a result, any transaction that takes place will be founded on mutual recognition and the knowledge by both parties that if something goes wrong, each knows how to contact the other to effect a remedy. However, where the buyer is passing through a town and is unlikely to make a return visit, the potential buyer takes different factors into account than the local buyer. An outsider will use what intuition their life experience has taught them to assess whether to trust each seller in the market. In this set of circumstances, it is unlikely that the transient buyer is concerned about authenticating the identity of any of the store holders. The buyer will evaluate the physical signals they observe about the seller of CDs. Their response, and whether to trust the seller, will be one part of the process in deciding to buy. Another consideration will be the potential loss they may suffer if they buy a CD that fails to work. If the buyer considers it is worth taking the risk, because the likely loss is negligible, then they may buy from the unknown seller if the other signals they have processed confirm the seller is to be trusted. Similarly, the seller, if they do not know the identity of the buyer, will enter the transaction if the medium of exchange is to be trusted. Whether the buyer pays in cash or by way of a cheque or credit card, the buyer is able to carry out a procedure that goes some way to establishing the authenticity of the medium of exchange.

For instance, where a cheque is offered, certain formalities are required to guarantee payment of the amount written on the cheque by the issuing bank:

(a)   The buyer writes on the cheque the correct date, the amount in figures and in numerals, and signs the cheque with their manuscript signature in the presence of the seller.

(b)   The seller then writes down the unique number (to be found on the reverse of the cheque guarantee card that in turn corresponds to the bank account as printed on the face of the cheque) on the reverse of the cheque, ensures the information written by the seller on the cheque is correct, and then compares the signature on the cheque guarantee card against the signature written by the buyer in the presence of the seller.

Once these formalities are satisfactorily completed, the seller can rest assured that in normal circumstances the issuing bank will honour the cheque and cause the seller's bank account to be credited with the amount on the cheque. Whichever method of exchange is used, whether it is cash, credit card or cheque, the seller is not checking the identity of the buyer. They are merely seeking to establish the validity of the means of exchange. The buyer is assumed, in most circumstances, to be the legitimate user of the cheque and cheque guarantee card. However, neither the cheque nor the accompanying cheque guarantee card is evidence that the person in possession of these items is the person whose name appears on the documents.

The signature of a testator on a will serves to adopt the content of the will, and the witnesses make a statement to the effect that they witnessed a person purporting to be the testator, sign the document. With a cheque, the signature serves to link the name of the person printed on the cheque with the person that claims they have the authority to draw money from the account indicated on the cheque. The existence of the cheque guarantee card with a manuscript signature on the reverse serves to reinforce the link between the card and the cheque. The signature, even if the signature on the reverse of the cheque guarantee card matches the signature on the cheque, does not identify the person signing the cheque.[1]

Yet this is precisely what the legislation relating to electronic signatures seeks to assert when a person uses such a signature. Often, the legislation may also explicitly state that when a person causes an electronic signature to be associated with an electronic document or message, they are also associating themselves with the content of the document. In the physical world, this does not happen, because a signature will serve a different function, depending on the nature of the document, as described above. What has been lost in the rush to enact legislation is the fact that the function of a signature is generally determined by the nature and content of the document to which it is affixed. A signature can have a variety of purposes, as indicated by D. Bruce Farrend:

'Clearly, a document may serve more than one function, in which case a signature on that document would also serve more than one function. A lengthy commercial agreement may contain certifications as to matters of fact (representations), promises to do certain things (covenants), acknowledgements (receipts), authorizations (grant of power of attorney) and other matters. However, the point I am getting at is that the function of the signature is, as a general statement, determined by the document itself. I cannot imagine how a random act of signature may give rise to legal consequences in a commercial setting.'[2]

---

1 See an instructive and amusing story of how little people rely on a manuscript signature for the many millions of transactions conducted every day, available from www.zug.com/pranks/credit/index.html where a visitor shared their experiences by experimenting with variations of their signature with a number of transactions, including evidence of the transaction slip. A return visit to this website in 2007 for the purposes of this revised text indicated that the prankster had, in the intervening years, extended their repertoire: www.zug.com/pranks/credit_card/. Even if the examples illustrated on this website are fictitious, they probably indicate the experience of many people that use credit cards and cheque cards. First viewed on 18 August 2003, revisited 1 March 2007.

2 D. Bruce Farrend 'Policy Considerations Behind Legislation Recognizing Electronic Signatures' (July 1998) available online at www.ulcc.ca/en/cls/index.cfm?sec=4&sub=4g.

The nature of an electronic signature

1.3 Of the types of electronic signature in use: typing a name on an electronic document; clicking the 'I accept' button placed on a website; tapping numbers into a keyboard; using a biodynamic version of a manuscript signature or a manuscript signature that has been scanned, and the use of a digital signature, the digital signature exercises most of the technical discussion in this text. To understand the reason for this, it is important to realise that most of the governments that have enacted legislation, based on a particular technology, intend the signature to perform two functions: to authenticate the person using the signature and to demonstrate that the person using the signature has adopted the content of the message. This can be achieved by any other form of electronic signature, yet a manuscript signature may not even perform one of these functions, least of all both. A digital signature using a private key and a public key pair is associated with a message or document by means of a hash result of the data included in the message. The digital signature is a product of the message. It is a message making the following statement:

'The private key, which made this signature, is associated with the public key used to verify it, and the message has not changed since the signature was made.'

A digital signature does not confirm the owner of the key caused the private key to be used to affix the signature to the document or message. Put another way, it does not make the statement that the person whose private key was used, was the person that caused the signature to be associated with the document or message. As a result, provisions in statutes that provide that an electronic signature is capable of authenticating the identity of the person whose private key was used, are creating a presumption on the user of an electronic signature that does not exist when using a manuscript signature. With the greatest possible respect to Farley J of the Ontario Superior Court of Justice (Commercial List), who approved an interim order to enable electronic voting to take place, it cannot be correct to suggest that '… an electronic signature with the integrity of passwords would be easier to verify' because the electronic signature, even when used with a password, does not verify that the person entitled to use the signature actually carried out the act to cause the association between the electronic signature with the document or message.[1]

1   *Re Newbridge Networks Corporation* (2000) 186 DLR (4th) 188 (Ont Sup Ct) at 191.

Public policy explained

1.4 In many cases, the legislation providing for electronic signatures has shifted the risk of forgery from the recipient of a signature to the purported signing party. The risk, or burden of proof, is normally on the person that relies on the signature to prove the signature was genuine. A new presumption has been created that presumes an electronic signature is genuine. The presumption covers more than just the authentication of the electronic signature. In many cases it also covers the integrity of the message and the confirmation that the content of the electronic document or message has been adopted by the purported signing party. There are two arguments that are used for placing a burden on the person using a private key to create a digital signature, with the concomitant consequences they would face for the loss of control over their private keys:

(a) If a person using a private key wants to benefit from their signature being recognized, it follows that they should carry the risk.

(b) Ergo, the person nearest the risk is best placed to manage it, and consequently it is justified to place the risk of failure on that person, and they are the ones who can best insure the risk (however, if they cannot prove they were careful with their private key, they will not be covered).

But these arguments cannot be right. It is the recipient who wants the advantage of a machine to verify the signing party, not the signing party. Commercial entities cannot take the risk of insisting on machine verifiable signatures, because they will turn business away by rejecting those people that will not use an electronic signature. Only the government has the power to insist that the signing party takes the risk, and it has begun to undertake this task by providing for the reversal of the burden of proof in a number of Statutory Instruments. A signing party can understand and deal with risks like losing possession of a credit card or door key, for instance. Whilst it is correct that a signing party to a digital signature is nearest the risk, the nature of the risk is completely different from the risk of losing a card or a door key, with the result that consumers (and indeed very many business people) have no comprehension of the complexity of the environment within which an electronic signature (in particular, a digital signature) exists. As a result, the burden should stay with recipients, who are mostly commercial entities and governments. If they want to reverse the burden, they should consider developing devices that are adequately secure for the purpose in order to justify the transfer of risk. Such devices would not be cheap, and they would have to be subsidised by those who want the benefit of a reversed burden of proof.

The manuscript signature

1.5 It is thought that the act of a person fixing their name to a document is well understood by lawyers and non-lawyers alike. However, a close look at the case law demonstrates the range of issues that have arisen in relation to what seems, at first glance, a relatively simple concept. The means by which judges have tested the validity of a signature has altered over time. From concentrating on the form a signature takes, judges went on to question its validity by considering the function the signature performs.[1] The analysis in the move from form to function applies equally to the analysis of electronic signatures.

1   Professor Chris Reed, 'What is a Signature?' 2000 (3) *The Journal of Information, Law and Technology (JILT)*, 1.3, online at www2.warwick.ac.uk/fac/soc/law/elj/jilt/2000_3/reed/.

Dictionary definitions

1.6   The Oxford English Dictionary offers a number of definitions of a signature.[1] The earliest references relate to signatures of a public nature that are intended to have legal effect. The first definition of a signature as a noun is that of 'A writing prepared and presented to the Baron of Exchequer by a writer to the signet, as the ground of a royal grant to the person in whose name it is presented'. An illustration for 1534 refers to 'To pass with writings and signaturis to be subscrivit be the Kingis grace'. The remaining references for this entry also relate to royal signatures in the public domain. The second and third definitions continue with the same meaning. Item 2(a) is defined as 'The name (or special mark) of a person written with his or her own hand as an authentication of some document or writing', and is illustrated from Hollyband of 1580, referring to 'the signature or marke of a Notaries', with the next illustration from Coke dated 1633 referring to 'A bill superscribed with the signature or signe manuall, or royall hand of the King.' The third reference, item 2(b) 'The action of signing one's name, or of authenticating a document by doing so' is also illustrated by an early reference to Lord Keeper Williams from 1621 'Some things wee must offer to the kings signature when the clarkes are not to bee found.'

The law dictionaries vary in their treatment of the way in which a signature is defined. Some provide a definition that is similar to that offered by the Oxford English Dictionary, such as:

An indication, by sign, mark, or generally by the writing of a name or initials, that a person intends to bind himself to the contents of a document.[2]

Signature, a sign or mark impressed upon anything; a stamp, a mark; the name of a person written by himself either in full or by initials as regards his Christian name or names, and in full as regards his surname, or by initials only ... or by a mark only, though he can write ... or by rubber stamp ... or by proxy.

A person signs a document when he writes or marks something on it in token of his intention to be bound by its contents. In the case of an ordinary person, signature is commonly performed by his subscribing his name to the document, and hence 'signature' is frequently used as equivalent to 'subscription'; but any mark is sufficient if it shows an intention to be bound by the document; illiterate people commonly sign by making a cross.[3]

1. A person's name or mark written by that person or at that person's direction. 2. *Commercial law.* Any name, mark, or writing used with the intention of authenticating a document.[4]

Other legal dictionaries provide judicial examples of the meaning to be attributed to a signature, with case examples.[5]

1   *Oxford English Dictionary*, (Electronic version), Second Edition, 1989 and Additions, 1993–7.
2   J. E. Penner *Mozley & Whiteley's Law Dictionary* (Butterworths, 12th edn, 2001).
3   John Burke *Jowitt's Dictionary of English Law* (Sweet & Maxwell, 2nd edn, 1977).
4   Bryan A. Garner *Black's Law Dictionary* (West Group, 7th edn, 1999).
5   Daniel Greenberg and Alexandra Millbrook *Stroud's Judicial Dictionary of Words and Phrases* (Sweet & Maxwell, 6th edn, 2000) the entry in this dictionary is of useful length, separating out different areas of law with good discussion; David Hay, General Editor *Words and Phrases legally defined* (3rd edn, 1990; Supplement 2002) the entries in this work set out the major judicial decisions.

The manuscript signature

1.7   The epitome of a signature is the act of an individual writing their name in their own hand on a document, usually in the form of a manuscript signature. More widely, it is the action of a person affixing a permanent imprint upon a document. In the world before the invention of electricity and computers, an imprint was required to have the characteristic of permanency because it was necessary to retain tangible evidence of intention. In addition, the parties to the document may consider it necessary to retain the evidence for a sufficient length of time in order to enforce any rights or obligations evidenced in the record. Before the development of the telegraph, a document would normally be considered something written on to a material, mainly paper. Although a number of people may be involved with the framing of a document and its subsequent manifestation in its final physical form, the document will have been created physically, with no intervention of any other form. Thus if an instruction was passed from one party to another by means of the operators of a semaphore, the sending operator could give evidence of the instructions received from the instructing party and the signals they used to transmit the message, and the receiving operator could give evidence of the signals they observed and noted down on paper. With the development of communications over the electric telegraph, the same principles would apply as with the semaphore, but the electronic pulses would be interpreted in the light of the code used by the sending and receiving operators. The use of the telegraph meant that the message was encoded into electronic pulses, but the pulses were not stored. The receiving operator transferred the evidence of the message to a carrier. In contrast, a computer transmits and stores the data in digital format, but the data is not visible to the human eye. It requires a combination of the interpretation and use of hardware and software to make the data visible to the human. In a world that relied on physical and permanent evidence of proof of intent, the requirement for an enduring record is understandable. The form a document can take includes, but is not restricted to, a passport, will, lease, contract, photograph, credit cards, tape recordings or television film. Whilst the legal consequences of a signature will differ when fixed to artefacts, such as items of pottery, paintings, sculpture and carvings on surfaces such as stone, marble, glass and wooden furniture, nevertheless a signature is capable of establishing the identity of the creator of the article and is also capable of authenticating the provenance of the object.

A document usually exists on a carrier, typically paper. The carrier is marked permanently with content, usually with ink, either in the form of handwriting or by means of a printing press. This process alters the carrier physically. The content imprinted on the carrier may include a range of information, depending on the nature of the document, including information about the person that created, issued or initiated the content. Over time, the carrier will include additional information as it is handled, including coffee stains, scratches, additional content, fingerprints and DNA. Finally, the content may be adopted by a person or legal entity that intends to sign the carrier with a signature: the reason for signing the document will depend on the nature of the document and the purpose for which the person is signing. When brought together, these components comprise the document in its entirety.

Document

1.8   In England and Wales, a document is defined in the Civil Evidence Act 1995, s 13 as:

> 'anything in which information of any description is recorded, and "copy", in relation to a document, means anything onto which information recorded in the document has been copied, by whatever means and whether directly or indirect.'

The Civil Procedure Rules 1998 also provide a meaning of a document in Pt 31, r.4 as '... anything in which information of any description is recorded' and a copy is, in relation to a document '... anything onto which information recorded in the document has been copied, by whatever means and whether directly or indirectly.' These definitions illustrate the emphasis on the recording of the content by the application of (usually text) on to (usually) paper, although a further statutory definition is provided in the Finance Act 1993 which specifically includes the use of the word 'computer': '"document" includes a document of any kind whatsoever and, in particular, a record kept by means of a computer.'[1] Various other definitions are offered by statute, including the specification of the types of storage medium, defining documents by reference to lists and references to the use of documents in digital format.[2] The modern definitions appear to exclude a very old form of document, that of the tally stick. Tally sticks were made of wood, and they were used as receipts for money and other items, and as a record of an obligation to make a payment. The amounts were added to the tally by the use of notches of differing widths, depths and intervals. Like a chirograph, they were a bipartite record, in that once the notches were made to the satisfaction of both parties the stick was split down the middle, providing each party with an identical copy of the record. Tally sticks also included the names of the parties and the nature of the agreement in ink on the wood, and some had a seal affixed to the side of the wood. Tally sticks were a sophisticated method of recording numbers, and in 1834, the Exchequer tallies stored at Westminster were burned after the passing of the statute abolishing the Receipt of the Exchequer. Apparently, it was this fire in which the tallies were consumed that spread to the Houses of Parliament. This was not without irony, for, as Clanchy has noted, at the same time 'the Record Commissioners were busy publishing lavish volumes with spurious Latin titles the earliest medieval records in parchment' they would not have burnt the Domesday Book or the Chancery rolls, yet the tallies were consumed into ashes because 'they were in a medium, wood, which was too uncouth for scholars to appreciate.'[3]

From the point of view of the common law, the meaning of a document has been restricted to its function as evidence, in particular to the process of disclosure. The concept of a document was the subject of *R v Daye*,[4] in which Darling J suggested that the meaning of a document should not be construed in a narrow sense at 340:

> 'I think that it is perfectly plain that the sealed envelope itself might be a document … I should myself say that any written thing capable of being evidence is properly described as a document and that it is immaterial on what the writing may be inscribed.'[5]

In the modern context, audio tapes were accepted as a discoverable document in *Grant v Southwestern and Country Properties Ltd*,[6] in which the meaning of a document was defined by its quality to convey information, and it did not matter what format the storage medium took.[7] The definition is considered wide enough to bring any medium into its ambit without causing difficulties.[8]

1   Section 40(1).
2   Chris Reed *Digital Information Law Electronic Documents and Requirements of Form* (Centre for Commercial Studies Queen Mary and Westfield College, 1996) 9–15.
3   M. T. Clanchy, *From Memory to Written Record England 1066–1307* (Blackwell Publishing, 2nd edition, 1993), 124; see Plate VIII for an example of the tally sticks issued by the Exchequer to Robert of Glamorgan, sheriff of Surrey and Sussex, as receipts for payments into the treasury in the financial year 1293–4.
4   [1908] 2 KB 333.
5   Hodge M. Malek, general editor, *Phipson on Evidence* (Sweet & Maxwell, 16th edn, 2005), 41-02 for a more detailed discussion.

6 [1975] Ch 185; [1974] 3 WLR 221; [1974] 2 All ER 465; 118 SJ 548 Ch D; 232 EG 333, Chancery Division.
7 Chris Reed *Digital Information Law Electronic Documents and Requirements of Form* Chapter 1; Stephen Mason, general editor, *Electronic Evidence: Disclosure, Discovery & Admissibility* (LexisNexis Butterworths, 2007), Chapter 8.
8 Charles Hollander QC *Documentary Evidence* (Sweet & Maxwell, 9th edn, 2006), 7.24.

Writing

1.9 Writing is defined in s 5, Schedule 1 of the Interpretation Act 1978 and 'includes typing, printing, lithography, photography and other modes of representing or reproducing words in visible form, and expressions referring to writing are construed accordingly.' This definition emphasises the need for the writing to be in visible form, which excludes information in a digital format. This means that information in digital format will only come within this definition if it comes within the method set out in the definition, '... and other modes of representing or reproducing words ...'[1] In his conclusion of whether information in digital format will amount to writing, Professor Reed suggested there were two possible approaches to this problem:

(a) The distinction is not between information affixed to a carrier or not, but between informal speech and formally recorded information, in the same way that the content of a message was recorded by means of telegraph, although the problem with this analysis is that there is no distinction between the use of the technology in a formal or informal capacity.

(b) The second possibility is to suggest that the requirement of 'writing' is merely evidential in nature, although the courts continue to maintain the position that tendering oral evidence cannot rectify the lack of formality.[2]

It is useful to note the range of functions that writing performs in relation to a physical carrier, as considered in the UNCITRAL Model Law on Electronic Commerce:[3]

> ... the following non-exhaustive list indicates reasons why national laws require the use of 'writings': (1) to ensure that there would be tangible evidence of the existence and nature of the intent of the parties to bind themselves; (2) to help the parties be aware of the consequences of their entering into a contract; (3) to provide that a document would be legible by all; (4) to provide that a document would remain unaltered over time and provide a permanent record of a transaction; (5) to allow for the reproduction of a document so that each party would hold a copy of the same data; (6) to allow for the authentication of data by means of a signature; (7) to provide that a document would be in a form acceptable to public authorities and courts; (8) to finalize the intent of the author of the 'writing' and provide a record of that intent; (9) to allow for the easy storage of data in a tangible form; (10) to facilitate control and subsequent

audit for accounting, tax or regulatory purposes; and (11) to bring legal rights and obligations into existence in those cases where a 'writing' was required for validity purposes.[4]

For the position in Scotland, the reader is referred to the Requirements of Writing (Scotland) Act 1995.

1 Chris Reed *Digital Information Law Electronic Documents and Requirements of Form*, 83–84 for other statutory definitions and further comments.

2 Chris Reed *Digital Information Law Electronic Documents and Requirements of Form*, 94–102.

3 The Model Law on Electronic Commerce was adopted by the Commission on 12 June 1996, following its 605th meeting, which in turn was adopted by the General Assembly in Resolution 51/162 at its *85th plenary meeting on 16 December 1996*, and includes an additional article 5 bis as adopted by the Commission at its 31st meeting in June 1998.

4 Guide to Enactment, paragraph 48.

Record

1.10 The need to define a record is of relatively recent origin. A definition is provided in s 13 of the Civil Evidence Act 1995 as 'anything in which information of any description is recorded' and this definition is also adopted in CPR Pt 31, r. 4: '"Copy" in relation to a document, means anything onto which information recorded in the document has been copied, by whatever means and whether directly or indirectly.' In respect to the use of 'record' in statute, the majority of provisions bring digital information within the ambit of a record, although a number of statutes may make assumptions that records are retained in hard copy. The case law illustrates that the meaning of 'record' is discussed in relation to the admissibility of a body of evidence and the purpose for which the record has been made.[1]

1 The reader is directed to a very helpful discussion by Chris Reed *Digital Information Law Electronic Documents and Requirements of Form*, 136–147.

Instrument

1.11 Of the references Professor Reed found where the word 'instrument' was used in a statute, only one statute, s 8(1) of the Forgery and Counterfeiting Act 1981, specifically referred to digital information, whilst other definitions that refer to 'document' do not necessarily exclude digital information.[1] The meaning given to the word 'instrument' was discussed in *R v Riley*[2] where the prisoner sent a telegram to a bookmaker after he knew the winner of the Newcastle Handicap run at 2.45pm on 27 June 1895 was named Lord of Dale. He contrived to make it appear that the telegram was sent from a sub-post office, which would mean the telegram would not arrive with the bookmaker until some time after the race was run. However, he actually sent the telegram from the head office after the news arrived in the office that Lord of Dale had won the race. The court held that a telegram amounted to an instrument for the purposes of s 38 of the Forgery Act 1861. In his judgment, Hawkins J suggested the word should be interpreted according to its ordinary meaning, and quoted a number of dictionary meanings before concluding that they covered an 'infinite variety of meanings.'[3] In his judgment, Willis J concurred, and went on to offer the following comment at 321:

> 'I cannot see anything in the nature of such a section which should make it necessary or desirable to restrict the application of the word 'instrument' to writings of a formal character, and I think it is meant to include writings of every description if false and known to be false by the person who makes use of them for the purpose indicated.'

Lord Russell of Killowen CJ and Vaughan Williams J had reservations about the meaning of the word in the context of the Act, although Vaughan Williams J accepted the word had been used in a narrow, restrictive meaning that referred to the formation of a legal document, to the wider meaning adopted by Hawkins and Willis JJ. Professor Reed's comment on this case, 'However, it must be recognised that in 1896 a non-written document would be abnormal, and the case cannot be considered as a very strong authority for the proposition that an electronic record cannot be an instrument'[4] must be correct, although there is a good reason to suggest that there is a reason why this case may appear to be helpful in the context of digital information. This is that it relates to the method by which the telegram came into being to begin with. As discussed above, the sending party may write down the message on a form or dictate it to an operator. The operator would then send a series of electronic pulses to the receiving operator, who in turn would interpret the code and write the text down by hand. This carrier forms the 'document' or 'instrument'. No consideration in this case was given to the transmission of the original text to the receiving operator, yet the telegram received by the bookmaker was considered to be a document. It could be argued that information in digital format is identical in concept to the pulses passed over a telegraph wire, with the exception that technology can now store the data, which was not possible with the telegraph.

1   Chris Reed *Digital Information Law Electronic Documents and Requirements of Form*, Chapter 4.
2   [1896] 1 QB 309; 65 LJMC 74; 74 LT 254; 44 WR 318; 18 Cox 285; 60 JP 519.
3   [1896] 1 QB 309 at 314.
4   Chris Reed *Digital Information Law Electronic Documents and Requirements of Form*, 186.

Statute

1.12   There does not appear to be a statutory definition of the term 'signature'. The Interpretation Act 1978 does not provide a definition, although Professor Reed noted there were 15 statutory definitions of 'signature' or 'signing' in force in 1996, 11 of which adopted an identical or similar variation to the following: '"signature" includes a facsimile of a signature by whatever process reproduced'.[1] This particular definition is sufficiently general to include a representation of a signature in electronic format. The most obvious example is that of a manuscript signature that is scanned and converted into digital form. Such a representation can be attached to a document produced on a computer, or it could be the image of the signature as sent and received by a facsimile machine.

1 Water Resources Act 1991 (c 57) Schedule 4, Part II, Proceedings of Flood Defence Committees, quoted in Chris Reed, *Digital Information Law Electronic Documents and Requirements of Form*, 225; Table 5.1, 262–263 for the full list.

The statutory requirement for a signature

1.13 It is estimated that over 6,000 statutes require a signature.[1] However, whether a personal signature is required depends upon the wording of the statute or from the context of the requirement.[2] With respect to legislation, Professor Reed notes the statutory provisions that relate to the provision of a signature fall into three broad categories:[3]

(a) Where documents that have been signed are admissible in evidence, or create evidential presumptions. The evidential presumptions are either the document is conclusive proof of its contents, or it is clear evidence of the facts set out in the document.

(b) Where documents have to be signed for the purpose of authentication, either expressly or from the context of the requirement.

(c) Where a signature is required to exercise a statutory power.

1 Chris Reed, *Digital Information Law Electronic Documents and Requirements of Form*, 239 and note 41; Chris Reed 'What is a Signature?', 3.1.2 and note 68. On 14 May 2003 the author conducted a search on the Lexis database using the same criteria used by Professor Reed: 'signature or signed or (under w/3 hand)'. The search was interrupted automatically, giving the reason that the search would 'Return more than 1,000 results'. The software only provided a result when a search of the statute database was made for the previous 20 years. This search gave 874 references. When the same search was run for all reported and unreported cases, a result was only provided by the software for the previous year, with 759 references. The author did not repeat this exercise for the current edition of this text. Mark Sneddon also carried out a similar exercise on the statutes and regulations of the Federal Territory of Victoria with similar results, see 'Legislating to facilitate electronic signatures and records: exceptions, standards and the impact on the statute book' *University of New South Wales Law Journal*, Volume 21, No 2, 1998.
2 Chris Reed, *Digital Information Law Electronic Documents and Requirements of Form*, 233–234 and notes 23 and 24.
3 Chris Reed, *Digital Information Law Electronic Documents and Requirements of Form*, 240–241. Professor Reed provides examples in notes 42–52.

Buying property

1.14 The law relating to contracts for the sale of land was overhauled when the Law of Property (Miscellaneous Provisions) Act 1989 was brought into force on 26 September 1989. By s 2 of the Act, a contract for the sale of land must be made in writing. The material part of s 2 reads as follows:

(1) A contract for the sale or other disposition of an interest in land can only be made in writing and only by incorporating all the terms which the parties have expressly agreed in one document or, where contracts are exchanged, in each.

(2) The terms may be incorporated in a document either by being set out in it or by references to some other document.

(3) The document incorporating the terms or, where contracts are exchanged, one of the documents incorporating them (but not necessarily the same one) must be signed by or on behalf of each party to the contract.

The members of the Court of Appeal had occasion to consider the requirement of a signature on a document for the sale of land in the case of *Firstpost Homes Ltd v Johnson*.[1] In this case, Geoffrey Hale, a director of the company, reached an oral agreement with Miriam Fletcher, the owner of land in Staffordshire whereby she agreed to sell the land. A letter was typed by Mr Hale's secretary on 9 April 1993 for Mrs Fletcher to sign. Mrs Fletcher's address was typed on the top right hand side of the letter and it was addressed to Mr Hale of Firstpost Homes Ltd, followed by the address of the company. The letter continued:

Dear Geoff, re: Land and rear of Fulfen Farm, Burntwood. Further to our recent discussions I now agree to sell you the above land shown on the enclosed plan which extends to 15–64 acres in consideration of the sum of £1,000 (One thousand pounds) per acre. Yours sincerely

Then there was a gap, and typed underneath the words 'M. Fletcher (Mrs)'. A plan, a copy of an Ordnance Survey plan showing the land in question, was attached to the letter by a paper clip. Mr Hale signed the plan at the foot. Mr Hale delivered the letter to Mrs Fletcher on Friday 1 April 1993 and returned on Sunday 11 April. Mrs Fletcher signed the letter and the plan. She died on 12 May 1993. The personal representatives refused to conclude the contract for the sale of the land and the company sought specific performance. His Honour Judge Farrer QC refused the application. The appeal was dismissed. In giving a substantial judgment, Peter Gibson LJ pointed out the legislature had intended to make radical changes, and the changes were intended to simplify the law and avoid disputes. Whilst the letter clearly indicated Mrs Fletcher intended to sell the land, it was not clear that she intended to sell the land to the company. As a result, it was the letter, and not the plan, that formed the document of sale, and only Mrs Fletcher had signed this document. It was argued by the company that the typed name and address of the company were sufficient to show it was signed by the company. However, Peter Gibson LJ rejected this submission, because it was based on previous authorities that in turn were based on earlier legislation, and not on the Law of Property (Miscellaneous Provisions) Act 1989. He considered it '... is an artificial use of language to describe the printing or the typing of the name of an addressee in the letter as the signature by the addressee when he has printed or typed the document ...'[2] and mentioned approvingly the comments made by Evershed MR and Denning LJ in *Goodman v J Eban Limited*.[3] He no longer considered the interpretation of the modern Act should be governed by the authorities in relation to the Statute of Frauds 1677 or s 40 of the Law of Property Act 1925. It was decided that the company had not signed the letter, and there was, therefore, no contract in place, although this decision was '... limited to a case where the party whose signature is said to appear on a contract is only named as the addressee of a letter prepared by him ...'.[4] Hutchinson and Balcombe LJJ agreed with this analysis, and Balcombe LJ reiterated the point, at 1577 E, that the '... policy of the section is to avoid the possibility that one or other party may be able to go behind the document and introduce extrinsic evidence to establish a contract, which was undoubtedly a problem under the old law.' The move from form to function has certainly been halted in the case of the sale of property, and perhaps, it may be considered, not before time.[5]

1   [1995] 1 WLR 1567, CA.
2   [1995] 1 WLR 1567 at 1575 F–G.
3   [1954] 1 QB 550; [1954] 1 All ER 763; [1954] 2 WLR 581, CA.
4   [1995] 1 WLR 1567 at 1576 E.
5   For signatures relating to the law of property, see J. T. Farrand *Emmet on Title* (Sweet & Maxwell, 19th edn) Chapter 2, Part 2, 2.041–2.043.

Disputing a manuscript signature

Defences

1.15 A manuscript signature cannot be disputed unless the following defences can be established:
(a)   The signature is a forgery.[1]
(b)   The signature was conditional.
(c)   The signature was obtained as a result of misrepresentation.
(d)   The signature was obtained in such circumstance that it was not the act of the person signing.[2]
(e)   Mental incapacity.
(f)   Mistake.
(g)   Where one party unilaterally added material terms to the writing after the other's signature.
(h)   Where the person signing the document did not realise the document they signed was a contractual document.
(i)   By statute as being unreasonable or unfair.

These defences are not dealt with in this text, other than a brief consideration of the disputes where a manuscript signature has been at issue. The reader is referred to the standard textbooks on the subject. It is well known that manuscript signatures are forged. To prevent this problem, and to test both the validity and the effectiveness of a manuscript signature, some documents require the signature to be affixed in the presence of a witness or an authorized official, such as a notary.

1   In the case of *Brown v National Westminster Bank Ltd* [1964] 2 Lloyd's Rep 187 QBD Commercial Court, the bank paid sums of money on 329 cheques to the value of £1234 7s to two individuals that were alleged to have forged Mrs Brown's signature. The bank admitted to paying out on 100 cheques that were forged, but put Mrs Brown to proof that the remaining cheques were forged. This was because the bank took measures, through the branch managers, to question certain cheques which Mrs Brown passed through her account. Mrs Brown failed to prove that she did not sign the remaining cheques.
2   Non est factum.

Evidence of the manuscript signature

1.16   Where a manuscript signature is challenged on a document, evidence will need to demonstrate the issues discussed below.

The identity of the person affixing the manuscript signature

1.17   Evidence will have to be adduced to show the signature affixed to the document is that of the signatory. In such cases, the signature in question will have to be compared to samples of the same signature. A signature may be forged or the signature could be that of the signatory, but they may have attempted to disguise their handwriting. Thus a handwriting analyst will need to have two kinds of samples: 'request samples' which are produced for the examination and duplicate the material in question, and naturally occurring samples, made by the signatory without realising the example will be examined. Two main factors can then be examined, that of pictorial impression, which includes matters such as slope, size, margins, spacing and the position of the writing in relation to lines. Second, the construction of the letters can be examined, such as the direction the letter 'o' is formed, the way the letter 't' is crossed, and the way in which the person has written letters that require more than one movement. Forgers tend to concentrate on the pictorial impression and fail to copy details of the way letters are constructed. Likewise, people trying to disguise their handwriting also concentrate on the pictorial impression, rather than changing the formation of their letters. Further analysis can be undertaken by considering the relative proportions of letters, the spaces between letters and pressure variations. Also, the attributes of the instrument used to affix the signature to the document can be considered, such as how smooth the signature has been signed, whether it is jagged or confident, whether there is a pause and where the instrument lifts off the surface. Further, the carrier itself can be examined, from the type of material used (physical properties, optical properties), any security features (watermarks), the printing process used (the use and identification of a photocopier, computer or printer) and other evidence such as perforations and microscopic analysis that might reveal imperfections that may link the carrier to the person. Further examination can include the comparison of typescript; impressions by means of Electrostatic Detection Apparatus; whether more than one type of material was used to affix information on the carrier; whether any alterations were made or entries obliterated, and the sequence in which intersecting lines have been written.

Where the party relying on the authenticity of the manuscript signature successfully demonstrates the similarity of the manuscript signature to the sample signatures, the evidential burden will then fall upon the alleged signatory to prove the signature was forged. Although this point was made in *Saunders v Anglia Building Society*[1] in relation to the defence where the signature was obtained in such circumstance that it was not the act of the person signing,[2] the principle applies to a forged signature.

1   [1971] AC 1004.
2   Non est factum.

The intention to sign

1.18   Where a person affixes their manuscript signature to a document, it must be shown that they intended to sign the document. The case of *L'Estrange v F Graucob Limited*,[1] which pre-dates the Unfair Contract Terms Act 1977 and Unfair Terms in Consumer Contracts Regulations 1994, SI 1994/3159, illustrates the attitude of Scrutton and Maugham LJJ to the effect a manuscript signature has on a document. In this case, Miss Harriet L'Estrange was the owner of a premises in Great Ormes Road, Llandudno, where she lived and carried on the business of a café. The defendants, of City Road, London, manufactured and sold automatic slot machines. In early 1933, Miss L'Estrange agreed to buy an automatic slot machine for cigarettes for a total of £81 5s 6d, payable over 18 months. She signed a form, printed on brown paper headed 'Sales Agreement'. This document included a number of contract terms written in very small print, one of which included 'This agreement contains all the terms and conditions under which I agree to purchase the machine specified above, and any express or implied condition, statement, or warranty, statutory or otherwise not stated herein is hereby excluded ...' The machine was installed on 29 March 1933. However, it failed to work properly, and despite attempts by the defendants to repair the machine, it failed to work at all. By 11 May 1933, Miss L'Estrange ceased to make use of the machine, agreed to forfeit her deposit and requested the defendants to remove the machine. On 25 May 1933, she initiated an action in the county court to recover the payments she had made. Judgment was made in her favour. The decision was reversed in the Divisional Court because Miss L'Estrange had signed the written contract, and had not done so by any misrepresentation. She was bound by the terms of the contract, and it was irrelevant that she did not read the contract or know its contents.[2] Miss L'Estrange intended to sign the document for the purchase of the vending machine.

This was not the case in *Pryor v Pryor*.[3] Anthony Pryor, of Plymouth, made a will on 5 November 1859. One of the attesting witnesses was his daughter, Mary Charles. The testator wanted his daughter's husband to sign the will as a witness, but because it was not known when he would return, he asked his daughter to sign her husband's name instead of her own. She did so. Sir C Creswell refused to admit the will to probate because the subscription was not intended to represent her signature.

1   [1934] 2 KB 394 Divisional Court. J R Spencer 'Signature, consent, and the rule in *L'Estrange v Graucob*' CLJ 104 notes that this was not the first case in which the rule was laid down, although it was the case that made the rule famous. See *Parker v The South Eastern Railway Company* (1877) 2 CPD 416; *The Luna* [1920] P 22 and *Blay v Pollard and Morris* [1930] 1 KB 628.

2   This decision, and the discussion of a fourth defence, that the signatory did not agree to the term, is discussed in J R Spencer 'Signature, consent, and the rule in *L'Estrange v Graucob*'.

3   (1860) LJR 29 NS P, M & A 114.

Intention to authenticate and adopt the document

1.19   Although a manuscript signature on a document may not be disputed, the person signing the document may wish the other party to infer they had the authority to sign the document. In *Ringham v Hackett*[1] Lawton LJ considered that 'A printed name accompanied by a written signature was prima facie evidence that the cheque was being drawn on the account it purported to be drawn on.'[2] The presumption may be rebutted by evidence. In this case, the name printed on the cheque was that of a partnership, and the signature by one partner to the cheque was sufficient evidence to intend the recipient to infer the cheque was drawn on the partnership.

In the case of *Central Motors (Birmingham) Ltd v P A & S N P Wadsworth*,[3] Central Motors required a cheque for the payment of a motor car in the name of the firm. In accordance with this request, Mr P Wadsworth gave Central Motors a cheque with his signature beneath the name of the firm, which was printed on the cheque, below that of the names of the defendants. It was held that Mr P Wadsworth, by providing a cheque signed in this way, provided sufficient evidence from the circumstances to personally authenticate the document as being a cheque of the firm. By signing the cheque, Mr P Wadsworth had the requisite intent to adopt the cheque as that of the firm.

1   (1980) 124 SJ 201.

2   (1980) 124 SJ 201 at 202(a).

3   [1982] CAT 231, May 28, 1982; (1983) 133 NLJ 555 Court of Appeal (Civil Division).

The functions of a signature

1.20 In summary, a signature can serve a number of functions, each of which can have varying degrees of importance.[1]

1   Mark Sneddon 'Legislating to facilitate electronic signatures and records: exceptions, standards and the impact on the statute book' Part 2 II A (i)–(iv); 'Digital Signature Guidelines', (Judicial Studies Board, July 2000), 3; Jos Dumortier, Patrick Van Eecke and Ilse Anné *The Legal Aspects of Digital Signatures* (Interdisciplinary Centre for Law & Information Technology, Katholieke Universiteit Leuven, 1998), Report 1, Part III, 50; 'Legal and Regulatory Issues for the European Trusted Services Infrastructure – European Trusted Services' Final Report by ISTEV June 1997, para 3; American Bar Association 'Digital Signature Guidelines' (August 1996), 4–9; Adrian McCullagh, Peter Little and William Caelli, 'Electronic Signatures: Understand the Past to develop the Future', University of New South Wales Law Journal, 1998, Volume 21, Number 2, 56 available online at http://www.austlii.edu.au/au/journals/UNSWLJ/1998/56.html; UNCITRAL Model Law on Electronic Commerce with Guide to Enactment 1996 with additional article 5 bis as adopted in 1998 (United Nations, New York 1999) paras 48 and 53; UNCITRAL Model Law on Electronic Signatures with Guide to Enactment 2001 (United Nations, New York 2002) para 29; 'Protections of the Acknowledgment' in 'A Position On Digital Signature Laws And Notarization', A Position Statement From The National Notary Association, September 2000, 3–5 available online at http://www.nationalnotary.org/userimages/digitalSignature.pdf.

The primary evidential function

1.21 It is suggested that the primary purpose of a signature serves to provide admissible and reliable evidence that comprise the following elements:
(a)   To provide tangible evidence that the signatory approves and adopts the contents of the document.
(b)   In so doing, the signatory agrees that the content of the document shall be binding upon them and shall have legal effect.
(c)   Further, the signatory is reminded of the significance of the act and the need to act within the provisions of the document.

Secondary evidential functions

1.22 A signature can also provide evidence of identification and proof of the following:
(a)   The signature can authenticate the identity of the person signing the document. One example would be to reinforce the causal link between the signature and a name printed on a document, such as a name printed on a cheque book or credit card.
(b)   The identity of a particular characteristic, or attribute, or status of the person such as a government Minister or company director.
(c)   Where a person signing acknowledges, verifies or witnesses the record, but does not necessarily agree to be bound by the content of the document.

(d)   The existence of the document provides a record of the intent of the signatory, and, in turn, physical evidence of the originality and completeness of the document itself, including the time, date and place of the act of the affixing of the signature to the document.

(e)   Where a person is a witness to the signing of a document, the signature of the witness can provide for the authenticity and the voluntary nature of the signature of a third party.

(f)   It can demonstrate that the content of the document has not been altered subsequently to the affixing of the signature.

(g)   A signature can provide evidence that the record is a true copy of another record.

Cautionary function

1.23   This function acts to reinforce the legal nature of the document, thereby encouraging the person affixing their signature that they should take care before committing themselves to the contents of the document.

Protective function

1.24   As a corollary to the cautionary function, the party receiving the document containing a manuscript signature recognises that the other party affirms the content of the document and they have given their full attention to the content of the document. They can also be assured of the identity of the signatory, and are consequently in receipt of the proof of the source and contents of the document. This function is linked to the evidentiary function.[1]

1   Mark Sneddon 'Legislating to facilitate electronic signatures and records: exceptions, standards and the impact on the statute book' Part 2 II A (ii).

Channelling function

1.25   The formality of a manuscript signature helps to clarify the point at which a person recognises the act has become legally significant. Also, the content of the document, by being recorded on a durable form, serves to concentrate the mind on the legally binding nature of the document, thus reducing the risks associated with oral recollections. This function is also linked to the evidentiary function.

Record keeping function

1.26   Closely related to the evidentiary function, a document contained on a carrier manifest in physical format serves as a durable record of the terms of the agreement. It also enables governments to impose taxes on documents and permit audits based on the existence of documents having a physical existence.

Challenges to manuscript signatures have occurred surrounding wills, more than any other area of law. Whilst some attempts have been made to restrict decisions to a particular set of circumstances, judges have given careful consideration to the intention behind the form the signature takes. Hence the function a signature performs is as equally important, if not more so, than the form in which it is manifest.

The public notary

1.27 The functions of a notary in England and Wales are not defined by any statute or other instrument, and are generally understood from a mixture of custom, case law and statutes that make references to the specific duties of a notary. The notary in England is an officer of the law appointed by the Court of Faculties. The duties of notaries are now regulated, in large part, by rules made by the Master of the Faculties under the provisions of s 57 of the Courts and Legal Services Act 1990, although it should be noted that the public notary in England and Wales does not enjoy the same underpinning from legal codes as that of the notary public in Europe, Latin America and other countries whose laws are based on Roman law.

The public notary holds a public office and has a duty to draw, attest or certify under his official seal, deeds and other documents; authenticate such documents to ensure they are acceptable, throughout the world, as proof of the matters attested; keep a protocol containing the originals of the instruments in public form and to issue authentic copies; administer oaths and declarations; certify transactions relating to negotiable instruments and to draw up protests and other formal papers relating to incidents that took place during a voyage and their navigation as well as the cargo in ships.[1] A public notary cannot delegate their powers, and it is clear that reliance is placed on the truth of the matters contained in a notarial certificate.

1 N. P. Ready *Brooke's Notary* (Sweet & Maxwell 12th edn 2002), 19.

The formalities of a notarial act

1.28 An act is the instrument that records the execution of a deed, contract or other document in writing, or where a fact or thing done has been verified. An act is authentic where the act has been executed as required by law and is certified by the proper officer. A notarial act is the act of a public notary, and such an act must be authenticated by the signature and official seal of the notary. The notarial act is capable of certifying the due execution in the presence of the notary, of a deed, contract or other document in writing. Alternatively, it can be an act that verifies a fact or thing done in the presence of the notary, or where the notary has certain knowledge of such a fact or thing done. Where notarial acts have full and automatic recognition in law, the act has such probative value that whatever the notary has certified is taken to be beyond dispute and proved, unlike the position in England.[1]

There are two types of notarial act: those in public form and those in private form. Public form acts are instruments created entirely by the notary, such as the creation of a contractual relationship. A notarial act in a private form comprises a certificate or attestation under the hand and seal of the notary, which is included as an appendix or placed upon a private document, which in turn is signed by one or more parties. In such instances, the notary is not the author of the instrument, nor, in most instances, does the notary concern themselves with the content of the documents to be authenticated.

1   N. P. Ready *Brooke's Notary* para 5-01 and Chapter 6.

The notarial protocol

1.29   One of the most important principles derived from the Bologna School in the thirteenth century, and one that remains a cornerstone of those countries whose legal systems are drawn from Roman Law, is that the original instrument that is executed before the notary remains with the notary in their protocol. The parties receive authentic copies of the instrument, but not the original. By comparison, duplicate copies are provided to both parties in England, because of the common law of evidence when proof of the document was only possible by producing the original.

The notary and electronic signatures

1.30   The Information Security Committee of the American Bar Association, Section of Science and Technology considered the concept of the Cyber Notary. A resolution relating to this concept was passed in August 1994. The premise for the development of a Cyber Notary is the reliance on:
(a)   Trust when transacting between parties over the internet.
(b)   The security of the transmission.
(c)   The integrity of the content of the communication.
(d)   The confidence that such transactions will receive legal recognition, so that a binding contract is enforceable.

It is argued by notaries that they have been trusted third parties for centuries in the physical world, and by turning their attention to the intangible world, they are best placed to certify and authenticate in the electronic environment all of those elements of a transaction upon which both parties will seek to rely to enforce the contract. Given the education and training required for a public notary, there is a compelling argument to trusting a Cyber Notary to carry out a range of activities in the electronic environment for instruments of high value. Cyber Notaries can undertake the role of a trusted third party, undertaking such activities as: the verification of a user to whom an individual certifying certificate is issued; certifying the identity, capacity and authority of users, and to authenticate the requirements required by form and law for any given transaction.

A Cyber Notary Association was set up in England and Wales, and there are similar associations around the world. In the previous edition, it was stated that 'However, it is debatable whether the valuable role that notaries have played in the law in the physical world will be successfully carried over to the virtual world'. These words have proved to be incorrect, and both Civil Law notaries[1] and the National Notary Association in the United States of America have taken great strides to use the technology of digital signatures to great effect.[2]

1   Dr Dominik Gassen, 'A system of trust: German civil law notaries and their role in providing trustworthy electronic documents and communication', *Digital Evidence Journal*, 2006, Volume 3 Number 2, 87–90.

2   The National Notary Association are presently revising the Model Notary Act of September 2002; for the developments with the Hague Conference on Private International Law, see 'The e-Apostille Pilot Program of the HCCH and NNA,' document drawn up by Christophe Bernasconi, First Secretary HCCH, Preliminary Document No 10 of March 2006 for the attention of the Special Commission of April 2006 on General Affairs and Policy of the Conference, available online at www.hcch.net/index_en.php?act=text.display&tid=37; for the current position in England and Wales, see Michael Lightowler, 'E-commerce for Notaries in England & Wales', *Digital Evidence Journal*, 2007, Volume 4 Number 1, 39–43.

Chapter 2

The form of a signature

2.1 It is thought that the act of a person fixing their name to a document is well understood by lawyers and non-lawyers alike. However, a close look at the history of literacy and subsequent case law demonstrates the range of issues that have arisen in relation to what seems, at first glance, a relatively simple concept. The means by which judges have tested the validity of a signature has altered over time. From concentrating on the form a signature takes, judges went on to question its validity by considering the function the signature performs.[1] The analysis in the move from form to function applies equally to the analysis of electronic signatures. This chapter will consider the characteristics of a signature and the degree to which something other than a manuscript signature is accepted as a 'signature' in a number of jurisdictions, mainly common law jurisdictions, with an emphasis on English law. It seems appropriate to introduce this chapter with the perceptive comments from the sound and authoritative dissenting judgment of Bell J in the South African case of *Van Vuuren v Van Vuuren*[2] at 121:

> '... the expression "to sign" a document has no strict legal or technical meaning different from the popular meaning, viz., to authenticate by that which stands for or is intended to represent the name of the person who is to authenticate. If you say to the most illiterate person "Sign this paper," if he cannot write, he will put a cross to it, and if he does not know how to do this the most experienced man of business cannot tell him to do more. If the party have learned a little writing, or if rheumatism of hard labour have cramped the nerves of his hand, and you ask him to sign a document, he will put the initial capital letters of his Christian and surname, while he will not venture upon writing the other more minute and therefore more difficult to be executed letters

of these names, and he will feel satisfied that he has "signed." If the man of business doubt this, and, seeing he can write so far as to be able to make the capital letters, think it will not be sufficient without the smaller letters, and insist upon his making them, should the party say he cannot, the lawyer will be content. On the other hand, should the party make the attempt and produce a scrawl more or less legible, so again the man of business will be content – whether the scrawl be legible or illegible, he will be satisfied that the man has "signed." Such is the popular and professional practice, and the decision of the Courts had been conformably to it.'

1　Professor Chris Reed, 'What is a Signature?' 2000 (3), *The Journal of Information, Law and Technology JILT* 1.3, online at www2.warwick.ac.uk/fac/soc/law/elj/jilt/2000_3/reed/.
2　2 Searle 116.

Methods of authentication before manuscript signatures

Objects as a means of authentication

2.2　Before the use of written charters became common, objects would be used to preserve memory and provide evidence of an act – certainly the act of obtaining title to a property. The object served to act as a symbol of the conveyance. For instance, Earl Warenne gave a gift to Lewes priory in 1147, and both he and his brother had hair from their head cut off by Henry of Blois, bishop of Winchester, before the altar for retention by the priory as evidence of the gift.[1] By the reign of Henry II, judges began to refuse to take cognizance of symbolic objects, other than sealed writings. However, the production of an object could still be adduced as evidence, and knives were used for this purpose, especially for a conveyance. In a case dating from 1213, the litigant objected to the production of a charter against him that did not have a seal, but instead had a knife attached to the document. This particular document was one half of a chirograph dated 1148, and is preserved at Durham cathedral.[2] One further example is the Conyers falchion, exhibited in Durham cathedral treasury. The sword was the symbol by which the head of the Conyers family held the manor of Sockburn from the bishop of Durham. The senior member was obliged to show the sword to the bishop as evidence of title until 1860. Although evidence suggests the sword dates from no earlier than the thirteenth century, nevertheless this example illustrates the importance of the object as a means of proving a gift or right.[3]

1　M. T. Clanchy, *From Memory to Written Record England 1066–1307*, 38 where he gives further examples.
2　M. T. Clanchy, *From Memory to Written Record England 1066–1307*, 39; 257–259 indicating knives were often used to convey land, and the blade had to be broken in the process.
3　M. T. Clanchy, *From Memory to Written Record England 1066–1307*, 40.

The sign of the cross

2.3   The presumption about what constitutes a signature is predicated on the concept of literacy. Evidence from anthropological studies of non-literate societies and sociological studies of people living in deprived areas of the industrialized world suggest that literacy itself is primarily a form of technology.[1] This is reflected in the history of literacy, because in medieval society, it was rare for the most educated people to write. Indeed, there was no value placed on a personal signature. Documents were ratified with a cross, because the cross was a solemn symbol of Christian truth. This method of authentication was retained after the conquest by the Normans,[2] and is illustrated in a grant dated 1068–76 by Waleran, of property at Bures St Mary, Suffolk, to St Stephen's Abbey, Caen, attested by William I, queen Matilda, John of Bayeaux, bishop of Rouen, and Roger and Robert Beaumont, with their names added by the scribe next to each cross.[3] Another example is a charter dating from around 1090 recording the gift of the manor of Tingewick in Buckinghamshire to the abbey of La Sainte Trinité du Mont at Rouen. The charter is authenticated by the crosses of king William Rufus, Ilbert and Hawise, his wife. Each cross is different, indicating they were affixed to the charter individually. The name of each person is inscribed by the scribe, adjacent to the cross.[4] A further example is that of a grant to the city of Narbonne of rights in Tortosa, made by the Count of Barcelona in 1148. The grant is authenticated with eight crosses, of a more elaborate nature than the crosses on the English document.[5] The history of the development of literacy has a bearing on the contemporary use of electronic signatures. There remains a great deal of confusion about the types of electronic signature that provide evidence of proving intent, and it is widely misunderstood that the term electronic signature is synonymous with a particular form of electronic signature, the digital signature. As Clanchy points out, the humanists are largely to blame for the propagation and reinforcement of myths about literacy, because before compulsory schooling was introduced in the nineteenth century, literacy in Europe and America was more widespread in remote rural Protestant areas, such as Iceland and Massachusetts. The teaching of the vernacular was the foundation of mass literacy, not the teaching of dead languages. In addition, it is suggested that innovation took place at the periphery, not at the centre.[6] Comparing this with the use of electronic signatures, the evidence illustrates that ordinary people do not use digital signatures, which both the IT industry and politicians have attempted to enforce upon people: a classic example of an unsuccessful attempt to enforce use of a technology from the centre that potential users spurn in favour of other forms of electronic signature that replicate the physical world more effectively.

1   M. T. Clanchy, *From Memory to Written Record England 1066–1307*, 7.
2   W. S. Holdsworth, *A History of English Law* Volume III (Methuen & Co, 3rd edn), 231.

3   P. D. A. Harvey and Andrew McGuinness, *A guide to British medieval seals* (University of Toronto Press, 1996), Figure 1.

4   Winchester College Manuscripts 11334, illustrated in M. T. Clanchy, *From Memory to Written Record England 1066–1307*, Plate 1.

5   In the possession of the Ville de Narbonnes-Archives municipals, illustrated in Fredric L. Cheyette, *Ermengard of Narbonne and the world of the Troubadours* (Cornell University Press, 2001), 84.

6   M. T. Clanchy, *From Memory to Written Record England 1066–1307*, 15–16.

The seal and chirograph

2.4   There was a time when a personal signature was not accepted as a lawful mark of authentication on a document unless the person signing the document was a Jew. A Christian was required to sign with a cross, or their signum was affixed to the document in the form of an impression of a seal.[1] Seal impressions were made in malleable metals, such as gold or silver, whilst the papacy used lead, although the use of metals prevents the impression from being attached directly to the document, which means the seal must be attached to the document in some other way, such as a piece of string. Sealing wax began to be used, which is an amalgam of beeswax and resin. The beeswax becomes malleable when gently heated, and the resin acts as an adhesive. In the sixteenth century, shellac was introduced as a material, and remains popular today. By 1300 in England, the use of seals had permeated society to such an extent that serfs and villeins were using documents, especially to convey property. Seals were first used by kings and those of exalted rank, yet by the reign of Henry II, the chief justice, Richard de Lucy, remarked, when Gilbert de Balliol mentioned a seal, that 'It was not formerly the custom for every petty knight to have a seal, which befits only kings and important people.'[2] The use of the imprint of a seal as a means of demonstrating intent appears to have been widely adopted by 1300 which, with the combination of using writing to convey property, illustrates the move from memory to the written record, although this change did not necessarily indicate that literacy had increased, because clerks were employed to write the charters.[3] Evidence of this change is indicated in the making of a will. Until the thirteenth century, a will was, essentially, an oral act. By the end of the thirteenth century, a will tended to be a closed and sealed document, and the witnesses did not hear the testator declare their bequests, but witnessed the seal being imprinted on the document.[4] Interestingly, as the impression of a seal began to become more widespread and replaced the affixing of the cross, it was felt necessary to include the reason for adding the impression of the seal to the document, claiming that the gift may last in perpetuity, or to ensure its permanence.[5] Seals have a long history in China, Japan, and Korea, and continue to be used daily in these countries.[6]

Sometimes two copies of a document, whatever the subject, would be produced. This form of document was known as a chirograph, dating from the ninth century or earlier. A chirograph might record an agreement between two parties, including a marriage settlement, conveyance of land or repayment of a loan. The text is written twice, usually on two sides of the same parchment. When written on the same parchment, the two halves were separated by being torn or cut into two pieces, usually with a wavy line or a zigzag as a precaution against forgery or alteration. In addition, the scribe would add text across the division, such as the word CHIROGRAPHUM.[7] Each party would be given one of the halves of the parchment, duly authenticated by the impression of the seal of the other party, and each piece served to authenticate the other. This practice was so popular that chirographs became known as indentures. One example is a lease between Gloucester abbey and a widow, Emma, who had to perform ploughing and other duties as well as paying money for the rental. The charter is a bipartite chirograph dating from c.1230. The extant half of the document is the copy retained by the abbey. This copy has an imprint of Emma's seal, bearing her name and a cross as a central device.[8] Another chirograph exists from the same date or earlier, estimated by the Public Record Office to be between 1217 and 1232. This is a charter made by the earl of Chester and Lincoln with the men of Freiston and Butterwick in Lincolnshire, bearing the seals of at least fifty of the men.[9] Tripartite chirographs were also widely used in England for drawing up wills in the tenth and eleventh centuries.[10]

1   M. T. Clanchy, *From Memory to Written Record England 1066–1307*, 233; Dr Patricia M. Barnes and L. C. Hector, *A Guide to Seals in the Public Record Office*, (Her Majesty's Stationery Office, 2nd edn, 1968) illustrate, on page 3, that the meaning of 'seal' is the actual impression that was attached to a document, and the 'matrix' or 'die' is the implement which makes the impression. However, in this text, the words 'matrix' and 'die' will not be used for fear of making the subject far too technical.

2   M. T. Clanchy, *From Memory to Written Record England 1066–1307*, 51.

3   M. T. Clanchy, *From Memory to Written Record England 1066–1307*, 51, 53.

4   M. T. Clanchy, *From Memory to Written Record England 1066–1307*, 254.

5   M. T. Clanchy, *From Memory to Written Record England 1066–1307*, 316.

6   *Halsbury's Laws of England* (Butterworths, 4th edn, 2000), Volume 13, discusses seals in the context of deeds, paragraphs 26–32; an excellent and substantial discussion of seals is contained in *The Laws of Scotland Stair Memorial Encyclopaedia* (The Law Society of Scotland & Butterworths, 1995) Volume 7, paragraphs 852–1000.

7   M. T. Clanchy, *From Memory to Written Record England 1066–1307*, 87; for an example of an agreement between Colchester abbey and the burgesses dating from 1254, see Plate VII, in the Harvard Law Library MS 87, 2.254.

8   M. T. Clanchy, *From Memory to Written Record England 1066–1307*, 50 and note 21.

9   Dr Patricia M. Barnes and L. C. Hector, *A Guide to Seals in the Public Record Office*, Plate II.

10 Pierre Chaplais, *English Diplomatic Practice in the Middle Ages*, (Hambledon and London, 2003), 40–41.

Witnesses and scribes

2.5   Clanchy has observed that there would be occasions when the addition of the sign of the cross or the impression of a seal on a charter was not considered a sufficient means of authentication. Hence documents would include a list of witnesses attending the event in which the promise was made. In such cases, the emphasis would have been on the public ceremonial attendant upon the transaction.[1] It was also possible that parties would rely on the particular handwriting of a scribe to establish the authenticity of a document, as in the case of Samuel, son of Aaron of Colchester against Sewal, son of William de Spineto in 1218. Sewal's father made a bond with Samuel, and Sewal denied the seal on the chirograph was that of his father. Samuel insisted it was genuine, and made the point that the handwriting of the clerk was so distinctive as to be a better mark of authenticity. The test of distinctive handwriting was acknowledged in the Statute of Merchants 1285, requiring all merchants to have their debts recorded before the mayor of London, or before similar authorities in other cities and towns, as designated. Each bond was to be written by a nominated clerk, and each bond had to be enrolled in the hand of the clerk who was known.[2]

1   M. T. Clanchy, *From Memory to Written Record England 1066–1307*, 295.
2   M. T. Clanchy, *From Memory to Written Record England 1066–1307*, 307.

The format of the signature

2.6   Although politicians enact statutes with a view to regulating human affairs, human ingenuity always manages to circumvent procedures and rules laid down in an attempt to provide for certainty. As a result, judges have been required to exercise their powers to test the definition of a signature, and what is acceptable in the legal context. The case law illustrates that judges assessed the validity in relation to the functions a signature performed. Different factual problems required a broader understanding of the function a signature performed. Whatever the form a signature took, judges looked to the intent behind the use of the signature. Thus the range of forms a signature can take is wide, as demonstrated by the following discussion.

Manuscript

A MARK

Bills of exchange

2.7   An issue arose in 1798 in the case of *Adam v Kerr*,[1] whether a particular mark used by custom in Jamaica could be accepted as a valid signature. The particular point was not resolved, partly because Buller J only had the evidence of a bond that had been signed by two people, both of whom were dead. On the face of the decision, although the particular detail was not discussed by the learned judge, it can be inferred that the mark was accepted. Later, in

1830, the validity of a bill of exchange was the subject of the case of *George v Surrey*.[2] The bill was endorsed with the mark of Ann Moore, and the plaintiff added the words 'Ann Moore her mark'. A witness was called to prove the indorsement, who also stated that he had frequently seen Ann Moore make her mark and so sign instruments. He also pointed out a peculiarity to the mark, which implied that Ann Moore may have been consistent in the way she affixed her mark. Tindal CJ sitting in the Guildhall admitted the evidence as sufficient, although not after some hesitation. In South Africa, in the case of *Hanse v Jordan & Fuchs*,[3] £21 4s was due on a promissory note. The body of the note was written by one of the plaintiffs, and the signing of the note, it was claimed, was witnessed. The words 'zyn. Mark. A Hanse' were also inscribed on the note. The defendant claimed not to have added his mark, although the magistrate at first instance, having heard the case, believed the plaintiff's account of the facts, and reached the conclusion that the defendant had signed the note with a mark, even though he could write. On appeal, Buchanan J said, at 530, 'The defendant denied this [adding his mark to the note], but the mere fact that he can write, and only signed by his mark, is not sufficient ground upon which the Court can upset the finding of the Magistrate upon the fact.'

1   1 B & P 360; 126 ER 952.
2   1 M. & M. 516, 173 ER 1243.
3   1909 19 CTR 530.

Interest in property

2.8   In South Africa, the signing of a contract for the sale of an erf was achieved by the affixing of a mark or marks with the function of making the document an act of the signer, and of signifying assent to the content of the document in the case of *Chisnall and Chisnall v Sturgeon and Sturgeon*.[1] Flemming, DJP indicated, at 645 F, that 'An enquiry concerning assent must, of course, not be into what the signatory subjectively planned but what his acts signify to the other party.'

1   1993 (2) SA 642 (W).

Wills

2.9   Before the majority of people could read and write, the provisions of some statutes meant that where a person could not write their name, they were still required to provide a mark on the document they wished to adopt. Instances of the use of a mark by a person tend to apply to the signing of wills, as outlined in this part. This also applies to witnesses, as in the case of *Harrison v Harrison*,[1] where a witness signed a will by marking the document with a cross. It was held that the signature in the form of a mark did not cause the will to be void. In the later case of *Baker v Dening*,[2] John Dening wrote a will by which he devised part of his estate to William Dening. A codicil, dated subsequently to the will, revoked the terms of the will and devised the property to another person. The codicil was duly attested, but only had the devisor's mark, not his signature. After hearing the case at the Devonshire Assizes, Lord Denman CJ gave leave for an appeal. Upon appeal, it was agreed by Lord Denman CJ, Littledale, Patterson and Coleridge JJ that the mark of a person who is not capable of writing is satisfied by the requirements of the Statute of Frauds 1677. It was held that the rule applied even in cases where a person could write at the time they placed their mark on the document. The members of the court agreed that there was no need to undertake a collateral enquiry into whether a person could write at the material time. However, it was pointed out by Patterson J that when a document is signed by a mark, an enquiry may be undertaken as to the circumstances of the signing to ensure a will was properly attested.[3]

A similar problem was brought before the court in the case of *Re Field's Goods*.[4] In this case, the testator died on 17 May 1843, leaving a widow and two children, one of which was illegitimate. He had been paralysed for some time before he died, which caused him to be deprived of speech and almost total use of his limbs. Three days before he died, he made it known he wanted to make a will. His brother, a solicitor, wrote the will for him. The testator made a cross at the bottom of the first and second pages, and twice on the third page. The witnesses duly subscribed their names in his presence. The will was moved for probate and the motion was granted. In this instance, the form required of the Wills Act 1837 was carried out, in that the testator had actually put the mark on the document himself, and his actions were witnessed correctly.

By comparison, the decision by the House of Lords in the case of *Hindmarch v Charlton*[5] appears to be highly technical in the light of the latitude of previous decisions. In this case, the testator, Joseph Hindmarsh, who was in a hospital in Newcastle, requested Mr Wilson, a surgeon, to witness his will. He did so on the morning of 17 December 1857, writing 'Fred. Wm. Nap. Wilson', leaving out the cross on the 'F'. When Mr Wilson visited the patient during the afternoon with a colleague, Mr Wilson suggested the will should be witnessed by a second person. Dr White duly signed the will in the presence of Mr Wilson and Mr Hindmarsh. Mr Wilson then looked at the will for a second time, and noticed that he had, as usual, left the cross out of the letter 'F' in his signature. He then placed a line in the letter to cross the 'F' properly. The sole issue was whether, when he signed the will for the second time, the single mark he applied to the will, by crossing the line in the letter 'F', was a valid subscription of a witness. The three members of the House of Lords agreed that putting the cross to the letter 'F' was not a subscription. Had Mr Wilson not added the line, Lord Chelmsford noted, the omission on the first signature would not have made it imperfect.[6]

Finally, it should be noted that in the case of a will where an interested person adds a mark to the document, the presumption is that the will is not valid.[7] The act itself is not invalid, but strict proof is required, as noted by Lord Watson in the case of *Donnelly v Broughton*[8] where he pointed out, at 442, that '... the onus of proof may be increased by circumstances, such as unbounded confidence in the drawer of the will, extreme debility in the testator, clandestinely, and other circumstances which may increase the presumption even so much as to be conclusive against the instrument.' In this instance, the grand-niece of Renata Kawepo, a Maori chief, who resided in Omahu, in the district of Hawkes Bay and colony of New Zealand, produced a second will written out by her and signed by him with a cross. This will was dated 12 April 1888, two days before he died on 14 April 1888. The members of the Privy Council agreed with the members of the Court of Appeal, that the evidence surrounding the second will inferred that either Renata, if he did execute the second document, did not understand the contents, or that the will was manufactured in order to defeat the first will executed on 12 January 1887, which was prepared by a solicitor with the assistance of counsel, and was signed by the deceased and formally acknowledged to be his last will before a Justice of the Peace. Thus a mark can be a perfectly proper method of signing a document, but if it is carried out in circumstances that suggest improper influence has been used to obtain the mark, the document may have no legal effect.

1   (1803) 8 Ves Jun 185; 32 ER 324.
2   (1838) 8 AD & E 94; 112 ER 771.
3   A will was held to be sufficiently signed where a testatrix signed with a mark without her name appearing on the document: *Re Bryce's Goods* (1839) 2 Curt 325; 163 ER 427. This observation was also made in the 1929 New York case of *In the Matter of the Estate of Stegman*, 133 Misc. 745, 234 N.Y.S. 239 where probate was denied where a testator, who was able to write, subscribed a third will with a mark. The proponent failed to prove the third and final will was valid. Evans S said, at 747, 'This manner of execution is not rare but it is unusual, for a person to sign by a mark that is able to write. This fact in itself does not invalidate a will but it is obvious that it call for greater scrutiny on the part of the court.'
4   (1843) 3 Curt 752; 163 ER 890.
5   (1861) 8 HL Cas 160.
6   (1861) 8 HL Cas 160 at 171.
7   *Paske v Ollat* 2 Phill 323.
8   [1891] AC 435 PC.

United States of America

2.10   In the United States of America, the case law has covered a wider range of examples where judges have been required to determine the legal implications of various forms of mark and other signs, fingerprints, and an account number. A mark on a bill has been held sufficient,[1] as on deeds,[2] fingerprints[3] (also thumbprints in South Africa),[4] on insurance documents,[5] notices of appeal,[6] under the relevant Statute of Frauds (including a trademark),[7] with respect to trover and conversion,[8] and wills.[9] Of interest is a recent decision that accepts the proposition that the unique number issued by a bank can be a signature. In the New Jersey case of *Spevack, Cameron & Boyd v National Community Bank of New Jersey*,[10] the unique account number assigned by a bank to a depositor was determined to be as complete a signature as the depositor's written or printed name. Bilder observed, at 1169, that a signature may take many forms, and there was no reason why a bank account number could not be one of them:

'In this computer age the use of numbers as a means of identification has become pervasive. Indeed, numbers are more readily recognized and handled than signatures. The "signature" used by Homequity was its account number at Midlantic, the bank in which it deposited the check. That "signature" accurately identified the payee and the funds were properly credited to the payee's account. In fact, had Homequity written a name without the account number, the bank would have had to look up the number that corresponded with the same. In keeping with the electronic age, it is the numbers which have the primary significance.'

1   Federal (1838): *Zacharie v Franklin*, 37 U.S. 151, 12 Pet. 151, 1838 WL 3945 (U.S.La.), 9 L.Ed. 1035 the mark of Joseph Milah in a bill of sale comprising slaves, their children and stock and household furniture, had the same effect as a signature.

Indiana (1867): *Shank v Butsch*, 28 Ind. 19, 1867 WL 2925 (Ind.).

New Hampshire: *Willoughby v Moulton*, 47 N.H. 205, 1866 WL 1982 (N.H.) a promissory note for the purchase and sale of a horse signed by a mark may be valid against the person signing, even though there was no subscribing witness.

New York (1844): *Brown v The Butchers & Drovers' Bank*, 6 Hill 443, 41Am.Dec. 755 a person writing '1. 2. 8.' on the back of a bill of exchange as a substitute for his name was held to have endorsed the bill.

Tennessee: *Brown v McClanahan*, 68 Tenn. 347, 1878 WL 4292 (Tenn.), 9 Baxt. 347, 2 Leg. Rep. 59.

South Carolina (1864): *Zimmerman v Sale*, 37 S.C.L. 76, 3 Rich. 76, 1846 WL 2269 (S.C.App.L.) a mark that is not accompanied by the name of the person making the mark remains a signature.

2   Carolina (1891): *Devereux v McMahon*, 108 N.C. 134, 12 S.E. 902, 12 L.R.A. 205.

Kentucky (1898): *Blair v Campbell*, 45 S.W. 93, 19 Ky.L.Rptr. 2012 a deed signed with a mark by Francis Jackson Mann and duly acknowledged in 1856 before the county clerk of Grant County held sufficient as a signature, although attestation of a mark was not obligatory.

Stephens v Perkins, 273 S.W. 545 in the conveyance of property by the heirs of Whitmill Stephens to James Stephens, held that the marks of nine heirs was sufficient signature on the conveyance dated 6 January 1888. (1925)

Georgia (1903): *Horton v Murden*, 117 Ga. 72, 43 S.E. 786 a deed is sufficiently signed within the Civil Code 1895, s 3599 as follows: 'I, J. R., sign my hand to it X here.'

3   Illinois: *Matter of the Estate of Deskovic*, 21 Ill.App.2d 209, 157 N.E.2d 769, 72 A.L.R.2d 1261 (1st Dist. 1959).

New York (1937): *In the Mater of the Estate of Romaniw*, 163 Misc. 481, 296 N.Y.S. 925.

4   *Putter v Provincial Insurance Co. Ltd.* 1963 (3) SA 145 (W) a print of a thumb on a statement constitutes a signature within the meaning of s 2(4) Evidence Act, 14 of 1962.

5   Georgia (1972): *Thurmond v Spoon*, 125 Ga.App. 811, 189 S.E.2d 92 a mark affixed to a beneficiary card is a sufficient signature. See the dissenting judgment of Evans J, in failing to take a liberal approach to the issues in the case, he articulated the view that the name of the person

must be affixed to the document as well as a mark, and suggested the nature of the evidence was inconclusive.

Pennsylvania (1936): *Tomilio v Pisco*, 123 Pa. Super. 423, 187 A. 86 Frank Ross, too weak to sign his name, made an undecipherable series of curves and strokes: accepted as a signature.

6   North Carolina: *State v Byrd*, 93 N.C. 624, 1885 WL 1753 (N.C.).

Wisconsin (1899): *Finley v Prescott*, 104 Wis. 614, 80 N.W. 930, 47 L.R.A. 695 there was no requirement to have the signature of a person in the form of a mark witnessed. Marshall J commented, at 931, 'One is liable to be led astray on this question by a statement in Story, prom. Notes, p. 15, to the effect that if one signs by his mark the signature must be witnessed to be valid. How that eminent author came to make such a statement as to the law, unsupported by any authority, and contrary to substantially all authority except, perhaps, decisions in states expressly abrogating the common law on the subject, is not easily understood.'

7   Federal (1893): *Bibb v Allen*, 149 U.S. 481, 13 S.Ct. 950, 37 L.Ed. 819, 50 L.R.A. 240 telegrams containing orders for cotton sent in the form of Shepperton's Code, and directed the sales delivery for account of designated names, such as 'Albert,' 'Alfred,' 'Alexander,' 'Amanda,' 'Andrew,' 'Winston,' and such like, intended and understood to represent the firm name of B. S. Bibb & Co., held to be sufficient as a signature.

Federal 4th circuit: *Barber & Ross Co., v Lifetime Doors, Inc.*, 810 F.2d 1276 (4th Cir. 1987), 3 U.C.C. Rep.Serv.2d (CBC) 41 a trademark printed on a written sales brochure met the requirements of the Statute of Frauds and signature requirement.

Missouri: *Defur v Westinghouse Electric Corporation*, 677 F.Supp. 622 (E.D.Mo. 1988) writings with the defendant's trademark printed on them constituted writings signed by the defendant.

8   Massachusetts: *Foye v Patch*, 132 Mass. 105, 1882 WL 10891 (Mass.) the plaintiff added his mark to a written agreement settling ownership of a number of bricks, held to be a satisfactory signature.

9   Illinois (1930): *Cunningham v Hallyburton*, 342 Ill. 442, 174 N.E. 420 ill in bed, a nurse lifted Miss Cunningham on her left elbow, gave her a pen, and she signed her will in the form of a cross – held to be a signature.

In re Westerman's Will, 401 Ill. 489, 82 N.E.2d 474 the will of Minnie Westerman (her maiden name) dated 13 April 1942 revoked her earlier will dated April 9, 1942 and executed under her married name of Wilhelmina Frederichs when both wills were signed with her mark, notwithstanding she was not authorized to resume her maiden name in her second divorce proceedings. (1948)

New York (1809): *Jackson v Van Dusen*, 5 Johns 144.

Butler v Benson, 1 Barb. 533 (1847).

Jackson v Jackson, 39 N.Y. 153, 12 Tiffany 153, 1868 WL 6249 (N.Y.) after trying for some time to apply the pen to the paper to sign his name, the hand of the deceased trembled so much that he made a cross on his will.

In the Matter of the Estate of Galvin, 78 Misc.2d 22, 355 N.Y.2d 751 a mark added to a will by Karen N. Smith, daughter of the deceased, and at the request of the deceased, was a valid signature of the deceased. (1974)

In re Estate of McCready, 369 N.Y.S.2d 325, 82 Misc.2d 531 the mark of a person who is blind and with the assistance of another is a signature. (1975)

Pennsylvania (1877): *Main v Ryder*, 84 Pa. 217, 4 W.N.C. 173, 1877 WL 13243 (Pa.) Daniel Miner signed his will with a mark whilst touching the writing instrument held and controlled by another person. Note: in Pennsylvania, a new Act was enacted in 1833, requiring the manuscript signature of a testator, and a mark was no longer permitted, see *Assay v Hoover*, 5 Pa. St. 21 (1846); *Grabill v Barr*, 5 Pa. 441, 5 Barr. 441, 1846 WL 5049 (Pa.), 47 Am.Dec. 418; but see *Long v Zook*, 13 Pa. 400, 1850 WL 5764 (Pa.), 1 Harris 400 where Gibson J, in applying the revised Act of 1848, commenting that the 1833 Act probably defeated more true wills than false ones.

10   677 A.2d 1168 (N.J.Super.A.D. 1996), 291 N.J.Super. 577.

ILLEGIBLE WRITING

2.11   Illegible writing challenged in court is relatively rare. In the 1862 case of *Trotter v Walker*,[1] the surname on a notice of objection was not legible. The appeal court reversed the decision of the revising-barrister, and held the notice of objection was sufficient. Earle CJ observed, at 39:

> 'Lastly, it is one thing to say that the statute enjoins a legible signature, and another thing to say that such legibility is a condition precedent to the validity of the notice. Were we to hold this notice bad, questions would arise on the notice or claim of every man who might have written his name very badly or spelt it incorrectly. The object of the act of parliament, which calls to its aid persons of very imperfect education, might be defeated by adopting a rigorous construction, and furthered by a more benignant one.'

In Canada, it has been held that a manuscript signature of a Justice of the Peace does not render the information invalid if it is not legible, because of the presumption of regularity.[2] Whilst in the United States, judges have also been required to consider illegible scrawl.[3] In the 1890 Pennsylvanian case of *Appeal of Knox*,[4] it was held that a note written by the deceased and signed with her first name 'Harriet' was a signature. Mitchell J remarked, at 1023, that 'Custom controls the rule of names, and so it does the rule of signature.' He went on to note, in relation to the difficulty in reading a signature:

> 'So the form which a man customarily uses to identify and bind himself in writing is his signature, whatever shape he may choose to give it. There is no requirement that it shall be legible, though legibility is one of the prime objects of writing. It is sufficient if it be such as he usually signs, and the signatures of neither Rufus Choate nor Gen. Spinner could be rejected, though no man, unaided, could discover what the rugged marks made by either of those two eminent personages were intended to represent. Nor is there any fixed requirement how much of the full name shall be written. Custom varies with time and place, and habit with the whim of the individual. Sovereigns write only their first names, and the sovereign of Spain, more royally still, signs his decrees only, "I, the King," (Yo el Rey.) English peers now sign their titles only, though they be geographical names, like Devon of Stafford, as broad as a county. The great bacon wrote his name "Fr. Verulam," and the ordinary signature of the poet-philosopher of fishermen was "Iz: Wa." In the 56 signatures to the most solemn instrument of modern times, the declaration of independence, we find every variety from Th. Jefferson to the unmistakably identified Charles Carroll, of Carrollton. In the present day it is not uncommon for business men to have a signature for checks and banking purposes somewhat different from that used in their ordinary business, and, in familiar correspondence, signature by initials or nick-name or diminutive is probably the general practice.'[5]

In South Africa, Murray J reached the conclusion in the case of *Van Niekerk v Smit*[6] that a letter is properly signed when on headed notepaper with the name and address of the firm, even though indecipherable marks were made with a lead pencil, perhaps representing initials, over the concluding words in type 'Ferreira en van Zyl'. In the more recent case of *SAI Investments v Vander Schyff NO*,[7] it was held that extrinsic evidence was admissible to indicate the identity of an illegible signature on the agreement where the signature of the person signing as purchaser on the last page was indecipherable, and the names of the two witnesses who attested to such signature were also illegible. A similar finding was made on appeal in the case of *Van der Merwe v Kenkes (Edms) BPK*,[8] where the appellant was clearly identified in an agreement as the purchaser, but the signatures of both the purchaser and the seller were illegible. It was held that extrinsic evidence to indicate that the illegible signature was that of the appellant or her husband would be admissible.

1 13 C.B. (N.S.) 29; 143 ER 12.
2 *R v Kapoor* 52 C.C.C. (3d) 41.
3 Mississippi (1896): *Sheehan v Kearney*, 82 Miss. 688, 21 So. 41, 35 L.R.A. 102 illegible scrawl held as a signature.
   Pennsylvania (1936): *Tomilio v Pisco*, 123 Pa. Super. 423, 187 A. 86 Frank Ross, too weak to sign his name, made an undecipherable series of curves and strokes: accepted as a signature.
4 131 P. 220, 18 A. 1021, 6 L.R.A. 353, 17 Am.St.Rep. 798.
5 Note his comments at 1022 about *Vernon v Kirk* 30 Pa.St. 222; *Assay v Hoover*, 5 Pa. St. 21 and *Grabill v Barr*, 5 Pa. 441, 5 Barr. 441, 1846 WL 5049 (Pa.), 47 Am.Dec. 418 and the subsequent change of the law.
6 1952 (3) SA 17 (T).
7 1999 (3) SA 340 (N).
8 1983 (3) SA 909 (T).

GUIDING A HAND IN MAKING A MARK

2.12 The problems associated with people that are too ill or too weak to sign a document are well illustrated in the South African case of *Matanda v Rex*,[1] where a boy of 13 could not write. He made a statement to a magistrate, described thus by the magistrate, at 436: 'My practice, which we adopted in this case, is for the witness to come up to me, I hand the pen to him, he touches the pen and then I make the mark for him. I hold one end of the pen and he holds the other, after he is told to what he is deposing. He is not actually holding the pen at one end while I am making the mark. I hand him the pen, holding it myself. He fingers it. Then I take it and I make the mark, That is what happened in this case.' Similarly, in the 1975 New York case of *In re Estate of McCready*,[2] the mark of a person who was blind was made with the assistance of another, and considered a signature.

1 1923 AD 435 (B).
2 369 N.Y.S.2d 325, 82 Misc.2d 531.

Wills

2.13 On occasions, a person may be too ill to sign a document. When this happens, the question is whether there is any evidence to demonstrate the person intended to sign. In the case of *Wilson v Beddard*[1] the testator, John Parker Wilson, made a will dated 7 September 1826 and died the following day. The will was signed by the testator's mark, his hand being guided by another person. Before making the mark, the testator made faint strokes on each of the sheets containing the will. On the motion for a new trial, the Vice Chancellor, Sir L. Shadwell, agreed with the trial judge, Parke B, that the will was signed by the testator. It was decided that the act of making the faint strokes provided evidence that the testator intended to sign the will, and the fact that he was helped by another person to place his mark on the document did not make the mark any less of a signature.

1   (1841) 12 Sim 28; 59 ER 1041.

A NAME WITHOUT A SIGNATURE

2.14 There are occasions when promises are made that, after the event, it becomes clear there was never any intention of fulfilling them. Such was the case in *Knight v Crockford*,[1] where Crockford agreed to sell a public house named the Rising Sun in December 1791 to one Knight. When meeting for a second time at the house of Crockford, Crockford had already prepared an agreement, which began 'I, James Crockford, agree to sell, &c' and which Knight duly signed. Arrangements were then made to have an attorney draft a proper conveyance. However, when Knight's attorney requested a time to be set for the conveyance to be executed, Crockford refused to convey the property, because he had sold the premises to another person for more money. Eyre CJ, in the Common Please at Westminster, determined the draft agreement was a sufficient agreement, and although only Knight has affixed his signature to the document, the words 'I, James Crockford, agree to sell, &c' written by Crockford were considered a signature within the meaning of the Statute of Frauds.

1   1 Esp 190; 170 ER 324.

MISTAKE AS TO THE NAME

Wills

2.15 Sometime humans make mistakes, and it can fall to judges to examine the facts in the light of the evidence and reach a decision based on the law and the equity of the situation. In response to slight complications, and probably to render an equitable result, the judges have, on occasion, disregarded minor issues, as in the case of *Re Clarke's Goods*.[1] In this instance, the schoolmaster in the parish the testatrix lived, one Sidney, wrote the will in his own handwriting and was also one of the attesting witnesses. The will was dated 19 February 1844 and the testatrix was described as 'Susannah Clarke'. She executed the will with a mark, against which was written 'Susannah Barrell, her mark', Barrell having been her maiden name. Both of the attesting witnesses died before the testatrix. It was thought that the inclusion of the maiden name was a mistake. In this instance, Sir C. Cresswell was satisfied that the mark was that of Susannah Clarke, and thought the additional words next to the mark did not matter.

A similar set of facts came before Sir C. Cresswell in *Re Douce's Goods*,[2] where Thomas Orme, a schoolmaster, wrote a will for the testator, Thomas Douce, who could not read or write. Thomas Orme mistakenly described the deceased as John Douce of Witherby, in the county of Leicester, labourer, and wrote against the mark made by the testator 'The mark of John Douce.' Sir C. Cresswell was satisfied the will was that of Thomas Douce, because the evidence of one of the attesting witnesses was corroborated by the internal evidence of the will, that set out the name of the testator's children. He concluded that the wrong name appearing on the will was fully explained, and declared the will entitled to probate.

1   (1858) LJR 27 NS P & M 18; 1 Sw & Tr 22; 164 ER 611.
2   (1862) 2 Sw & Tr 592; 164 ER 1127.

VARIATIONS OF A NAME

Voting

2.16   Administrative mistakes tend not to be considered an adequate reason for preventing people from casting their vote. In *R v Thwaites*[1] the names of a number of men entitled to vote were listed on the burgess roll incorrectly; when they voted, they signed the voting papers with their correct names. It was held that the men had a right to vote, and although they voted in the wrong names in comparison to the names listed on roll, they were the men mentioned in the burgess roll and this was a mere case of misnomer within the provisions of s 142 of the Municipal Corporation Act of 5 & 6 Will. 4 c76. 1853.

1   22 LJQB 238.

Wills

2.17   Whilst humans use names to identify themselves, there are times when some people will adopt alternative names for a variety of reasons, or even forget to write their present name, as in the case of *In the Goods of Glover*,[1] where a woman signed her will with the name of her first husband, 'Susan Reeve', and then placed the will into an envelope marked by her 'The will of Susan Glover.' It was held that the signature was sufficient. This also should be no reason for failing to honour the intentions of a person where they use a substitute name. In the case of *Re Reddings Goods*,[2] Charlotte Redding died a spinster on 12 October 1850. She resided, amongst other places of habitation, with a Mr John Holmes at Wells for 12 years. During the first seven years she was known by the name of Charlotte Higgins, but, without giving a reason, assumed and passed by the name of Charlotte Redding for the last five years of her life. Whilst residing with Mr Holmes and passing by the name of Higgins, she had her will prepared. It was drawn up in the name of Higgins and she duly signed the will at the foot 'C. Higgins' on 21 October 1843. When she changed her name to Redding, she gave instructions for her name to be altered in her will. The name at the beginning of the will was turned into 'Redding' and the signature at the foot of the will was almost erased with a knife, although the words could be distinguished. She then, in the presence of the same two people that witnessed her first signature, signed her name 'C. Redding' at the foot of the will, but the witnesses did not re-subscribe. It transpired, after her death, that her proper name was Redding. In this instance, Sir Herbert Jenner Fust noted the second execution of the will was not valid, but permitted probate to pass in the name of 'Higgins' on the basis that it was the mark of the testatrix, because her original signature had not been completely erased from the document.

In Scotland, a letter written and sent from one sister to another was capable of constituting a holographic will, and the subscription of her Christian name 'Connie' only was also a sufficient authentication.[3] The relevant text of the letter, sent on 17 May 1936, read 'You will wonder what on earth the enclosed card is. Well, to-morrow I am going for an excursion to Keswick and have taken out the Insurance. Take care of the Card and if I'm killed Billy will get £1000. If I'm injured I get £8 for 26 weeks. By the way while speaking of dying! Should anything happen to me, (which it will one day) I haven't made a Will, but everything I have is for Billy. Knowing he will do the right thing.' Lord Patrick offered his opinion at 140 '… I am of opinion that a signature by initials or by a Christian name is as effective as a fuller signature, provided only that there be proof or admission that the granter was in use to sign documents of the kind under consideration in the particular shorter form which has been used.' Lord Mackintosh further commented, at 141–142 'The case of *Home Speirs* [*Speirs v Home Speirs* (1879) 6 R 1359, 16 SLR 784] was before the Court in the seven-Judge case of *Taylor's Executrices v Thom* [1914 SC 79], and in the exhaustive review of the whole topic of the authentication of holograph testamentary writings which was there undertaken it did not come in for any adverse comment. I think, therefore, that the letter in which the passage now founded on occurs was, when subscribed "Connie," sufficiently authenticated to enable the letter to be treated for all purposes as a valid holograph writing.'

1   11 Jur. 1022.
2   (1850) 14 Jur 1052; 2 Rob Ecc 338; 163 ER 1338. The two law reports differ whether the testatrix signed her first name with the initial 'C' or 'Charlotte'.
3   *Draper v Thomason* 1954 SC 136, 1954 SLT 222.

United States of America

2.18   A range of variations of a name have been tested in US courts, including the use of a fictitious name on deeds,[1] and using the name of another without permission on a promissory note.[2] More commonly, mistaken or partial names have appeared in matters relating to a lien,[3] the Statute of Frauds,[4] mortgages,[5] the name of a partnership on an arbitration bond,[6] and on a writ,[7] and it is not surprising that the range of human behaviour is more widely reflected in the cases of wills,[8] although the liberal approach in extending the meaning of a signature was not extended to the 1914 Pennsylvanian case of *In re Brennan's Estate*,[9] where a testamentary paper ending with 'your miserable father' was held not to have been executed correctly.

1   Arkansas (1947): *Walker v Emrich*, 212 Ark. 598, 206 S.W.2d 769.
      New York: *David v Williamsburgh City Fire Insurance Company*, 83 N.Y. 265, 38 Sickels 265, 1880 WL 12653 (N.Y.), 38 Am.Rep. 418 where a person adopts a fictitious name with intent to covey title, he is bound by the name he adopts when executing a conveyance of the property.
2   New Hampshire: *Grafton Bank v Flanders*, 4 N.H. 239, 1827 WL 744 (N.H.) a person putting the name of another on a promissory note without authority from any person of that name is liable for the note.
3   Federal 2nd circuit: *In the Matter of Excel Stores, Inc.*, 341 F.2d 961 (1965) the use of the name 'Excel Department Stores' instead of the correct name 'Excel Stores, Inc' was held to be a minor error and not seriously misleading when the contract was properly signed by an appropriate officer of the company.
4   Massachusetts (1853): *Fessenden v Mussey*, 65 Mass. 127, 1853 WL 4969 (Mass.) in an auction for a church pew, the name 'Benj. Mussey' as recorded at the time of the auction held to be a signature, even though it omitted the middle letter of the defendant's name.
      Walker v Walker, 175 Mass. 349, 56 N.E. 601 a marriage contract was deemed to be signed where the defendant signed the document with her first name only. (1900)
      Missouri (1907): *Great Western Printing Co., v Belcher*, 127 Mo.App. 133, 104 S.W. 894 the words 'Guaranteed. Belcher' written in lead pencil across the face of the original account for the payment of $44.50 in respect of posters is a signature, even though the signature did not include first name.
5   California: *Middleton v Findla*, 25 Cal. 76, 1864 WL 629 (Cal.) a grantor that signs a deed by a wrong name (Edmund Jones) with his correct name in the body of the deed (Edward Jones) does not invalidate the conveyance.
      Indiana: *Zann v Haller*, 71 Ind. 136, 1880 WL 6236 (Ind.), 23 Am.Rep. 193 a woman signing a mortgage deed with her first name only, 'Catharine', accepted as a signature.
6   New York (1812): *Mackay v J. and L. Bloodgood*, 9 Johns. 285 the affixing of the name and seal of a firm by one partner binds the other partner.
7   Maine: *Sawtelle v Wardwell*, 56 Me. 146, 1868 WL 1770 (Me.) surname of attorney on the back of a writ of endorsement a sufficient signature, although see the dissenting judgment of Kent J.
8   Kentucky (1894): *Word v Whipps*, 28 S.W. 151, 16 Ky. Law Rep. 403 in the absence of fraud or suspicious circumstances, the misspelling of a name does not affect the validity of a signature, 'A. J. Whpps' written instead of 'A. J. Whipps.'
      Wells v Lewis, 190 Ky. 626, 228 S.W. 3 the signature 'Ant Nanie' appended to a letter as a testamentary writing is a sufficient signature. (1921)
      Pennsylvania (1890): *Appeal of Knox*, 131 P. 220, 18 A. 1021, 6 L.R.A. 353, 17 Am.St.Rep. 798.

Texas (1921): *Barnes v Horne*, 233 S.W. 859 a letter by the deceased to his brother considered a will, and signed at the end with the shortened version of his name 'Ed' accepted as a signature.

9   91 A. 220, 244 Pa. 574.

THE USE OF INITIALS

Statute of Frauds

2.19   The use of initials has been held sufficient to be a mark or signature to indicate the intent of a party under the provisions of the Statute of Frauds, as in the case of *Phillimore v Barry*.[1] Messrs Fector and Minet of Dover stored a quantity of rum, the cargo of a Danish prize, which was to be sold by auction in various lots on 28 April 1808. Before the day of the sale, the defendants wrote to Fector and Minet to buy 13 puncheons of the rum. As a result, Mr John Minet Fector of the firm bid for several lots, which were duly knocked down to him. The auctioneer wrote down in the printed catalogue the initials 'I.M.F' opposite each lot sold to the defendant. On 11 May 1808, the defendants subsequently wrote a letter to Fector and Minet, recognising and approving the purchase. Unfortunately, the warehouse accidentally caught fire on 18 May 1808, and a quantity of gunpowder stored in the building exploded, destroying the rum. There was no evidence that the deposit was paid. The defendants claimed the contract was void under the Statute of Frauds on the basis that there was no memorandum in writing. It was also submitted that the auctioneer was not the authorized agent of the defendants, and even if he were, the inclusion of the initials against each lot could not be considered a memorandum of agreement. It was also contended that the rum remained at the risk of the sellers for 30 days, and the property did not vest with the defendant. Lord Ellenborough held that Mr Minet was the agent to the defendants, and that his initials as written by the auctioneer in the catalogue, together with the defendant's letter confirming the sale, constituted a sufficient memorandum in writing to satisfy the Statute of Frauds. He also held that the property vested absolutely in the purchasers from the moment of sale, and the provision of storage for 30 days was part of the consideration for which the purchase money was to be paid. Whilst the finding by Lord Ellenborough was not relevant to whether the initials represented a signature, nevertheless they were considered part of the evidence to demonstrate a contract existed between the parties.

In *Chichester v Cobb*,[2] the defendant wrote a letter to Mary Ann Williams, as follows:

'Kensington, 21st July 1865

My dear M. A. – So soon as all pecuniary and necessary arrangements are made to constitute an unquestionable legal marriage as proposed, I will be prepared to pay over for your behalf 300*l.*, and concur in every practicable measure by which an equitable share, or its equivalent, in the settled property can be assured to you. I shall expect to see Edward here this evening, as requested in my note to him of last evening. – Yours ever affectionately, E.C.'

After the marriage, the defendant refused to pay the £300. Blackburn and Shee JJ in the Queen's Bench agreed the initials constituted a sufficient signing of the contract or memorandum to satisfy the Statute of Frauds.

1   1 Camp 512; 170 ER 1040.
2   (1866) 14 L.T.N.S. 433.

Judicial use

2.20   There is one recorded case where a judge in England and Wales signed a bill of indictment with his initials. In *R v Morais*,[1] a bill of indictment was signed in manuscript 'Cor. The Honourable Mr. Justice Roch' and underneath, in the judge's handwriting, the words 'Leave to prefer' and his initials, 'J. R.' with the date '23.9.87.' and the words 'A Justice of the High Court.' This form of signature was held not to be a signature by Lord Lane, CJ in the Court of Appeal. A new trial was ordered. Of significance, no case law on signatures was cited or referred to in the appeal.

Judicial officers in the United States have used initials, although the decisions do not always approve of the use of initials in the absence of a full signature.[2] In the 1933 Federal case of *George A. Ohl & Co., v A. L. Smith Iron Works*[3] the use of a judge's initials followed by 'D.J.' was held as a signature authenticating a bill of exceptions, and the initials 'D. J.' were added for the purpose of indicating his judicial office. Hughes CJ commented on the use of initials at 176–177:

'Signature by initials has been held to be sufficient under the Statute of Frauds and the Statute of Wills, and in other transactions. It has been held in some states that a different rule obtains in the case of the official signature of certain judicial officers, but the Congress has not established such a rule for the judges of the federal courts. Nor, in the absence of special statutory requirement, is there a uniform custom in relation to official signatures. It may be assumed that a requirement of the officer's signature, without more, means that he shall write his name or his distinctive appellation; but the question remains as to what writing of that character is to be deemed sufficient for the purpose of authenticating his official act. There is no rule that he shall adhere to the precise form of his name as it appears in his commission. The full name of the officer may or may not be used. Not infrequently Christian names are omitted, in part or altogether, or are abbreviated or indicated by initials. In some of the most important communications on behalf of the federal government, only the surname of the officer is used. When an officer authenticates his official act by affixing his initials he does not entirely omit to use his name;

he simply abbreviates it; he uses a combination of letters which are part of it. Undoubtedly that method is informal, but we think that it is clearly a method of "signing." It cannot be said in such a case that he has utterly failed to "sign," so that his authentication of his official act, in the absence of further statutory requirement, is to be regarded as absolutely void.'

The cases of *Origet v United States*[4] and *Kinney v United States Fidelity & Guaranty Company*[5] were neither cited nor referred to as being overruled, although the comments by Hughes CJ appear to make it clear that initials are acceptable. The initials of a judge on a judgment were held to be sufficient in the Illinois case of *Robertson v Robertson*,[6] in which Karns J made it clear, at 715, that spurious arguments were not welcome, in that '... plaintiffs' arguments attacking the form of the judgment are without merit.' In the 1905 Nebraska case of *Griffith v Bonawitz*,[7] the initials of two judges, P. A. Buller and A. J. Flatung, were written on the back of a number of ballots, and held to signatures. Ames C suggested, at 329, that 'If history teaches any lesson relative to the subject, or relative to any subject, for that matter, it is that electors are far less likely to be guilty of malconduct than are election and returning boards, supervisors and inspectors.' He went on to indicate further at 329:

'Buller was sworn as a witness, and testified to having written the letters on the ballots himself with no sinister intent, which, indeed, is not suspected. He further testified that he wrote them as, and intending them for, his signature, and that he was accustomed to so using them, instead of his full name, upon his letters and some of his business documents – particularly weight or scale certificates or checks. The object for which the indorsements are required is evident. It is for the purpose of the identification and authentication of the ballots, so as to render it certain that none not officially issued shall be used for voting. That this object was as effectively accomplished, and is likely so to be, by the means adopted, as it would have been by the use of the full name, or of the surname and the first two initials, is not disputed or doubted; and we think the spirit, if not the letter, of the statute, was satisfied.'

1   [1988] 3 All ER 161, CA.
2   Federal (1888): *Origet v United States*, 125 U.S. 240, 8 S.Ct. 846, 31 L.Ed. 743 the initials 'A. B.' held not to be a signature of the judge, nor sufficient authentication of a bill of exceptions.
        Kinney v United States Fidelity & Guaranty Company, 222 U.S. 283, 32 S.Ct. 101, 56 L.Ed. 200 a paper in the record styled 'Exceptions to the Charge to the Jury' upon which the initials 'J. P. McP., Trial Judge' are placed is not a bill of exceptions. (1911)
        Kentucky (1934): *Wurts v Newsome*, 253 Ky. 38, 68 S.W.2d 448 there was no signature where a judge signed a ballot with his surname and initial, or with his initials.
3   288 U.S. 170, 53 S.Ct. 340, 77 L.Ed. 681.
4   125 U.S. 240, 8 S.Ct. 846, 31 L.Ed. 743.
5   222 U.S. 283, 32 S.Ct. 101, 56 L.Ed. 200.
6   462 N.E.2d 712 (Ill.App. 5 Dist. 1984).
7   73 Neb. 622, 103 N.W. 327.

Wills

2.21 Initials have been used in wills, as in the case of *Re Savory's Goods*,[1] where the testatrix executed the will by writing her initials in the presence of two witnesses who duly attested. The solicitor was not satisfied that her initials would suffice, so directed her to make her mark again. She did so, in the presence of the same two witnesses. However, as the first witness signed the will for a second time, the ink ran out. The second witness traced over their name. In this case, Sir Herbert Jenner Fust held that the second execution must fail, because the second witness did not affix their signature to the will, but the first was quite sufficient, even though the testatrix only signed with her initials.[2]

In South Africa, initials appended to a will were held to be signed in accordance with Ordinance 15 of 1845 in the case of *In re Trollip*.[3] The decision in *Van Vuuren v Van Vuuren* 2 Searle 116 was overruled, and the decision in the case of *In re Ebden's Will* 4 Juta 495, approved. De Villiers CJ, observed pertinently, at 245, that 'If a mark is a sufficient signature, *à fortiori* initials must be sufficient.'

A modern example of a will in which initials were accepted as sufficient evidence of a signature is that of the Canadian case of *Re Schultz*[4] in which the testator wrote a holograph will, beginning 'I, Lawrence Ivan Schultz', the words of which were crossed out, and the following line continued 'this is the last will and testament of me, L. I. S., of Y.G., in the Province of Saskatchewan in the country of Canada made of this day December 28, 1983.' It was accepted that the document was a holograph will, based on the proposition that the testator identified his wife and children by their initials, and it was therefore to be concluded that he intended his initials to form his signature.

1   15 Jur 1042.
2   See also *In the Goods of Clark* 2 Curt. 329, 163 ER 428 where the deceased, too ill to sign his will, requested his wife, Mary Butler, to sign for him, which she did, with her mark. Sir Herbert Jenner Fust in the Prerogative Court considered this to be a sufficient compliance with the Act, although the executrix lost a legacy that was granted to her under the terms of the will; *In the Goods of Christian* 2 Rob. Ecc. 110, 163 ER 1260 where H. H. Christian, a Rear Admiral in the Royal Navy, died on 31 August 1849, leaving a will that included the signature of a witness in the form of initials, which Sir Herbert Jenner Fust in the Prerogative Court determined was a sufficient subscription; for a line of cases with respect to wills, see *Re Blewitt's Goods* (1879–81) 5 PD 116.
3   1895 12 SC 243.
4   (1984) 8 DLR (4th) 147.

Rights in property

2.22 In *Hill v Hill*,[1] a lease was executed on 18 December 1936 in respect of a property situated at 9 Nimmings Road, Blackheath, Birmingham, between the landlord, James Frederick Hill and Mr F. Hill, his son. The son lived at this address and carried on a business as a newsagent, stationer, tobacconist and fancy goods dealer. His father lived next door. The term began on 25 December 1936 for five years at a rental of £52 payable over 52 equal instalments of £1. Each week, the figure of 20s was recorded as being paid by Mr Hill, and his father initialled each entry with the initials 'F. H.' As the lease drew near its end, both parties hastened to renew the lease by a short written memorandum prepared by the son. The son gave the new rent book the heading 'Renewed lease, December 25, 1941.' As before, the father initialled each payment of rent, with the exception of one week's payment, when another person acknowledged receipt of the payment by placing their initials in the rent book. The father died in January 1943. The will was proved on 29 January 1943. The son then gave notice to exercise an option, under the terms of the original lease, to buy the property. It was held that the initials inserted by the father not only referred to and authenticated the words 'Renewed lease, December 25, 1941' but also served to acknowledge receipt of the rent. Morton LJ observed:

'The description: "Renewed lease, December 25, 1941," is a loose one, but it fits nothing else than those two linked documents, which together constitute, in rather loose parlance, a renewed lease, being a lease with its renewal notice.'[2]

Somvervell LJ concluded the memorandum was an offer by the son to renew the lease, which in turn was accepted orally by the father, and the rent book of 1942 with the father's initials was itself a memorandum of the agreement.

1   [1947] 1 Ch 231.
2   [1947] 1 Ch 231 at 241.

Guarantees

2.23   Directors adding their initials to a clause providing a guarantee in a contract were held bound by the guarantee under the provisions of s 2 of the Contracts Enforcement Act 1956 in the New Zealand case of *Doughty-Pratt Group Limited v Perry Castle*.[1]

1   [1995] 2 NZLR 398 (CA).

Voting

2.24   In the nineteenth century, under the provisions of s 32 of the Municipal Corporation Act of 5 & 6 Will. 4 c76, voting papers had to be signed with the name of the burgess voting. In 1852, in the case of *R v Avery*,[1] it was held that a person can sign as they ordinarily write their signature, such as, in this instance, the surname and initial of the Christian name. During the appeal in this case, the Attorney General used an argument that is familiar today, implying that the register of the electoral roll is perfect, amongst other things, at 439–430:

'The "name" of a party, according to its general acceptation, implies both the christian names and surname at full length. That is the only way in which it would appear on the burgess-roll, and it should be so signed to the voting paper.

[Lord Campbell, CJ – The legislature expressly requires that in regard to the person voted for, but it has used different language as to the voter.]

Effect cannot be given to the policy and spirit of the act without so reading it. If an initial be sufficient, it would be equally competent to leave out the christian name altogether. Suppose the initial applied to two persons, as John Smith and James Smith, who were both on the roll, whose name is to be ticked off? The mayor is only entitled by section 34 to ask three questions, neither of which would avoid the difficulty.

[Lord Campbell, CJ – The same difficulty would arise if there were two John Smiths on the roll and they each signed in full.]'

This particular argument put forward by the Attorney General did not succeed.

1   21 LJQB 430.

United States of America

2.25   In the United States of America, decisions relating to the use of initials cover a range of situations, including bills,[1] cheques,[2] the Statute of Frauds,[3] trusts[4] and wills,[5] although the evidence does not always indicate the initials served as a means of authentication, as in the 1945 Wisconsin case of *North American Seed Co., v Cedarburg Supply Co.*,[6] where the initials 'H. Z.' for Harvey Zirtzlaff, were placed in such an odd position, that it was determined they did not serve as a signature in accordance with s 207 of the Restatement of Contracts.

Attempts are made on occasions to retrieve a small scintilla of hope from an otherwise impossible position, which was what was attempted in the federal eighth circuit case of *Vess Beverages, Inc., v The Paddington Corporation*.[7] Vess made and sold soft drinks in St Louis, and Paddington is an international firm that imported and distributed liquor. Vess took over production of the Steidl wine cooler, a brand owned by Paddington, but a year after the agreement, sales of the wine cooler had declined and there was little or no profit in the product. Vess expressed an interest in buying the wine cooler, and negotiations began in June 1986. Correspondence ensued, and a number of meetings took place between representatives of the parties. Eventually, when Vess thought it had an agreement, it transpired that the wine cooler was sold to another entity. Vess took action against Paddington for repudiation of the contract. Vess attempted to show there was a memorandum in writing sufficient to conform to the Statute of Frauds, in the form of a note as part of a list of those attending a meeting. The person taking the note added the initials of those attending to the paper. The argument that these initials constituted a signature was not successful. It was held that they did not qualify as a means of authentication. Had each person present added their own initials with the purpose of agreeing with the content, this would have been different, as pointed out by Magill CJ at 655: 'If each participant had signed his own initials to signify that the notes were an accurate expression of the oral agreement, or if Keller alone had signed them to indicate that the notes were his, this would be a different case.'

1   New York (1845): *Palmer v Stevens*, 1 Denio 471.
2   New York (1831): *The Merchants' Bank v Spicer*, 6 Wend. 443 the initials of the defendant, 'P. W. S.', on a check held to be a sufficient indorsement.
3   Federal (1852): *The Salmon Falls Manufacturing Company v Goddard*, 55 U.S. 446, 14 How. 446, 1852 WL 6760 (U.S.Mass.), 14 L.Ed. 493 where the initials 'R. M. M.' and 'W. W. G.' sufficient to be signatures.
    Federal 5th Circuit (1934): *Jones v Fox Film Corporation*, 68 F.2d 116 the initials 'J. T. J' for John T. Jones held to be a signature.
    Federal 7th Circuit: *Monetti, S.P.A. v Anchor Hocking Corporation*, 931 F.2d 1178 (7th Cir. 1991) the initials 'SS/mh' typed by a secretary held to be the signature of Steve Schneider, who dictated the letter to the secretary.
    Iowa (1923): *Burns v Burrows*, 196 N.W. 62 the initials 'R. A. S.' held to be a signature of R. A. Santee.
    Massachusetts (1946): *Irving v Goodimate, Co.*, 320 Mas. 454, 70 N.E.2d 414, 171 A.L.R. 326 where the initials 'RL/s' of the president of the company were typed at the bottom of a letter.
    Sanborn v Flagler, 9 Allen 474, 91 Mass. 474, 1864 WL 3510 (Mass.) initials of both parties, 'J. H. F.' and 'J. B. R.', were signatures.
    Michigan (1933): *Archbold v Industrial Land Co.*, 264 Mich. 289, 249 N.W. 858 an instrument signed 'Approved: J. S. L.' and 'O.K. with me: O. T. B.' and 'O.K. with me: O. T. M.' held to be signed by O. G. Bowker and J. S. Lille, respectively president and vice-president of the Industrial Land Company, and O. T. Morse, vice-president of the American Blower Corporation.
    Borkowski v Kolodziejski, 332 Mich. 589, 52 N.W.2d 348 defendant signed his name with the initials 'L. S.' after it. (1952)
    Missouri: *Kamada, M.D., v RX Group Limited*, 639 S.W.2d 146, (Mo.App. 1982) initials on a lease sufficient.
    New Jersey (1857): *Smith v Howell*, 11 N.J.Eq. 349, 1857 WL 4462 (N.J.Ch.), 3 Stockt. 349 the initials of Walter Kirkpatrick used by him as his signature to form a trust.
    Crabtree v Elizabeth Arden Sales Corporation, 305 N.Y. 48, 110 N.E.2d 551 the initials of Robert P. Johns, executive vice-president and general manager, 'RPJ' subscribed to a payroll card, held to be a signature for the purposes of establishing an employment contract. (1953)
    Washington (1907): *Degginger v Martin*, 48 Wash. 1, 92 P. 674 the initials of an agent, J. M. Martin, were added by him in his own hand underneath his typewritten name, contract held to be sufficiently executed.
4   California (1943): *Weiner v Mullaney*, 59 Cal.App.2d 620, 140 P.2d 704 the initials of George J. Mullaney, 'G. J. M.', typed at the end of several letters to his sister comprised a signature sufficiently signed in the formation of a trust.
5   Virginia (1915): *Pilcher v Pilcher*, 117 Va. 356, 84 S.E. 667, L.R.A. 1915D 902 a will written by the testator 'I give to my wife, Alice McCabe Pilcher, all of my property, real and personal. E. M. P.' held to be sufficiently signed.

6   247 Wis. 31, 18 N.W.2d 466, 159 A.L.R. 250.
7   941 F.2d 651 (8th Cir. 1991).

Statute of Frauds

2.26 People use many variations of their name when signing a document, and the use of first name or family name is not unusual. The question about what could be construed as a signature was argued before Lord Denham CJ and Patteson, Coleridge and Wrightman JJ in the case of *Lobb and Knight v Stanley* in 1844.[1] Interestingly, the comments made both by counsel and Patteson J in this case seem to imply that contemporaries would have preferred to tighten up the meaning of a signature as it stood in the mid-nineteenth century. However, by this time, it is clear the authorities were too well established to be reviewed or ignored. In this instance, one Stanley, a certified bankrupt, gave a written promise signed by him after his bankruptcy. Three undated letters were produced, one of which read 'Mr Stanley begs to inform Mr Lobb that he will be glad to give him a promissory note or bill for the amount of Mr Stanley's account, payable at three months, as Mr Stanley has of late been put to heavy expenses, and hopes this arrangement will be satisfactory to Mr Lobb. 3 Crescent. Thursday morning.' At the trial before Lord Denman CJ, a verdict was found for Lobb, and leave was given to appeal. It was submitted by Whately, counsel for Stanley, that all the previous decisions relating to what was meant to be a signature were not correct: 'Those decisions, however, are scarcely to be defended on principle; and, if the question were new, probably a different doctrine would be adopted.'[2] This view was noted and commented upon by Patteson J:

> 'It is true that the word "signed" occurs in the statute: and, if this had been the first time that we were called upon to put a construction on that word, and if the decisions on the Statute of Frauds had not occurred, I should perhaps be slow to say that this was a signature.'[3]

Lord Denham CJ agreed, that in one sense the letters were not signed. However, he then considered the intrinsic evidence of the documents, and pointed out that '... it is a signature of the party when he authenticates the instrument by writing his name in the body. Here, it is true, the whole name is not written, but only "Mr Stanley". I think more is not necessary.'[4] Coleridge J reinforced the significance of the mechanism by which the document was authenticated, when he pointed out that 'Is it not enough if a party, at the beginning of a document, writes his name so as to govern what follows? Does he not then use his name as a signature?'[5] It was unanimously agreed that Stanley signed the documents. Stanley wrote the letters himself. He identified himself by surname in the body of the letters. By identifying himself in this way, he demonstrated his intention that the recipient should rely on the promise contained in the letter. The signature was, in effect, his assertion, by writing his surname, that the contents of the letters are to be acted upon by the recipient.

For examples where a note written in the third person has been accepted, see the 1811 case of *Morrison v Turnour*,[6] whether a note written in the third person is capable of amounting to a contract and signed within the Statute of Frauds was eventually withdrawn by the defendant, but the Lord Chancellor, Lord Eldon did offer the following comments at 182–183 'I fully agree, that this Court has gone much further than a wholesome attention to this Statute with reference to the specific performance of agreements will justify; but upon this particular point has not gone further than Courts of Law: what is the construction of the Statute, what within the legal intent of it will amount to a signing, being the same question in equity and law.' Also note the case of *Propert v Parker*,[7] where a contract for the purchase of a leasehold house was written by the defendant, but not signed by him. It started the agreement in the third person 'Mr Wilmot Parker has agreed.' In an action for specific performance, counsel for the defendant cited *Morrison v Turnour* in support of the objection. Sir John Leach, the Master of the Rolls, considered the contract was sufficient under the Statute of Frauds, and the addition of the name of the defendant was a sufficient signing.

1   (1844) 5 QB 574; 114 ER 1366.
2   (1844) 5 QB 574 at 579.
3   (1844) 5 QB 574 at 582.
4   (1844) 5 QB 574 at 581.
5   (1844) 5 QB 574 at 582.
6   18 Ves. 175, 34 ER 1204; 18 Ves. Jun. 175, 34 ER 284.
7   [1830] 1 Russ & M 625; 39 ER 240.

Deeds

2.27   In Scotland, Lord Dervaird held that a deed executed by the subscription of the granter's surname alone is not of itself improbative or invalid in the case of *American Express Europe Ltd v Royal Bank of Scotland plc*,[1] following the decision in *Gordon v Murray*[2] (where it was upheld that the subscription to an assignation, being 'Fullerton of that Ilk' without a Christian name, was valid). The case of *Earl of Traquair v Janet Gibson*[3] in which the use of initials was used, was also canvassed. For the modern position in Scotland, see s 7(2) of the Requirements of Writing (Scotland) Act 1995.

1   1989 SCLR 333, 1989 SLT 650, OH.
2   (1765) Mor. 16818.
3   (1724) Mor. 16809.

THE USE OF A TRADE NAME

2.28 The use of a trade name by a party may be sufficient to indicate an intention to enter into a contract. In the case of *Cohen v Roche*,[1] Mr G W Roche traded as Roche & Roche as an auctioneer in Fulham at premises known as South Kensington Auction Gallery. On 18 December 1925, Mr Roche held an auction of modern and antique furniture. One of the lots, number 145 was described as 'set of 8 genuine Hepplewhite chairs, comprising 2 elbow chairs and 6 standard ditto, with carved back and splat and reeded legs.' This lot was entered by Mr Roche personally and was knocked down to Mr Frederick Cohen, who traded in the name of Fredericks, as a dealer in antique furniture, for £60. As each lot was knocked down, Mr Roche wrote a note against the entry in the catalogue. In this instance, he wrote the words '£60. Fredericks.' against the entry for lot 145. Mr Roche subsequently refused to deliver the chairs to Mr Cohen, who then took action for delivery up of the goods. In his defence, Mr Roche claimed that there was no signature by him and even if there was a signature, there was no memorandum of the terms of the contract. In reaching his judgment, McCardie J followed the decision in *Saunderson v Jackson*[2] and *Schneider v Norris*.[3] The printed name of the firm on the front page of the auction catalogue constituted a signature by Mr Roche. He considered that the insertion of the name in the catalogue served to authenticate the catalogue, and this authentication was reinforced '… in that the defendant himself wrote down in his auctioneer's book the price realized by lot 145, and also entered the names of the purchasers.'[4] The next question was whether there was sufficient memorandum of the terms of the contract so as to comply with s 4 of the Sale of Goods Act 1893. He thought it plain that Mr Roche intended to add the name of each buyer next to the lot they bought, which he did, and the name of Fredericks could indicate nothing else. It was written next to the description of lot 145 and above and below it were entered the names of the buyers of other lots. After discussing a number of conflicting decisions on this point, McCardie J reached the conclusion that there was a sufficient and duly signed memorandum of the sale, and as a result, there was an enforceable contract between the parties.

1 [1927] 1 KB 169.
2 (1800) 2 Bos & Pul 238; 126 ER 1257.
3 (1814) 2 M & S 237; 105 ER 388.
4 [1927] 1 KB 169 at 175 and 176.

A PARTIAL SIGNATURE

Wills

2.29 Sudden changes in life expectancy can cause a person, as they near the end of their life, to review the arrangements for the disposal of their worldly goods. On such occasions, ensuring the disposition is made in the proper form can be overtaken by the imminent demise of the testatrix. In *Re Chalcraft's Goods*,[1] Ellen Chalcraft, on the day she died, signed a document drawn up by Helen Chalcraft, one of her daughters, as follows '96, Osborne Road, Acton. I wish my house to be sold and £500 made over to Mr C F West for purchase of 33, Stilecroft Gardens, E. Chal' and signed by two witnesses. The facts are that Mrs Chalcraft, who had four daughters and one son, had been suffering from cancer for some time. Towards the end of her life, it was agreed that she would go to live with one of her daughters and her husband, Mr and Mrs West, in a new house they intended to buy. However, they could not afford to fund the new house without additional financial help from Mrs Chalcraft. It was also intended that her unmarried daughter, Helen Chalcraft, who had been looking after her mother for some time, should also live with Mr and Mrs West. A few days before her health deteriorated, Mrs Chalcraft wrote to her solicitor, instructing him to sell her house for £700 and to pay £500 towards the new house that Mr and Mrs West were buying. As Mrs Chalcraft's life ebbed away, she was in great pain, and her doctor administered greater doses of morphia to alleviate the pain. When it was recognised that she did not have long to live, Helen Chalcraft summoned two neighbours to act as witnesses to sign a proposed codicil. Mrs Chalcraft was not able to speak. In the presence of those in the room, Helen Chalcraft wrote out the content of the document, and asked her mother to nod her head if she agreed with the content of the document, which she did. The pad was then held out to Mrs Chalcraft, who then took hold of the pen and began to write. She wrote 'E. Chal', but never completed her name, because she died. The signature came to an abrupt end. The judge, Willmer J, had a number of issues to reach a conclusion upon, one of which was whether the testatrix knew of and approved the contents of the document, and another, whether what the deceased wrote was intended to be her signature. In the light of the evidence of her intention to sell her house and give a portion of it to one of her daughters to buy another house, it was inferred that Mrs Chalcraft intended it to be a testamentary document and thus the contents were known to and approved by the deceased. Willmer J found making a decision as to whether the partial signature could be considered to be her signature within the provisions of the Wills Act 1837 to be a '... very difficult point to decide.'[2] He suggested that there must be a question of degree involved in any decision, and he should interpret the words used by the Lord Chancellor in *Hindmarch v Charlton*[3] broadly. Considering all the facts of the case, he asked whether he could '... draw the inference that what she wrote was intended by her to be the best that she could do by way of writing her name.'[4] Taking into account the circumstances the deceased found herself in at the end of her life, Willmer J decided that the mark she made, 'E. Chal', did amount to a signature.

1   [1948] P 222.
2   [1948] P 222 at 232.

3   (1861) 8 HL Cas 160 at 167 'I will lay down this as my notion of the law: that to make a valid subscription of a witness, there must be the name or some mark which is intended to represent the name.'
4   [1948] P 222 at 233.

WORDS OTHER THAN A NAME

Wills

2.30   Occasionally, people will not refer to each other by name, but by reference to their relationship with each other. A good example is between parents and children, where a child may continue to call their parties 'mum' and 'dad', 'mater' or 'pater' or some other form of address for the rest of their lives. Equally, parents may well do the same with their children, especially when writing to them. They may not sign a letter or card with their name, but with the words 'mother' or 'father'. In the case of *Re Cook's Estate Murison v Cook*,[1] the testatrix drew up a holograph will on two sheets of notepaper, which was duly properly attested by two competent witnesses. The document began 'I, Emmie Cook of 38 Maida Vale, W 9 declare this to be my last will …' and after disposing of her property, the will ended 'Please Leslie be kind to Dot. Your loving mother.' Leslie was her son and Dot referred to one of her daughters. The question was whether the words 'Your loving mother' constituted a signature within the meaning of the Wills Act 1837. Collingwood J, having cited various authorities, came to the conclusion that the testatrix intended the words 'Your loving mother' to identify herself as the person attesting. The most persuasive comment to support his decision in this context was the opinion of Lord Campbell LC in *Hindmarch v Charlton*, who offered the opinion that 'there must be either the name or some mark which is intended to represent the name.'[2] This case illustrates the concern that judges have in establishing whether the person signing the document intended the words they used to apply to the terms of the document they signed, and in the United States there is a line of case law to illustrate the use of similar words and phrases,[3] although the 1940 Californian case of *Brendan v Brendan*[4] demonstrated this liberal approach can only be taken so far. In this instance, a letter was typewritten by a father to his son, and his wife added further handwritten script on the reverse of the letter: 'Dad signed this with his signature and also 'Dad' below. The signature in case you might want to use it. Lawfully. Mother.' The word 'Mother' was capable of being a legally binding signature, but taken not to be because is was assumed, in the absence of any evidence, that the language illustrated that she did not believe the word 'Dad' was a legally binding signature.

1   [1960] 1 All ER 689.
2   (1861) 8 HL Cas 160 at 167.
3   Arkansas (1906): *Arendt v Arendt*, 80 Ark. 204, 96 S.W. 982 after William Arendt shot himself, a letter addressed to his wife was discovered, including the statement 'Whatever I have

in wordly goods, it is my wish that you should possess them.' At the end of the letter, he signed with a shortened version of his first name, 'Will.' Held to be a signature by the members of the jury and affirmed on appeal.

Cartwright v Cartwright, 158 Ark. 278, 250 S.W. 11 the abbreviation 'Lus' a sufficient signature to a letter testamentary in its effect. (1923)

California (1923): *In re Henderson's Estate*, 196 Cal. 623, 239 P. 938 'From A Loving Mother' a sufficient signature.

In re Button's Estate, 277 P. 758 *reversed* 287 P. 964 words 'Love from Muddy' a valid signature. (1930)

Kentucky (1894): *Word v Whipps*, 28 S.W. 151, 16 Ky. Law Rep. 403 in the absence of fraud or suspicious circumstances, the misspelling of a name does not affect the validity of a signature, 'A. J. Whpps' written instead of 'A. J. Whipps.'

Wells v Lewis, 190 Ky. 626, 228 S.W. 3 the signature 'Ant Nanie' appended to a letter as a testamentary writing is a sufficient signature. (1921)

Pennsylvania (1890): *Appeal of Knox*, 131 P. 220, 18 A. 1021, 6 L.R.A. 353, 17 Am.St.Rep. 798.

In re Kimmel's Estate, 278 P. 435, 123 A. 405, 31 A.L.R. 678 a testamentary letter ending with 'Father' held to be signed. (1924)

Texas (1921): *Barnes v Horne*, 233 S.W. 859 a letter by the deceased to his brother considered a will, and signed at the end with the shortened version of his name 'Ed' accepted as a signature.

4   103 P.2d 622.

AN IDENTIFYING PHRASE

Statute of Frauds

2.31   In contrast to the previous examples above, the use of the phrase 'mother' was not held to be a signature in the earlier case of *Selby v Selby*.[1] In this instance, a son was promised an annuity by his mother, evidence of which could be inferred from letters written by her upon the occasion of his marriage. The question was whether a letter addressed to the son, beginning 'My Dear Robert' and ending in the words 'Do me the justice to believe me the most affectionate of mothers', was sufficiently signed within the meaning of the Statute of Frauds 1677. The Master of the Rolls held that it was not sufficient that a party to a document can be identified in such a way, because the Statute required the document to be signed. He rejected the proposition that where the writer of the document has been identified, so it could be construed that there was a signature within the meaning of the Statute. The son failed to recover the arrears of the annuity.

It is instructive to compare the decision of the Master of the Rolls in *Selby v Selby* to that of the comment made by Maule J in *Morton v Copeland*, that a 'Signature does not necessarily mean writing a person's Christian and surname, but any mark which indicates it as the act of the party'[2] and the decision by Lord Hunter in *Rhodes v Peterson*[3] from Scotland. In this case, Mrs Dorothy Macandrew died on 4 July 1969, leaving two sons and one daughter. On 18 October 1966 she wrote a letter to her daughter in her own handwriting. Part of the letter read 'I want you to have 63 Merchiston and all the contents, the furniture, linen, silver and my treasures, etc., when I am gone so that I can rest in peace in the knowledge that you are not homeless …' and signed the letter 'Lots of Love. Mum.' Lord Hunter was required to determine whether the word 'Mum' was sufficient to establish the holograph will was duly signed. He noted some latitude in the law of Scotland towards the meaning of what is meant by a signature, and went on to observe, at 100(a):

> 'It clearly is not essential that the subscription should consist of a surname preceded by either an initial or initials or a Christian name or names, nor is it essential that the surname should appear at all or, indeed, that there should be comprised in the subscription or signature any of the Christian names or surnames written in full.'

Lord Hunter also commented that the use of a familiar or pet name could be a valid signature provided it was proved that the writer signed their name usually in such a way. He went on to suggest, at 100(b), that the use of such a form of signature was '… as apt to signify that the writing is the completed and concluded expression of the writer's intention as a signature by initials or by abbreviated Christian name.' In particular, he considered it settled authority that where a holograph writing consisted of a name other than the Christian name or names or initials followed by the surname of the writer, that there must be sufficient evidence to identify whatever name was used by the writer (in this case, 'Mum'), was used regularly. The form by which a person identifies themself does not necessarily affect the validity of the document, especially where a person writes a document with their own handwriting and uses a phrase as a means of identification.

The facts of these cases do not appear to offer any features to distinguish them. In the earlier case, it may be inferred, perhaps, that the Master of the Rolls was content to let the son in question make his own way in life, unaided by financial help that was promised in a letter at the time he was married.

1   (1817) 3 Mer 2; 36 ER 1.
2   (1855) 16 C B 516 at 535. A footnote was added to this comment: 'Provided it be proved or admitted to be genuine, and be the accustomed mode of signature of the party.'; 139 ER 861.
3   (1972) SLT 98.

ABBREVIATION OF A NAME

Solicitors Act 1974

2.32   Professional firms tend to accumulate long names over time, although the present fashion is to adopt a shortened version, in line with current marketing strategies. Long names can be tedious, and one partner in the firm of Bartlett Gluckstein Crawley & de Reya sought to reduce the requirement of signing the firm's name in full, and one of their client's decided to challenge this practice.[1] In this instance, Mr F X Byrne was sent a bill of costs. The bill had a printed heading with the full name of the partnership, its address and the names of the partners. The bill was signed 'Bartletts' by a partner. The full name was printed below the signature but not immediately beneath it. The bill was sent with a letter headed with the firm's full name, which was also signed in the same abbreviated name. Mr Byrne refused to pay on the basis that the signature on the bill did not comply with s 69(2) of the Solicitors Act 1974. The firm brought an action to recover the costs. Sitting at Westminster county court, His Honour Judge McDonnell gave judgment for Mr Byrne. He agreed the sum was owed, but considered the bill was not signed in accordance with the required form. On appeal to the Court of Appeal, Civil Division, Fox LJ determined that the bill was properly signed, and offered the following comments:

> 'There had been legislation relating to solicitors' bills of costs over several centuries. The question was whether as a matter of construction it could be said that the bill was signed "in the name of the firm".
>
> Those words could not require that the whole name of the firm, which in the present case was a long one, had to be set out in full. If a solicitor was required to sign in his own name he did not have to sign all his names in full nor write all his initials.
>
> If the name of the firm had been printed immediately below the signature 'Bartletts' it could hardly have been doubted that the bill was signed in the name of the firm.
>
> There was a signature on the bill of costs by a solicitor of the Supreme Court. That signature was intended to authenticate the bill and the defendant treated it as a bill issued with the authority of the firm itself....
>
> The signature could only be regarded as a signature in the name of the firm, and anyone reading it would take it to be a convenient and obvious contraction of the full name of the firm.'[2]

Bush J agreed with this analysis and the appeal was allowed. Interestingly, between the trial and the appeal, a fresh bill of costs was prepared and delivered to Mr Byrne, signed with the full name of the firm. It was paid before the hearing in the Court of Appeal.

1   (1983) *The Times* 14 January; (1983) 127 SJ 69, Court of Appeal (Civil Division).
2   (1983) *The Times* 14 January.

Impression of a mark

A SEAL IMPRINT

Wills

2.33   The impression of a seal on documents has a long history, especially on wills, and their use continues today. A seal as a means of authentication will invariably accompany documents issued by the Crown, and seals will occasionally be used to demonstrate that an envelope has not been opened. An early case after the passing of the Statute of Frauds where a seal was the subject of a decision is that of *Lemayne v Stanley*.[1] In this instance, the devisor wrote his will in his own hand, beginning 'In the name of God, Amen, I John Stanley make this my last will and testament', and added his seal to the will, but did not sign it. Three witnesses subscribed the will in his presence. The members of the court unanimously held that this was a good will, because he had written it himself and identified himself in the will by name. However, they did not agree on the question of whether the imprint of the seal was sufficient to satisfy the requirement for a signature. Three members of the court, North, Wyndham and Charlton JJ, with Levinz J dissenting, considered signing is no more than a mark, and sealing was a sufficient mark. However, the report, which was prepared by Thomas Vickers in 1797 and is a record made by Sir Creswell Levinz, who was a judge in the Court of Common Pleas, is ambiguous. The report states the majority held the mark was sufficient because 'for *signum* is no more than a *mark*, and sealing is a sufficient *mark* that this is his *will*' (italics in the original). The second part of this sentence may be construed either to mean the sealing was sufficient to authenticate that it was the devisor's will, or that the sealing was sufficient because the devisor wrote the will in his own hand and clearly identified himself.[2]

However, this decision may well not have been acceptable to many judges, for in the case of *Smith v Evans*,[3] the decision by North, Wyndham and Charlton JJ in *Lemayne v Stanley* was denounced as 'a very strange doctrine' by Lord Chief Baron Parker and Clive and Smythe BB. It was considered that signing with a seal would open the possibilities of forgery, a comment that reflected a change in judicial attitude from the middle ages, reflecting upon the reduced importance given to a seal in England and Wales than in China, Japan and Korea. The Barons were reported as stating: '... if the same thing should come in question again, they should not hold that sealing a will only was a sufficient signing within the statute.'

In a later case, that of *Warneford v Warneford*,[4] Raymond CJ ruled that the sealing of a will was also a signing within the Statute of Frauds 1677. The report of this case is merely a statement of the decision, which does not make it a persuasive authority. In any event, this case pre-dated the comments made in *Smith v Evans*. The reporting of decisions such as this were clearly in the mind of a later Chief Justice when he commented upon this issue in *Ellis v*

Smith.[5] That a seal could be a substitute for a signature was clearly quashed by Willes CJ:

> 'Nor do I think, sealing is to be considered as signing; and I declare so now, because, if that question ever comes before me, I shall not think myself precluded from weighing it thoroughly and decreeing, that it is not signing, notwithstanding *obiter dicta*, which in many cases were *nunquam dicta*; but barely the words of reporters; for upon examination I have found many of the sayings ascribed to that great man, Lord Chief Justice *Holt*, were never said by him.' (Italics in the original).[6]

A practical reason for rejecting the use of a seal was given by Sir John Strange, at 15, where he stated: '... that sealing is signing, I am not convinced; for sealing identifies nothing; it carries no character ... and most seals are affixed by the stationers, who prepare the paper.' It seems the court in the case of *Ellis v Smith* finally had sufficient weight of authority, comprising, as it did, the Lord Chancellor, Master of the Rolls, Chief Justice and Chief Baron, to prevent future submissions that a seal could be a substitute for a signature.

A further variation of the use of a seal occurred in the case of *Re Emerson's Goods*.[7] Thomas Emerson died on 14 April 1881. He previously prepared a document in his own handwriting, ending the content of the document with the words 'Signed, sealed, and delivered by me, the first day of February, 1881.' Mr Emerson affixed his seal marked with his initials by impressing wax upon the paper at the foot and at the end of the document in the presence of the subscribing witnesses. He also placed one of his fingers on the wax impression and stated before the witnesses 'This is my last will, and this is my hand and seal.' Warren J granted probate on the basis that the testator used the words 'this is my hand', intending this statement to be his signature. This decision was followed by Warren J in the case of *Re Lemon's Goods*,[8] where the testator was too ill to write, so he stamped his initials in wax on the paper in the presence of the witnesses.

1   (1681) 3 Lev 2; 83 ER 545.
2   In the case of *Dormer v Thurland* (1728) 2 Eq Ca Abr 663, 22 ER 557; 2 P Wms 506; 24 ER 837, a will had to be signed and sealed to be effective, and because it was signed but not sealed, it was declared void for want of being sealed.
3   (1751) 1 Wils K B 313; 95 ER 636.
4   (Easter 13 Geo 1) 2 Strange 764; 93 ER 834.
5   (1754) 1 Ves Jun 11; 1 Ves Jun Supp 1; 30 ER 205; 34 ER 666.
6   (1754) 1 Ves Jun 11 at 13.
7   (1882–83) 9 LR Ir Ch 443.
8   (1896) 30 IrLTR 127.

Interest in property

2.34   A seal used to be attached to an indenture respecting an interest in property, and Lord Eldon, when Lord Chancellor, took up the discussion relating to the use of a seal in the case of *Wright v Wakeford*,[1] where both a signature and a seal were used. The facts are that by indentures of a lease and release dated 3 and 4 March 1788, Giles Stibbert sold premises to Robert Hudson, with the agreement of Thomas Wood the elder and Thomas Wood the younger. The indentures were signed, sealed and delivered. However, the memorandum of attestation only stated that they were signed and delivered. Bearing in mind the value of the estate, at £15,988, this became a technical issue of great importance to both parties. After the death of Thomas Wood the elder, who was a party to the indenture, the two attesting witnesses endorsed a further memorandum, dated 13 November 1810, stating they witnessed the signing at the same time as the original document was sealed and delivered. Eldon LC rejected the proposition that a subsequent attestation was acceptable. He accepted that the document may have been signed, sealed and delivered, but it was not attested to this effect. As a consequence, he held that the members of a jury could not presume that the act of signing was done in the presence of the attesting witnesses. In comparison to the other cases cited in relation to whether a seal is sufficient as a signature, the decision in this case was decided upon the technical issue of regularity of the attestation. However, Lord Eldon took the opportunity, at 458–459 to make further observations about the use of a seal as a means of authentication:

'It is true, at one time it was decided, that sealing was signing (*Lemayne v Stanley*, 3 *Lev*. 1. *Warneford v Warneford*, 2 *Sir*. 764); and when it was urged, that the Legislature meant more than sealing, first, from the circumstance, that sealing is not mentioned as to Wills: secondly, as the Legislature must have proposed some evidence from the hand-writing of the party, the objection was, that a person may sign by his mark: an act affording no material testimony; and upon such reasoning it was decided originally, that sealing was signing: but upon a review of that the contrary has been held for a long time; and, so far as sealing from being equivalent to signing, that it is determined, that sealing is not necessarily; and that sealing without signing is not a sufficient execution of a Will (see *Ellis v Smith*, 1 *Ves, jun*. 11; and that attestation by a mark is good, *Harrison v Harrison*, *Addy v Grix*, 8 *Ves*. 185, 405): the converse holding as to a deed; which cannot be without sealing and delivery: if signed, it may be a writing: but, if delivered, it may be a good deed, whether signed, or not, and, if it is to be executed under a power with signature and sealing, both are required.'

This decision may have been unique to the facts of the case, given the value of the estate in question, and can be distinguished from *Re Emerson's Goods*[2] for this reason.

By comparison, another technicality arose in *Lord Lovelace's Case*,[3] where a swaynemoote roll was authenticated with one seal by an officer of the forest by the assent of all the verders, regarders and other officers. In this instance, it was held that a single seal was a good obligation of them all. Similarly, in *Ball v Dunsterville*,[4] one partner executed a deed for himself and his partner, by authority of the partner and in his presence. This act was a sufficient execution, even though only one seal was used. In *Cooch v Goodman*,[5] two people entered into a lease in their capacity as governors of a hospital. The defendant signed the lease and added his seal, and the lessors affixed a common seal to the lease, but did not sign it. No decision was made, because the seal was that of a corporation, not of the individuals, which meant the action was brought by the wrong parties. Lord Denman CJ commented, at 598, that a single seal may serve a number of people: 'It is true that one piece of wax may serve as a seal for several persons, if each of them impress it himself, or one for all, by proper authority, or in the presence of all, as was held in *Ball v Dunsterville* (4 T.R. 313), following *Lord Lovelace's Case* (W. Jones, 268).'

More recently, the case of *First National Securities Ltd v Jones*[6] considered the effect on a legal charge sealed with a circle printed on the document containing the letters 'L.S'. with the signature of the first defendant affixed across the seal. This was held to be sufficiently executed where the seal has been placed with the intention of serving the purpose of a seal. Buckely LJ said at 118 C–D:

'... it is a very familiar feature nowadays of documents which are intended to be executed as deeds that they do not have any wax, or even wafer, seal attached to them, but have printed at the spot where formerly the seal would probably have been placed, a printed circle, which is sometimes hatched and sometimes the letters "L.S." within it, which is intended to serve the purpose of a seal if the document is delivered as the deed of the party executing it.

In the present case there is not only the circle with the letters "L.S." within it upon the document, printed as part of the printed version of the document, but also there is the feature that the mortgagor has placed his signature across the circle. In my judgment those features and the attestation, in the absence of any contrary evidence, are sufficient evidence to establish that the document was executed by the first defendant as his deed.'

Goff LJ indicated that the intent behind the act was important, at 119 E 'In my judgment, in this day and age, we can, and we ought to, hold that a document purporting to be a deed is capable in law of being such although it has no more than an indication where the seal should be' and Sir David Cairns suggested what the modern view might be on the use of seals at 121 B 'Moreover, while in 1888 the printed indication of a locus sigilli was regarded as being merely the place where a seal was to be affixed, I have no doubt that it is now regarded by most business people and ordinary members of the public as constituting the seal itself.' The decision reached in this more recent case mirrors the approach taken by the members of the court in *Re Sandilands*,[7] where a deed had pieces of green ribbon attached to places where the seals should be, but no wax or other material to receive an impression. It was held there was sufficient evidence that the deed was sealed. Bovill CJ said at 413 'Here is something attached to this deed which may have been intended for a seal, but which from its nature is incapable of retaining an impression' whilst Byles J also offered the opinion at 413 that 'The sealing of a deed need not be by means of a seal; it may be done with the end of a ruler or anything else.'

1   (1811) 17 Ves Jun 455; 34 ER 176.
2   (1882–83) 9 LR Ir Ch 443.
3   W. Jones, 268, 82 ER 140; W. Jones, 270, 82 ER 141.
4   4 T.R. 313; 100 ER 1038.
5   (1842) 2 QB 580; 114 ER 228.
6   [1978] Ch 109, [1978] 2 All ER 221, CA.
7   (1871) LR 6 CP 411.

Court records

2.35   However, despite the reluctance by some judges to accept a seal as a signature in the eighteenth century, the members of the Exchequer of Pleas decided a seal was sufficient in relation to office copies from the Insolvent Court, being a court of record, in the case of *Doe d Phillips, Jones and Morris v Evans and Lloyd*.[1] It was possible for an office copy to be adduced as evidence without further proof, although it had to be signed by an officer of the court. Having discussed the relevant statutory provisions in his judgment, Bayley B came to the conclusion that where an office copy was sealed with the seal of the Insolvent Debtors' Court, 'The seal of the Court then becomes the signature of the Court and of the officer.'[2] It seems that this decision provided for the authentication of the insolvent petition either where the document contained the signature of the officer or his deputy and the seal of the court, or where the document only contained the seal of the court. Given the comment by Bayley B, it appears that the seal of the court was sufficient for the purpose of authentication.

In *R v St Paul, Covent Garden Inhabitants*,[3] relating to the settlement of an illegitimate child, it was not considered necessary that an order of the justices be sealed with wax. Two justices of the peace for the City and liberty of Westminster, John Johnson and J. T. Pratt, signed the order. The form of order was made on a preprinted form. The parish officers of St Martin in the Fields had a printer print from time to time a large number of the forms, and on each sheet a stationer was employed to impress two marks in ink with wooden blocks, and these impressions, when made at the foot, were intended to serve as seals for the justices when they signed such orders. The impressions represented an equestarian figure of St Martin sharing his cloak with a beggar, which were the size of an ordinary seal. The court in the Quarter

Sessions held that the impression in ink made by such blocks was a sufficient seal to make the order, when signed and delivered by the justices, a good and valid order.

In the United States, seals have generally been upheld, although there seems to have been a divergence between adopting the word 'seal' as an acknowledgment that a document has been sealed, and refusing to accept a document has been sealed unless an impression of a seal has been effected.[4] For a list of cases relating to the adoption of seals, see Richard A. Lord.[5] Recognition of the Japanese seal is illustrated in the Pennsylvanian case of *Zenith Radio Corporation v Matsushita Electric Industrial Co., Ltd.*,[6] where Becker DJ said, at 1224, that a Japanese seal 'should be given weight equivalent to a signature,' (also referred to in the colloquial form as a 'chop' although it appears it was probably a mitomein seal). For an unusual form of seal, the 1916 New York case of *Matter of the Probate of the Will of Severance*[7] illustrates the inherent flexibility of what constitutes a seal. In this instance, the testator affixed a holiday seal (containing the inscription 'Merry Christmas. American Red Cross, 1912 Happy New Year') to his will and inscribed it with his initials. It was held to constitute a subscription where the testator intended the holiday seal and inscription as a signature.

1   (1833) 1 C & M 450; 149 ER 476; (1833) LJ Ex 2 NS 179.
2   (1833) 1 C & M 450 at 461.
3   (1844) 5 QB 671; 114 ER 1402; (1845) 7 QB 232; 115 ER 476.
4   Richard A. Lord, *A Treatise on the Law of Contracts*, (Lawyers Cooperative Publishing, 4th edn., 1990), Volume 1, 68–71.
5   Richard A. Lord, *A Treatise on the Law of Contracts*, 2:2 to 2:4.
6   505 F.Supp. 1190 (1980).
7   96 Misc. 384, 161 N.Y.S. 452.

THE USE OF A PRINTED NAME

Statute of Frauds

2.36   The legal constraints relating to commerce were gradually lifted and amended during the nineteenth century, and the case of *Saunderson v Jackson*[1] at the turn of the century illustrated how the judges began to deal with the practical issues relating to contractual disputes where the claimed signature was affixed by virtue of the change in technology. In this instance, Jackson and Hankin sold gin to Saunderson. At the time the order for the gin was given to Jackson, a bill of parcels was delivered to Saunderson. The first part was printed as follows: 'London. Bought of Jackson and Hankin, distillers, No 8 Oxford Street' and there followed in manuscript writing '1000 gallons of gin, 1 in 5 gin £350 7s.' Some four weeks or so later, Jackson sent a letter to Saunderson 'Sir, we wish to know what time we shall send you a part of your order, and shall be obliged for a little time in delivery of the remainder; must request you to return our pipes. We are, your humble servants, Jackson and Hankin.' A trial was held before Lord Eldon CJ at the Guildhall, because Saunderson claimed the gin was not delivered on time or within a reasonable time. He directed the members of the jury to find for Saunderson, reserving consideration of the legal principles for a later hearing. At the later hearing, Lord Eldon indicated that the single question was 'Whether if a man be in the habit of printing instead of writing his name, he may not be said to sign by his printed name as well as his written name?'[2] He concluded that the letter in itself was not sufficient to establish the terms of the contract, but because the jury connected the letter with the bill of parcels, these two items, taken together, provided sufficient evidence to demonstrate the terms of the contract. As there was a clear nexus between the documents, and because Jackson signed the letter, this provided sufficient evidence of the contract. The bill of parcels was not sufficient evidence on its own to be considered as a note or memorandum of the contract.

The later case of *Schneider v Norris*[3] distinguished the facts in *Saunderson v Jackson*.[4] In this instance, Messrs John Schneider and Co bought cotton yard and piece goods from Thomas Norris and Co, who acted as agents. The bill of parcels read as follows: 'London, 24 October 1812. Messrs John Schneider and Co bought of Thomas Norris and Co, Agents. Cotton yard and piece goods. No 3 Freeman's Court, Cornhill', all of which was printed, except the words 'Messrs John Schneider and Co', which were handwritten by an agent or employee of the defendant. When, on 23 December, the plaintiffs demanded the yarn, the defendant refused to deliver it, because the principle had refused to perform the contract. At the subsequent trial, the defendants did not accept a contract had been formed, and relied on the absence of any note or memorandum in writing of the contract, as required by the Statute of Frauds 1677. Lord Ellenborough CJ overruled this objection and Schneider and Co obtained a verdict. On appeal, Lord Ellenborough reiterated his opinion at the trial, and considered that the printed name of the defendants, as it appeared on the bill, was recognized as a signature. This occurred when the name 'Messrs John Schneider and Co' was added to the bill of parcels that included the printed name of Norris and Co. By writing the name of the firm on the bill, Schneider's identified themselves with the other party to the transaction. Le Blanc and Bayley JJ concurred with this decision, and Dampier J added that the act of a person handwriting the name of the plaintiffs on the bill served to authenticate it as a memorandum of the bargain struck between the parties, and went on to explain, at 290: 'The defendant has ratified the sale to Schneider and Co by inserting their name as buyer to a paper in which he recognizes himself as seller.' Thus the names of the two firms on the same bill provided evidence of the agreement.

There is a fine distinction between these two cases. The additional manuscript comments to the bill of parcels in *Saunderson v Jackson* referred to the price and quantity of the order. This was not considered sufficient evidence, in the absence of the signed letter, to demonstrate a contract existed. In comparison, the additional manuscript comments to the bill of parcels in *Schneider v Norris* contained the name of one of the parties to the contract. This meant that both parties to the contract in *Schneider v Norris* were identified in the bill of parcels, and this was sufficient to establish a commercial relationship between the parties.

At the same time as these cases were being determined, another problem occurred of a similar nature in circumstances where one of the parties retained evidence of the orders they received in loose cases and memorandum books. In 1809, the case of *Allen v Bennet*[5] illustrated the problem. In this case, one W. Wright, the agent for H. and G. Bennett of Liverpool, agreed to sell to Mr Allen various quantities of rice and tobacco. Mr Wright wrote the orders into a book owned by Mr Allen. The book was described as 'a sort of waste book, containing various memoranda of different natures.' The name of Mr Allen, the plaintiff, was not written upon or in any part of the book. After the orders were taken, correspondence took place between the parties, but H. and G. Bennett failed to deliver the goods ordered by Mr Allen. It was considered the orders entered by the agent for Bennett were made in that capacity, and in conjunction with the exchange of correspondence, this was sufficient as a memorandum and a signature by Bennett. Mansfield CJ observed a wider question that occupied the courts on this issue at the time, when he said, at 176: '... every one knows it is the daily practice of the Court of Chancery to establish contracts signed by one person only, and yet a court of equity can no more dispense with the statute of frauds than a court of law can, there is no reason therefore to set aside the verdict, and the rule must be discharged.'

A similar set of facts occurred in 1856 in the case of *Sarl v Bourdillon*,[6] where the defendant, about to proceed to India, ordered goods from the plaintiff. Having selected the goods, a list was entered into an order book retained for the purpose, with the words 'Order Book' printed in gold letters on the outside and the names 'Sarl & Son' written on the flyleaf at the beginning. At the foot of the entry, the plaintiff wrote his name and address 'Capt. Bourdillon, 29 Inverness Terrace, Bayswater.' The defendant failed to pay for the goods, and claimed there was no sufficient memorandum of the sale as required by s 17 of the Statute of Frauds. It was held that the names of the contracting parties sufficiently appeared to satisfy the statute.[7] The judgments did not explain the reasoning for this decision. Jervis CJ indicated at the end of the submissions by counsel that there was only one point worth considering at length, and merely commented, at 195, that 'We also think that the names of the contracting parties sufficiently appear to satisfy the statute of frauds.' Cresswell J proceeded to deliver the judgment of the court more fully at a later date, and he said, at 195: 'In this case, inasmuch as the defendant declined to go to the jury, and insisted that there was no evidence of a memorandum to satisfy the statute of frauds, it may be assumed that the defendant wrote his name in the plaintiff's book, intending it as a signature to an order to the plaintiffs, whose order-book it was, and whose names were written in the beginning of it in the usual way. This, with the observations made in the course of argument, disposes of all the objections raised [the learned judge then dealt with a separate issue].' It is interesting to note that Cresswell J mentioned that the name 'Sarl & Son' was written in the beginning of the order book *in the usual way*. It might be inferred from this comment that Cresswell J was referring to the usual method of taking an order, and that it was common knowledge that notebooks containing pages to enter orders were widely used. If this was the case, the importance of this decision should not go unnoticed, because a decision the other way would have caused business people to alter the way they conducted business, and it is usually the case that judges in England and Wales looked to the common custom in reaching a decision.[8]

A variation of this theme, which also indicated the way people conducted their daily business, is the case of *Jones Brothers v Joyner*.[9] Mr J. P. Joyner, a publican, ordered a quantity of hops from the Jones brothers, who were hop growers. The order was written down in a notebook owned by the Jones Brothers, as follows: 'April 22 – Mr. J. P. Joyner, Worcester. – 2 Pos. of Hops 1989, at 7*l*. 5s. per cwt., awaiting order. Cash on delivery. – J. P. Joyner.' J. P. Joyner signed the order. The paper book in which this order was placed was, in turn, slipped into a leather cover, upon which the name 'James Jones' was stamped. When the paper memorandum book was full, it could be withdrawn and a fresh one inserted in the same leather cover. Mr Joyner contended there was no sufficient memorandum to satisfy s 4 of the Statute of Frauds, re-enacted by s 4 of the Sale of Goods Act 1893, because the name of the plaintiff did not appear in the memorandum signed by him. The Jones Brothers contended that the name on the cover constituted a sufficient signing. Sir Richard Harington, sitting at the Worcester County Court, held that the cover and the book were two distinct articles, distinguishing the decision in the case of *Sarl v Bourdillon*. The decision at first instance was reversed on appeal before Darling and Bucknell JJ. Darling J focused on the relationship between the notebook and the cover, at 769: '... when the memorandum was made they were only one. Take the case of the letter and envelope. First of all the letter is written, it is placed in an envelope, and the name of the other person appears on the envelope. In such a case there may be two distinct articles, which are used as one. Further, I think it makes no difference that the words "order book" do not appear. In fact, the orders were placed in a book which was used for that purpose.'[10]

1   (1800) 2 Bos & Pul 238; 126 ER 1257.
2   (1800) 2 Bos & Pul 238 at 239.
3   (1814) 2 M & S 237; 105 ER 388.
4   (1800) 2 Bos & Pul 238; 126 ER 1257.
5   3 Taunt. 169, 128 ER 67; the spelling of Bennet differs as between the name of the case and the description of the firm in the report.
6   1 C.B. (N.S.) 188; 140 ER 79.
7   *Jacob v Kirk* 2 M & R 221; 174 ER 269 was argued on different facts.
8   *Joshua Buckton and Co (Limited) v London and North-Western Railway Company* (1917–1918)

34 TLR 119 a contract signed with the printed name of the firm 'Joshua Buckton and Co. (Limited)' accepted by Astbury J as a regular business practice, at 121: '… having regard to the long practice of signing these consignment notes and to the fact that notes so signed have been accepted and recognized by the Court as fulfilling the requirements of the section,' the printed name was a signature under the provisions of s 7 of the Railway and Canal Traffic Act 1854 (now repealed).

9   (1900) 82 L.T.N.S. 768 In April 1899.

10 Compare the decision in *Champion v Plummer* 5 Esp. 239; 170 ER 798; 1 Bos. & P. (N.R.) 252; 127 ER 458; *Allen v Bennet* 3 Taunt. 169, 128 ER 67; *Jacob v Kirk* 2 M & R 221; 174 ER 269.

Interest in property

2.37   The principles set out in *Schneider v Norris*[1] were subsequently followed by Hall VC in *Tourret v Cripps*[2] where Mr R L Cripps wrote in his own hand on a sheet of memorandum paper an offer to lease parts of 14 and 15 Mortimer Street, Cavendish Square. The memorandum was not signed by Mr Cripps, but contained, at its head, the words 'From Richd. L Cripps' and his address. Tourret, who took an action against Cripps for specific performance, accepted the offer. The plaintiff was granted judgment with costs, constituting, as it did, in the words of Hall VC a '… good contract under the statute, as well as according to the ordinary understanding of mankind.'[3] It was plain that the letter was in the handwriting of Cripps, it contained his name and it was actually sent by him, thus the court inferred that his intention was to accept the lease, and his name at the head of the letter authenticated this intention.

1   (1814) 2 M & S 237; 105 ER 388.

2   (1879) 48 L J Ch 567; 27 WR 706. These cases were reviewed by Buckley J in *Hucklesby v Hook* 82 LT 117.

3   (1879) 48 L J Ch 567 at 568.

Public notices

2.38   The use of a printed name was also challenged when used by officers working for local authorities. In *Bridges (Town Clerk of Cheltenham) v Dix*[1] the Cheltenham council required the town clerk to execute certain works. When the owner of the property refused, the council sent a notice to the owner on a printed form, duly filled in, with the name of the town clerk printed at the foot of the notice. The council subsequently undertook the work and then sought to recover their costs. Matters dealing with the authenticity of the notice was set out in s 266 of the Public Health Act 1875, as follows:

'Notices, orders, and other such documents under the Act may be in writing or print, or partly in writing and partly in print, and if the same require authentication by the local authority the signature thereof by the clerk to the local authority, or their surveyor or inspector, shall be sufficient authentication.'

An objection was taken that the signature of the clerk was a requisite and that it should be affixed by hand. The magistrates accepted this argument and refused to make an order for payment. Pollock B and Charles J heard the appeal in the Queens Bench Division. They allowed the appeal and came to the conclusion that if a signature was required, a manual signature was not necessary: '... all that was necessary was that the notice should be authenticated as coming from the town clerk, and that sufficiently appeared in this notice.'[2] The printed signature was held to be sufficient. This observation was also to be noted by Romer LJ in *Goodman v J Eban Limited*,[3] where he pointed out that the recipient could confirm the authenticity of the notice by confirming its contents directly with the clerk.

1   (1890–91) 7 TLR 215.
2   (1890–91) 7 TLR 215 at 216(a).
3   [1954] 1 QB 550 at 564; [1954] 1 All ER 763; [1954] 2 WLR 581, CA.

Cheques

2.39   The decision in *Goodman v J Eban Limited*[1] was followed in *Ringham v Hackett*[2] where a partner in a firm signed a cheque and an action was successfully taken against the other partner of the firm. The name of the firm was printed on the cheque, and Lawton LJ considered that 'A printed name accompanied by a written signature was prima facie evidence that the cheque was being drawn on the account it purported to be drawn on.'[3] Whilst it can be presumed the account name printed on the cheque is the account of the firm, it does not follow that the signature has been authorized. In this instance, Megaw LJ indicated that each partner was liable for the actions of the other partner, and the cheque was sound for this reason. The comments by Slade and Griffiths LJJ in *Central Motors (Birmingham) Ltd v P A & S N P Wadsworth*[4] reinforce the development of the line of authorities in relation to the meaning attached to a signature. Slade LJ observed that a signature was not limited to the manuscript writing of a name, and it is possible that the identity of a firm can be adduced from the printed name of the firm on a cheque.

The decision in the South African case of *Akasia Finance v Da Souza*[5] reinforces the suggestion that the name of the account holder printed on a cheque does not constitute the signature of a company. In this instance, the name of the company was not held to be a signature under the provisions of the Companies Act 61 of 1973. Leveson J made it clear, at 338 G–H, why he did not consider the name printed on the cheque could be a signature:

'At the foot of each cheque, where the signature of the drawer is normally to be found, appear the words, "Domestic Homes (Pty) Ltd, Registration No 73/0541." The words are printed and are plainly printed by machine.

It is well known that for several years past banks have been issuing cheque books to their customers with the customer's name machine-printed thereon in the same space as the cheques in the present case. The printing is usually computer-controlled. This is done as part of a design to facilitate the modern banking system. Of importance is the fact that the printing is not done by the customer. It is therefore not the company's signature in the sense that, if put there by a person authorised by a corporate customer, it would constitute the company's signature or seal under the provisions of the Companies Act 61 of 1973.'

1   [1954] 1 QB 550; [1954] 1 All ER 763; [1954] 2 WLR 581, CA.
2   (1980) 124 SJ 201.
3   (1980) 124 SJ 201 at 202(a).
4   [1982] CAT 231, May 28, 1982; (1983) 133 NLJ 555 Court of Appeal (Civil Division).
5   1993 (2) SA 337 (W).

United States of America

2.40   Generally, judges in the United States, in combination with the open-minded approach adopted in various model acts to provide a degree of uniformity to the law, have followed English judgments. The range of illustrations includes printing on bank notes,[1] bills of lading,[2] bonds,[3] brokers contracts,[4] court papers[5] (although printed names have not always been accepted),[6] and a printed name can be the subject of forgery (including a name on a rubber stamp),[7] promissory notes (subject to suitable evidence),[8] public documents,[9] Statute of Frauds (with rare exceptions) generally,[10] with respect to letterheads,[11] and in matters pertaining to voting.[12] The burden of proving a printed name was adopted is on the party asserting the nature of the signature, as illustrated by the 1949 Californian case of *Felt v L. B. Frederick Co. Inc.*[13] In addition, care must be taken over proving the link between the printed name or letterhead, and the intent to authenticate, as in the 1949 Californian case of *Marks v Walter G. McCarthy Corporation*,[14] where the letterhead stationery of the name of a hotel used for the purpose of providing carbon copies was held not to be sufficient to show intention to adopt the letterhead as a signature, as indicated by Shenk J at 822: 'Here the defendant's letterhead was printed on its stationery at some earlier time for a purpose unconnected with the transaction in suit.' However, Carter J gave a strong dissenting judgment in this case which has much to recommend it.

1   Federal, 7th circuit (1923): *Hill v United States*, 288 F. 192 facsimile signatures of the governor and cashier of the Federal Reserve Bank of St Louis on bank notes are true and genuine signatures.
2   Pennsylvania: *Carna t/d/b/a/ T.C. Trucking Company v Bessemer Cement Company*, 558 F.Supp. 706 (1983) the preprinted company name on bill of lading held to be a sufficient signature.
3   California (1874): *Pennington v Baehr*, 48 Cal. 565, 1874 WL 1399 (Cal.) a bond signed by a printed facsimile of the President of the Reclamation Fund Commissioners held to be sufficient. It is reported that the Attorney-General argued, at 567 that 'A printed *fac simile*,

... could be more easily forged than an autograph; and such a signature would be no more protection than no signing at all.'

Williams v McDonald, 58 Cal. 527, 8 P.C.L.J. 23, 58 Cal. 527, 1881 WL 1946 (Cal.) a resolution of intention with the printed name of the clerk affixed was sufficient because he intended the printed name to be adopted.

4   Nebraska (1915): *Berryman v Childs*, 98 Neb. 450, 153 N.W. 486 where the plaintiffs signed a contract with their printed name, they are entitled to the benefit of the contract.

5   California (1874): *Hancock v Bowman*, 49 Cal. 413, 1874 WL 1548 (Cal.) a judgment is not void because the name of the plaintiff's attorney is printed on the complaint.

Ligare v California Southern Railroad Company, 76 Cal. 610, 18 P. 777 a summons signed with the printed signature of the clerk accompanied with the seal of the court held to be sufficient signature. (1888)

Smith v Ostly, 53 Cal.2d 262, 1 Cal.Rptr. 340, 347 P.2d 684 a name printed on a notice of appeal can be adopted as a signature providing the petitioner intended to authenticate the document. (1959)

Indiana (1885): *Hamilton v State*, 103 Ind. 96, 2 N.E. 299, 53 AmRep. 491 the name of the prosecuting attorney appearing in print on an indictment is sufficient.

Iowa (1908): *Cummings v Landes*, 117 N.W. 22, 140 Iowa 80 an original notice is signed when the name of the attorney is printed thereon.

Minnesota: *Ames v Schurmeier*, 9 Minn. 221, 1864 WL 1409 (Minn.), 9 Gil. 206 a summons in a civil action is void where the name of the plaintiff or their attorney is printed where handwriting is required.

Herrick v Morrill, 37 Minn. 250, 33 N.W. 849, 5 Am.St.Rep. 841 a summons in a civil action may be subscribed by the printed signature of the plaintiff or his attorney. (1887)

New York (1866): *Barnard v Heydrick*, 49 Barb. 62, 32 How. Pr. 97, 2 Abb.Pr.N.S. 47 a summons issued by an attorney with his name typed at the end is subscribed by him within the meaning of the provisions of the Code of Procedure (see cases cited and discussion of decision of Ingraham J in *The Farmers' Loan and Trust Company v Dickson*, 9 Abb.Pr. 61).

Wisconsin (1882): *Mezchen v More*, 54 Wis. 214, 11 N.W. 534 a summons in a civil action with the printed names of the attorneys is subscribed.

6   New York (1859): *The Farmers' Loan and Trust Company v Dickson*, 9 Abb.Pr. 61 a summons issued by an attorney with his name typed at the end was a nullity.

7   Massachusetts (1855): *Commonwealth v Ray*, 3 Gray 441, 69 Mass. 441, 1855 WL 5701 (Mass.) a printed or engraved name can be forged.

Wellington v Jackson, 121 Mass. 157, 1876 WL 10902 (Mass.) a person who knows a signature is forged on a promissory note, but who acknowledges it as his own, assumes the note to be his, just as if it was signed with his authority.

Oklahoma (1939): *Boyer v State*, 68 Okl.Cr. 220, 97 P. 779 a person can forge a name if they use a rubber stamp.

8   Illinois: *Weston v Myers*, 33 Ill. 424, 1864 WL 2948 (Ill.) a printed name adopted on an instrument for value.

Minnesota: *Brayley v Kelly*, 25 Minn. 160, 1878 WL 3577 (Minn.) a printed name on a promissory note was not considered admissible as the act of the party without further evidence.

Oregon (1926): *Toon v Wapinitia Irrigation Co.*, 117 Or. 374, 243 P. 554 a printed signature attached to an interest coupon payable to bearer is sufficient to authenticate the instrument.

9   North Carolina (1976): *State of North Carolina v Watts*, 289 N.C. 445, 222 S.E.2d 389 the mechanical reproduction of the name of an authorized officer placed on a public record of the Division of Motor Vehicles is properly authenticated where the officer intends to adopt the mechanical reproduction as his signature.

Wisconsin (1882): *Potts v Cooley*, 13 N.W.Rep. 682 a tax certificate the word 'Assigned May 19, 1877. J. P. Carpenter, County Clerk' partly written by hand and partly printed on the face of the certificate is sufficient for the purposes of the statute.

10 Arizona (1960): *Bishop v Norell, doing business as Al Norell Company Realtors*, 88 Ariz. 148, 353 P.2d 1022 a name and address printed on a listing agreement is signed in accordance with the statute provided it is done with the intention of signing.

Georgia (1972): *Kohlmeyer & Company v Bowen*, 126 Ga.App. 700, 192 S.E.2d 400, the name of a securities brokerage firm printed on a confirmation statement for the sale of securities was held to be intended as a means of authentication and thus met the signature requirement under the Statute of Frauds. Note the dissenting judgment of Evans J and his comments in respect of *Evans Implement Company v Thomas Industries, Inc.*, 117 Ga.App. 279, 160 S.E.2d 462.

Illinois (1920): *Prairie State Grain and Elevator Company v Wrede*, 217 Ill.App. 407 the name 'Ben. B. Bishopp, Grain Broker' printed on a memorandum is adopted and signed by him, especially because he had used such a signature for years as if it had been personally placed on the memorandum.

Kansas (1970): *Southwest Engineering Company Inc., v Martin Tractor Company Inc.*, 205 Kan. 684, 473 P.2d 18 the name 'Ken Hurt, Martin Tractor, Topeka, Caterpillar' printed on a memorandum with the details of specifications for a generator written by hand was sufficient authentication.

Michigan (1886): *Grieb v Cole*, 60 Mich. 397, 27 N.W. 579, 1 Am.St.Rep. 533 a warranty printed on the back of a purchase order with the vendor's printed signature binds the warrantor.

Missouri: *Defur v Westinghouse Electric Corporation*, 677 F.Supp. 622 (E.D.Mo. 1988) a Relocation Policy/Home Sale Program had the defendant's name printed on every page, held to constitute a writing signed by the defendant.

New York (1849): *Velie v Osgood*, 8 Barb. 130 names printed at the foot of a contract to buy a pew held not to be a sufficient subscription within the Statute of Frauds.

Goldowitz v Henry Kupfer & Co., 80 Misc.Rep. 487, 141 N.Y.S. 531. (1913)

New York: *Pearlberg v Levisohn*, 112 Misc. 95, 182 N.Y.S. 615. (1920)

United Display Fixture Co., Inc., v S. & W. Bauman, 183 N.Y.S. 4. (1920)

Cohen v Arthur Walker & Co., Inc., 192 N.Y.S. 228 the printed name of the defendant corporation on an order for goods is sufficient compliance with the statute. (1922)

Mesibov, Glinert & Levy, Inc., v Cohen Bros. Mfg. Co. Inc., 245 N.Y. 305, 157 N.E. 148 no proof of intent is demonstrated when a paper with the name of a firm is printed at the top and not signed. (1927)

New York (1966): *Reich v Helen Harper, Inc.*, 3 UCC Rep.Serv. 1048, 1966 WL 8838 (N.Y.City Civ.Ct.) sales confirmation sent on stationery imprinted with the name of the seller's agent upon which the name of the seller's principle was handwritten was signed within the meaning of the UCC.

11 Federal 3rd circuit: *Associated Hardware Supply Co., v The Big Wheel Distributing Co.*, 355 F.2d 114. (1966)

Federal 7th circuit: *Monetti, S.P.A. v Anchor Hocking Corporation*, 931 F.2d 1178 (7th Cir. 1991).

Connecticut: *Merrill Lynch, Pierce, Fenner & Smith, Inc., v Cole*, 189 Conn. 518, 457 A.2d 656 (Conn. 1983).

Georgia (1974): *Evans v Moore*, 131 Ga.App. 169, 205 S.E.2d 507.

Georgia (1981): *Troutt v Nash AMC/Jeep, Inc.*, 157 Ga.App. 399, 278 S.E.2d 54 the seller's standard printed form, with the seller's company name, address, and other information on the letterhead amounted to a signature.

Illinois: *Automotive Spares Corp., v Archer Bearings Company*, 382 F.Supp. 513 (1974) Bauer J at 515 'This Court recognizes the need to use common sense and commercial experience in regards to this signature question. Often times merchants exchange documents which control the transaction that do not bear their signature.'

Maryland (1882): *Drury v Young*, 58 Md. 546, 1882 WL 4502 (Md.), 42 Am.Rep. 343.

Mississippi: *Dawkins and Company v L & L Planting Company*, 602 So.2d 838 (Miss. 1992) a letter on the buyer's letterhead with the name of the sender typewritten at the bottom of the document is a sufficient signing to meet the merchant's exception to the Statute of Frauds.

New York (1980): *B & R Textile Corp., v Domino Textiles, Inc.*, 77 A.D.2d 539, 430 N.Y.S.2d 89, 29 UCC Rep.Serv. 396.

Ohio (1979): *Alarm Device Manufacturing Company v Arnold Industries, Inc.*, 65 Ohio App.2d 256, Ohio App., 417 N.E.2d 1284 the letterhead on the seller's invoice was sufficient to satisfy the Statute of Frauds.

12 Kentucky (1911): *Lamaster v Wilkerson*, 143 Ky. 226, 136 S.W. 217 the names of trustees of a common graded school district attached their names in print on a notice prepared by them of the time and place of holding an election to issue bonds by the district to build a schoolhouse: held the printed names were sufficient providing they authorized the printing of their names and adopted them as their legal signatures.

Massachusetts: *Henshaw v Foster*, 9 Pick. 318, 26 Mass. 312, 1830 WL 25334 (Mass.) in the election of governor, votes may be printed.

New Jersey (1984): *Matthews v Deane*, 201 N.J.Super. 583, 493 A.2d 632 names printed on recall petitions are valid.

13 92 Cal.App.2d 157, 206 P.2d 676.

14 33 Cal.2d 814, 205 P.2d 1025.

THE USE OF A LITHOGRAPHED NAME

2.41   The use of printed forms to reduce wasted time is an accepted way of doing business. However, there are occasions when a manuscript signature is required under statute, more particularly with respect to the rules governing the running of a firm of solicitors. In the case of *R v Cowper*[1] the name of the firm of solicitors was lithographed in bulk on to a county court bill of particulars. Spaces were left blank to fill in the form as necessary. A claim was made in respect of £2 16s 5d for a debt and 4s for solicitor's costs. At the hearing, the registrar refused an order for the 4s costs because the solicitors had not signed the particulars in accordance with the County Court Rules, 1889, order VI, r 10. The matter was then heard before the Divisional Court, which upheld the decision of the registrar. An appeal was subsequently heard in the Court of Appeal before Lord Esher MR and Fry LJ. Lord Esher pointed out that the name of a firm was included on the particulars to ensure the court may control its officers. He pointed out, at 535, that 'If that was the object, how is it affected by the objection, that the name appears in a lithograph form?' and concluded that if the forms were misused, such misuse would inevitably be found out and punished. Further, he went on to demonstrate the reason for the rule, at 535:

'The whole object of the rule seems to me to be to get the document authenticated as coming from a solicitor's office, and if the solicitor has authorized the issue of the lithograph form that object is attained. He means it to be his signature and sends it forth as his, and that seems to me sufficient compliance with the Act.'

However, Fry LJ disagreed with Lord Esher. He thought that blank forms that can be filled up at any time did not offer any guarantee that a particular form was personally considered by the solicitor or any person authorized to act on his behalf. Also, and more compellingly, he argued, at 536, that '… the signature required is intended to be something to authenticate the particulars and the accuracy of the copies, and to make the solicitor responsible for them as an officer of the Court.' Thus attempts by solicitors to ease the burden of filling in forms has not always met with agreement from the bench, and in this case, because the members of the Court of Appeal did not agree, the decision of the Divisional Court was not changed. In comparison, a lithographed name on bonds has been held to be a valid signature in the United States, although the position would not be any different in England and Wales.[2]

1   (1890) 24 QBD 60, 533 CA.
2   California (1906): *Hewel v Hogin*, 3 Cal.App. 248, 84 P. 1002 the lithographic signatures of a secretary of an irrigation district, adopted by him and appearing on the interest coupons on irrigation bonds issued by the district, were sufficient evidence of his signature to the bonds. McLaughlin J observed, at 254, in relation to the argument that the lithographic signatures were signed, that '… there is nothing in the point …'
   Missouri (1874): *McKee v Vernon County*, 3 Dill. 210, 16 F.Cas. 188, No. 8851 railroad bonds are valid where the signature of the presiding justice and clerk of the county are lithographed on the bond.
   Mississippi (1897): *Town Council of Lexington v Union National Bank*, 75 Miss. 1, 22 So. 291 railroad bonds are valid with the signature of the clerk of the council lithographed on the bond.

THE USE OF A RUBBER STAMP

2.42   An early record of the use of a stamp, although not made with rubber, is that of the signature of the monarch from the Tudor period in England. Apparently the signet of Mary Tudor occurs with a stamp signature of the queen, of which more than 20 specimens appear on signet warrants. Also, there are examples of rubber stamps being used instead of seals in the nineteenth century by the sheriffs of Devonshire, Cardiganshire, Lincolnshire, Suffolk and Yorkshire for official documents.[1]

1   Dr Patricia M. Barnes and L. C. Hector, *A Guide to Seals in the Public Record Office*, 47 note 2 and 52.

Wills

2.43   The case of *Jenkins v Gainsford and Thring*[1] illustrates the problems that humans must overcome, such as people suffering from ataxia by way of example, and what measures they take to resolve them. Towards the end of his life, one John Jenkins of Botley Hall, in the county of Southampton, had great difficulty in writing and signing his name. As a result, he had cause to be made an engraving of his signature. Thereafter, when he was required to sign a letter or other document, he would direct Henry Atkins, who acted as his amanuensis for many years, to affix an impression of his name to the document by using the engraving. Mr Jenkins left a will, duly executed, on 14 April 1862. He also executed two codicils dated respectively 5 November 1862 and 6 November 1862. An affidavit by Henry Atkins accompanied the codicils, stating the manner in which they were executed. Mr Atkins was one of the subscribing witnesses to both codicils to the will. He was ordered and directed by the testator to affix the signature to the codicil using the engraving, in the presence of the other subscribing witness, Ann Budd. After the signature was affixed, the testator placed his hand on the codicil and acknowledged the signature as his own and said the codicil was to be a codicil to his will. The two witnesses then attested and subscribed the codicil. The same procedure was followed on both occasions. Sir C. Cresswell held that the codicils were duly executed. He observed that a testator has sufficiently signed by making their mark, and went on to note at 96:

> 'Now, whether the mark is made by a pen or by some other instrument cannot make any difference, neither can it in reason make a difference that a fac-simile of the whole name was impressed on the will instead of a mere mark or X.'

The instrument or stamp was intended to stand for and represent the signature of the testator. The form the signature took was not relevant, so much as the evidence surrounding the affixing of the stamp, which went to show that the testator intended to be bound by the content of the codicils.

1   (1863) 3 Sw & Tr 93; 164 ER 1208; (1862–63) 11 WR 854.

Voting

2.44   The members of the Court of Common Pleas came to an identical decision in the later case of *Bennett v Brumfitt*[1] under the repealed Parliamentary Voters Registration Act 1843, s 17. The usual signature of William Brumfitt was engraved in facsimile and made into a stamp, which was subsequently used to sign a notice of objection. Bovill CJ observed at 31:

> 'The ordinary mode of affixing a signature to a document is not by the hand alone, but by the hand coupled with some instrument, such as a pen or pencil. I see no distinction between using a pen or a pencil and using a stamp, where the impression is put upon the paper by the proper hand of the party signing.'

The point was made that it is the personal act of the signatory that is relevant. Byles and Willes JJ agreed, and as to the genuineness of a signature, Keating J could not see why, a signature '… is better authenticated by a signature by means of a pen than by means of an impression of a stamp affixed by the party's own hand.'[2]

1   (1867–68) 3 LRCP 28.
2   (1867–68) 3 LRCP 28 at 32.

Judicial use

2.45 The development of technology permits actions that are repetitive in nature to be less onerous in their execution. Thus the use of a rubber stamp can alleviate the requirement that a manuscript signature be affixed to numerous documents by the same person in circumstances where the intention is to authenticate a document. Changes in technology included the adoption of stamps in the courts. In *Blades v Lawrence*[1] a case was transferred to the City of London court by the order of a master. The order was, in the words of Blackburn J, issued in the ordinary way '... according to the practice long established at Judge's Chambers, by the clerk of the judge, having on it the signature of the judge, stamped by the clerk.'[2] The judge in the London court, R. M. Kerr, inquired into the circumstances under which the order was made, and because the judge had not signed the order, he refused to hear the case and ordered the entry to be struck out. It was then unanimously held by Cockburn CJ, Blackburn, Quain and Archibald JJ that such an order was properly authenticated and it was not for the judge of the London court, in the words of Cockburn CJ, 'to determine the validity or invalidity of the order bearing the proper authentication on its face'.[3] Where it was doubted that the order was genuine, the judge should have applied to a superior court to set the order aside. In this instance, the judge was ordered to pay the costs of the case, and Cockburn CJ observed 'The judge's conduct has been so perverse as to amount almost to contumacy,'[4] illustrating the strength of feeling apparent amongst the members of the court over the action taken by Mr Kerr in this instance.

Consideration has been given to the judicial use of rubber stamps in Ireland in the case of *The State v His Honour Judge P. J. Roe*,[5] where it was determined that a justice of the peace may sign a committal warrant by means of a rubber stamp. Gavan Duffy P said, at 186–187:

> 'As to the rubber stamps, if one man may sign by a mark, another may use a rubber facsimile as a signature; but, where the device is questioned by a man entitled to call for proof, the affixing of the stamp by the Justice must be proved, either by the Justice himself or by another witness who can swear positively to the making by the Justice of the particular signature questioned; and that may not be easy evidence for a Court clerk to give, if a Justice makes a habit of stamping his name on a sheaf of documents at one time. If the fact be that pressure of work makes the use of a rubber stamp a necessity, or almost a necessity, for a very busy Justice, one would expect to see the need expressly recognised in the code, with stringent rules for the safe custody of the stamp and a peremptory veto upon any delegation of its use to a clerk or any other person.'

The acceptance of the use of a rubber stamp is also illustrated in the Canadian case of *R v Burton*[6] in which an informant affixed a facsimile signature to an information by means of a rubber stamp, which in turn was sworn before a Justice of the Peace, who signed the information with a manuscript signature. The information was held to be a sufficient signature in absence of proof that the officer who signed the jurat failed to comply with the duties imposed upon him. In reaching his decision, Lacourciere J observed, at 387: 'In my opinion the use of a rubber stamp signature by the informant is a practice that should be discouraged and indeed deprecated, as it detracts from the solemnity of an important step in the machinery of law, and may give rise to public suspicion that the officer taking the oath has done less than his duty. The partially stamped information, however, is not a nullity, in the absence of proof that the officer who signed the jurat failed to comply with the requirements set out above.' In comparison, an Ontario Court of Appeal held in the case of *Re R v Welsford*[7] that an information charging an accused with a summary conviction offence under a provincial statute is a nullity if the jurat bears a facsimile rubber stamp signature of the Justice of the Peace. For cases in the United State of America, see below.

1   (1873–74) 9 LRQB 374; (1874) 43 LJR QB 133.
2   (1873–74) 9 LRQB 374 at 377.
3   (1873–74) 9 LRQB 374 at 376.
4   (1873–74) 9 LRQB 374 at 380.
5   [1951] I.R. 172.
6   [1970] 3 C.C.C. 381, [1970] 2 O.R. 512, 8 C.R.N.S. 269 (Ont. H.C.J.).
7   [1967] 2 O.R. 496, [1968] 1 C.C.C. 1, 2 C.R.N.S. 5.

Statute of Frauds

2.46   The use of a stamp for this purpose was also challenged in the later case of *Evans v Hoare*[1] where an employer authorized a clerk to draw up a contract of employment, which was signed by the employee, as follows:

'5, Campbell-terrace, Cannhill Road, Leytonstone, E. Feb 19, 1890. Messrs Hoare, Marr, and Co., 26, 29, Budge Row, London, EC. Gentlemen, In consideration of your advancing my salary to the sum of £130 per annum, I hereby agree to continue my engagement in your office for three years, from and commencing January 1, 1890, at a salary at the rate of £130 per annum as aforesaid, payable monthly as hitherto. Yours obediently, George E Evans.'

The jury found a verdict for Mr Evans, but the assistant judge of the Mayor's Court did not accept there was a memorandum signed by the firm in accordance with s 4 of the Statute of Frauds, so gave judgment for the defendants. Upon appeal, before Denman and Cave JJ, this decision was reversed on the basis that the clerk was authorized by the firm to draw up the document, reference was made to the firm by the use of 'your' in the text and the name of the firm was included at the top of the document. The comments by Cave

J reflected the difference in procedure between the passing of the statute and the time this case was heard:

> 'The Statute of Frauds was passed at a period when the legislature was somewhat inclined to provide that cases should be decided according to fixed rules, rather than to leave it to the jury to consider the effect of the evidence in each case. This, no doubt, arose to a certain extent from the fact that in those days the plaintiff and the defendant were not competent witnesses... No doubt, in attempting to frame a principle, one is obliged to depart somewhat from the strict lines of the statutes.'[2]

In the later case of *McDonald v John Twiname Ld*,[3] the plaintiff entered into an apprenticeship with the company, but an authorized representative from the company failed to sign the agreement. The name of the company was stamped on the document with a rubber stamp. In this instance, Evershed MR and Birkett LJ agreed that not only had the document been signed by the company, but there was sufficient evidence to show they adopted, acted upon and affirmed the existence of the agreement.

1 [1892] 1 QB 593; (1892) 66 LTRep NS 345.
2 [1892] 1 QB 593 at 597. For a more robust and less polished version of this part of the decision by Cave J, see (1892) 66 LTRep NS 345, 347.
3 [1953] 2 QB 304, CA.

Ecclesiastical use

2.47 A similar problem occurred in *De Beauvais v Green*.[1] A new incumbent was installed at Whiteshill, in the County of Gloucester, after the death of the previous incumbent. The Bishop of Gloucester had occasion to have a report made of state of the buildings of the benefice, and required the new incumbent to pay a total of £248 9s 6d for the repairs. The new incumbent objected to paying this repair bill. One of the points raised in argument was that the Bishop failed to sign the relevant order in triplicate in his own hand, as required by ss 35 and 60 of the Ecclesiastical Dilapidations Act 1871, but authorized the use of a stamp for this purpose. It was held by Lawrence J that the order by the Bishop was sufficient in form to satisfy the requirements of the relevant sections.

1 (1905–06) 22 TLR 816.

Solicitors Act 1974

2.48 Solicitors, in the normal course of events, are required to sign bills of costs. In the case of *Goodman v J Eban Limited*,[1] where a sole practitioner sought to recover £50 9s 6d for professional services provided to the defendant company, the solicitor affixed his name by means of a rubber stamp. The solicitor sent a bill of costs to the defendants on 23 June 1952. The bill was accompanied by a letter which ended in the words typewritten at the bottom of the letter 'Yours faithfully, Goodman, Monroe & Company.' Below the name, the words 'Goodman, Monroe & Co', a facsimile of the solicitor's handwriting had been affixed by the solicitor to the letter by means of a rubber stamp. The defendants refused to pay the solicitor because the bill of costs did not satisfy the requirements of s 65(2)(i) of the Solicitors Act 1932. It was held, with Denning LJ dissenting, that the bill had been signed for the purposes of s 65. However, Evershed MR observed, at 554, that '… as a matter of good practice, the 'signature' of a bill of costs, or of a letter enclosing such a bill, by means of a rubber stamp seems to me in general undesirable.' He went on to comment that the purpose of the statute was to impose a personal responsibility for any bill of costs delivered, and the client was to have the assurance by means of personal authentication that the bill was a proper bill. Romer LJ noted that the rubber stamp did not, on the face of it, constitute a signature,[2] although he accepted that when the matter was considered in the light of authority and the function that a signature is intended to perform, the conclusion must be that the rubber stamp did constitute a signature. He also concluded that a repetition of the name of the firm under the typewritten name would be otiose if it was only to repeat the typed name of the firm. It was plain that Mr Goodman intended the rubber stamp to '… be regarded as a signature for the purpose of authenticating the letter.'[3] Should the client doubt its authenticity, all they had to do was ask Mr Goodman, by telephone or letter.[4] Romer LJ might have also adopted, had he been aware of it, the reasoning of Clay J in the 1934 Kentucky case of *Wurts v Newsome*,[5] where a judge signed ballots by means of a rubber stamp. Clay J stated, at 450:

'The opportunities for fraud when a rubber stamp is used are no greater than the opportunities for fraud by forgery. It would be just as difficult to ascertain that the ballots had not been signed, and have a rubber stamp prepared, as it would be to employ one to imitate the signature of the judge who failed to sign. Besides, the statute, though designed to prevent fraud, has operated in several instances to defeat the popular will. In numerous contests that have come before this court, the successful candidate has lost by the failure of one of the judges, either through ignorance, mistake, or fraud to sign the ballots. In the circumstances we are not inclined to go further and adopt a construction so technical as to make the situation even worse. A rubber stamp identifies the ballot just as clearly as the written signature of the judge. If not placed on the ballot either by him, or some one else in his presence, and at his direction while the election is being conducted, that may be shown in a context just as it may be shown that the written signature appearing on the ballot was not his act. We therefore conclude that the signing of the ballots by a rubber stamp was a substantial compliance with the statute, and that all the ballots so signed should have been counted.'

In his dissenting judgment, Denning LJ suggested he would restrict his comments to whether a solicitor's bill could be stamped with a rubber stamp, but later asked a series of rhetorical questions relating to the signing of a bill of exchange, cheques and the transfer of shares. He also mentioned the leading cases without reference, and failed to apply them. The main argument he used to defend his dissenting judgment seems to be that a person must make their mark, whatever the format, by themselves. By so doing, this action is supposed to demonstrate that they have given their personal attention to the document. In attacking the way in which rubber stamps were used, he introduced extraneous opinions to support his assertion, which was no more than prejudice and irrelevant to the matter being dealt with, at 561:

> 'This is such a common knowledge that a "rubber stamp" is contemptuously used to denote the thoughtless impress of an automaton, in contrast to the reasoned attention of a sensible person.'

He overlooked several points. A rubber stamp is used to sign hundreds of letters or forms for the convenience and saving in labour, as the case law in this chapter illustrates, rather than the contemptuous use by a thoughtless automaton, the purpose of which is different to a solicitor's bill. Also, he clearly did not appreciate, and if he did, did not acknowledge, the fact that some people do not have the ability to sign documents. He obviously did not agree with Romer LJ, that if the client thought somebody other than Mr Goodman, or without his authority affixed the rubber stamp, the client could easily have contacted him to resolve the matter. He failed to see that this was the case of a single solicitor, running his own firm, using a very basic technology in an attempt to make his life slightly easier. The issue was not the widespread use of rubber stamps in various other activities. In this judgment, Denning LJ refused to distinguish between the form a signature took and the function it was to perform, which has been the main thrust of judicial decision making over the past 200 years. Interestingly, the use of a stamp by judges and bishops during the nineteenth century was not raised or discussed in this case. If Denning LJ thought the personal signature of a solicitor was so necessary on a bill of costs, it may be equally as desirable when a judge orders a case to be transferred to another court, as in *Blades v Lawrence*.[6]

The decisions from other jurisdictions, together with the rationale articulated for accepting rubber stamps, is also an instructive counterpoint to the comments by Denning LJ. In Canada, the judgment in *Goodman v J Eban Limited* was discussed in *R v Burton*.[7] In this case, an informant affixed a facsimile signature to an information by means of a rubber stamp, which in turn was sworn before a Justice of the Peace, who signed the information with a manuscript signature. It was held to be a sufficient signature in absence of proof that the officer who signed the jurat failed to comply with the duties imposed upon him.

In the 1976 North Carolina case of *State of North Carolina v Watts*,[8] the mechanical reproduction of the name of an authorized officer placed on a public record of the Division of Motor Vehicles was held to be properly authenticated where the officer intended to adopt the mechanical reproduction as his signature. Branch J indicated why the physical reality of mechanical means of rendering a signature had become relevant at 392: 'The purpose of authentication and certification of records is to avoid the inconvenience and sometimes the impossibility of producing original public documents in court. Obviously the admission of certified records tends to expedite the trial of cases. It is just as obvious that to require the manual signing of every record certified from the Division of Motor Vehicles would be extremely time consuming and expensive.' The comments made by Branch J were reinforced by Hallett J in *Re United Canso Oil & Gas Ltd*[9] where proxy forms submitted with a facsimile or mechanically rendered signature were considered to be sufficient. Hallett J explained the rationale at 289 paragraph 17: ' Today's business could not be conducted if stamped signatures were not recognized as legally binding. The affixing of a stamp conveys the intention to be bound by the document so executed just as effectively as the manual writing of a signature by hand. I would point out that no one questions the validity of millions of payroll cheques signed by facsimile signatures.' He also addressed the fallacious argument that one form of signature was more prone to fraud than any other at 305 paragraph 64:

'In my opinion, in view of the obvious opportunities for fraud with respect to votes to be cast by registered shareholders where a bare signature is normally accepted, I cannot see any reason to differentiate between the degree of proof required by a chairman to be satisfied that a proxy has actually been executed by the registered individual shareholder (the degree of proof being virtually nothing) and the degree of proof urged upon the court by the Buckley group with respect to proxy voting of brokers for their clients. In the absence of evidence that there was no authority for the execution of proxies by brokers by facsimile signature, the proxy vote should be accepted and counted as is apparently the practice. To conclude otherwise, the chairman is presuming dishonesty on the part of the brokers who tendered the proxies on behalf of their clients. In the absence of evidence, such a conclusion is unwarranted.'

1   [1954] 1 QB 550; [1954] 1 All ER 763; [1954] 2 WLR 581, CA.
2   [1954] 1 QB 550 at 563.
3   [1954] 1 QB 550 at 564.
4   [1954] 1 QB 550 at 563–564.
5   253 Ky. 38, 68 S.W.2d 448.
6   (1873–74) 9 LRQB 374; (1874) 43 LJR QB 133.
7   [1970] 3 C.C.C. 381, [1970] 2 O.R. 512, 8 C.R.N.S. 269 (Ont. H.C.J.).
8   289 N.C. 445, 222 S.E.2d 389.
9   (1980) 12 B.L.R. 130; 76 A.P.R. 282; 41 N.S.R.(2d) 282 (T.D.).

Administrative use

2.49 The inconvenience of affixing a manuscript signature to documents was also tested in *British Estate Investment Society Ltd v Jackson (H M Inspector of Taxes).*[1] During a hearing before Danckwerts J on 13 and 14 November 1956 in the Chancery Division, the Society challenged a finding by the Commissioners for the Special Purposes of the Income Tax Acts that it was trading in real property, and appealed against past assessments. Documents relating to the finding were bound into separate volumes and numbered. Each document in each volume was numbered consecutively and fastened together by metal rods passing through holes in the margin of each document and through two pieces of stiff millboard at each end. The rods were sealed at each end with a metal seal. Whilst it was possible to tear a document from the volume, additional documents could not be inserted unless the seal was cut and the rods removed. At the end of each volume, a certificate was produced to authenticate the content of each volume. An Additional Commissioner signed the various certificates with a rubber stamp, which was kept by the Additional Commissioner or by the Clerk to the Commissioners. Although the Additional Commissioner personally affixed his signature by using the rubber stamp, the Society did not accept this evidence. The Society contended first, the documents should have been signed by the Additional Commissioner in accordance with s 36 of the Income Tax Act 1952, second that the certificates should have been personally signed by the Additional Commissioner and finally, the documents were not contained in books as required in the statute. In opening his judgment, Danckwerts J expressed his opinion as to the merits of the appeal, with the following robust comment: 'The appeal as brought today has absolutely no merits of any conceivable kind, and in my opinion it has been a disgraceful waste of the time of the Court and public money to have pursued the matter here.'[2] He went on to indicate that the points raised by the Society were made upon the most technical grounds conceivable.[3] On the matter of the stamped signature, he observed, before referring to *Goodman v J Eban Limited*:[4]

> 'Of course, this is a case, if ever there was a case, in which the signing by means of a stamped signature is proper, because everybody knows that Commissioners of this kind have to deal with numerous documents, and it is an onerous duty if they have to be signed by the writing of the Commissioner himself.'[5]

Before dealing with the other issues raised in the case, Danckwerts J commented upon the submission by counsel for the Inspector of Taxes relating to the evidential presumption in relation to the regularity of the signature affixed to a document by an officer. He said:

> '... one would presume that when a document appears to be signed it has been duly signed by the officer who purports to sign it, is a perfectly good one. It seems to me that the presumption in law is that the document has

been properly signed until the contrary has been shown by a person who desires to upset that conclusion.'[6]

Interestingly, it was the Society who put in evidence, without objection by the Crown, letters between the Society's solicitors and the Clerk to the Commissioners of Taxes for the City of Manchester relating to the affixing of the signature by rubber stamp and how the stamp was controlled. Danckwerts J correctly indicated that the Commissioners were, in such circumstances, entitled to take the statements that appeared in the letters as being true.

Almost at the same time as the actions relating to the previous case were being played out, so the facts relating to a similar case were also being acted in another geographical location. In the case of *Lazarus Estates Ltd v Beasley*,[7] documents in the form prescribed by the Housing Repairs and Rents Act 1954 were signed with the name of the company by means of a rubber stamp. No objection was taken as to the validity of the signature in the county court, and the matter could not be addressed on appeal. However, Denning LJ could not resist commenting, at 710, that:

'The statutory forms require the documents to be "signed" by the landlord, but the only signature on these documents (if such it can be called) was a rubber stamp "Lazarus Estates Ltd." without anything to verify it. There was no signature of a secretary or of any person at all on behalf of the company. There was nothing to indicate who affixed the rubber stamp. It has been held in this court that a private person can sign a document by impressing a rubber stamp with his own facsimile signature on it: *Goodman v J Eban Limited* [[1954] 1 QB 550; [1954] 2 WLR 581; [1954] 1 All ER 763, CA], but it has not yet been held that a company can sign by its printed name affixed with a rubber stamp.'

This comment by Lord Denning was not to the point, and in the light of the extensive case law relating to this topic, from both England and Wales and the United States of America, it may be safe to indicate that Lord Denning's remarks on the topic are irrelevant. Of interest is the case of *Fitzpatrick v Secretary of State for the Environment*,[8] in which enforcement notices signed with the rubber stamp of the appropriate official bearing their facsimile signature were held to be valid in accordance with the provisions of s 234(2) of the Local Government Act 1972. The members of the Court of Appeal reached their decision without reference to any relevant case law.

1   (1954–1958) 37 Tax Cas 79; [1956] TR 397; 35 ATC 413; 50 R & IT 33.
2   (1954–1958) 37 Tax Cas 79 at 83.
3   (1954–1958) 37 Tax Cas 79 at 84.
4   [1954] 1 QB 550; [1954] 1 All ER 763; [1954] 2 WLR 581, CA.
5   (1954–1958) 37 Tax Cas 79 at 86.
6   (1954–1958) 37 Tax Cas 79 at 87.
7   [1956] 1 QB 702.
8   [1990] 1 PLR 8, CA.

United States of America

2.50   Rubber stamps have the virtue of being able to tender a facsimile version of a manuscript signature, which means they have been used extensively. The use of rubber stamps as a means of authenticating documents in the United States has only been tempered with the need to ensure the version of the signature in the form of an impression of a rubber stamp was used with the intent to authenticate the document. The range of uses to which rubber stamps have been put, and which judges have accepted with minor exceptions, include bank notes,[1] bills of lading,[2] cheques,[3] matters pertaining to the fifth amendment,[4] elections,[5] finance statements,[6] when affixed to letters,[7] public documents,[8] and receipts.[9] The judicial use of rubber stamps appears to have been widely taken up in various states of the United States and with varying degrees of success. In the federal seventh circuit case of *United States of America v Juarez*,[10] a search warrant signed with a rubber stamp by a magistrate was held not to be valid. Tone CJ offered the opinion of the court at 1114:

> 'Defendant also contends that the search warrant should be invalidated because the magistrate used a signature stamp instead of signing it personally. We do not approve the use of a signature stamp by a magistrate. Its use creates the appearance that the user lacks the sensitivity a federal judicial officer should have to the important values which the warrant is designed to protect. Nevertheless, in this case the magistrate testified unequivocally that he remembered placing the signature stamp on the warrant, and the District Court credited this testimony. We cannot say that it was clearly erroneous for the court to have done so. We therefore do not find that it was in error to refuse to declare the warrant invalid and thereby exclude the evidence seized pursuant to the warrant, despite our condemnation of the magistrate's practice.'

In comparison, at a state level, the use of rubber stamps has been widely accepted,[11] and Hood AJ indicated how widely rubber stamps were used in the 1943 Columbia case of *McGrady v Munsey Trust Co.*,[12] where the chief deputy clerk personally applied a facsimile representation of their signature to a summons. Hood AJ indicated the general use of the methods in his comments at 106: 'This practice was adopted many years ago and is a matter of great convenience since more than 4,000 landlord and tenant complaints are filed in the trial court each month.' The legal and practical position of rubber stamps was put into context by Lattimore J in the 1930 Texas case of *Stork v State*,[13] in which the facsimile signature of a Justice of the Peace affixed by rubber stamp to affidavit and liquor search warrant was held to be a sufficient signing. Lattimore J considered a number of cases, and stated, at 735:

> 'The writer is of opinion that when it appears without question, as in this case, that the magistrate in person took the affidavits of those who swore to same, and also so issued the search warrant, and that to each he affixed

his name, it would be a matter of no moment whether he so affixed said name by one stroke as by the use of a stencil or rubber stamp, or whether he sat down at a typewriter and wrote his name with same upon such document, or that he wrote it out in what we commonly call longhand, provided that in each such case the facts must allow the name to have been affixed by the officer himself, or under his immediate authority and direction and in his presence.'

1   Federal 7th circuit (1923): *Hill v United States*, 288 F. 192 the facsimile signatures of the president and cashier of the Federal Reserve Bank of St. Louis on a banknote were held to be true and genuine signatures.

2   Pennsylvania: *Carna t/d/b/a/ T.C. Trucking Company v Bessemer Cement Company*, 558 F.Supp. 706 (1983) the reprinting (presumably by the use of a rubber stamp, but the report does not make this clear) of a company name on a Bill of Lading was held to be signed.

3   Pennsylvania (1897): *Robb v The Pennsylvania Company for Insurance on Lives and Granting Annuities*, 40 W.N.C. 129, 3 Pa.Super. 254, 1897 WL 3989 (Pa.Super. 1897) affirmed by 186 Pa. 456, 40 A. 969, *for dissenting opinion, see* 186 Pa. 456, 41 A. 49.

4   Federal 2nd circuit: *Biegeleisen v Ross*, 158 F.3d 59 (2nd Cir. 1998) a valid IRS levy based on a notice signed with a signature stamp rather than a manuscript signature does not violate the Due Process Clause of the Fifth Amendment.

5   Kentucky (1934): *Wurts v Newsome*, 253 Ky. 38, 68 S.W.2d 448 held to be a valid signature where a judge signs ballots by means of a rubber stamp.

6   Colorado: *In the Matter of Colorado Mercantile Co.*, 299 F.Supp. 55 (1969) a financing statement submitted with a stamped signature was acceptable, even though the requirement at the time of filing was for a manual signature.

    Conneticut (1965): *In re Bengston*, 1965 WL 8262 (Bankr.D.Conn.), 3 UCC Rep.Serv. 283 a name printed in ink (understood to mean stamped with a rubber stamp) on a standard form financing statement satisfied the requirement that the secured party signed the financing statement.

    Texas (1979): *Brooks v The State of Texas*, 599 S.W.2d 312 a pen packet reflecting convictions for theft in value over $50 and burglary where the facsimile signature of the clerk is affixed by means of a rubber stamp did not bar admission of the pen packet at the penalty stage.

    Connecticut (1900): *In re Deep River National Bank*, 73 Conn. 341, 47 A. 675 the signature of Clinton B. Davis, affixed to a promissory note 'D., Treasurer' was held to be a valid signature.

7   Federal 6th circuit (1897): *National Accident Society v Spiro*, 78 F. 774, 24 C.C.A. 334 the facsimile signature of an officer of the company affixed to a printed letterhead of the company was sufficiently proven.

    Wisconsin: *Kocinski v The Home Insurance Company*, 154 Wis.2d 56, 452 N.W.2d 360 (Wis. 1990) a facsimile signature stamped on a document with a rubber stamp satisfied the requirement that the document be subscribed.

8   Arizona (1943): *Maricopa County v Osborn*, 60 Ariz. 290, 136 P.2d 270 the facsimile signature of the treasurer applied by rubber stamp was sufficient for refunding bonds.

    Carolina (1938): *Smith v Greenville County*, 188 S.C. 349, 199 S.E. 416 the facsimile signature using a rubber stamp by a county treasurer on a tax execution is the signature of the treasurer.

    Florida (1941): *State v City of Fort Lauderdale*, 149 Fla. 177, 5 So.2d 263 facsimile signatures affixed to city hospital revenue certificates and the attached coupons are valid.

    New York (1912): *Tenement House Department of City of New York v Weil*, 76 Misc. Rep. 273, 134 N.Y.S. 1062 an order issued under the Tenement House Law containing a facsimile signature affixed by an official by means of a rubber stamp was held to be valid.

    Brooklyn City Railroad Company v City of New York, 139 Misc. 691, 248 N.Y.S. 196 a notice of claim with the signatures of an officer and of a notary public affixed to the document with a rubber stamp were sufficient. (1930)

North Dakota (1980): *Andre v North Dakota State Highway Commissioner*, 295 N.W.2d 128 a record of a speeding violation with the words (on three lines) 'STAT. FEE JUL 24 1979 THOMAS EWING' stamped on the back of the paper was determined to be adequate for the intended purpose of informing the State Highway Department of an admission or adjudication of a traffic violation.

State of North Dakota v Obrigewitch, 356 N.W.2d 105, (N.D. 1984) an order of suspension and driving record held to be valid where a rubber stamp was used to affix the signature of the director of the Drivers License Division of the State Highway Department.

Oklahoma (1938): *Moss v Arnold*, 63 Okl.Cr. 343, 75 P. 491 the facsimile signature of Fred D. Lowe, the chairman of the Board of County Commissioners, applied by means of a rubber stamp was deemed sufficient to authenticate requisitions.

State of Oklahoma ex rel. Independent School District Number One of Tulsa County v Williamson, 1960 OK 126, 352 P.2d 394 (Okla. 1960) the Uniform Facsimile Signature of Public Officials Act is not invalid and officials may use facsimile signatures on public bonds as a substitute for manuscript signatures as required by law.

Utah (1967): *Salt Lake City v Hanson*, 19 Utah 2d 32, 425 P.2d 773 the signatures of a police officer and city judge to a complaint, affixed by means of a rubber stamp, are sufficient.

9   Georgia (1906): *Bell Bros., v Western & A. R. Co.*, 125 Ga. 510, 54 S.E. 532 a freight receipt for the car containing cabbages signed by stencil with the name of the agent of the defendant company was not accepted because there was no proof that the agent signed the receipt, adopted the signature, or that it was his custom to sign his name to receipt by this type of stamp.

Massachusetts: *Boardman v Spooner*, 13 Allen 353, 95 Mass. 353, 1866 WL 5009 (Mass.), 90 Am.Dec. 196 a bill of sale of goods bearing the purchaser's name stamped upon it is not sufficient proof to show that the stamp was adopted as a signature.

10 549 F.2d 1113 (1977).

Maine (1924): *Mahoney v Ayoob*, 124 Me. 20, 125 A. 146, 37 A.L.R. 85 where a disclosure commissioner indorsed a capias signed with his facsimile signature impressed with a rubber stamp, held not to be a signature, because the signature was not 'under his hand.'

11 Florida (1966): *State of Florida v Hickman*, Fla., 189 So.2d 254 the facsimile signature of a Justice of the Peace affixed to a warrant by a rubber stamp is valid, even when affixed by the chief clerk under the authority of the justice.

Illinois (1896): *Streff v Colteaux*, 64 Ill.App. 179, 1896 WL 2352 (Ill.App. 1 Dist.) a declaration may be signed with the names of the plaintiff's attorneys by means of a rubber stamp.

Illinois (1973): *People of the State of Illinois v Stephens*, 297 N.E.2d 224 a search warrant signed by a magistrate with a rubber stamp was not invalid.

Iowa (1904): *Loughren v B. F. Bonniwell & Co.*, 125 Iowa 518, 101 N.W. 287, 106 Am.St. Rep. 319 the subscription by a justice with a rubber stamp bearing the facsimile of his signature is sufficient for a notice, even when carried out by another, but with his authority.

Massachusetts (1861): *Wheeler v Lynde*, 1 Allen 402, 83 Mass. 402, 1861 WL 6171 (Mass.) it is a signature where an attorney at law signs the back of a writ by means of a rubber stamp.

New Mexico (1928): *Costilla Estates Development Co., v Mascarenas*, 33 N.M. 356, 267 P. 74 the signature of a court clerk by means of a rubber stamp as a method of indorsement of filing papers was held sufficient.

Pennsylvania (1975): *Commonwealth Department of Transportation v Ballard*, 17 Pa. Cmwlth. 310, 331 A.2d 578 the signature of a traffic court judge by means of a rubber stamp was not inadmissible where the seal of the court was also applied to the record.

Texas (1961): *Ex parte Spencer*, 171 Tex.Cr.R. 339, 349 S.W.2d 727 a complaint is valid where the complainant and the deputy clerk both affixed their signatures by means of a facsimile rubber stamp.

Ex parte Britton, 382 S.W.2d 264 a facsimile stamped signature of the Governor on extradition papers does not affect the validity of the warrant. (1964)

Parsons v The State of Texas, 429 S.W.2d 476 a complaint was sufficiently signed with the facsimile signature of the complainant with a rubber stamp. (1968)

Estes v State, 484 S.W.2d 711 facsimile signature applied to a document from the Department of Corrections by means of a rubber stamp was a sufficient signature. (1972)

Huff v The State of Texas, 560 S.W.2d 652 the facsimile signature of the country district clerk stamped on certified copies of a judgment and sentence was held to be valid. (1978)

Paulus v The State of Texas, 633 S.W.2d 827 (Tex.Crim.App. 1981) there was no error when an indictment is signed with the facsimile signature of the foreman of a jury by means of a rubber stamp.

Benavides v State of Texas, 763 S.W.2d 587 (Tex.App. – Corpus Christi 1988) a penitentiary packet stamped with a rubber stamp producing a facsimile of an original signature is an acceptable means of signing legal documents.

Kemp v State of Texas, 861 S.W.2d 44 (Tex.App. – Houston 14th Dist. 1993) the use of a rubber stamp to produce a facsimile of a county judge's signature on a list of previous criminal records did not affect the authenticity of the signature.

In re Barber, 982 S.W.2d 364 (Tex. 1998) the signature of a judge affixed by a rubber stamp is a signature on a judgment, even when affixed to the document by an intermediate authority at the direction of the judge.

Wisconsin (1882): *Dreutzer v Smith*, 56 Wis. 292, 14 N.W. 465 a rubber stamp with a facsimile of the signature of the County Clerk of Door County affixed to a tax deed was considered to be writing the name.

12   32 A.2d 106.
13   114 Tex.Crim. 398, 23 S.W.2d 733.

Mechanical marks by human action

2.51   The application of legal principles applies to new technology in the same way as it applies to more established ways of conducting business. However, this does not prevent challenges to the way in which business is conducted when using new technology, as the following discussion illustrates.

TYPEWRITING

2.52   Once the typewriter had developed sufficiently to be a useful tool that enabled the typist to type faster then a human could write, the machine began to be widely used, although, it must be said, not at quite the same rapidity as the computer.[1] An early example of litigation respecting the value of a typed signature was a case involving a remonstrance in 1905 in Indiana, that of *Ardery v Smith*.[2] In this instance, an attorney had the authority to sign a remonstrance against the issue of a liquor license for and on behalf of voters, and being afflicted with erysipelas in his right hand, he caused the names to be typed in his presence and under his supervision. It was held to be immaterial that the names were added by means of a typewriter. Roby J summed up the position, at 841:

'In an opinion given in 1842 by William Wirt, then Attorney General, the question submitted being whether the Secretary of the Treasury was authorized by a statute requiring warrants to be drawn and signed by him to have his name impressed thereon by means of copper plate, the following language was used: "There would be great difficulty in maintaining the proposition, as a legal one, that, when the law required signing, it means that it must be done with pen and ink. No book has laid down the proposition, or even given color to it. I believe that a signature made with straw dipped in blood would be equally valid and obligatory, and, if so, where is the legal restriction on the implement which the signer may use? If he may use one pen, why may he not use several – a polygraph, for example, or types, or a stamp? The law requires signing merely as an indication and proof of the parties' assent." 1 Opinions of Attorneys General, 670. The quotation is an apt one, as applied to the facts now under consideration. The typewriter is a modern convenience. The signature made by it was in this case the signature of the attorney; the operator being in fact his agent, exactly as the keys and the types were his agents.'

From an evidential point of view, judges have required proof of intention that a particular typed name was adopted by the person whose name was typed on the document.[3] Crane J illustrated the difficulty in the 1911 New York case of *Landeker v Co-operative Bldg. Bank*,[4] of linking the application of the typewritten name to proof that the name was typed with authority and intent. Crane J said, at 781, that 'The mere production of the contract with the typewritten name of the grantor is insufficient to meet the requirements of the statute, unless the authority and intent in signing the name is shown.'[5] Interestingly, a number of cases dealing with typewritten signatures are of relatively recent origin, and it is to be wondered, when reading some of the reports, whether the points ought to have been taken at all, given the long and liberal history adopted by the common law in relation to the form a signature takes.[6] Examples include arbitration,[7] mechanics' lien,[8] Statute of Frauds,[9] mortgages,[10] pleadings,[11] secured transactions,[12] taxation[13] and wills.[14]

In New Zealand, the concept is called the 'authenticated signature fiction' and is illustrated by the case of *Bilsland v Terry*,[15] where an agreement for the sale of land had the names of both parties set out in the document, but it was only signed with the manuscript signature of one party. It was held to be a sufficient signing to satisfy s 2 of the Contracts Enforcement Act 1956 under the rule known as 'authenticated signature fiction'. Quilliam J, commented, at 50:

'Upon the authority, therefore, of the cases I have cited I find that the agreement was a sufficient memorandum in writing to satisfy the Contracts Enforcement Act, and is binding on the parties. I should mention that it was contended by Mr Luck that the conclusion I was invited to draw upon the basis of the authorities I have cited was plainly wrong, and that if I were to adopt it I should be introducing into the realm of conveyancing a hazard which should not be there. I realise that the rule to which I have referred is probably unknown to many conveyancers, but this alone is hardly a reason for not applying it where the facts render it applicable. The rule appears to be well established and I can see no reason why I should ignore it.'

This decision was followed in *Short v Graeme Marsh Ltd*,[16] but not in *Carruthers v Whitaker*[17] (*Bilsland v Terry* was not referred to in this judgment). The *Bilsland v Terry* and *Short v Graeme Marsh Ltd* cases were later distinguished in *Stuart v McInnes*,[18] where a contract for the sale of land was held not to be enforceable where neither party signed the agreement. Wilson J discussed the 'authenticated signature fiction' at 733–734:

'Although, over the years, the basis for the authenticated signature fiction seems to have changed somewhat, the line of cases in England which includes *Tourret v Cripps*, *Evans v Hoare* and *Leeman v Stocks* has now settled the law on this topic. From these cases it is clear that, in England, the principle applies if, and only if, these conditions obtain:

(1)   the contract, or the memorandum containing the terms of contract, must have been prepared by the party sought to be charged, or by his agent duly authorised in that behalf, and must have that party's name written or printed on it.

(2)   It must be handed or sent by that party, or his authorised agent, to the other party for that party to sign.

(3)   It must be shown, either from the form of the document or from the surrounding circumstances, that it is not intended to be signed by anyone other than the party to whom it is sent and that, when signed by him, it shall constitute a complete and binding contract between the parties.

I think the justification for the fiction is to be found in the last condition. Where the form of the memorandum or the surrounding circumstances show the intention that the contract shall be binding on both parties although not signed by the one who prepared it, the terms of the statute are not really applicable with reference to that one, so the fiction is introduced to meet the case. It is easy to see the justice of the result, but I confess to a regret that the solution found was to describe as a signature something that is not a signature and was never intended to be such. It might have been preferable to hold that such memoranda were outside the ambit of the statute in regard to the party whose signature was not contemplated as being necessary.'

He went on to discuss the decisions in *Bilsland v Terry* and *Short v Graeme Marsh Ltd* at 734 to 735, which he declined to follow. The same decision was reached in *Van der Veeken v Watsons Farm (Pukepoto) Ltd*,[19] where a contract for the sale of property called for the signature of both parties, and the authenticated signature fiction was considered not relevant to the fact of this case; the decision in *Bilsland v Terry* was also distinguished. It seems the current position in New Zealand is governed by *TA Dellaca Ltd v PDL Industries Ltd*,[20] where the approaches taken in *Bilsland v Terry* and *Short v Graeme Marsh Ltd* were rejected. The members of the court favoured the approach taken by Wilson J in *Stuart v McInnes* and Beattie J in *Van der Veeken v Watsons Farm (Pukepoto) Ltd*. Tipping J commented, at 99: 'I agree with their observations that go further than the approach summarised by Wilson J really amounts to an unacceptable judicial repeal of the Contracts Enforcement Act 1956. The authenticated signature fiction is itself quite a significant departure from the literal terms of the Act.'

In Canada, the use of a typed signature in combination with an authorized manuscript signature of a departmental lawyer was the issue in the case of *R v Fredericton Housing Limited*.[21] The question was whether the typewritten signature of the Deputy Attorney General of Canada was acceptable on a statement of claim, together with the manuscript signature of a lawyer in the department. A statement of claim was subscribed by typing as follows:

'D. S. Maxwell
Deputy Attorney General of Canada
Per   'F. J. Dubrule'
            F. J. Dubrule'

The manuscript signature 'F. J. Dubrule' was affixed to the statement of claim by Mr Storrow, a solicitor in the Tax Litigation Section of the Department of Justice of which section Mr Dubrule was the director. It was held that the signature 'F. J. Dubrule' subscribed by Mr Storrow was in fact the signature of Mr Dubrule, duly authorized by him, and the typed name 'D. S. Maxwell', when authenticated by the subscription of the signature of Mr Dubrule, became the signature of the Deputy Attorney General of Canada. Cattanach J made a useful observation, at 223, in discussing the difference between using a rubber stamp to affix a signature and a typewriter: 'If the typewritten name "D. S. Maxwell" is not "writing" (as I think it is) it is most certainly a mechanical method of affixing and I cannot distinguish in principle an affixing by keys striking a ribbon from a rubber stamp with ink on it.'

1   For an interesting summary of the development and history of the typewriter, see www. en.wikipedia.org/wiki/Typewriting.
2   35 Ind.App. 94, 73 N.E. 840.
3   Federal, 10th circuit (1954): *Roberts v Johnson*, 212 F.2d 672 a witness to a form designating a beneficiary signed with a typewritten name. It was held that it must be proven to be intended to be the signature of the witness.
      Maine (1969): *Maine League Federal Credit Union v Atlantic Motors*, 250 A.2d 497, 6 UUC Rep.Serv. 198 the evidence demonstrated that there was no intent to adopt a typewritten name on a financing statement. It was only through inadvertence that the document was not signed with a manuscript signature.

Missouri: *First Security Bank of Brookfield v Fastwich*, 612 S.W.2d 799 (Mo.App. 1981) the burden of establishing the typed signature of a corporation arises when it has been put in issue by a specific denial. The burden is on the party claiming under the signature, but he is aided by the presumption that it is genuine, or authorized.

4   130 N.Y.Supp. 780.

5   See also the 1911 Californian case of *Little v Union Oil Company of California*, 73 Cal.App. 612, 238 P. 1066; the Maryland case of *Cambridge, Inc., v The Goodyear Tire & Rubber Company*, 471 F.Supp. 1309 (1979) where a typewritten name of a lease did not bind where it was not intended to bind as a legal signature, and the 1926 Pennsylvania case of *Tabas v Emergency Fleet Corporation*, 9 F.2d 648 *affirmed United States Shipping Board Emergency Fleet Corporation v Tabas*, 22 F.2d 398 the government of the United States is not deemed to have executed a contract because its name is typed on paper in the absence of evidence to show it authorized or adopted such signature.

6   Although see the Maine case of *In re Carlstrom*, 3 UCC Rep.Serv. 766, 1966 WL 8962 (Bankr. D.Me.) where a typewritten name on a financing statement was not accepted as a signature. See the astounding comments of Conrad, Referee in Bankruptcy, negating the concept that a symbol can be considered a signature, and his hostile comments on the decision in *Benedict, Trustee in Bankruptcy of Lillian E. Hargrove d/b/a Hargrove Typesetting Services v Lebowitz*, 346 F.2d 120 (1965).

7   Illinois: *Just Pants, an Illinois limited partnership v Wagner*, 617 N.E.2d 246 (Ill.App. 1 Dist. 1993) the typewritten name of an arbitrator at the end of a memorandum of decision can serve to execute and give legal effect to the contents.

8   New Jersey (1956): *J. D. Loizeaux Lumber Company v Davis*, 124 A.2d 593, 41 N.J. Super. 231 the name of the plaintiff typed on a materialman's notice of intention was held to be intended to be a signing as well as to serve other functions disclosed by the printed material.

9   Federal, 9th circuit: *In the Matter of Save-On-Carpets of Arizona, Inc.*, 545 F.2d 1239 (1976) a typewritten signature on a UCC financing statement satisfied the signature requirement of the Statute of Frauds.

Alaska (1976): *A & G Construction Co., Inc., v Reid Brothers Logging Co., Inc.*, Alaska 547 P.2d 1207 the name 'Glenn W. Reid' typed at the bottom of a letter was considered to be signed.

Florida (1972): *Ashland Oil, Inc., v Pickard*, Fla., 269 So.2d 714 the typed words on notepaper with the letterhead of the company and with the word 'Harold L. Slam, President' typed at the bottom is a signature.

Maryland (1967): *Dubrowin v Schremp*, 248 Md. 166, 235 A.2d 722.

Massachusetts (1946): *Irving v Goodimate, Co.*, 320 Mas. 454, 70 N.E.2d 414, 171 A.L.R. 326 the name of the employer typed at the end of a letter to an employee is a sufficient signature.

Minnesota (1965): *Radke v Brendon*, 271 Minn. 35, 134 N.W.2d 887 a prospective vendor's letter including the prospective purchaser's name and typewritten name of the vendor is tantamount to a written signature, given the intent.

Mississippi: *Dawkins and Company v L & L Planting Company*, 602 So.2d 838 (Miss. 1992) a letter written on a buyer's letterhead including the typewritten name of the sender is a sufficient signing to meet merchant's exception to the Statute of Frauds.

New York (1919): *Cohen v Wolgel*, 107 Misc. Rep. 505, 176 N.Y.S. 764 *affirmed* 191 A.D. 883, 180 N.Y.S. 933.

New Mexico: *Watson v Tom Growney Equipment, Inc.*, 721 P.2d 1302 (N.M. 1986) a name typed on a purchase order was held to be a sufficient signature, because the signatory had deliberately filled out other details on the order form.

Wisconsin (1912): *Garton Toy Co., v Buswell Lumber & Mfg. Co.*, 150 Wis. 341, 136 N.W. 147.

10   Federal 2nd circuit: *Benedict, Trustee in Bankruptcy of Lillian E. Hargrove d/b/a Hargrove Typesetting Services v Lebowitz*, 346 F.2d 120 (1965) the insertion of the chattel mortgagee's name in the body of a financing statement was held to be a sufficient signing to satisfy the Con-

necticut Uniform Commercial Code. The intent to authenticate was established by the act of a secretary in typing his name at his direction and subsequently filing the statement.

11 Indiana (1953): *City of Gary v Russell*, 112 N.E.2d 872 a notice of claim was sufficiently signed when the plaintiff's name was typewritten at the end.

North Dakota (1916): *Hagen v Gresby*, 159 N.W. 3, 34 N.D. 349, 5 L.R.A. 1917B, 281 the typewritten name and address of an attorney on a summons is sufficient. The attorney, F. B. Lambert, had not written a summons with a manuscript signature since 1896.

12 Federal 4th circuit (1969): *Calaway v Admiral Credit Corporation*, 407 F.2d 518 a financing statement with a typed name was not invalid for lack of manuscript signature where a type-written signature was provided.

Federal 5th circuit: *In the Matter of Bufkin Brothers, Inc.*, 757 F.2d 1573 (1985) a secured creditor's typewritten corporate name on a continuation statement was sufficient to validate the statement.

Connecticut (1963): *In re Horvath*, 1963 WL 8592 (Bankr.D.Conn.), 1UCC Rep.Serv. 624 a typewritten name considered a signature.

Georgia (1976): *Peoples Bank of Bartow County v Northwest Georgia Bank*, 139 Ga.App. 264, 228 S.E.2d 181 the printed name of the bank on a financing statement for Angus beef cattle served to reinforce a manuscript signature that was not easily identified.

13 Massachusetts (1942): *Assessors of Boston v Neal*, 311 Mass. 192, 40 N.E.2d 893 an application for abatement that was inadvertently not signed with a manuscript signature, accompanied with a letter signed by W. C. Larson, Treasurer of the First People's Trust, held that the application signed with a typewriter was sufficient.

14 California (1949): *Estate of Moore*, 92 Cal.App.2d 120, 206 P.2d 413 a will signed with a type-written name cannot be considered to be signed in the absence of evidence to show it was typed by the testator or that it was typed in his presence and at his direction by another.

15 [1972] NZLR 43.

16 [1974] 1 NZLR 722.

17 [1975] 2 NZLR 667.

18 [1974] 1 NZLR 729.

19 [1974] 2 NZLR 146.

20 [1992] 3 NZLR 88.

21 [1973] F.C. 196; [1973] CTC 160.

TELEGRAM

Statute of Frauds

2.53 The development of telegraphy in the early nineteenth century brought about the same types of dispute that occur in the era of the internet, and judges were required then, as they are required now, to adapt old laws to new technologies, as has been discussed above. The telegram and its various technologies, including telex, was widely used from the outset. The authors of the entry in Wikipedia illustrate the nature of the telegram succinctly, with the exception of the inaccuracy about the legal position regarding correspondence conducted by email:

'Telegraphy messages sent by the telegraph operators using Morse code were known as telegrams or cablegrams, often shortened to a cable or a wire message. Later, telegrams sent by the Telex network, a switched network of teleprinters similar to the telephone network, were known as telex messages. Before long distance telephone services were readily available or affordable, telegram services were very popular. Telegrams were often used to confirm business dealings and, unlike email, telegrams were commonly used to create binding legal documents for business dealings.'[1]

In *Godwin v Francis*[2] an offer to buy a property was accepted by telegram. It was held that the telegram, together with other correspondence, was sufficient to satisfy the Statute of Frauds, and the signature of the telegraph clerk was considered a sufficient signature. In response to the argument that the instructions for the sending of the telegram cannot be a signature of the contract, because the paper was a mere instruction to the telegraph clerk, Bovill CJ responded, at 301–302:

> 'Assuming that argument to be correct (though I am not prepared to adopt it), that would be instructions to the company to do that which in the ordinary course of their business is done. Now, the ordinary course of business is to transmit, to write out, an exact copy of that which is intended to be conveyed, and to forward it. The acceptance of the plaintiff's offer is in the body of the document. The telegraph clerk copies it, signs it, and sends it to the plaintiff, the name of the seller appearing thereon. A correspondence ensues between the parties on the footing that there had been a binding contract for the sale of the estate; and, if the defendant had authority, it is clear that what was done did constitute a binding contract. But, independently of that, I am prepared to hold that the mere telegram written out and signed in the way indicated by the telegraph clerk, if done with the authority of the vendors, would have been a sufficient signature within the Statute of Frauds.'

It was necessary to resolve the distinction between the contents of the document containing the message to be sent and subsequently presented to the telegraph office, and the document received by the recipient. In this respect, Willes J observed, at 302–303 that 'The message was left, signed by the defendant, at the office of the Telegraph Company. A copy was sent by the company to the plaintiff, and authenticated by them in the usual way. If the message so sent had been contained in a letter sent by post, there can be no doubt that would have been a sufficient contract to satisfy the statute. That is because the General Post Office has been held to be the common agent of the parties employing it.' Brett J also noted, at 303 '... I think there is evidence that the defendant, when he signed the instructions, intended that to operate as his signature to the contract, and that it constituted a binding contract signed by him, if he had authority to enter into it. Then, it was objected that the defendant's name appearing on the paper received by the plaintiff was insufficient, because the defendant had no power to delegate to the telegraph clerk an authority to sign his name. I think, however, it must be assumed as against him that he had authority to delegate to the clerk the power to sign for him, and that the signature so placed was binding upon him.'

A number of cases dealing with the exchange of telegrams were dealt with in a similar way as some forms of electronic signature are dealt with today: the point was not raised in argument, and therefore the issue of the efficacy of the signature not challenged, inferring an acceptance of the proof of intent of the parties in the case.[3] Clearly, new technology did form part of the decision-making process of judges, and they made it clear that the introduction of technology was not an excuse to prevent the application of legal principles to new technology. In *McBlain v Cross*,[4] it was held that the signature in a telegram was sufficient to come within the Statute of Frauds. Willes J was not going to let technology impede the way the law was interpreted, commenting, at 806 that 'If we did not hold such to be the law, the convenience which the modern invention of the electric telegraph has bestowed upon mankind would be in a great measure subverted.'

Similarly, Vaughan Williams J had the foresight to issue a novel form of order in the case of *In re English, Scottish, and Australian Chartered Bank*.[5] In this case, the principle business of the bank was in Australia, but it was ordered that the bank had to be wound up in England. A scheme of reconstruction was proposed, and Vaughan Williams J directed that meetings of shareholders and creditors be held to ascertain their wishes. The majority of the creditors were in Australia, and because of the need for speed, Vaughan Williams J made an entirely new form of order directing a form of proxy to be sent by the Official Receiver by telegraph to Australia, appointing specified persons to vote for or against the scheme at the meeting to be held in London. A number of objections were taken on the result of the vote in the meeting, and one of the objections was that the judge had no power to order the Australian proxies to be communicated by telegram to the meeting, but the proxies ought to have been produced at the meeting. It was held that the judge had the power under s 91 of the Companies Act 1862, in combination with s 2 of the Joint Stock Companies Arrangement Act 1870, to direct the particulars of the Australian proxies to be communicated by telegraph, and there was no need for the proxies to be physically produced at the meeting. Lindley LJ commented, at 410: 'Now, that is an entirely new form of order. I need hardly say that it is adapted to the necessities of the time – it is ingeniously using the improved methods of communication by telegraph, which it would be folly to shut out and not use if you can do it' and Smith, LJ said, at 417 'I wish to add a few remarks upon a point which for the first time arises in this case, that is as to whether or not the electric telegraph can be made use of to carry out what was eminently needed, and indeed was absolutely necessary to do justice in this case.'

1   http://en.wikipedia.org/wiki/Telegraphy   and   http://en.wikipedia.org/wiki/Electrical_ telegraph.

2   (1870) LR 5 CP 295; 22 LT Rep NS 338.

3   In *Henkel v Pape* (1870) 6 L.R.Exch. 7 and *L. Roth and Co. (Limited) v Taysen, Townsend, and Co.*
    (1896–97) 12 TLR 211, CA contracts were formed by exchange of telegrams; the signature
    point not raised in either case, but can be inferred that it was accepted; in *Sadgrove v Bryden*
    [1907] 1 Ch 318, the words 'Consent, Shaw' sent by cablegram, which was, in turn, stamped
    with a 10 shilling stamp as power of attorney, was held sufficient to validate a form of proxy
    signed in advance but not dated in accordance with the provisions of s 80 of the Stamp Act
    189; in *Behnke v Bed Shipping Co* [1927] 1 KB 649 a contract for the sale and purchase of a
    ship was conducted by letter, telegram and telephone, and it was held that a name added to a
    telegram is a signature where it is adopted or recognized by the party to be charged.
4   (1872) LT 804.
5   [1893] 3 Ch 385.

United States of America

2.54   Telegrams were as widely used in the US as in any other jurisdiction,
and in 1869, the process involved in sending and receiving a telegram was
outlined by Sargent J in the New Hampshire case of *Howley v Whipple*.[1] In
this instance, the decision centred on the requirements to provide for the
proper evidentiary foundation necessary in adducing evidence of a telegram
into proceedings. In addition, it also follows that telegrams may constitute
adequate memorandum of the contract, and a contract can be construed by
reference to several letters and telegrams.[2] The use of telegrams covered a
range of situations, including bills,[3] judicial use[4] and the Statute of Frauds.[5]
Generally, members of the judiciary have taken a robust view of telegrams,
as illustrated in the 1912 Missouri case of *Leesley Bros., v A. Rebori Fruit Co.*,[6]
where it was held that an exchange of two telegrams between the parties to
buy and sell a car load of onion sets was held to be in substantial compliance
with the Statute of Frauds. Nixon PJ remarked at 142: 'to hold otherwise
would certainly embarrass present business methods and increase the expense
and impair the usefulness of the telegraph as a necessary instrumentality in
modern commerce.' This view was shared by Wolff, Referee in the 1961 New
York case of *La Mar Hosiery Mills, Inc., v Credit and Commodity Corporation*,[7]
where he held that a name included in a telegram constituted a signature. He
commented, at 190:

> 'It does not matter whether the telegram as delivered was copied from
> one written by an officer or employee of the defendant or was telephoned
> to the telegraph company by someone in the defendant's behalf. Precisely
> what happened here was not shown. The defendant could not well be
> heard to disclaim responsibility for the telegram and it is to the credit of
> the defendant that it has not attempted to do so. The telegram with the
> typed signature of defendant's name emanated from the defendant which
> is responsible for it. The signature on the telegram in suit, although
> typed in the office of the telegraph company, is therefore defendant's
> authorized signature within the requirements of the statute of frauds. In
> view of the way in which business is done nowadays, any other view would

be unrealistic and would produce pernicious consequences, impeding the conduct of business transactions.'

The 1970 case of *Yaggy v The B.V.D. Company, Inc.*,[8] from North Carolina reinforced this point, where a telegram sent to the plaintiff accepting the latter's offer to purchase property was binding on the defendant. It was held that the defendant's name in print and affixed to the telegram by the same mechanical process employed by the telegraph company in reproducing other portions of the message constituted a signing within the Statute of Frauds. In the Pennsylvania case of *Hessenthaler v Farzin*,[9] it was held that a mailgram that the vendor sent to a prospective purchaser of real estate confirming acceptance of sale constituted a signed writing. Hoffman J, after revising a number of cases, indicated, at 993 that 'We agree with these authorities that the proper, realistic approach in these cases is to look to the *reliability* of the memorandum, rather than to insist on a formal signature.' He went on, at 994:

'The detail contained in this mailgram is such that there can be little question of its reliability. Appellants were careful to begin the mailgram by identifying themselves. They then made certain that their intention would be properly understood by declaring their acceptance, and identifying both the property and the consideration involved. In light of the primary declaration of identity, combined with the inclusion of the precise terms of the agreement, we are satisfied that the mailgram sufficiently reveals appellants' intention to adopt the writing as their own, and thus is sufficient to constitute a "signed" writing for purposes of the Statute. Moreover, this result is consistent with the holdings of courts in other jurisdictions that have addressed the question of whether or not a telegram can be a signed writing for purposes of the Statute.'

1   48 N.H. 487 (1869).
2   Florida (1920): *Meek v Briggs*, 80 Fla. 487, 86 So. 271.
3   Kentucky (1918): *Selma Savings Bank v Webster County Bank*, 206 S.W. 870, 182 Ky. 604, 2 A.L.R. 1136.
4   Kentucky: *Blackburn v City of Paducah*, 441 S.W.2d 395, (Ky. 1969) a telegram sent by Judge John B. Blackburn resigning from his post constituted a writing and was signed. The Board of Commissioners accepted the resignation and subsequently another police judge was appointed to fill the vacancy. When the appellant later attempted to act in this capacity, he was arrested. Clay, Commissioner, remarked, at 398 'Perhaps we have belaboured the obvious too much. Here the appellant selected the medium to the transmittal of his message, composed its content and authorized his signature thereto. It is difficult to understand how he can now question the legal efficacy of the written instrument he had drafted for the sole purpose of tendering his resignation.'
     Oklahoma: *State ex rel. West v Breckinridge*, 34 Okla. 649, 126 P. 806, 1912 OK 283 where the resignation of the County Attorney by telegram acceptable.
5   Alabama: *McMillan, Ltd v Warrior Drilling and Engineering Company, Inc.*, 512 So.2d 14 (Ala. 1986) the name in telegram was a signature.

California (1900): *Brewer v Horst and Lachmund Company*, 127 Cal. 643, 60 P. 418, 50 L.R.A. 240 two telegrams buying and selling hops were held sufficient for purposes of Statute of Frauds.

Florida (1961): *Heffernan v Keith*, Fla., 127 So.2d 903 a telegram is signed by the telegraph company with authority of the sender.

Florida (1972): *Ashland Oil, Inc., v Pickard*, Fla., 269 So.2d 714 a telegram constitutes a signed memorandum.

Massachusetts (1972): *Providence Granite Co., Inc., v Joseph Rugo, Inc.*, Mass., 291 N.E.2d 159, 362 Mass. 888.

Michigan (1890): *Ryan v United States*, 136 U.S. 68, 10 S.Ct. 913, 34 L.Ed. 447.

Montana (1980): *Hillstrom v Gosnay*, Mont., 614 P.2d 466 provided the necessary intent to authenticate the signature on a telegram is shown, the typewritten signature is a proper subscription.

Nebraska: *Hansen v Hill*, 340 N.W.2d 8 (Neb. 1983) a telegram accepting an offer to buy land to which the vendor's name has been affixed was considered signed under the Statute of Frauds.

New York (1862): *Dunning & Smith v Roberts*, 35 Barb. 463 the manipulations of a telegraph operator, upon the oral instructions of a person to send a dispatch for him, are the equivalent to a signing by that person within the Statute of Frauds.

Trevor v Wood, 9 Tiffany 307, 36 N.Y. 307, 1867 WL 6445 (N.Y.), 3 Abb.Pr.N.S. 355, 93 Am.Dec. 511, 1 Transc.App. 248 where dealers in bullion bought and sold bullion by exchange of telegrams, the telegrams are sufficiently signed under the Statute of Frauds. (1867)

But see Vermont (1992): *Pike Industries, Inc. v Middlebury Associates*, 398 A.2d 280 *affirmed on other grounds* 436 A.2d 725, *cert denied*, 455 U.S. 947 where the contents of a telegram were held not to be signed because the name of the party was not included in the body of the text.

6   162 Mo.App. 195, 144 S.W. 138.
7   28 Misc.2d 764, 216 N.Y.S.2d 186.
8   70 N.C.App. 590, 173 S.E.2d 496, 72 Am.Jur.2d.
9   564 A.2d 990 (Pa.Super. 1989).

TELEX[1]

2.55   When compared to the jurisprudence developed in Europe and America relating to the formation of contract, Japan is less concerned for contracts to be in writing and conform to a Statute of Frauds, but defines a contract as a judicial act to join two opposing wills.[2] As a result, the formation of a contract does not necessarily require either party to sign a contract. It is instructive, however, to observe that the methods of communication do not appear to pose a problem in determining whether a contract has been formed in Japan. In the case of *Fawlty & Co Ltd v Matsui Shoten K.K.*,[3] the defendant, a New Zealand company, agreed to ship 600 quarters of GAQ quality frozen heifer meat to Kobe port. The defendant attempted to cancel the contract and refused to accept delivery, which meant the plaintiff had to sell the meat at a loss. The contract was negotiated by a mix of letters sent by airmail and telex. The court held that there was a contract for the purchase and sale of the meat. Although the court did not have to determine whether the communications sent and received by telex were signed by the parties, nevertheless the court must have reached the conclusion that a contract had been formed in the light of the totality of the evidence, including the content of the correspondence conducted by telex. The inference is, that if signatures were necessary in Japan, it is probable that a signature sent by telex will have been acceptable.

In the English case of *Clipper Maritime Ltd v Shirlstar Container Transport Ltd, The Anemone*,[4] Staughton J had to determine whether a valid contract existed to perform a guarantee. Clipper Maritime let their vessel *Anemone* on time charter to Afram Line Ltd for a trip from Europe to West Africa. Shirlstar were in the business of leasing and operating containers. By May 1983, Shirlstar was owed US$275,000 by Transaltic, an associated company to Clipper Maritime. Owners of ships became reluctant to let their ships to such a charterer without security. The charter in respect of *Anemone* was negotiated by the owners' brokers on behalf of the charterers. It was agreed at an early stage there would be a guarantee, and the charter was eventually drawn up and dated 24 December 1983. The owners alleged that US$107,115.92 was due under the charter and claimed this amount from Shirlstar. Shirlstar denied they entered into a contract of indemnity. Evidence relating to the contract between the parties was partly contained in three telexes, one of which was dated 23 December 1983 and two of which were dated 6 January 1984. It was determined by Staughton J that the context in which the telexes were exchanged demonstrated a contract existed, even if only implied from the circumstances by which the correspondence took place.[5] Although the point did not arise, Staughton J offered extra-judicial comments in relation to the nature of the exchange of telexes in the context of s 4 of the Statute of Frauds 1677:

> 'I reached a provisional conclusion in the course of the argument that the answerback of the sender of a telex would constitute a signature, whilst that of the receiver would not since it only authenticates the document and does not convey approval of the contents.'[6]

This conclusion followed the analysis of older cases. When a person sends a telex, it can be assumed they did so either because they intended the contents to be acted upon, or had the authority so to do. Upon receipt of the answerback, the sender may wish to revoke the original document, although to retract the document effectively may be difficult. Whether a document can be effectively revoked in this way will depend upon the circumstances of the case. When the transmission of a telex is completed, the recipient will have received the document in much the same way as if the document had been sent through the post. The recipient cannot be said to approve the content until it takes such action that demonstrate its approval. A number of issues were not examined in the judgment. Although none of these issues were in dispute in this case, they could arise in the future, as pointed out by Professor Reed:[7]

> 'It does not consider the effect of the cases which appear to require a mark to be made;

the identification messages of telex machines (and fax machines and computers) only identify the sending *machine*, not the sender;

it is quite possible to program a telex (or a fax machine or a computer's modem) to send a false identification message; and

if the message is stored on disk by the recipient, it is possible to edit the contents and amend the identification message to take account of the alteration.' (Italics in the original)

The acceptance of communications by telex in Australia occurred in 1985;[8] it has a long history of recognition in the United States of America at the federal level,[9] and Newman CJ made it clear, in the federal second circuit case of *Apex Oil Co., v Vanguard Oil & Services Co.*,[10] that the hasty formation of contracts did not pose a problem for the courts. It was held that an exchange of communications by telex satisfied the merchants exception to the Statute of Frauds, and he indicated, at 423, that 'Parties seeking the opportunity to make money with hurriedly arranged and briefly documented transactions ought not to expect appellate courts to provide them with extra protection against the risk that on occasion they will be held to the terms of an agreement that not every fact-finder would have found had been made.' Decisions at state level in relation to the Statute of Frauds follow this trend,[11] exemplified in the early 1948 Californian case of *Joseph Denunzio Fruit Co., v Crane*,[12] where signatures included in messages exchanged by teletype purporting to accept for sale three cartloads of grapes by a food broker on behalf of a buyer constituted a signature. O'Connor DJ observed at 128:

'As the court understands the modus operandi of the teletype machines in modern business practice, and particularly in connection with this lawsuit, Raymond R. Crane and A. B. Rains, Jr., each had a teletype machine in his office and as the machine was operated in one office, it would type the message or memorandum simultaneously in the other office; each party was readily identifiable and known to the other by the symbols or code letters used, and there is no contention that the messages did not originate in the office of one and terminate in the office of the other. The question is just what does constitute a "signature" or "signing" to satisfy the Statute of Frauds in California.

The court must take a realistic view of modern business practices, and can probably take judicial notice of the extensive use to which the teletype machine is being used today among business firms, particularly brokers, in the expeditious transmission of typewritten messages.'

In Thailand, case number 3046/2537 (1994) (Sale of Movable Property (Section 456 of the Civil & Commercial Code)) (known as the 'sticky rice' case) involved a Swiss company, Woodhouse Drake and Carrey SA buying Thai parboiled rice under a F.O.B. contract from Thaimapan Trading Co.

Ltd. Both parties communicated with each other by way of exchange of telex. Woodhouse Drake agreed to receive the parboiled rice at the Bangkok Port where the Thaimapan Trading office was located. Thaimapan Trading breached the sales contract by refusing to deliver the rice after Woodhouse Drake's vessel arrived at the Bangkok Port. Woodhouse initiated legal action for damages caused by Thaimapan Trading failing to deliver the rice. The position adopted by Thaimapan Trading was they neither knew of nor had ever transacted with Woodhouse Drake. The Court of First Instance, Appellate Court and Supreme Court all dismissed Woodhouse Drake's case. There were four main legal issues: first, the negotiations by telex could create a contact, but second, it was held that the requirements to create a valid contract were missing, namely partial payment, providing a deposit, and the signature of the person liable for the contract. Third, the plaintiff raised a new ground of appeal in the Supreme Court, that the telex correspondence was signed with a mark, not a signature, and the mark should be accepted as a form of signature. This argument was dismissed on two grounds, in that it was not raised at the trial, and in any event, the court failed to find the mark in the telex as claimed. The final issue was related to the third point, in that the writing requirements relating to a person's signature under Thai law requires a mark to be witnessed by two people affixing their manuscript signatures to the document, or the cross must be affixed before a competent authority. This decision was criticized at the time, but it is generally acknowledged that the Electronic Transaction Act B.E. 2544 (2001) that was passed after this case was decided, would provide a suitable remedy in similar circumstances in future.[13]

1   See http://en.wikipedia.org/wiki/Telegraphy#Telex for an overview of the technology.

2   Noboru Kashiwagi and E. Anthony Zaloom in The Business Guide to Japan, edited by Gerald Paul McAlinn, (1996), 89–101, re-published in Kenneth L. Port and Gerald Paul McAlinn, *Comparative Law: Law and the Legal Process in Japan* (Carolina Academic Press, 2nd edn, 2003), 459.

3   320 Hanrei Jiho 4 (November 10, 1962), Kobe District Court; translated by Luke Nottage in Kenneth L. Port and Gerald Paul McAlinn, *Comparative Law: Law and the Legal Process in Japan*, 480–483.

4   [1987] 1 Lloyd's Rep 546.

5   [1987] 1 Lloyd's Rep 546 at 556(b).

6   [1987] 1 Lloyd's Rep 546 at 554(b).

7   Professor Chris Reed, 'What is a Signature?' 4.1.

8   *Torrac Investments Pty Ltd v Australian National Airlines Commission* [1985] ANZ Conv R 82.

9   Federal, 2nd circuit: *Interocean Shipping Company v National Shipping and Training Corporation*, 523 F.2d 527 (1975) a signature typed into a telex under authority was sufficient to bind the principle.

10   760 F.2d 417 (1985).

11   New York: *Miller v Wells Fargo Bank International Corp.*, 406 F.Supp. 452 (1975) footnote 36 at 483 discusses the validity of a signature by way of a telex, and raised the issue as to whether a test key on telex is capable of being a signature.

Pennsylvania: *The Ore & Chemical Corporation v Howard Butcher Trading Corp.*, 455 F.Supp. 1150 (1978) the exchange of telex between parties can constitute a written contract.

Texas: *Hideca Petroleum Corporation v Tampimex Oil International Ltd.*, 740 S.W.2d 838 (Tex. App. – Houston 1st Dist.1987) the negotiation of sale for Dubai crude oil largely by means of exchange of telex.

12   79 F.Supp. 117 *reversed on other grounds upon rehearing* 89 F.Supp. 962.

13   Noppramart Thammateeradaycho, Case Note – Thailand, *Digital Evidence Journal*, 2006, Volume 3 Number 2, 118–120.

FACSIMILE

2.56   Not all jurisdictions accept the submission of documents by facsimile transmission, as in Brazil;[1] and one jurisdiction, Finland, case 16.11.2006/3044 KHO: 2006:87 is presently awaiting a ruling from the European Court of Justice respecting the validity of a grant sent by facsimile transmission.[2] In essence the case is about the admissibility and legal enforceability of documents transmitted by facsimile transmission. The main question in the case is whether an (European Agricultural Guidance and Guarantee Fund) export refund can be paid to the applicant irrespective of the fact that export declaration was delivered by facsimile transmission. Before making its decision, the Finnish Ministry of Agriculture and Forestry asked for the views of the EU Commission. The Commission replied that according to C-278/98 and C-27/94, an export refund cannot be paid if the export declaration is delivered by facsimile transmission. The Finnish Ministry of Agriculture and Forestry decided the matter in accordance with the Commission's reply and refused the export refund. The applicant appealed. The matter is now in the Finnish Supreme Administrative Court and they have asked for preliminary ruling from the European Court of Justice if Commission Regulation (EC) No 800/1999 art 5 can be interpreted in a way that accepts a facsimile transmission as an admissible export declaration. The response will be of interest, bearing in mind Case C-398/00, Judgment of the Court (18.6.2002), where the Court of Justice held that where there are no provisions that require the presentation of specific forms of original documents or original signatures or specific forms of transmission, communicating by way of facsimile transmission or email must be regarded as an acceptable form for communication with the Commission. A similar proposition was accepted in Case C-170/00, Judgment of the Court (24.1.2002), where a letter was sent by facsimile transmission by the Commission to a member state. Advocate-General Geelhoed considered the question of the admissibility of documents sent by facsimile transmission at 62 to 71 of his Opinion to this case dated 20 September 2001. The Finnish Government took the view that there was no obligation to accept a facsimile transmission, but Geelhoed pointed out, at 64, that Community law, both in the directives on electronic signatures and electronic commerce, 'now recognises electronic communication in a number of fields as equivalent to traditional paper communication.'

Documents sent by facsimile transmission may also not be accepted because of the nature of the document tendered and the propensity of the method of communication to increase the possibility of fraud, especially relating to property transactions, as in the Danish case of U.2006.1341V,[3] where mortgage bank N delivered a mortgage for the purpose of cancellation. The scanned signatures of A and B were affixed to the cancellation endorsement. By notice circulated to all judicial districts, N had authorised A and B to jointly endorse the mortgage by means of scanned manuscript signatures. The endorsements were added or attached to the original mortgage. The registration judge refused to cancel the mortgage because the signatures were not added by means of a manuscript signature in accordance with s 9(1) of the Danish Registration of Property Act. The High Court upheld this decision. In this respect, the registry took the view that under section 261(2) of the Danish Administration of Justice Act, the endorsement must be signed, see the Danish weekly law reports (UfR) 2001.1980/IH, since section 10 of the Registration of Property Act does not derogate from the general principle that pleadings to the court must be signed. According to established case law, pleadings must further be available in their original form, and photocopies or facsimiles were therefore not considered sufficient. Section 148(a) of the Administration of Justice Act provides, by Act no 447 of 9 June 2004, for the use of digital notifications by means of digital signatures, but the Act has yet to come into force.

The matter of a signature affixed to a document and sent by facsimile transmission was discussed in a recent case relating to criminal procedure in Poland.[4] The Supreme Court (Criminal Chamber) decided it is generally possible to send a document containing a manuscript signature by facsimile transmission, but the signature is not regarded as an original signature of the sender. In this instance, the court stated that the lack of a manuscript signature can be remedied, and if remedied (there is procedure under which the court may enable the remedy of some formal shortcomings within seven days), the appeal is deemed effectively delivered as of the day on which the facsimile transmission was received by the court.

However, documents sent by facsimile transmission have been accepted in other jurisdictions, especially common law jurisdictions. The use of a facsimile transmission to send a copy of a document to a recipient was considered in Singapore in 1989 in the case of *Chua Sock Chen v Lau Wai Ming*[5] in relation to the service of a notice to complete a transaction. Grimberg JC held that a notice to complete was properly served when sent by means of a facsimile transmission and where the original papers were subsequently sent by post to arrive the day after transmission. The learned judge responded to the argument that the notice sent by facsimile transmission was not a good service for the purposes of condition 29(2) and (3) of the Singapore Law Society's Conditions of Sale 1981 at 1126 B–C: 'I am unable to accept that contention. Neither of the two conditions I have quoted calls for the giving or servicing of notice to complete by a stipulated method. In these days of instantaneous communication it would be unrealistic and retrogressive, in the absence of clear words to the contrary under condition 29(2) and (3) by fax or telex is bad.' Although the decision on the substance of the case was reversed on appeal, the members of the court of appeal offered no comments in relation to this aspect of the decision by Grimberg JC, which leads to the inference that his comments were adopted.

A similar issue arose in England and Wales in the case of *Re a debtor (No 2021 of 1995), Ex p, Inland Revenue Commissioners v The debtor; Re a debtor (No 2022 of 1995), Ex, Inland Revenue Commissioners v The debtor.*[6] On Friday 9 June 1995 the Commissioners of Inland Revenue sent a completed form of proxy by first class post with directions to the chairman of a meeting of creditors to vote against the debtors' proposals for voluntary arrangements. On the morning of the meeting, the Commissioners sent a facsimile transmission of the completed form of proxy to the chairman's office. Although not stated in the report of the case, it is probable that the form transmitted included the manuscript signature of the relevant official. When it was received, the chairman sought to verify the contents of the transmission by telephoning the Commissioners office, but he was not able to speak to the officer handling the case. He refused to act upon the instructions sent by facsimile transmission. The original form of proxy arrived the following day. The Commissioners appealed the decision at first instance, where the district judge decided that the proxy sent by facsimile transmission was not signed as required by r 8.2(3) of the Insolvency Rules 1986 (SI 1986/1925). The question was, should the facsimile transmission of the form of proxy have been accepted and acted upon by the chairman. In reaching his decision, Laddie J noted that given there was no direct authority on this point, he had to approach the issue from first principles. Having reviewed *Jenkins v Gainsford and Thring*[7] and *Goodman v J Eban Limited*,[8] he observed that:

> '... in the overwhelming majority of cases in which the chairman of a creditors' meeting received a proxy form, the form will bear a signature which he does not recognise and may well be illegible. Authenticity could only be enhanced if the creditor carrying suitable identification signed the form in person in the presence of the chairman. Even there the possibility of deception exists.'[9]

Interestingly, he went on to suggest '... that the function of a signature is to indicate, but not necessarily prove, that the document has been considered personally by the creditor and is approved of by him.'[10] Laddie J then took the matter one stage further, and made the following observation, which is directly related to the concept of an electronic signature:

> 'It may be said that a qualifying proxy form consists of two ingredients. First, it contains the information required to identify the creditor and his voting instructions and, secondly, the signature performing the function set out above. When the chairman receives a proxy form bearing what

purports to be a signature, he is entitled to treat it as authentic unless there are surrounding circumstances which indicate otherwise.'

In reaching the conclusion that a proxy form is acceptable when sent by facsimile transmission,[11] Laddie J noted that two things happen at the same time. The contents of the form are sent, and so is the signature applied to the form, described thus:

'The receiving fax is in effect instructed by the transmitting creditor to reproduce his signature on the proxy form which is itself being created at the receiving station. It follows that, in my view, the received fax is a proxy form signed by the principal or by someone authorized by him.'[12]

This decision was reached in November 1995 without, it seems, the benefit of the knowledge of the decision by Waller J in *Standard Bank London Ltd v Bank of Tokyo Ltd*,[13] which was delivered on 13 March 1995. The decision by Waller J is based on a tested telex between banks, which is a slightly different concept to a facsimile transmission, because a tested telex provides for a separate method of authenticating the content of the transmission. Nevertheless, in both cases, an emphasis was placed on the fact that a document sent by such means can be considered authentic and reliable, provided the recipient was not aware of any particulars that might indicate the document cannot be so trusted. A case similar to that determined by Waller J in *Standard Bank London Ltd v Bank of Tokyo Ltd* was heard before Tay Yong Kwang JC in Singapore in 2003, in which he held, in the case of *Industrial & Commercial Bank Ltd v Banco Ambrosiano Veneto SpA*,[14] that a message using an authentication code sent through the SWIFT (Society for Worldwide Interbank Financial Telecommunication) system has the legal effect of binding the sender bank according to its contents, and where a recipient bank undertakes further checks on credit standing or other aspects, it does not detract from this proposition. The effect of the comments made by Laddie J, taken together with the comments by Waller J, suggest a move towards a responsibility by a recipient to consider all the circumstances of the means of authentication before acting upon the authority – certainly when documents are sent electronically.

More recently, the Vice Chancellor, Sir Andrew Morritt, was required to reach a decision on the identical point in the case of *PNC Telecom plc v Thomas*,[15] as to whether the service of a notice sent by facsimile transmission for an extraordinary general meeting on a members' requisition under s 368 of the Companies Act 1985 was valid. By s 368, notice to call a meeting is required to be deposited at the registered office of the company. The claimant argued that the notice was not valid on three counts, because it was sent by facsimile transmission, and the use of a facsimile transmission was not permitted within the meaning of 'deposited' in s 368; that the Companies Act 1985 (Electronic Communication) Order 2000 (SI 2000/3373) had made service by electronic means in respect of some sections of the 1985 Act, but not for s 368, and there was a requirement to know that the notice received at the registered office was genuine, which meant that it was not permissible to send a notice by facsimile transmission. Sir Andrew referred to a number of authorities in which a facsimile transmission had been accepted by the courts, and rejected all of the arguments put forward by the claimant. He considered the deposit of the notice by facsimile transmission was valid, and robustly responded, at 94 a–b, to the illogical claim about the reliability of such a means of transmitting a document thus: 'For the reasons given by Laddie J in the last citation, there is nothing inherent in a fax transmission to make it more or less reliable than the post. It is true that a fax may be falsified by a cut and paste operation but forgery and falsification is equally possible, usually by other means, in connection with postal and personal transmission too.'

The same position with respect to facsimile transmissions holds in Canada, where, in the case of *Re United Canso Oil & Gas Ltd*[16] proxy forms submitted with a facsimile or mechanically rendered signature were held to be sufficient. Hallett J at 289 paragraph 17 made the point clear: 'Today's business could not be conducted if stamped signatures were not recognized as legally binding. The affixing of a stamp conveys the intention to be bound by the document so executed just as effectively as the manual writing of a signature by hand. I would point out that no one questions the validity of millions of payroll cheques signed by facsimile signatures.' This view is echoed in the Singapore decision of Lim Teong Qwee JC in the case of *Masa-Katsu Japanese Restaurant Pte Ltd v Amara Hotel Properties Pte Ltd*,[17] in which he held that a facsimile transmission of a request to extend the term of a lease was a valid form of communicating. He commented, at 18:

'The written request dated 4 October 1997 was in fact received by the landlord. It was received by fax on 10 October 1997. It was not suggested that it was received other than at the landlord's office where it could be attended to immediately. It was undoubtedly in writing when it was received. Communication by fax is not uncommon. It is fast. It is efficient. It accords with the practice of the business community. It seems to me that where as in this case a written request is to be made it is sufficiently made as much where the request is written on paper that is physically transported to the office of the person to whom the request is made as where it is transmitted by fax and received in written form at that person's office.'

Consideration was also given to a signature sent by way of facsimile transmission in the German case of GmS-OGB 1/98 before the Gemeinsamer Senat der obersten Gerichtshöfe des Bundes (Joint Senate of the Federal High Courts) in 2000. In this instance, The Joint Senate of the Federal High Courts was requested to decide on the question whether or not a facsimile transmission sent directly from a computer (Computerfax) with a scanned signature, complied with the requirements of written form for formal court pleadings. In the normal course of events, various rules of German procedural law require formal court pleadings to be signed with a manuscript signature, and a number of Federal High Courts have provided decisions on this in the past.[18] The court held that it was sufficient to transfer pleadings electronically in this manner, providing the documents are signed with a scanned signature or if the document transmitted indicates that the document could not be signed personally because of method of transmission. The members of the court, comprised the President, Dr. Franßen, and Dr. Geiß, Dr. Ebling, v. Wulffen, Dr. Wißmann, Nobbe, Dr. Hohrmann and Dr. Siol. They reached the conclusion on the basis that the formal requirements of procedural law do not serve as an end in themselves, and the purpose of requiring court proceedings to be in written form is to identify the sender and ensure the document was sent with the sender's knowledge and intent. As a result, the intention of the sender is not seriously in doubt because of the method of transmission.[19]

Similarly, in Hungary, case number BDT 2001/496, pre-dating the entry into force of 2001. évi XXXV. Törvény az elektronikus aláírásról (Digital Signature Act 2001), considered the legal effect of facsimile transmissions. In this instance, the reasoning of the court set forth the principle that a signature is not always an essential element of the written form of a document. The provisions of s 38(2) of Law-Decree no. XI of 1960 on the entry into force and execution of the Hungarian Civil Code, in effect before the enactment of the Digital Signature Act 2001, provided that if a statute provides a contract to be valid only if drawn up in writing, in the absence of an alternate provision of law, an agreement concluded by way of postal mail, telegram, and transmitting by telex shall be considered as a contract drawn up in writing (transmissions by facsimile and the use of digital signatures were not on the list). In the view of the members of the court, this rule also applied to computer facsimiles. Facsimiles sent from a computer are prepared electronically and are sent via facsimile to the addressee, thus appearing in writing only when received by the addressee. Such documents accurately reflect the thoughts of the person producing them, yet they do not contain the signature of the person sending the document, but that did not prevent a facsimile sent by computer of generating legal effects in the same way as telegrams and telex. The position in Lithuania is similar, as demonstrated by *UAB "Bite Lietuva" v Communications Regulatory Authority*,[20] in which the Supreme Administrative Court, in its ruling of 13 April 2006, held that the copy of an administrative decision sent by facsimile transmission constituted a proper form of notification by the governmental institution of its decision.

In the United States, a federal court on the ninth circuit found itself severely constrained by a set of extremely strict rules laid down by the Bureau of Land Management in the case of *Gilmore v Lujan* respecting documents sent by facsimile transmission.[21] In this instance, an application was sent by facsimile transmission because the original postal application had not arrived on time.

The Bureau refused to accept the documents sent by facsimile transmission because the papers were not signed with a manuscript signature. Upon appeal, this decision was upheld because the signature was required to be as manuscript signature only, and no other form was permitted. The Bureau of Land Management required applications to be holographically signed in ink by each potential lessee, and machine or rubber stamped signatures were not acceptable. The rule was altered after the case of *W. H. Gilmore*,[22] where Gilmore protested the lease was awarded to an applicant that used a rubber stamp as a signature. The regulations were deliberately altered to only permit manuscript signatures thereafter. Although the regulations required the signature to be in ink, nevertheless the Board determined, in the later case of *Jack Williams*,[23] that a signature signed with a lead pencil was adequate. Nelson CJ criticized the decision, indicating, at 142, that:

> 'Justice Holmes observed that citizens dealing with their government must turn square corners .... Gilmore turned all but the last millimetre, but that millimetre, whose traverse is jealously guarded by the BLM, was his undoing. Relief to Gilmore in this narrow case would expose BLM to no fraud or risk of fraud, as his bona fides are beyond question. If Gilmore and those other few luckless applicants whose documents are stored rather than delivered by the Postal Service are to get any relief, it must come at the hands of the BLM. As shown by this case, those hands are more iron than velvet. We can only suggest to BLM that the body politic would not be put at risk by the granting of relief in these narrow and rare situations.'

The use of facsimile transmissions have been challenged in other situations, such as arbitration[24] and elections.[25] In addition, cases have occurred under the Statute of Frauds,[26] although not always successfully. In particular, the practice of programming the machine to include the name of the sender on the top or bottom of each page automatically was challenged in the New York case of *Parma Tile Mosaic & Marble Co., Inc. v Estate of Fred Short, d/b/a Sime Construction Co.*[27] In this instance, it was held that the automatic imprinting by the facsimile machine of the name of the sender at the top of each page transmitted did not satisfy the requirement that writing shall be subscribed. Smith J offered the following opinion:

> 'The act of identifying and sending a document to a particular destination does not, by itself, constitute a signing authenticating the contents of the document for Statute of Frauds purposes and reject plaintiff's argument that such an inference is warranted here. It is undisputed that MRLS' fax machine, after being programmed to do so, automatically imprinted "MRLS Construction" on every page transmitted, without regard to the applicability of the Statute of Frauds to a particular document. We also reject plaintiff's contention that the intentional act of programming

a fax machine, by itself, sufficiently demonstrates to the recipient the sender's apparent intention to authenticate every document subsequently faxed. The intent to authenticate the particular writing at issue must be demonstrated.'[28]

It is respectfully suggested that this decision by the members of the Court of Appeals in New York does not accord with the case law (see their references at 635) and the argument that no contract was made (at 635) does not follow from the nature of the document sent by facsimile transmission, which read: '… this company would be willing to guarantee payment on regular terms for goods delivered … [Upon deliver of the tile] (y)ou would then bill Sime Construction for those goods delivered. MRLS would guarantee payment for goods delivered to the Nehemiah Project in the event Sime Construction does not pay within terms … Please consider all the above in making your decision.'[29]

In Canada, forms of proxy sent by facsimile transmission were the subject matter of the British Columbia case of *Beatty v First Exploration Fund 1987 and Company, Limited Partnership*.[30] In this case, it was held that forms of proxy sent by facsimile transmission were sufficient to meet the signature requirements under a limited partnership agreement. Hinds J indicated, at 383 that 'The faxed proxies were not themselves signed, but they bore the photographic reproduction of the original of the limited partner who executed the particular proxy.' He went on to say at 383, that 'The law has endeavoured to take cognizance of, and to be receptive to, technological advances in the means of communication. The development of that approach may be observed in a number of cases, including the following.' At 385 he addressed the argument relating to the theoretical possibility that such transmissions might be the subject of fraud, which is hardly an argument to use when the authenticity of the document in question has not been challenged:

'It was argued by counsel for the Fund that validating faxed proxies would increase the risk of fraud, create uncertainty, and give an unfair advantage to those limited partners who had access to a telecopier or fax machine. I reject that argument. Faxed proxies are, in effect, a photocopy of an original copy. They reveal what is depicted on an original copy, including an exact replica of the signature of the person who signed the original proxy. I observe no greater opportunity for the perpetration of a fraud by the use of faxed copies than by the use of original copies. The same observation applies to the matter of uncertainty.'

1   RMS-AgR-ED 24257 DF (Distrito Federal Interlocutory Appeal Relating to Writ of Mandamus) Supremo Tribunal Federal (Brazilian Supreme Court) and AI 564765 RJ – Rio De Janeiro, Supremo Tribunal Federal (Brazilian Supreme Court) Interlocutory Appeal, both are reported by Professor Carlos Alberto Rohrmann, Case Note: Brazil, *Digital Evidence Journal*, 2006, Volume 3 Number 2 109–114.

2   The original text in Finnish is available online at http://www.finlex.fi/fi/oikeus/kho/vuosikirjat/2006/200603044.

3   Danish Western High Court, 27 February 2007; to be published in English translation in the *Digital Evidence Journal*, 2007, Volume 4 Number 2.

4   Resolution from 20 December 2006, I KZP 29/06, not published.

5   [1989] SLR 1119, the decision on the substance of the case was reversed on appeal [1992] 2 SLR 465.

6   [1996] 2 All ER 345, Ch D.

7   (1863) 3 Sw & Tr 93; 164 ER 1208.

8   [1954] 1 QB 550; [1954] 1 All ER 763; [1954] 2 WLR 581, CA.

9   [1996] 2 All ER 345, Ch D at 351 (b–c).

10   [1996] 2 All ER 345, Ch D at 351(d).

11   Laddie J made it clear that the decision he made was only in relation to Part 8 of the Insolvency Rules 1986, and said 'Different considerations may apply to faxed documents in relation to other legislation' at 352(d–e).

12   [1996] 2 All ER 345, Ch D at 351(h).

13   [1995] CLC 496; [1996] 1 C.T.L.R. T-17.

14   [2003] 1 SLR 221.

15   [2003] BCC 202, [2004] 1 BCLC 88, [2002] EWHC 2848, 2002 WL 31676421.

16   (1980) 12 B.L.R. 130; 76 A.P.R. 282; 41 N.S.R.(2d) 282 (T.D.).

17   [1999] 2 SLR 332.

18   Federal Social Court, Beschluß vom 15.10.1996–14 BEg 9/96; Federal Administrative Court, Beschluss vom 19.12.1994–5 B 79/94.

19   Michael Knopp, Case Note, *e-Signature Law Journal* (now the *Digital Evidence Journal*), 2005, Volume 2 Number 2, 117–118.

20   Case number AS14–77-06.

21   947 F.2d 1409 (9th Cir. 1991).

22   41 IBLA 25 (1979).

23   91 IBLA 355 (1986).

24   New York (1989): *In the Matter of American Multimedia, Inc., v Dalton Packaging, Inc.*, 143 Misc.2d 295, 540 N.Y.S.2d 410 an order was transmitted by facsimile machine that only contained the first of two pages of an order form, stating that all orders were subject to the terms and conditions on the reverse of the form, which was not sent. It was held that the terms did apply, because the petitioner had filed over 100 such orders in the previous three years.

25   New Jersey: *Madden v Hegadorn*, 565 A.2d 725 (N.J. Super.L. 1989), 236 N.J.Super. 280, *affirmed* 571 A.2d 296 (N.J. 1989), 239 N.J.Super. 268 a document sent by facsimile transmission containing a manuscript signature was deemed effective for filing a nomination petition, and any technical defects were cured when the candidate filed the original documents the day after the facsimile transmission. Troast JLD commented on the technology of facsimile transmissions at 728: 'Facsimile technology is relatively new. It is common knowledge that "fax" machines electronically scan documents, reduce the documents to a series of digital signals and transmit them over telephone lines to a receiving machine which reassembles the signals and then reproduces the original documents.'

26   New York (1996): *WPP Group USA, Inc., v The Interpublic Group of Companies, Inc.*, 644 N.Y.S.2d 205, 228 A.D.2d 296 it was premature to decide whether the Statute of Frauds was satisfied where an unsigned facsimile transmission on the letterhead of the sender was sent. For the merchant's exception see the New York case of *Bazak International Corp., v Mast Industries, Inc.*, 140 Ad.2d 211, 528 N.Y.S.2d 62, 6 UCC Rep.Serv.2d 375, *appeal granted by* 72 N.Y.2D 808, 529 N.E.2d 425, 533 N.E.2d 57 (N.Y. 1988), *Order reversed by* 73 N.Y.2D 113, 535 N.E.2d 633, 538 N.Y.2d 503, 57 USLW 2520, 82 A.L.R.4th 689, 7 UCC Rep.Serv.2d 1380 (N.Y. 1989) where annotated telecopies ('telecopies' is a trademark sometimes used for a facsimile machine) of headed purchase order forms signed by the alleged purchaser and sent to the alleged seller and retained without objection came within the merchant's exception to the Statute of Frauds.

27   155 Misc.2d 950, 590 N.Y.S.2d 1019 (Supp. 1992), *motion for summary judgment affirmed*, 209

A.D.2d 495, 619 N.Y.S.2d 628 *reversed* 663 N.E.2d 633 (N.Y. 1996), 640 N.Y.S.2d 477 (Ct. App. 1996), 87 N.Y.2D 524.
28   663 N.E.2d 633 (N.Y. 1996) at 635.
29   590 N.Y.S.2d 1019 (Supp. 1992) at 1020.
30   25 B.C.L.R.2d 377 (1988).

The writing material

2.57   In the days before the development of techniques to identify microscopic indentations or traces of lead on paper, the material used to write on a document could cause conceptual problems. The nature of the writing material used to affix a signature was raised in the case of *Geary v Physic*.[1] An objection was taken where a promissory note was signed using a pencil. At the trial, the Lord Chief Justice, Abbott CJ, thought the promissory note was sufficiently indorsed, and directed the members of the jury to find a verdict for the plaintiff. He also permitted the plaintiff to challenge this finding. The matter was subsequently argued before Abbott CJ, Bayley and Holroyd JJ. In his judgment, the Lord Chief Justice pointed out, 'There is no authority for saying that where the law requires a contract to be in writing, that writing must be in ink.'[2] This decision was made before the development of the forensic analysis of materials and the use of technology as a means of detecting changes to materials. Although it is now possible to detect the erasure of a manuscript signature if it were to be affixed using a pencil, the principle established by this decision remains sound. The rationale for this decision is the principle that a signature was affixed to the document with an intent that it should be acted upon. Hence the type of writing material used was irrelevant, providing it was not removed from the document. This decision may also be considered correct on the premise that the promissory note was only valid for a limited period of time, and the use of a pencil to sign the note may not have been considered relevant because there was no requirement to retain a permanent record of the note.

A similar issue arose in *Lucas v James*,[3] where a series of remarks on a draft under-lease were written in pencil, including the words 'I agree to these terms, subject to the above observations. W. M. James'. In this instance, the plaintiff sought specific performance, whilst the defendant denied an agreement had been reached, arguing in part that the comments made by him on the draft, being made in pencil, were not intended to be binding. Although the claim failed for other reasons, the Vice-Chancellor, Sir James Wigram, made the extra-judicial remark that these words, taken in conjunction with a previous comment made by the defendant on the same draft, would, on the face of it, bind him to the terms of the under-lease.[4] The Vice-Chancellor made it clear that the remarks made in pencil demonstrated a willingness to be bound by the amended document. In this instance, the use of pencil on the document was deemed perfectly acceptable as evidence of the writer's intent to agree the terms of the document.

Whether the nature of a document has been changed sufficiently as the result of alterations made in pencil was the subject of *Co-operative Bank plc v Tipper*.[5] Mr and Mrs Tipper entered into a personal guarantee with the bank, but it transpired that the document erroneously described the defendants personally as both the customer (ie the principal debtor) and the guarantor. The bank applied to the court to rectify the error after Mr and Mrs Tipper's company went into liquidation. Mr and Mrs Tipper opposed the application of the bank on the basis that where a document is altered in a material way, the document becomes void, and therefore unenforceable. In this instance, a person unknown working for the bank used a pencil to strike out the names of Mr and Mrs Tipper and added the name and address of the company. His Honour Judge Roger Cooke concluded that the proper evidential inference to draw was that the alterations constituted a drafting amendment. The changes made in pencil were not intended to alter the substance of the document, but were meant to propose that the names be put in the correct place in the document. As a result, the use of pencil did not alter the content of the document because the use of a pencil constituted a series of suggestions to correct errors in the document.

The use of a lead pencil has also been the subject of a number of decisions in the United States of America, include bills of exchange,[6] Statute of Frauds,[7] wills[8] and deeds, as in the 1920 Missouri case of *Kleine v Kleine*,[9] in which John Kleine granted his sister a lease on a portion of land, and it was signed with a lead pencil. It was held to be a valid instrument. Graves J, indicated, at 610 what he thought of Kleine and his motive for using a lead pencil in this instance:

'Kleine's testimony in the case tends to leave a bad taste in the judicial mouth. Among other things, he requested that the lease be signed with a lead pencil, and says that he "figured" that it was no good when he signed it, "because there was no starting point." All this was after the sister had put her money into the improvements.'

The learned judge went on, at 611, to observe that 'The real issue in the case is not the views expressed by John Kleine, to the effect that he signed the lease (in lead pencil, at his own suggestion) because he thought it invalid, owing to the absence of a starting point. He seems not only to have had that idea, but the other erroneous view, entertained by many laymen, that a deed must be signed with a pen and ink.' His comments illustrate the frustration by many lawyers of the erroneous and endlessly inaccurate comments made by lay people respecting the legal issues relating to all manner of things, especially electronic signatures and digital evidence.

However, it is the use of a lead pencil on a judicial document in 1823 that serves to illustrate the fallacy about the use of lead pencil as a means of affixing a signature to a document, and also in relation to whether a document is open to attack. In the Columbia case of *United States v Thompson*,[10] it was held that an indictment for assault and battery for violently beating a slave and signed by a Justice of the Peace with a lead pencil was not a sufficient signature. The reason given by Cranch CJ was that 'it is liable to be so easily obliterated.' This is a false conclusion based on an erroneous premise. The logic of the reasoning runs as follows: a material that can be erased was used to affix the signature to the document; ergo the signature is not valid because it is possible to erase the signature. It is correct that the material impressed on to paper by a lead pencil can be erased, but the possibility that the writing can be erased does not prevent the document from having been signed. In this instance, the document was signed with the manuscript signature of a Justice of the Peace. The evidence of the signature was clear for all to see, which meant the signature was sufficient. Had the signature been erased, then the integrity of the document would have been questioned, and, depending on the strength or weakness of the evidence tendered and tested before the court, a decision could be made as to the authenticity of the document, which in turn would enable the trier of fact to determine whether the document had been signed or not. This argument is often used by lawyers with respect to documents in electronic and digital format. The argument runs like this: because it is possible to forge an email, facsimile transmission or electronic signature (any form of electronic signature); ergo the email, facsimile transmission or electronic signature should not be admitted because of the possibility of forgery. This argument was successfully used in the German case reference AG Bonn Urteil vom 25.10.2001 3 C 193/01 Beweiskraft von E-Mails, JurPC Web-Dok. 332/2002,[11] where the claimant sued the defendant for a broker's fee for acting as an intermediary for the sale of cigarettes. The claim was dismissed on the basis that there was no sufficient proof, because the emails submitted in evidence had no value as evidence because it is generally known that emails can be easily altered or forged. This argument is also fallacious. Any paper document can be forged, such as a letter from a commercial entity or a government, and lawyers are required to sift through documentary evidence regularly to test the authenticity of documents. The forgery of evidence is hardly new, and if this argument was to be accepted by judges, which it seems to be in some cases, then by logical extension, any item of documentary evidence could be excluded because it was possible to forge. If it is suggested an item of evidence is forged, the question should be raised before trial, so that the party relying on the evidence has the opportunity to adduce evidence to prove the document is genuine. It is submitted that unsound arguments based on a flawed foundation have no place in a court.

1   (1826) 5 B & C 234; 108 ER 87.
2   (1826) 5 B & C 234 at 237.
3   (1849) 7 Hare 410; 68 ER 170.
4   (1849) 7 Hare 410 at 419.
5   [1996] 4 All ER 366 Ch.
6   New York (1844): *Brown v The Butchers & Drovers' Bank*, 6 Hill 443, 41Am.Dec. 755 the endorsement of a bill of exchange using a lead pencil is sufficient.

Vermont (1831): *Clossen v Stearns*, 4 Vt. 11, 1831 WL 2104 (Vt.), 23 Am.Dec. 245 the endorsement of a promissory note by means of a lead pencil held to be valid.

7   Missouri (1907): *Great Western Printing Co., v Belcher*, 127 Mo.App. 133, 104 S.W. 894 the words 'Guaranteed. Belcher' written in lead pencil across the face of the original account for the payment of $44.50 in respect of posters is a signature, even though the signature did not include first name.

New York (1817): *Merritt v Clason*, 12 Johns. 102, 7 Am.Dec. 286, 12 N.Y.S.C. 1814-15 92 *affirmed as The Executors of Clason v Bailey*, 14 Johns. 484 where a memorandum of a contract was written down in a notebook using a lead pencil, the document is a sufficient memorandum within the Statute of Frauds.

South Carolina (1844): *Draper v Pattina*, 29 S.C.L. 292, 2 Speers 292, 1844 WL 2584 (S.C.App.L.) a memorandum written using a lead pencil was not a valid objection.

8   Pennsylvania (1890): *Appeal of Knox*, 131 P. 220, 18 A. 1021, 6 L.R.A. 353, 17 Am.St.Rep. 798 an instrument written in lead pencil was sufficient to be admitted as a will.

9   219 S.W. 610, 281 Mo. 317.

10   2 Cranch C.C. 409, 28 F.Cas. 89, 2 D.C. 409, No 16484.

11   Available online at http://www.jurpc.de/rechtspr/20020332.htm.

Oral adoption of the content of a document

Statute of Frauds

2.58   It appears that the oral adoption of a contract under the Statute of Frauds is a rare occurrence, although in 1857, it was decided in the case of *Smith v Neale*[1] that a written proposal containing the terms of the contract, signed by one party and assented to by the other party by word of mouth was sufficient to satisfy s 4 of the Statute of Frauds. Other unusual methods of proving intent include the tape recording of a conversation, as in the Colorado case of *Ellis Canning Company v Bernstein*,[2] where a contract was reduced to tangible form when an oral conversation was recorded, and the tape recording held to be sufficient to satisfy the provisions of the Statute of Frauds; and authentication over the telephone in the Delaware case of *Parshalle v Roy*[3] where a proxy authorized by datagram (a datagram is a procedure in which a registered shareholder uses a toll-free telephone number to communicate their vote in telegraphic or 'datagram' form) was held not to be valid where there is insufficient evidence to demonstrate the authenticity and genuineness of the process to link the voter to the vote cast.

1   2 C. B. (N. S.) 67; 140 ER 337.
2   348 F.Supp. 1212 (1972).
3   Del.Ch., 567 A.2d 19 (1989).

Wills

2.59   On occasion, instances occur when a will does not conform to form as determined by statute, and judges have to apply underlying principles to reach a judgment. In the case of *Gryle v Gryle*[1] a will was executed in the presence of two witnesses. The testatrix later said, '... this is my will ...' in the presence of a third witness. However, she did not add her seal on this second occasion, or adopt the signature she affixed to the will on the first occasion by declaring to the third witness that the signature she placed on the document before the first two witnesses was of her handwriting. In this instance, the Lord Chancellor considered the will was void. This was because the signing did not conform to the required form. The will was not re-sealed by the testatrix in the presence of the third witness, nor did she declare her first signature to be her handwriting. Giving no absolute opinion on the matter, he agreed to the suggestion by counsel for the plaintiff that the case be stood over with a view to obtaining evidence of acts that may have been done that might amount to the confirmation of the will.[2]

This matter was raised again in the later case of *Ellis v Smith*.[3] The testator made his first will in England. He later travelled to New York, America, and made a second will. It appears three witnesses subscribed the second will, and the testator declared it to be his will before the witnesses, but did not sign it. A trial could not take place because the original of the will was not in England. As a result, the Lord Chancellor, Lord Hardwick, permitted the case to go before the Court of King's Bench for the court's opinion. The members of the court doubted whether such a declaration was sufficient to comply with s 5 of the Statute of Frauds 1677, but were bound by previous decisions. Parker CB expressed the view that such an admission would '... let in inconveniencies and perjuries, which the statute designed to prevent;'[4] whilst Willes CJ would have preferred more time to consider the point, and agreed that '... the cases admitting the attestation at three different times have gone too far ... and an inlet is made for great frauds and impositions.'[5] Sir John Strange MR accepted the issue was settled, but continued '... yet I think it a dangerous determination, and destructive of those barriers the statute erected against perjury and frauds'[6] and Lord Hardwick LC reluctantly suggested the authorities were stronger than the court's ability to shake them, offering the opinion that they '... go too far, and open a way to frauds ... and the Courts should go no farther.'[7] It was reluctantly, but unanimously agreed, that where the testator acknowledges his handwriting, this act can be deemed to be as being equivalent to the signing of the document.[8]

The comments offered by the members of the court in this case were used by the members of the Judicial Committee of the Privy Council in the case of *Casement v Fulton*[9] to restrict the concept that a person may orally acknowledge his signature and adopt the content of a document. General Sir William Casement was struck down with cholera on 14 April 1844, and recognising the dangers of not recovering, he made his last will in writing on 16 April 1844 in his house in Cassipore, near Calcutta. He left the whole of his property to his wife. He duly read over and signed the will in the presence of Mr Nicholson, a medical attendant and Lieutenant Colonel Hawkins. As there was no place upon which the will could be placed to be signed, Mr Nicholson took the will and subscribed his name to it at a table in the adjoining room, which stood in site of the couch where the general was placed. Both Mr Nicholson and Colonel Hawkins then waited for Mr Roberts, who arrived some two hours later. Colonel Hawkins then produced the will and requested Mr Roberts to attest it. Before doing so, Mr Roberts required general Casement to acknowledge his signature. Before all three men, he acknowledged his signature and stated that the document was his will. Mr Roberts then subscribed to the will in the same manner as Mr Nicholson. Mr Nicholson then acknowledged his subscription to the will in the presence of general Casement and Mr Roberts, but did not sign it for a second time. The respondents were the next of kin of the deceased. The question in this instance was whether or not the subscription of the two witnesses was made in accordance with the requirements of s 7 of the Indian Will Act 1838,[10] which required:

> '... that no Will shall be valid unless it shall be in writing, and executed in manner hereinafter mentioned (that is to say), it shall be signed at the foot or end thereof by the Testator, or by some other person in his presence, and by his direction, and such signature shall be made or acknowledged by the Testator, in the presence of two or more witnesses, present at the same time; and such witnesses shall subscribe the Will in the presence of the Testator, but no form of attestation shall be necessary.'

The recommendation by the Privy Council was given by Lord Brougham, in which the sentence of the Supreme Court at Calcutta was affirmed, in that the requirements of the Act had not been sufficiently complied with in this case. In his judgment, Lord Brougham indicated that the members of the Privy Council intended to prevent any further extension of the precedent, as expressed by the members of the court in *Ellis v Smith*.[11] He made it clear that, regardless of the lack of any impropriety in the behaviour of the participants to this set of facts, further extensions of the rule were to end:

> 'We are thus fully warranted in refusing to carry one step further, a construction which so great a weight of authority lamented, and showed to have been ill-advised in its inception, and we are left in no doubt how these eminent Judges would have dealt with the present attempt to extend the latitude already given. They never would have held, that a witness acknowledging his subscription in the presence of his fellow-witness was equivalent to his signing in that fellow-witness's presence.'[12]

There was a conflict between being fair in the circumstances, against providing for legal certainty. This decision can be distinguished by the fact that the two attesting witnesses signed the document at separate times, although in the modern case of *Weatherhill v Pearce*,[13] it appeared that the two attesting witnesses did not sign the document together in the presence of the testatrix, yet the handwriting of the testatrix was held to be a sufficient signature for the purposes of s 9 of the Wills Act 1837.

1   (1741) 2 Atk 176; 26 ER 509.

2   The Lord Chancellor mentioned the case of *Lee v Libb* 3 Mod 262, 87 ER 173; 1 Show KB 68, 88, 89 ER 454, 468; Comberbach 174, 90 ER 413; Carthew 35, 90 ER 625; Holt KB 742, 90 ER 1308; 3 Salkeld 395, 91 ER 893. In this case, two witnesses, instead of the required three, signed a codicil. Dolben J is reported to have said '… he was very sorry that they could not help the plaintiff, for two witnesses do as much shew the intent of the devisor, as twenty …' Comberbach 174 at 176.

3   (1754) 1 Ves Jun 11; 1 Ves Jun Supp 1; 30 ER 205; 34 ER 666.

4   (1754) 1 Ves Jun 11 at 11.

5   (1754) 1 Ves Jun 11 at 14.

6   (1754) 1 Ves Jun 11 at 14.

7   (1754) 1 Ves Jun 11 at 16.

8   Followed by the Master of the Rolls in *Addy v Grix* (1803) 8 Ves Jun 504; 32 ER 450; see also *Wood v Smith* [1993] Ch 90, CA, Civil Division; [1992] 3 All ER 556 CA Civil Division where a holograph will beginning 'My Will by Percy Winterbone …' was written out by the testator. He then asked the two witnesses to sign the document. When asked to sign the document by one of the witnesses, he declared he had already signed at the top of the document with the inclusion of his name at the beginning. The members of the Court of Appeal agreed that the declaration he made to both witnesses was sufficient evidence to establish that his writing of his name amounted to a signature. In the judgment of the court given by Scott LJ, he reiterated the point at 111E, that: 'The object of a signature by a testator … is to authenticate the written document in question as the will of the testator.'

9   [1845] 5 Moore 130 PC; 13 ER 439.

10 This section was a copy of s 9 of the Wills Act 1837, with the omission of the words 'shall attest'.

11 (1754) 1 Ves Jun 11; 1 Ves Jun Supp 1; 30 ER 205; 34 ER 666.

12 [1845] 5 Moore 130 PC at 138–139.

13 [1995] 2 All ER 492, Ch D.

No signature on the document

2.60   Two further illustrations demonstrate the willingness of judges to imply a document has been signed in the absence of a manuscript signature. In the case of *Rist v Hobson*,[1] an agreement for the sale and purchase of an estate had been drawn up but not signed by either party. The vendor sought an order for specific performance, and Sir John Leach VC reached the conclusion that where the agreement was in writing, it would be presumed the document was signed unless evidence to the contrary was adduced to rebut the presumption. It is not clear from the report whether the agreement had been committed to writing by either of the parties in this instance. However, in the later case of *Bleakley v Smith*,[2] the agreement had been written in the hand of one of the parties. Mr Bridges agreed to sell five houses in Liverpool to John Bleakley. The only evidence to this agreement was a memorandum, written by Mr Bridges: 'July 26th, 1839. John Bleakley agrees with J R Bridges to take the property in Cable Street for the net sum of £248 10s.' Mr Bridges died on 10 February 1840, but had not conveyed the property. In an action against Mr Bridge's executors, the Vice Chancellor made a declaration that the memorandum was a valid and binding contract and ordered specific performance and execution of a conveyance of the properties. In this instance, the Vice Chancellor merely stated that, in his opinion, the agreement was sufficiently signed to take it out of the Statute of Frauds. In all probability, the reason for so finding was partly because the memorandum was drawn up in the hand of Mr Bridges and he had received the purchase price. In such circumstances, there was sufficient evidence to show he intended to sell the properties. It appears that the obligation was considered to be 'entire', thus permitting an order for specific performance.[3]

These cases illustrate that, despite failing to comply with the formal requirements, the content of a document can be authenticated where there is sufficient evidence to show the person signing the document adopted the content.

1   (1824) 1 Sim & St 543; 57 ER 215.
2   (1840) 11 Sim 149; 59 ER 831.
3   H. G. Beale, general editor, *Chitty on Contracts The Law of Contracts* (29th edn, 2004, Sweet & Maxwell) para 12-123; 42 *Halsbury's Laws* Sale of Land (4th edn Reissue) para 36.

Signature by authority

2.61   Authorizing a third party to bind another is acceptable for an individual, firm or the holder of a state office. In addition, because a corporation aggregate cannot sign on its own behalf, an authorized officer of the corporation must sign on behalf of the entity. The main issues are whether the person signing the document has the relevant authority to sign a document, and whether the form the signature took was sufficient in the circumstances of the case. Although in cases involving bankruptcy, a document signed on behalf of a debtor has been held to require signature by the debtor in person.[1]

The Statute of Frauds continued to be used as a defence, even in disputes where it was clear, on the case law, that the contract was evidenced in a written memorandum. An example of such a case is that of *Johnson v Dodgson*.[2] Mr D Morse, a travelling salesman for Johnson, Johnson & Co, hop merchants in London, visited John Dodgson in Leeds. As a result of this visit, Dodgson agreed to buy hops from Johnson. At the time of the sale, Mr Morse wrote a memorandum in his own sample book, which he retained:

> 'Leeds, 19th October, 1836. Sold John Dodgson – 27 pockets Playsted, 1836, Sussec, at 103s. The bulk to answer the sample. 4 pockets Selme, Beckley's, at 95s. Samples and invoice to be sent per Rockingham Coach. Payment in bankers' at two months.'

At the request of Dodgson, he then signed this memorandum 'Signed for Johnson, Johnson & Co, D. Morse.' Later that evening, Mr Dodgson wrote a letter to Johnson, confirming the details of the sale, signing the letter with his name. The hops were delivered and rejected as not conforming to the sample. At a trial before Lord Abinger CB, the members of the jury found that the hops did conform to the sample. Thereafter, Dodgson argued that because he did not sign the entry in the sample book, and his letter did not sufficiently convey the terms of the contract, there was no sufficient memorandum of the contract of writing to satisfy the Statute of Frauds. This point was reserved to be heard before Lord Abinger CB, Parker and Bolland BB. It was unanimously decided that the requirements of the statute were complied with. The written memorandum comprised two documents: the entry in the sample by Mr Morse, who bound his employer by signing as their agent, and the letter written, signed and sent by Dodgson. It was the opinion of Parke B that Dodgson's intention was to ensure the entry in the sample book was a memorandum of the agreement, and this intention was evidenced by Dodgson's insistence that Mr Morse sign the entry with his signature.[3]

Further challenges include *Morton v Copeland*,[4] where it was held that an agent on behalf of an author may give consent. In *Durrell v Evans*,[5] a case on appeal from the Court of Exchequer, the appellate court comprising Crompton, Byles, Blackburn, Keating and Mellor JJ reviewed the case law, and concluded that an agent selling hops can be in possession of sufficient authority to bind the parties. In the case of *R v The Justices of Kent*[6] the Reverend Joseph Weld appealed against an assessment levied by the Commissioners of the Rother Levels on 29 May 1872. The notice of appeal was signed by the clerk to the Reverend Weld's attorney, with the authority of the appellant. It was unanimously held that a personal signature was not necessary in this instance.[7] However, in 1845, it was held by Tindal CJ, Maule and Erle, JJ in the case of *Toms v Cuming*,[8] that a duplicate of the original notice of objection had to be signed by the objector in accordance with s 100 of 6 & 7 Victoria, c18. In this instance, Henry Toms served a notice of objection to the name of Samuel Angel being retained on the list of persons entitled to vote in the election of members of the borough of Totnes. Toms signed the original notice, and the copy was signed by William Bernard Hannaford by the direction of Toms, and in his presence. This was not held to be sufficient upon a construction of s 17 of the Act.

In the Australian case of *R v Moore, ex p Myers*,[9] Mr L M Myers was a licensed pawnbroker and manager of the Mont de Piété Company carrying on business of pawnbroking in various branches licensed for the business. Under s 21 of The Pawnbrokers Statute 1865, pledge-tickets were to be signed with the signature of the pawnbroker. Pledge-tickets were given to customers, and each manager was authorized to sign the ticket under the printed words 'Lewis M Myers, per'.[10] On appeal from being convicted by the justices at South Melbourne for not signing the tickets, it was held by Higinbotham J for the court that a statute '... is satisfied by proof of the making of a mark upon the document by or by the authority of the signatory.'[11] Further, Lord Coleridge CJ observed in *France v Dutton*[12] that a principal can authorise a third party to sign a document on their behalf, provided that the third party is empowered to undertake the particular act, and acts within the scope of that authority.[13] This line of cases was subsequently followed in *London County Council v Agricultural Food Products Ld*; *London County Council v Vitamins Ld*[14] and *Tennant v London County Council*[15], and in *Fung Ping Shan v Tong Shun*,[16] the members of the Privy Council held that a party that signs a deed in the name of another cannot avoid liability, nor can they bind the other party if they are not their lawful agent.[17]

1   *Hyde v Johnson* (1836) 2 Bing (NC) 776; 132 ER 299 and *Re Prince Blücher* [1931] 2 Ch 70, CA.
2   (1837) 2 M & W 653; 150 ER 918.
3   (1837) 2 M & W 653 at 660; 150 ER 918 at 922.
4   (1855) 16 C B 516; 139 ER 861.
5   (1862) 1 H & C 174; 158 ER 848.
6   (1873) LR 8 QB 305.
7   For an example of signing with authority to an indenture, see *R v The Inhabitants of Longnor* 1 Nev. & M. 576; 4 B. & Ad. 647; 110 ER 599.
8   7 Man. & G. 88, 135 ER 38.
9   (1884) 10 VLR 322 Cases at Law.
10 Lord Denning observed, in *London County Council v Agricultural Food Products Ld*; *London County Council v Vitamins Ld* [1955] 2 QB 218 at 222 that 'Such a signature is called a signature by procuration, by proxy, "per pro" or more shortly "p.p." All of these expressions are derived from the Latin "per peocurationerm," which means by the action of another.'
11 (1884) 10 VLR 322 at 324.
12 [1891] 2 QB 208.
13 [1891] 2 QB 208 at 211.
14 [1955] 2 QB 218.
15 [1957] 121 JP & LGR 379. See the comments by Sir W Page Wood LJ in *Re London and Mediterranean Bank ex p Birmingham Banking Company* (1867–68) 3 L R Ch App 651 at 654.
16 [1918] AC 403 PC.
17 A selection of cases in the United States of America include the following:
    Georgia (1857): *Reinhart v Miller*, 22 Ga. 402, 1857 WL 1927 (Ga.), 68 Am.Dec. 506 a woman about to be married declared that she would not marry her intended husband unless he signed a marriage settlement, which she authorized her brother to sign for her, and upon marrying, it was presumed the deed was executed upon the couple being married, and that she knew it before the marriage, and by the act of marriage she ratified her brother's signing.
    Minnesota (1886): *Conlan v Grace*, 36 Minn. 276, 30 N.W. 880 a grantor can adopt a signature where it is written with their authority.
    Kentucky (1934): *Pardue v Webb*, 253 Ky. 838, 70 S.W.2d 665 ballots signed by a clerk at the request of and in the presence of the judge of the election was a substantial compliance with the statute.
    Maine (1854): *Achorn v Matthews*, 38 Maine 173, 1854 WL 1786 (Me.) a writ signed by authority of justice held to be sufficient.

Agency

2.62   In *Re Whitley Partners, Limited*,[1] the company was limited by shares. It was registered on 10 November 1873, and the name of Mr Callan appeared as a subscriber to 100 shares. The articles were signed by Mr Oakley in the name of Mr Callan, who was given authority to do so by Mr Callan verbally and by telegram. The company was not successful, and was duly wound up. Mr Callan was served with orders of payment for calls, and refused to pay, alleging he did not sign the articles. It was held at first instance and on appeal that the relevant sections of the Companies Act 1862 did not prevent an agent signing on behalf of a principal, although the signature should have been 'P. Callan by Oakley his attorney' but such irregularity did not make the signature invalid where there was authority to affix it. Bowen LJ observed at 340 'In every case where an Act requires a signature it is a pure question of construction on the terms of the particular Act whether its words are satisfied by signature by an agent.' The learned judge distinguished *Hyde v Johnson* (1836) 2 Bing (NC) 776; 132 ER 299.

Auctioneers act on behalf and with the authority of bidder and seller, as illustrated in *Sims v Landray*[2] where a sale of real estate took place at auction. A lot was knocked down to the defendant, who was unknown to the auctioneer. The auctioneer's clerk, by the direction of the auctioneer, filled in the defendant's name and address into the memorandum of sale. The defendant was required to pay a deposit and sign the memorandum, but claimed he did not have his chequebook with him, and made an appointment to attend the office of the vendor's solicitor later that day to sign the contract and pay the deposit. He failed so to do. Romer J indicated that the only question was whether the memorandum had been signed by the defendant, and held it was, because his name was affixed to the memorandum with the authority of the auctioneer. In another case of the auction of property, that of *Leeman v Stocks*,[3] the vendor of a premises included his property in an auction. Neither the vendor nor his solicitor attended the auction. The auctioneer borrowed from another solicitor, who was not acting for any of the parties, but was interested in another property, a farm for sale by private treaty. The solicitor edited the document and added the date for completion, 16 September 1950. The auctioneer inserted the vendor's name, W. E. Stocks. The plaintiff made the highest bid, at £1,140, whereupon the auctioneer added the name and address of the buyer, together with a description of the premises and price, and the name of the buyer's solicitor. The buyer then signed the document. On 9 October 1950, the vendor's solicitor informed the buyer's solicitor that there was no contract. The buyer brought an action against the vendor for specific performance. It was held that the auctioneer was an agent for both parties and the document was intended to be binding on both parties, and the document constituted a sufficient memorandum in writing under the provisions of s 40 of the Law of Property Act 1925, and by implication, the addition of the name of the vendor by the auctioneer was valid.

1   32 Ch D 337, CA.
2   [1894] 2 Ch 318.
3   [1951] 1 Ch 941.

Chapter 3

International initiatives

The approach taken by a government in determining how legislation is to be enacted can affect the infrastructure of the electronic environment. Some jurisdictions favour the use of smart cards to carry the cryptographic functions for the signature process, whilst others encourage the development of a public key infrastructure, with a certification authority acting as a trusted third party. Other governments have enacted legislation that seeks to be neutral, thus allowing for the changes in technology that are bound to alter over time.

United Nations Commission on International Trade (UNCITRAL)

3.1 Sets of uniform rules have been prepared by UNCITRAL, the Model Law on Electronic Commerce, the Model Law on Electronic Signatures,[1] together with the 2005 United Nations Convention on the Use of Electronic Communications in International Contracts. The Model Laws are intended to provide help, guidance and a tool for national states to use in forming legislation. Whilst states are encouraged to incorporate both the Model Law on Electronic Commerce and the Model Law on Electronic Signatures fully into their domestic legislation, changes can be made to the content. The Model Laws are complementary to each other, although many states will have enacted legislation relating to electronic signatures before the final version of the Model Law on Electronic Signatures was adopted. The following discussion is intended to bring the salient issues to the attention of the reader.

1   The Model Law on Electronic Commerce was adopted by the Commission on 12 June 1996, following its 605th meeting, which in turn was adopted by the General Assembly in Resolution 51/162 at its *85th plenary meeting on 16 December 1996*, and includes an additional article 5 *bis* as adopted by the Commission at its 31st meeting in June 1998. The Commission at its 727th meeting on 5 July 2001 adopted the Model Law on Electronic Signatures.

Model Law on Electronic Commerce

3.2   The objectives of the Model Law on Electronic Commerce are set out in the accompanying Guide to Enactment, as follows:

(a)   To provide a set of rules acceptable to the international community relating to electronic communications.

(b)   To illustrate how obstacles to electronic commerce can be removed by national legislators, such as rules relating the use of 'written', 'signed' or 'original' documents, and to help create legal certainty in the electronic environment.

(c)   To help remedy any disadvantages because inadequate legislation creates obstacles to international trade.

(d)   To act as a tool for interpreting existing international conventions and other instruments that may create legal obstacles when using electronic commerce.

(e)   To foster efficiency in international trade.[1]

The Model Law is predicated upon the recognition that most legal requirements relate to documentation based on paper. It was thought that new rules might have to be developed to take into account the many distinctive differences between paper-based documents and electronic data. A new approach was established, called the 'functional equivalent approach', based on the analysis of the purposes and functions of a paper carrier. The functions a paper carrier provides for include:

(a)   To provide that a document would be legible by all.

(b)   To provide that a document would remain unaltered over time.

(c)   To allow for the reproduction of a document so that each party would hold a copy of the same data.

(d)   To allow for the authentication of data by means of a signature.

(e)   To provide that a document would be in a form acceptable to public authorities and courts.[2]

It was considered necessary that the approach would not require higher standards of security and related costs than already existed in the paper-based environment. Hence the adoption of a flexible standard, because data in digital format is not the equivalent of a paper document. Documents in paper and digital format are different in nature, and neither can perform the same functions as the other. Thus the Model Law seeks to establish the functions that a paper-based document will perform and then provides criteria which, if met, will enable electronic data to be recognised in the same way as a paper document. Part One, Chapter I of the Model Law deals with electronic commerce in general. Chapter II provides for the legal requirements relating to data messages.

1   Introduction to the Model Law Part A, paragraphs 1–6.
2   Introduction to the Model Law Part B, paragraph 16.

LEGAL RECOGNITION OF DATA MESSAGES

3.3 Article 5 provides for the legal recognition of data messages as follows:

'Article 5.   Legal recognition of data messages

Information shall not be denied legal effect, validity or enforceability solely on the grounds that it is in the form of a data message.

Article 5 bis. Incorporation by reference (as adopted by the Commission at its thirty-first session, in June 1998)

Information shall not be denied legal effect, validity or enforceability solely on the grounds that it is not contained in the data message purporting to give rise to such legal effect, but is merely referred to in that data message.'

The provisions of article 5 establish the principle that electronic data should not be treated any differently from paper documents because of the form it takes. Article 5 bis provides guidance when reference is made to other documents in the text of another document. This occurs frequently in the paper-based world, and the aim is to ensure it can also be effective in the electronic environment. Thus the commentary in paragraph 46-2 to the Guide to Enactment suggests that advantage can be taken of the ability to have links to databases, code lists or glossaries, by making use of abbreviations. In addition, the use of embedded uniform resource locators that can direct a reader to a referenced document by way of a hypertext link is another method of referring to other, related documents.[1] An example could be where an individual or legal entity uses an individual identity certificate provided by a certificate authority.[2] This is a signed structured message that seeks to assert the existence of an association between a particular set of data that identifies a key holder with a particular public key. It is probable that the certificate authority may well incorporate, by reference, the terms and conditions of use that limit its liability for the individual identity certificate.

1   Guide to Enactment, paragraph 46-5.
2   The reader should be aware that there are different classes of certificate, and it is not always clear what a particular certification authority means by a certificate and how they distinguish between types of certificate. See Roger Clarke 'Conventional Public Key Infrastructure: An Artefact Ill-Fitted to the Needs of the Information Society' prepared for submission to the 'IS in the Information Society' Track of the European Conference in Information Systems, Bled, Slovenia, 27–29 June 2001 available online at www.anu.edu.au/people/Roger.Clarke/II/PKIMisFit.html.

WRITING

3.4 The term 'writing' is considered in article 6:

'Article 6. Writing

(1) Where the law requires information to be in writing, that requirement is met by a data message if the information contained therein is accessible so as to be usable for subsequent reference.
(2) Paragraph (1) applies whether the requirement therein is in the form of an obligation or whether the law simply provides consequences for the information not being in writing.
(3) The provisions of this article do not apply to the following: [...].'

The purpose of article 6 is to define the basic standard that an electronic data message must meet. It is not a requirement that electronic data should conform to the functions of writing affixed to a carrier. Rather it is a provision that the electronic data should be: made available by being rendered into a format that can be interpreted and read, that is, 'accessible,' and the data must also be 'useable for subsequent reference'. This refers to two functions. The ability of a human to read the content of the data, and the processing of the data by a computer.

SIGNATURE

3.5   Matters pertaining to the signature are set out in article 7, as follows:

'Article 7. Signature

(1) Where the law requires a signature of a person, that requirement is met in relation to a data message if:
   (a) a method is used to identify that person and to indicate that person's approval of the information contained in the data message; and
   (b) that method is as reliable as was appropriate for the purpose for which the data message was generated or communicated, in the light of all the circumstances, including any relevant agreement.
(2) Paragraph (1) applies whether the requirement therein is in the form of an obligation or whether the law simply provides consequences for the absence of a signature.
(3) The provisions of this article do not apply to the following: [...].'

The provisions of article 7 do not claim to establish any standards or procedures to be used as substitute for a signature, because it was felt that there was a risk that the legal framework would be tied to a particular state of technological development. The aim of article 7 is to provide a basic standard of authentication between two parties, whether the parties are linked by an agreement, or where they have no previous relationship. It sets out general conditions under which electronic data can be regarded as authentic and enforceable, focusing on two of the functions of a manuscript signature: that is to identify the author of a document and to confirm the author approved the content of the document. There are two elements to this process:

(a) The first element, set out in paragraph (1)(a), provides a method is to be used to identify the person, and to indicate their approval of the information contained in the data message. The person sending the message becomes the originator of the data message.

(b) The second element is set out in paragraph (1)(b). The method used to generate or communicate the message must be sufficiently reliable and appropriate, bearing in mind the circumstances, for its intended purpose. The Guide sets out a number of legal, technical and commercial factors that should be taken into account when determining whether the method used was sufficiently reliable and appropriate:

   (1) the sophistication of the equipment used by each of the parties;
   (2) the nature of their trade activity;
   (3) the frequency at which commercial transactions take place between the parties;
   (4) the kind and size of the transaction;
   (5) the function of signature requirements in a given statutory and regulatory environment;
   (6) the capability of communication systems;
   (7) compliance with authentication procedures set forth by intermediaries;
   (8) the range of authentication procedures made available by any intermediary;
   (9) compliance with trade customs and practice;
   (10) the existence of insurance coverage mechanisms against unauthorized messages;
   (11) the importance and the value of the information contained in the data message;
   (12) the availability of alternative methods of identification and the cost of implementation;
   (13) the degree of acceptance or non-acceptance of the method of identification in the relevant industry or field both at the time the method was agreed upon and the time when the data message was communicated; and
   (14) any other relevant factor.[1]

The legal effectiveness of the method used to apply an electronic signature depends, according to the Guide to Enactment to the Model Law on Electronic Signatures,[2] on demonstrating its reliability to the person trying the fact. However, the reliability of the method does not demonstrate a link between the owner of the electronic signature and the act of affixing the signature to a document in digital format. The Guide to Enactment to the Model

Law on Electronic Commerce notes that when an electronic document is signed by means of a functional equivalent of a manuscript signature, it does not follow that the electronic data is legally valid. The relevant provisions set out in national law govern this matter.[3]

1 Guide to Enactment, paragraph 58.
2 Guide to Enactment, paragraph 76.
3 Guide to Enactment, paragraph 61.

Model Law on Electronic Signatures

3.6 This Model Law is predicated on the principles underlying article 7 of the Model Law on Electronic Commerce, and is intended to assist states in setting out a legal framework for electronic signatures. The Model Law considers technical reliability and legal effectiveness, whilst setting out a number of basic rules of conduct for the parties to an electronic signature (sending party, receiving party and third party certification authority). The objectives of the Model Law include the encouragement of facilitating the use of electronic signatures and providing equal treatment for all documents whether they are in electronic format or on a physical carrier.[1] In this respect, the Model Law has focused on the roles or functions relating to public key cryptography, which usually implies a trusted third party acts to certify the identity of an entity by means of an individual identity certificate. However, it should be noted that trust in a key could be established bilaterally, without the services of a trusted third party. These functions consist of the signatory function, relying function and certification function. Whilst the signatory and relying functions remain constant, the certification function may differ, depending on the system used. Whilst other techniques, such as biometric measurements, are not specifically covered in the Model Law, the aim has been to deal with the legal issues at an intermediate level between the generality of the Model Law on Electronic Commerce and the specific issues when considering a particular electronic signature technique.

As the Model Law is predicated on article 7 of the Model Law on Electronic Commerce, it was not a foregone conclusion that a new Model Law would be created. Consideration was given to incorporating the new rules into the Model Law on Electronic Commerce as a new Part III, but because so many states had already implemented the Model Law on Electronic Commerce, it was felt that a separate instrument was more appropriate. To provide for consistency, the following articles have been reproduced from the Model Law on Electronic Commerce: articles 1 (Sphere of application); 2 (a), (c) and (d) (Definitions of 'data message', 'originator' and 'addressee'); 3 (Interpretation); 4 (Variation by agreement) and 7 (Signature). The notes in the Guide to Enactment make it explicit that the Model Law only offers a framework within which laws can be structured, and it is not intended to set forth all the requirements that may be necessary to implement any given electronic signature law. For instance, it does not set out the rules and regulations that may be necessary to implement electronic signature techniques. Nor does it deal with liability, leaving the national law to determine what liability a party may be subject to in accordance with applicable law. However, the Model Law does set out criteria against which an adjudicator might assess the conduct of the parties.

1   The history of this Model Law illustrates differences had to be resolved before the final version was agreed. The reader is referred to Part C, paragraphs 12–25 of the Guide that accompanies the Model Law for more information.

CONSUMER PROTECTION

3.7   The comments in the Guide to Enactment indicate that the Model Law has not been drafted with any special provisions in mind regarding the protection of consumers.[1] There was no reason why conditions relating to consumers should be excluded from the scope of the Model Law, especially because it was considered that the Model Law could be beneficial to a consumer. This does not prevent the consumer from being protected independently, as provided for in article 1:

'Article 1. Sphere of application

This Law applies where electronic signatures are used in the context of commercial activities. It does not override any rule of law intended for the protection of consumers.'

It is for individual states to determine whether they should exclude or modify rules in relation to consumers and their use of electronic signatures.

1   Guide to Enactment, paragraph 91.

DEFINITIONS

3.8   The Model Law provides a number of definitions in article 2, as described below.

Electronic signature

3.9   The definition of an electronic signature is set out in article 2(a):

'"Electronic signature" means data in electronic form in, affixed to or logically associated with, a data message, which may be used to identify the signatory in relation to the data message and to indicate the signatory's approval of the information contained in the data message;…'

This definition is intended to include all traditional uses of a manuscript signature, and emphasises the use of an electronic signature as a functional equivalent of a manuscript signature.[1] There are two elements to this definition of an electronic signature. The first element provides for the link between different types of electronic data: electronic signature data that is 'in, affixed to or logically associated with, a data message'.

(a) The word 'in' operates where the signature data is contained in a message or document. It can be seen when it is opened and read, or when it is printed. When used 'in' the data message, the signature data consists of additional text in the document or message.

(b) There does not appear to be any difference in meaning between the words 'affixed to' and 'logically associated'. The use of the phrase 'affixed to' probably means signature data contained in a file sent as an attachment to an email. However, this example falls into the meaning 'logically associated' in any event.[2]

(c) The phrase 'logically associated' with a message or document is where signature data is contained in a separate file from the data that has been signed. It is not visible in the data itself. The signature data can only be verified where a signature verification application is used. This uses the data that purports to have been signed, the purported signature file and the verification key to determine whether the verification is valid. The signature data will only be verified if the relevant logical association is demonstrated: if the purportedly signed data was in fact signed with the signature key corresponding to the verification key used.

The second element provides for the purpose of the associated data, that of identifying the signatory and the signatory's approval of the content of the message. The data specifically provides for the identification of the signatory.

(a) The first part of this element permits the use of associated data that 'may be used to identify the signatory in relation to the data message'. The use of the word 'may' acknowledges that there is a difference between the legal notion of a signature and the different technical functions that can be used to create an electronic signature, but can also be used for other purposes.[3] Whether an electronic signature merely acts to authenticate interactions between protocols, or identify the sender, will be determined by the ability to establish a connection between the signature and the person affixing the signature to the data.

(b) The second part of the element provides for the associated data to 'indicate the signatory's approval of the information contained in the data message'. The aim of this part of the element is to cover the traditional use of the manuscript signature. The comments in the Guide to Enactment indicate the nature of the problem: '... defining an electronic signature as capable of indicating approval of information amounts primarily to establishing a technical prerequisite for the recognition of a given technology as capable of creating an equivalent to a handwritten signature.'[4] However, it is to be observed that the tool that can be used for the production of a signature with legal meaning can also be used for other purposes, such as to authenticate or identify an entity. Thus the context and intention of the tool must be taken into account before it can be inferred that a document has been 'signed'. A message or document may include data that seeks to link the person to the message or document without indicating their approval of the content.

1   Guide to Enactment, paragraph 93.
2   The definition of what constitutes an electronic signature was discussed on various occasions at meetings of the Working Group on Electronic Commerce. A proposed change to the definition was agreed at a session in Vienna between 8 and 19 February 1999. The change is noted in A/CN.9/457 dated 25 February 1999 at paragraph 28: '"Electronic signature" means data in electronic form which (a) is included in, affixed to or logically associated with a data message.' No reason was ascribed to the inclusion of two phrases that appear to have similar meanings.
3   Guide to Enactment, paragraphs 93 and 94.
4   Guide to Enactment, paragraph 93.

Certificate

3.10   Article 2(b) provides a definition of a certificate:

'"Certificate" means a data message or other record confirming the link between a signatory and signature creation data;'

The Guide to Enactment to the Model Law points out that a 'certificate' as defined is no different from any other meaning of a document, other than it is in digital format. The aim of such a document is to confirm facts. Thus the purpose of a certificate is to 'recognize, show or confirm a link between the signature creation data and the signatory'.[1] According to the commentary, the link is created when the signature creation data is generated. This must be wrong. The link is created when the possessor of the signature key seeks a certificate for the verification key, and perhaps accepts obligations to procure the issue of the certificate. The signature creation data is, when using asymmetric cryptography, the cryptographic key pair. The private key is the operative element in the process and it is the private key that is referred to in the phrase 'signature creation data'. However, it is also meant to include the confirmation of the link between the signatory and their public key.

1   Guide to Enactment, paragraph 96.

Data message

3.11   The definition provided in article 2(c) is as follows:

'"Data message" means information generated, sent, received or stored by electronic, optical or similar means including, but not limited to, electronic data interchange (EDI), electronic mail, telegram, telex or telecopy; and acts either on its own behalf or on behalf of the person it represents;'

This definition is drafted to cover a broad range of data, including records. It does not follow that a data message has to be communicated. The definition seeks to include all forms of document not on paper, as well as future developments in technology.[1]

1   Guide to Enactment, paragraphs 98 to 100.

Signatory

3.12   Article 2(d) provides the following definition of a signatory:

'"Signatory" means a person that holds signature creation data and acts either on its own behalf or on behalf of the person it represents;'

The meaning of 'person' includes all types of person, including physical, corporate and other forms of legal entity. The digital environment permits a legal entity to have an electronic signature in its own name. A legal entity can sign documents in two ways. The method most frequently used is when authorized officers affix their manuscript signatures to a document with the requisite authority. Alternatively, the organization can use its own signature, with the impression of the seal. Whether an electronic signature has been added to digital data with authority is a matter for the law governing the relationship between the person whose actions affix the electronic signature and the legal entity.[1]

1   Guide to Enactment, paragraphs 102 and 103.

Certification service provider

3.13   Article 2(e) provides the following definition of a certification service provider:

'"Certification service provider" means a person that issues certificates and may provide other services related to electronic signatures;'

The commentary mentions that the certification service provider will have to provide a certification service to come within this definition, although it can supply other services. It does not have to undertake the work directly, but can subcontract the service. The definition does not include entities that issue certificates for internal purposes. It is only intended to cover activities of commercial providers of such services.[1]

1   Guide to Enactment, paragraph 104.

Relying party

3.14 The definition of a relying party is to be found in article 2(f):

'"Relying party" means a person that may act on the basis of a certificate or an electronic signature.'

The inclusion of what is meant by a 'relying party' is meant to provide symmetry in the definition of the various parties involved in a transaction involving an electronic signature. Interestingly, the commentary also suggests that the word 'act' should be interpreted broadly, covering a positive action and a failure to act. This issue was the subject of discussion, and concern was expressed that in some legal systems the word 'act' would not cover acts of omission.[1] The comments in the Guide to Enactment illustrate the intention is to create an obligation upon a recipient to undertake acts of due diligence, as further demonstrated by the terms of article 11:

'Article 11. Conduct of the relying party

A relying party shall bear the legal consequences of its failure:

(a) To take reasonable steps to verify the reliability of an electronic signature; or
(b) Where an electronic signature is supported by a certificate, to take reasonable steps:
  (i) To verify the validity, suspension or revocation of the certificate; and
  (ii) To observe any limitation with respect to the certificate.'

It is not certain that a recipient should be made to undertake due diligence, although there may be good reasons of public policy to enforce organizations such as banks to take steps to authenticate the identity of their customers. However, taking into account the discussion of this issue in the chapter on evidence, it may be appropriate for both sending and receiving parties to be aware of the risks and limitations that attend the use of electronic signatures. The comments in the Guide to Enactment suggest the recipient should bear in mind whether it is reasonable to rely on a certificate in the circumstances.[2] Furthermore, the Model Law is not intended to overrule any rules with respect to the protection of consumers, but it was thought that imposing such a duty on consumers would play a role in educating recipients about the standard of conduct expected of recipients.[3] Bearing in mind the complexity of the infrastructure surrounding electronic signatures, especially digital signatures, perhaps the failure to carry out an act is something that should be borne in mind when assessing the evidence in the event of a dispute, depending on the circumstances of the case.[4] This aspect of the meaning for the word 'act' should be considered in the light of the provisions of article 4:

'Article 4.   Interpretation

1. In the interpretation of this Law, regard is to be had to its international origin and to the need to promote uniformity in its application and the observance of good faith.

2. Questions concerning matters governed by this Law which are not expressly settled in it are to be settled in conformity with the general principles on which this Law is based.'

The commentary indicates that article 4 is based upon the United Nations Convention on Contracts for the International Sale of Goods, and is reproduced from article 3 of the Model Law on Electronic Commerce. The aim of paragraph 1 is to ensure the interpretation of the Model Law is by reference to its international origin, with the aim of ensuring uniformity in its interpretation. It is hoped that the Law, once incorporated into national law, will not be subject only to local legislation.[5] The Model Law may act as a guide in dealing with a dispute, but national courts will be required to implement national law, especially national consumer law. Although the concept of utilizing a device to create a signature means the signing party should look to control its use and protect it from unauthorized use, it is debatable whether a duty should be imposed upon a recipient to verify the certificate and the link between the certificate, public key and identity of the sending party.

1   Report of the Working Group on Electronic Commerce on the work of its thirty-seventh session (Vienna, 18–29 September 2000) A/CN.9/483 paragraphs 105–108.
2   Guide to Enactment, paragraph 148.
3   Guide to Enactment, paragraph 149.
4   Guide to Enactment, paragraph 106.
5   Guide to Enactment, paragraphs 108 and 109.

THE REQUIREMENT FOR A SIGNATURE

3.15   The Model Law, by way of the provisions set out in articles 3 and 6, seeks to ensure that whatever the form a signature takes, whether in electronic format or a manuscript signature placed on a physical document, it is subject to the same treatment. For an electronic signature to be acceptable, it must fulfil the requirements of articles 6 and 7. In addition, provisions are made for the conduct of the various parties that may be connected to an electronic signature, including that of the signatory (article 8) and the certification service provider (articles 9 and 10).

International Chamber of Commerce

3.16   The International Chamber of Commerce produced the first version of a set of guidelines entitled 'General Usage for International Digitally Ensured Commerce' (GUIDEC) on 6 November 1997. This was revised in October

2001. The introduction to the first version of the Guide sets out one of the aims respecting electronic signatures:

'The GUIDEC aims to draw together the key elements involved in electronic commerce, to serve as an indicator of terms and an exposition of the general background to the issue. It also addresses one of the key problems in talking about electronically signed messages, in that they are not signed physically, but require the intervention of an electronic medium. This in turn alters the function of the signer, and introduces problems which a physical signature does not encounter, most especially the possibility of use of the medium by a third party. The GUIDEC therefore adopts a specific term, "ensure", to describe what elsewhere is called a "digital signature" or "authentication", in an attempt to remove the element of ambiguity inherent to other terms employed.'

The revised version continued to expand on the use of digital signature technology, as indicated in the aims:

'The aim of the GUIDEC

The GUIDEC framework attempts to allocate risk and liability equitably between transacting parties in accordance with existing business practice, and includes a clear description of the rights and responsibilities of subscribers, certifiers, and relying parties.

The aim of the GUIDEC is to enhance the ability of the international business community to execute trustworthy digital transactions utilizing legal principles that promote reliable digital authentication and certification practices.

The GUIDEC treats the core concepts, best practices and certification issues in the context of international commercial law and practice. In so doing, the document assumes practices in which transacting parties are expert commercial actors, operating under the lex mercatoria. The document does not attempt to define rights and responsibilities for transactions involving consumers. Nor is it intended to outline practices for transactions in which overriding national or other public interests may demand additional transactional security, such as notarial or other public intervention, although many notarial principles are enshrined in the document. In this regard, it is also important to note that the GUIDEC does not attempt to set out rules for certification of information relating to authority, legal competence, etc, which notaries are often called upon to certify.

Although the GUIDEC is organized primarily as an outline for parties involved in public key based systems (ie digital signatures), the fact that it draws upon existing law means most of its principles will apply for other technologies.'

The guidance offered, which has no legal force, sets out some best practices that might be considered when deciding to form contracts electronically. However, in the introduction to the second version, the main objective is set out in part I(1) as follows:

> 'The principle objective of the GUIDEC is to establish a general framework for the authentication of digital messages, based upon existing law and practice in different legal systems. In so doing, the GUIDEC provides a detailed explanation of principles, particularly as they relate to information system security issues, public key cryptographic techniques and emerging biometric capabilities. It also provides succinct standard practices or recommendations relating to secure authentication and processing of digital information.'

The assumptions that underpin the Guide are set out in part III:

> 'The movement to open network communications systems, such as the Internet, poses significant challenges to the implementation of a global electronic trading system. Among the most significant barriers to global electronic commerce over open networks are those pertaining to the security of the information involved (ie its integrity, availability and confidentiality). The application of security and reduction of the risk of fraud and unauthorized access is vital to the growth of the number and volume of international commercial transactions over networked computers.

> Appropriate information security enables a level of trust and confidence to be present in the transfer of information between parties. Industry recognizes the need for a reliable framework for identifying and certifying parties to a transaction and authenticating the transaction itself.'

It is interesting to note that the security of information has become paramount – as if the security of information was not relevant in the past, when contracts were formed by using the latest technologies, such as telegram, telex and facsimile transmissions. It is as if people have never faced such problems in the past. Part IV of the Guide traverses the UNCITRAL Model Laws, the European Union Directive on electronic signatures, the 1998 OECD Ottawa Ministerial Declaration, and the United States legislation, the Electronic Signatures in Global and National Commerce Act (Public Law 106–229). Parts V to VIII deal with the broad principles of electronic contracting, and parts IX and X deal with best practices, comprising authenticating a message and certification respectively.

The provisions of part IX respecting the appropriate practice when authenticating a message are discussed within the confines of a digital signature. No other means of proving intent seems to be considered. Item 4 provides 'A signatory **must** authenticate a message by a means **appropriate under the circumstances**.' (Bold in the original). First, it is to be noted that the guidance issued under the United Nations Convention on the Use of Electronic Communications in International Contracts has ameliorated the requirement that a reliability test must be considered by a court. Second, it is most unusual for a person signing a message or communication to be required to authenticate a message. Authentication was not required with telegrams, so it is to be wondered why it is necessary in the digital environment. In the comment on 'clarification,' to this point, the word 'must' is amplified:

> '"must": The consequence of a failure to authenticate a message properly is that the message may be disregarded. In general commercial practice and unless otherwise agreed, a message may be ignored if the manner of authenticating it either contravenes an agreement by the parties, is not suited to impart the legal efficacy intended by the parties for the message, or if reliance on the message as authenticated would not be reasonable under the circumstances.'

Even before the advent of the internet, contracts would be formed between businesses and individuals and business at a distance. The most striking example is that of contracts conducted by way of the post: such issues were commonplace well before the internet, and it is to be wondered why businesses need such guidance when they have been dealing with such issues for over a hundred years. Further evidence of the reliance on digital signatures and the public key infrastructure is manifest in the provisions of part X. Paragraph 1 discusses the effect of a certificate issued by a certification authority:

> 'A person may **rely** on a valid certificate as accurately representing the fact or facts set forth in it, if the person has no notice that the certifier has failed to satisfy a material requirement of authenticated message practice.' (Bold in the original)

This statement is bold indeed, and is predicated, as pointed out in the commentary, on the proposition that the parties 'are acting in good faith and without deception or negligence in conducting their business.' This statement on its own undermines the entire rationale of the reason for implementing the Guide, because if the parties are known to each other and recognise the communications sent between each other, there is no need for a Guide and no need for either to have digital signatures: the email address alone, together with the content, will suffice (as it does in reality) to provide sufficient evidence that the authenticity of the communications is not in doubt.

United Nations Convention on the Use of Electronic Communications in International Contracts

3.17 This United Nations Convention was adopted in the 53rd plenary meeting of the UN on 23 November 2005, and at the date of writing, is open for signature by all states from 16 January 2006 to 16 January 2008, and a number of states have signed the Convention to date.[1] The development of the Convention was based on the UN resolution 2205 (XXI) of 17 December 1966, which established the Commission on International Trade Law with the mandate to undertake the harmonization and unification of the law of international trade, and a decision in the thirty-fourth session in 2001 to prepare an international instrument dealing with issues of electronic contracting, which also aimed at removing obstacles to electronic commerce in existing uniform law conventions and trade agreements. Working Group IV (Electronic Commerce) was requested to prepare a draft Convention. The preamble sets out the reasoning for the Convention:

> '*Reaffirming* their belief that international trade on the basis of equality and mutual benefit is an important element in promoting friendly relations among States,
>
> *Noting* that the increased use of electronic communications improves the efficiency of commercial activities, enhances trade connections and allows new access opportunities for previously remote parties and markets, thus playing a fundamental role in promoting trade and economic development, both domestically and internationally,
>
> *Considering* that problems created by uncertainty as to the legal value of the use of electronic communications in international contracts constitute an obstacle to international trade,
>
> *Convinced* that the adoption of uniform rules to remove obstacles to the use of electronic communications in international contracts, including obstacles that might result from the operation of existing international trade law instruments, would enhance legal certainty and commercial predictability for international contracts and help States gain access to modern trade routes,
>
> *Being of the opinion* that uniform rules should respect the freedom of parties to choose appropriate media and technologies, taking account of the principles of technological neutrality and functional equivalence, to the extent that the means chosen by the parties comply with the purpose of the relevant rules of law,
>
> *Desiring* to provide a common solution to remove legal obstacles to the use of electronic communications in a manner acceptable to States with different legal, social and economic systems,'

In summary, the Convention covers the following:

(a)   Contracts between parties whose places of business are in different states, but excluding contracts for personal, family or household purposes, amongst other forms of contract (articles 1 and 2).

(b) Parties may exclude the application of the Convention or derogate or vary the effect of any of its provisions (article 3).

(c) Location and information requirements (articles 6 and 7).

(d) Requirements to recognise contracts in electronic format and to recognise various requirements of form, including methods of identifying the parties and indicate intention (articles 8 and 9).

The technical issues relating to the formation of contract are covered by articles 10, 11, 12, 13 and 14.

1   Article 16(1); signatories to date are: the Central African Republic on 27 February 2006; China on 6 July 2006; Lebanon on 22 May 2006; Madagascar on 19 September 2006; Senegal on 7 April 2006; Sierra Leone on 21 September 2006; Singapore on 6 July 2006 and Sri Lanka on 6 July 2006.

Signature provisions

3.18   Article 9(3) sets out the provisions for a signature:

'3.   Where the law requires that a communication or a contract should be signed by a party, or provides consequences for the absence of a signature, that requirement is met in relation to an electronic communication if:

(a) A method is used to identify the party and to indicate that party's intention in respect of the information contained in the electronic communication; and

(b) The method used is either:

   (i) As reliable as appropriate for the purpose for which the electronic communication was generated or communicated, in the light of all the circumstances, including any relevant agreement; or

   (ii) Proven in fact to have fulfilled the functions described in subparagraph (a) above, by itself or together with further evidence.'

It can be observed that article 9(3) changes the emphasis in respect to electronic signatures in comparison to the provisions in the Model Laws. Weight is now on the reliability of the method used to sign a document, the purpose for which the communication is generated or communicated, and, more importantly, whether the method of signature used actually fulfilled the functions, either on its own, or if taken together with further evidence. The provisions of article 9(3) indicate that a significant change has taken place, away from the approaches taken in the Model Laws, and is, in consequence, far more realistic. This new approach allows for any form of electronic signature to be used, in keeping with the decisions made by judges across the globe before this Convention was agreed. The commentary to the Convention reflects this change in view.[1]

Of note are the comments respecting the reliability of the signature method. The emphasis is on assessing the evidence when considering the methods used under article(9)(3)(a), but the comments continue to imply that it is necessary to have sufficient technical evidence in place to validate a particular signature. For instance, paragraph 162 provides as follows:

'162.   Legal, technical and commercial factors that may be taken into account in determining whether the method used under paragraph 3(a) is appropriate, include the following: (a) the sophistication of the equipment used by each of the parties; (b) the nature of their trade activity; (c) the frequency at which commercial transactions take place between the parties; (d) the kind and size of the transaction; (e) the function of signature requirements in a given statutory and regulatory environment; (f) the capability of communication systems; (g) compliance with authentication procedures set forth by intermediaries; (h) the range of authentication procedures made available by any intermediary; (i) compliance with trade customs and practice; (j) the existence of insurance coverage mechanisms against unauthorized communications; (k) the importance and the value of the information contained in the electronic communication; (l) the availability of alternative methods of identification and the cost of implementation; (m) the degree of acceptance or non-acceptance of the method of identification in the relevant industry or field both at the time the method was agreed upon and the time when the electronic communication was communicated; and (n) any other relevant factor.'

The criteria is, according to the commentary at paragraph 163, proposed 'with a view to ensuring the correct interpretation of the principle of functional equivalence in respect of electronic signatures. The 'reliability test', which appears also in article 7, paragraph 1(b), of the UNCITRAL Model Law on Electronic Commerce, reminds courts of the need to take into account factors other than technology, such as the purpose for which the electronic communication was generated or communicated, or a relevant agreement of the parties, in ascertaining whether the electronic signature used was sufficient to identify the signatory.' On the face of it, this test is unrealistic. If a document has been signed in good faith electronically, and the parties to the contract acknowledge the contract is authentic and valid, there should be no need for any court to take the matter any further. If the authenticity of the document is not in dispute between the parties, the method by which the document is generated is irrelevant: if there is a dispute, the parties define the issues to be adjudicated, and unless a party raises the issue of the authenticity of the document, it is not for the court to raise the issue on its own initiative.

However, further guidance is given in paragraph 164 in an attempt to pre-empt a party from using the proposed test to prevent the signature from being admitted, even though there is no dispute that the communication was sent and received and the communication signed:

'164.   However, UNCITRAL considered that the Convention should not allow a party to invoke the "reliability test" to repudiate its signature in cases where the actual identity of the party and its actual intention could be proved. The requirement that an electronic signature needs to be "as reliable as appropriate" should not lead a court or trier of fact to invalidate the entire contract on the ground that the electronic signature was not appropriately reliable if there is no dispute about the identity of the person signing or the fact of signing, that is, no question as to authenticity of the electronic signature. Such a result would be particularly unfortunate, as it would allow a party to a transaction in which a signature was required to try to escape its obligations by denying that its signature (or the other party's signature) was valid—not on the ground that the purported signer did not sign, or that the document it signed had been altered, but only on the ground that the method of signature employed was not "as reliable as appropriate" in the circumstances. In order to avoid these situations, paragraph 3(b)(ii) validates a signature method—regardless of its reliability in principle—whenever the method used is proven in fact to have identified the signatory and indicated the signatory's intention in respect of the information contained in the electronic communication.'

In comparison to the Model Laws, the provisions of article 9(3) of the Convention are far more realistic and pragmatic, and for that reason, are to be welcomed.

1   *United Nations Convention on the Use of Electronic Communications in International Contracts* (including explanatory notes by the UNCITRAL secretariat on the United Nations Convention on the Use of Electronic Communications in International Contracts) (United Nations, New York, 2007), paragraphs 147–164.

Chapter 4

European Union Directive on electronic signatures

4.1 The European Union took an active stance on issues relating to the information society by 1996. In September 1996, the European Parliament passed a resolution asking the Commission to prepare proposals covering security and confidentiality, authentication and to safeguard privacy,[1] and in November 1996 the Council of Ministers requested the Member States and the Commission to prepare consistent measures to ensure the integrity and authentication of electronically transmitted documents.[2] Further initiatives continued, with the OECD adopting 'Guidelines for cryptography policy' on 27 March 1997,[3] which set out general principles to guide countries in formulating policies related to the use of cryptography. A European Ministerial Conference took place in Bonn in July 1997, entitled 'Global Information Networks: Realising the Potential', which led to the Bonn Ministerial Declaration, the objective of which was 'to broaden the common understanding of the use of Global Information Networks, to identify barriers to their use, to discuss possible solutions and to undertake an open dialogue on further possibilities for European and international co-operation.' The Declaration covered the topic of electronic signatures, specifically digital signatures:

'Digital signatures

38. Ministers emphasise the need for a legal and technical framework at European and international level which ensures compatibility and creates confidence in digital signatures, a reliable and transparent way of ensuring data, document and message integrity and authentication both for electronic commerce and for electronic transactions between public bodies and citizens.

39. Ministers call upon industry and international standards organisations to develop technical and infrastructure standards for digital signatures to

ensure secure and trustworthy use of networks and respect privacy and data protection requirements.

40. Ministers will initiate the necessary steps to remove barriers to the use of digital signatures in law, business and public administration, and to provide legal and mutual recognition of certificates.'

The Commission subsequently produced a communication in response to the resolution from the Parliament, 'Ensuring security and trust in electronic communications Towards a European Framework for digital signatures and encryption'.[4] This document made it explicit that the only method of electronic signatures that was under consideration was that of the digital signature. In arguing the case, assertions were made in the Executive Summary without reference to any evidence, or the accuracy of the premise upon which the assertion was made, such as: 'As cryptographic services and products are more and more demanded,' and 'As, in addition, they need a specific regulatory framework to take into account their legal implications.' In addition, one comment made was factually incorrect: 'Digital signatures could even bring significant law enforcement benefits as they allow for example messages to be attributed to a particular reader and/or sender' because no form of electronic signature, including the digital signature, is capable of proving the person whose private key was used, was the person who caused the digital signature to be affixed to a document or communication. On the subject of digital signatures, it was asserted that the failure for digital signatures to be offered as a service was predicated on 'the absence of legal recognition of digital signatures.'[5] There was a fear that the European Union needed to regulate electronic signatures, especially as some nation states had already begun to pass laws on the topic. As can be expected, there was discussion about the technical requirements of digital signatures, including liability for certification service providers and interoperability.

1   European Parliament Resolution A4-244/96, 19.9.96, OJ320, p. 164, 28.10.96 Europe and the global information society – Recommendations to the European Council.
2   Council Resolution 96/C 376/01 of 21 November 1996 on new policy-priorities regarding the information society, OJ C 376, 12.12.96, p. 1.
3   Conference Conclusions 'A Borderless World: Realising the potential of global electronic commerce', 7–9 October 1998, Ottawa, Canada (Directorate for Science, Technology and Industry Steering Committee for the Preparation of the Ottawa Ministerial Conference, SG/EC(98)14/REV6); A Global action plan for electronic commerce prepared by business with recommendations from governments, 7–9 October 1998, Ottawa, Canada (Directorate for Science, Technology and Industry Steering Committee for the Preparation of the Ottawa Ministerial Conference, SG/EC(98)11/REV2).
4   Communication from the Commission, 'Ensuring security and trust in electronic communications Towards a European Framework for digital signatures and encryption' COM(97) 503 final, 08.10.1997.
5   Part II, paragraph 3.

The Directive

4.2 On 1 December 1997, the Council invited the Commission to submit a proposal for a European Parliament and Council Directive on digital signatures. The proposal was to be offered as soon as possible. A draft proposal was produced by May 1998,[1] and submitted by the Commission on 16 June 1998.[2] This draft removed the term 'digital signature' with the term 'electronic signature', although the text reflects the emphasis on digital signatures and the infrastructure that is required to prop up the intricate technical edifice comprising digital signatures. Action was taken fairly quickly. The Council consulted the Economic and Social Committee on 30 July 1998,[3] and the Committee of the Regions, which had reviewed the proposal by early 1999.[4] By 14 April 1999, the proposal had been reviewed and a number of amendments were proposed by the Parliament.[5] The definition of 'electronic signature' was, as proposed by the Commission:

> '"electronic signature" means a signature in digital form in, or attached to, or logically associated with, data which is used by a signatory to indicate his approval of the content of that data and meets the following requirements: (the requirements are those as set out in the Directive that pertain to an advanced electronic signature).'

The proposed amendment read:

> '"electronic signature" means a signature in electronic form in, or attached to, or logically associated with, data which is used by a signatory to indicate his approval of the content of that data and meets the following requirements:'

In comparison, the final version, at article 2(1) reads:

> '"electronic signature" means data in electronic form which are attached to or logically associated with other electronic data and which serve as a method of authentication.'

Apparently there was a difference of opinion over what legal effect an electronic signature would have when created using products (secure signature-creation devices) that meet a minimum level of technical security.[6] This matter was the subject of debate at the Council meeting of 27 November 1998. The security requirements relating to these products were enumerated in Annex III. The opposition to setting out such criteria was voiced in the main by the United Kingdom and the Netherlands. The reason for the objection was the concern that the industry could not meet the conditions laid down in the Annex. At the time, it was suggested that the matters might be resolved by making the contents of Annex III a strong recommendation, or by reducing the requirements relating to the products.[7] In the event, the content of Annex III was split between requirements and recommendations for secure signature-creation devices. The views expressed by some countries may also have influenced the decision to revise the meaning of an electronic signature and produce more than one version of an electronic signature: which seems a somewhat bizarre concept, because a document is either signed or it is not signed.

The Directive was adopted by the European Parliament and Council on 13 December 1999 and came into force on 19 January 2000.[8] Member states were required to implement the Directive by 19 July 2001,[9] and a review of the operation of the Directive was to be prepared and delivered to the European Parliament and to the Council by 19 July 2003.[10] One further development took place in 2005 with the establishment of an Expert Group on electronic commerce,[11] the mission of which is set out in article 2:

'The Commission can consult the Group on any questions relating to the directive on electronic commerce. This covers, among others, the following areas:

— administrative cooperation in the context of Article 3(4) to procedure to restrict the freedom to provide services against a given information society service provider,
— information on codes of conduct drawn up at Community level by trade, professional and consumer associations or organisations, designed to contribute to the proper implementation of Articles 5 to 15 of the Directive (Article 16 of the Directive),
— codes of conduct on on-line advertising by regulated professions (Article 8 of the Directive),
— national case law, especially related to the liability provisions, including decisions taken in out-of-court dispute settlement (Articles 17 and 19(5) of the Directive),
— areas currently outside the scope of the liability section of the Directive but referred to in Article 21, such as: "notice and take down" procedures, hyperlinks and search engines,
— scope of the subsequent evaluation reports on the application of the Directive on electronic commerce (Article 21 of the Directive).

The chairman of the Group may suggest that the Commission consults the Group on any related matter.'

The composition of the Group is set out in article 3, and the Group is given a remit to set up working groups to study specific subjects on the basis of the mandate; to invite experts and observers with specific knowledge to participate in the work of the Group and the working groups. It will be of interest to see how the members of this Group view their duties and what recommendations they consider in the future.

1   Proposal for a European Parliament and Council Directive on a common framework for electronic signatures, COM(1998) 297 final, 13.05.1998.

2   Proposal for a European Parliament and Council Directive on a common framework for electronic signatures, OJ C 325, 23.10.98, p. 5.

3   Opinion of the Economic and Social Committee on the 'Proposal for a European Parliament and Council Directive on a common framework for electronic signatures' OJ C 40, 15.2.1999, p. 29.

4   Opinion of the Committee of the Regions on the 'Proposal for a European Parliament and Council Directive on a common framework for electronic signatures' OJ C 93, 6.4.1999, p. 33.

5   Electronic signatures, Proposal for a European Parliament and Council Directive on a common framework for electronic signatures, OJ C 104, 14.4.1999, p. 49.

6   Recital 15 and definition in Article 2.

7   Jos Dumortier and Patrick Van Eecke 'Electronic Signatures The European draft Directive on a common framework for electronic signatures' CLSR Vol 15 no 2 1999, 106–112, 111–112.

8   Directive 1999/93/EC of the European Parliament and of the Council of 13 December 1999 on a Community framework for electronic signatures, OJ L 13, 19.01.2000, p. 12.

9   Article 13(1).

10 Article 12(1). The contract to prepare a review for the Commission was prepared by Jos Dumortier, Stefan Kelm, Hans Nilsson, Georgia Skouma and Patrick Van Eecke, *The Legal and Market Aspects of Electronic Signatures* (Interdisciplinary centre for Law & Information Technology, Katholieke Universiteit Leuven, Service Contract C 28.400); see also an earlier report *The implementation of the European Directive on electronic signatures status report* (Landwell and Interdisciplinary centre for Law & Information Technology, Katholieke Universiteit Leuven, 2002).

11 Commission Decision of 24 October 2005 establishing an expert group on electronic commerce (2005/752/EC), OJ L 282, 26.10.2005, p. 20.

The aim

4.3   Although the Directive appears to be technologically neutral,[1] the provisions relating to advanced electronic signatures clearly illustrate a bias towards smart cards.[2] The Directive seeks to strengthen the confidence in, and general acceptance of, the new technologies, and by doing so, to assist the use of electronic signatures across the European Union.[3] This is achieved by ensuring certificate authorities[4] are free to provide their services without requiring prior authorization in a member state,[5] and providing a common legal framework for the recognition and admissibility of electronic signatures, although the provisions of the Directive do not prevent parties making private arrangements in relation to the terms and conditions under which they will accept electronically signed data, subject to the restrictions set out in national law.[6]

1   Recital 8.
2   See the definition of advanced electronic signature, by which the signature must meet four requirements, the third of which is Article 2(2)(c), 'it is created using means that the signatory can maintain under his sole control', which would be difficult to apply to a computer.
3   Article 1.
4   Called certification-service-providers in the Directive.
5   Recitals 10 and 12.
6   Recitals 16, 20 and 21.

The legal recognition of electronic signatures

4.4 The Directive provides for two types of electronic signature. An electronic signature and an advanced electronic signature. There is a significant difference between the two types, and one that is not readily imported into a legal framework based on common law. The provisions of article 5 are central to the provisions of the Directive, providing that an electronic signature cannot be denied legal effectiveness or be held inadmissible because it is in electronic form. This principle applies to all forms of electronic signature, and recital 21 makes it clear that the provisions of the Directive do not touch upon the powers of national courts regarding the rules of evidence. The case of *I Up 505/2003*,[1] decided by the Supreme Court of the Republic of Slovenia in 2003, illustrates the force of this provision, where a student appealed against the decision of the dean for the rejection of a grade, and the student, not having heard from the office of the dean, sent an email to ask for a response. Not having any response to his email, the student initiated an action under the provisions of the Administrative Dispute Procedure, which is regulated by the Administrative Dispute Act.[2] The court of first instance decided that the student's request was not fulfilled by sending the email. However, on appeal, the Supreme Court decided that the condition of filing a new request for issuing a decision was fulfilled by sending the email, on the basis that data in electronic form was not to be refused validity just because it was in electronic form.

This point is further illustrated by two cases from Finland.[3] In 2004, the Market Court determined that an administrative appeal in a public procurement matter sent as an attachment to an email required an advanced electronic signature.[4] An advanced electronic signature was necessary because Chapter 5, section 24 of the Administrative Judicial Procedure Act (586/1996, 26.7.1996 Hallintolainkäyttölaki) requires a signature, and it could be fulfilled by providing an advanced electronic signature under the provisions of section 9 of the Act on Electronic Services and Communication in the Public Sector (13/2003, 24.1.2003 Laki sähköisestä asioinnista viranomaistoiminnassa), which in turn refers to section 18 of the Act on Electronic Signatures (14/2003, 24.2.2003 Laki sähköisistä allekirjoituksista). The Market Court decided the appeal was not delivered because the court did not have the facilities for lodging appeals by email and the email failed to include an advanced electronic signature. More recently, the Insurance Court dealt with a matter concerning an administrative appeal claim in which the claimant appealed a decision of the social security authority to the unemployment benefits board, by sending the appeal by email.[5] The claim was dismissed because the claimant failed to provide a manuscript signature on paper after submitting the electronic version of the document, which was not signed.

Chapter 5, section 24 of the Administrative Judicial Procedure Act requires an appeal to be signed:

'24 § Henkilö- ja osoitetiedot sekä allekirjoitus
Valituskirjelmässä on ilmoitettava valittajan nimi ja kotikunta. Jos valittajan puhevaltaa käyttää hänen laillinen edustajansa tai asiamiehensä tai jos valituksen laatijana on joku muu henkilö, valituskirjelmässä on ilmoitettava myös tämän nimi ja kotikunta.

Valituskirjelmässä on lisäksi ilmoitettava postiosoite ja puhelinnumero, joihin asiaa koskevat ilmoitukset valittajalle voidaan toimittaa.

Valittajan, laillisen edustajan tai asiamiehen on allekirjoitettava valituskirjelmä.

Section 24 – Personal information and signature
(1) The appeal document shall indicate the name and domicile of the appellant. If the right of the appellant to be heard is exercised by his legal representative or attorney or if the appeal document has been drawn up by someone else, the document shall indicate also his name and domicile.

(2) The appeal document shall further indicate the postal address and telephone number where the notices relating to the matter can be served on the appellant.

(3) The appellant, his legal representative or attorney shall sign the appeal document.'[6]

However, section 9 of the Act on Electronic Services and Communication in the Public Sector (13/2003) provides as follows:

'9 § Kirjallisen muodon ja allekirjoitusvaatimuksen täyttyminen
Vireillepanossa ja asian muussa käsittelyssä vaatimuksen kirjallisesta muodosta täyttää myös viranomaiselle toimitettu sähköinen asiakirja. Jos asian vireillepanossa tai muussa käsittelyssä edellytetään allekirjoitettua asiakirjaa, allekirjoitusvaatimuksen täyttää myös sähköisistä allekirjoituksista annetun lain 18 §:ssä tarkoitettu sähköinen allekirjoitus.

Viranomaiselle saapunutta sähköistä asiakirjaa ei tarvitse täydentää allekirjoituksella, jos asiakirjassa on tiedot lähettäjästä eikä asiakirjan alkuperäisyyttä tai eheyttä ole syytä epäillä. Jos viranomaiselle toimitetussa sähköisessä asiakirjassa on selvitys asiamiehen toimivallasta, asiamiehen ei tarvitse toimittaa valtakirjaa. Viranomainen voi kuitenkin määrätä valtakirjan toimitettavaksi, jos viranomaisella on aihetta epäillä asiamiehen toimivaltaa tai sen laajuutta.

Section 9 – Meeting the requirements for written form and signature
In the lodging and consideration of a matter, the required written form is also met by an electronic document delivered to the authorities. If a

signed document is required in the lodging or consideration of a matter, an electronic signature referred to in section 18 of the Act on electronic signatures meets the requirements for signature.

An electronic document delivered to the authorities does not have to be signed, if the document includes sender information and there is no uncertainty about the originality or integrity of the document. If an electronic document delivered to the authorities includes a clarification of the authority of an agent, the agent does not have to deliver a power of attorney. However, if there is uncertainty about the agent's authority or the scope of the authority, the authorities may order the agent to deliver a power of attorney.'[7]

The Insurance Court overruled the board and referred the matter back, concluding that it is not necessary to supplement the application by providing a manuscript signature where the electronic message contains sufficient information regarding the sender such that there is no reason to doubt the authenticity or integrity of the document.

Article 5 provides for a hierarchy of electronic signatures that is not to be found in the physical realm, elevating one form of signature to be something grander and apparently more relevant than any other form of electronic signature:

'1. Member States shall ensure that advanced electronic signatures which are based on a qualified certificate and which are created by a secure-signature-creation device:

(a) satisfy the legal requirements of a signature in relation to data in electronic form in the same manner as a handwritten signature satisfies those requirements in relation to paper-based data; and

(b) are admissible as evidence in legal proceedings.

2. Member States shall ensure that an electronic signature is not denied legal effectiveness and admissibility as evidence in legal proceedings solely on the grounds that it is:

— in electronic form, or
— not based upon a qualified certificate, or
— not based upon a qualified certificate issued by an accredited certification-service-provider, or
— not created by a secure signature-creation device.'

1   A case report will be published in the *Digital Evidence Journal*, 2007, Volume 4 Number 2.

2   Official Gazette of the Republic of Slovenia, no. 50/1997 as amended. The new Administrative Dispute Act (Official Gazette of the Republic of Slovenia, no. 105/2006) came into force on 1 January 2007.

3   The author is grateful to Jan Ollila, Managing Partner, and Eva Storskrubb of Dittmar & Indrenius for bringing these cases to his attention, and to Eva Storskrubb for reviewing this part of the text.

4 Combined cases 106/04/JH (140/04/JH and 147/04/JH, judgment MAO: 161/04, 162/04, 163/04 of 27.8.2004) available online in Finnish at www.finlex.fi.
5 Case1486:2006 judgment 19.10.2006 available online in Finnish at www.finlex.fi.
6 Unofficial translation © Ministry of Justice, Finland, available online at www.finlex.fi/en/laki/kaannokset/1996/en19960586 including amendments up to 435/2003.
7 Unofficial translation © Ministry of Justice, Finland, available online at www.finlex.fi/pdf/saadkaan/E0030013.PDF.

The electronic signature

4.5 The Directive provides for the definition of an electronic signature in article 2(1):

> '"electronic signature" means data in electronic form which are attached to or logically associated with other electronic data and which serve as a method of authentication;'

The definition is very broad, in keeping with the wide nature of what is capable of constituting a signature in digital terms, and therefore includes any means that is capable of demonstrating proof of intent. This definition will include any of the forms of electronic signatures discussed elsewhere in this text. The elements of an electronic signature comprise:
(a) Data in electronic form.
(b) The data must be attached to or logically associated with other electronic data.
(c) The function of the electronic signature is to act as a method of authentication.

The definition of an electronic signature fails to link the need for the electronic signature to authenticate the data to which it is attached or logically associated,[1] although it may be fair to infer that the data is added by the person signing the document or communication with the intention of approving or being bound to the text. Note also that the process of authentication is between protocols, not between human beings and it is not clear whether the authentication relates to the origin of the data, or acts to verify the identity of a person or entity. The provisions of recital 21 require an electronic signature to be capable of being used in evidence in legal proceedings. The legal recognition of the signature is to be based upon objective criteria, and it does not need to be linked to an individual identity certificate issued by a certification authority to be admissible. This definition appears to be wide enough to permit secret codes (such as a PIN), and biometric measurements in electronic format. The third element of an electronic signature provides for a method of authentication, although it is not certain what data is to be authenticated. In the event an individual identity certificate is used, and providing it conforms to the definition of a certificate, it can act to confirm the identity of the person or legal entity, although it does not follow that a certificate is able to undertake this task. To perform this task, the certificate needs to link the 'signature-verification data' to an entity. A link can be made between different sets of data under the terms of a protocol, but it is not capable of linking the data with the entity, nor is it possible to confirm the identity of the entity.

1   A point also noted by Graham J H Smith *Internet Law and Regulation* (Sweet & Maxwell, 3rd edn 2002), 10-084.

The advanced electronic signature

4.6   An advanced electronic signature is a more elaborate construct than an electronic signature.[1] There is no definition of an advanced electronic signature, but article 2(2) sets out a number of characteristics relating to performance:

> '"advanced electronic signature" means an electronic signature which meets the following requirements:
>
> (a)   it is uniquely linked to the signatory;
> (b)   it is capable of identifying the signatory;
> (c)   it is created using means that the signatory can maintain under his sole control; and
> (d)   it is linked to the data to which it relates in such a manner that any subsequent change of the data is detectable;'

It appears from this definition that an advanced electronic signature is only capable of existing in a format that an individual has total physical control over, as set out in article 2(2)(c) above. Each of the four attributes are discussed below.

1   Arguably, there is yet another form of signature, a 'qualified electronic signature' consisting of an advanced electronic signature based on a qualified certificate, using a secure-signature-creation device that must comply with the requirements set out in Annex I, II and III: Report on the operation of Directive 1999/93/EC on a Community framework for electronic signatures, COM(2006) 120 final, 15.3.2006, 2.3.2.

UNIQUELY LINKED TO THE SIGNATORY

4.7   No form of electronic signature can conform to this part of the definition. For instance, a user relinquishes control over their scanned signature once it has been sent. A digital signature is not linked to the person creating it: the unique link is made with the private key, not the user. Nobody is capable of committing a private key to memory, because it is far too complicated. This means that private keys are retained on a computer, disk or smart card. In conclusion, it is not possible to create an electronic signature that can be uniquely linked to the signatory. Any court that recognizes such a signature arguably suspends reality: and, it might be argued, surrealism does not have a part to play in courts or the formation of legislation.

CAPABLE OF IDENTIFYING THE SIGNATORY

4.8 Any form of electronic signature is capable of identifying the person that signed it.

CREATED USING MEANS THAT THE SIGNATORY CAN MAINTAIN UNDER HIS SOLE CONTROL

4.9 Any form of electronic signature can be created under the sole control of the user, but when a private key to a digital signature is used, a recipient will not know whether it was the owner that actually used the private key. It is also arguable, given the ease by which a key on a computer can be misused, whether the signatory can ever maintain that the electronic signature is under their sole control when located on a computer, and if loaded on a smart card, the ease by which a smart card can be stolen or 'borrowed' by another person is so significant as to undermine the suggestion that the signature can remain under the sole control of the person whose signature it is.[1] This is also accepted by the members of the Forum of European Supervisory Authorities for Electronic Signatures, where the concept of 'sole control' was discussed in a 2004 paper:[2]

'c) "sole control"

Creation and storage of signature-creation data

Most requirements on the creation and storage of signature-creation data have their foundation in Annex III and Annex II j who do not apply on advanced electronic signatures. However, the advanced electronic signature must be "created using means that the signatory can maintain under his sole control". This does not require the use of a special hardware device as a signature-creation device, but it requires – especially in the case where the private key is stored in software – the use of security measures by the signatory to maintain his control over the key (eg encryption of the file which stores the private key, restriction of access to the computer and this file).

What does "sole control" mean in the context of (automatically signing) systems which are maintained by several system administrators (this is also relevant for systems that sign qualified certificates)? If the certificate is issued to a certain natural person, the security concept and the configuration of the server must ensure that only this person has control over the private key. How the person executes her control is defined in the security concept. If the certificate is issued to a legal person (which is not possible in most countries) the personnel of the legal person maintains "sole control" over the private key by its security concept.'

In a 2005 paper 'Public Statement on Server Based Signature Services',[3] the members of the Forum elaborated on 'sole control' in relation to server-based signature services:

'Sole control

The meaning of "sole control" in Article 2 of the Directive has been discussed in the FESA working paper on advanced electronic signatures. According to that paper, the use of special hardware as signature creation device is not required. However, the signatory must take measures to maintain control over his key. The security concept and the system configuration of the server must ensure that only the signatory, who is either a natural or a legal person, has control over the corresponding signature creation data.

If signatures are created automatically at a server, the signatory is usually not present in person. However, the signatory has control over security measures, and has the responsibility to select suitable security measures.

For server based signature services, the signatory is not present in person either. But neither can he select suitable security measures. He can only choose whether or not to enlist the services. The signatory can decide whether or not security measures taken by the service provider are sufficient for him. For making this decision, the signatory needs at least:

• access to a comprehensible version of the security concept, and
• confidence that the service provider sticks to the security concept (confidence can be strengthened by audits performed by a trusted third party like an independent auditor or a supervisory authority).

In addition, sole control requires certain cryptographic qualities of algorithms and of signature creation data that have been discussed in the working paper mentioned above.

Under these premises, FESA members believe that sole control at least of the signature creation data can be achieved and that advanced electronic signatures can be created by a server based signature service.'

The authors of these papers indicate the tenuous nature of the digital environment, and how it cannot be under the sole control of anybody. In addition, the authors of the second paper include a footnote to the final sentence, thus: 'Note that according to German law, "sole control" implies physical control and that therefore in Germany, server-based signature services cannot be used for creating advanced electronic signatures and definitely not for creating qualified electronic signatures.' The position in Germany must be correct, otherwise the meaning of 'sole control' becomes distorted beyond measure.

1   S. C. Rennie and J. R. Rudland, 'Differences in medical students' attitudes to academic misconduct and reported behaviour across the years—a questionnaire study', *J Med Ethics* 2003; 29:97–102, in which medical students admitted they would forge signatures on work submitted.

2   'Working Paper on Advanced Electronic Signatures' (Forum of European Supervisory Authorities for Electronic Signatures 12 October 2004).
3   'Public Statement on Server Based Signature Services' (Forum of European Supervisory Authorities for Electronic Signatures, 17 October 2005).

LINKED TO THE DATA TO WHICH IT RELATES IN SUCH A MANNER THAT ANY SUBSEQUENT
CHANGE OF THE DATA IS DETECTABLE

4.10   The only form of electronic signature that is capable of complying with this element is the digital signature, but even a digital signature is not immune from attack.

The Directive has determined that the legal effect of an advanced electronic signature is greater than that of an ordinary electronic signature, in that an advanced electronic signature is considered to have satisfied the same requirements of a handwritten signature, where a 'handwritten signature satisfies those requirements in relation to paper-based data.' This point is reinforced in recital 20, which reads 'advanced electronic signatures which are based on a qualified certificate and which are created by a secure-signature-creation device can be regarded as legally equivalent to handwritten signatures only if the requirements for handwritten signatures are fulfilled.' The requirements for a manuscript signature are not set out. As a result, the comparison must be made to the legal status of manuscript signatures in domestic law for each member state. In this respect, some domestic laws may differentiate between manuscript signatures according to the purpose of the signature.[1] For an advanced electronic signature to meet the requirements of a manuscript signature, it is necessary for it to comply with the functions that a manuscript signature fulfils, discussed elsewhere in this text.[2] The rules that apply to electronic signatures will apply equally to advanced electronic signatures, and a court can determine the validity of either form of signature in the same way. At best, the use of an electronic signature should seek to replicate the function of cautioning the person using the electronic signature by *'conveying the same sense of legal significance to the user* that a manual signature does'. (Italics in the original)[3] It should be noted, however, that the Law Commission's Advice on the Formal Requirements in Commercial Transactions points out that any electronic signature, however insecure, will meet the requirement that a signature should demonstrate the intention of the signatory to authenticate a document or message.[4] As a matter of English law, an advanced signature can have no greater validity than any other, although 'validity' is the wrong purpose. The test should have been 'prudence of reliance'. One further problem will remain. From the point of view of security engineering, the Directive fails calamitously by excluding from relevance the system within which the secure signature creation data are used. The evidence of the security and structure of the system within which the secure signature creation data are used must be of prime concern to anybody relying on a key pair.

1   Vincenzo Sinsi 'Digital Signature Legislation in Europe' JIBFL Volume 16 No 1 January 2001, 17–22.

2   For the position in the Netherlands, see M. H. M. Schellekens, *Electronic Signatures Authentication Technology from a Legal Perspective* (T M C Asser Press, 2004), 3.2.2.

3   Mark Sneddon 'Legislating to facilitate electronic signatures and records: exceptions, standards and the impact on the statute book' University of New South Wales Law Journal available online at www.austlii.edu.au/au/journals/UNSWLJ/1998/59.html Part 2 III A (iii) (c).

4   Law Commission 'Electronic Commerce: Formal Requirements in Commercial Transactions Advice from the Law Commission', December 2001, 3.28.

QUALIFIED CERTIFICATE

4.11   To be admissible, an advanced electronic signature requires a qualified certificate, and must also be created by a secure-signature-creation device. A qualified certificate is defined in article 2(10):

'"qualified certificate" means a certificate which meets the requirements laid down in Annex I and is provided by a certification-service-provider who fulfils the requirements laid down in Annex II;'

The requirements that a qualified certificate must meet are set out in Annex I, as follows:

'Requirements for qualified certificates

Qualified certificates must contain:

(a)   an indication that the certificate is issued as a qualified certificate;

(b)   the identification of the certification-service-provider and the State in which it is established;

(c)   the name of the signatory or a pseudonym, which shall be identified as such;

(d)   provision for a specific attribute of the signatory to be included if relevant, depending on the purpose for which the certificate is intended;

(e)   signature-verification data which correspond to signature-creation data under the control of the signatory;

(f)   an indication of the beginning and end of the period of validity of the certificate;

(g)   the identity code of the certificate;

(h)   the advanced electronic signature of the certification-service-provider issuing it;

(i)   limitations on the scope of use of the certificate, if applicable; and

(j)   limits on the value of transactions for which the certificate can be used, if applicable.

The term 'certificate' is defined in article 2(9) as meaning 'an electronic attestation which links signature-verification data to a person and confirms the identity of that person' and 'signatory' is defined in article 2(3) as 'a person who holds a signature-creation device and acts either on his own behalf or on behalf of the natural or legal person or entity he represents.' What constitutes 'signature-verification data' is defined in article 2(7):

'signature-verification-data' means data, such as codes or public cryptographic keys, which are used for the purpose of verifying an electronic signature;

The definition of 'signature-verification data' more accurately describes the mechanism of the protocol. A code or public key can act to verify an electronic signature, but there is no nexus between how the key is used and the identity of the person or entity whose key it purports to be. The qualified certificate must contain the information set out in Annex I, and the certificate must be provided by a certification-service-provider who fulfils the stipulations set out in Annex II of the Directive. The criteria set out in Annex I omits some of the requirements of article 9 of the UNCITRAL Model Law on Electronic Signatures, particularly the provisions included in article 9(d):

'(d) Provide reasonably accessible means that enable a relying party to ascertain, where relevant, from the certificate or otherwise:
  (i) The method used to identify the signatory;
  (ii) Any limitation on the purpose or value for which the signature-creation data or the certificate may be used;
  (iii) That the signature-creation data are valid and have not been compromised;
  (iv) Any limitation on the scope or extent of liability stipulated by the certification service provider;
  (v) Whether means exist for the signatory to give notice pursuant to article 8, paragraph 1 (b), of this Law;
  (vi) Whether a timely revocation service is offered;'

CERTIFICATION-SERVICE-PROVIDER

4.12 Article 2(11) defines a certification-service-provider as 'an entity or a legal or natural person who issues certificates or provides other services related to electronic signatures.' This definition is very wide, in that it includes any entity that offers any service in relation to the provision of an advanced electronic signature, including organizations that offer registration services and time-stamping services. A certification-service-provider can only issue qualified certificates if it complies with the lengthy requirements laid down in Annex II, as follows:

'Requirements for certification-service-providers issuing qualified certificates

Certification-service-providers must:

(a) demonstrate the reliability necessary for providing certification services;

(b) ensure the operation of a prompt and secure directory and a secure and immediate revocation service;

(c) ensure that the date and time when a certificate is issued or revoked can be determined precisely;

(d) verify, by appropriate means in accordance with national law, the identity and, if applicable, any specific attributes of the person to which a qualified certificate is issued;

(e) employ personnel who possess the expert knowledge, experience, and qualifications necessary for the services provided, in particular competence at managerial level, expertise in electronic signature technology and familiarity with proper security procedures; they must also apply administrative and management procedures which are adequate and correspond to recognised standards;

(f) use trustworthy systems and products which are protected against modification and ensure the technical and cryptographic security of the process supported by them;

(g) take measures against forgery of certificates, and, in cases where the certification-service-provider generates signature-creation data,[1] guarantee confidentiality during the process of generating such data;

(h) maintain sufficient financial resources to operate in conformity with the requirements laid down in the Directive, in particular to bear the risk of liability for damages, for example, by obtaining appropriate insurance;

(i) record all relevant information concerning a qualified certificate for an appropriate period of time, in particular for the purpose of providing evidence of certification for the purposes of legal proceedings. Such recording may be done electronically;

(j) not store or copy signature-creation data of the person to whom the certification-service-provider provided key management services;

(k) before entering into a contractual relationship with a person seeking a certificate to support his electronic signature inform that person by a durable means of communication of the precise terms and conditions regarding the use of the certificate, including any limitations on its use, the existence of a voluntary accreditation scheme and procedures for complaints and dispute settlement. Such information, which may be transmitted electronically, must be in writing and in readily understandable language. Relevant parts of this information must also be made available on request to third-parties relying on the certificate;

(l) use trustworthy systems to store certificates[2] in a verifiable form so that:

— only authorised persons can make entries and changes,
— information can be checked for authenticity,
— certificates are publicly available for retrieval in only those cases for which the certificate-holder's consent has been obtained, and
— any technical changes compromising these security requirements are apparent to the operator.'

The requirements set out in Annex II mirror the requirements of article 9(f) of the UNCITRAL Model Law on Electronic Signatures, in that the provider is required to 'utilize trustworthy systems, procedures and human resources in performing its services' and includes a number of the points set out in article 10 respecting the factors to consider in assessing the trustworthiness of the provider, with the exception of an independent audit and any form of accreditation. However, these matters are, arguably, covered in item (e), which requires the provider to comply with a set of recognized standards, whether national or international in nature.[3]

The requirement in paragraph (a) requires the provider to demonstrate their reliability, which must be a difficult proposition, unless a provider is registered or accredited by a recognized third party. However, the Directive does not permit member states to require a provider to be accredited, as set out in recital 12 and article 3(1), although voluntary schemes are permitted and a supervision system is required in accordance with article 3(3). This leads to the provisions set out in paragraph (k), which requires the provider to inform the prospective subscriber whether there are any voluntary accreditation schemes before they enter into the contract, although the provider does not have to be a member of such a scheme.[4] The provision in item (l), that the provider has a trustworthy system to store certificates in a verifiable form so that information can be checked for authenticity is a puzzle, in that it is not certain what is meant by authentic. It might be that the information contained in the certificate is the authentic information supplied to the subscriber, but it is not certain.[5] As for the requirement of trustworthiness, article 3(5) of the Directive provided that the Commission may establish and publish reference numbers of generally recognized standards for electronic signature products, and both the European Committee for Standardization (CEN) and the European Telecommunications Standards Institute (ETSN) have provided a long list of standards, all of which are available on their respective websites.

Finally, for an advanced electronic signature to be admissible, it must be created by a secure-creation-device, which is defined in article 2(6) as a device that meets the requirements of Annex III. The requirements for such a device are set out in Annex III, paragraph 1, which sets out the technical and procedural criteria:

'Requirements for secure signature-creation devices

1. Secure signature-creation devices must, by appropriate technical and procedural means, ensure at the least that:

(a) the signature-creation-data used for signature generation can practically occur only once, and that their secrecy is reasonably assured;

(b) the signature-creation-data used for signature generation cannot, with reasonable assurance, be derived and the signature is protected against forgery using currently available technology;

(c) the signature-creation-data used for signature generation can be reliably protected by the legitimate signatory against the use of others.'

The provisions of sub-paragraph (a) are somewhat confusing, as indicated by Lorna Brazell,[6] but it seems right, despite the structure of the language used, to infer that the device is only to produce a signature that can only occur once, being the message digest unique to the message that is signed. Although sub-paragraph (b) requires the signature to be free from forgery using currently available technology, nevertheless what is not clear is at what point in time the signature must not be capable of being forged: at the time the signature is created, or the time during which it is used to create signatures. The weakness of all digital signature technologies is exposed by sub-paragraph (c), which requires the data to be protected by the signatory against the use by others: the only methods is the use of a password, even if the signature is placed on a smart card, which means the digital signature is as strong as the password used to protect the private key. The device must also comply with the requirements of paragraph 2, in that such devices 'must not alter the data to be signed or prevent such data from being presented to the signatory prior to the signature process.'[7]

1 Article 2(4) defines signature-creation data as 'unique data, such as codes or private cryptographic keys, which are used by the signatory to create an electronic signature.'

2 Article 2(9) defines certificate as 'an electronic attestation which links signature verification data to a person and confirms the identity of that person.'

3 The EU has set up a number of bodies to consider the issue of standards, the authority of which stems from Directive 98/34 of the European Parliament and of the Council laying down a procedure for the provision of information in the fields of technical standards and regulations and of rules on information services, OJ L 204, 21.7.1998, p. 37, as amended by Directive 98/48 of the European Parliament and of the Council, OJ L 217, 5.8.1998, p. 18, and three European Standards Organisations are recognized, CEN, CENELEC and ETSI: see Commission Decision of 14 July 2003 on the publications of reference of generally recognised standards for electronic signature products in accordance with Directive 1999/93/EC of the European Parliament and of the Council 2003/511/EC, OJ L 175, 15.7.2003, p. 45, which lists the following standards in the Annex: CWA 14167-1 Security Requirements for Trustworthy Systems Managing Certificates for Electronic Signatures – Part 1: System Security Requirements; CWA 14167-2 Security Requirements for Trustworthy Systems Managing Certificates for Electronic Signatures – Part 2: Cryptographic Module for CSP signing operations with backup – Protection profile (CMCSOB-PP) and CWA 14169 Secure Signature-creation devices 'EAL 4+'.

4   Article 2(13) defines voluntary accreditation: "'voluntary accreditation" means any permis-
     sion, setting out rights and obligations specific to the provision of certification services, to
     be granted upon request by the certification-service-provider concerned, by the public or
     private body charged with the elaboration of, and supervision of compliance with, such rights
     and obligations, where the certification-service-provider is not entitled to exercise the rights
     stemming from the permission until it has received the decision by the body.
5   Lorna Brazell, *Electronic Signatures Law and Regulation* (Sweet & Maxwell, 2004) 5-052 for
     further discussion.
6   Lorna Brazell, *Electronic Signatures Law and Regulation*, 5-056.
7   Article 3(4) requires secure signature-creation-devices to conform to the requirements in
     Annex III. Member states are required to designate bodies to be responsible for the conform-
     ity assessments of secure signature-creation-devices. The Commission, under the provisions
     of article 3(4), have established the criteria for member states to determine whether a body
     is suitable enough to be responsible for such a task. The criteria is set out in Commission
     Decision of 6 November 2000 on the minimum criteria to be taken into account by Member
     States when designating bodies in accordance with article 3(4) of Directive 1999/93/EC of
     the European Parliament and of the Council on a Community framework for electronic
     signatures 2000/709/EC OJ L 289, 16.11.2000 p. 42.

Regulation and supervision of certification service providers

4.13   Articles 3, 4 and 8 refer to market access, data protection and the
internal market with respect to the powers of member states to regulate and
supervise certification service providers. A member state is not permitted to
require certification services to be the subject of prior authorization, although
member states are required to establish a system of supervision of certification
service providers.[1] If voluntary schemes are introduced, they are required, in
accordance with the provisions of article 3(2), to be objective, transparent,
proportionate and non-discriminatory. Certification services providers are not
to be restricted when providing services originating in another member state,
and products must be able to circulate freely.[2] Certification services providers
are required to adhere to the principles of data protection, and member states
cannot prevent certificate service providers from indicating in a certificate a
pseudonym instead of the name of the signatory.[3]

1   Article 3(1) and (3).
2   Article 4.
3   Article 8.

Liability

4.14   Certification services providers that issue or guarantee qualified
certificates are liable, in accordance with the provisions of article 6:

'Liability

1.   As a minimum, Member States shall ensure that by issuing a certificate
as a qualified certificate to the public or by guaranteeing such a certificate

to the public a certification-service-provider is liable for damage caused to any entity or legal or natural person who reasonably relies on that certificate:

(a) as regards the accuracy at the time of issuance of all information contained in the qualified certificate and as regards the fact that the certificate contains all the details prescribed for a qualified certificate;

(b) for assurance that at the time of the issuance of the certificate, the signatory identified in the qualified certificate held the signature-creation data corresponding to the signature-verification data given or identified in the certificate;

(c) for assurance that the signature-creation data and the signature-verification data can be used in a complementary manner in cases where the certification-service-provider generates them both;

unless the certification-service-provider proves that he has not acted negligently.

2. As a minimum Member States shall ensure that a certification-service-provider who has issued a certificate as a qualified certificate to the public is liable for damage caused to any entity or legal or natural person who reasonably relies on the certificate for failure to register revocation of the certificate unless the certification-service-provider proves that he has not acted negligently.

3. Member States shall ensure that a certification-service-provider may indicate in a qualified certificate limitations on the use of that certificate, provided that the limitations are recognisable to third parties. The certification-service-provider shall not be liable for damage arising from use of a qualified certificate which exceeds the limitations placed on it.

4. Member States shall ensure that a certification-service-provider may indicate in the qualified certificate a limit on the value of transactions for which the certificate can be used, provided that the limit is recognisable to third parties.

The certification-service-provider shall not be liable for damage resulting from this maximum limit being exceeded.'

In essence, the only defence a certification service provider has, is to prove they are not negligent. This means they will be required to provide proof that the systems, administration procedures and records are maintained such that it has reached a suitable standard of care. This does not prevent a certification service provider from limiting their liability in respect of qualified certificates in relation to use to which the certificate is put (article 6(2)), or the value of a transaction (article 6(3)), although the limits imposed may be void as against consumers because the terms are considered unfair.[1]

1   Article 6(5); Council Directive 93/13/EEC of 5 April 1993 on unfair terms in consumer contracts, OJ L 95, 21.4.1993, p. 29.

Relying party

4.15   The Directive does not address what action, if any, a recipient of an advanced electronic signature should take to satisfy themselves that signature can be relied upon. However, Annex IV provides a list of recommendations for secure signature verification:

'During the signature-verification process it should be ensured with reasonable certainty that:

(a)   the data used for verifying the signature correspond to the data displayed to the verifier;

(b)   the signature is reliably verified and the result of that verification is correctly displayed;

(c)   the verifier can, as necessary, reliably establish the contents of the signed data;

(d)   the authenticity and validity of the certificate required at the time of signature verification are reliably verified;

(e)   the result of verification and the signatory's identity are correctly displayed;

(f)   the use of a pseudonym is clearly indicated; and

(g)   any security-relevant changes can be detected.'

It can certainly be implied that it is anticipated that a recipient will undertake some action to verify the reliability of the signature, nevertheless, there is no specific duty on a recipient to undertake any such act. Had it been intended to impose such on the recipient, no doubt it would have been made explicit in the Directive. Given the complexity of this issue, as discussed elsewhere in this text, it was probably considered right to leave this to the judges to resolve in the event of disputes, mainly because the European Union did not want to make any difficult decisions: because dealing with the exceedingly difficult position of the recipient, had any serious thought been given to the issue, would undoubtedly have caused the failure of the passing of the Directive.

Review of the Directive

4.16   In accordance with the provisions of article 12(1), the Directive was reviewed in 2003. The final report was published in October 2003.[1] The study concluded that most member states had, 'more or less' faithfully transposed the Directive into national legislation, and the language used in the Directive had been taken up by EEA member countries, Switzerland, the Accession and Candidate countries.

A number of areas were identified as being 'problematic,' such as:[2]

(a) The development of supervision schemes that appeared to require prior authorization and thereby infringing the provisions of article 3(1).

(b) The rules on voluntary accreditation appeared to be misunderstood, and were used by member states as a means of controlling certification service providers and were not, in practice, voluntary in nature.

(c) There were divergences of interpretation and implementation of electronic signatures in the public sector (article 3(7)), including the requirement that communicating with public authorities is only possible in some member countries through the use of a digital signature based on qualified certificates issued by an accredited certification service provider.

(d) Most member states were reluctant to designate domestic bodies for assessment of secure-creation devices. This was due to a number of problems that are glaringly obvious. One is partly because of the paucity of vendors, and partly because the vendors were reluctant to have their products assessed, because the assessment only lasts for a short period of time, after which the produce must be reassessed. Also, the assessment process is extremely expensive and time-consuming, which required large resources. Not surprisingly, the expense did not justify the product.

(e) The non-discrimination principle set out in article 5(2) had been transposed in a patchy manner, and where it had been transposed, it had not always been covered in its entirety.

(f) The legal effects of a qualified electronic signature (a digital signature subject to the further provisions of the Directive) appeared to be explicitly recognised by member states. In addition, the transposition of the provisions of the Annexes varied, which led to a fragmented market, and some member states had, apparently, made the recommendations set out in Annex IV into obligatory requirements at a national level.

(g) The provisions relating to liability were transposed in their entirety with few exceptions, and some member states extended the liability provisions.

(h) All member states set out the rules on foreign qualified certificates in their territory, with Ireland, Malta and the United Kingdom not distinguishing between domestic and foreign qualified certificates.

(i) The implementation of the provisions of article 8 relating to data protection does not appear to pose any problems, although some member states had failed to implement article 8(2) correctly. Every member country with the exception of Estonia and Bulgaria permitted the use of a pseudonym in a certificate.

(j)   The lack of interoperability at both a national and cross-border level was considered an obstacle for the acceptance and proliferation of digital signatures. No evidence was provided to substantiate this assertion.

The authors of the report set out their recommendations in paragraph 1.2.2. It was felt the Directive did not need to be amended, partly because of the lengthy process that must be undertaken to amend it, and partly because the compromises reached in the final version of the Directive were only reached after long and difficult negotiations between the member states. The recommendations overwhelmingly related to the technical issues relating to the infrastructure of digital signatures, and do not require further elaboration in this text.

1   Jos Dumortier, Stefan Kelm, Hans Nilsson, Georgia Skouma and Patrick Van Eecke, *The Legal and Market Aspects of Electronic Signatures* (Interdisciplinary Centre for Law & Information Technology, Katholieke Universiteit Leuven, Service Contract C 28.400); Stefan Kelm, 'On the implementation of the 1999 European Directive on electronic signatures,' *e-Signature Law Journal* (now the *Digital Evidence Journal*) 2005, Volume 2 Number 1, 5–13.
2   Paragraph 1.2.1.

Take-up of advanced electronic signatures

4.17   In March 2006, the Information Society and Media Commissioner issued a press release[1] after the publication of a report from the Commission to the European Parliament and Council.[2] The content of the press release made it clear that people were reluctant to obtain advanced electronic signatures (digital signatures), and this, apparently, resulted in 'slowing down the growth in goods and services.' No evidence was offered to substantiate this assertion, although more regulation was promised if it was considered necessary. This comment echoed the observation of the authors of the 2003 report, that 'There is currently no natural market demand for Qualified Certificates and related services.'[3] Clearly nothing had changed in three years. In any event, the press release indicated that the imposition of electronic 'Identity' cards that included a digital signature would act as a means by which digital signatures would increase in the future, and people will be increasingly forced to use public services online in combination with their electronic 'Identity' cards. The Report on the operation of the Directive is a review of the operation of the Directive in accordance with the provisions of article 12, and is partly based on a study published in 2003.[4] The first part of the Report is mainly descriptive, and claims, at paragraph 2.3.4, that there is 'no representative case law that allows for any assessment of the recognition of electronic signatures in practice.' It is anticipated that the case law illustrated in this text illustrates the inaccuracy of this comment. The Report reviews the use of various forms of electronic signature and outlines the work undertaken by the various standards bodies. The reasons for the slow take-up of digital signatures is partly addressed in paragraph 3.3.2:

'3.3.2. Technological challenges

There is no simple answer to why the market for electronic signatures has not developed faster, but the market is facing a number of technical challenges. One frequently highlighted problem that could contribute to the slow take-up of advanced or qualified electronic signatures in Europe is the complexity of the PKI technology. The often stressed advantage of PKI is that this technology uses the system of the "trusted third party" which allows parties that have never met to trust each other on the internet. In many of the current applications there seems, however, to be little interest from the service providers, essentially for liability reasons, to allow their customers to use their authentication device for other services. This is probably why the use of different one-time passwords (OTPs) is still dominating the market and there is little indication of this changing in the near future.'

Other reasons for the failure of people to use digital signatures includes the lack of mutual recognition between certification service providers, including technical, legal and organizational problems. In addition, the smart card, although the most widely used form upon which to carry a digital signature, is acknowledged to be expensive and requires a physical infrastructure. Also, another reason cited is the legal requirements to archive documents, sometimes for up to 30 years, which produces a significant strain on resources. It will be observed that there is no consideration given to finding out why ordinary people and businesses do not feel the need to use digital signatures. The Report went to indicate, at paragraph 4, that even if the take-up of digital signatures could not be achieved by legislation, other methods could be found to achieve the same result:

'Even if the demand for the deployment of PKI is something that cannot be created by legislation, the Commission still sees the introduction of electronic signatures as an important tool for the development of the information society services and to encourage secure electronic commerce.'

To this effect, two Directives have been passed that require a form of advanced electronic signature.[5] In addition, the internal rules of procedure of the Commission were amended, setting out the conditions of validity of electronic documents for the Commission's purposes. It applies to electronic documents established or received and held by the Commission and electronic signatures will be used to attest the validity of electronic documents when necessary.[6] The concluding paragraph, 5.2, indicates that the Commission will make further efforts to encourage the take-up of digital signatures, in the face of overwhelming evidence that nobody seems to want to use them, nor has any use for them: e-commerce is clearly developing in the absence of digital signatures.

1   IP/06/325 dated 17 March 2006.

2   Report on the operation of Directive 1999/93/EC on a Community framework for electronic signatures, COM(2006) 120 final, 15.3.2006.

3   Jos Dumortier, Stefan Kelm, Hans Nilsson, Georgia Skouma and Patrick Van Eecke, *The Legal and Market Aspects of Electronic Signatures*, page 8; see also Simson L. Garfinkel, Jeffrey I. Schiller, Erik Nordlander, David Margrave, and Robert C. Miller, 'Views, Reactions and Impact of Digitally-Signed Mail in e-Commerce' (Financial Cryptography and Data Security Ninth International Conference, February 28–3 March 2005, Roseau, The Commonwealth of Dominica) available online at www.simson.net/ref/2004/fc2005_smime_submitted.pdf.

4   Jos Dumortier, Patrick Van Eecke and Ilse Anné *The Legal Aspects of Digital Signatures* (Interdisciplinary Centre for Law & Information Technology, Katholieke Universiteit Leuven, 1998).

5   Council Directive 2001/115/EC of 20 December 2001 amending Directive 77/388/EEC with a view to simplifying, modernizing and harmonizing the conditions laid down for invoicing in respect of value added tax, OJ L 15, 17.1.2002, p. 24; Directive 2004/17/EC of the European Parliament and of the Council of 31 March 2004 coordinating the procurement procedures of entities operating in the water, energy, transport and postal services sectors, OJ L 134, 30.4.2004, p. 1 and Directive 2004/18/EC of the European Parliament and of the Council of 31 March 2004 on the coordination of procedures for the award of public works contracts, public supply contracts and public service contracts, OJ L 134, 30.4.2004, p. 114.

6   2004/563/EC, Euratom: Commission Decision of 7 July 2004 amending its Rules of Procedure, OJ L 251, 27.07.2004 p. 9.

Canada

Anila Srivastava, Valerie C. Mann and
Thomas S. Woods

Introduction

5.1   As this chapter will outline, Canada has developed a relatively flexible
and adaptive interpretation of common law principles that accommodates and
recognizes the exchange of information and the conduct of commerce in an
electronic age. The legislative background of electronic signatures in Canada
is reviewed, in part in comparison to the international context, together with
the ways that Canadian courts have dealt with electronic signature issues as
they have arisen in litigation in Canada.

Legislative background

5.2   Understanding the application and interpretation of statutory provisions
regarding electronic signatures requires a basic understanding of the division of
legislative powers in Canada. The *Constitution Act, 1867*[1] distributes legislative
powers between the federal and provincial[2] governments. A preliminary step
in legal analysis is to determine which level of government has jurisdiction
in any particular area or issue. This is often not easy to discern, given that
different levels of government will often claim jurisdiction over different
aspects of a particular subject matter. For example, the federal government
legislates with respect to criminal law, although the provinces legislate with
respect to the administration of justice within the provinces and quasi-criminal
matters such as motor vehicle offences. The federal government legislates with
respect to those undertakings that are of national scope or importance such as
banking, telecommunications, broadcast, and shipping, but the provinces and
territories legislate with respect to property and civil rights in the provinces.
Electronic signatures are, depending on context, governed by both federal
and provincial evidence legislation; by provincial contract and consumer

protection legislation; and by provincial rules of court for the purposes of civil procedure.

The province of Québec belongs to the civil law tradition, while the other nine provinces and three territories belong to the common law tradition. However, the Supreme Court of Canada, the court of final appeal, interprets the civil and common law traditions harmoniously and in accordance with the Constitution and *Charter*.[3] Statutory requirements and definitions must therefore be read for their plain meaning, and purposively, but they are interpreted in light of existing case law.

1   The division of legislative powers is set out in ss 91 to 95 of the *Constitution Act 1867* (U.K.), 30 & 31 Vict., c. 3, reprinted in R.S.C. 1985, App. II, No. 5.

2   In this chapter, the words 'province' and 'provincial' are used compendiously to refer to all of the Canadian provinces, the Yukon Territory, the Northwest Territories, and Nunavut.

3   *Canadian Charter of Rights and Freedoms*, Part I of the *Constitution Act 1982*, being Schedule B to the Canada Act 1982 (U.K.), 1982, c. 11.

A signed document

5.3   The definitions of 'document', 'writing' and 'signature', and the requirements for enforceability of contracts (original document, in writing, signed or sealed), were all derived from the English common law.[1] These definitions have evolved with technology: first the telegraph, then telex, then the facsimile machine, then the internet. In addition, courts interpret the terms flexibly in accordance with a principled, as opposed to rule-based, approach to evidence. The requirements for contracts have similarly evolved to respond to changing commercial reality. Thus, long before the enactment of electronic evidence legislation, original evidence rules were reinterpreted liberally to permit the reception into evidence of business records, copies, and documentary evidence in non-paper forms.[2]

1   The English Statute of Frauds was adopted verbatim, or with minor modifications, by all common law provinces.

2   This is merely a codification of Canadian case law which as early as 1978 had already accepted computer printouts as business records: *R v McMullen* (1978), 42 C.C.C. (2d) 67 (Ont. H.C.), aff'd (1979), 100 D.L.R. (3d) 671 (Ont. C.A.).

Document

5.4   Most federal and provincial evidence statutes or rules of civil procedure define 'document' expansively, in keeping with the liberal common law interpretation. What is defined as a 'document' in one enactment or jurisdiction may be defined as a 'record' in another. For example, in British Columbia a 'document' includes 'any device by means of which information is recorded or stored'[1] and a 'record' includes 'books, documents, maps, drawings, photographs, letters, vouchers, papers and any other thing on which information is recorded or stored by any means whether graphic, electronic, mechanical or otherwise'.[2] In contrast, in Ontario, 'record' includes 'any information that is recorded or stored by means of any device';[3] while 'document' includes 'a sound recording, video tape, film, photograph, chart, graph, map, plan, survey, book of account and information recorded or stored by means of any device'.[4]

The federal legislation and rules, and those of most provinces, tend to follow the Ontario legislation and rules. An exception is Saskatchewan, where newly enacted evidence legislation defines 'document' narrowly as 'a record in any tangible form that is capable of being photographed'. 'Record' retains the expansive meaning of 'any information that is recorded or stored by means of any device or electronic means'.[5]

1   *Evidence Act*, R.S.B.C. 1996, c. 124, s 42.
2   *Interpretation Act*, R.S.B.C. 1996, c. 238, s 29.
3   *Evidence Act*, R.S.O. 1990, c. E.23, s 35(1).
4   *Rules of Civil Procedure*, R. 30.01(1).
5   *Evidence Act*, S.S. 2006, c. E-11.2.

Writing

5.5   The definition of 'writing' is consistent across all jurisdictions. A typical definition is that found in the federal *Interpretation Act*: '"writing", or any term of like import, includes words printed, typewritten, painted, engraved, lithographed, photographed or represented or reproduced by any mode of representing or reproducing words in visible form'.[1]

1   R.S.C. 1985, c. I-21, s 35(1).

Signature

5.6   'Signature' is not a statutorily defined term. Where a statute requires a signature, Canadian courts have followed the liberal common law approach and accepted any name, sign, or mark as a signature as long as it can be associated with the person whose signature it is alleged to be. A signature indicates, but does not prove, that the person signing has considered and approved the document. As discussed later in this chapter, contracts can be and are enforceable without the requirement of any sign or mark at all.

Domestic and International context for Canadian legislation

5.7   The Uniform Law Conference of Canada (ULCC) exists to harmonize the laws of the provinces of Canada, and, where appropriate, the federal laws. It also recommends changes to existing legislation, whether those arise from inconsistencies between jurisdictions, gaps in existing law, or problems created by judicial interpretation. The ULCC produced a model *Uniform Electronic Commerce Act*[1] (UECA) in August 1999. The UECA drew heavily on the principles of the 1996 UNCITRAL *Model Law on Electronic Commerce* (UNCITRAL MLEC), but differs significantly in definitions and provisions. Between 2000 and 2002, all ten provinces and the Yukon Territory enacted electronic commerce or electronic transactions statutes based on the UECA.[2]

In 2001, the federal, provincial, and territorial ministers responsible for consumer affairs approved a common 'Internet Sales Contract Harmonization Template' to harmonize consumer protection in electronic commerce across the country. The template covers disclosure, contract formation, cancellation rights and credit card charge-backs and has been adopted by amendment or regulation to existing consumer protection legislation in most provinces.[3] There is no law in Canada directly modelled on the 2001 UNCITRAL Model Law on Electronic Signatures (UNCITRAL MLES), though parallel provisions may be found in the above-noted electronic commerce statutes or consumer protection amendments.

The ULCC also produced a model *Uniform Electronic Evidence Act* (UEEA) in September 1998, from which most provinces derived amendments to their evidence statutes.[4] Since the UEEA relates to the law and rules of evidence rather than to a particular sphere of law or activity, it bears little resemblance to either of the UNCITRAL Model Laws. The focus is on admissibility and on the clarification, codification, or extension of the common law. Canada has not ratified the UN Convention on the Use of Electronic Communications in International Contracts.

1 Text available online at: www.ulcc.ca/en/us/index.cfm?sec=1&sub=1u1.
2 See the relevant appendix for a list of electronic commerce statutes.
3 For example, *Consumer Protection Act*, C.C.S.M., c. C2000, ss 127–135 and *Internet Agreements Regulation*, Man. Reg. 176/2000; *Alberta Fair Trading Act*, R.S.A. 2000, c. F-2 and *Internet Sales Contract Regulation*, Alta. Reg. 81/2001; *Ontario Consumer Protection Act, 2002*, S.O. 2000, c. 30, Sch. A, ss 37–40 and *General Regulation*, O. Reg. 17/05, ss 31–33.
4 Text and commentary available online at: www.ulcc.ca/en/us/index.cfm?sec=1&sub=1u2.

The Canadian legislation

5.8 Canadian legislation regarding electronic signatures is, generally speaking, enabling and minimalist. Rather than requiring either evidence of the reliability of individual signatures or electronic signature certification, the legislation presumes reliability when the system that produces or stores the signature is reliable. The legislation is technology-neutral, in that it does not specify any technological requirements, or any standard of reliability that must be achieved, for legal recognition of electronic signatures. Such technological requirements or standards are set out in regulations enacted pursuant to an enabling statute. The difference in level of legislation is significant, because, as subordinate legislation, regulations are not drafted and enacted by elected provincial legislatures or the federal Parliament, but are made by delegated administrative entities.[1] This means that regulations can be made and amended quickly in response to technological change. It also means, however, that regulations may not be exposed to the broad and thoughtful scrutiny that non-subordinate legislation, theoretically, undergoes before enactment.

The enabling approach is consistent with the liberal accommodation of technological change in Canadian case law long before the enactment of electronic evidence and electronic commerce statutes. Canadian courts have been quick to recognize the electronic functional equivalents of traditional paper systems, media and methods, and have barely hesitated in granting legal efficacy to those electronic equivalents where there is a legal requirement for writing, a signature or original documents. Electronic evidence and electronic commerce statutes codify, rather than depart from, a common-sense and judicial recognition that in some cases, the technological methods are inherently more, not less, reliable than traditional pen and paper methods.

The Canadian legislation is starkly minimalist in comparison to the UNCITRAL Model Laws. There is no requirement for technical authentication of signatures; no requirement that the signature identify the sender, be under the sole control of the sender, or associate the sender with the record; nor is there any requirement to provide assurance of record integrity. Any such requirements are left to regulation by the appropriate delegated authority. At the time of writing, such regulation has been slight,[2] with the exception of federal legislation regarding secure electronic signatures, discussed below.

1 Legislation by regulation is common in Canada. The power to make regulations must be expressly set out in the governing or enabling statute. The enabling provision must explicitly state what sections or topics within the statute are subject to regulation. The power to make regulations must be delegated either to the Lieutenant-Governor in Council, acting on advice of the Cabinet or Executive Council, or to the Minister responsible for the statute.

2 Most of the current regulations simply list those statutes or government departments subject to or exempt from the legislation pursuant to the requirement in UECA s 6(2) that governments must expressly consent to the use of information in electronic form.

Uniform Electronic Evidence Act

5.9 While the focus of this chapter falls upon how electronic signatures operate to create enforceable electronic contracts, some preliminary observations about electronic documents and evidence are in order. Any disputes arising under electronic transactions statutes will likely be informed by the definitions and concepts in the UEEA. It is likely that the general presumption of confidence in electronic records expressed in the UEEA will inform the interpretation of specific provisions in the UECA.

There is no definition of 'electronic document' in the UEEA. As noted above, the definition of 'document' and 'record' varies among Canadian jurisdictions and in the absence of a statutory definition, the common law applies. The UEEA defines 'electronic record' as 'data that is recorded or stored on any medium in or by a computer system or other similar device, that can be read or perceived by a person or a computer system or other similar device. It includes a display, printout or other output of that data'. In contrast to the UNCITRAL definition of 'data message', the electronic record contemplated by the UEEA does not include telexes or facsimile transmissions, unless those are computer-generated.

The UEEA manifests a general confidence in the use of electronic records in legal proceedings. It reflects the law's continuing retreat from historical insistence upon 'best evidence' by dispensing with the need for an original. The UEEA substitutes evidence of the reliability of the system that produces the record for evidence of the reliability of the individual record:

'4(1) In any legal proceeding . . . where the best evidence rule is applicable in respect of an electronic record, it is satisfied on proof of integrity of the electronic records system in or by which the data was recorded or stored.'

Electronic records further benefit from a set of rebuttable presumptions that, again, substitute evidence of the integrity and reliability of the computer system that produced the record, and the record-keeping system within which it operates, for evidence of the reliability of individual records:

'5   In the absence of evidence to the contrary, the integrity of the electronic records system in which an electronic record is recorded or stored is presumed in any legal proceeding:

(a)   by evidence that supports a finding that at all material times the computer system or other similar device was operating properly or, if it was not, the fact of its not operating properly did not affect the integrity of the electronic record, and there are no other reasonable grounds to doubt the integrity of the electronic records system;

(b)   if it is established that the electronic record was recorded or stored by a party to the proceedings who is adverse in interest to the party seeking to introduce it; or

(c)   if it is established that the electronic record was recorded or stored in the usual and ordinary course of business by a person who is not a party to the proceedings and who did not record or store it under the control of the party seeking to introduce the record.'

The UEEA thus incorporates a fairly simple test of reliability and integrity, and seeks to ensure that the introduction of electronic records in evidence is not made expensive, difficult or open to frivolous attacks.

Uniform Electronic Commerce Act

5.10   The UECA defines 'electronic signature' as 'information in electronic form that a person has created or adopted in order to sign a document and that is in, attached to or associated with the document.' Some provinces have replaced 'document' with 'record'.[1] This definition differs significantly from that in the UNCITRAL MLES: 'data in electronic form in, affixed to or logically associated with, a data message, which may be used to identify the signatory in relation to the data message and to indicate the signatory's approval of the information contained in the data message.' The Canadian definition neither implies nor requires identification of the signatory through a signature; nor does it imply or require the element of approval of information contained in the record to which the signature is attached.

The UECA consists of three parts. Part 1, 'Provision and Retention of Information', sets out the basic rules of functional equivalency for the traditional legal requirements of writing, signatures and the provision and retention of originals. Part 1 also sets out the presumptions that apply when people have expressly or by implication agreed to use electronic documents. Section 2(3) expressly excludes certain instruments (wills, trusts, powers of attorney, and documents creating or transferring interests in land) from the application of the statute. Section 6(1) confirms that the application of the statute is permissive rather than mandatory; a person is not required to 'use or accept information in electronic form', although 'consent to do so may be inferred from the person's conduct'. On the other hand, consent by a government to use or accept information in electronic form must be express (s 6(2)).

The UECA provisions regarding satisfaction of requirements for writing and requirements for signature parallel those of both UNCITRAL MLEC and UNCITRAL MLES as follows:

'5.   Information shall not be denied legal effect or enforceability solely by reason that it is in electronic form.

. . .

7.   A requirement [. . .] that information be in writing is satisfied by information in electronic form if the information is accessible so as to be usable for subsequent reference.

. . .

10.   (1) A requirement [. . .] for the signature of a person is satisfied by an electronic signature.

(2) For the purposes of subsection (1), the [authority responsible for the requirement] may make a regulation that:

(a)   the electronic signature shall be reliable for the purpose of identifying the person, in the light of all the circumstances, including any relevant agreement and the time the electronic signature was made; and

(b) the association of the electronic signature with the relevant electronic document shall be reliable for the purpose for which the electronic document was made, in the light of all the circumstances, including any relevant agreement and the time the electronic signature was made.'

These provisions parallel UNCITRAL MLEC articles 5, 6(1), and 7(1) and UNCITRAL MLES article 6(1).

The UECA departs from the pre-conditions for reliability set out in UNCITRAL MLEC article 7, which states that a signature requirement is met in relation to a data message if a method is used to identify the person signing and to indicate the person's approval of the message, and if the method is as reliable as appropriate for the purpose and circumstances. The UECA delegates the responsibility for imposing conditions on the recognition of electronic signatures to the authority responsible for the requirement. A regulation under the provincial equivalent of the UECA might impose requirements similar to those in the UNCITRAL MLEC. At the time of writing, no provinces have enacted such regulations under their electronic commerce or electronic transactions statutes, although some provincial statutes have been amended to set out requirements for secure electronic signatures.[2]

The ULCC commented that s 10 originates in UNCITRAL MLEC article 7, but that the working group took the view that the legal effect of the signature should be left to the general law. Since the element of approval was not essential to the function of a signature at common law, there was no need to import it into the electronic signature definition. The working group did believe that the element of identification and association in some way was essential, but it believed that this element was sufficiently implied by the definition of electronic signature. Though there is no case law addressing this point, it is possible that Canadian courts will decline to interpret the definition as imposing a requirement for identification and association.

The UECA does not contain any deeming provisions for conditions under which an electronic signature will be deemed to be reliable, unlike those in article 6(3) of the UNCITRAL MLES. This is in part because, as mentioned above, the definition of electronic signature neither implies nor requires an element of approval on the part of the signatory. More significantly, the set of conditions creating deemed reliability in the UNCITRAL MLES require that any alteration to the signature, or to the information for which the signature provides assurance or approval, can be detected after signing. There are no such provisions in the UECA. This more relaxed approach is in keeping with the presumptions of integrity and regularity set out in the UEEA and also with the common law proclivity for statutory minimalism enhanced by judicial interpretation.

The Canadian legislation and the common law of contract and evidence assume that it is always open to a party to adduce evidence establishing the reliability or non-reliability of a document or signature, whether electronic or conventional. That reliability will always be established with regard to both the purpose for which the document or signature is being proffered, and the circumstances at the time the document or signature was created. Arguably, paper-based documentary evidence suffers from as many issues of authentication as electronic evidence.

The only provisions regarding detection of alterations in the UECA are those relating to the legal requirement for original document form. These provisions closely parallel those in UNCITRAL MLEC article 8:

'11. (1) A requirement under . . . law that requires a person to present or retain a document in original form is satisfied by the provision or retention of an electronic document if:

(a) there exists a reliable assurance as to the integrity of the information contained in the electronic document from the time the document to be presented or retained was first made in its final form, whether as a paper document or as an electronic document;

(b) where the document in original form is to be provided to a person, the electronic document that is provided to the person is accessible by the person and capable of being retained by the person so as to be usable for subsequent reference; and

(c) where the document in original form is to be provided to the Government,

(i) the Government or the part of Government to which the information is to be provided has consented to accept electronic documents in satisfaction of the requirement; and

(ii) the electronic document meets the information technology standards and acknowledgement rules, if any, established by the Government or part of Government, as the case may be.

(2) For the purpose of paragraph (1)(a),

(a) the criterion for assessing integrity is whether the information has remained complete and unaltered, apart from the introduction of any changes that arise in the normal course of communication, storage and display;

(b) the standard of reliability required shall be assessed in the light of the purpose for which the document was made and in the light of all the circumstances.'

The UECA, unlike the UNCITRAL MLEC article 13, does not contain provisions regarding when electronic communications will be attributed to a party and when the usual rules of attribution will not apply.

Part 2 of the UECA, 'Communication of Electronic Documents', sets out rules for the formation and operation of contracts; the effect of using electronic agents for automated transactions; and the deemed time and place for sending and receiving electronic documents.

Because the statutory definition of electronic signature neither implies nor requires an element of approval, no legal rights or obligations flow from the mere presence or absence of an electronic signature. Like UNCITRAL MLEC article 11, the UECA is permissive about electronic contracting. Unlike UNCITRAL MLEC, UECA transposes the traditional common law principles of offer and acceptance to the realm of electronic commerce:

> '20. (1) Unless the parties agree otherwise, an offer or the acceptance of an offer, or any other matter that is material to the formation or operation of a contract, may be expressed:
>
> (a)   by means of an electronic document; or
> (b)   by an action in electronic form, including touching or clicking on an appropriately designated icon or place on a computer screen or otherwise communicating electronically in a manner that is intended to express the offer, acceptance or other matter.
>
> (2) A contract shall not be denied legal effect or enforceability solely by reason that an electronic document was used in its formation.'

At common law, many types of contracts can be entered into orally or by conduct, with no requirement of writing or signature. Whether an electronic signature meets legal requirements for enforceability of an agreement depends entirely on context and not on the form or even presence of a signature. An electronic transaction may be enforceable without the requirement for a signature at all, let alone any particular form of secure or digital electronic signature. Contracts that are not in writing, especially those entered into by conduct, are much harder to enforce. Section 20(1)(b) thus provides much-needed certainty in the area of electronic commerce.

The statutes in the common law provinces all contain a substantially similar provision to s 20 of the UECA.[3] The legislative emphasis is not on the form of the transaction, but how it functions as evidence of the intentions of the parties. Under such provisions, an electronic contract that is an exact reproduction of a printed contract, including the signatures of the contracting parties, is neither more nor less enforceable than a contract created by clicking the 'I Agree' or 'I Accept' button displayed on a computer screen. Significantly though, these latter forms of contract require 'an action'. The wording of the provision suggests that passive 'shrink-wrap' contracts would be unenforceable. Case law decided prior to the enactment of electronic transactions statutes supports this interpretation.[4]

Nonetheless, a party could later resist enforcement of an agreement by establishing that he or she did not sign or send the document; that the document received was not the same as the message sent; or that the document was sent in error. This is particularly so in jurisdictions where amendments have been made to consumer protection legislation regarding electronic transactions. Such amendments typically require suppliers to provide a copy of an internet sales contract 'in writing or electronic form' after the contract is entered into. The requirements of provision can be met by traditional writing, email, facsimile, or any other method than enables the supplier to prove that the consumer has received it. The amendments also enhance consumer protection with pre-purchase disclosure requirements, cancellation rights, and credit card protection rights.[5] As noted above, s 2(3) expressly excludes certain instruments (wills, trusts, powers of attorney, and documents creating or transferring interests in land) from the application of the statute, and any electronic transaction relating to such contracts would likely be held to be non-enforceable.

Part 3 of the UECA deals with contracts for the carriage of goods. Section 25(2) imposes a requirement for reliability on electronic documents that grant rights to or impose obligations on one person to the exclusion of others. The section does not set out any technological requirements or standards, and s 25(3) provides, as elsewhere in the act, for a purposive and contextual rather than prescriptive assessment of reliability.

The Québec statute differs significantly from the statutes in the common law provinces.[6] Although Québec participated in the ULCC conferences leading up to the drafting of the Uniform Acts, the legislature enacted a comprehensive statute to deal globally with the creation, transmission, and storage of electronic information for the whole information technology sector. The statute combines the objects of both the UECA and the UEEA and addresses issues such as privacy[7] that were not addressed in either Uniform Act. Much of the detail left to regulation in the Uniform Acts is expressly set out in the Québec statute; for example, the statute provides a legal framework for the accreditation and registration of certification authorities, and for the liability of those authorities, network service providers, and intermediaries. The Québec statute makes no express provision for electronic contracting, but commentators suggest that the general provision for legal equivalence will suffice:

'5. The legal value of a document, particularly its capacity to produce legal effects and its admissibility as evidence, is neither increased nor diminished solely because of the medium or technology chosen.

Legal value.

A document whose integrity is ensured has the same legal value whether it is a paper document or a document in any other medium, insofar as, in the case of a technology-based document, it otherwise complies with the legal rules applicable to paper documents.

Admissibility.

A document in a medium or based on technology that does not allow its integrity to be confirmed or denied may, depending on the circumstances, be admissible as testimonial evidence or real evidence and serve as commencement of proof, as provided for in article 2865 of the Civil Code.

Requirement.

Where the law requires the use of a document, the requirement may be met by a technology-based document whose integrity is ensured.'

1   For example, British Columbia *Electronic Transactions Act*, S.B.C. 2001, c. 10, s 1.
2   For example, the *Electronic Court Documents Regulation*, B.C. Reg. 60/2005, enacted under the *Evidence Act*, R.S.B.C. 1996, c. 124, ss 41.2(2) and 41.3(3), sets out a list of 'electronic court systems' and a list of persons who may electronically sign a record produced by any of these systems. The regulation does not define or set out technological requirements for secure electronic signatures, although the enabling statute contemplates such regulations.
3   The exceptionally lean New Brunswick *Electronic Transactions Act*, S.N.B. 2001, c. E-5.5 contains no provisions regarding formation and operation of contracts, although it does provide for the formation of contracts by electronic agents. Nor does it contain any carriage of goods provisions. It appears that the drafters chose not to include provisions that they believed would merely codify well-established common law.
4   See cases discussed below under 'Enforceability of Contracts.'
5   For example, *Consumer Protection Act*, C.C.S.M., c. C2000, ss 127–135 and *Internet Agreements Regulation*, Man. Reg. 176/2000; *Alberta Fair Trading Act*, R.S.A. 2000, c. F-2 and *Internet Sales Contract Regulation*, Alta. Reg. 81/2001; *Ontario Consumer Protection Act*, 2002, S.O. 2000, c. 30, Sch A, ss 37–40 and *General Regulation*, O. Reg. 17/05, ss 31–33. There is some uncertainty about the extra-territorial scope of consumer protection statutes although most state expressly that they apply to any consumer transaction within the province: Roger Tassé, *On-Line Consumer Protection: A Study on Regulatory Jurisdiction in Canada* (Ottawa: Industry Canada, 2001). These provisions have yet to be judicially interpreted in light of older case law confirming choice of law and jurisdiction clauses and exclusive arbitration clauses in electronic contracts; see also cases discussed below under 'Enforceability of Contracts.'
6   *An Act to establish a legal framework for information technology*, R.S.Q. c. C-1.1.
7   For example, s 44 prohibits the use of a person's biometric data to verify or confirm identity without that person's express consent. Other provinces have excluded biometric data from the application of the relevant electronic transactions statute, and may also enhance privacy protection through the relevant privacy statute: Alberta, *Electronic Transactions Act*, S.A. 2001, c. E-5.5 , s 5(2) and *Freedom of Information and Protection of Privacy Act*, R.S.A. 2000, c. F-25; Ontario, *Electronic Commerce Act, 2000*, S.O. 2000, c. 17, s 29.

Secure electronic signatures

5.11   It has been noted that both Uniform Acts take a minimalist and enabling approach to electronic signatures, documents, and commerce. Neither act defines, requires, or provides for digital or secure electronic signatures although, as noted, the appropriate delegated authority may make regulations where permitted by statute. Some jurisdictions have therefore amended particular statutes to expressly state requirements or presumptions of reliability of electronic signatures. Such amendments are far less prescriptive than those in either the UNCITRAL MLEC or UNCITRAL MLES. This vagueness reflects the common law preference for judicial interpretation rather than legislative prescription, and in the context of electronic commerce, allows much-needed flexibility and responsiveness to technological change.

'Secure electronic signature' is the preferred statutory term for what the UNCITRAL MLES calls 'digital signature'. When reading Canadian cases or commentary, it is important to keep in mind that 'digital signature' is not a statutorily-defined term. It sometimes means, generically, any electronic signature and sometimes any electronic signature with technological attributes that ensure identification of the signer, association with an electronic record and integrity of the record. Occasionally, 'digital signature' means only a secure electronic signature based on encryption-based authentication systems, such as public key cryptography. It is important to assess the meaning of 'digital signature' in context. For example, s 41.3 of the British Columbia *Evidence Act*, R.S.B.C. 1996, c. 124, defines 'secure electronic signature' and creates a presumption of identification of the signatory when certain requirements are met:

'41.3   (1) In this section, 'secure electronic signature' means an electronic signature that is applied to a prescribed electronic record:

(a)   by a prescribed person, and

(b)   in accordance with any prescribed terms, conditions or restrictions.

(2)   If an electronic court document is accompanied by a secure electronic signature, the electronic court document is presumed, in the absence of evidence to the contrary, to have been signed by the person who is identified in, or can be identified through, the secure electronic signature.

(3)   For the purposes of this section, the Lieutenant Governor in Council may make regulations:

(a)   prescribing classes of persons who may apply electronic signatures to electronic records,

(b)   prescribing the classes of electronic records to which electronic signatures may be applied,

(c)   respecting terms, conditions or restrictions relating to the application of electronic signatures to electronic records, and

(d)   conferring a discretion in respect to the matters set out in paragraphs (a) to (c).'

This provision provides only for authentication (the reliable association of an electronic signature with the person who is identified by it). Further, what makes the electronic signature 'secure', and what other presumptions, if any, may flow from such a signature, remain to be prescribed by regulation.[1] The provisions thus fall far short of the pre-conditions for deemed reliability found in UNCITRAL MLES article 6(3).

The *Canada Evidence Act*[2] goes one step further by providing for integrity as well as authenticity:

'31.4 The Governor in Council may make regulations establishing evidentiary presumptions in relation to electronic documents signed with secure electronic signatures, including regulations respecting:

(a) the association of secure electronic signatures with persons; and

(b) the integrity of information contained in electronic documents signed with secure electronic signatures.'

The most significant legislation regarding secure electronic signatures is the federal *Personal Information Protection and Electronic Documents Act* (PIPEDA).[3] PIPEDA contains two quite distinct parts: Part 1 deals with protection of personal information collected by businesses in the course of commerce. Part 2, which came into force on 1 May 2000, provides for electronic communications and transactions with federal government bodies. The remaining parts deal with consequential amendments to other federal statutes such as the *Canada Evidence Act*.

The purpose of Part 2 is 'to provide for the use of electronic alternatives . . . where federal laws contemplate the use of paper to record or communicate information or transactions'.[4] PIPEDA defines an electronic document as 'data that is recorded or stored on any medium in or by a computer system or other similar device and that can be read or perceived by a person or a computer system or other similar device [including] a display, printout or other output of that data'. This is the UEEA definition. An electronic signature is 'a signature that consists of one or more letters, characters, numbers or other symbols in digital form incorporated in, attached to or associated with an electronic document.' This definition is considerably more precise than 'information in electronic form' as set out in the UECA definition. Finally, 'secure electronic signature' means an electronic signature that results from the application of a technology or process prescribed by regulations'. Section 48(2) of PIPEDA requires that any such process can only be prescribed if it can be proved that:

'(a) the electronic signature resulting from the use by a person of the technology or process is unique to the person;

(b) the use of the technology or process by a person to incorporate, attach or associate the person's electronic signature to an electronic document is under the sole control of the person;

(c) the technology or process can be used to identify the person using the technology or process; and

(d) the electronic signature can be linked with an electronic document in such a way that it can be used to determine whether the electronic document has been changed since the electronic signature was incorporated in, attached to or associated with the electronic document.'

These reliability attributes parallel the reliability requirements of unique association, authenticity, verification, and document integrity set out in UNCITRAL MLEC and UNCITRAL MLES.

Section 43 of PIPEDA permits the use of an electronic signature where a signature is required, if the federal statute is listed in a schedule to the act and if the regulations have been complied with. Somewhat surprisingly, the *Secure Electronic Signature Regulations* (the Regulations), enacted in 2005, depart radically from the permissive tenor of all other Canadian legislation by prescribing a detailed technological standard for secure electronic signatures.[5] The regulatory impact statement published in conjunction with the Regulations asserts that only a secure electronic signature based on asymmetric (public key) cryptography and certified by a public certification authority can 'provide the requisite characteristics of a secure electronic signature'.[6] Since Canada has no recognized standards for accrediting certification authorities, such authorities will have to be accredited and listed from time to time on a government website and in other publicly accessible sources such as the *Canada Gazette*.

Once the technological requirements prescribed by the Regulations have been met, there is a statutory presumption of authenticity, ie that the data has been signed by the person who is identified in or through the digital signature certificate.[7] However, the statute does not create a presumption of reliability and integrity of the data or document itself. In this way, PIPEDA differs from UNCITRAL MLES article 6.

At the time of writing, the only federal statute prescribed in the schedule to PIPEDA is the *Federal Real Property and Federal Immovables Act*.[8] However, some federal statutes in addition to the *Canada Evidence Act* (discussed above) have directly incorporated the PIPEDA definitions by amendment to the statute, rather than having the statute designated under the PIPEDA schedule. This allows for a more tailored application of the secure electronic signature provisions. For example, amendments to the *Canada Business Corporations Act* (CBCA) have adopted the definitions of electronic document and secure electronic signature from PIPEDA.[9] Under the amendments, a person may provide a statutory declaration or affidavit in electronic form if both the person providing it and the person before whom it is made sign the document with a secure electronic signature. The CBCA may also adopt the Regulations themselves, or the requirements embodied in the Regulations, to ensure signature authenticity, verification, and document integrity.[10]

---

1   At the time of writing, the only regulation enacted pursuant to this section is the *Electronic Court Documents Regulation*, B.C. Reg. 60/2005. The regulation sets out a list of 'electronic

court systems' and a list of persons who may electronically sign a record produced by any of these systems, but does not define or set out technological requirements for secure electronic signatures.

2   R.S.C. 1985, c. C-5.

3   S.C. 2000, c. 5.

4   PIPEDA, s 31.

5   S.O.R./2005-30.

6   Available online at: www.canadagazette.gc.ca/partII/2005/20050223/html/sor30-e.html.

7   *Secure Electronic Signature Regulations*, s 5.

8   S.C. 1991, c. 50. This statute applies to the acquisition, administration and disposition of real property and immovables by the federal government.

9   R.S.C. 1985, c. C-44, ss 252.6–252.7.

10 Provincial legislators may also enact provisions similar or identical to the PIPEDA require-ments without expressly incorporating them by reference. For example, see British Columbia *Land Title Act*, R.S.B.C. 1996, c. 250, ss 168.1–168.91.

Canadian case law

5.12 Perhaps not surprisingly, the volume of Canadian case law in this evolving area is relatively slight. However, what has been decided to date does illuminate the Canadian position. It generally reveals a modern and pragmatic approach to electronic commerce generally and the electronic signature requirements that are incidental to it.

Enforceability of contracts

5.13 The leading case on the enforceability of 'click-wrap' contracts is *Rudder v Microsoft Corp.*[1] The case was decided well before Ontario's *Electronic Transactions Act, 2000* came into force, but its reasoning is consistent with the electronic contracting provisions in the UECA and related provincial statutes. The defendant Microsoft sought a stay of proceedings against a proposed class action on behalf of about 89,000 MSN subscribers on the basis that subscribers had agreed, by clicking on an 'I Agree' icon, to submit to the exclusive jurisdiction and venue clause in an online agreement. The plaintiffs argued that such terms were obscured and analogous to fine print in a paper contract. There was no electronic commerce legislation in force at the time, and the judge did not consider whether clicking on the icon constituted a signature. He noted, however, that potential subscribers were presented with the membership terms twice during the sign-up process and thus were offered two opportunities to disagree and terminate the process. The second time the terms were displayed, the potential member was given clear notice: 'If you click 'I Agree' without reading the membership agreement, you are still agreeing to be bound by all of the terms of the membership.' The judge concluded that to give effect to the plaintiffs' arguments would 'move this type of electronic transaction into the realm of commercial absurdity' and, as well, 'lead to chaos in the marketplace, render ineffectual electronic commerce and undermine the integrity of any agreement entered into through this medium' (at para 16).

The reasoning in *Rudder* was applied in *Kanitz v Rogers Cable Inc.*[2] where the court upheld an arbitration clause added to a user agreement by posting a notice of the change on the Rogers website. The court upheld the clause, observing that people seeking to avail themselves of electronic services should reasonably expect that their legal relationship with the party that is providing electronic services will be defined and communicated to them through the electronic service itself. Although this case is often cited for the proposition that 'web wrap' contracts are enforceable, it is factually akin to *Rudder*. The customers had initially entered into a written user agreement that included an amendment provision. The original agreement expressly allowed Rogers to change, modify, add or remove portions of the agreement and to give notice by posting notice on its website, or sending notice by email or postal mail.

The status of a true 'shrink wrap', 'web wrap' or 'browse wrap' contract in the post-UECA period is not clear in Canada. For example, a 'shrink wrap' licence was held not to be enforceable in *North American SystemShops Ltd. v King*,[3] decided years prior to legislation and prior to widespread use of the internet. The case was expressly decided on copyright and licence principles rather than contract principles. In the absence of satisfactory evidence, the court concluded that the copyright symbol and licence were not visible to the defendant prior to removing the shrink wrap. *North American SystemShops* was distinguished in the more recent case of *Paterson Ross and Santan Management Ltd. v Alumni Computer Group Ltd.*[4] where the court noted that the packaging clearly displayed a warning that opening it had legal implications. Further, the plaintiff filled out and returned a written warranty card after opening the package. While the plaintiff argued that he was not familiar with electronic transactions, the judge in *Paterson Ross* considered the need to ensure commercial efficacy even in novel environments. The judge observed that the plaintiff ordered the product over the telephone, received and opened the software package, and then returned a written warranty card. The entire transaction occurred through several different media, and the court considered that it would be 'incongruous' for the plaintiff to expect to take the benefit of that part of the agreement recorded on paper (the warranty) while not being bound by other terms.

The court in *Canadian Real Estate Association v Sutton (Québec) Real Estate Services Inc.*[5] granted an interlocutory injunction preventing the respondent from downloading real estate listings from the applicant's website for reposting on its own website. The terms of use on the applicant's website did not require users to take any affirmative action to express agreement with those terms of use before entering the site. Without expressly deciding whether the respondent was bound by the terms of use, the court noted that the respondent was aware of the terms of use and indeed had similar terms of use posted on its own website. As in *Paterson Ross*, the court noted the defendant's familiarity with the environment in which the transaction took place.

However, notice remains a primary factual consideration. The court in *Aspencer1.com Inc. v Paysystems Corporation*[6] declined to enforce an exclusive arbitration clause added by the defendant company by posting a notice on its website. The court found that the notice method used by the defendant provided no proof that the plaintiff had consented to the new terms.

Class proceedings or consumer protection statutes may override valid arbitration clauses in electronic contracts.[7] All provinces in Canada have robust class proceedings statutes and the Federal Court Rules allow for such actions in the federal court system. In certifying a class action, the court is to consider, amongst other factors, whether a class proceeding is preferable to other available forms of proceeding. Certification of a class action effectively renders a valid arbitration clause inoperative.[8]

Similarly, in *Dell Computer Corporation v Union des consommateurs*,[9] an arbitration clause was not enforced because it referred consumers to an external website which was viewed by a hyperlink from Dell's website. Québec's Civil Code article 1435 has a consumer protection provision that provides 'In a consumer contract . . . an external clause is null if, at the time of formation of the contract, it was not expressly brought to the attention of the consumer . . . unless the other party proves that the consumer . . . otherwise knew of it.' Setting aside the arbitration clause, the court certified a class proceeding. Although the case will be decided under Québec's Civil Code, the decision of the Supreme Court of Canada may clarify the status of arbitration clauses in electronic contracts across the country.

1   (1999), 2 C.P.R. (4th) 474, 47 C.C.L.T. (2d) 168 (Ont. Sup. Ct.).
2   (2002), 58 O.R. (3d) 299 (Sup. Ct.).
3   (1989), 68 Alta. L.R. (2d) 145 (Q.B.).
4   [2000] M.J. No. 630 (Q.B.) (QL).
5   [2003] J.Q. No. 3606 (Qué. Sup. Ct.) (QL).
6   [2005] J.Q. No. 1573 (Qué. Sup. Ct.) (QL).
7   For an in-depth analysis of this subject, see David T. Neave and Jennifer M. Spencer, 'Class Proceedings, a New Way to Trump Mandatory Arbitration Clauses?' (2005) 63 Advocate 495.
8   For example, see *MacKinnon v National Money Mart Co.*, 2004 BCCA 473; *Frey v BCE Inc.*, 2006 SKQB 331.
9   2005 QCCA 570, leave to appeal to SCC granted, [2005] S.C.C.A. No. 370 (appeal heard and reserved 13 December 2006).

Electronic signatures as evidence

5.14   There is little case law in Canada directly addressing the validity of electronic signatures. In *City Park Co-operative Apartments Inc. v David Dubois*,[1] the court accepted that the 'electronic signature' of an apartment entry-exit key contradicted the defendant's affidavit evidence. The entry-exit key provided access to the building and each entry or exit was recorded by the building's security computer and attached uniquely to the key. The use of the term 'electronic signature' is perhaps questionable, but the judge's meaning is clear: this is an example of digital evidence demonstrating that the holder of a token used the token, thus going to show that the evidence of the holder of the token was incompatible with the digital evidence. In *R v Blumes*,[2] the accused challenged a parking ticket by seeking a declaration that the vehicle registration and licensing document showing him to be the vehicle's owner was inadmissible. The document contained a paragraph stating that it was certified by an officer of the Insurance Corporation of British Columbia, but it was not possible to determine whether the signature below that certification was an original signature, rubber stamp, or facsimile signature. The judge noted that the British Columbia *Electronic Transactions Act*[3] defines and provides for electronic signatures, but preferred to decide the matter under provisions of the British Columbia *Motor Vehicle Act* that deem this method of certification valid.[4]

In a trademark infringement action, the plaintiffs sought an order that the defendants were in contempt of a court order enjoining them from using the impugned trade names.[5] Evidence of the contempt included emails sent to potential customers over specific signature blocks, some of which infringed the plaintiff's trade name and some of which did not. In finding for the plaintiffs, the court rejected the personal defendant's claim that he was ignorant about email addresses and signatures, and unaware that his email would go out with the forbidden trade names as part of the signature block.

As noted above, the *Canada Business Corporations Act* has been amended to permit some transactions to occur in electronic form. In *Re Newbridge Networks Corp.*,[6] the applicant corporation applied for an order approving an electronic voting procedure for approximately 4,300 option-holders throughout Canada and the world. The decision was issued before Ontario's *Electronic Commerce Act* came into force, but the court considered actual and proposed amendments to the relevant federal and provincial statutes. The court found those amendments overly restrictive and too focused on the present state of technology. Instead, the court looked behind the mechanics of the procedure to the underlying requirements of reliability, safeguarding and notice, and observed that statutory provisions should retain the flexibility to accommodate future technological change. In the particular circumstances, the electronic notice and voting procedures were the functional equivalent of receiving notice and being able to vote by mail. The court observed that 'on balance the electronic procedure envisaged is a safer and more reliable system than is that which relies on the mails or other delivery systems'[7] with built-in password integrity and instantaneous delivery. The court equated the use of a password signifying the user's choice with the traditional form of signing a paper proxy vote.

Even in the absence of statutory definitions of 'electronic signature' that imply or require approval, the court will apply common law principles in determining the admissibility, or in assessing the reliability, of documents to which electronic signatures are attached. In *Macdonald v Sun Life Assurance Co. of Canada*,[8] a medical expert retained by the defence was not permitted to testify after he stated that his signature stamp had been affixed to a medical report without his authority. The question of his signature arose when it became clear that the report he referred to during his testimony differed substantially from the one served on the plaintiff and filed with the court. The court did not consider any relevant legislation, but determined the issue on the basis of existing principles.

1   [2006] O.J. No. 4428 (Sup. Ct.) (QL).
2   2002 BCPC 45 (B.C. Prov Ct., Traffic Div.); see also *R v Pearce*, 2000 BCSC 0376; *R v Parkinson*, [2002] O.J. No. 5478 (Ct. J.) (QL).
3   S.B.C. c. 10, ss 1 and 11.
4   R.S.B.C. 1996, c. 318, s 82(7).
5   *Dursol-Fabrik Otto Durst GmbH Co. KG v Dursol North America Inc.*, 2006 FCC 1115.
6   (2000), 48 O.R. (3d) 47, [2000] O.J. No. 1346 (QL) (Sup. Ct.) (QL).
7   (2000), 48 O.R. (3d) 47, [2000] O.J. No. 1346 (QL) (Sup. Ct.) (QL) at para 6.
8   [2006] O.J. No. 4428 (Sup. Ct.) (QL).

Conclusion

5.15   The adoption of electronic evidence and commerce laws in Canada is relatively recent, but has kept pace with legislative change in other parts of the world. The Canadian legislation responds to present-day technological and business realities while retaining sufficient flexibility to deal with further technological change. By delegating much of the detail to regulation, legislatures have signalled an expectation that the legislation itself is a framework for interpretation, rather than a detailed prescriptive code. Though not faced with many opportunities to interpret the law on electronic signatures and documents, Canadian courts have tended towards a liberal interpretation that flows from and remains consistent with the common law of contract and evidence.

Chapter 6

England and Wales, Northern Ireland and Scotland

The Electronic Communications Act 2000

6.1 The first draft of a bill, the Electronic Communications Bill, was published in July 1999. This Bill was withdrawn when it attracted a great deal of wrath regarding key escrow (which is now expressly excluded in the Act by s 14) and provisions that were later incorporated into the Regulation of Investigatory Powers Act 2000. The Electronic Communications Act received the Royal Assent on 25 May 2000, and extends to Northern Ireland.[1] The Act is in three parts:

(a) Part I: Cryptography service providers. This part of the Act provides for the establishment of a statutory register of approved providers of cryptography support services. It has not been implemented, and a voluntary scheme is in place.[2] Further, by the terms of s 16(4), Part I was repealed on 25 May 2005 because no order was made under s 16(2) by the end of the period of five years beginning with the day on which the Act was passed.

(b) Part II: Facilitation of electronic commerce, data storage, etc. This part is concerned with the legal recognition and admissibility of electronic signatures; permits the removal of statutory restrictions, which impose a requirement that a transaction must be in writing, and facilitates the use of electronic means to store information in an electronic format.

(c) Part III: Miscellaneous and supplemental. This part makes a number of amendments to the Telecommunications Act 1984 regarding the modification of telecommunications licences, and also covers the usual matters including interpretation; the short title, commencement and the territorial extent of the Act.

Sections 7, 11 and 12 came into force on 25 July 2000 in accordance with the provisions of the Electronic Communications Act 2000 (Commencement No 1) Order 2000 (SI 2000 No 1798); section 4(2) was amended by section

82, Schedule 4(10) of the Regulation of Investigatory Powers Act 2000, and section 15(1) was amended by section 406(1), Schedule 17(158) of the Communications Act 2003, and sections 11 and 12 were repealed by section 406(7), Schedule 19(1) of the Communications Act 2003.

Unless there is a specific statutory requirement for a document to be signed, English law does not require any document to be signed to be both valid and effective. Thus in many instances, it was possible to sign a document with an electronic signature before the passing of the Act. The signature at the end of an email, as in the case of *Hall v Cognos Limited*[3] was sufficient, providing the person signing the document intended to sign it and intended their signature to affect the authenticity of the document. If the identity of the person signing the document is in doubt, further evidence can be adduced to identify the person who affixed their signature to the document.[4]

1   Section 16(5).
2   Scheme, available online at www.tscheme.org.
3   Industrial Tribunal Case No 1803325/97.
4   Graham J H Smith *Internet Law and Regulation* para 10-076; Lorna Brazell, *Electronic Signatures Law and Regulations* (Sweet & Maxwell, 2004), 6-062 to 6-063.

The international context

6.2   The Explanatory Notes to the Act were prepared by the Department of Trade and Industry. The commentary, at paragraph 19, suggested the Bill was consistent with the EU Electronic Signatures Directive, although it only implemented some of the provisions of the Directive. It was also suggested that the Bill was compatible with the Cryptography Guidelines published by the Organization for Economic Co-operation and Development (OECD) on 19 March 1997; the United Nations Commission on International Trade Law Model Law of Electronic Commerce (UNCITRAL), and the draft Uniform Rules on Electronic Signatures and Certification Authorities.

The definition of an electronic signature

6.3   The Act provides, in s 7(2), the following definition of an electronic signature, which incorporates additional features that are not included in the definition set out in the Directive:

'(2)   For the purposes of this section an electronic signature is so much of anything in electronic form as:
  (a)   is incorporated into or otherwise logically associated with any electronic communication or electronic data; and
  (b)   purports to be so incorporated or associated for the purpose of being used in establishing the authenticity of the communication or data, the integrity of the communication or data, or both.'

An electronic communication is defined in s 15(1)[1]:

> '"electronic communication" means a communication transmitted (whether from one person to another, from one device to another or from a person to a device or vice versa):
>
> (a)   an electronic communications network; or
> (b)   by other means but while in an electronic form;'

Whilst an electronic signature does not have the same characteristics as a manuscript signature, it is the equivalent of a manuscript signature where it performs a similar function. The better view is to consider an electronic signature as a link between protocols of electronic devices that communicate, each with the other. The attention should be focused on the treatment of messages before they are transmitted and after they are received. By way of example, consider the steps taken in relation to a document in electronic format:

(a)   Alice uses a computer to type a letter. She has two options. She can print it out and sign it manually before arranging for it to be delivered to its destination. This can be by means of the post, hand delivery or any other method. When the document is produced in printed format and is signed with a manuscript signature, the electronic version remains (unless expunged), but no longer governs the content. The paper version becomes the document that will govern the relationship between the parties. Alternatively, Alice can decide to sign the letter with a digital signature.

(b)   Signing the letter with a digital signature follows a protocol. The letter is in the form of a number of bits. For instance, Alice may instruct her computer to perform a mathematical calculation on the file. She will do this by typing in a password and clicking an icon to instruct the computer to carry out the necessary actions. The program will then decrypt the private key with the password and calculate the signature. The calculation, called a signature, is then associated with the document by the computer. Clearly, there is a direct association between the computer in which the file has been created and the mathematical calculation that is used to sign the document. The signature is proof, in mathematical terms, that a value, known as a secret key, was present in the computer at the time the calculation was made. Thus there is an association between the secret key and the signing of the document, although it must be remembered that the encryption key is just a value, which must have been available to the system that originated the signature and does not identify the individual. Thus it does not follow that Alice caused the computer to undertake the mathematical calculation. There is no nexus between the signing of the document by the computer and any action on the part of Alice (it would be different if Alice accepts that it was her action that caused the connection to occur).

(c)   The problems may occur where a person can gain access to the computer by means of malicious software, such as, for instance, a Trojan horse that causes the computer to display one message on the screen, whilst signing another document. It is possible for a third party to have written a suitable plug-in that infiltrates the computer, permitting a person to enter the computer remotely without authority and use the private key to sign documents without Alice's consent or her knowledge. Should the computer have been taken over in this way, the status of the computer changes from being trusted to un-trusted. However, the owner or user may not be aware that the computer cannot be trusted.

(d) Consider another scenario. Alice creates a document and then saves it. Assume Alice attaches it to an email to be sent at a time in the future. Assume the document is automatically signed with a digital signature as Alice sends it, without any action. It does not follow that the signature appended automatically can authenticate that it was Alice who signed the document.[2]

(e) It is possible in principle to produce an electronic signature that can be trusted, and link the individual to the document. By having a computer that is not connected to any external connections, and never has been so connected at any time, and that incorporates no components that have ever been incorporated in a machine which has ever had any external connections, and by retaining complete physical control over access to the computer by anyone except Alice, it is possible to provide for the nexus between the electronic signature and Alice. However, this then requires the user to rely on the security of the software and hardware, which in turn poses even more problems.

The definition of an electronic signature illustrates that there is no attempt to equate the electronic signature to a manuscript signature. However, it can be the equivalent of a manuscript signature where it performs a similar function, even though the two types of signature are conceptually different. The manuscript signature exists in the corporeal world and requires the physical application of matter to alter the surface of a carrier. An electronic signature can only be defined within the operational boundaries of the binary numbers used by computers.

1   As amended by s 406(1), Schedule 17(158) of the Communications Act 2003.
2   To a certain extent, this matter will be dealt with by the organization. Access controls will be included in the infrastructure to determine which messages should be signed and by whom. The only problem is if an insider with sufficient rights of access alters the configurations. On this and other matters of a similar nature, see William List 'Using Digital Signatures The Issues' a Contemporary Briefing (IT Faculty of the Institute of Chartered Accountants, 2001).

The elements of an electronic signature

SO MUCH OF ANYTHING IN ELECTRONIC FORM

6.4   This is a wide-ranging provision that should ensure new concepts yet to be invented are covered by the term 'electronic form.'

INCORPORATION OR LOGICAL ASSOCIATION

6.5   The first element, 'so much of anything in electronic form' must either be incorporated or logically associated with any electronic communication or electronic data. This part of the requirement differs slightly from article 2(1) of the Directive, which refers to 'attached to or logically associated with…' However, the meaning of the word 'attached' is defined as 'joined functionally', which implies a similarity to the meaning of 'incorporated', which in turn is defined as to 'be included as part of a whole' or 'embodied.'[1] This seems to be a semantic difference that does not affect the meaning of either the provisions of article (2)(1) of the Directive or s 7(2) of the Act. The signature could be incorporated by reference to the way it is created. For instance, with a digital signature, incorporation is possible when the computer takes part of the plaintext and encrypts it (creating the message authentication code), so the recipient can check if the message has been altered. In effect, the message authentication code is a separate part of the message, but is also incorporated into the message by taking the message and encoding it. Alternatively, a biometric measurement can be attached to a message. This is where the biometric measurement, if used, must be logically associated with the message, otherwise it will not serve any function. Although the discussion above is predicated on particular methods of producing electronic signatures, the underlying principles are the same for all methods, including a name typed into an email or an email address, although the functions of an electronic signature may differ between products and methods.

1   *Oxford English Dictionary*, (Electronic version), Second Edition, 1989 and Additions, 1993–7.

FOR THE PURPOSE OF ESTABLISHING AUTHENTICITY OR INTEGRITY

6.6   The thing in electronic form must be incorporated or logically associated with the communication or data for the purpose of being used to establish the authenticity or the integrity of the communication or data, or both. The Act includes an additional reference to 'integrity', that is not included in article 2(1) of the Directive. For the thing to be an electronic signature, it must be affixed to the data for a purpose: that is, to authenticate the communication or data or provide for the identity of the communication or data. This element restricts the purpose of the electronic signature to providing for authentication and integrity, which is a narrower focus than that set out in the Directive. The term authentication has two meanings in the context of information security, which is pertinent in the context of electronic signatures.[1] One refers to the authentication of the origin of the data, whilst the other verifies the identity of a person or entity. In the context of the Act, the meaning of authenticity relates to the single issue of verifying the person or entity, as provided for in s 15(2):

'(2) In this Act:
    (a)   references to the authenticity of any communication or data
           are references to any one or more of the following:
           (i)   whether the communication or data comes from a
                  particular person or other source;
           (ii)   whether it is accurately timed and dated;
           (iii) whether it is intended to have legal effect;
           and
    (b)   references to the integrity of any communication or data are
           references to whether there has been any tampering with or
           other modification of the communication or data.'

This definition relates to the evidential issues regarding the authentication of the communication or data. Where an electronic signature is in issue,
whichever party has the burden of proof will be required to submit evidence
in response to the guidance set out in s 15(2), together with any other extrinsic evidence that may be necessary to support the evidential burden.

1   Fred Piper and Sean Murphy *Cryptography A Very Short Introduction* (Oxford University
     Press, 2002), 92.

The legal presumption of an electronic signature

6.7   An electronic signature is admissible in evidence in relation to the
authenticity or integrity of the communication. Although the reference in
Article 5(2) in the Directive refers to 'legal effectiveness', a phrase not used in
the Act, an electronic signature will have to be admissible before it can become
legally effective.[1] In addition, it does not follow that the communication will
have a legal effect, unless it is intended to have such an effect.[2] The provisions
of s 7 also do not address whether the signature is genuine and leaves the
question of evidential weight to the courts. Section 7(1) of the Act provides
for the admissibility of the electronic signature in two ways:

'7(1) In any legal proceedings:
    (a)   an electronic signature incorporated into or logically associated
           with a particular electronic communication or particular
           electronic data, and
    (b)   the certification by any person of such a signature,
    shall each be admissible in evidence in relation to any question as to
    the authenticity of the communication or data or as to the integrity
    of the communication or data.'

First, an electronic signature is admissible under the provisions of s 7(1)(a)
where it is incorporated into or logically associated with a particular electronic
communication or data. Alternatively, in accordance with the provisions of
s 7(1)(b), the authenticity or the integrity of the communication or data can

be admissible where any person certifies the signature. The certificate would normally be provided by an entity such as a trusted third party, although it does not follow that such a certificate has to be provided by a trusted third party. For instance, it is perfectly possible for Bob to certify that Alice signed an email she sent when she typed her name at the bottom of the text. It seems, therefore, that if a recipient receives an electronic communication which is signed with an electronic signature, and the certifying certificate relating to the electronic signature can be verified, the communication in question is admissible in evidence, subject to the provisions of s 15(2) of the Act.[3]

The certification by any person mentioned in s 7(1)(b) is satisfactory if the statement made includes the criteria set out in s 7(3), as follows:

'(3)   For the purposes of this section an electronic signature incorporated into or associated with a particular electronic communication or particular electronic data is certified by any person if that person (whether before or after the making of the communication) has made a statement confirming that:
(a)   the signature,
(b)   a means of producing, communicating or verifying the signature, or
(c)   a procedure applied to the signature,
is (either alone or in combination with other factors) a valid means of establishing the authenticity of the communication or data, the integrity of the communication or data, or both.'

The person or organization certifying the electronic signature may need to certify before or after or both before and after sending the communication, that the signature is authentic and the integrity of the data or communication is therefore not to be questioned. From a practical point of view, the certification process will probably occur before the sending of the communication, although there may be circumstances where the certification process can occur after the communication is sent. The actual certification will probably be an assertion, that ought to be substantiated by suitable evidence, by the person or organization certifying the signature that there is an association that links the verification key (if a digital signature) with an entity, and certifies that the use of the verification key is a valid way of verifying whether a private key issued to the person named was used in creating the signature. The link between the components of the key pair, if this were to be challenged, would have to be the subject of expert evidence. It is possible for a certificate in isolation to be sufficient in some instances. In all probability, where a party seeks to adduce evidence of a certificate as establishing the authenticity or integrity of the communication or message or both, additional evidence may be required. Hence the addition of the phrase 'alone or in combination with other factors' in s 7(3). It is the provision of this extrinsic evidence that is necessary to provide evidence of the user's identity. From the practical point of view, it may be difficult to obtain such evidence if the communication in question is the subject of legal action years after it was sent. Even if such a certificate is accepted as evidence of the facts contained in the certificate, it will not link the act of signing with the individual or entity whose signature it is. Whether the certification is provided electronically or physically, it may have to be the subject of proof that part of the content of the certificate is acceptable as to the truth of the content, because the information relating to the subscribing party will be a hearsay statement in relation to any facts not within the knowledge of the certification-service-provider. It should be noted that the provisions of s 7 do not consider whether the signature is genuine, or if it demonstrates the necessary intent by the signing party. The section, in dealing with admissibility, leaves the question of evidential weight to the courts.

1   Law Commission 'Electronic Commerce: Formal Requirements in Commercial Transactions Advice from the Law Commission', para 3.27; Graham J H Smith *Internet Law and Regulation* at 10-089 points out that no further legislation was required to provide for the admissibility of electronic signatures, and it would be unfortunate if s 7 introduced, by implication, a restriction of such admissibility.
2   Section 15(2)(a)(iii).
3   It should be noted that all this evidence would have been admissible anyway, just as it has been in the past.

Advanced electronic signature

6.8   There is no specific provision for the concept of an advanced electronic signature in the Act. However, the government have set out the extent of the liability that a certification-service-provider faces when they issue a key pair that conforms to the criteria of an advanced electronic signature under the provisions of the Electronic Signatures Regulations 2002 (SI 318/2002), which came into force on 8 March 2002. The liability of a certification-service-provider is dealt with in more detail elsewhere, but it is interesting to note that a certification-service-provider who issues a qualified certificate will be liable to the relying party unless it can be demonstrated that the provider was not negligent.[1] The burden of proof is reversed from the normal standard for negligence, where the person suffering loss is usually required to prove negligence. This leads to the possibility that organizations that decide to issue qualified certificates may seek an indemnity from the subscribing party against claims by a receiving party.

1   Regulation 4(1)(d) and 4(3)(d).

The power to modify legislation

6.9   There are many thousands of references in statutes and statutory instruments, which require the use of paper or can be interpreted to require the use of paper, as well as the use of manuscript signatures. Amending such provisions with an overall catch-all clause was not possible, nor desirable. However, it is pertinent to observe a comment by the Law Commission in relation to this issue: 'Whilst section 7 deals with admissibility, it does not provide that electronic signatures will satisfy a statutory signature requirement. It does not, therefore, assist in determining to what extent existing statutory signature requirements are capable of being satisfied electronically.'[1] In any event, power has been delegated to Ministers to modify, by order made by statutory instrument, the provisions of any enactment or subordinate legislation, or instruments made under such legislation, for which they are responsible. The government recognize the need for a co-ordinated approach between departments in enacting such subordinate legislation. Following the recommendation noted in paragraph 10.45 to the Performance and Innovation Unit Report e-commerce@its.best.uk,[2] the Central IT Unit in the Cabinet Office was given the task of developing guidelines to ensure Departments follow a consistent approach.

The authority granted to Ministers is provided by s 8(1). Ministers have the power to modify by statutory instrument the provisions of:[3]

'(a) any enactment or subordinate legislation, or
(b) any scheme, licence, authorisation or approval issued, granted or given by or under any enactment or subordinate legislation,
in such manner as he may think fit for the purpose of authorising or facilitating the use of electronic communications or electronic storage (instead of other forms of communication or storage) for any purpose mentioned in subsection (2).'

1 Law Commission 'Electronic Commerce: Formal Requirements in Commercial Transactions Advice from the Law Commission' para 3.27.
2 September 1999.
3 By s 8(7), matters under the care and control of the Commissioners of the Inland Revenue or Customs and Excise are not included, because there are corresponding powers in s 132 of the Finance Act 1999, which have already been exercised by way of statutory instruments relating to electronic tax and VAT returns.

LIMITATION OF POWERS

6.10 The power granted to the Minister is limited by the terms of s 8(3), where consideration must be given to the arrangements for record keeping. Changes must not be made that make the new arrangements for record keeping less satisfactory than before the changes were made. A further limitation is set out in s 8(6), which provides that an order 'shall not require the use of electronic communications or electronic storage for any purpose.' This subsection is qualified by s 8(6)(b), which permits a period of notice to expire before effect is given to a variation or withdrawal of an election or other decision.

PURPOSES FOR WHICH MODIFICATION CAN BE MADE

6.11 Modification of an enactment can be made for the following purposes, by permitting the use of electronic means as follows:

(a) The doing of things that may need to be evidenced in writing or where a document, notice or instrument is required.[1]

(b) Alternative means of delivery where the post or other specified means of delivery is required.[2]

(c) Where there is a requirement for a matter to be authorised by a person's signature or seal, or where it is required to be delivered as a deed or witnessed.[3]

(d) Where a statement may be required to be made under oath or to be contained in a statutory declaration.[4]

(e) Where records have to be kept, maintained or preserved in relation to any account, record, notice instrument or other document.[5]

(f) The provision, production or publication relating to any information or other matter.[6]

(g) The making of any payment.[7]

1   Section 8(2)(a).
2   Section 8(2)(b).
3   Section 8(2)(c).
4   Section 8(2)(d).
5   Section 8(2)(e).
6   Section 8(2)(f).
7   Section 8(2)(g).

THE PROVISIONS A MINISTER MAY MAKE

6.12 The Act provides the Minister with a power to provide for a range of issues when drafting a statutory instrument. The list is set out in s 8(4). The provisions of s 8(4)(g) cross refer to s 8(5). These two sections provide Ministers with the powers to determine such issues as matters relating to the legal presumption and the burden of proof. Section 8(4)(g) reads as follows:

'(g) provision, in relation to cases in which the use of electronic communications or electronic storage is so authorised, for the determination of any of the matters mentioned in subsection (5), or as to the manner in which they may be proved in legal proceedings;'

Section 8(5) provides:

'(5) The matters referred to in subsection (4)(g) are:
   (a) whether a thing has been done using an electronic communication or electronic storage;
   (b) the time at which, or date on which, a thing done using any such communication or storage was done;

(c)   the place where a thing done using such communication or
storage was done;

(d)   the person by whom such a thing was done; and

(e)   the contents, authenticity or integrity of any electronic data.'

These two sections, taken together, indicate a Minister has a great deal of control over how electronic communications are to be handled, and what presumptions will apply when using electronic communications. The combined effect of s 8(4) and 8(5) permits a minister to impose rebuttable or irrebuttable presumptions, with the potential for shifting the risks from the relying party to the purported signing party. This has the potential for doing great injustice, and as a result causing much harm to the prospects of electronic commerce. Arguably, the power is wider than just replacing paper documents with an electronic equivalent. An example would be replacing the circulation of statutory accounts to shareholders by post or as attachments to an email, with an electronic notice of their availability at a nominated uniform resource locator.

If electronic signatures are to become effective, provisions must be given to a fair and reasonable set of presumptions in relation to the evidential provisions that apply to both the sending and relying parties. Commercial organizations and government departments are able, at any rate in principle, to provide for the effective security of electronic signature creation devices because they have access to the necessary skills and resources. However, others, including smaller businesses and consumers, do not have a sufficient need or knowledge of the electronic environment to decide whether to utilize electronic signature technology at present. This may change, and it will be for governments to lay down sensible foundations to ensure both a sending party and a relying party can use digital signature technology properly and effectively.

The Electronics Communications Act 2000 has not altered the underlying flexibility of the meaning of a signature. An electronic signature does not have to be in the specific form of digital signature for it to be accepted as a signature. By typing a name to an electronic document, all the person needs to do is intend the name they type to act as a means of authentication, and intend the recipient to act upon the content of the document. The act of typing a name in this fashion comes within the provisions of s 7(2) of the Electronic Communications Act 2000, because the typed signature is incorporated with the content of the document for the purpose of establishing the authenticity of the communication. No further requirements are necessary to make a typed signature admissible. Whether a name in an email can be construed as a form of electronic signature is discussed at length elsewhere in this text in relation to the case of *J Pereira Fernandes SA v Mehta*.[1]

---

1   [2006] 1 WLR 1543; [2006] 2 All ER 891; [2006] 1 All ER (Comm) 885; [2006] All ER (D) 264 (Apr); [2006] IP & T 546; *The Times* 16 May 2006; [2006] EWHC 813 (Ch).

Regulation of Investigatory Powers

6.13 The Regulation of Investigatory Powers Act 2000 (RIPA), which extends to Northern Ireland, received the Royal Assent on 28 July 2000. The following provisions of RIPA were brought into force from 25 September 2000:[1]

(a) Part II, ss 26 to 48.

(b) Part IV s 61; s 62 in part; ss 63 and 64; ss 71 and 72 to the extent that they relate to Part II, s 5 of the Intelligence Services Act 1994 or to Part III of the Police Act 1997.

(c) Part V, ss 74 to 78; ss 80 and 81; s 82(1) and (2) for the purposes of giving effect to those provisions in Schedules 4 and 5 that are brought into force by virtue of s 82.

(d) Schedule 1; in Schedule 4, paragraphs 4, 6 and 8; in Schedule 5, the entries relating to ss 6 and 7 of the Intelligence Services Act 1994, the Police Act 1997 and the Crime and Disorder Act 1998.

The following provisions have also been brought into force:

(a) As from 2 October 2000: Schedule 3; Schedule 4 to the extent that it is not in force by virtue of article 2, and subject to article 5; Schedule 5, to the extent that it is not in force by virtue of article 2, and subject to article 6.

(b) As from 24 October 2000: s 1(3).

The Explanatory Notes point out that rationale of RIPA is to ensure the powers are used in accordance with human rights, and sets out the main purposes, as follows:

(a) The interception of communications.

(b) The acquisition of communications data (eg billing data).

(c) Intrusive surveillance (on residential premises or in private vehicles or both).

(d) Covert surveillance in the course of specific operations.

(e) The use of covert human intelligence sources (such as agents, informants, undercover officers).

(f) Access to encrypted data.[2]

The Act is also intended to ensure, in respect to each of these powers, that the law provides for the purposes for which they may be used, which authorities can use the powers, who should authorise each use of the power, the use that can be made of the material gained, independent judicial oversight, and means of redress for the individual.[3]

1   Regulation of Investigatory Powers Act 2000 (Commencement No 2 and Transitional Provisions) Order 2000 SI 2000/2543.
2   Paragraph 3.
3   Paragraph 3.

Surveillance Commissioner

6.14   The Office of the Surveillance Commissioner was established under the provisions of the Police Act 1997. The Prime Minister is responsible for appointing a Chief Commissioner to perform a number of statutory responsibilities under Part III of the Act.[1] These responsibilities have been extended to cover oversight of RIPA Parts II and III, except where they relate to interception of communications and the intelligence services. Interception of communications will be dealt with by a separate Interception of Communications Commissioner under s 57 of RIPA, who is be appointed by the Prime Minister. The Chief Surveillance Commissioner and the Assistant Surveillance Commissioners appointed under the authority of s 63 of RIPA hold, or have held, high judicial office, and are responsible for: establishing the oversight arrangements, considering appeals against decisions by the Commissioners from authorising officers, and reporting to the Prime Minister and Scottish Ministers on the matters with which the office is concerned. The Commissioners' remit is set out on the website thus:

'To review authorisations under the Act by Chief Officers of Police, the National Criminal Intelligence Service, the National Crime Squad and HM Customs, for operations involving entry on, or interference with, property or wireless telegraphy, without the consent of the owner. In 2000 the Chief Commissioner's responsibilities were extended to include keeping under review (except in relation to the interception of communications and the intelligence services) the exercise and performance of powers and duties conferred or imposed by or under Part II (covert surveillance) and Part III (encryption) of RIPA and its Scottish equivalent RIP(S)A. This legislation addresses the issue of interference with a person's right to privacy.'[2]

It is of interest to note that 'judicial oversight' might seem to require the making of an application to an independent judge (not specially selected for the purpose by a Minister) and acting in their judicial capacity, supported by admissible evidence. In this case, the use of the phrase 'oversight arrangements' is used in a different sense, namely the employment in an administrative capacity of a judge or former judge appointed by a Minister to an office not protected by the special protection from dismissal normally accorded to judges.[3]

1   Police Act 1997, s 91.
2   www.surveillancecommissioners.gov.uk/about_establishment.html.
3   See Police Act 1997, s 91(7).

The infrastructure

6.15   The infrastructure set up under RIPA includes the provision of:

(a) A Tribunal by ss 65–69. The jurisdiction of the Tribunal is set out in s 65(2)–(8), and a set of Rules came into force on 2 October 2000.[1]

(b) A Technical Advisory Board by s 13, which in turn was established by a statutory instrument in 2001.[2]

(c) Other matters that have been dealt with by way of statutory instrument include the disclosure and interception of messages;[3] setting out the offices, ranks and positions that are designated persons for the granting of authorizations under ss 28 and 29;[4] setting out the matters that must be notified to an ordinary Surveillance Commissioner with respect to intrusive surveillance;[5] setting out the criteria by which communications can be intercepted;[6] providing for suitable arrangements to record covert human intelligence sources under s 29(5);[7] setting out matters relating to a source under the age of sixteen;[8] providing for the ability of deputies to cancel authorizations;[9] dealing with the surveillance detecting television receivers;[10] designating the Home Office as an authority whose activities may require the carrying out of intrusive surveillance,[11] and provisions relating to the obligations imposed upon providers of public postal services or public telecommunications services for the purposes of providing assistance in relation to interception warrants.[12]

A series of Codes have also been developed and are now in operation, covering covert surveillance, dealing with covert human intelligence sources and the interception of communications.[13]

1 The Investigatory Powers Tribunal Rules 2000 SI 2000/2665.
2 The Regulation of Investigatory Powers (Technical Advisory Board) Order 2001 SI 2001/3734.
3 The Wireless Telegraphy (Interception and Disclosure of Messages) (Designation) Regulations 2000 SI 2000/2409.
4 The Regulation of Investigatory Powers (Prescription of Offices, Ranks and Positions) Order 2000 SI 2000/2417; The Regulation of Investigatory Powers (Authorisations Extending to Scotland) Order 2000 SI 2000/2418.
5 The Regulation of Investigatory Powers (Notification of Authorisations etc.) Order 2000 SI 2000/2563.
6 The Telecommunications (Lawful Business Practice)(Interception of Communications) Regulations 2000 SI 2000/2699.
7 The Regulation of Investigatory Powers (Source Records) Regulations 2000 SI 2000/2725.
8 The Regulation of Investigatory Powers (Juveniles) Order 2000 SI 2000/2793.
9 The Regulation of Investigatory Powers (Cancellation of Authorisations) Regulations 2000 SI 2000/2794.
10 The Regulation of Investigatory Powers (British Broadcasting Corporation) Order 2001 SI 2001/1057.
11 The Regulation of Investigatory Powers (Designation of Public Authorities for the Purposes of Intrusive Surveillance) Order 2001 SI 2001/1126.
12 The Regulation of Investigatory Powers (Maintenance of Interception Capability) Order 2002 SI 2002/1931.
13 The Regulation of Investigatory Powers (Covert Surveillance: Code of Practice) Order 2002 SI 2002/1933; The Regulation of Investigatory Powers (Covert Human Intelligence Sources: Code of Practice) Order 2002 SI 2002/1932; The Regulation of Investigatory Powers (Interception of Communications: Code of Practice) Order 2002 SI 2002/1693.

Disclosure of a key

6.16 Part III of RIPA, which is not yet in force, provides for the investigation of data protected by encryption.[1] Authorized persons can serve notices on individuals or bodies that require the disclosure of protected information, which is defined in s 56(1) as:

'any electronic data which, without the key to the data:

(a) cannot, or cannot readily, be accessed, or
(b) cannot, or cannot readily, be put into an intelligible form;'

1 The Home Office began a consultation process on a draft code of practice for the Investigation of Protected Electronic Information in 2006.

The power to require disclosure

6.17 The relevant power to require disclosure is provided in s 49. Disclosure can be required where protected information has come into the possession of a person by means of the exercise of a statutory authority, or where by any other lawful means not involving the exercise of statutory powers, it comes into the possession of the intelligence services, the police or the customs and excise. A person must have the appropriate permission to serve a s 49 notice, and the provisions of Schedule 2 has introduced levels of authority, depending on the power under which the protected information was or is likely to be obtained.[1]

1 Section 49(11) and Schedule 2.

THE DISCLOSURE NOTICE

6.18 A notice requiring the disclosure of protected information may be served where the disclosure is necessary for the interests of national security, the purpose of preventing or detecting crime, or in the interests of the economic well-being of the United Kingdom.[1] The imposition of the notice must be proportionate to what is sought to be achieved by imposing it;[2] it must not be reasonably practicable to obtain possession of the protected information in an intelligible form without issuing a notice,[3] and the key must be in the possession of an individual.[4]

1 Section 49(2)(b)(i) and 49(3). See Yaman Akdeniz, Nick Taylor and Clive Walker 'Regulation of Investigatory Powers Act 2000 (1): BigBrother.gov.uk: State surveillance in the age of information and rights' [2001] Crim LR 7 at 85–86 for comments relating to the provisions of s 49(3).
2 Section 49(2)(c).
3 Section 49(2)(d).
4 Section 49(2)(a).

The meaning of a key

6.19 What constitutes a key is widely defined, and includes codes and passwords. The definition in s 56(1) is as follows:

'in relation to any electronic data, means any key, code, password, algorithm or other data the use of which (with or without other keys):

(a) allows access to the electronic data, or

(b) facilitates the putting of data into an intelligible form;'

In the context of digital signatures, any person or organization that obtains and uses private keys should ensure the key is only suitable for the purposes of a digital signature, and it cannot be used for any other purpose.[1] If a key can be used for purposes other than a digital signature, it may be the subject of a s 49 notice. Also, it will be important to ensure keys used for digital signatures are stored separately from any other types of private key used for other purposes.

1   It is possible for encrypted data to be encoded in such a way that it can be decoded in two separate ways, one to reveal the secret message and the other to reveal an innocuous message: Derrick Grover, 'Dual encryption and plausible deniability', *Computer Law & Security Report*, Volume 20, Number 1, 2004, 37–40.

Possession of a key

6.20 A person has possession of a key in accordance with the provisions of s 56(2). A person may be deemed to have a key, although they do not have the key themselves. The definition is as follows:

'References in this Part to a person's having information (including a key to protected information) in his possession include references-

(a) to its being in the possession of a person who is under his control so far as that information is concerned;

(b) to his having an immediate right of access to it, or an immediate right to have it transmitted or otherwise supplied to him; and

(c) to its being, or being contained in, anything which he or a person under his control is entitled, in exercise of any statutory power and without otherwise taking possession of it, to detain, inspect or search.'

This is a fairly important provision, because the officers of an organization, whatever the legal form the organization takes, are the ones responsible for the proper management of the private key.[1] This is because any s 49 notice served will be served on an officer or senior manager. Control must, therefore, be exercised over the acquisition and use of private keys. For instance, a person at the highest level in an organization should be made responsible for this issue. Considerations in whether to use private keys will cover, but not be limited to:

(a) Deciding if information sent electronically needs to be encrypted. If it does, whether there are more appropriate means of delivering the information to the intended recipient.

(b) Deciding if documents or messages need to be digitally signed. If so, then the next question is whether a risk analysis has been conducted to determine the likely costs of resolving a dispute if a signature has been misused, bearing in mind the discussion elsewhere in this text relating to liability.

(c) If private keys are to be used, whatever the purpose, sufficient consideration must be given to storage, access for appropriately authorized officers and employees, and the provision of checks and balances to provide for security.

1 Ross Anderson *Security Engineering: A Guide to Building Dependable Distributed Systems* (Wiley Computer Publishing, 2001) Chapter 22 for a discussion on the principles involved in this process.

Format of the notice

6.21 The format a notice must take is set out in s 49(4), and it includes the provision of the time by which the notice is to be complied with, which must allow a reasonable period for compliance, depending on the circumstances of the case:

'(4) A notice under this section imposing a disclosure requirement in respect of any protected information-

(a) must be given in writing or (if not in writing) must be given in a manner that produces a record of its having been given;

(b) must describe the protected information to which the notice relates;

(c) must specify the matters falling within subsection (2)(b)(i) or (ii) by reference to which the notice is given;

(d) must specify the office, rank or position held by the person giving it;

(e) must specify the office, rank or position of the person who for the purposes of Schedule 2 granted permission for the giving of the notice or (if the person giving the notice was entitled to give it without another person's permission) must set out the circumstances in which that entitlement arose;

(f) must specify the time by which the notice is to be complied with; and

(g) must set out the disclosure that is required by the notice and the form and manner in which it is to be made;

and the time specified for the purposes of paragraph (f) must allow a period for compliance which is reasonable in all the circumstances.'

Upon whom the notice is served

6.22   Where a notice is to be served on a body corporate or a firm and it is obvious that more than one person may be in possession of the key, then the notice will be directed to a senior officer, partner or senior employee.[1] However, where it is considered the circumstances were such that purpose of the notice would be defeated if it were to be served on the most appropriate person (for instance, they are the subject of an investigation), then the notice can be served on another individual.[2]

1   Section 49(5) and (6).
2   Section 49(7).

Exclusion of electronic signatures

6.23   Where a key is used only for the purpose of generating a digital signature, it does not have to be disclosed in response to a notice, providing it has not been used for any other purpose.[1] It might be useful to recall that a key pair has more than the single function of producing a digital signature. The same key pair can be used to encrypt a message, depending on the algorithm used. An electronic signature is defined in s 56(2) and means:

'anything in electronic form which:
(a)   is incorporated into or logically associated with, any electronic communication or other data;
(b)   is generated by the signatory or other source of the communication or data; and
(c)   is used for the purpose of facilitating, by means of a link between the signatory or other source and the communication or data, the establishment of the authenticity of the communication or data, the establishment of its integrity, or both;'

This exemption may be less effective than it seems. In a commercial context, where more than one person may properly have access to a key, the person served with the notice may not be able to be sure that a key, despite being intended for signature purposes, has never been used to decrypt a message encrypted with the corresponding public key. Although it is arguably for the prosecution to prove that a key has been used for such a purpose, and is therefore subject to seizure, the mere assertion of this fact by the person demanding access to the key would place the recipient of the notice in a position of impossible difficulty in resisting the demand.

1   Section 49(9).

The effect of the notice

6.24   Where a person is served with a s 49 notice, they may use any key in their possession to obtain access to the information or to put it into intelligible form, and is required to disclose the information in intelligible form if the notice so requires.[1] However, the person to whom the notice is addressed may instead disclose the relevant key to the person serving the notice.[2] There may be times when the person to whom the notice is directed does not have the key, or cannot gain access to the key. In such instances, they must give up what keys they actually have, although they do not have to disclose every key they have in their possession.[3]

1   Section 50(1).
2   Section 50(2).
3   Section 50(3) and the effects of s 50(4), (5) and (6). See also s 50(7) and (8).

When the key is required

6.25   There may be occasions when the key is required, rather than the unencrypted plain text.[1] In such circumstances, the provisions of s 51 will apply. The criteria is set out in s 51(4), in that a direction to produce the key cannot be given unless it is believed that the circumstances are such that the purpose would be defeated if the notice did not provide for the key to be delivered up, and asking for the key is proportionate:

'(4)   Subsections (5) to (7) apply where a person ('the person given notice'):
  (a)   is entitled or obliged to disclose a key to protected information for the purpose of complying with any disclosure requirement imposed by a section 49 notice; and
  (b)   is in possession of more than one key to that information.'

When deciding whether to demand the key, s 50(5) sets out the matters to be taken into account, including the nature and extent of the protected information and any adverse effects asking for the key might have on the business carried on by the person to whom the notice is directed.

1   Section 50(3)(c).

Contribution to costs

6.26   Where there is a cost to complying with a s 49 notice, s 52 provides for the Secretary of State to make an appropriate contribution.

Failure to comply with a notice

6.27   A person is guilty of an offence if they knowingly fail to comply with a s 49 notice, and are liable on conviction on indictment, to imprisonment for a term not exceeding two years or to a fine, or both; on summary conviction, to imprisonment for a term not exceeding six months or to a fine not exceeding the statutory minimum, or both.[1] The provisions of this section are important. The presumption of possession is set out in s 53(2) and (3):

'(2) In proceedings against any person for an offence under this section, if it is shown that that person was in possession of a key to any protected information at any time before the time of the giving of the section 49 notice, that person shall be taken for the purposes of those proceedings to have continued to be in possession of that key at all subsequent times, unless it is shown that the key was not in his possession after the giving of the notice and before the time by which he was required to disclose it.'

The provisions of this section have the following effect:

(a) The prosecution have the persuasive burden to prove that the accused was in possession of a key to protected information at any time before the giving of the s 49 notice. This element of the definition of the offence requires the prosecution to prove possession, not merely that a key generating third party sent the key, say. Also, the second element relates to time. The key can be proved to be in the possession of the accused at any time up to the giving of the s 49 notice. This part of the offence means that it is possible for a key to have expired and to have been deleted, if such was the policy. It has been argued that the presumption that the key remains with the person, as a continuing state of affairs, may be unfair.[2] In any event, the key management policy becomes an important document, as does the physical implementation of its provisions.

(b) The second part to the offence places an express burden on the accused to offer a reason for a key not being in their possession: 'unless it is shown that the key was not in his possession after the giving of the notice and before the time by which he was required to disclose it.' Proving that a key was not in their possession at the material time will require the accused to adduce sufficient evidence to demonstrate that the key was no longer in their possession after the notice was served by before the time elapses that the key must be disclosed.

The Act offers further guidance relating to the defence the accused is permitted to raise in the provisions of s 53(3):

'(3) For the purposes of this section a person shall be taken to have shown that he was not in possession of a key to protected information at a particular time if:
   (a) sufficient evidence of that fact is adduced to raise an issue with respect to it; and
   (b) the contrary is not proved beyond a reasonable doubt.'

Section 53(3) provides for the standard of proof the accused is required to meet to raise doubts about whether they had the key in their possession when the notice was given. The burden will be satisfied on a balance of probabilities, but the quality of the evidence in relation to the relevant security policy will be highly relevant. A person can raise in the defence that they did not have enough time to make the disclosure within the time frame set out in the s 49 notice, or that they did disclose the key or information as soon after the time as practicable.[3] The accused will not bear a persuasive burden, merely an evidential burden to raise sufficient evidence to demonstrate the key was not in their possession at the time the notice was given. Once the accused introduces evidence to prove their case, it will then be for the prosecution to prove beyond reasonable doubt that the evidence introduced by the accused does not demonstrate the key left their possession.

1   Section 53(1) and 53(5).
2   Yaman Akdeniz, Nick Taylor and Clive Walker 'Regulation of Investigatory Powers Act 2000 (1): BigBrother.gov.uk: State surveillance in the age of information and rights,' 87.
3   Section 53(4).

Tipping off

6.28   A s 49 notice may require the person to whom the notice is given, and every other person who becomes aware of its contents, to keep the giving of the notice, its contents and the things undertaken in responding to it, a secret in accordance with the provisions of s 54(1):

'(1)   This section applies where a section 49 notice contains a provision requiring-
(a)   the person to whom the notice is given, and
(b)   every other person who becomes aware of it or of its contents,
to keep secret the giving of the notice, its contents and the things done in pursuance of it.'

The criteria for the imposition of a secrecy requirement are set out in s 54(3), and the punishment is provided in s 54(4). Where the person is guilty of an offence and liable, they may be sentenced as follows: on conviction on indictment, to imprisonment for a term not exceeding five years or to a fine, or both; on summary conviction, to imprisonment for a term not exceeding six months or to a fine not exceeding the statutory minimum, or both. A range of defences are provided by:
(a)   Section 54(5), where it is a defence to show that the disclosure was caused by the operation of software which is designed to indicate when a key to protected information has ceased to be secure, and the person to whom the notice is served could not reasonably have been expected to take steps to prevent the disclosure.
(b)   Section 54(6) and (7) where disclosure is made by or to a professional legal adviser in connection with giving advice about the effect of the provisions of this part of the Act, or in any proceedings.
(c)   Section 54(9) where the disclosure is made to a Commissioner or authorised by a Commissioner, the terms of the notice, by or on behalf

of the person who gave the notice, or by the person to which the data relates.

(d) Section 54(10) provides for a defence where the person can show they neither knew or had reasonable grounds for suspecting that the notice contained a requirement to keep secret what was disclosed.

It should be noted, however, that the effectiveness of the 'tipping off' offence is debatable. Some people, when they sign their email correspondence, might include a disclaimer such as 'I will always explain why I revoke a key, unless the UK government prevents me using the RIP Act 2000.' To illustrate the point, assume a correspondent using this qualification revokes a key. Further assume they are asked for the reason and reply that they cannot give one. It must be doubtful whether they can be convicted of tipping off, though this is what they have done, after all, there has been no suggestion that a disclosed key cannot lawfully be revoked.

Controlling the use of private keys

6.29 It is incumbent on the organization to control the use of private keys, for whatever purpose they are used. Consideration must be given to ensuring employees and contractors are aware of the security policy and their rights, if they have been granted any rights, for using private keys. This should be the case whether they have access to a single computer, a laptop or any system that includes private keys. Users should also understand the uses to which different types of key can be put.

A vexing topic is how to control the use of private keys by members of staff. A s 49 notice, even of a private key issued to and used by an employee in their private capacity, may be directed to an officer of the organization where it is known that the key was used from within the organization's infrastructure. It is possible for a member of staff to compromise an entire organization by conducting illicit business (whether legitimate or criminal) over the infrastructure without the knowledge of the organization. If a risk analysis is undertaken, one of the issues that must be considered is the use of private keys by members of staff in their private capacity. On the face of it, members of staff should not have any requirement to encrypt or digitally sign any message or document of a private nature during the course of their employment for private purposes. However, it is very well known that employees use email in particular to send personal correspondence. It is for the organization to determine whether employees are permitted to send and receive personal correspondence by way of email. Regardless whether employees are permitted or not to use email for personal use, the organization must consider the ramifications of the adoption of either option:

(a) If private use of email is permitted, careful attention must be made to the drafting of the appropriate policy, keeping it up to date and the provisions of adequate training.

(b) If the organization does not permit employees to use email for private correspondence, it is necessary to enforce the rule, otherwise it is of no significance.

Whether personal use of email is permitted or not, the organization will, in the interests of protecting itself, have to consider monitoring traffic over the infrastructure to identify if and when employees use private keys to encrypt or apply a digital signature to a message or document.

Lawful monitoring

6.30 The Regulation of Investigatory Powers Act 2000 makes it unlawful for communications to be intercepted, unless a warrant has been authorized by an approved authority; an existing statutory power is used to obtain stored communications; the reason for monitoring is governed by the Telecommunications (Lawful Business Practice) (Interception of Communications) Regulations 2000 or both the sender and recipient (or the intended recipient) explicitly consent to the interception.[1] Communications can be intercepted under the provisions of the Telecommunications (Lawful Business Practice) (Interception of Communications) Regulations 2000.[2] If an organization decides to monitor or record communications, it must do so in line with the requirements of the regulations.

1   Regulation of Investigatory Powers Act 2000 s 3.
2   SI 2000/2699, which came into force on 24 October 2000.

Monitoring communications

6.31 Monitoring is permitted in the following circumstances:

USERS MUST BE INFORMED

6.32 An organization can monitor or record communications on their telecoms systems without consent, provided that all reasonable efforts have been made to inform every person who may use the system that their communications may be intercepted. Employees and third parties must be informed that the monitoring or recording of communications is taking place. Should the organization decide to monitor, it is important to have evidence to prove the employees have been informed that their communications will be subject to monitoring.

THERE MUST BE A BUSINESS PURPOSE

6.33 Where a communication is intercepted in the course of transmission, it must be relevant to the business. A communication that is relevant to a business is defined in regulation 2(b) as follows:

'(i)   a communication:
    (aa) by means of which a transaction is entered into in the course of
          that business, or
    (bb) which otherwise relates to that business, or
(ii) a communication which otherwise takes place in the course of the
      carrying out of that business;'

This definition is quite wide, because it covers communications that are entered into in the normal course of running a business, relate to the business in some other way, and take place as a result of running the business other than communications that are entered into in the normal course of running a business. The relevance of this definition is important. For instance, where a communication is clearly private and not related to the employer's business, it does not appear to come within the definition of a communication that is relevant to the business unless the organization has prohibited employees from using email for personal and private purposes. Where the communication has breached the policy by, for example, sending confidential information or pornography (or using a private key without permission), then the communication becomes relevant to the business because it is in breach of the policy.

MONITORING OR RECORDING COMMUNICATIONS

6.34 Regulation 3(1) authorizes the monitoring or recording of communications for the following purposes:

(a)   To establish the existence of facts relevant to a business.[1] For instance, this may include keeping records of share transactions or emails relating to entering a contract.

(b)   To ascertain compliance with regulatory or self-regulatory practices or procedures relevant to the business.[2] This includes the monitoring of communications to ensure, for instance, that employees are complying with either external or internal regulatory rules or guidelines.

(c)   To ascertain or demonstrate standards which are or ought to be achieved by persons using the system.[3] It is possible, for instance, to monitor to provide for quality control or staff training.

(d)   In the interests of national security;[4] to prevent or detect crime.[5] If fraud or corruption is suspected, monitoring can take place to ascertain any facts in relation to such a crime.

(e)   To investigate or detect the unauthorized use of telecommunications systems.[6] It is possible to monitor to ensure employees do not breach the rules or policies on the use of email or the internet.

(f)   To ensure the effective operation of the system.[7] This permits the organization to monitor for viruses or other threats to the system.

The range of reasons for monitoring enables the organization to implement a policy to prevent members of staff from using personal private keys.

1   Regulation 3(1)(a)(i)(aa).
2   Regulation 3(1)(a)(i)(bb).
3   Regulation 3(1)(a)(i)(cc).
4   Regulation 3(1)(a)(ii).
5   Regulation 3(1)(a)(iii).
6   Regulation 3(1)(a)(iv).
7   Regulation 3(1)(a)(v).

MONITORING BUT NOT RECORDING

6.35 A business is also authorized to monitor communications on their systems for the purpose of determining whether or not the communications are relevant to the business.[1] This permission covers the checking of an employee's communications when they are on leave or absent for any other reason. Business must continue in the absence of any employee, and it is reasonable to expect employers to insist that all correspondence is opened for the efficient running of the organization.

1   Regulation 3(1)(b).

MONITORING AND EMPLOYEES

6.36 The Information Commissioner has produced a revised version of the Employment Practices Code, and the Employment Practice Code Supplementary Guidance. The aim of the Code is to help employers comply with the provisions of the Data Protection Act 1998 and to encourage the adoption of good practice. The Code has been issued under s 51 of the Data Protection Act 1998, which requires the Information Commissioner to promote good practice, including compliance with the requirements of the Act.

THE HUMAN RIGHTS ACT 1998

6.37 The Human Rights Act 1998 incorporates the European Convention on Human Rights, and article 8 of the Convention sets out the individual's right to respect for privacy and family life. The Human Rights Act only applies directly against employers in the public sector, although private organizations are affected, because an employment tribunal can take into account whether a breach of human rights has occurred when deciding claims for unfair dismissal or discrimination. The case of *Copland v The United Kingdom*[1] illustrates the direct effect of the Convention on the state. In this case, heard before the European Court of Human Rights, Lynette Copland was employed by Carmarthenshire College in 1991. In 1995 she became the personal assistant to the College Principal, and from the end of 1995 she was required to work closely with the Deputy Principal. During the course of her employment in 1999, her use of the telephone, email and internet were monitored at the request of the Deputy Principal. Mrs Copland was not informed that her use of the communications network was monitored, and the College did not have a policy in force at the material time regarding the monitoring of telephone, email or internet use by employees. It was agreed that Carmarthenshire College is a statutory body administered by the state and possesses powers under ss 18 and 19 of the Further and Higher Education Act 1992 relating to the provision of further and higher education. The government accepted that the College was a public body for whose actions the state was directly responsible under the provisions of the Convention. The arguments used by the government for the right to monitor were set out in paragraphs 33 to 35 of the judgment:

> '33. In the event that the analysis of records of telephone, email and internet use was considered to amount to an interference with respect for private life or correspondence, the Government contended that the interference was justified.
>
> 34. First, it pursued the legitimate aim of protecting the rights and freedoms of others by ensuring that the facilities provided by a publicly funded employer were not abused. Secondly, the interference had a basis in domestic law in that the College, as a statutory body, whose powers enable it to provide further and higher education and to do anything necessary and expedient for those purposes, had the power to take reasonable control of its facilities to ensure that it was able to carry out its statutory functions. It was reasonably foreseeable that the facilities provided by a statutory body out of public funds could not be used excessively for personal purposes and that the College would undertake an analysis of its records to determine if there was any likelihood of personal use which needed to be investigated. In this respect, the situation was analogous to that in *Peck v the United Kingdom*, no. 44647/98, ECHR 2003-I.
>
> 35. Finally, the acts had been necessary in a democratic society and were proportionate as any interference went no further than necessary to establish whether there had been such excessive personal use of facilities as to merit investigation.'

The applicant did not accept that her communications had not been read, and argued that 'the conduct of the College was neither necessary nor proportionate. There were reasonable and less intrusive methods that the College could have used such as drafting and publishing a policy dealing with the monitoring of employees' usage of the telephone, internet and email.' (paragraph 38). It was held that the applicant had a reasonable expectation of the privacy of calls made from her work telephone, including her use of email and the internet, because she had not been given a warning that her communications would be liable to monitoring. As a result, this amounted to an interference with her right to respect for her private life and correspondence within the meaning of article 8 of the Convention. In addition, the monitoring was not carried out in accordance with the law at the material time. It was held there had been a breach of article 8, which is hardly surprising. The state was ordered to pay the applicant €3,000 in respect of non-pecuniary damages and €6,000 in respect of costs and expenses.

Where the organization makes it clear that employees' communications may be subject to interception, and such interception and monitoring is carried out within the law (ie interception is for a legitimate business reason and is proportionate to the stated purpose), it is unlikely that an employee will have an action against the organization for breach of the right to privacy (article 8) and correspondence (article 10). Where the use of email facilities for private communication is forbidden, it can be argued that the organization can intercept personal email so as to detect unauthorized personal use of the facilities.

By comparison, it is instructive to note that the members of the Working Party on the protection of individuals with regard to the processing of personal data (Working Party),[2] in their paper 'Working document on the surveillance of electronic communications in the workplace' dated 29 May 2002,[3] aspire to extend the principles laid down by the European Court of Human Rights in relation to the provision of secrecy of correspondence, and propose that 'Workers have a legitimate expectation of privacy at the workplace, which is not overridden by the fact that workers use communication devices or any other business facilities of the employer.'[4] Although the authors go on to make the comment 'However the provision of proper information by the employer to the worker may reduce the workers' legitimate expectation of privacy', nevertheless they make it plain that their view is: 'The general principle of secrecy of correspondence covers communications at the workplace. This is likely to include electronic email and related files attached thereto.'[5] The authors of this document reject the view of other commentators, that where a worker is warned in advance about the possibility of their communications being intercepted, they can expect to lose the right to privacy for correspondence and any protection under the provisions of article 8 of the Convention.

However, where the organization permits employees to use email to send personal messages, interception is prohibited because it will not be related to the purpose of the business. If the organization monitors private communications sent and received by way of email in such circumstances, it is probable that the employer will be in breach of the right to privacy and correspondence. An added complication is where an organization permits its employees to send and receive personal correspondence by way of email, and employees subsequently abuse the resource. Employers should take great care to ensure that they have the entitlement to investigate misuse of the facility by employees who breach the duty of trust and confidence between employee and employer, such as using a private key to encrypt or affix a digital signature to a message without permission. For instance, the organization should make sure it has the power to intercept and monitor private email correspondence where there is sufficient evidence to indicate the employee is using the facility to the employer's detriment.

1 No. 62617/00, [2007] ECHR 253.
2 Set up in pursuance of articles 29 and 30 of Directive 95/46/EC of the European Parliament and of the Council of 24 October 1995 on the protection of individuals with regard to processing of personal data and on the free movement of such data OJ L 281 of 23.11.1995 p. 31. Their tasks include the provision of expert opinion at member state level to the Commission on questions relating to data protection. Membership of the Working Party comprises the commissioners, or senior members of the relevant body from member states. The Working Party produces various documents, including opinions and working documents.
3 5401/01/EN/Final WP55.
4 Paragraph 2.2 (a).
5 Paragraph 2.2 (b).

Standards from the Information Commissioner

6.38 The Code defines monitoring as '… activities that set out to collect information about workers by keeping them under some form of observation, normally with a view to checking their performance or conduct. This could be done either directly, indirectly, perhaps by examining their work output, or by electronic means.'[1] There is no definition of what is meant by monitoring. However, the Information Commissioner gives examples of what is considered to be monitoring, which includes:

(a) Randomly opening individual worker's emails to look for evidence of malpractice. In this instance, the unfairness is manifest. Failure to open a worker's networked communications as set out in the relevant policy will undoubtedly be a breach of the Act.

(b) Using automated checking software to collect information about workers, for example to find out whether particular workers are sending or receiving inappropriate emails. An example will be to filter the use of language for particular words to establish whether particular workers are sending or receiving inappropriate emails in contravention of the relevant policy.

(c) Examining logs of websites visited to check that individual workers are not downloading pornography.

1 The Employment Practices Code, 55.

WHAT THE INFORMATION COMMISSIONER CONSIDERS IS NOT MONITORING

6.39 The Information Commissioner does not consider the following as monitoring:

(a) Looking back through customer records in the event of a complaint, to check that the customer was given the correct advice.

(b) Checking a collection of emails sent by a particular worker which is stored as a record of transactions, in order to ensure the security of the system or to investigate an allegation of malpractice.

(c) Looking back through a log of telephone calls made that is kept for billing purposes, to establish whether a worker is suspected of disclosing trade secrets or has been contacting a competitor.

The Information Commissioner has set out the standards that are expected to be enforced in relation to the monitoring of emails and use of the internet. When establishing a policy and deciding to monitor, the organization should take into account the benchmarks and the notes to the benchmarks published by the Information Commissioner.

THE 'IMPACT' ASSESSMENT

6.40 Where the organization decides to monitor, it is crucial to ensure the adverse effects of monitoring are justified by the benefits to the employer and others. For this reason, an 'impact assessment' should be made before monitoring workers. The aim should be to judge whether any monitoring that takes place represents a proportionate response to the problem. The development of the 'impact assessment' involves the following criteria, taken from the Code, each of which is further amplified in the Code:

(a) Identifying clearly the purpose(s) behind the monitoring arrangement and the benefits it is likely to deliver.

(b) Identifying any likely adverse impact of the monitoring arrangement.

(c) Considering alternatives to monitoring or different ways in which it might be carried out.

(d) Taking into account the obligations that arise from monitoring.

(e) Judging whether monitoring is justified.

The issues to be covered in the 'impact assessment' when considering the monitoring of email are set out in the Supplementary Guidance, at paragraph 3.2.7. The ninth bullet point bears careful consideration, and is reproduced in full below:

'Is there a ban on personal use of the email system or a restriction on the types of messages that can be sent? Such a ban or restriction does not in itself justify the employer knowingly opening messages that are clearly personal. However an employer designing monitoring [it is not clear what "employer designing monitoring" means] is entitled to work on the assumption that messages in the system are either all likely to be business ones or, if personal, are only likely to be of a particular type. If personal use is prohibited it may be possible to detect personal messages from the header or address information and take action against the sender or recipient without opening them.'

Further consideration is given to this in paragraph 3.2.8, which states:

'Accessing the contents of a worker's personal emails or other correspondence will be particularly intrusive. This should be avoided wherever possible. It is particularly important if the worker has a genuine expectation of privacy. This might be confined to emails where the words 'private' or 'personal' have been included in the message header if workers have been clearly instructed to mark personal emails in this way. If the content of personal emails is to be accessed, the employer must have a pressing business need to do so, eg grounds to suspect the worker of work-related criminal activity. This must be sufficient to justify the degree of intrusion involved and there must be no reasonable, less intrusive alternative.'

Bearing in mind the increasing numbers of workers that have been detected in sending out confidential information or running businesses from the workplace, it seems that this particular point is making two statements. First, organizations are, it appears, now required to let employees use the corporate infrastructure to send and receive private communications. It is extraordinary that such a right did not exist with mail sent and received by the organization before the advent of the internet, when correspondence passed through the postal services or by way of facsimile transmission. Organizations would not permit employees to write and send postal correspondence or messages by facsimile transmission at the expense of the organization, so why is email any different?

Second, even if an email is marked personal, it is difficult for the employer, without opening the email, to determine whether the worker is sending trade secrets out or distributing pornography (or something much worse), under the cover of personal correspondence. It seems most bizarre that workers can use such a simple device to hide criminal behaviour. It will not always be immediately apparent if a particular worker should be subject to monitoring for criminal behaviour, because such behaviour may only become apparent when another member of staff opens emails when the worker is on holiday. The case of *Miseroy v Barclays Bank plc*,[1] illustrates the nature of this problem. Mr Hilary Miseroy was employed by Barclaycard in the Fraud Prevention Department between 14 March 1988 and 13 September 2002. The Staff Manual dated 16 June 2000 included a policy in relation to the supply and trafficking of drugs and money laundering. In addition, the Group IT Security Policies, dated July 2002, included instructions about the use of the corporate email facilities. Clear guidance was set out by Barclays in both these areas. In July 2002, Maureen Crane, a Senior Fraud Analyst, was informed that an individual within her team appeared to be receiving a disproportionate number of emails during the day. A formal investigation was subsequently initiated. The Information, Risk and Security Department carried out an audit of the emails sent and received by three employees. The audit indicated that Mr Miseroy sent a significant number of emails. As a result, he was also included in the investigation. After a series of investigatory meetings, it was concluded that Mr Miseroy had abused the email facilities, as follows:

(a) He sent out an unwarranted number of personal emails. On some days eight or more exchanges had taken place in quick succession.

(b) Some of the emails he sent out included content that was derogatory, offensive and sexist. During his first interview, he accepted that the comments he made were not appropriate. Later, he contended that there was a great deal of social activity and laddish banter between employees working within the Fraud Department and he did not consider that anybody had been offended.

(c) A number of emails were exchanged between him and Andrew West, a manager in a different department, between 26 April and 30 April 2002. The content of these emails referred to the purchase of cannabis from a friend of Mr Miseroy, who in turn passed the drug to Mr West. Similar emails had been passed between Mr Miseroy and Mr West between 15 February and 10 April 2002. In an email dated 15 February, Mr Miseroy wrote to Mr West: 'I've brought it in with me. Fag-break about 10.30?' In a further email sent on 18 February, Mr Miseroy asked 'quality ok?'

(d) It was also determined that Mr Miseroy disclosed confidential information regarding Barclay's operations and customers.

Mr Miseroy was summarily dismissed for gross misconduct on 13 September 2002. In his defence, Mr Miseroy maintained he was treated differently from Mr West, who was given a final written warning. However, the following factors did not help his case: Mr Miseroy faced a greater number of charges than Mr West relating to the transmission of inappropriate emails; he lied at the first investigatory meeting; it was Mr Miseroy who supplied drugs on Barclay's premises, not Mr West; Mr West was remorseful and contrite in responding to the charge made against him, and provided explanations for his behaviour; Mr Miseroy did not accept that he was wrong in sending out emails with content that was inappropriate. Further, he did not seem to accept that his emails relating to the supply of cannabis represented a serious threat to the reputation of Barclays Bank. When he appealed internally against the decision to dismiss him, Mr Miseroy argued about the future classification of cannabis as a Class C drug and discussed whether it was possible for him to enter a binding contract for the sale of cannabis by means of an exchange of emails. Such explanations led Mr Tim Kiy, the Marketing Director of Barclaycard Corporate who heard Mr Miseroy's appeal, to conclude that Mr Miseroy failed to understand the reputational risk that his actions posed for the company. The members of the Tribunal accepted that the dismissal of Mr Miseroy was within the range of reasonable responses of a reasonable employer in relation to the circumstances of the case.

1   Employment Tribunal Case No 1201894/2004.

CORE PRINCIPLES

6.41 The content of paragraph 3.1 of the Code sets out a number of core principles, all of which are elaborated upon. They are:
(a) It will usually be intrusive to monitor your workers.
(b) Workers have legitimate expectations that they can keep their personal lives private and that they are also entitled to a degree of privacy in the work environment.
(c) If employers wish to monitor their workers, they should be clear about the purpose and satisfied that the particular monitoring arrangement is justified by real benefits that will be delivered.
(d) Workers should be aware of the nature, extent and reasons for any monitoring, unless (exceptionally) covert monitoring is justified.
(e) In any event, workers' awareness will influence their expectations.

MONITORING NETWORKED COMMUNICATIONS

6.42 The provisions of paragraph 3.2 deals with the issues relating to monitoring communications. The guidelines for monitoring use are set out below:
(a) If you wish to monitor electronic communications, establish a policy on their use and communicate it to workers. The features that should be included in the policy are elaborated in the Code. You should set out how the policy is enforced and the penalties that exist for a breach of the policy.
(b) Ensure that where monitoring involves the interception of a communication, it is not prevented by the provisions of the Regulation of Investigatory Powers Act 2000.
(c) Consider, preferably using an 'impact assessment', whether any monitoring of electronic communications can be limited to that necessary to ensure the security of the system and whether it can be automated.
(d) If emails and internet access or both are, or are likely to be, monitored, consider, preferably using an 'impact assessment', whether the benefits justify the effect on the worker. If so, inform workers about the nature and extent of all monitoring of email and use of the internet.
(e) Wherever possible avoid opening emails, especially ones that clearly show they are private or personal.
(f) If it is necessary to check the email accounts of workers in their absence, make sure that they are aware that this will happen.
(g) Inform workers of the extent to which information about their use of the internet and email is retained in the system and for how long.

Each of the above recommendations is followed by a number of key points. Some of the key points made in relation to a number of the above recommendations will pose a serious problem to many organizations. It will be very difficult to prevent improper use of the infrastructure if all of these key points are held to be reasonable in the future. The most important are noted below.

(a) Whenever possible avoid opening emails, especially ones that clearly show they are private or personal

Key points and possible actions:
(i)   Ensure that email monitoring is confined to address/heading unless it is essential for a valid and defined reason to examine content.
(ii) Encourage workers to mark any personal email as such and encourage them to tell those who write to them to do the same.
(iii) If workers are allowed to obtain access to personal email accounts from the workplace, such emails should only be monitored in exceptional circumstances.

(b) If it is necessary to check the email accounts of workers in their absence, make sure that they are aware that this will happen

Key points and possible actions:
(i)   If email accounts need to be checked in the absence of workers, make sure they know this will happen.
(ii) Encourage the use of a marking system to help protect private or personal communications.
(iii) Avoid, where possible, opening emails that clearly show they are private or personal communications.

(c) Inform workers of the extent to which information about their internet access and emails is retained in the system and for how long

Key points and possible actions:
(i)   Check whether workers are currently aware of the retention period of email and internet usage.
(ii) If it is not already in place, set up a system (eg displaying information online or in a communication pack) that informs workers of retention periods.

The issue relating to the retention of emails is revisited in the Supplementary Guidance, where it is stated in paragraph 3.2.11 that 'It is important to ensure that workers are aware of retention periods and, in particular, that they are not misled into believing that information will be either deleted or retained when this is not the case.'

Guidance from the European Union

SURVEILLANCE OF ELECTRONIC COMMUNICATIONS

6.43 The Working Party adopted a 'Working document on the surveillance of electronic communications in the workplace' on 29 May 2002,[1] which is meant to complement the matters discussed in Opinion 8/2001.[2] The authors of this document highlight the need to balance different rights and interests in the light of, amongst other considerations, proportionality. The employee's right of privacy has to be balanced against the right of the employer to control the functioning of the organization and take necessary action to defend any action by an employee that will harm the employer's legitimate interests. In addition, any method of surveillance should not be used in such a way as to intrude on the rights and freedoms of employees.[3] Guidelines offered in relation to the general principles of monitoring the use of email and the internet cover the following:

(a)   Any action must be necessary, which places a burden on the employer to ensure the purpose of monitoring is absolutely necessary, and traditional methods of supervision are not appropriate. It is accepted that the detection of viruses is a necessary component of any email system, as is the requirement that other employees should be able to read emails when an employee is on holiday or out of the office because they are ill.[4]

(b)   Data must be collected for a specified, explicit and legitimate purpose and not processed contrary to those purposes.[5]

(c)   The employer must be transparent about its activities. As a result, the employer has an obligation to inform employees fully about any monitoring undertaken. This includes the provision of an email and internet use policy which is freely available to employees, including the provision of reasons why monitoring is taking place; the details of any surveillance undertaken must be provided and the nature of any enforcement procedures that will be taken if the disciplinary code is transgressed.[6]

It must be clear that monitoring must be adequate, relevant and not excessive. As a result, the policy should be specifically written to cover the specific needs of the organization.

1   5401/01/EN/Final WP55.
2   5062/01/EN/Final WP 48 adopted on 13 September 2001.
3   Chapter 1.
4   Paragraph 3.1.1.
5   Paragraph 3.1.2.
6   Paragraph 3.1.3.

Covert monitoring

6.44   The Information Commissioner considers the covert monitoring of behaviour can only be justified in very limited circumstances. It is suggested that covert monitoring may be necessary where being open with employees is likely to prejudice the prevention or detection of crime, or the apprehension or prosecution of offenders. The Code sets out guidance for covert monitoring in paragraph 3.4:

(a) Senior management should normally authorize any covert monitoring. They should satisfy themselves that there are grounds for suspecting criminal activity or equivalent malpractice and that notifying individuals about the monitoring would prejudice its prevention or detection.

(b) Ensure that any covert monitoring is strictly targeted at obtaining evidence within a set time frame and that the covert monitoring does not continue after the investigation is complete.

(c) Do not use covert audio or video monitoring in areas which workers would genuinely and reasonably expect to be private.

(d) If a private investigator is employed to collect information on workers covertly, make sure there is a contract in place that requires the private investigator to only collect information in a way that satisfies the employer's obligations under the Act.

(e) Ensure that information obtained through covert monitoring is used only for the prevention or detection of criminal activity or equivalent malpractice. Disregard and, where feasible, delete other information collected in the course of monitoring unless it reveals information that no employer could reasonably be expected to ignore.

The organization should document the above points and only use the covert monitoring for the purpose. The organization should also be aware of the interconnection between the provisions of the Regulation of Investigatory Powers Act 2000 and the Anti-Terrorism, Crime and Security Act 2001, because there may be times when the employer is required to monitor covertly under the provisions of these Acts.

Chapter 7

Germany

Dr Martin Eßer

Legal framework

7.1 Electronic signatures in Germany are governed by comprehensive legislation. Basically two sets of rules have to be distinguished: the first set consists of the Signature Act and the Signature Decree, which provides for a secure signature infrastructure and technical standards. It is the prerequisite of the second set, which consists of a large number of statutes prescribing the cases in which the written form can be replaced by the electronic form using an electronic signature. The federal legislator enacts relevant statutes, and the Länder (Germany's 16 federal states) enact respective decrees. As far as federal laws are concerned, the BGB (German Civil Code, 'Bürgerliches Gesetzbuch') and the ZPO (Code of Civil Procedure, 'Zivilprozessordnung'), contain the most important provisions for contracts and procedures. Other provisions regarding the electronic form are contained in the VwVfG (Administrative Procedure Act, 'Verwaltungsverfahrensgesetz'), the VwGO (Rules of the Administrative Courts, 'Verwaltungsgerichtsordnung') and the StPO (Code of Criminal Procedure, 'Strafprozessordnung'). Numerous decrees of the Länder provide the cases and the conditions under which electronic signatures can be used in legal proceedings in the relevant federal state.

Legislation regarding signature infrastructure

SIGNATURE ACT 2001

7.2 The first German Signature Act was enacted in 1997. After the European Union Directive on electronic signatures (1999/93/EC)[1] and an evaluation report by the German government in 1999, the Signature Act was completely revised in 2001.[2] The purpose of the legislation, both the 1997 Act and the revised Act, is to provide a secure signature infrastructure. The legislation provides for standards to be observed by certification service providers and to be met by technical equipment used for the signature process.

The provisions of §§ 4 to 14 of the Signature Act 2001 (SigG) govern the obligations of certification service providers, in particular the allocation of qualified signature certificates to end users and the duties to provide information to the end user. § 11 SigG governs the certification service provider's liability towards third parties, with respect to having good faith in the qualified certificate, qualified time stamp or information issued by the service provider. In the event that a third party suffers any damage as a result of relying on a signature, the service provider becomes liable if it failed to meet the requirements of the Signature Act and the Signature Decree or both, or where the technical equipment of the service provider fails.

Under the former Signature Act 1997, a certification service provider required an authorisation from the supervisory authority before starting certification services. Under the Signature Act 2001, and in accordance with the European Union Directive on electronic signatures (1999/93/EC), such prior authorisation is no longer mandatory. Service providers are only obliged to notify their activities to the Bundesnetzagentur ('Federal Network Agency') as the public supervisory authority, at the latest when they begin to offer their services (§ 4 III SigG). However, the German legislator made use of the leeway conceded by the European Directive and inserted an optional accreditation for service providers in § 14 SigG. Such accreditation is advantageous for the certification service provider and the user of accredited qualified signatures, because only certificates issued by accredited providers contain a root certificate of the Bundesnetzagentur as seal of approval by the supervisory authority and accreditation (§ 15 SigG). The root certificate reveals to anyone using the signature that a certain security level was met. It may also constitute a selling point for certification service providers. Furthermore, the Signature Act 2001 provides, in § 17 SigG, that secure signature units ('sichere Signaturerstellungseinheiten') have to be used for the storage of the signature key and the signature process for qualified electronic signatures. Secure signature units may be approved by inspection authorities designated by the Bundesnetzagentur (§ 18 SigG).

Amendments to the Signature Act 2001 were made in 2005[3] and 2007.[4] Among other changes to the Signature Act, the first amendment in 2005 clarified that only users of qualified electronic signatures have to hold a certificate assigned to them. This resolved any doubt if users of advanced signatures need such certificates. Other amendments to the Signature Act 2001 are of minor importance and will not be addressed here for the purpose of conciseness.

1   Directive 1999/93/EC of the European Parliament and of the Council of 13 December 1999 on a Community framework for electronic signatures, OJ L 13, 19.01.2000, p. 12.
2   Federal Law Gazette ('Bundesgesetzblatt') I 2001, 876. The Signature Act 2001 (SigG) can be found online at www.bundesrecht.juris.de/sigg_2001/index.html.
3   Federal Law Gazette ('Bundesgesetzblatt') I 2005, 2 and 170.

4 Federal Law Gazette ('Bundesgesetzblatt') I 2007, 179. This amendment affected the change of the name of the competent public supervisory authority from 'Regulierungsbehörde für Telekommunikation und Post – RegTP' to 'Bundesnetzagentur für Elektrizität, Gas, Telekommunikation, Post und Eisenbahnen – BNetzA'.

SIGNATURE DECREE 2001

7.3 According to § 24 SigG, the federal government is entitled to enact a Signature Decree in order to specify the duties of the certification service provider at the beginning of its services, during its operations and at the end of its operations. Therefore the Signature Decree 2001 (SigVO)[1] stipulates in particular how a person applying for a qualified certificate has to be identified (§ 3 SigVO), that the certification service provider is required to supply a directory of certificates (§ 4 SigVO), how users have to be informed (§ 6 SigVO) and how certificates must be revoked (§ 7 SigVO). Furthermore, the Signature Decree 2001 addresses the content and the limit of validity of qualified certificates issued by the certification service provider according to the Signature Act, and determines details of the securities to be provided by certification service providers. In accordance with § 17 SigG, the Signature Decree 2001 lays down requirements regarding secure signature units. § 18 SigVO sets up a procedure to declare equality of foreign electronic signatures.

1 The Signature Decree 2001 (SigVO) can be found online at www.bundesrecht.juris.de/bundesrecht/sigv_2001/gesamt.pdf.

PUBLIC SUPERVISORY AUTHORITY

7.4 Pursuant to § 3 SigG, the competent public supervisory authority is the Federal Network Agency ('Bundesnetzagentur für Elektrizität, Gas, Telekommunikation, Post und Eisenbahnen – BNetzA') with its headquarters located in Bonn.[1]

1 Information about the Bundesnetzagentur in English can be found online at www.bundesnetzagentur.de.

Legislation regarding the use of electronic signatures

7.5 Since 2001, some important statutes have been amended with regard to the use of electronic signatures, such as the Formanpassungsgesetz[1] that was amended at the same time as the fundamental revision of the Signature Act in 2001. On 1 April 2005, the Justizkommunikationsgesetz[2] entered into force. This law contains modifications of form requirements in respect of the ZPO (Code of Civil Procedure). After previous amendments were made to the German contract and procedural law as well as to the administrative law, it completes the adjustment of legal requirements for the use of electronic documents by establishing rules for the use of electronic documents in court procedure. At the same time, the evidence rule in the former § 292 a ZPO is replaced by the new § 371 a ZPO which provides for the application of the rules on documentary evidence to apply to electronic documents. The provision leads to the equivalence of electronic documentary evidence with documentary evidence. The provisions of § 416 ZPO applies to documents manually signed by a physical person. Pursuant to §§ 371 a, 416 ZPO a document signed electronically by a physical person constitutes prima facie evidence that the physical person is the originator of the document (prima facie evidence of authenticity). Such evidence can only be rebutted by serious doubts that the physical person did not sign the document electronically. In a trial, the other party has the burden of submitting sufficient facts to support serious doubts. The rules of evidence rules also apply to documents signed electronically by public authorities (§§ 371 a, 437 ZPO). Further provisions, § 298 and § 298 a ZPO, concern the transformation of electronic documents to paper and vice versa, and obtaining access to electronic records. The use of electronic files, § 298 a ZPO, is subject to decrees passed by the Länder, some of which have already been created for single pilot projects.

1   Complete title of the law: 'Gesetz zur Anpassung der Formvorschriften des Privatrechts und anderer Vorschriften an den modernen Rechtsverkehr'; Federal Law Gazette ('Bundesgesetzblatt') I 2001, 1542.
2   Federal Law Gazette ('Bundesgesetzblatt') I 2005, 837.

BGB (GERMAN CIVIL CODE)

7.6   The BGB (German Civil Code, 'Bürgerliches Gesetzbuch') contains an essential rule for the use of qualified electronic signatures in legal acts. Pursuant to § 126 III BGB, the written form can be replaced by an electronic form: '[...] If the written form is prescribed by law, the document must be signed by the issuer with his name in his own hand, or by his notarially certified mark. [...] The written form may be replaced by the electronic form, unless otherwise provided by statute'.[1] The term 'electronic form' is defined in § 126 a BGB: '[...] If the electronic form is to replace the written form prescribed by law, the issuer of the declaration must add his name to it and provide the electronic document with a qualified electronic signature in accordance with the Signature Act. In the case of a contract, the parties must each provide a counterpart with an electronic signature [...]'.[2] In principle, the written form may be replaced by the electronic form, but as mentioned in § 126 BGB, the legislator has made some exceptions by which replacement by the electronic form is excluded and written form is required for effectiveness, for instance, in the termination of employment by notice of termination or separation agreement,[3] a written letter of reference on employment,[4] declaration of bond,[5] debt commitment,[6] debt acknowledgement[7] and entering a consumer loan contract.[8]

1   Excerpt from § 126 BGB.
2   Excerpt from § 126 a BGB.

3   § 623 BGB.
4   § 630 BGB.
5   § 766 BGB.
6   § 780 BGB.
7   § 781 BGB.
8   § 492 BGB.

ZPO (CODE OF CIVIL PROCEDURE)

7.7 The provisions of the ZPO (Code of Civil Procedure, 'Zivilprozeßordnung') regarding electronic signatures are very important, because other statutes of judicial procedure refer to the ZPO in this respect. The legislator inserted provisions on electronic documents established by the parties for the purposes of a trial and for the production of evidence by third parties (§ 130 a ZPO), on judicial electronic documents (§ 130 b ZPO), the creation of hard copies from such electronic documents (§ 298 ZPO) and electronic file management (§ 298 a ZPO).[1]

The provisions of § 130 a ZPO stipulate that if written form is required for pleadings (and exhibits to pleading), claims and declarations of the parties or if written form is required for information, statements, opinions and declarations of third parties, an electronic document shall suffice under the condition that the electronic document is suitable for processing by the court. The responsible person is required to attach a qualified electronic signature to the electronic document. This means that practically all correspondence with the court may be done electronically. If an electronic document submitted to court is not suitable for processing by the court, this has to be notified to the sender by the court without delay including the applicable technical specifications. Before electronic documents can be exchanged with the court, the federal government and the governments of the Länder need to specify in decrees from which point in time electronic documents may be submitted to the court. Pursuant to § 130 a II ZPO, the admission of electronic forms may be restricted to certain courts. An electronic document is submitted to the court as soon as the court's equipment dedicated to receive electronic documents recorded the electronic document.[2]

The provisions of § 130 b ZPO correspond to § 130 a ZPO and enable courts to produce electronic documents: 'As far as this Act stipulates for a handwritten signature of the judge, judicial officer, the clerk of the court, or the bailiff, the record as an electronic document shall suffice if the responsible person prints her name at the end of the document and attaches a qualified electronic signature to it.' As a consequence of §§ 130 a, 130 b ZPO case files may be managed electronically (§ 298 a ZPO). But electronic case file management requires the federal government and the government of the Länder to prescribe the point in time from which in their domain case files will be administrated electronically, as well as the applicable organisational and technical framework requirements for the creation, administration and storage of electronic case files. The governments of the Länder can assign this authority to the provincial justice administrations by decree. The admission of electronic case files may be restricted to certain courts or proceedings. Paper documents and other documents submitted to courts are converted into electronic documents to replace the original. The electronic document must contain the details such as when and by whom they have been converted into electronic form. The documents are stored until the binding completion of the trial if they are required in paper form.

The courts may produce hard copies of electronic documents for the case files. Pursuant to § 298 ZPO, the hard copy must contain the following annotations: (a) the result of the integrity check of the document, (b) who is identified as the signature holder by the signature check and (c) which point in time is identified as the time of attachment of the signature according to the signature check. Even if a hard copy was created, the electronic document must be stored at least until the binding completion of the trial.[3]

1   Amendments made by the Justizkommunikationsgesetz 2005. The complete ZPO can be found (in German language) online at www.gesetze-im-internet.de/bundesrecht/zpo/gesamt.pdf.
2   § 130 a III ZPO.
3   § 298 III ZPO.

OTHER IMPORTANT PROCEDURAL RULES

7.8   The newly created §§ 55 a and 55 b VwGO (Code of Administrative Courts Procedure, 'Verwaltungsgerichtsordnung') contain provisions equivalent to §§ 130 b, 298, and 298 a ZPO for trials at the administrative courts. The same applies to the newly created §§ 52 a and 52 b FGO (Code of Financial Courts Procedure, 'Finanzgerichtsordnung') for trials at the finance courts, to §§ 65a and 65b SGG (Code of Social Courts Procedure, 'Sozialgesetzbuch') for trials at the social courts, to §§ 46 c and 46 d ArbGG (Code of Labour Courts Procedure, 'Arbeitsgerichtsgesetz') for trials at labour courts.

Unlike the procedural rules mentioned above, the newly created provision § 41 a StPO (Code of Criminal Procedure, 'Strafprozessordnung') does not mirror all provisions of the ZPO with regard to electronic case files. § 41 a StPO contains a provision similar to § 130 a ZPO, allowing the submission of electronic documents to the court during trials. Due to the fundamental criminal procedure principals, the StPO does not contain provisions for the electronic formation of case files.

Case law

7.9   A summary of relevant electronic signature cases is provided below.

(a) Decision of the BFH (Federal Finance Court, 'Bundesfinanzhof') dated 14 September 2005, file number VII B 138/05, regarding § 52 a FGO: For an appeal to be submitted in due form it must contain a qualified electronic signature if submitted electronically. Otherwise it is inadmissible. In this case the appeal was submitted by an ordinary, signed email and was thus held to be inadmissible.

(b) Decision of the BFH dated 18 October 2006, file number XI R 22/06, regarding former § 77 a FGO: If submitted electronically, also under § 77 a FGO, the appeal had to be submitted with a qualified electronic signature. If such signature contained a monetary restriction, which restricts the kind of transactions it can be used for (€ 100, - in this case), such restriction does not impair the validity of the signature for the purposes of legal appeals.

(c) Decision of the OVG Rheinland-Pfalz (Higher Administrative Court Rheinland-Pfalz, 'Oberverwaltungsgericht Rheinland-Pfalz') dated 21 April 2006, file number 10 A 11741/05, regarding § 55 a VwGO: An electronically submitted document has no legal effect and is not suited to meet a procedural deadline if it is not provided with a qualified electronic signature. In this case the deadline for appeal was not met for that reason.

(d) Decision of the Bayerischer VGH (Higher Administrative Court Bavaria, 'Bayerischer Verwaltungsgerichtshof') dated 8 November 2005, file number 12 ZB 05.2821, regarding former § 86 a VwGO: Former § 86 a VwGO also required a qualified electronic signature for an appeal submitted in electronic form to be admissible. In this case the appellant submitted by ordinary, signed email which was insufficient. The appeal did not qualify as 'in writing' under § 152 VwGO.

(e) Decision of the Hessischer VGH (Higher Administrative Court Hesse, 'Hessischer Vewaltungsgerichtshof') dated 3 November 2005, file number 1 TG 1668/05, regarding former § 86 a VwGO. The decision is similar to the decision of the Bayerischer VGH dated 8 November 2005 mentioned above.

(f) Decision of the VG Sigmaringen (Administrative Court Sigmaringen, 'Verwaltungsgericht Sigmaringen') dated 27 December 2004, file number 5 K 1313/05, regarding former § 86 a VwGO: If submitted in electronic form, an objection against an administrative decision must be provided with a qualified electronic signature to be admissible. Otherwise it is not qualified as 'in writing' under § 70 VwGO. In this case an objection sent by ordinary email was insufficient.

(g) Decision of the BSG (Federal Social Court, 'Bundessozialgericht') dated 18 November 2003, file number B 1 KR 1/02 S, regarding §§ 90, 92 SGG: A claimant going to court must provide his mailing address with the statement of claim. A mere email address is insufficient. In the case a woman who claimed to be homeless provided just an email address and a cell telephone number. Her claim was held inadmissible.

(h) Decision of the BGH (Federal Supreme Court, 'Bundesgerichtshof') dated 10 October 2006, file number XI ZB 40/06, regarding § 130 ZPO: A scanned manuscript signature is not sufficient to be qualified as 'in writing' under § 130 VI ZPO if such a signature is printed on a document which is then sent by facsimile transmission. Referring to a prior decision, the court pointed out that it would have been sufficient if the scanned signature was implemented into a computer fax or if a document was manually signed before being sent by facsimile transmission to court.

Chapter 8

United States of America

Thomas M. Dunlap

8.1 To ensure a method for secure electronic commerce, lawmakers the world over sought a method of electronic authentication that provided the equivalent contractual and legal status of a handwritten signature. An electronic signature was the solution. Sometimes confused with 'digital signatures', which are really a species of electronic signature, many experts believe that electronic signatures are far superior to traditional ink signatures with respect to security due to the difficulty in forging them and in the ease of authentication.[1]

The Uniform Commercial Code (UCC) is clear that 'writings' are not exclusively limited to ink on paper, but rather are 'embodiments of communication reduced to tangible form.'[2] In addition, the UCC states that a signature is a symbol coupled with the intent of a party to authenticate a writing.[3] As courts have held that documents sent by facsimile transmission including signatures are legally binding and valid,[4] logically, an electronic record intended as a signature will meet the same requirement. Even before Congress or any states had taken steps to create a statutory scheme for electronic contracts, courts had specifically held that electronic signatures were valid for the purposes of enforcing contractual obligations. More than ten years before the first Federal legislation was introduced, in the case of *In re RealNetworks, Inc. Privacy Litig.*,[5] the Federal District Court for the Northern District of Illinois held that a licensing agreement on a website will constitute a writing if the agreement can be printed and stored. Similarly, in *CompuServe Inc. v Patterson*,[6] the Sixth Circuit Court of Appeals recognized the validity of an electronic contract between an internet service provider and one of its customers. Since these early decisions technology and legislation have come a long way to refine electronic signature law.

---

1   Marianne Menna, *From Jamestown to the Silicon Valley, Pioneering a Lawless Frontier: The Electronic Signatures in Global and National Commerce Act*, 6 VA J. L. & Tech. 12 (2001); Miriam

A Parmentier, *Legislative Development: Directive 1999/93 on a Community Framework for Electronic Signatures*, 6 Colum. J. Eur. L. 251 (2000).

2   U.C.C. § 1-201(46) (1998).

3   Uniform Commercial Code, § 1-201(39) (Nat'l Conference of Comm'rs on Unif. State Laws 1998).

4   *Madden v Hegadorn*, 565 A.2d 725 (N.J. Super. 1989), *aff'd* 571 A.2d 296 (N.J. 1989).

5   *In re RealNetworks, Inc. Privacy Litig.*, 2000 U.S. Dist. LEXIS 6584 (N.D. Ill. 2000), 2000 WL 631341 (N.D.Ill. 2000).

6   *CompuServe Inc. v Patterson*, 89 F.3d 1257 (6th Cir. 1996).

Electronic Signatures in Global and National Commerce Act

8.2   Commerce in the United States is regulated and controlled through both federal and state legislation. Under the power granted to Congress in the United States constitution, the federal government has the right and responsibility to create laws regulating commerce between the different states, with foreign nations, and with the Indian tribes indigenous to the United States. The right to regulate intrastate commerce remains with the governments of individual states, which are further not precluded from promulgating laws that affect the Federal domain of interstate commerce, providing Congress has not made any law which would otherwise pre-empt the state regulation. With the primary exception of antitrust matters and the specific regulation of certain industries,[1] contract law has generally been considered a matter reserved to state level regulation.

Many states have enacted laws providing for the enforceability of electronic signatures. These statutes followed the Federal legislation signed into law on 30 June 2000 by President Clinton[2], and effective 1 October 2000, and is officially titled the Federal Electronic Signatures on Global and National Commerce Act, more commonly known as 'E-Sign.' E-Sign, found at 15 U.S.C. § 7001, governs electronic signatures in interstate commerce.[3] E-Sign does not specify a single digital signature technology. In fact there are a number of different definitions for an electronic signature. The most pervasive and generally understood definition describes electronic signatures as a paperless method of entering into an electronic contract. To consent to an electronic contract, an individual may be required to click an 'Accept' or 'Agree' button or use a private key to encrypt data that serves as a unique identifier for the signing party by means of a Public Key Infrastructure (PKI). These signatures, under E-Sign, are as binding as inked original signatures.

E-Sign went into effect with the essential purpose of promoting electronic commerce by providing a country-wide Federal law that electronic contracts are valid, legally binding documents, and strengthening consumer protection. Under E-Sign, a contract relating to an electronic transaction may not be denied legal effect, validity or enforceability solely because an electronic signature or record was used in its formation. E-Sign defines an electronic signature as 'an electronic sound, symbol or process, attached to or logically associated with a contract or other record and executed or adopted by a person with the intent to sign the record.'[4] The use of a PIN, a digital signature or even a typed name, could be considered an electronic signature. The contractual issue is whether the electronic signature can be attributed to the person signing and specifically attached to the related record. E-Sign is technologically neutral in that it does not endorse any particular technology but merely requires that the basic requirements of the underlying statute are met.

As a result of numerous congressional subcommittee hearings, the E-Sign statute, while broad in its topical coverage, is very narrow with regard to its effect on substantive law. The National Association of Attorneys General has opined that this broad federal pre-emption would 'unduly hinder the ability of the states to protect their citizens against consumer fraud.'[5] E-Sign is an 'overlay' law, as it does not amend any laws, but provides that any transactions in or affecting interstate or foreign commerce involving a signature, contract or other record 'may not be denied legal effect, validity, or enforceability solely because it is in electronic form.'[6] E-Sign does not affect any other Federal or state statute or common law that applies to electronic transactions. With respect to consumer transactions, Congress was careful to narrow the scope even further, forbidding businesses that are currently required to make certain information available to consumers in writing to supply the information in electronic form unless the consumer has consented to receive such information in electronic form, and only after the consumer has been fully informed about the possibility of receiving such information in writing and what consent is required to receive the information in electronic form.[7]

E-Sign further states that a contract or other record may not be denied legal effect solely because it involved the action of an electronic agent, provided the action of any such electronic agent is legally attributable to the person to be bound.[8] An 'electronic agent' is defined as 'a computer program or an electronic or other automated means used independently to initiate an action or respond to electronic records or performance in whole or in part without review or action by an individual at the time of the action or response.'[9]

Much like the corresponding state versions, E-Sign does not apply to family law issues, wills and trusts, notice of the cancellation of utilities, real estate issues (including repossession, default, acceleration, foreclosure), court orders or notices, the cancellation or termination of health insurance or benefits or life insurance benefits, recall of a product, material failure of a product that risks endangering health or safety, or any document required to accompany any transportation or handling of toxic or dangerous materials or to the Uniform Commercial Code, other than §§ 1-107 and 1-206, and articles 2 and 2A.[10]

E-Sign also contains records retention standards. It states that if a law or regulation requires the retention of records for a particular transaction, the retention requirement may be met by retaining an electronic record, provided certain conditions are met.[11] One of the most important and challenging of these requirements is that the record remains capable of being reproduced for later reference. Therefore, it is important to ensure that the document remains retrievable despite changing technology.

E-Sign provides that if notarization or acknowledgment of a signature or record is required, that requirement is satisfied if the electronic signature of the person notarizing the record is 'attached to or logically associated with the signature or record.'[12]

E-Sign addresses the electronic creation and execution of notes secured by real estate by creating a category of electronic documents known as 'transferable records.' E-Sign defines a 'transferable record' as an electronic record that:

> '(A) would be a note under Article 3 of the Uniform Commercial Code if the electronic record were in writing;
> (B) the issuer of the electronic record expressly has agreed is a transferable record; and
> (C) relates to a loan secured by real property.'[13]

E-Sign states specifically that a transferable record may be executed with an electronic signature and sets forth conditions for determining who is a holder in due course of the transferable record. Among other things, E-Sign requires that there be only a single authoritative copy of the transferable record which is unique, identifiable and unalterable.[14] This is a requirement that is dependent on technology that will be able to ensure that only one authoritative copy exists. In the past, some writers on the subject of E-Sign have opined that the technology is not yet in place to meet this requirement. However, since the implementation of E-Sign, a number of companies have stepped up to provide systems and cryptography that seem to meet the 'authoritative copy' requirement. There are industry groups in the process of developing standards for such technology. This requirement does not preclude making other copies of the transferable record, provided it is clear which copy is for informational purposes and which copy is the 'authoritative' copy.

While there have been significant gains and much optimism from industry groups in recent years, except for certain financial services companies, as of 2001, E-Sign was slow to take off with limited compliance.[15]

---

1   See The Sherman Act, 15 U.S.C. § 1 et seq (2007); See also Carmack Amendment, 49 U.S.C. § 11707 (2007).

2   President Clinton manually signed the Act 'the traditional way, with a felt-tip pen' and then re-signed it for ceremonial purposes, using a digital signature encoded on a smart card. *Electronic Signatures Given Legal Standing*, N.Y. Times, July 1, 2000, at C3. As the Act was not effective immediately, E-Sign could not be invoked to validate the electronic signature used to make it law in the first place.

3   Electronic Signatures Act of 2000, Pub. L. No. 106-229, 114 Stat. 464 (codified as 15 U.S.C. § 7001 et seq (2007)).

4   Electronic Signatures Act of 2000, supra note 3, at § 7006(5).

5   Hearing Before the Subcommittee on Technology, Terrorism and Government Information

of the Committee on the Judiciary United States Senate, 106th Congress, 2nd Session (28 March 2000).
6   Electronic Signatures Act of 2000, supra note 3, at § 7001(a).
7   Section 7001(c)(1)(C) states that the consumer must 'consent electronically, in a manner that reasonably demonstrates that the consumer can access information in the electronic form that will be used to provide the information that is the subject of the consent.'
8   Electronic Signatures Act of 2000, supra note 3, at § 7001(h).
9   Electronic Signatures Act of 2000, supra note 3, at § 7006(3).
10   Electronic Signatures Act of 2000, supra note 3, at § 7003.
11   Electronic Signatures Act of 2000, supra note 3, at § 7001(d).
12   Electronic Signatures Act of 2000, supra note 3, at § 7001(g).
13   Electronic Signatures Act of 2000, supra note 3, at § 7021.
14   Electronic Signatures Act of 2000, supra note 3, at § 7021(c).
15   Thomas E Crocker, Before the Subcommittee on Domestic Monetary Policy, Technology and Economic Growth Committee on Financial Services U.S. House of Representatives (28 June 2001).

Uniform Electronic Transactions Act

8.3   The Uniform Electronic Transactions Act (UETA)[1] acts as a model for state legislatures to enact law for contracts governed by state law. While many states have adopted UETA in some form, there is hardly any uniformity in the states' enactment of such laws. The state versions of UETA often contain numerous exceptions and modifications. In fact, state legislation became so diverse and changed so quickly, that the Federal government stopped tracking such laws in 2003.[2]

Because the objectives of E-Sign and UETA are the same, that is to facilitate e-commerce by providing a system to enforce and validate electronic signatures, it begs the question of why these practically co-extensive laws co-exist. At least one commentator has observed:

'Without a uniform standard, many jurisdictions ruled inconsistently, while other jurisdictions did not consider the issue. This disparate treatment threatened the legitimacy of on-line agreements and deprived both consumers and businesses of the certainty and predictability expected from well-developed markets. The law's formalities evolved outside of the digital world, and the process of adapting them to it has proven to be more difficult than expected. Congress reacted to this trend by enacting broad legislation to give nationwide validity to electronic records and signatures.'[3]

UETA is one of a number of Uniform Acts proposed by the National Conference of Commissioners on Uniform State Laws (NCCUSL).[4] The primary purpose of UETA is to align various state laws in a number of electronic commerce issues, including the validity of electronic signatures to support valid electronic contracts and retention of paper records. The scope of the act is strictly limited to commercial matters.[5]

Prior to UETA, almost every state required banks to keep a physical record of all checks that had been processed. A number of states have laws governing the maintenance of other records and contracts as well. The aim of UETA, as a model act, was to align states legislation on a national basis to allow for a uniform method for electronic retention of paper records, making the electronic copy as valid as an ink version in intrastate commerce. By the end of 2001, over 38 states had enacted UETA. In 2002 California and Hawaii passed legislation that amended their existing UETA laws. The Act passed by California directly complies with E-Sign, whilst the legislation passed by Hawaii added provisions regarding electronic commerce security. Virginia has revised its electronic signature law to prohibit a signature from being denied legal effect or enforceability solely because it is in electronic form. As of March 2007, 47 states and the District of Columbia had enacted some form of UETA.[6]

UETA defines an 'electronic record' as 'a record created, generated, sent, communicated, received, or stored by electronic means' and 'electronic signature' as 'an electronic sound, symbol, or process attached to or logically associated with a record and executed or adopted by a person with the intent to sign the record.'[7] In the comments to this section, the authors noted that 'in the paper world, it is assumed that the symbol adopted by a party is attached to or located somewhere in the same paper that is intended to be authenticated, eg, an allonge firmly attached to a promissory note, or the classic signature at the end of a long contract. These tangible manifestations do not exist in the electronic environment, and accordingly, this definition expressly provides that the symbol must in some way be linked to, or connected with, the electronic record being signed.'[8]

UETA does not require parties to conduct business electronically; rather, it allows transactions 'between parties each of which has agreed to conduct transactions by electronic means.'[9] Absent a formal contract, the context, parties' conduct and surrounding circumstances act as the primary determiners of whether or not the parties agree to conduct a transaction electronically. Any consent provision to an electronic transaction must be conspicuously displayed and separately consented to in the contract. Alternatively, the parties to an electronic transaction could agree in a separate document to consent to conduct a given transaction electronically. Conversely, E-Sign requires a specific electronic consent from a consumer before an electronic notice may replace a legally required written notice.

UETA also deals with the evidentiary weight a court may give to an electronic signature.[10] Similar to E-Sign, UETA also contains provisions for electronic agent notarization, transferability of records and contract formation. Unlike E-Sign, UETA is similar to the Uniform Commercial Code in that it allows parties to modify its provisions in a contract unless specifically prohibited by UETA. Section 8 provides that 'An electronic record is not capable of retention by the recipient if the sender or its information processing system inhibits the ability of the recipient to print or store the electronic record.'

Additionally, any such contract that could not be stored or printed would not be enforceable, thus creating a unique statutory electronic contract defence under s 8(c). Specifically, this section would prevent the proponent of an electronic contract that could not be saved on a local machine or printed by the other party, wherein the author can prevent both printing and saving of a document.

Section 12(a) of UETA states that if a record must be legally retained, an electronic record is a viable substitute for paper if it accurately reflects the original information and remains accessible for later reference. Part (a) may be satisfied by using a third party for storage. An example of this type of requirement can be found in statutes enacted by many states using digital certificate programs for notaries that allow a certificate to be affixed to a document through prompts in the software program being used (sometimes referred to as 'e-notarization'). The certificate serves to identify the notary signing the document, seal the document and ensure that it has not been tampered with after leaving the notary's possession. The document is then forwarded electronically to its next destination or to the end user.

Some states have created particular requirements for electronic signatures, known as 'digital signature' acts. These acts exceed the scope of UETA in an effort to make the transaction more secure, usually by requiring that some form of encryption be employed. Conversely, both E-Sign and UETA have remained technologically neutral in respect of legitimizing electronic signatures. While E-Sign clearly pre-empts any state law requiring contracts or signatures to be in non-electronic form, provision is made in E-Sign for a limited exemption to federal pre-emption so that a state may modify, limit or supersede some E-Sign provisions if the superseding law is an enactment of UETA. While E-Sign specifically mandates pre-emption by its provisions, unless the state has enacted UETA, whether the E-Sign actually pre-empts state digital signature acts or other state laws has been and continues to be the subject of much debate.

One of the only cases in the United States that has dealt squarely with the issue of pre-emption, did so only in dicta. In *People v McFarlan*,[11] Justice Lewis Bart Stone of the Supreme Court of New York compared UETA with the New York Electronic Signatures and Records Act, finding 'that ESRA is not the same as, a clone of, or even similar to UETA. . . . E-Sign, thus, to the extent it was so enacted pre-empts ESRA.' While not reaching the merits of the constitutional argument, the Justice noted that as much the United States Supreme Court held in *Printz v United States*,[12] regarding the imposition by Congress of mandatory background checks for handgun purchases, E-Sign's 'effective imposition of a federal rule on state records . . . may well constitute a violation against the rule against commandeering the activities of a state to achieve a federal purpose.'

As technology becomes more reliable, common and acceptable in commerce, digital signature law in the United States has become more pervasive.

UETA and E-Sign have already changed the face of business and will continue to evolve through legislative mandate and judicial interpretation.

1   Originally promulgated in 1999 as a Model Act by the National Conference of Commissioners on Uniform State Laws.

2   See the former www.uetaonline.com, a site that formerly maintained a state by state comparison, but has since been removed because states have amended their laws too frequently.

3   Carl Carl, Corey Ciocchetti, Wes Barton and Nathan Christensen, 'Are Online Business Transactions Executed By Electronic Signatures Legally Binding?', 2001 Duke L. & Tech. Rev. 0005 (2001).

4   The National Conference of Commissioners on Uniform State Laws is a non-profit unincorporated association, comprised of state commissions on uniform laws from each state, the District of Columbia, the Commonwealth of Puerto Rico, and the U.S. Virgin Islands which was formed in 1892 to promote the uniformity of state laws. As of 2007, only four states have not adopted some form of UETA (Georgia, Illinois, New York and Washington), however, these states have similar laws governing electronic signatures.

5   'The Scope of this Act is inherently limited by the fact that it only applies to transactions related to business, commercial (including consumer) and governmental matters. Consequently, transactions with no relation to business, commercial or governmental transactions would not be subject to this Act. Unilaterally generated electronic records and signatures which are not part of a transaction also are not covered by this Act.' Uniform Electronic Transactions Act, pmbl. (Nat'l Conference of Comm'rs on Unif. State Laws 1999).

6   National Conference of State Legislatures website, UETA Enactments, at www.ncsl.org/programs/lis/CIP/ueta-statutes.htm.

7   Electronic Signatures Act of 2000, Pub. L. No. 106–229, 114 Stat. 464 (Codified as 15 U.S.C. § 7001 et seq (2007)), at § 7002.

8   Uniform Electronic Transactions Act, § 2 cmt. 7 (Nat'l Conference of Comm'rs on Unif. State Laws 1999). This correlation is consistent with the regulations promulgated by the Food and Drug Administration. 21 C.F.R. §11 (1997).

9   Electronic Signatures Act of 2000, supra note 7, at § 7001.

10 15 U.S.C. 7013 states that: 'In a proceeding, evidence of a record or signature may not be excluded solely because it is in electronic form.'

11 744 N.Y.S.2d 287 (N.Y. Misc. 2002) cert. denied, 802 N.Y.S.2d 359 (2005).

12 521 U.S. 898 (1997).

Chapter 9

International comparison of electronic signature laws

9.1 The framework within which legislation is drafted will invariably depend on the decisions made by politicians. Whilst the existence of the UNCITRAL Model Law on Electronic Commerce and Model Law on Electronic Signatures have acted as a guide for many states when enacting legislation, other factors help shape the formation of legislation, such as the regional requirements provided by the European Union in the form of the Directive on electronic signatures.[1] In an early report by the Internet Law and Policy Forum,[2] it was suggested it is possible for there to be a tension between legislation that seeks to be technologically neutral and the establishment of legal rules to provide for electronic authentication. In any event, as legal rules are developed, governments will invariably have to amend legislation relating to electronic signatures in the light of the development of new technologies and decisions by the courts.

1 Directive 1999/93/EC of the European Parliament and of the Council of 13 December 1999 on a Community framework for electronic signatures, OJ L 13, 19.01.2000, p. 12.
2 Stewart Baker and Matthew Yeo 'Survey of International Electronic and Digital Signature Initiatives' available online at www.ilpf.org/groups/survey.htm and Chris Kuner, Rosa Barcelo, Stewart Baker and Eric Greenwald, 'An Analysis of International Electronic and Digital Signature Implementation Initiatives A Study Prepared for the Internet Law & Policy Forum' (September, 2000), available online at www.ilpf.org/groups/analysis_IEDSII.htm.

Approaches to legislation

Functional equivalent concept

9.2 Many civil law jurisdictions have established legislation that is prescriptive in nature, with the intention of establishing a particular type of technology as a means to replace a manuscript signature in the electronic environment.

The digital signature is considered to have a greater legal effect than that of an electronic signature in any other format, as in the case of Japan,[1] Malaysia,[2] Nepal,[3] the Philippines[4] and South Korea.[5] For instance, many of the states in Latin America have developed laws based on the UNCITRAL Model Law on Electronic Signatures and the European Union Directive on electronic signatures,[6] and the laws passed by Azarbaijan,[7] Egypt,[8] India,[9] and the Russian Federation[10] only appear to provide for digital signatures, but other forms of signature also appear to be acceptable by agreement, such as the provisions of the relevant Russian Code.[11] It is not clear, judging by the English translation of the legislation in Ukraine,[12] whether the provisions only relate to a digital signature, or include other forms of electronic signature: if advising on the legal force of documents signed electronically in the Ukraine, further advice will be necessary, although this comment also refers to all other jurisdictions mentioned in this text. Although there is an emphasis on the digital signature as the functional equivalent of a manuscript signature, generally the legislation also permits the use of other forms of electronic signature, which also suggests a two-tier approach as discussed below.

1   Law Concerning Electronic Signatures and Certification Services (Law No.102 of 2000).
2   Digital Signature Act 1997; Md. Abdul Jalil and Leo D. Pointon, 'e-Contract law – Malaysia', *Computer Law & Security Report*, 2004, Volume 20 Number 2, 117–124.
3   The Electronic Transactions Ordinance, 2005.
4   Electronic Commerce Act of 2000, Republic Act No 8792.
5   Electronic Signature Act 1999·2·5 Act No. 5792.
6   Mercedes Rivolta and Patricia Prandini 'Argentine public key infrastructure development – a comparative study of PKI experiences in Latin America' Chief of Cabinet Office, Argentine Federal Government (ID #G131 25 April 2002).
7   Electronic Signatures and Electronic Documents 2004.
8   Law No 15/2004 on E-signature and Establishment of the Information Technology Industry Development Authority; HH Judge Ehab Maher Elsonbaty, 'The electronic signature law: between creating the future and the future of creation,' *e-Signature Law Journal* (now the *Digital Evidence Journal*), 2005, Volume 2 Number 1, 60–64.
9   Information Technology Act 2000, although the law has been substantially revised, although the amendments were not passed at the time of writing. The revisions reduce the reliance on digital signatures.
10   Federal Law No. 1-FZ on Electronic Digital Signature.
11   Victor Naumov and Tatiana Nikiforova, 'Electronic signatures in Russian law', *e-Signature Law Journal* (now the *Digital Evidence Journal*), 2005, Volume 2 Number 2, 100–104.
12   On the electronic digital signature No. 852-IV of May 22, 2003.

ARGENTINA

Digital signature equivalence

9.3   Thus the Ley De Firma Digital N° 25.506 passed by Argentina in 2001,[1] which is similar to those passed by Brazil,[2] Chile,[3] Colombia,[4] Costa Rica,[5] and laws of the Dominican Republic,[6] Ecuador,[7] Mexico,[8] Panama,[9] Peru,[10] Uruguay[11] and Venezuela,[12] provides for the functional equivalent of a manuscript signature in article 3, in that a digital signature is considered to be the equivalent of a manuscript signature:

'ARTICULO 3º — Del requerimiento de firma. Cuando la ley requiera una firma manuscrita, esa exigencia también queda satisfecha por una firma digital. Este principio es aplicable a los casos en que la ley establece la obligación de firmar o prescribe consecuencias para su ausencia.

ARTICLE 3. — On the requirement of signature. When the law requires a handwritten signature, this requirement is also met by a digital signature. This principle is applicable to those cases in which the law establishes the obligation of signing or prescribes consequences for the absence of a signature.'

Where a digital signature is used, the legislation requires it to be verified by a third party by way of the Application Authority, and the verification will not only identify the signing party, but is required to detect any alteration to the document after it has been signed. In addition, there is a requirement that the digital signature be controlled by the signing party and be under their absolute control, as provided for in article 2:

'ARTICULO 2º — Firma Digital. Se entiende por firma digital al resultado de aplicar a un documento digital un procedimiento matemático que requiere información de exclusivo conocimiento del firmante, encontrándose ésta bajo su absoluto control. La firma digital debe ser susceptible de verificación por terceras partes, tal que dicha verificación simultáneamente permita identificar al firmante y detectar cualquier alteración del documento digital posterior a su firma.

Los procedimientos de firma y verificación a ser utilizados para tales fines serán los determinados por la Autoridad de Aplicación en consonancia con estándares tecnológicos internacionales vigentes.

ARTICLE 2. — Digital Signature. A digital signature is the result of applying a mathematical procedure to a digital document, that requires information controlled exclusively by the signing party and which is under his absolute control. The digital signature must be verifiable by third parties, such that this verification will simultaneously permit the identification of the signing party and detect any alteration of the digital document after it has been signed.

The signature and verification procedures to be used for this purpose shall be those established by the Application Authority in accordance with current international technological standards.'

1   The English translation is from the Firma Digital website at www.pki.gov.ar.
2   Medida Provisoria Nº 2.200-2, de 24 de Agosto de 2001 Institui a Infra-Estrutura de Chaves Públicas Brasileira – ICP-Brasil, e dá outras providências; Cristina de Hollanda 'Electronic

Signatures and Digital Certification: The Liability of Registry Authorities under Brazilian Legislation' *e-Signature Law Journal* (now *Digital Evidence Journal*), 2004, Volume 1 Number 1, 23–24; Professor Carlos Alberto Rohrmann, 'Electronic Signatures and court proceedings in Brazil' *Digital Signature Journal*, 2006, Volume 3 Number 1, 5–9.

3   Ley Sobre Documentos Electronicos, Firma Electronica y Servicios de Certificación de Dicha Firma No 19.799, 25 de marzo 2002 and Ley de bases sobre contratos administrativos de suministro y de prestación de servicios Nº 19.886 11 de julio de 2003.

4   Ley Por No 527 de agosto 18 de 1999 medio de la cual se define y reglamenta el acceso y uso de los mensajes de datos, del comercio electrónico y de las firmas digitales, y se establecen las entidades de certificación y se dictan otras disposiciones and Ley 588 de julio 5 de 2000 Por medio de la cual se reglamenta el ejercicio de la actividad notarial.

5   Ley número 8454, de Certificados, Firmas Digitales y Documentos Electrónicos.

6   Ley 126-02 sobre Comercio Electrónico, Documentos y Firmas Digitales de fecha 20 de septiembre de 2002.

7   Ley de Comercio Electrónico, Firmas y Mensajes de Datos, Ley No. 67.

8   The Commercial Code (Articles 80 and 89–114) and Civil Code (Articles 1803, 1805, 1811 and 1834) have been amended to provide for electronic transactions.

9   Ley No 43 de 31 de julio de 2001 Que define y regula los documentos y firmas electrónicas y las entidades de certificación en el comercio electrónico, y el intercambio de documentos electrónicos.

10 Ley No 27269 Ley de Firmas y Certificados Digitales.

11 Ley No 16.002, Ley No 16.736 and Ley No 17.243.

12 Decreto con Fuerza de Ley No.1.204 Sobre Mensajes de Datos y Firmas Electrónicas.

Other forms of electronic signature

9.4   By comparison, other forms of electronic signature are not recognized as the functional equivalent of a manuscript signature unless the parties recognize it. This is somewhat ironic, given that the most basic of all electronic signatures, the 'I accept' icon on websites, is probably one of the most popular and most used of any form of electronic signature. This state of affairs in Argentina is illustrated in the cases of *Huberman Fernando Pablo c/Industrias Audiovisuales Argentinas SA s/despido*,[1] and *Cooperativa de Vivienda Crédito y Consumo Fiduciaria LTDA c/Becerra Leguizamón Hugo Ramón s/incidente de apelación*,[2] the details of both of which are outlined elsewhere in this text.

If a party relies on such a signature, it is for them to prove its validity, as provided for in article 5:

'ARTICULO 5º — Firma electrónica. Se entiende por firma electrónica al conjunto de datos electrónicos integrados, ligados o asociados de manera lógica a otros datos electrónicos, utilizado por el signatario como su medio de identificación, que carezca de alguno de los requisitos legales para ser considerada firma digital. En caso de ser desconocida la firma electrónica corresponde a quien la invoca acreditar su validez.

ARTICLE 5. — Electronic signature. An electronic signature is a set of integrated electronic data, linked or associated logically to other electronic data, used by the signing party as his means of identification, which lacks any of the necessary requirements to be considered a digital signature. If an electronic signature is not recognized, it is up to the party that invokes it to prove its validity.'

1   (29884/02 S. 56885 – CNTRAB – SALA VI – Buenos Aires, 23 de febrero de 2004 (Published in www.elDial.com.ar Cite: elDial AA1E25).
2   CNCOM – SALA A 16645/2006 – Buenos Aires Junio 27 de 2006 (Published in www.elDial.com.ar Cite elDial – AA379B).

The minimalist approach

AUSTRALIA

9.5   The Attorney General of Australia requested an expert group to report on a proposed legal framework for electronic commerce, which was duly published in 1998. The expert group conducted a wide-ranging survey of the laws that had been or were to be enacted, and reached a conclusion that it was appropriate not to take a prescriptive approach towards the legal recognition of electronic signatures for a number of reasons:

'A legislative electronic signature regime is not required

Consideration of the legal issues raised by electronic commerce is sometimes complicated by the discussion of electronic signatures, a term which is used to refer to a range of technologies intended to ensure the security and certainty of electronic commerce, and in particular one of these technologies, namely digital signatures. Many jurisdictions overseas have enacted or drafted legislation to facilitate the use of electronic signatures. We have analysed a number of these enacted or proposed legislative regimes in Chapter 3. These legislative regimes go beyond ensuring the legal effect of electronic signatures and their functional equivalence with paper-based signatures.

It is our view that the enactment of legislation which creates a detailed legislative regime for electronic signatures needs to be considered with caution. There is the risk, particularly given the lack of any internationally uniform legislative approach, that an inappropriate legislative regime may be adopted without regard to market-oriented solutions. Given the pace of technological development and change in this area, it is more appropriate for the market to determine issues other than legal effect, such as the levels of security and reliability required for electronic signatures. Accordingly, we have recommended that legislation should deal simply with the legal effect of electronic signatures. While a number of articles in the Model Law deal with electronic signature issues that go beyond legal effect, it is our view that these issues should be left to the existing law in Australia. Whether the existing Australian law deals with these issues adequately or not, the same situation should apply to both paper-based commerce and electronic commerce. At this stage we are not persuaded of the need to give a legislative advantage to electronic commerce not available to traditional means of communication. If a clear need to deal with these issues appears in the future the recommended legislation can be amended.'[1]

The Australian government followed the recommendations of the expert group and adopted article 7 of the UNCITRAL Model Law on Electronic Commerce. This decision was made on the premise that there is no internationally uniform legislative approach to this issue, and it is important merely to deal with the legal effect of electronic signatures. By taking this approach, the Australian government have decided to allow the market to determine the issues that do not have a legal effect, such as levels of security and reliability. The view taken by the expert group is reflected in the provisions of s 10 of the Electronic Transactions Act 1999 (Cth) of the Commonwealth of Australia:

'10   Signature

Requirement for signature

(1)   If, under a law of the Commonwealth, the signature of a person is required, that requirement is taken to have been met in relation to an electronic communication if:

(a)   in all cases—a method is used to identify the person and to indicate the person's approval of the information communicated; and

(b)   in all cases—having regard to all the relevant circumstances at the time the method was used, the method was as reliable as was appropriate for the purposes for which the information was communicated; and

(c)   if the signature is required to be given to a Commonwealth entity, or to a person acting on behalf of a Commonwealth entity, and the entity requires that the method used as mentioned in paragraph (a) be in accordance with particular information technology requirements—the entity's requirement has been met; and

(d)   if the signature is required to be given to a person who is neither a Commonwealth entity nor a person acting on behalf of a Commonwealth entity—the person to whom the signature is required to be given consents to that requirement being met by way of the use of the method mentioned in paragraph (a).'

No form of electronic signature is set out or required in this instance. The focus is on the method used to communicate intention and to ensure the method chosen is appropriate for the purposes of the information. Hence an 'I accept' icon can be equally as effective when used to indicate the agreement for the purchase of goods or services from a trader operating a website, as the complexity associated with the use of a digital signature. The important issue is whether the intent is manifest and the method is appropriate to the particular transaction. The case of *Faulks v Cameron*[2] is interesting from the perspective of the method and whether the method used is appropriate to the particular transaction, because in this case, involving a separation between two people, there was an exchange of emails, and the plaintiff successfully sought to submit that the email correspondence constituted a separation agreement. Inevitably whether the method is appropriate seems to be somewhat irrelevant, given the propensity of individuals to use whatever form of communication is available, without thought to the legal consequences of the actual method of communication: it was ever thus, and seems somewhat unusual that legislators should begin to impose such requirements in the internet age, especially as such requirements were not imposed in the age of the telegram.

1 'Electronic commerce: Building the legal framework' Report of the electronic commerce expert group to the Attorney General 31 March 1998 Executive Summary.
2 [2004] 32 Fam LR 417; [2004] NTSC 61.

CANADA

9.6 The Uniform Law Conference of Canada has prepared two important documents that have helped shape legislation in Canada, the Uniform Electronic Evidence Act and the Uniform Electronic Commerce Act. The primary focus of the Uniform Electronic Evidence Act is to replace the concept of an original document with the proof of the reliability of a system instead of the reliability of an individual record, and using standards to demonstrate the reliability of a system. The Uniform Electronic Commerce Act provides a single, media neutral, definition of an electronic signature in s 1(b):

'(b) "electronic signature" means information in electronic form that a person has created or adopted in order to sign a document and that is in, attached to or associated with the document.'

However, the Uniform Act also permits, in s 10(2), a standard of reliability to be imposed where it is considered necessary by the relevant authority:

'Signatures

10. (1) A requirement under [enacting jurisdiction] law for the signature of a person is satisfied by an electronic signature.

(2) For the purposes of subsection (1), the [authority responsible for the requirement] may make a regulation that,
    (a) the electronic signature shall be reliable for the purpose of identifying the person, in the light of all the circumstances, including any relevant agreement and the time the electronic signature was made; and

(b)   the association of the electronic signature with the relevant electronic document shall be reliable for the purpose for which the electronic document was made, in the light of all the circumstances, including any relevant agreement and the time the electronic signature was made.

(3)   For the purposes of subsection (1), where the signature or signed document is to be provided to the Government, the requirement is satisfied only if

   (a)   the Government or the part of Government to which the information is to be provided has consented to accept electronic signatures; and

   (b)   the electronic document meets the information technology standards and requirements as to method and as to reliability of the signature, if any, established by the Government or part of Government, as the case may be.'

The provisions of this clause seek, as noted by the comments to the Uniform Act make clear, to link a person to a document, and this section seeks to ensure an electronic signature functions as a signature in law. The person creating or adopting the document in electronic format must have the requisite intent and their intent must be associated to the document in some way. In this respect, the Uniform Act does not incorporate the test of appropriate reliability, as set out in the UNCITRAL Model Law.

GUERNSEY

9.7   The Electronic Transactions (Guernsey) Law 2000 also takes a minimalist approach to electronic signatures, providing a single definition in s 22(1):

'"signature in electronic form" means a signature wholly or partly in electronic form attached to or logically associated with information in electronic or non-electronic form, and references to a signature being in electronic form shall be construed accordingly;'

The Law does not, in s 8 'Requirement of form,' require any particular type of electronic signature to satisfy the law where a signature is required.

THE UNITED STATES OF AMERICA

9.8   The enactment of the Electronic Signatures in Global and National Commerce Act, 15 U.S.C. §§ 7001–7003 in 2000 has provided for a broad definition of an electronic signature, set out in s 106(5):

'(5)   ELECTRONIC SIGNATURE. – The term "electronic signature" means an electronic sound, symbol, or process, attached to or logically associated with a contract or other record and executed or adopted by a person with the intent to sign the record.'

Whilst the Act provides various safeguards for consumers in relation to the provision of electronic records, the definition of an electronic signature permits any format of electronic signature to be acceptable, and this is reflected in the case law discussed elsewhere in this text.

The two-tier approach

UNCITRAL

9.9   The United Nations has adopted the two-tier approach between the two Model Laws. Article 7 of the Model Law on Electronic Commerce provides for an electronic signature relates to the form such a signatures takes and whether it is appropriate in the circumstances:

'Article 7.   Signature

(1)   Where the law requires a signature of a person, that requirement is met in relation to a data message if:

   (a)   a method is used to identify that person and to indicate that person's approval of the information contained in the data message; and

   (b)   that method is as reliable as was appropriate for the purpose for which the data message was generated or communicated, in the light of all the circumstances, including any relevant agreement.

(2)   Paragraph (1) applies whether the requirement therein is in the form of an obligation or whether the law simply provides consequences for the absence of a signature.'

The Model Law on Electronic Signatures has taken one step further by incorporating the provisions of article 7 of the Model Law on Electronic Commerce and adding a provision relating to the reliability of a signature:

'Article 6   Compliance with a requirement for a signature

1.   Where the law requires a signature of a person, that requirement is met in relation to a data message if an electronic signature is used that is as reliable as was appropriate for the purpose for which the data message was generated or communicated, in the light of all the circumstances, including any relevant agreement.

2.   Paragraph 1 applies whether the requirement referred to therein is in the form of an obligation or whether the law simply provides consequences for the absence of a signature.

3.   An electronic signature is considered to be reliable for the purpose of satisfying the requirement referred to in paragraph 1 if:

(a) The signature creation data are, within the context in which they are used, linked to the signatory and to no other person;

(b) The signature creation data were, at the time of signing, under the control of the signatory and of no other person;

(c) Any alteration to the electronic signature, made after the time of signing, is detectable; and

(d) Where a purpose of the legal requirement for a signature is to provide assurance as to the integrity of the information to which it relates, any alteration made to that information after the time of signing is detectable.'

4. Paragraph 3 does not limit the ability of any person:

(a) To establish in any other way, for the purpose of satisfying the requirement referred to in paragraph 1, the reliability of an electronic signature; or

(b) To adduce evidence of the non-reliability of an electronic signature.'

The provision of certainty as to the legal effect that follows the use of an electronic signature is left for the enacting state, although the Model Law seeks to expressly establish the legal effects that will result where the technical characteristics set out in article 6(3)(a) to (d) apply, and which a digital signature is capable of conforming to.

EUROPEAN UNION

9.10 The European Union Directive on a common framework for electronic signatures also adopts a two-tier approach. The Directive distinguishes between an electronic signature and a qualified certificate. The electronic signature is defined in article 2(1) as:

'"electronic signature" means data in electronic form which are attached to or logically associated with other electronic data and which serve as a method of authentication;'

An electronic signature is admissible in evidence if it complies with the definition in article 2(1), although it only serves as a tool to authenticate data. In contrast, a qualified certificate is capable of identifying a person or entity, providing it meets the technical requirements of Annexe I. A definition is not given in article 2(2), but a list of characteristics that relate to performance criteria:

'"advanced electronic signature" means an electronic signature which meets the following requirements:

(a) it is uniquely linked to the signatory;

(b) it is capable of identifying the signatory;

(c) it is created using means that the signatory can maintain under his sole control; and

(d) it is linked to the data to which it relates in such a manner that any subsequent change of the data is detectable;'

To be admissible, an advanced electronic signature must have a qualified certificate and it is required to be created by a secure-signature-creation device. The necessary technical requirements are set out in Annex I and a qualified certificate must be provided by a certification-service-provider who fulfils the stipulations set out in Annex II. The provisions relating to the advanced electronic signature suggest that such a signature can only be capable of being made with a private key stored on a medium that an individual has total physical control over, such as a smart card.

The Directive has been implemented by Austria;[1] Belgium;[2] Bulgaria,[3] Cyprus,[4] Czech Republic;[5] Denmark;[6] Estonia, although it only refers to digital signatures,[7] Finland has produced a paired down version of the Directive;[8] France;[9] Germany has amended the original law, with additional material relating to the two types of signature provided for in the Directive,[10] Greece,[11] Hungary,[12] Ireland,[13] Italy amended its earlier law dating from 1997 (the first in Europe),[14] Latvia,[15] Lithuania,[16] Luxembourg,[17] Malta,[18] the Netherlands,[19] Poland,[20] Portugal,[21] Romania,[22] Slovak Republic,[23] Republic of Slovenia,[24] Spain,[25] Sweden,[26] and the United Kingdom (comprising England & Wales, Northern Ireland and Scotland).[27] The laws passed by Gibraltar,[28] Iceland,[29] Norway[30] and Turkey[31] also follow the Directive.

---

1 Signaturgesetz – SigG, BGBl. I Nr. 190/1999.

2 9 Juli 2001 Wet houdende vaststelling van bepaalde regels in verband met het juridisch kader voor elektronische handtekeningen en certificatiediensten; Johan Vandeddriessche, 'Introduction to the Belgian laws on e-signatures' together with an unofficial translation of the law *e-Signature Law Journal* (now the *Digital Evidence Journal*) 2004, Volume 1 Number 2, 75–82.

3 Закон за Електронния Документ и Електронния Подпис (Обн., ДВ, бр. 34 от 2001 г.); George G. Dimitrov, 'Legal aspects of electronic signatures in Bulgaria' *e-Signature Law Journal* (now the *Digital Evidence Journal*) 2004, Volume 1 Number 2, 85–90.

4 Law on the Legal Framework for Electronic Signatures and Associated Matters of 2004, Law No. 188(I)/2004; Olga Georgiades, unofficial translation of Law No 188(I)/2004, *e-Signature Law Journal* (now the *Digital Evidence Journal*) 2005, Volume 2 Number 1, 42–50.

5 Zákon č. 227/2000 Sb., o elektronickém podpisu o změně některých dalších zákonů (zákon o elektronickém podpisu).

6 Lov om elektroniske signaturer Nr. 417.

7 Digitaalallkirja seadus Vastu võetud 8. märtsil 2000. a. (RT I 2000, 26, 150) jõustunud 15. detsembril 2000 and Tsiviilseadustiku üldosa seadus Vastu võetud 27. märtsil 2002. a (RT I 2002, 35, 216) jõustunud 1. juulil 2002.

8 Laki sähköisistä allekirjoituksista 24.1.2003/14.

9 Loi No 2000-230 du 13 mars 2000 portant adaptation du droit de la preuve aux technologies de l'information et relative á la signature électronique, further decrees have also been issued.

10 Gesetz über Rahmenbedingungen für elektronische Signaturen (Signaturgesetz – SigG) vom 16.5.2001 (BGBl. I S. 876); VwVfG Verwaltungsverfahrensgesetz [I B 25]; BGB Bürgerliches Gesetzbuch (BGB) and ZPO Zivilprozessordnung.

11 Presidential Decree 150/2001.

12 2001. évi XXXV. Törvény az elektronikus aláírásról.

13 Electronic Commerce Act 2000.

14 The first law to be passed is Legge 25 marzo 1997, n.59 *Delega al Governo per il conferimento di funzioni e compiti alle regioni ed enti locali, per la riforma della Pubblica Amministrazione e per la semplificazione amministrativa*; Decreto del Presidente della Repubblica 28 dicembre 2000, n. 445 *Testo unico delle disposizioni legislative e regolamentari in materia di documentazione amministrativa*. See Dr Tommaso Scannicchio 'Important Decision of the Italian Supreme Court of Cassazione in the Matter of Electronic Documents: Italian Supreme Court of Cassazione – September 6, 2001 case 11445/2001' *The Journal of Information Law and Technology* (JILT) 2002 (2) www.elj.warwick.ac.uk/jilt/02-2/scannicchio.html, Alessandro Del Ninno 'Electronic Signatures in Italy – The New Italian Rules' [2002] CTLR Issue 5 117; Dr Luigi Martin and Dr Roberto Pascarelli, 'Electronic signature: value in law and probative effectiveness in the Italian legal system' *e-Signature Law Journal* (now the *Digital Evidence Journal*) 2004, Volume 1 Number 1, 17–22; Franco Ruggieri 'A technician's views on the digital signature in Italy,' *e-Signature Law Journal* (now the *Digital Evidence Journal*) 2005, Volume 2 Number 1, 53–59.

15 Elektronisko dokumentu likums.

16 Elektroninio parašo įstatymas 2000 m. liepos 11 d. Nr. VII-1822, pakeistas 2002 m. birželio 6 d.

17 Loi du 14 août 2000 relative au commerce électronique modifiant le code civil, le nouveau code de procédure civile, le code de commerce, le code pénal et transposant la directive 1999/93 du 13 décembre 1999 relative à un cadre communautaire pour les signatures électroniques, la directive 2000/31/CE du 8 juin 2000 relative à certains aspects juridiques des services de la société de l'information, certaines dispositions de la directive 97/7/CEE du 20 mai 1997 concernant la vente à distance des biens et des services autres que les services financiers.

18 Electronic Commerce Act 2002; Rimantas Petrauskas, Rytis Cesna and Sylvia Mercado-Kierkegaard, 'Legal regulation of electronic signatures in Lithuania' *e-Signature Law Journal* (now the *Digital Evidence Journal*) 2005, Volume 2 Number 2, 111–114.

19 Wet van 8 mei 2003 tot aanpassing van Boek 3 en Boek 6 van het Burgerlijk Wetboek, de Telecommunicatiewet en de Wet op de Economische Delicten inzake elektronische handtekeningen ter uitvoering van richtlijn nr. 1999/93/EG van het Europees Parlement en de Raad van de Europese Unie van 13 december 1999 betreffende elektronische handtekeningen (PbEG L 13) (Wet elektronische handtekeningen), Staatsblad 2003, 199; Guido Boer, 'Electronic administrative communications in The Netherlands' *e-Signature Law Journal* (now the *Digital Evidence Journal*) 2004, Volume 1 Number 2, 67–70; Simone van Esch, 'The electronic prescription of medication in a Netherlands hospital,' *Digital Evidence Journal* 2006, Volume 3 Number 2, 73–77.

20 Ustawa z dnia 18 września 2001 r. o podpisie elektronicznym.

21 Decreto-lei no. 290-D/99, de 2 de Agosto, Decreto-lei no. 375/99, de 18 de Setembro, Decreto-lei no. 146/2000, de 18 de Julho, Decreto-lei no. 234/2000, de 25 de Setembro and Decreto-lei no. 62/2003, de 3 de Abril.

22 Lege nr. 455 din 18 iulie 2001 privind semnătura electronică.

23 Zakon c. 215/2002 Z.z.o elektronickom podpise a o zmene a doplneni niektorych zakonov.

24 Zakon o elektronskem poslovanju in elektronskem podpisu (uradno prečiščeno besedilo), Uradni list Republike Slovenije št. 98/2004 and Zakon o elektronskem poslovanju na trgu, Uradni list Republike Slovenije št. 61/2006.

25 Ley 59/2003, de 19 de diciembre, de firma electrónica; Eduardo Gómez de la Cruz, 'The electronic signature in Spain', *e-Signature Law Journal* (now the *Digital Evidence Journal*) 2005, Volume 2 Number 2, 115–116.

26 Lag (2000:832) om kvalificerade elektroniska signaturer.
27 Electronic Communications Act 2000 and Electronic Signatures Regulations 2002 (SI 318/2002).
28 Electronic Commerce Act 2001.
29 Lög nr. 28/2001 um rafrænar umdirskriftir.
30 Lov om elektronisk signatur av 15. juni 2001 nr. 81, with the exception of Annex IV.
31 Eleltronik Imza Kanunu Kanun No 5070; Pekin & Pekin, 'The electronic signature law in Turkey' *e-Signature Law Journal* (now the *Digital Evidence Journal*), 2004, Volume 1 Number 1, 31–34.

SINGAPORE

9.11 The two-tier approach has also been adopted by Singapore in the Electronic Transactions Act 1998. This legislation also differentiates between electronic signatures and secure electronic signatures. The Act provides that an electronic signature can be proved in any manner, as provided for in s 8:

'8. Electronic signatures

(1) Where a rule of law requires a signature, or provides for certain consequences if a document is not signed, an electronic signature satisfies that rule of law.

(2) An electronic signature may be proved in any manner, including by showing that a procedure existed by which it is necessary for a party, in order to proceed further with a transaction, to have executed a symbol or security procedure for the purpose of verifying that an electronic record is that of such party.'

This definition usefully provides for the use of the 'I accept' icon on websites. The inclusion of the word 'symbol' can extend to any form of electronic data, indicated by the decision of Prakash J in *SM Integrated Transware Ltd v Schenker Singapore (Pte) Ltd* with respect to the name forming part of an email address,[1] but also appears to specifically include the popular method of accepting a contract over the internet. Providing the person selling retains evidence of the acceptance of the sale, the assumption will be that the person whose details appear in the order form will be that of the person that clicked on the 'I accept' icon.

The definition of a secure electronic signature, in contrast, very similar to the advanced electronic signature set out in article 2(2) of the European Union Directive on electronic signatures:

'17. Secure electronic signature

If, through the application of a prescribed security procedure or a commercially reasonable security procedure agreed to by the parties involved, it can be verified that an electronic signature was, at the time it was made:

(a) unique to the person using it;

(b) capable of identifying such person;

(c) created in a manner or using a means under the sole control of the person using it; and

(d) linked to the electronic record to which it relates in a manner such that if the record was changed the electronic signature would be invalidated,

such signature shall be treated as a secure electronic signature.[2]

Of interest is the provision for two types of security procedure that can apply to a secure electronic signature: a prescribed procedure and a commercially reasonable procedure, thus allowing for a degree of flexibility as to the precise technical method to be used.

1   [2005] 2 SLR 651, [2005] SGHC 58.
2   Section 17.

BERMUDA

9.12 Bermuda drew from the UNCITRAL Model Law on Electronic Commerce, the European Directive on electronic signatures and legislation from other jurisdictions, in particular that of Singapore,[1] when drafting the Electronic Transaction Act 1999, which provides for two types of signature, depending on the use to which they are put. The definition of an electronic signature, is provided in s 2:

> "'electronic signature" means a signature in electronic form in, attached to, or logically associated with, information that is used by a signatory to indicate his adoption of the content of that information and meets the following requirements:
>
> (i)   it is uniquely linked to the signatory;
>
> (ii)   it is capable of identifying the signatory;
>
> (iii) it is created using means that the signatory can maintain under his sole control, and
>
> (iv)   it is linked to the information to which it relates in such a manner that any subsequent alteration of the information is revealed.'

Reference is made, in Part II s 11, to the form an electronic signature should take that will meet the criteria where a signature is required by law, when used to identify a person intending to sign or otherwise adopt the content of a document in electronic format. This clause is based on article 7 of the Model Law:

> '1   (1) Where the signature of a person is required by law, that requirement is met by an electronic record if:

(a)   a method is used to identify that person and to indicate that the person intended to sign or otherwise adopt the information in the electronic record; and

(b)   that method is as reliable as is appropriate for the purpose for which the electronic record was generated or communicated, in the light of all the circumstances, including any relevant agreement.'

This provision permits the use of different types of electronic signature, other than a digital signature. However, Part IV of the Act, in referring to electronic signatures, indicates clearly that an electronic signature, to satisfy the requirements of s 11(1)(a) and (b), where a signature is required by law, such a signature must be associated with an accredited certificate, making it a digital signature in all but name:

'19   An electronic signature that is associated with an accredited certificate issued by an authorised certification service provider under section 20 is deemed to satisfy the requirements of s 11(1)(a) and (b).'

Bermuda has taken the view that a digital signature must be used where the law requires a signature.

1   Explanatory memorandum.

CHINA

9.13   China has also adopted the two-tier approach in the Electronic Signatures Law of the People's Republic of China of 2004.[1] Article 2 provides a definition of electronic signature and data message, both of which are widely drafted:

'"Electronic signature" in this law means data in electronic form in or affixed to a data message, which may be used to identify the signatory in relation to the data message and to indicate the signatory's approval of the information contained in the data message.

"Data message" means information generated, sent, received or stored by electronic, optical, magnetic or similar means.'

Confusingly, article 3 provides that the parties are free to determine whether to use electronic signatures in civil activities, which implies that the type of signature referred to in article 2 is a digital signature, although digital signatures are clearly referred to in chapter 3 article 13, even if the word 'digital' is not used:

'Article 13: An electronic signature is deemed to be a reliable electronic signature if the following requirements are met:

(1)   The signature creation data, when used to an electronic signature, is linked to the signatory and to no other person;

(2) The signature creation data is under the control of the signatory and of no other person when signing;

(3) Any alteration to an electronic signature, made after the time of signing, is detectable;

(4) Any alteration to the content or form of a data message, made after the time of signing, is detectable.

The parties may choose the form of electronic signature that meets the agreed reliability requirements.'

Although article 14 provides that 'The reliable electronic signature has the same legal effect as the handwritten signature or seal,' nevertheless this approach has not prevented judges concluding that data sent by way of text messages between mobile telephones is capable of being admitted into evidence, as in *Yang v Han*.[2]

1   Minyan Wang and Minju Wang, 'Introduction to the Electronic Signatures Law of the People's Republic of China' together with an unofficial translation, *e-Signature Law Journal* (now the *Digital Evidence Journal*) 2005, Volume 2 Number 1, 35–41; Felix W. H. Chan, 'China's Electronic Signature Act 2005: A Great Leap Forward of Backward?' [2005] C.T.L.R. Issue 2, 47–50; Minyan Wang, 'Do the regulations on electronic signatures facilitate international electronic commerce? A critical review' *Computer Law & Security Report*, 2007, Volume 23 Number 1, 32–41; paragraph 3.4.

2   Beijing Haidian District People's Court, 14 July 2005.

IMPLEMENTATION OF THE TWO-TIER APPROACH ELSEWHERE

9.14   Other counties adopting the two-tier approach include Anguilla,[1] the Bahamas,[2] Barbados,[3] Brunei Darussalam,[4] Dubai,[5] Hong Kong,[6] Iran,[7] Isle of Man,[8] Jersey,[9] Jordan,[10] Myanmar,[11] New Zealand,[12] Pakistan,[13] Netherlands Antilles,[14] South Africa,[15] Switzerland,[16] Taiwan,[17] Thailand,[18] Turks and Caicos Islands,[19] Vanuatu[20] and Vietnam.[21]

1   Electronic Transactions Act 2006.
2   Electronic Communications and Transactions Act 2003.
3   Electronic Transactions Act, 2001-2.
4   Electronic Transactions Order, 2000.
5   Law of Electronic Transactions and Commerce No. 2/2002.
6   Electronic Transactions Ordinance 2000.
7   Electronic Commerce Act 2004; Dr Ahad Gholizadeh, 'The evidential value of the data-message in Iran', *Digital Evidence Journal*, 2006, Volume 3 Number 2, 78–86.
8   Electronic Transactions Act 2000.
9   Electronic Communications (Jersey) Law, 2000.
10 Electronic Transaction Law No. 85 of 2001.
11 Electronic Transactions Law (The State Peace and Development Council Law No. 5/2004).
12 Electronic Transactions Act 2002.
13 Electronic Transactions Ordinance, 2002.
14 Landsverordening overeenkomsten langs elektronische weg (P.B. 2000, 186).
15 Electronic Communications and Transactions Act 2002.

16 Bundesgesetz vom 19. Dezember 2003 über Zertifizierungsdienste im Bereich der elektro-
    nischen Signatur (ZertEs) and Verordnung vom 3. Dezember 2004 über Zertifizierungsdi-
    enste im Bereich der elektronischen Signatur (VZertEs).
17 Electronic Signatures Law 2001.
18 Electronic Transactions Act B.E. 2544 (2001).
19 Electronic Transactions Ordinance 2000.
20 Electronic Transactions Act No 24 of 2000.
21 Law on E-Transactions (No. 51/2005/QH11).

Presumptions

9.15 Where a law adopts the aim of substituting an electronic signature as a
functional equivalent of a manuscript signature, a number of presumptions may
be included in the legislation. Illustrated below are some of the presumptions
set out in various laws.

Validity of the signature

9.16 The Ley De Firma Digital N° 25.506 passed by Argentina, provides
that where a digital signature is used, it is valid, providing it complies with the
provisions of article 9:

'ARTICULO 9° — Validez. Una firma digital es válida si cumple con los
siguientes requisitos:

(a) Haber sido creada durante el período de vigencia del certificado
     digital válido del firmante;
(b) Ser debidamente verificada por la referencia a los datos de
     verificación de firma digital indicados en dicho certificado según el
     procedimiento de verificación correspondiente;
(c) Que dicho certificado haya sido emitido o reconocido, según el
     artículo 16 de la presente, por un certificador licenciado.

ARTICLE 9. — Validity. A digital signature is valid if it complies with
the following requirements:

(a) That it was created during the period of time in which the signing
     party's digital certificate was valid;
(b) That it has been duly verified by reference to the digital signature
     verification data indicated in this certificate according to the
     corresponding verification procedure;
(c) That such certificate was issued or recognized, according to article
     16 of the present law, by a licensed certification authority.'

In China, a 'reliable' electronic signature has the same legal effect as a
manuscript signature or a seal in accordance with the provisions of article 14
of the Electronic Signatures Law of the People's Republic of China of 2004,
although the provisions of article 13 will also have to be met.

Integrity of the digital signature

9.17   Article 8 of the Argentine Ley De Firma Digital N° 25.506 establishes a presumption that the verification procedures applied to a digital signature demonstrate it has not been modified:

'ARTICULO 8° — Presunción de integridad. Si el resultado de un procedimiento de verificación de una firma digital aplicado a un documento digital es verdadero, se presume, salvo prueba en contrario, que este documento digital no ha sido modificado desde el momento de su firma.

ARTICLE 8. — Integrity presumption. If the result of the verification procedure of a digital signature applied to a digital document is true, it is presumed, unless otherwise specified, that this digital document has not been modified as from the moment it was signed.'

Presumption the user affixed the digital signature

9.18   Some legislation tends to avoid setting out clearly the presumptions relating to an electronic signature, especially of a digital signature, although a number of countries have provided that a message is to be attributed to the sender in given circumstances, and Israel has made such a presumption explicit.[1] For instance, by article 3 of the Japanese Law Concerning Electronic Signatures and Certification Services (Law No.102 of 2000), a record shall be genuinely complete when signed by the sender:

'Chapter 2: Presumption of the authenticity of an electro-magnetic record

Article 3:

An electro-magnetic record which is made in order to express information (with the exception of one drawn by a public official in the exercise of his official functions) shall be presumed to be authentic if an electronic signature (limited to those that, if based on the proper control of the codes and objects necessary to perform the signature, only that person can substantially perform) is performed by the principal in relation to information recorded in the electro-magnetic record.[2]'

This provision highlights the need for a user to control their private key very carefully, as well as provide for the proper security of their computer to prevent a signature from being misused. In Argentina, any person using a digital signature will be presumed to have sent it, even where it is sent automatically, according to article 10 of the Argentine Ley De Firma Digital N° 25.506:

'ARTICULO 10. — Remitente. Presunción. Cuando un documento digital sea enviado en forma automática por un dispositivo programado y lleve la firma digital del remitente se presumirá, salvo prueba en contrario, que el documento firmado proviene del remitente.

ARTICLE 10. — Sender presumption. When a digital document is sent automatically by a programmed device and bears the sender's digital signature it shall be presumed, unless otherwise specified, that the signed document was originated by the sender.'

This position is also set out in the Electronic Transactions Order 2000 of Brunei Darussalam, which has a two-tier model. The Electronic Transactions Order provides for electronic signatures, as defined in s 2:

'"electronic signature" means any letters, characters, numbers or other symbols in digital form attached to or logically associated with an electronic record, and executed or adopted with the intention of authenticating or approving the electronic record;'

An electronic signature is capable of satisfying a rule of law that requires a signature, as provided in s 8:

'Electronic signatures.

8. (1) Where any rule of law requires a signature, or provides for certain consequences if a document is not signed, an electronic signature satisfies that rule of law.
    (2) An electronic signature may be proved in any manner, including by showing that a procedure existed by which it is necessary for a party, in order to proceed further with a transaction, to have executed a symbol or security procedure for the purpose of verifying that an electronic record is that of such party.'

However, there is also provision for a secure electronic signature, as provided by s 17 in Part V of the Order:

'Secure electronic signature.

17. If, through the application of a prescribed security procedure or a commercially reasonable security procedure agreed to by the parties involved, it can be verified that all electronic signature was, at the time it was made —
     (a) unique to the person using it;
     (b) capable of identifying such person;
     (c) created in a manner or using a means under the sole control of the person using it; and

(d) linked to the electronic record to which it relates in a manner such that if the record was changed the electronic signature would be invalidated,

such signature shall be treated as a secure electronic signature.'

The Order appears to distinguish between a secure electronic signature and a digital signature, because the term digital signature is defined in s 2 and references are made to the effect of digital signatures in Part VI, although s 18(4) provides that a secure electronic signature can comprise a digital signature. The importance of the secure electronic signature is revealed in the presumptions set out in s 18:

Presumptions relating to secure electronic records and signatures.

'18. (1) In any proceedings involving a secure electronic record, it shall be presumed, unless evidence to the contrary is adduced, that the secure electronic record has not been altered since the specific point in time to which the secure status relates.

(2) In any proceedings involving a secure electronic signature, it shall be presumed, unless evidence to the contrary is adduced, that —

(a) the secure electronic signature is the signature of the person with whom it correlates; and

(b) the secure electronic signature was affixed by that person with the intention of signing or approving the electronic record.

(3) In the absence of a secure electronic record or a secure electronic signature, nothing in this Part shall create any presumption relating to the authenticity and integrity of the electronic record or an electronic signature.'

This clause clearly demonstrates that the user of a secure electronic signature is presumed to have affixed the signature to any electronic data and that there is a direct link between the user and the signature. The Electronic Signature Act 1999· 2· 5 Act No. 5792 of Korea also provides for such a presumption in article 3(2):

'(2) In case that a certified digital signature is affixed on an electronic message, it shall be presumed that such a digital signature is the signature, signature and seal, or name and seal of the signer of the electronic message concerned and that there has been no alteration in the contents of such message since it was signed digitally.'[3]

However, this presumption is somewhat negated as far as the recipient is concerned, as article 25-2 illustrates:

'Article 25-2 (Obligation of Users)

The users shall take the following measures in order to verify whether or not a certified digital signature is true by referring to the particulars, etc. of the authorized certificate as set forth in Article 15 (2) 1 through 6:

1. A measure to ascertain whether the authorized certificate remains valid;
2. A measure to ascertain whether the authorized certificate has been suspended or revoked; and
3. A measure to ascertain such matters as set forth in Article 15 (2) 7 and 8.'[4]

The matters provided in article 15 are, in essence, a requirement to undertake complete due diligence to authenticate the certificate, and become a verifying party before relying on the presumption set out in article 3(2).

The Electronic Transactions Act 1999 (Cth) of the Commonwealth of Australia is predicated on the recommendations of the expert report, recommendation 12 of which reads as follows:[5]

'In general, issues of attribution and message integrity should be left to determination by agreement between the parties. Disputes can be decided by the courts.

For cases where parties do not determine these issues by agreement, default provisions on attribution should be enacted stating that a person purporting to be the originator of a data message should only be bound if in fact the data message was sent by that person or with their authority. The onus is on the addressee of the data message to prove that it was sent by the originator or with their authority.

Legislation should also provide that where parties agree on rules of attribution and message integrity a party cannot rely on the agreed rules unless it is fair and reasonable to do so in all the circumstances.'

In consequence of this recommendation, s 15 of the Act deals with attribution of electronic communications generally in the widest terms:

'15   Attribution of electronic communications

(1)   For the purposes of a law of the Commonwealth, unless otherwise agreed between the purported originator and the addressee of an electronic communication, the purported originator of the electronic communication is bound by that communication only if the communication was sent by the purported originator or with the authority of the purported originator.

(2)   Subsection (1) is not intended to affect the operation of a law (whether written or unwritten) that makes provision for:
    (a)   conduct engaged in by a person within the scope of the person's actual or apparent authority to be attributed to another person; or
    (b)   a person to be bound by conduct engaged in by another person within the scope of the other person's actual or apparent authority.'

The Singapore Electronic Transactions Act 1998 also provides a presumption that the signature is that of the person with whom it is associated, and a further presumption that the person affixed their signature with the intention of signing or approving the document sent, as provided for in s 18(2):

'(2) In any proceedings involving a secure electronic signature, it shall be presumed, unless evidence to the contrary is adduced, that:
  (a) the secure electronic signature is the signature of the person to whom it correlates; and
  (b) the secure electronic signature was affixed by that person with the intention of signing or approving the electronic record.

The nexus between the electronic signature and the act of affixing it to a document or message is the subject of a rebuttable presumption in s 9 of the Electronic Commerce Act of 2000, Republic Act No 8792 of the Philippines:

'Sec. 9. Presumption Relating to Electronic Signatures. – In any proceedings involving an electronic signature, it shall be presumed that:

(a) The electronic signature is the signature of the person to whom it correlates; and
(b) The electronic signature was affixed by that person with the intention of signing or approving the electronic document unless the person relying on the electronically signed electronic document knows or has notice of defects in or unreliability of the signature or reliance on the electronic signature is not reasonable under the circumstances.'

In this instance, it appears that the recipient may act upon receipt of an electronic document or message where an electronic signature has been affixed, whilst s 9(b) implies that the recipient may be required to take action and thereby become a verifying party before relying on the signature. However, the provision is that a recipient only needs to take any action where they know or have notice of any defects or unreliability that would make it unreasonable to rely on the signature. The provision is not a mandatory requirement to authenticate the electronic signature. However, if the recipient were to rely on the signature to their detriment in circumstances that they should have been aware that they might not be able to trust the signature, then they will have the burden of proving its authenticity by the provisions of s 11(b).

The discussion of the presumption that where a person obtains a digital signature, they are presumed to have affixed the signature is, considering the claims made for digital signatures, sound. By making it clear to the person obtaining a digital signature that they will have to prove they did not use their private key, the law puts an emphatic and clear duty on the signing party to put robust security measures in place to protect the private key. This means, in circumstances where a digital signature is used, but where the signatory claims they did not affix the signature to the document or communication, the signatory is, in effect, refusing to be bound by a promise because they claim a third party sent the communication or document without permission or authorization, which in turn means their defence is that they were negligent in failing to provide for the proper security of their private key. For all the fuss about the so-called advanced electronic signature in the European Directive[6] and the vast array of technical criteria that have to be followed before a digital signature can be called an advanced electronic signature, the recipient has not a single jot of comfort – they do not benefit from the presumption that the person whose signature it purports to be, is presumed to have sent the document or communication. The recipient is no better off, and they have to decide whether to become a verifying party by undertaking due diligence to verify the signature, and if they succeed at this (their success will depend on their own ability and depth of technical knowledge to ensure they carried out the verification process thoroughly), they then become a relying party, with all the ramifications that follow.

1   Article 3, Electronic Signature Law, 5761–2001.
2   Taken from the translation available at www.meti.go.jp.
3   Amended by Act No. 6585, December 31, 2001.
4   This Article newly inserted by Act No. 6585, December 31, 2001.
5   'Electronic commerce: Building the legal framework'; Sharon Christensen and Rouhshi Low, 'Electronic Signatures and PKI Frameworks in Australia' *e-Signature Law Journal* (now the *Digital Evidence Journal*) 2004, Volume 1 Number 2, 56–59.
6   Directive 1999/93/EC of the European Parliament and of the Council of 13 December 1999 on a Community framework for electronic signatures, OJ L 13, 19.01.2000, p. 12.

Presumption of ownership

9.19   In article 7 of the Ley De Firma Digital N° 25.506 of Argentina, it is presumed that a digital signature belongs to the holder of the certificate:

'ARTICULO 7° — Presunción de autoría. Se presume, salvo prueba en contrario, que toda firma digital pertenece al titular del certificado digital que permite la verificación de dicha firma.

ARTICLE 7. — Authorship presumption. Unless it is otherwise proved, every digital signature is presumed to belong to the holder of the digital certificate that permits the verification of the digital signature in question.'

A similar presumption is also included in article 3 of the Israeli law:[1]

'3.   An electronic message signed with a secure electronic signature is admissible in any legal procedure, and will constitute prima-facie evidence that:

(1) the signature is that of the owner of the signing device;
(2) the electronic message is that which was signed by the owner of the signing device.'

It is refreshing to observe that some politicians in some countries are willing to make the implicit explicit.

1   Electronic Signature Law, 5761–2001.

Certification authorities

9.20   It is a matter of public policy whether a state sets up an implementation scheme to provide for a technical framework for electronic authentication, or permits a voluntary scheme to operate. A scheme may include some or all of the following:

(a) The provision of national and international standards for products and services relating to electronic authentication.
(b) The provision of a framework to regulate the supervision, accreditation and certification of some or all authentication products and services. Where such a framework is in place, it may be one that is established by the state or a voluntary accreditation scheme.
(c) The provision of guidelines, best practice and other matters that relate to the provision of authentication infrastructures.[1]

1   Chris Kuner, Stewart Baker, Rosa Barcelo and Eric Greenwald 'An Analysis of International Electronic and Digital Signature Implementation Initiatives'.

Licensed certification authorities

9.21   The states of Latin America have, to a large extent, adopted a licensing system for certification authorities. For instance, the Argentine government started a public key infrastructure project in 1996, which includes a fully operational root certification authority, a licensed certification authority (the Ministry of Economy) and other bodies that have started to issue licences. It is anticipated that the experience of developing the public key infrastructure for the public sector may be the basis for introducing the project on a national basis in the future.[1] Chapter III of the Ley De Firma Digital N° 25.506 establishes the regime for certification authorities, and article 17 provides for certification authorities to be licensed:

'ARTICULO 17. — Del certificador licenciado. Se entiende por certificador licenciado a toda persona de existencia ideal, registro público de contratos u organismo público que expide certificados, presta otros servicios en relación con la firma digital y cuenta con una licencia para ello, otorgada por el ente licenciante.

La actividad de los certificadores licenciados no pertenecientes al sector público se prestará en régimen de competencia. El arancel de los servicios prestados por los certificadores licenciados será establecido libremente por éstos.

ARTICLE 17. — Of the licensed certification authority. A licensed certification authority is any person, public registry of contracts or a government agency which issues certificates and renders other services related to digital signatures and holds a license for this purpose, issued by the Licensing Institution.

The activity of the licensed certification authority which does not belong to the public sector shall be governed by a competitive regime. The licensed certification authorities shall freely establish their fees.'

The provisions relating to the certification authority include its functions,[2] methods for becoming licensed,[3] the duties,[4] rights and duties of the holder of a digital certificate,[5] provisions relating to the control of the licensing regime,[6] and matters relating to the Application Authority, auditing and the formation of an Advisory Commission.[7]

Malaysia has opted for a compulsory licensing regime, as set out in Part II to the Digital Signature Act 1998. The advantages of a compulsory licensing regime can be seen in the provisions of Part IV of the Act, which set out the duties of licensed certification authorities and subscribers, including the need of both parties to use trustworthy systems,[8] the conditions that must be fulfilled when issuing a certificate,[9] the warranties and obligations a certification authority must adhere to[10] and the duties of the subscriber.[11] Of particular note is the duty of the subscriber as set out in clause 43:

'43. By accepting a certificate issued by a licensed certification authority, the subscriber named in the certificate assumes a duty to exercise reasonable care to retain control of the private key and prevent its disclosure to any person not authorised to create the subscriber's digital signature.'

The duty of the subscribing party to provide for the proper security of their private key, enforced by contractual measures as between the certification authority and subscribing party, is thus enshrined in law in Malaysia. More recently, Taiwan has also established a compulsory licensing regime by article 11 of the Electronic Signatures Law 2001.

1   Mercedes Rivolta and Patricia Prandini 'Argentine public key infrastructure development – a comparative study of PKI experiences in Latin America' Part III.
2   Article 19.
3   Article 20.
4   Article 21.
5   Chapter IV articles 24 and 25.
6   Chapter V.

7 Chapters VI, VII and VIII.
8 Section 27.
9 Section 29.
10 Sections 34 to 37.
11 Sections 30 to 42.

Voluntary licensing

9.22 The government of Singapore has adopted a voluntary licensing regime, and certification authorities can apply to be licensed by the Controller of Certification Authorities in accordance with the Electronic Transactions (Certifications Authority) Regulations 1999, issued under the authority of s 42 of the Electronic Transactions Act 1998. However, all certification authorities, whether they are licensed or not, are subject to the relevant provisions of the Act. In particular, Part VIII sets out the duties that affect every certification authority.

Recognition of foreign certificates

9.23 Legislation either remains silent on the matter of the recognition of foreign certificates, or expressly provides for the recognition of foreign certificates with requirements attached. Where recognition is not mentioned in legislation, the inclusion or exclusion of evidence relating to the certificate will be a matter for procedural rules and the exercise of the judicial function. In addition, the effect of any terms relating to applicable law, jurisdiction and time and place of when and where the contract was formed will also be the subject of substantial law and decisions by the courts. Where legislation expressly provides for the recognition of certificates issued by certification authorities beyond the boundary of a nation state, the provisions may merely give legal effect to the certificate, or require the certification authority to conform to requirements laid down in the legislation. An example of such a requirement is provided for in article 16 of the Ley De Firma Digital N° 25.506 of Argentina, which provides as follows:

'ARTICULO 16. — Reconocimiento de certificados extranjeros. Los certificados digitales emitidos por certificadores extranjeros podrán ser reconocidos en los mismos términos y condiciones exigidos en la ley y sus normas reglamentarias cuando:

(a) Reúnan las condiciones que establece la presente ley y la reglamentación correspondiente para los certificados emitidos por certificadores nacionales y se encuentre vigente un acuerdo de reciprocidad firmado por la República Argentina y el país de origen del certificador extranjero, o

(b) Tales certificados sean reconocidos por un certificador licenciado en el país, que garantice su validez y vigencia conforme a la presente ley. A fin de tener efectos, este reconocimiento deberá ser validado por la autoridad de aplicación.

ARTICLE 16. — Recognition of foreign certificates. Digital certificates issued by foreign certification authorities shall be considered valid in the same terms and conditions required by law and its regulation, when:

(a) They meet the conditions established by the present law and its corresponding regulation decree for the certificates issued by national certification authorities and there is in force a reciprocity agreement signed by the Argentine Republic and the country of origin of the foreign certification authority; or

(b) They are recognized by a local licensed certification authority that guarantees their validity in accordance with the present law. In order to have effect, the Application Authority should validate this recognition.'

Similar provisions apply in the Dominican Republic,[1] and in Colombia article 43 of the Ley Por No 527 de agosto 18 de 1999 medio de la cual se define y reglamenta el acceso y uso de los mensajes de datos, del comercio electrónico y de las firmas digitales, y se establecen las entidades de certificación y se dictan otras disposiciones makes an almost identical requirement:

'Artículo 43. Certificaciones recíprocas. Los certificados de firmas digitales emitidos por entidades de certificación extranjeras, podrán ser reconocidos en los mismos términos y condiciones exigidos en la ley para la emisión de certificados por parte de las entidades de certificación nacionales, siempre y cuando tales certificados sean reconocidos por una entidad de certificación autorizada que garantice en la misma forma que lo hace con sus propios certificados, la regularidad de los detalles del certificado, así como su validez y vigencia.

Article 43. Reciprocal certifications. The digital signature certificates issued by foreign certification entities can be recognized in the same terms and conditions required by the law for the issuance of local certificates by national certification entities; provided said certificates are recognized by an authorized certification entity who guarantees equally as it does with its own certificates, the regularity of the details in the foreign certificate, as well as its validity and effect.'[2]

The European Union will also recognise certificates or classes of certificates that are issued as qualified certificates from foreign certification authorities under the provisions of the Directive for electronic signatures,[3] providing they meet the criteria laid down in the Directive, have been accredited under a voluntary scheme established in a member state, or they are already established within the Community, or they benefit from a bilateral or mutual agreement between the Community and third countries or international organizations, as provided in article 7:

'Article 7

International aspects

1. Member States shall ensure that certificates which are issued as qualified certificates to the public by a certification-service-provider established in a third country are recognised as legally equivalent to certificates issued by a certification-service-provider established within the Community if:
    (a) the certification-service-provider fulfils the requirements laid down in this Directive and has been accredited under a voluntary accreditation scheme established in a Member State; or
    (b) a certification-service-provider established within the Community which fulfils the requirements laid down in this Directive guarantees the certificate; or
    (c) the certificate or the certification-service-provider is recognized under a bilateral or multilateral agreement between the Community and third countries or international organisations.'

A number of other jurisdictions have similar provisions to the European Union, including Bermuda,[4] Brunei Darussalam[5] and Singapore.[6] Provision for the recognition of foreign certificates is included in s 19 of the Information Technology Act 2000 passed in India[7]:

'19 Recognition of foreign Certifying Authorities.

(1) Subject to such conditions and restrictions as may be specified by regulations, the Controller may with the previous approval of the Central Government, and by notification in the Official Gazette, recognise any foreign Certifying Authority as a Certifying Authority for the purposes of this Act.
(2) Where any Certifying Authority is recognised under sub-section (1), the Digital Signature Certificate issued by such Certifying Authority shall be valid for the purposes of this Act.'

A similar provision is provided in s 40 of the Electronic Communications and Transactions Act 2002 passed by South Africa, as well as under article 15 of the Electronic Signatures Law 2001 passed by Taiwan, subject to permission from the competent authority. In this instance, the regulations have already been put in place.[8] In comparison, s 31 of the Electronic Transactions Act B.E. 2544 (2001) passed by Thailand is relatively relaxed about the legal effect of certificates from foreign jurisdictions, and requires a court to examine the evidence relating to the certificate in the light of the provisions enacted in the Electronic Transactions Act:

'Section 31.   A certificate or an electronic signature shall be deemed to be legally effective without having to consider:

(1)   the geographic location where the certificate is issued or the electronic signature created or used; or
(2)   the geographic location of the place of business of the issuer of the certificate or signatory.

A certificate issued in a foreign country shall have the same legal effect as a certificate issued in the country if the level of reliability used in issuing such certificate is not lower than as prescribed in this Act.

An electronic signature created or used in a foreign country shall have the same legal effect in the country as an electronic signature created or used in the country if the level of reliability used in creating or using such electronic signature is not lower than as prescribed in this Act.

In determining whether which certificate or electronic signature offers reliability pursuant to paragraph two or paragraph three, regard shall be had to recognized international standards and any other relevant factors.'[9]

1   Article 59, Ley de Comercio Electrónico, Documentos y Firmas Digitales No. 126-02.
2   Taken from Official Translation No 7, 13 – 1/99 of the Bill by the National Federation of Colombian Coffee Growers, available online from www.qmw.ac.uk/~tl6345/colombia_en_final.htm.
3   Directive 1999/93/EC of the European Parliament and of the Council of 13 December 1999 on a Community framework for electronic signatures, OJ L 13, 19.01.2000, p. 12.
4   Section 21, Electronic Transactions Act 1999.
5   Section 43, Electronic Transactions Order, 2000.
6   Section 43, Electronic Transactions Act 1998.
7   The Information Technology (Certifying Authority) Regulations 2001 were passed in July 2001 under the provisions of s 89 of the Act.
8   'Regulations governing permission of foreign certification service providers' dated 3 April 2002, available in translation from www.wflc.lawbank.com.tw/Eng/Fnews/FnewsContent.asp?msgid=945&msgType=en&keyword=undefined.
9   Translation of the Act from www.dmsc.moph.go.th/moph2000/et_Eng.pdf.

Liability

9.24   Various provisions are made in legislation for the liability of the certification authority, the holder of the electronic signature and, to a lesser extent, the recipient of an electronic signature. Where legislation fails to deal adequately, or at all, with the issues of liability, the general law that applies to these issues will be considered by national courts.

Liability of the certification authority

9.25   The Electronic Transactions Order 2000 passed by Brunei Darussalam provides for a presumption in relation to the information listed in a certificate issued by a certification authority, which few other jurisdictions have implemented. With the exception of information that has not been verified by the certification authority, the information will be presumed to be correct, as provided in s 21:

'Presumptions regarding certificates.

21.   It shall be presumed, unless evidence to the contrary is adduced, that the information listed in a certificate issued by a licensed certification authority is correct, except for information identified as subscriber information which has not been verified, if the certificate was accepted by the subscriber.'

Thus any contract term that purports to negate this aspect of a certificate will have no effect in Brunei Darussalam, and any certification authority attempting to avoid this provision by refraining from verifying information provided by an applicant will probably negate the requirements of their certification practice statement, or, if there is no such provision in their certification practice statement, any certificate they issue without verifying the information supplied by the applicant will mean the certificate has very little value. Also, the Order provides a further assurance of reliance in s 23:

'Reliance on certificates forseeable.

23.   It is foreseeable that persons relying on a digital signature will also rely on a valid certificate containing the public key by which the digital signature can be verified.'

By comparison, the Dominican Republic, by article 42 of Ley 126-02 sobre Comercio Electrónico, Documentos y Firmas Digitales de fecha 20 de septiembre de 2002, have excluded the foreseeability as a requirement:

'Art. 42. — Responsabilidad de la entidad de certificación.

Salvo acuerdo entre las partes, las entidades de certificación responderán por los daños y perjuicios que causen a toda persona.

ARTICLE 42. — Liability of the certifying entity.

Excepting by agreement between the parties, the certifying entities shall be liable for the damages and harm which they cause to any person.'

Liability of the sender

9.26   Where legislation provides for electronic signatures that are the functional equivalent of a manuscript signature, such as the Ley De Firma

Digital N° 25.506 of Argentina, the provisions relating to the holder of a digital certificate are expressed in the form of duties in article 25:

ARTICULO 25. — Obligaciones del titular del certificado digital. Son obligaciones del titular de un certificado digital:

(a) Mantener el control exclusivo de sus datos de creación de firma digital, no compartirlos, e impedir su divulgación;
(b) Utilizar un dispositivo de creación de firma digital técnicamente confiable;
(c) Solicitar la revocación de su certificado al certificador licenciado ante cualquier circunstancia que pueda haber comprometido la privacidad de sus datos de creación de firma;
(d) Informar sin demora al certificador licenciado el cambio de alguno de los datos contenidos en el certificado digital que hubiera sido objeto de verificación.

ARTICLE 25. — Duties of the digital certificate holder. These are duties of the holder of a digital certificate:

(a) To keep exclusive control of his digital signature creation data, not to share it, and to prevent it from being publicly known;
(b) To use a technically reliable digital signature creation device;
(c) To request the licensed certification authority to revoke his certificate if faced with any circumstance which might have compromised the privacy of his signature creation data;
(d) To inform the licensed certification authority without delay of any change in any of the data which has been subject to verification contained in the digital certificate.

In China, article 27 of the Electronic Signatures Law of the People's Republic of China of 2004 provides for the liability of the signing party:

'Where the signatory knows that the signature creation data has been compromised or may have been compromised, but fails to notify the relevant parties without undue delay and to cease to utilize the signature creation data, or where the signatory does not provide genuine, complete and accurate information to the certification service provider, or is responsible for any other faults, he shall be responsible for any damages suffered by the relevant relying parties and the certification service provider.'

The liability is contingent upon the signing party being aware that the signature creation data has been compromised or may have been compromised, although article 15 required the signatory to exercise reasonable care to protect the signature creation data. The Dominican Republic has provided a slightly more detailed approach to the duties of a signing party in article 53 of the Ley 126-02 sobre Comercio Electrónico, Documentos y Firmas Digitales de fecha 20 de septiembre de 2002:

'Art. 53. — Deberes de los suscriptores. Son deberes de los suscriptores:

(a) Recibir de las claves por parte de la entidad de certificación o generar las claves, utilizando un sistema de seguridad exigido por la entidad de certificación;

(b) Suministrar información completa, precisa y verídica a la entidad de certificación;

(c) Aceptar los certificados emitidos por la entidad de certificación, demostrando aprobación de sus contenidos mediante el envío de éstos a una o más personas o solicitando la publicación de éstos en repositorios;

(d) Mantener el control de la clave privada y reservada del conocimiento de terceras personas;

(e) Efectuar oportunamente las correspondientes solicitudes de suspensión o revocación.

Párrafo. — Un suscriptor cesa en la obligación de cumplir con los anteriores deberes a partir de la publicación de un aviso de revocación del correspondiente certificado por parte de la entidad de certificado.

ARTICLE 53. — Duties of the signers. The duties of the signers are:

(a) To receive the passwords from the certifying entity, or to generate the passwords, using a security system required by the certifying entity;

(b) To provide complete, precise, and accurate information to the certifying entity;

(c) To accept the certificates issued by the certifying entity, demonstrating approval of its contents by means of the sending of same to one or more persons or requesting the publication of same in repositories;

(d) To maintain the control of the private reserved password from the knowledge of third persons;

(e) To perform opportunely the corresponding requests for suspension or revocation.

Paragraph. — A signer ceases to be obligated to comply with the abovegoing duties as of the publication of a notice of revocation of the corresponding certificate by the certifying entity.'

The provisions of article 53 set out, in slightly more explicit detail, the duties expected of a person where they decide to obtain and use a digital signature, the definition of which includes a link to the password, as defined in article 2(i) as:

'(i) Firma digital: Se entenderá como un valor numérico que se adhiere a un mensaje de datos y que, utilizando un procedimiento matemático conocido, vinculado a la clave del iniciador y al texto del mensaje, permite determinar que este valor se ha obtenido exclusivamente con la clave del iniciador y el texto del mensaje, y que el mensaje inicial no ha sido modificado después de efectuada la transmisión;

(i) Digital signature: It will be understood as a numerical value attached to a data message and which, by using a known mathematical procedure, linked to the password of the initiator and to the text of[1] the message, allows one to determine that this value has been obtained exclusively with the inititator's password and the text of the message, and that the initial message has not been modified after the transmission has been effected;'

The liability of a sender, once their duties are set out, is provided for in article 55:

'Art. 55. — Responsabilidad de los suscriptores.

Los suscriptores serán responsables por la falsedad o error en la información suministrada a la entidad de certificación y que es objeto material del contenido del certificado. También serán responsables en los casos en los cuales no den oportuno aviso de revocación o suspensión de certificados en los casos indicados anteriormente.

ARTICLE 55. — Liability of the signers. The signers shall be liable for falseness or error in the information supplied to the certifying entity and which is the material object of the contents of the certificate. They shall also be liable in those cases in which they do not give prompt notice of revocation or suspension of certificates in the cases indicated above.'

In comparison, the Australian Commonwealth Electronic Transaction Act 1999 (Cth) provides for a presumption in s 15:

'15 Attribution of electronic communications

(1) For the purpose of a law of the Commonwealth, unless otherwise agreed between the purported originator and the addressee of an electronic communication, the purported originator of the electronic communication is bound only if the communication was sent by the purported originator or with the authority of the purported originator.'

This provision only binds the sending party where the originator accepts they sent the communication, or authorized the sending of the communication. There is no presumption that the electronic signature is that of the sending party. It seems, therefore, that the recipient is required to prove the signing party signed; but it may be that proof of verification puts an evidential burden on the purported signing party to introduce evidence that they did not sign the communication.

1   The word 'ot' in the original translated text altered to read 'of.'

Liability of the recipient

9.27   For obvious reasons, the liability of the recipient is shaped by the warp and weft of political and commercial obstructionism. Often, a recipient has no precise rights or obligations, but attempts are made using obscure methods to impose quasi-contractual duties that are virtually impossible to comply with. Neither governments nor commercial certification authorities wish to make explicit what they seek to achieve implicitly: that is, to cause the recipient to become a verifying party, with all the responsibility that such a role implies, although the provisions of article 21 of the Dubai Law of Electronic transactions and Commerce No 2/2002 do go some way to set out such a duty:

'1.   A person is entitled to rely on an Electronic Signature or an Electronic Certificate to the extent that it is reasonable to do so.

2.   Where an Electronic Signature is supported by a Certificate, the Relying Party in respect of such signature shall bear the legal consequences of its failure to take reasonable and necessary steps to verify the validity and enforceability of the Certificate, as to whether it is suspended or revoked, and of observing any limitations with respect to the Certificate.

3.   In determining whether it was reasonable for a person to rely on an Electronic Signature or a Certificate, regard shall be had, if appropriate, to:
   a.   the nature of the underlying transaction which was intended to be supported by the Electronic Signature;
   b.   the value or importance of the underlying transaction, if this is known;
   c.   whether the Relying Party in respect of the Electronic Signature or certificate has taken appropriate steps to determine the reliability of the Electronic Signature or the Certificate;
   d.   whether the Relying Party in respect of the Electronic Signature or certificate took reasonable steps to verify if the Electronic Signature was supported by a Certificate, or if it should be expected to be so supported;
   e.   whether the Relying Party in respect of the Electronic Signature or Certificate knew or ought to have known that the Electronic Signature or the Certificate had been compromised or revoked;

f. any agreement or course of dealing between the Originator and the Relying Party, or any trade usage which may be applicable;

g. any other relevant factor.

4. If reliance on the Electronic Signature or the Certificate is not reasonable in the circumstances, having regard to the factors in paragraph (2) of this Article, the party relying on the Electronic Signature or Certificate assumes the risk of the Electronic Signature or the Certificate not being valid.'

Exceptions in the commercial arena includes IdenTrust and Bolero, both of which operate a system that binds the three parties (user, certification authority and receiving party) to a relationship governed by contractual terms. By comparison, the British government have produced a number of Statutory Instruments that effectively push the burden to the signing party to ensure their certificate is not misused, by presuming the signing party has affixed the digital signature to a document or communication sent to a government department, thus denying any suggestion that the government, as a recipient, should undertake due diligence and thereby become a verifying party, as required in the commercial sector.[1]

The Argentine government, in article 23 of Ley De Firma Digital N° 25.506 have responded by imposing a mild form of limitation on the recipient of a digital signature in the form of a rule against relying on the validity of the certificate:

'ARTICULO 23. — Desconocimiento de la validez de un certificado digital. Un certificado digital no es válido si es utilizado:

(a) Para alguna finalidad diferente a los fines para los cuales fue extendido;

(b) Para operaciones que superen el valor máximo autorizado cuando corresponda;

(c) Una vez revocado.

ARTICLE 23. — Lack of recognition of the validity of a digital certificate. A digital certificate is not valid if it is used:

(a) For a purpose different from that for which it was issued;

(b) For transactions that exceed the maximum value authorized when applicable;

(c) Once it has been revoked.'

In comparison, the provisions of the Singapore Electronic Transactions Act 1998 permits the recipient to presume that the document or message that is signed with a digital signature has been affixed by the person or entity to whom the digital signature is associated with, although it is a presumption that can be rebutted, as provided in s 22:

'22. Unreliable digital signatures

Unless otherwise provided by law or contract, a person relying on a digitally signed electronic record assumes the risk that the digital signature is invalid as a signature or authentication of the signed electronic record, if reliance on the digital signature is not reasonable under the circumstances having regard to the following factors:

(a) facts which the person relying on the digitally signed electronic record knows or has notice of, including all facts listed in the certificate or incorporated in it by reference;

(b) the value or importance of the digitally signed electronic record, if known;

(c) the course of dealing between the person relying on the digitally signed electronic record and the subscriber and any available indicia of reliability or unreliability apart from the digital signature; and

(d) any usage of trade, particularly trade conducted by trustworthy systems or other electronic means.

The provisions of s 22 have, it appears, been influenced by article 13 of the UNCITRAL Model Law on Electronic Commerce. Whilst the provisions of this section appear to be reasonable, the reference in s 22(a) of the phrase 'including all facts listed in the certificate or incorporated in it by reference' seems to imply that to rely on the signature, the recipient will have to consider becoming a verifying party before relying on the signature. Section 22 of the Electronic Transactions Order 2000 issued by Brunei Darussalam has an almost identical provision to that mentioned above.

Where the certification authority is regulated, as in Malaysia, s 63 of the Digital Signature Act 1998 takes a pragmatic view where a recipient is not sure of the authenticity of the signature:

'63. (1) Unless otherwise provided by law or contract, the recipient of a digital signature assumes the risk that a digital signature is forged, if reliance on the digital signature is not reasonable under the circumstances.

(2) Where the recipient determines not to rely on a digital signature under this section, the recipient shall promptly notify the signer of its determination not to rely on a digital signature and the grounds for that determination.'

The provisions of this section appear to have taken into account the comments made by Romer LJ in *Goodman v J Eban Limited*, where he pointed out that 'If in fact his clients entertained any doubt as to the authenticity of the letter, nothing could be easier than to ask him, by telephone or letter, to confirm it.'[2] If in doubt, the recipient is advised to make a telephone call, send an email or use such old fashioned technology as a facsimile transmission or the postal services to confirm the signature with the person that sent the message or document. By confirming the signature in this fashion, the recipient does not have to consider becoming a verifying party, and the terms 'verifying party' and 'relying party' used by certification authorities thereby become meaningless.

1   Note the reversal of the burden in the various Statutory Instruments issued by the British government during the past three years.
2   [1954] 1 QB 550 at 564.

Chapter 10

The form of an electronic signature

10.1 Whilst it is possible for an electronic signature to perform the same functions of a manuscript signature, the document to be signed does not exist as a physical object in the same way as the content of a document rendered on to a paper carrier. Although an electronic document appears to be a thing that is beyond the physical, nevertheless an electronic document depends on the existence of a record in material form. This can be manifest by being recorded on a hard drive, stored in memory or made visible on the screen. It is not necessarily intended that an electronic signature should be manifest in a physical form, which leads to the conclusion that evidence to provide intent becomes vitally important in the event it is disputed that a signature was affixed to a document or communication.

Digital documents

Information relating to the carrier

10.2 When a manuscript signature is affixed to a physical carrier, two changes occur. First, the signature alters the carrier physically with the addition of a substance, such as ink, to the surface. Second, the signature increases the amount of information about the carrier, and thereby the document. An electronic signature, on the other hand, only tends to alter the information relating to the digital document. It does not necessarily alter the carrier in the same way as a manuscript signature, although an inline Pretty Good Privacy signature, for instance, is read with the message. The information associated with the carrier is termed the metadata. The metadata refers to the data about data. It is a digest of the structure and subject matter of a resource. For instance, the metadata in relation to a piece of paper may be:

(a) Explicit from perusing the paper itself, such as the title of the document, the date, who wrote it, who received it and where the document is located.

(b) Implicit, which includes such characteristics as the kinds of type used, such as bold, underline or italic; perhaps the document is located in a coloured file to denote a particular type of document; labels may also act as pointers to allow the person using the document to deal with it in a particular manner, such as a confidential file, for instance.

With digital documents, the implicit data needs to be made explicit if it is to be used to help interpret the purpose of the document. Such data can include, and be taken automatically from the originating application software, or supplied by the person that originally created the record. As a result, a digital record will normally contain two main types of information, the content of the document and its internal structure, and the metadata, which describes the record and each of the constituent parts.

The nature of a document in digital format

10.3 A digital document can be evident as a physical document, where it is created using a computer and produced in physical format by being printed. However, it must be noted that the nexus between the printed document and the document stored in digital format will alter. First, the printed form of the document will capture the content of the document at the time it is printed. The physical manifestation of the electronic document can then be marked with a manuscript signature, and it then becomes a document in the physical sense. The information about the physical carrier will then alter over time. However, unless the metadata relating to the document stored in digital form is retained in such a way as to link the document, as printed, with the act of printing, the nexus between the printed version of the document and the electronic version may change. Such alterations to the metadata will take place when the original document stored in digital form is deleted or the content is modified or rewritten. In such circumstances, the content on the printed carrier may differ from the content stored in digital form. Whilst this will not matter when a standard letter, by way of example, is altered to change the name and address of the recipient, it will be of substantial concern when the document is a contract, and the printed version differs from the digital version. The information relating to the content of the document, the metadata, then becomes crucial in any investigation. Alternatively, a person cannot observe a digital document that is stored in a digital form without using a computer with a screen. Even when a document is apparent to the eye on a screen, the viewer is not looking at the underlying digital format of the carrier. This is because it is in binary form, which in turn is translated into a readable format on the screen.

Reference to electronic documents in this text will primarily be references to documents stored in digital format that are invisible to the human eye.

Forms of electronic signature

10.4 Electronic signatures are manifest in a variety of forms, all of which can demonstrate the intent of the signing party to authenticate the data. The terms 'electronic signature' and 'digital signature' tend to used interchangeably.[1] This creates confusion.[2] In essence, a digital signature is data appended to, or a cryptographic transformation of, a data unit that allows a recipient of the data to prove the source and integrity of the data unit. The digital signature mechanism defines two processes, that of the purported signing of a data unit by the person initiating the signature, which is a private action, and verifying a signed data unit by using the procedures and information publicly available.[3] A digital signature is a signature that is specifically based on asymmetric cryptography, coupled with a one-way hash function. Thus a digital signature is a particular type of signature that is brought about by the use of a public key infrastructure.[4] It is argued that the digital signature provides a higher degree of certainty for the relying party. However, little attention is paid to illustrating the significant technical and legal obstacles to this assertion, the verification process is opaque, and the possibility that a digital signature can be removed from a document in electronic format without trace.[5]

By comparison, the term electronic signature is anything in electronic form that can be used to demonstrate a signing entity intended their signature to have legal effect. An electronic signature, especially when defined in legislation, tends to represent a generic response to the concept of authentication, and is to be understood in such a context. A signature can be manifest in different forms, and the term 'electronic signature' is used to reflect methods other than the use of a public key infrastructure to sign a message or document, such as the typing of a name on an electronic document, or the capture of the dynamics of a manuscript signature.

For the sake of clarity, the term 'electronic signature' is used to denote the generic concept of a signature that is brought about by the use of a computer or computer-like device, and includes a digital signature as one form of electronic signature. However, this does not prevent the terms used to describe electronic signatures from adding to or increasing the confusion, as illustrated in the Texas case of *In re Piranha, Inc., Debtor, Berger v Piranha, Inc.*,[6] where an electronic signature was attached to a form sent to the Securities and Exchange Commission purporting to be the resignation of a director. In this instance, it was established that the legislation did not prevent the person whose signature was used from challenging the signature and contending he did not execute, adopt or authorize the use of the signature. The report does not make it clear what type of electronic signature is under discussion, but consideration of the relevant regulation appears to indicate that a typed name is sufficient:

'Part 232—Regulation S-T—General Rules and Regulations for Electronic Filings

§ 232.302 Signatures.

(a) Required signatures to, or within, any electronic submission (including, without limitation, signatories within the certifications required by §§240.13a–14, 240.15d–14 and 270.30a–2 of this chapter) must be in typed form rather than manual format. Signatures in an HTML document that are not required may, but are not required to, be presented in an HTML graphic or image file within the electronic filing, in compliance with the formatting requirements of the EDGAR Filer Manual. When used in connection with an electronic filing, the term "signature" means an electronic entry in the form of a magnetic impulse or other form of computer data compilation of any letters or series of letters or characters comprising a name, executed, adopted or authorized as a signature. Signatures are not required in unofficial PDF copies submitted in accordance with §232.104.

(b) Each signatory to an electronic filing (including, without limitation, each signatory to the certifications required by §§240.13a–14, 240.15d–14 and 270.30a–2 of this chapter) shall manually sign a signature page or other document authenticating, acknowledging or otherwise adopting his or her signature that appears in typed form within the electronic filing. Such document shall be executed before or at the time the electronic filing is made and shall be retained by the filer for a period of five years. Upon request, an electronic filer shall furnish to the Commission or its staff a copy of any or all documents retained pursuant to this section.

(c) Where the Commission's rules require a registrant to furnish to a national securities exchange or national securities association paper copies of a document filed with the Commission in electronic format, signatures to such paper copies may be in typed form.'

In comparison, the Florida case of *Florida Department of Agriculture and Consumer Services v Haire*[7] is less than clear about the form of electronic signature described in the report. It was decided that a judge may affix an electronic signature to a warrant. It is possible to infer that the signature was a digital signature, but it is not clear, especially in the light of the 'Administrative Procedures for electronic filing in civil and criminal cases', issued by the United States District Court Middle District of Florida. The current version of the Procedures are dated January 17, 2006, which pre-dates this case, so the reference to electronic signatures in this case is somewhat nebulous if the precise form of electronic signature is to be divined. The Administrative Procedure sets out the rules pertaining to electronic signatures. When an attorney submits documents to the court that require their signature, they type their name on the form, as illustrated in II(C)(1), and reference to electronic signatures for judges is made at II(E)(1): 'Signature of Judge: An order may be signed by the Judge electronically or by hand. The Judge or the Clerk shall electronically file all orders.' This comment does not explain which form of signature a judge may use, although there is a strong inference that the same form is acceptable as required from an attorney.

The confusion is also highlighted in the Dominican Republic case of *Verizon Dominicana, C. por A., v Enilsa Rodríguez Pérez*, September 8, 2006, in which the Supreme Court of Justice upheld the decision of *Verizon Dominicana, C. por A. v Genara Ramírez Mariñez* dated April 13, 2005 in which it was decided that a PIN, when blocking the numbers 0 and 1 for making long distance calls, can be compared to a digital signature, and that it is the user who voluntarily decides to accept the terms and conditions of this service. It was stated in the report that the person who agreed to accept the service is the only person to know the PIN, because the PIN is a secret and the only number allocated to each telephone line. First, the difference between the use of a PIN and digital signature is considerable. Second, the decision in this case, together with the reasoning (what little there is), illustrates the assumptions made about the security of a password or PIN that cannot be justified by the ease by which numbers and passwords can be obtained illicitly. Further, in Spain, a Resolution of the Dirección General de los Registros y del Notariado,[8] refers to the validity of communications made by electronic means between the Notary and the register. The Resolution states as follows:

'The incorporation of the new electronic technologies, computers and telematic means to notarial and register activities, on the one side, can not, under any circumstances, change the current faculties granted to Notaries and registers in order to assure the legality of the transactions and, on the other side, this incorporation should serve to reduce costs and fees for the users of this electronic system. Moreover, the electronic document is legally equivalent and has the same effects as if the referred document would have issued in paper.

Therefore, a public deed issued by a Notary with an electronic record and sent to the Trade Registry with the corresponding electronic signature of the Notary who issues the document, is considered a completely legal, valid and effective document as any other issued in paper.'

Unfortunately, the Resolution does not refer explicitly to a digital signature, but it is probably correct to infer, bearing in mind that notaries across the world have embraced digital signature technology for very good reasons, that this does refer to a digital signature.

Some examples of electronic signatures are discussed below.

1 This is also pointed out in paragraph 2.2 of the Final Report of the EESSI Expert Team 20 July 1999 European Electronic Signature Standardization Initiative available from www.ictsb.org/EESSI/Documents/Final-Report.pdf; the OECD also points this out in the OECD, A Global action plan for electronic commerce prepared by business with recommendations from governments, 7–9 October 1998, Ottawa, Canada (Directorate for Science, Technology and Industry Steering Committee for the Preparation of the Ottawa Ministerial Conference, SG/EC(98)11/REV2), note on page 16; see also GUIDEC II, 'General Usage for International Digitally Ensured Commerce' for further discussion of terms available at www.iccwbo.org/home/guidec/guidec_two/foreword.asp. GUIDEC II does not use the term 'electronic signature' but 'digital signature', thus adding to the confusion. In addition, the Draft Guide to Enactment of the UNCITRAL Model Law on Electronic Signatures, dated 12–23 March 2001 (A/CN.9/WG.IV/WP.88) also appears to refer to digital signatures and electronic signatures interchangeably, see paragraphs 31 to 62 available from www.legalminds.lp.findlaw.com/list/intpil/msg00295.html. The European Union adds to the confusion even more by refusing to refer to the term 'digital signature' in Directive 1999/93/EC of the European Parliament and of the Council of 13 December 1999 on a Community framework for electronic signatures, OJ L 13, 19.01.2000, p. 12, and yet further confusion is rendered with the title of at least one legal textbook: Dennis Campbell, editor, E-Commerce and the Law of Digital Signatures (Oceana Publications, 2005).

2 Also noted by Carlisle Adams and Steve Lloyd Understanding PKI Concepts, Standards, and Deployment Considerations, 184–185.

3 Final Report of the EESSI Expert Team Annex B, available from www.ictsb.org/EESSI/Documents/Final-Report.pdf.

4 See also paragraph 33 to UNCITRAL Model Law on Electronic Signatures, Guide to Enactment.

5 Adrian McCullagh, William Caelli and Peter Little 'Signature Stripping: A Digital Dilemma' 2000 (1) Journal of Information, Law and Technology (JILT) www2.warwick.ac.uk/fac/soc/law/elj/jilt/2001_1/mccullagh/.

6 297 B.R. 78 (N.D.Tex. 2003), 2003 WL 21468504 (N.D. Tex.), affirmed 83 Fed.Appx. 19.

7 836 So.2d 1040 (Fla.App. 4 Dist. 2003), corrected opinion Haire v Florida Department of Agriculture and Consumer Services, Nos SC03-446 & Sc03-552, February 12, 2004, available online at www.law.fsu.edu/library/flsupct/sc03-446/op-sc03-446-corrected.pdf.

8 (DGRN)(Registry and Notarial General Office, Spain) dated 18 January 2006.

Typing a name in an electronic document

10.5 The use of electronic signatures pre-dates any form of legislation, and in the latter decade of the twentieth century, adjudicators found themselves applying well established legal principles to new technologies when presented in the form of electronic signatures, just as judges in the nineteenth century were confronted with the increasing use of printing, typewriting and telegrams: all, it must be said, without the need for special legislation to be enacted. Case law applying electronic signature statutes in the United States of America indicates that the act of typing a name into a document on screen was considered just as acceptable a method of proving intent as any other form of signature, although not uniformly accepted in all jurisdictions before the introduction of relevant legislation.[1]

1   The reader is referred to the discussion later in this chapter dealing with the United States of America for examples.

AUSTRALIA

Statute

10.6   The Supreme Court of the Northern Territory had cause to consider the effectiveness of an electronic signature under Australia's electronic transactions legislation in an action for an adjustment of property interests Under Division 3 of Part 2 of the De Facto Relationships Act 1991 (NT). In *Faulks v Cameron*,[1] the parties lived together in a de facto relationship for some two years before they separated. In 2003, the plaintiff informed her former partner that she was in the process of preparing a separation statement. The defendant had, by this time, moved out of the country, and the only means of communication the plaintiff had with her former partner was by email, because he did not provide a postal address. One of the issues in this case was whether a separation agreement between two de facto partners had been formed for the purposes of the De Facto Relationships Act 1991 (NT). Section 45(2) of the Act provides that where the court is satisfied that there is a separation agreement between the partners, is in writing and signed by the other partner, the court may make an order under Division 3 or 5 of Part 2, but may not make an order that is inconsistent with the terms of the agreement. In her application, the plaintiff submitted that the email correspondence constituted a separation agreement, or in the alternative, if the court did not consider the email correspondence constituted a separation agreement, regard should be given to what was agreed by this form of correspondence. First, the learned judge reached the conclusion that, even though the evidence was not overwhelming, there was an agreement between the former partners, and that it was enforceable at common law. The second issue was whether the email correspondence had been signed. The defendant signed his name at the bottom of the text 'Regards, Angus,' and in applying the provisions of s 9 of the Electronic Transactions (Northern Territory) Act 2000 (NT) to the name typed at the bottom of the email, Acting Master Young concluded, at 64: 'I am satisfied that the printed signature on the defendant's emails identifies him and indicates his approval of the information communicated, that the method was as reliable as was appropriate and that the plaintiff consented to the method. I am satisfied that the agreement is 'signed' for the purposes of s 45(2).' This decision has been criticised as failing to offer any substantial judicial analysis or guidance on the potential scope and application of the legislation,[2] but in the light of previous decisions relating to other forms of signature using different technologies, it is debatable whether any further analysis was required.

1   [2004] 32 Fam LR 417; [2004] NTSC 61.

2   Sharon Christensen, Stephen Mason and Kathryn O'Shea, 'The international judicial rec-
     ognition of electronic signatures – has your agreement been signed?' Communications Law,
     Volume 11 Number 5, 2006, 150–160.

CHINA

10.7   In China, the case of *Shanghai Yaken Enterprise-Image Designing Co.
Ltd. v Wel-Mart China Investment Co. Ltd*[1] illustrates that the courts are dealing
with email, although appear to be a little uncertain at present. This is a first
decision, and it appears a final decision has yet to be made. The plaintiff,
Shanghai Yaken enterprise-image designing Co. Ltd. (Yaken) presented two
emails as evidence to prove that Yaken sent an order form by email with an
electronic signature to Wel-Mart China Investment Co. Ltd. (Wel-Mart).
However, the defendant Wel-Mart did not believe the validity of the order
form sent by email. As to the main issue in this case, whether the electronic
order form by email is valid or not, apparently the judge had not made the
final decision at the time of publication. In another case, *Yang v Han*,[2] Mr
Yang claimed that the defendant Miss Han asked to borrow RMB 11,000
from him. Yang agreed to loan the money to Miss Han, but Miss Han failed
to return the money. As evidence, Mr Yang exhibited several messages sent
from Miss Han's mobile telephone about the loan. It was confirmed that the
messages were transmitted from Miss Han's mobile telephone number. In this
case, the judge supported the plaintiff's claim based on the evidence of the
mobile telephone message between the parties. The court judged that these
messages, as a form of electronic text according to the Electronic Signature
Law, could serve as evidence to support Mr Yang's claim.

1   Shenzhen City Luohu District People's Court, 25 September 2005.
2   Beijing Haidian District People's Court, 14 July 2005.

ENGLAND AND WALES

Employment

10.8   In England and Wales, the first case of this nature occurred in the
Industrial Tribunal case of *Hall v Cognos Limited*.[1] Cognos employed Mr Hall
as a sales executive under the terms of the Standard Employment Agreement
used by Cognos. He was provided with a car for business and personal use.
Mr Hall was reimbursed for all reasonable expenses incurred for travel,
accommodation and other costs in accordance with the relevant policy, which
the learned chairman determined was incorporated into the contract. The
policy stated that all expenses over six months old would not be paid. Mr
Hall failed to submit any travel expenses between 1 December 1995 and 3
June 1996. By January 1997 Mr Hall wanted his expenses paying. A series of
emails were exchanged on 15 January between Mr Hall, Sarah McGoun and

Keith Schroeder, Mr Hall's line manager. Mr Hall asked if he could submit a late expenses claim to Ms McGoun. Ms McGoun in turn referred Mr Hall to Keith Schroeder, and Mr Schroeder, in response to the question as to 'whether [the late submission] is OK with you?' replied, 'Yes, it is OK.' Mr Hall subsequently submitted his expenses, although he did not provide all the necessary forms immediately. He also inflated his claims. His employers refused to make any payment and dismissed him.

Counsel for Cognos argued that because an email was not in writing and signed, the exchange of emails did not have any effect on the terms of the employment agreement. Mr C. T. Grazin, the learned chairman sitting on his own, declined to accept this proposition, attractive as it appeared to him. He held that the emails were in writing and signed once they were printed out. Despite there being no reference or discussion to any relevant case law or the statutory definitions of 'writing' and 'document,' the learned chairman reached the right conclusion at 5:

> 'I am satisfied than an email is "in writing and signed by the parties" once it is printed out. The position might (it is not necessary to make any finding on this point) be different if the email was only retained temporarily on the computer's hard disk storage system. The documents that were, however, produced from the computer are clearly in writing and bear the signatures of both "Sarah" and "Keith". The fact that those signatures are printed, rather than hand-written, is not in my view material. For those reasons, I reject Mr Pym's submission that the relevant email messages are incapable, as a matter of law, of having any modifying effect on the specific contract between the parties.'

A further argument put forward on behalf of Cognos was that Mr Schroeder did not have the authority to respond to Mr Halls' request, nor was he authorized to agree to it. This was rejected on the basis that as Mr Halls' line manager, Mr Schroeder was vested with the appropriate authority to deal with such a request, and as a result, Mr Hall could rely on Mr Schroeder's response. This meant Mr Schroeder's response acted to bind Cognos. As a result, the exchange of emails between Mr Hall and his line manager acted to vary the policy, and Cognos was obliged to pay Mr Hall his reasonable expenses. Both parties subsequently agreed the claim would relate to 9,960 miles at 9 pence per mile, and it was ordered that the employer pay Mr Hall £896.40.

1   Industrial Tribunal Case No 1803325/97.

ISRAEL

Contract

10.9   Whether a signature contained in an email constitutes a valid contract was considered by Noa Grossman J in *Computer Sky Edv v Prime Medical*

Company Ltd.[1] It was held that a contract that was signed through email correspondence is valid. In essence, the reasoning of the decision was as follows:

> 'Negotiations are also carried out today through electronic communications. An offer, a request for an offer and the reception of an offer can all be performed via email correspondence. The correspondence as a whole is what creates the actual agreement. Unlike a printed contract that incorporates the parties' will into one document, a contract reached by way of reciprocating electronic communications is a mosaic of all the parties' communications.'

1   Tel-Aviv Peace Court Civil Case 29488/04, (4 August 2005, unpublished decision).

LITHUANIA

10.10   Two rulings of the Lithuanian courts, in the Court of Appeal[1] and in the Supreme Court of Lithuania[2] accept email communications (signed by the name) as evidence in civil proceedings, although there are presently no cases recorded where the courts will explicitly accept names written in the emails as a form of electronic signature.

1   10 April 2006, case No. 2A– 95/2006.
2   6 March 2006, case No. 3K-3-169/2006.

UNITED STATES OF AMERICA

Insurance

10.11   Of interest, the first two cases that appeared to have reached the courts in the United States are from the insurance sector, illustrating, perhaps, that this particular sector, in seeking to extend the use of the new technology, was the first to be caught up in spurious claims relating to the application of the law to the technology: many people may have forgotten or not even been aware of the history of judicial decision making in respect of emerging technologies during the nineteenth century. In 1990, insurance agents brought an action against an insurer on the case of *Wilkens v Iowa Insurance Commissioner*, alleging that the insurer failed to comply with section 515.52 of the Iowa Code,[1] in that an agent, Larry Hertel, countersigned insurance policies by typing his name into the document on the computer. The Insurance Commissioner determined that signatures generated on a computer did meet the requirements of the statute, and the members of the Court of Appeals of Iowa agreed. Section 4.1(7) of the 1989 Iowa Code provided, at the material time, the following:

> '*Written – in writing – signature*. The words "written" and "in writing" may include any mode of representing words or letters in general use. A

signature, when required by law, must be made by the writing or markings of the person whose signature is required. If a person is unable due to a physical handicap to make a written signature of mark, that person may [make substitutions] in lieu of a signature required by law...'

Sackett J giving the judgment of the court indicated, at 3, that the sole issue was proving intent, not the method or technology used to effect the signature:

'We find the fact that the signature is computer-generated rather than hand-signed does not defeat the purpose of the act. The issue is not how the name is placed on a sheet of paper; rather the issue is whether the person whose name is affixed intends to be bound. No one argues that the agent whose name was affixed did not intend to be bound. We find the signature requirements of the statute were met.'

This litigation was followed in 1993 with the South Carolina case of *Cylburn v Allstate Insurance Company*.[2] In this instance, the plaintiff took legal action against his insurer for breach of contract. The plaintiff's house burned down approximately two years after he stopped paying insurance premium payments. The plaintiff claimed that the policy had not been legally cancelled, which meant he had been denied insurance cover. The arguments in the case primarily focused on the interpretation of the South Carolina Code, in particular § 38-75-730(b), where cancellation arises when premiums are not paid – the cancellation is not effective unless the insured is provided with written notice of cancellation not less than ten days before the proposed effective date of cancellation. At the trial, the members of the jury determined that the defendant had sent notice of cancellation of the policy to the plaintiff for failing to pay the premium. However, the jury were also asked to decide whether the insurance company had sent a written notice to their insurance agent, indicating the policy was cancelled. It appears that the insurance company sent computer disks to its agents to bring them up-to-date with changes, and the members of the jury concluded that this method of providing written notice was not sufficient. At appeal, it was decided, after a brief indication that other forms of technology, such as videotapes and tape recordings were considered as 'writings,' that the computer disk sent by mail to the agent was equally as acceptable. Blatt SDJ indicated, at 956–957, that the form of technology was hardly a problem in reaching a decision based on sound legal principles:

'The storage of information on tape recordings and videotapes is not that much different from that on floppy diskettes for computers, but rather is more a difference in the devices used to read the information. The information can be retrieved and printed as "hardcopy" on paper. In today's "paperless" society of computer generated information, the court is not prepared, in the absence of some legislative provision or otherwise, to find that a computer floppy diskette would not constitute a "writing" within the meaning of [S.C.Code 1976] § 38-75-730.'

1   457 N.W.2d 1 (Iowa App. 1990).
2   826 F.Supp. 955 (D.S.C. 1993).

Public administration

10.12   Challenges involving the name typed into an email began to occur in 1997. The first challenge appears to be the Massachusetts case of *Doherty v Registry of Motor Vehicles*, relating to public documents and concerning the interpretation of revisions to the relevant code.[1] The plaintiff's driving licence was suspended by the Massachusetts State Police following the plaintiff's arrest for operating a motor vehicle while under the influence of intoxicating liquor and for refusing to take a breathalyzer test. The police officer submitted his report to the Registry of Motor Vehicles in the form of an email. When submitting a report, an officer is required to make such reports under the penalties of perjury. The plaintiff contended that because the email did not contain the officer's manuscript signature, the Registrar of Motor Vehicles could not act on the content of the email. The relevant text is taken from the memorandum of decision as follows:

'The report is not signed by anyone. At the bottom of the report, there are statements indicating the identity of various state police troopers and their functions. The report states that "Thomas Kelley" is the officer before whom the refusal was made and that "Tpr. Kevin Hogaboom" is the other person who witnessed the refusal. At the bottom of the report there is the following statement: "This is the report of TROOPER THOMAS KELLEY and was made by TROOPER THOMAS KELLEY under the penalties of perjury. Data entry and transmission were done by KELLY, THOMAS by or at the direction of TROOPER THOMAS KELLEY."'

Agnes J held that the email was signed where the statement was made under the penalties of perjury, even where the report did not contain a manuscript signature:

'I conclude that a police officer who files or transmits (or who has another file or transmit) a report that is required by law to be made to the Registry of Motor Vehicles or to some other agency or individual by means of Email or some other electronic method in which there is a statement that identifies the officer making the report and a statement that it is "made under the penalties of perjury" has "signed" the document and is subject to a prosecution for perjury if the report is willfully false in a material manner even though the report does not contain a handwritten signature.'

In reaching his decision, he considered the effect of the legislation, which was amended in 1995, and relevant case law. Amongst other conclusions, he noted that the legislature removed the requirement that the police officer's report had to be in writing; that the format of the report may be approved by the registrar, and the legislature inserted a new phrase to permit the mode of communication to include electronic means of transmission. In essence, the changes were meant to give effect to the use of email in such circumstances.

The judiciary also use electronic signatures, as demonstrated in the Florida case of *Florida Department of Agriculture and Consumer Services v Haire*,[2] in which it was decided that a judge may affix an electronic signature to a warrant. Warner J observed, at 1059–1060:

> 'When a judge issuing a warrant directs the use of an electronic signature, it is clear that the judge is attesting to the act of issuing the warrant. Accordingly, we find no prohibition to the use of an electronic signature, so long as it is the judge who authorizes and is in control of its use.
>
> The record here, however, discloses that in once instance an issuing magistrate authorized the Department to affix his signature to search warrants. We disapprove of a procedure which would permit the Department itself to prepare and electrically sign warrants with the judge's signature. However, technologically there is no reason why the Department could not provide the judge with software, expertise, and assistance to issue such warrants without the judge actually permitting the Department to electronically sign the warrants on the judge's behalf.'

1   No 97/CV0050 (Suffolk, SS Massachusetts District Court, May 28, 1997), available online at www.loundy.com/CASES/Doherty_v_RMV.html.
2   836 So.2d 1040 (Fla.App. 4 Dist. 2003), corrected opinion *Haire v Florida Department of Agriculture and Consumer Services*, Nos SC03-446 & Sc03-552, February 12, 2004, available online at www.law.fsu.edu/library/flsupct/sc03-446/op-sc03-446-corrected.pdf.

Employment

10.13   In the United States, the status of emails and electronic signatures arose in the employment context in the federal first circuit case of *Campbell v General Dynamics Government Systems Corporation*.[1] Gerard DeMuro, president of the company, sent an email to the employees (no mention is made in the report whether every employee had an email account) of the company regarding the implementation of a new dispute resolution policy. The subject heading read 'G. DeMuro – New Dispute Resolution Policy.' The content of the email included an introductory paragraph, described at 548:

> 'DeMuro pointed out that General Dynamics was "a leader in a very competitive marketplace," that its success depended on its employees, and that it was committed to "open, forthright and honest communications," especially in the context of "addressing and resolving employee issues

concerning legally protected rights and matters." Subsequent paragraphs explained that the company had developed the Policy as a means to handle legal issues arising out of workplace disputes. The email then limned the Policy's four-step approach to dispute resolution, describing the last step as "[a]rbitration by a qualified and independent arbitrator.'"

The email stated that the policy would become effective on 1 May 2001, the day following transmission. Two links were included in the email to relevant documents, and the recipient was urged to click on the links to peruse the documents. On 30 December 2002, the plaintiff's employment was terminated because of persistent absenteeism and tardiness. The plaintiff began action by filing an administrative complaint with the appropriate agency on the basis of discrimination, but withdrew the complaint and initiated legal action against General Dynamics in a Massachusetts state court. General Dynamics moved the action to the federal district court. Given the facts of this particular case, it was held that the email was not sufficient to put the employee on notice that a new policy had been introduced that terminated a right that extinguished the right to apply to a judicial forum to resolve employment claims. The email as a means of communication was not at issue, although one of the arguments used by the plaintiff was that the email communication was not a writing and therefore the policy did not satisfy the written provisions of the relevant statute. In this instance, the content of the email and the surrounding circumstances demonstrated the communication in itself was not effective. In particular, the email:

(a) Did not mention whether or how the revised policy would affect the employee's right to obtain access to a judicial forum with respect to employer-employee disputes.

(b) Failed to specify that the policy contained an agreement to arbitrate that would become binding upon continued employment.

(c) Did not indicate whether the term 'workplace disputes' included those giving rise to federal claims.

(d) The text of the policy was not part of the email, although it was posted on the intranet.

(e) Employees were not required to respond acknowledging receipt of the policy or to signify that they had read and understood its terms.

(f) The Policy used contractual language, whilst the text of the email played down the obligations set out in the Policy and the vocabulary used was completely different in tone to the language used in the Policy. As Selya CJ said at 558, 'To be blunt, the email announcement undersold the significance of the Policy and omitted the critical fact that it contained a mandatory arbitration agreement.'

In the judgment of the court given by Selya CJ, he indicated at 555 that the underlying issue related to the sufficiency of the notice, which: '... turns on whether, under the totality of the circumstances, the employer's communication would have provided a reasonably prudent employee notice of the waiver. This is an objective standard ..... Factors relevant to this analysis include, but are not limited to, the method of communication, the workplace context, and the content of the communication.' In the judgment of the court, it was made clear that an email may be an appropriate method of conveying such information, and in the light of the context of the conventions and routines employed by General Dynamic, it was noted that communication by email was a preferred method of communication within the company, although personnel matters were not routinely dealt with by email, and although the court did not uphold the requirement that an employee needs to take affirmative action in such an instance, nevertheless, in this case, the failure of the company to require a response to the email was significant. Selya CJ put these conclusions into the context of this particular set of facts at 557:

'The upshot is that the record supports the conclusion that email was a familiar format for many forms of intra-office communication, but it does not suggest that email was a traditional means either for conveying contractually binding terms or for effectuating waivers of employee's legal rights. Given that circumstance, we cannot say that delivery of an email heralding the birth of a new policy would raise a red flag vivid enough to cause a reasonable employee to anticipate the imposition of a legally significant alteration to the terms and conditions of his employment.'

Finally, he offered the following caveat at 559: 'We caution that this holding should not be read as a general denunciation of email as a medium for contract formation in the workplace.'

1   321 F.Supp.2d 142 (D.Mass. 2004), *affirmed* 407 F.3d 546 (1st Cir. 2005).

Statute of Frauds

10.14 Email is a particularly useful means of communicating and negotiating the terms of contracts. However, most organizations that use email for this purpose usually fail to comprehend the need to educate their workforce on the mechanisms by which a contract is formed, which means that disputes have occurred relating to whether the content of an exchange of emails was sufficient to demonstrate a contract was formed,[1] and if so, whether the emails were sufficiently signed under the relevant Statute of Frauds. For instance, two federal cases, the facts of which pre-date the passing of the Electronic Signatures in Global and National Commerce Act, 15 U.S.C. § 7001–7003, were decided in 2002 and 2005 respectively. In the seventh circuit case of *Cloud Corporation v Hasbro, Inc.*,[2] in an action for breach of contract, the contract was modified by an exchange of email communications during 1996 between employees of each company, in which it was decided that the sender's name in an email satisfied the requirements of the Illinois Statute of Frauds. The report of this case is inconclusive respecting the form in which the signature took. At 296, Posner CJ for the court stated that '... we conclude without having to rely on the federal Act that the sender's name on an email satisfies the signature requirements of the statute of frauds,' but it is not clear whether the learned judge refers to the name of the employee typed in the body of the text, possibly at the end of the email, or whether it is a reference to the name contained in the email address. In reaching this conclusion, Posner CJ considered the federal eighth circuit case of *Toghiyany d/b/a First Class Refurbishing v Amerigas Propane, Inc.*,[3] in which it was concluded that emails did not include a signature. The report of this case is ambiguous, and Posner CJ commented on this at 296 '... it is unclear whether the court thought the absence of a signature fatal or thought that it was that absence combined with the absence of an essential term – the duration of the contract – that triggered the statute of frauds.' The second federal case is *Lamle v Mattle, Inc.*,[4] in which the name of an employee added to an email sent in 1997 was held to be a valid writing and signature to satisfy California's Statute of Frauds. It was observed that if the email had been sent after 1 January 2000, there would have been no question of its sufficiency under the Uniform Electronic Transactions Act, Cal. Civ. Code §§ 1633.7. The case was therefore decided on the basis of Californian common law, and Dyk CJ observed at 1362 that 'We can see no meaningful difference between a typewritten signature on a telegram and an email.'

Prior to the federal court cases noted above, the case of *Shattuck v Klotzbach* came before the Superior Court at Plymouth in Massachusetts.[5] The parties discussed the sale of a property by an exchange of emails, and in an action to enforce the contract, it was held that the emails contained sufficient terms concerning the purchase and sale of the property to form an agreement. In addition, it was also held that the names of the parties typed at the end of each email was a signature, and where the husband signed on behalf of his wife where both husband and wife were aware of the negotiations, his signature was good for his wife. Murphy J indicated, at 361, that 'Taken as a whole, a reasonable trier of fact could conclude that the emails sent by the defendant were "signed" with the intent to authenticate the information contained therein as his act.' This was followed by the New York case of *On Line Power Technologies, Inc., v Square D Company*,[6] where it was held that an exchange of emails provided sufficient evidence to suggest the parties intended to enter into an agreement for the payment of commissions, and it was made clear that the emails contained valid electronic signatures under N.Y. State Technology Law § 104 (2003) and 15 U.S.C. § 7001 (2003). The form of the signature is not clear. The description given is that the name 'Steven J. Maling, NE Regional Service Sales Manager for Square D' was included in the relevant emails, and the emails originated from the email address of the company. There are three possibilities: the name was typed at the end of the email, or it was included in the email address or it was both typed at the end of the email and included as part of the email address. Another New York case was also heard in the same year, that of *Rosenfeld v Zerneck*,[7] where it was held that the content of an exchange of emails was not sufficient to create a binding agreement to buy and sell property, but was specifically recognized by Kramer J that a name typed at the end of an email constitutes an electronic signature and satisfies the Statute of Frauds.

The further New York case of *Bazak International Corp. v Tarrant Apparel Group*,[8] concerned allegations of breach of contract and unjust enrichment relating to the cancellation of a transaction over a quantity of jeans. The parties met to discuss the contract, and also entered into email correspondence. The lawyers for Tarrant contended the email correspondence did not satisfy the requirement for a confirmation in writing under section 2-201(2) UCC because the statute does not specifically mention email as a recognized form of writing. This argument was rightly and comprehensively dispensed with, and it was held that email does constitute a 'writing' under the New York Statute of Frauds. In addition, it was also confirmed that where the name of the sender is typed at the bottom of an email and typed on the company's letterhead, the signature satisfies the requirements of the Statute. Marrero DJ offered the following observations at 383: 'Tarrant contends that Bazak's October 3 email cannot satisfy UCC Section 2-201(2)'s 'writing in confirmation' requirement because the statute does not specifically mention email as a recognized form of writing.' He later continued:

'Although emails are intangible messages during their transmissions, this fact alone does not prove fatal to their qualifying as writings under the UCC. Aside from posted mail, the forms of communication regularly recognized by the courts as fulfilling UCC "writing" requirement, such as fax, telex, and telegraph, are all intangible forms of communication during portions of their transmission. Just as messages sent using these accepted methods can be rendered tangible, thereby falling within the UCC definition, so too can emails.'

1   Federal 5th circuit: *Hugh Symons Group, plc v Motorola, Inc.*, 292 F.3d 466 (5th Cir. 2002) the contents of an exchange of emails following oral discussions were not sufficient evidence of an agreement to satisfy the Statute of Frauds in Texas.

Federal 8th circuit: *General Trading International, Inc. v Wal-Mart Stores, Inc.*, 320 F.3d 831 (8th Cir. 2003) the contents of an exchange of emails were not sufficient evidence to constitute an agreement to reduce the purchase price for the purposes of the merchants' exception to the Arkansas Statute of Frauds.

Illinois: *Bell Fuels, Inc. v Chevron U.S.A. Inc.*, 2000 WL 305955 (N.D.Ill.) the contents of an exchange of emails were insufficient evidence of an exclusive distributorship to satisfy the Statute of Frauds.

Central Illinois Light Company v Consolidated Coal Company, 235 F.Supp.2d 916 (C.D.Ill 2002) the content of an exchange of email only indicate the parties were negotiating.

Kentucky: *Commonwealth Aluminum Corporation v Stanley Metal Associates*, 186 F.Supp.2d 770 (W.D.Ky. 2001) correspondence between a manufacturer and supplier comprising a series of letters, facsimile transmissions and emails, held to satisfy the Statute of Frauds. The correspondence was sufficient to establish an enforceable contract, and all other arguments were not discussed. By implication, the signatures on the emails must have been acceptable to the court.

Massachusetts: *Singer v Adamson*, 2003 WL 2364985 (Mass. Land Ct.) where an exchange of emails were not sufficient to demonstrate a meeting of the minds.

New Jersey: *Ballas v Tedesco* 41 F.Supp.2d 531 (D.N.J. 1999) an exchange of emails did not satisfy the statutory requirements of a written instrument signed by the defendants; no reason given.

New York: *Page v Muze, Inc.*, 270 A.D.2d 401; 705 N.Y.S.2d 383; 2000 N.Y. Slip Op. 02646 an unsigned email made an equivocal reference to terms and was not shown to have satisfied the subscription requirement of UCC former 8-319.

Sel-Lab Marketing, Inc. v Dial Corp., 48 UCC Rep.Serv.2d 482, 2002 WL 1974056 (S.D.N.Y.) an exchange of emails did not conform to the Statute of Frauds partly on the grounds that only one of the emails was signed, but not by the party to be charged. (The learned judge did not appear to consider whether the name in the email address could be an electronic signature).

Ohio: *In the Matter of Estate of Georgskey*, 2001 WL 824326 (Ohio App. 11 Dist.) an exchange of emails between siblings relating to an oral agreement to buy the family home on the death of a parent was insufficient to satisfy the Statute of Frauds.

Washington: *Hansen v Transworld Wireless TV-Spokane, Inc.*, 111 Wash. App. 361, 44 P.3d 929, 47. U.C.C. Rep.Serv.2d 460 (Div. 3 2002), *review denied*, 148 Wash.2d 1004, 60 P.3d 1211 (2003) (Wash.App. Div. 3 2002) an exchange of email messages did not satisfy the writing requirement of the Statute of Frauds because they were merely internal documents regarding continuing negotiations, even assuming the emails satisfied the signature requirements of the Uniform Commercial Code Statute of Frauds.

2   314 F.3d 289 (7th Cir. 2002).
3   309 F.3d 1088 (8th Cir. 2002).
4   394 F.3d 1355 (Fed. Cir. 2005).
5   14 Mass. L. Rptr 360; 2001 WL 1839720 (Mass. Super.).
6   2004 WL 1171405 (S.D.N.Y.).
7   776 N.Y.S.2d 458 (Sup. 2004).
8   378 F.Supp.2d 377 (S.D.N.Y. 2005).

Contractual terms

10.15 The findings in these cases are significant, even if the Industrial Tribunal decision from England and Wales is not binding on any court. This is partly because the format of the document is irrelevant. First, the effect this should have on the advice that lawyers give their clients is highly pertinent, whether dealing with commercial contracts, employment contracts or any other form of relationship that is possible to create or vary in writing. Consider, by way of example, a standard clause added to most contracts in the following terms: 'the contract shall not be altered unless done so in writing and signed by both parties.' If the words 'in writing and signed' remain as a standard element in such a clause, it will leave open the probability that contracts, no matter how long they have taken to negotiate, or their apparent length, are susceptible to being varied by an exchange of emails, perhaps between two fairly junior employees. This may well occur because most organizations have now lost control of their means of communication, because all, or virtually all, employees in some sectors have the ability to communicate with the outside world by means of email and other forms of technology, contrary to the position before the introduction of such facilities. This problem will be mitigated to a certain extent in contracts which provide a list of nominated personnel within each organization that have the authority to agree alterations and variations. In such circumstances, if a junior employee agrees an alteration without reference to those who are authorized to agree such changes, any dispute will centre on what, if any, authority was vested in the junior employee, and whether their actions acted to bind the organization. From the point of view of the organization, it is imperative to ensure that its employees are made aware of the effect that a promise can have if made by exchange of email. To mitigate this problem, it may be wise to establish whether the parties are content for a contract to be altered by exchange of emails, and if not, to include an amended version of the standard clause, such as: 'the contract shall not be altered unless done so in writing on paper and signed with the manuscript signature of both parties' or some similar form of words.

Hall v Cognos Limited illustrates the ease by which a contract can be varied, as does the Ohio case of *Amedisys, Inc., v JP Morgan Chase Manhattan Bank, as Trustees, In re National Century Financial Enterprises, Inc.*.[1] In this instance, a regular exchange of emails took place between Amedisys and National Century over the amount of funding Amedisys would need from week to week. It was held that the exchange of email messages were sufficient to satisfy a clause in an agreement between the parties specifying that its terms could be modified only in writing. The clause read:

'Section 10.6   Amendments; Waivers; Consents

No modification, amendment or waiver of, or with respect to, any provision of this Agreement, and all other agreements, instruments and documents thereto, nor consent to any departure by the Seller or the Subservicer from any of the terms or conditions thereof, shall be effective unless it shall be in writing and signed by each of the parties hereto. Any waiver or consent shall be effective only in the specific instance and for the purpose for which it is given ....'

After a brief discussion on the meaning of what constituted 'writing,' the learned judge, Calkoun BJ stated the decision of the court at 596 'In this case, Amedisys sent a weekly email to NCFE to notify how much funding Amedisys wanted for that week. Further, Amedisys was provided, on a weekly basis, with reconciliation reports showing its requested funding amounts. The Court finds that these weekly emails are reconciliation requirements satisfying the writing and signature requirements of the Sale Agreement. Further, the Court finds that these emails modified the Sale Agreement where Amedisys received funds from the sale of the accounts receivable on its terms when it so directed the NCFE Defendants instead of receiving funds automatically upon the sale of the accounts receivable.'

A further point centres on whether the use of email is appropriate and reasonable in the circumstances. Whether the use of email is a reasonable means of communication between two parties, or any number of parties, will depend on a range of factors, as indicated by Marrero DJ in *Bazak International Corp. v Tarrant Apparel Group*, where he commented, at 387–388: 'Nonetheless, whether email is an appropriate and reasonably expected form of communication between the two particular parties before the court is a question of fact. Here, the issue's resolution requires a factual inquiry into trade usage and course of dealing ...... Neither party directly addresses whether email is an appropriate method of communication in the re-sale trade generally or in Tarrant and Bazak's particular relationship. Yet later email correspondence from Tarrant to Bazak (the "GMAC email") provides evidence in light of which a reasonable jury could find that the parties did accept email as an appropriate form of communication.' This view corresponds with that expounded in *Campbell v General Dynamics Government Systems Corporation*, although this issue was never debated with other forms of communication, such as the use of telegrams or telex. It is to be wondered why correspondence by email should be subject to different criteria than any other form of communication, especially when email is a more readily available method of communication than telegrams, telex of facsimile transmissions.

1   310 B.R. 580 (Bkrtcy.S.D.Ohio 2004).

Wills

10.16   One further case serves to illustrate the fluid notion of an electronic signature and the use to which is can be put. In the Tennessee case of *Taylor v Holt*,[1] Steve Godfrey prepared his last will and testament on his computer and affixed his computer generated signature at the end, described in the report as his 'stylized cursive signature'. Two neighbours, Hershell Williams and Teresa Williams, witnessed the will by each signing their name below the signature applied by Mr Godfrey, and dated the document next to their respective signatures. He died approximately one week later. Doris Holt, Mr Godfrey's girlfriend, submitted the will for probate. Donna Godfrey Taylor, Mr Godfrey's sister, filed a complaint alleging, in part, that the will was not signed and claiming that Mr Godfrey had died intestate. Doris Holt was granted summary judgment holding there were no undisputed material facts and that all the legal requirements concerning the execution and witnessing of the will had been met. This decision was upheld on appeal. Swiney J noted, at 4:

'In the case at hand, Deceased did make a mark that was intended to operate as his signature. Deceased made a mark by using his computer to affix his computer generated signature, and, as indicated by the affidavits of both witnesses, this was done in the presence of the witnesses. The computer generated signature made by Deceased falls into the category of "any other symbol or methodology executed or adopted by a party with intention to authenticate a writing or record," and, if made in the presence of two attesting witnesses, as it was in this case, is sufficient to constitute proper execution of a will. Further, we note that Deceased simply used a computer rather than an ink pen as the tool to make his signature, and, therefore, complied with Tenn. Code Ann. § 32-1-104 by signing the will himself.'

The phrase 'stylized cursive signature' could mean that it was a biodynamic version of a manuscript signature, alternatively, he could have inserted a file with his scanned signature, and further in the alternative, he could have typed his name using the keyboard, then altered the font to change the look of the signature. The report also does not indicate the form of signature used by the witnesses, but it is probable that they merely typed their names into the document, using the keyboard. If this was the case, and if it becomes generally acceptable to sign a will using an electronic signature, it is possible to foresee that it will be necessary to consider what evidence there is to confirm the witnesses whose names were placed on the will actually attended the signing of the will and affixed their electronic signatures to the document. If such a state of affairs becomes the norm, it is probable that in proving probate, the witnesses will have to give evidence, which may serve to defeat the witnessing of the will.

In reaching its decision, the members of the court considered the formalities for the execution and witnessing of a will in Tennessee, as provided for in the Tennessee Code § 32-1-104, which states:

'32-1-104. Will other than holographic or nuncupative. —

The execution of a will, other than a holographic or nuncupative will, must be by the signature of the testator and of at least two (2) witnesses as follows:

(1)   The testator shall signify to the attesting witnesses that the instrument is the testator's will and either:
   (A)   The testator sign;
   (B)   Acknowledge the testator's signature already made; or
   (C)   At the testator's direction and in the testator's presence have someone else sign the testator's name; and
   (D)   In any of the above cases the act must be done in the presence of two (2) or more attesting witnesses.
(2)   The attesting witnesses must sign:
   (A)   In the presence of the testator; and
   (B)   In the presence of each other.'

On the face of these provisions, it seems possible to sign a will with an electronic signature, and the members of the court prayed in aid the definition of a signature under § 1-3-105 of the Tennessee Code. However, this section refers to a holographic will, not any other form of will:

'32-1-105. Holographic will. —

No witness to a holographic will is necessary, but the signature and all its material provisions must be in the handwriting of the testator and the testator's handwriting must be proved by two (2) witnesses.'

This decision was reached in 2003, after the passing of Senate Bill No. 376,[2] the Uniform Electronic Transactions Act, section 3 of which limits the scope of the use of electronic signatures, and specifically excludes wills:

'SECTION 3. SCOPE.

(a)   Except as otherwise provided in subsection (b), this act applies to electronic records and electronic signatures relating to a transaction.
(b)   This act does not apply to a transaction to the extent it is governed by:
    (1)   a law governing the creation and execution of wills, codicils, or testamentary trusts;'

It appears that the members of the court interpreted some of the legislation, but failed to consider all of the relevant legislation, which means this decision cannot be very persuasive. Nevertheless the facts of the case demonstrate that there are circumstances when a will might need to be considered as a result of being written on a computer, and it is conceivable that a court many be required to consider the content of an email that is clearly testamentary in character – perhaps an email sent by a service man or woman whilst on active duty.[3]

1   CA Tennessee Knoxville 18 August 2003 No E2003-00901-COA-R3-CV, available online at www.tsc.state.tn.us/opinions/tca/PDF/034/taylordg.pdf.
2   Public Acts, 2001, Chapter No. 72 Senate Bill No. 376, passed on 9 April 2001 and approved on 11 April 2001.
3   Jeremy Malcolm, a lawyer in Australia signed his will using digital signatures, see Angus Kidman, 'Australian makes digital will', *ZDNet Australia*, 20 January 2004, available online at www.news.zdnet.co.uk/emergingtech/0,1000000183,39119199,00.htm; *e-Signature Law Journal* (now the *Digital Evidence Journal*) 2003, Volume 1 Number 1, 42; Michael Cameron Wood-Bodley, 'Wills, data messages, and the Electronic Communications and Transactions Act' *The South African Law Journal*, 2004 Volume 21, 526–528; W.H. Hurlburt QC, 'Electronic Wills and Powers of Attorney: has their day come?', Alberta Law Reform Institute, available online at www.ulcc.ca/en/poam2/index.cfm?sec=2001&sub=2001ha and www.ulcc.ca/en/poam2/e-wills-power-attorney.pdf.

Evidence

10.17 Under the hearsay provisions for evidence in the United States of America, a third party statement is not admissible into evidence. The advent of email as a method of communication has led to some new and interesting challenges, as exemplified in the federal ninth circuit case of *Sea-Land Service, Inc. v Lozen International, LLC*.[1] Sea-Land agreed to transport three 40-foot containers of grapes from Hermosillo, Mexico, to Felixstowe, England. The containers were to travel for part of the journey by rail. Unfortunately, Sea-Land's railroad agent placed the containers on the wrong train, and the grapes did not arrive at the port in sufficient time for the sailing of the vessel they were due to be transported in. Sea-Land began the action to recover the full amount of its contract with Lozen to transport the containers of grapes, and Lozen counterclaimed for breach of contract and for loss of cargo, because it had to sell the grapes domestically at a lower price. At the hearing for summary judgment, the learned judge excluded an internal email written by an employee of Sea-Land and forwarded to Lozen by another employee of Sea-Land. On appeal, it was held that the email was not hearsay as an admission of a party opponent. Graber CJ indicated the position at 821:

> 'The original email, an internal company memorandum, closes with a electronic "signature" attesting that the message was authored by "Mike Jacques," Sea-Land's "Rail Reefer Services Coordinator" at the time the email was written. Jacques is listed as one of Sea-Land's employees in Exhibit 9, a letter from Sea-Land to Lozen that the district court *did* admit into evidence. The original email also appears to concern a matter within the scope of Jacques' employment.
>
> More importantly, however, Jacques' original email was forwarded to Lozen by Laurie Martines, a second Sea-Land employee. She copied the entire body of Jacques' internal memorandum into her email and prefaced it with the statement "Yikes, Pls note the rail screwed us up ....," Martinez thereby incorporated and adopted the contents of Jacques' original message, because of her remark "manifested an adoption or belief in [the] truth" on the information contained in the original email.'

One further issue that may exercise the minds of judges in the future is how to determine the actual act that constitutes the acceptance by the sender of the electronic signature. In the case of a manuscript signature, the person furnishes evidence of their intent by physically writing on a carrier, and providing there is sufficient text to link the person to the document, the proof of intent is demonstrated. However, in the digital context, the moment of authentication may not be when the person actually types in their name or adopts the signature text at the end of the email (or put in automatically when a new email is begun where the program is set up to include a signature at the end of the email). The Missouri case of *International Casings Group,*

Inc. v Premium Standard Farms, Inc.[2] illustrates this point. A new contract for the purchase of hog casings was partly established by an exchange of emails between the parties. The emails in question are set out in the report in full at 865–868. Kent Pummill signed some of his emails 'Kent' and some he sent without adding his name, whilst Tom Sanscki sent all of his emails without any form of salutation. First, Laughrey J concluded there was sufficient evidence to establish the existence of a contract that contained all the essential terms. Second, having rehearsed the statutory provisions governing electronic signatures, he concluded that the signatures satisfied the UCC Statute of Frauds, providing each person had the intention to authenticate the document. The learned judge appeared to make it clear that where an email includes the name of the sender in the header or at the bottom of the email, the act of pressing the send icon on a computer constituted the authentication of the document and a valid electronic signature under the Missouri and North Carolina Electronic Transactions Act. The comments made by Laughrey DJ recorded at 873:

> 'There is overwhelming evidence that Sanecki's and Pummill's emails are authentic and that the information contained in them was intended by each to accurately reflect their communications with the other. Although they do not all contain a typed name at the bottom of the emails, each email contains a header with the name of the sender. Given the testimony at the preliminary hearing, it is clear that Sanecki and Pummill, by hitting the send button, intended to presently authenticate and adopt the content of the emails as their own writing. This is enough to satisfy the UCC given the breadth of the definition of signature, as well as the UETA which specifically refers to a "process attached to or logically associated with a record."'

The learned judge took the opportunity to list relevant case law at 874, and distinguished the decision in *Toghiyany d/b/a First Class Refurbishing v Amerigas Propane, Inc.*[3] where emails were held not to include a signature. Examining the *Toghiyany* decision, Laughrey J noted that the contract was not enforceable because it lacked a durational term; the definition of 'signature' in the UCC did not apply to *Toghiyany* because the sale was not governed by the UCC, and the case was decided before the Missouri UETA was passed.

1   285 F.3d 808 (9th Cir. 2002).
2   358 F.Supp.2d 863 (W.D.Mo. 2005), 2005 WL 486784.
3   309 F.3d 1088 (8th Cir. 2002).

The 'click wrap' method of indicating intent

10.18 Clicking the 'I accept' or 'I agree' icon to confirm the intention to enter a contract when buying goods or services electronically is now a very popular method of demonstrating intent. In itself, the action of clicking the icon has the effect of satisfying the function of a signature. This is certainly implied in the Canadian case of *Rudder v Microsoft Corp.*,[1] and has been widely accepted in the United States of America.[2] The Law Commission has suggested that this form of signature is the technological equivalent of a manuscript signature using a cross.[3] It is suggested with respect that the analysis proposed by the Law Commission is sound. This analysis is also in keeping with the decisions made by judges over the past two hundred years regarding the form that a manuscript signature may take. In English law, the validity of the signature depends on the function it performs, not necessarily the form a signature takes. Even if the act of clicking on an icon to order goods or services is deemed to be less secure than that provided by a manuscript signature, it does not follow that the reliability of the signature will affect its validity. Should a dispute occur between a buyer and a seller where one of the issues relates to the pressing of the icon, and the parties fail to resolve the matter, they will have to contemplate taking legal action. Before the matter reaches a court, both parties will have to pay particular attention to the quantity and quality of the evidence available to them. In all probability, the reliability of the signature will depend on the ability of one or both of the parties to adduce sufficient forensic evidence of a high enough quality to demonstrate either the icon was clicked or it was not. Even if the relying party can prove that the icon was clicked, it will not follow that the purported buyer clicked it. The nexus between the action of clicking the icon and the identity of the person who purported to order the items may be difficult to resolve, bearing in mind the security risks associated with using the internet.

This type of conflicting evidence, coupled with a denial that the email communications were sent by the sender, occurred in Germany in the three cases of OLG Köln, 19 U 16/02; LG Konstanz, 2 O 141/01 A; AG Erfurt, 28 C 2354/01.[4] The three individual defendants were asked to pay for items bought in internet auctions. The winning bids were sent from email accounts where the user can write the email on the website of the provider of the address. Each of the defendants had access to the address by means of a password, but denied taking part in the bidding process. All three cases were dismissed, because the relying party failed to prove to the satisfaction of the courts that the defendants sent the declarations, which meant the plaintiff failed to prove that a contract had been concluded. By the same token, exactly the same problem may occur with the use of digital signatures. Whether a user denies clicking on an icon or using their private key to sign a document or message, the problem will be the same: proving that the sending party carried out the action. In this respect, the difference between a digital signature and clicking an icon is a narrow one.

1   (1999), 2 C.P.R. (4th) 474, 47 C.C.L.T. (2d) 168 (Ont. Sup. Ct.), FSR (1996) 367. See also
     Kanitz v Rogers Cable Inc. (2002), 58 O.R. (3d) 299 (Sup. Ct.).
2   For instances where the mode of acceptance is implicit by the nature of the claim:

Federal 6th circuit: *CompuServe, Incorporated v Patterson*, 89 F.3d 1257 (6th Cir. 1996) inferred that 'I accept' or 'I agree' icon accepted as a means of proving intent (not at issue).

California: *America Online, Inc., v Superior Court of Alemeda County*, 90 Cal.App.4th 1, 108 Cal. Rptr.2d 699, 01 Cal. Daily Op. Serv. 5191, Daily Journal D.A.R. 6367.

Florida: *America Online, Inc., v Booker*, 781 So.2d 423 (Fla.App. 3 Dist. 2001).

Illinois: *In re RealNetworks, Inc., Privacy Litigation*, 2000 WL 631341 (N.D.Ill.).

Lieschke v Realnetworks, Inc., 2000 WL 198424 (ND Ill.).

DeJohn v. The .TV Corporation Int'l, 245 F.Supp.2d 913 (C.D.Ill. 2003) domain name registration 'I agree' upheld as a means of expressing assent.

New Jersey: *Caspi v Microsoft Network, L.L.C.*, 323 N.J. Super. 188, 732 A.2d 528 (N.J.Super. A.D. 1999).

Texas: *Barnett v Network Solutions, Inc.*, 38 S.W.3d 200 (Tex.App.-Eastland 2001).

Where the 'I accept' icon is specifically commented upon:

California: *Hotmail Corporation v Van$ Money Pie Inc.*, 1998 WL 388389, 47 U.S.P.Q.2d 1020 a default judgment upholding a breach of a click-through agreement.

Colombia: *Forrest v Verizon Communications, Inc.*, 805 A.2d 1007 (D.C. 2002) clicking an 'Accept' icon sufficient to prove intent.

Kansas: *Mortgage Plus, Inc., v DocMagic, Inc. d/b/a Document Systems, Inc.*, 2004 WL 2331918 (D.Kan.), 55 UCC Rep.Serv.2d 58 a clickwrap licence held valid.

Massachusetts: *I.Lan Systems, Inc., v Netscout Service Level Corp.*, 183 F.Supp.2d 328 (D.Mass. 2002) a click-wrap licence upheld by the court. Young, CJ, said, at 338 'The only issue before the Court is whether clickwrap license agreements are an appropriate way to form contracts, and the Court holds that they are. In short, i.Lan explicitly accepted the clickwrap license agreement when it clicked on the box stating "I agree."'

Missouri: *Davidson & Associates, Inc., v Internet Gateway*, 334 F.Supp.2d 1164 (E.D.Mo. 2004) two agreements that required the user to express assent by clicking 'I Agree' and 'Agree' expressly upheld.

New Jersey: *Bergraft v e-Bay, Inc.*, (N.J. Super. Ct. Oct. 1, 2003) the act of clicking the 'I accept' icon acted to bind the parties to the terms of the User Agreement. The Order is available online from the website of Assistant Professor Eric Goldman www.eric_goldman.tripod.com/caselaw/begraftvebay.pdf

New York: *Moore v Microsoft Corporation*, 293 A.D.2d 587, 741 N.Y.S.2d 91, 48 UCC Rep.Serv.2d software user was bound by licence agreement where terms were prominently displayed on computer screen before software could be installed and where the user was required to indicate assent by clicking the 'I agree' icon.

Ohio: *Bell v Hollywood Entertainment Corporation*, 2006 WL 2192053 (Ohio App. 8 Dist.), an arbitration clause was held to be effective where an applicant applied for a job online and answered all the questions, signing the document by clicking the 'Yes' icon specifically to agree the binding nature of the clause relating to arbitration.

Pennsylvania: *Verizon Communications, Inc. v Pizzirani*, 462 F.Supp.2d 648 (E.D.Pa. 2006), under New York law, an employee signified his acceptance of a contractual term containing a restrictive covenant not to engage in competitive activities as set out in the relevant agreement by clicking on an icon with the words 'I ACKNOWLEDGE' each time he accepted an Award as an incentive.

Rhode Island: *Groff v America Online, Inc.*, 1998 WL 307001 (R.I.Super.) 'I Agree' icon upheld.

3   Law Commission 'Electronic Commerce: Formal Requirements in Commercial Transactions Advice from the Law Commission' December 2001 para 3.37; see also paras 3.36 and 3.38.

4   Michael Knopp, Case Note, OLG Köln, 19 U 16/02; LG Konstanz, 2 O 141/01 A; AG Erfurt, 28 C 2354/01, *e-Signature Law Journal* (now the *Digital Evidence Journal*), Volume 2 Number 2, 2005, 119–120.

Personal Identification Number (PIN)

10.19 The PIN has become a very widely used form of authentication, especially to obtain access to a bank account through the use of an ATM (automated teller machine or automatic teller machine or automated banking machine or cash machine), or to confirm a transaction with a credit card or debit card.[1] Invariably, a claim by the user that one or more transactions conducted on the account were not authorized by them will require the relying party to prove the transaction was authorized by the account holder. The fact a withdrawal or other form of transaction took place may not be in issue, and in any event, the bank can adduce the evidence under the relevant business records or the Bankers' Books exemptions. The central issue will probably be whether it was the customer or somebody else that was responsible for withdrawals made from the customer's account using the correct PIN. The United States case of *Judd v Citibank*,[2] illustrates the nature of the problem. In 1980, Dorothy Judd discovered two withdrawals were made from her account by use of a cash card and PIN in the sum of US$800 when she was at work. Marmarellis J indicated that the case turned on issues of evidence, burden and credibility. He determined the issue by considering whether the plaintiff had proven her case by a fair preponderance of the credible evidence. In this instance, the issue was whether to believe the person or the print-out of the transactions from the machine. The judge determined that the plaintiff had proved her case 'by a fair preponderance of the credible evidence' and judgment was awarded in the amount of the loss plus interest and disbursements.

In England and Wales, PC John Munden was charged with attempting to obtain money by deception after he complained that he was not responsible for making six transactions from ATM machines, all of which appeared on his statement in September 1992. He was subsequently prosecuted at Mildenhall Magistrates' Court in Suffolk in February 1994 and convicted. He appealed against his conviction before Turner J, sitting with two Magistrates at Bury St Edmunds Crown Court. It appears that the defence attempted to obtain information about the computer systems, records and operational procedures of Halifax Building Society, but the Halifax apparently refused to provide such evidence, except in the form of a report by a third party. In these circumstances, the court decided that PC Munden's conviction could not stand, and he was acquitted. In Germany, an appeal from a civil action was brought before the Bundesgerichtshof (the Federal Supreme Court) in 2004.[3] In this instance, the plaintiff's purse was stolen. It contained her cash card, and an hour or so later, cash was withdrawn at two different ATMs using the correct PIN. The plaintiff took action against her bank to recover the money, and the bank refused to reimburse the customer, because, it was alleged, of her negligence, which excluded the bank's liability under its general terms and conditions for the issue of cash cards. The court of first instance found for the plaintiff, and a regional court reversed the decision on appeal. The plaintiff appealed to the Federal Supreme court on a point of law. The only issue before the Federal Supreme Court concerned the burden of proof. The decision of the regional court was confirmed. It was held that the rules on prima facie evidence applied. This was because the facts proved in the matter (the withdrawal of cash in conjunction with a stolen bank card and the use of the correct PIN) characteristically resulted from a different set of facts (the storage of PIN with the card). The court also held that in order to prove her case, the plaintiff had to show that the same result could occur in another way, in order to rebut the prima facie evidence.

In comparison, two judges in separate jurisdictions have reached different conclusions on similar facts. In a Greek case of 5526/1999,[4] the claimant's bank cash card was stolen from his car, amongst other items. Although the claimant immediately informed the police and the bank, the bank failed to put a stop on the account in time, and funds were subsequently removed from his account. The bank sought to enforce the terms and conditions that applied to the issuance of the card, relying on the strict liability of the customer where the card was used without authority. In this instance, the term was considered unfair, because it was contrary to the main principle of fault allocation in Greek law, and second, because such terms are contrary to good faith. The customer was not held to be at fault. Compare this decision to the South African case of *Diners Club SA (Pty) Ltd v Singh*[5] where Levinsohn J held, at 659, that a contract term by which the customer was liable, irrespective of who used the PIN, was not against public policy. This is a very wide and sweeping decision that cannot, it is respectfully suggested, be maintained in the light of the relative ease by which a PIN can be obtained without the consent or authority of the cardholder. In the Papua New Guinea District Court, Seneka J found for Mathew Roni against the Bank of South Pacific.[6] Mr Roni discovered the loss of his Save Card, and informed the bank immediately he knew of the loss. It was not in dispute that the bank put a stop to all withdrawals, but it subsequently transpired that a number of transactions occurred after the time the bank put a stop on the account, some of the transaction took place at almost the same time in separate geographical locations using the correct PIN. The learned judge reached the conclusion that the bank was negligent.

In the Dominican Republic, the Instituto Dominicano de Telecomunicaciones is an autonomous entity that regulates telecommunications. Decisions made by the Instituto are only subject to appeal before the Supreme Court of Justice, in accordance to Article 79 of the Telecommunication Law No. 153-98. In the case of *Verizon Dominicana, C. por A., v Enilsa Rodríguez Pérez*, September 8, 2006, the Supreme Court of Justice upheld the Instituto decision of *Verizon Dominicana, C. por A. v Genara Ramírez Mariñez* dated April 13, 2005 in which is was decided that a PIN number, when blocking the numbers 0 and 1 for making long distance calls, can be compared to a digital signature, and that it is the user who voluntarily decides to accept the terms and conditions of the service. By agreeing to accept the service, it was determined that they are the only person to know the PIN, because the PIN is a secret and the only number allocated to each telephone line. No consideration seems to have been given with the ease by which a PIN can be obtained by a third party intent on using the services without authority.

In situations such as those illustrated above, the nature of the evidence and the types of attack that third parties can use to obtain the correct PIN will be highly relevant in reaching a decision between two conflicting claims.[7] However, not every dispute is about unauthorized transactions. Transactions can occur with the authority of the user, but the user may dispute the amount they authorized, as in the Danish case of U.2000.1853V, where, at a restaurant with late night opening hours, A authorized two Dankort card payments as he swiped his debit card through one of N's card terminals, entered his PIN, and agreed the amount that appeared on the display. The court was satisfied that one of the payments was erroneously accepted in the sum of DKK 10,500 instead of DKK 105. N was therefore ordered to pay back the difference. The court accepted, as a starting point, that when the appellant entered his PIN and approved an amount in the sum of DKK 10,500, the appellant made a binding payment to the respondent. However, that action did not rule out that it can be proved that payment of a higher amount was made by mistake.[8]

1   For instance, the use of PIN was explicitly recognized as a type of electronic signature by the Supreme Court of Lithuania in its ruling as of 20 February 2002, case No. 3K-3-390/2002.

2   N.Y.City Civ.Ct., 435 N.Y.S.2d 210.

3   BGH October 5. 2004, XI ZR 210/03.

4   Court of First Instance of Athens constituted by one judge 5526/1999, for a translation into English see Anastasia Fylla, Case Note – Greece, *Digital Evidence Journal*, Volume 4 Number 1, 47–48.

5   2004 (3) SA 630 (D).

6   *Roni v Kagure* [2004] PGDC 1; DC84 (1 January 2004).

7   Stephen Mason, general editor, Electronic Evidence: Disclosure, Discovery & Admissibility, (LexisNexis Butterworths, 2007), Chapter 4 'Evidentiary foundations' for a wider discussion of the evidence and the nature of the risks in relation to ATMs.

8   A full report of this case will be published in the *Digital Evidence Journal*, 2007, Volume 4 Number 2.

The name in an email address

10.20   The name in an email address is capable of identifying a person, especially where an email address in an organization, whether public or private, is allocated by setting out the name of the person followed by the domain name of the organization. There are other variations that can be used, such as when an email address describes the office or function of the person, rather then their name. However, even this, if allocated to a single person, can also function to identify a particular person. The link between the prefix of the email address and the person responsible for sending the email can be problematic: for instance, the sender may be able to choose the first part, and may decide to adopt letters or numbers or a combination of letters and numbers with a view to obfuscating their identity. Further, the true email address might be hidden by the sender. If it was not obvious who the sender was, and if correspondence ensues and a dispute occurs, it will be a matter of establishing what, if any, evidence there is pertaining to the source of the relevant emails as a preliminary point. It has been held in a number of jurisdictions that the name in an email address, or the combination of the name and the domain name in an email address can be a form of electronic signature.

AUSTRALIA

Limitation Act

10.21   The case of *McGuren v Simpson*[1] raised the issue as to whether correspondence by email was capable of constituting an acknowledgement that was in writing and signed for the purposes of the Limitation Act 1969 (NSW). Mr Simpson and Ms McGuren were in a relationship between 1992 and 2000. Mr Simpson received a cheque for A$23,000 when he was in prison in November 1993 in respect of a claim for damages for personal injuries he suffered in a motor vehicle accident. He endorsed the cheque in favour of Ms McGuren's sister, Jody McGuren, to enable her to bank the cheque in her account on behalf of Ms McGuren (Ms McGuren did not want to pay the cheque into her own account, otherwise it would have affected the state benefits she was receiving at the time). Mr Simpson claimed that the defendant used the money almost entirely for her own purposes and he sought recovery of the money from Ms McGuren. Ms McGuren asserted that she used the money in accordance with his instructions and with his approval. Mr Simpson's main item of evidence was in the form of an email sent to him by Ms McGuren. It read in part:

> 'Date: Wed, 29 Sep 1999 14 16.20+1000
> To: "Rob – yahoo"<Robert-john-simpson@yahoo.com.au>
> From: "McGuren, Kim" Kim.Mcguran@air.gov.au
>
> I am going to try and book a cab for 6pm at childcare does that suit you?
>
> It probably won't turn up but I may as well book it. So, what do you want to do: split up, – go to counselling or – just blame each other for every thing since everything is obviously the other person's fault, for the rest of our lives? Yes, I spent the money and I shouldn't have and yes, you have been violent and you shouldn't have so what now??'

Master Harrison dealt with an appeal from a Local Court Magistrate, and the main issue to determine was whether Mr Simpson's cause of action was statute barred under s 14 of the Limitation Act 1969 (NSW). The time limit is extended under the provisions of s 54 where the person against whom the cause of action lies confirms the cause of action by acknowledging it to the person who holds the action, providing the acknowledgment is in writing and signed by the maker. Mr Simpson's case was that Ms McGuren acknowledged the cause of action in the email she sent when she wrote the words 'Yes, I spent the money and I shouldn't have.' The Magistrate previously determined that the email was an electronic communication within the meaning of s 9(1) of the Electronic Transaction Act 2000 (NSW). However, the Act was not in force at the time the email was sent, which meant the provisions of the Act did not apply to the email, hence the Magistrate's decision was incorrect. Master Harrison dealt with the problem in the context of the common law. First, he concluded that the email constituted a written document. In so doing, he noted the expansive approach taken in other jurisdictions (at paragraph 20), and decided to construe the act to take into account the changes in technology (at paragraph 21), a view taken by judges in England and Wales and the USA in the nineteenth century: 'It is my view that ..... s 54 of the Act ought to be read to accommodate technological change and that, accordingly, the email sent by the plaintiff constitutes a written document.'

Second, he agreed with the decision of the Magistrate, that the email address was a signature for the purpose of s 54(4) of the Limitation Act 1969 (NSW), at paragraph 22:

'As Ms McGuren's name appears in the email and she expressly acknowledges in the email as an authenticated expression of a prior agreement, the email is recognisable as a note of a concluded agreement. Accordingly, the Magistrate was correct at law to conclude that Ms McGuren signed the email and that the requirements of s 54(4) of the Act were met. It was open to the Magistrate to find that Ms McGuren acknowledged the claim and she has admitted her legal liability to pay Mr Simpson that which he seeks to recover.'

1   [2004] NSWSC 35.

ENGLAND AND WALES

Statute of Frauds

10.22   The question arose in the case of *J Pereira Fernandes SA v Mehta*[1] whether the name forming part of an email address could be construed as a signature. J Pereira Fernandes SA is a Portuguese company that supplied bedding products in July 2002 to Bedcare (UK) Limited, a company of which Mr Mehta was a director. Bedcare (UK) Limited failed to pay for the products it had received, and was wound up on a Petition by J Pereira Fernandes SA by an Order made on 7 March 2005. The cause of the appeal before Judge

Pelling QC related to the presentation of a winding-up petition by J Pereira Fernandes SA on 12 January 2005. On 20 February 2005, an email was sent from the email address 'Nelmehta@aol.com' to Ian Simpson & Co, solicitors acting for J Pereira Fernandes SA.[2] Mr Mehta's name was not typed at the end of the email. On 9 November 2005, District Judge Harrison gave summary judgment to J Pereira Fernandes SA in the sum of £24,985.53 and ordered Mr Mehta to pay the costs of the claim, which were summarily assessed in the sum of £1,080.00. Mr Mehta was subsequently given permission to appeal by Holman J on 20 February 2006.

The email contained the following text:

'... I would be grateful if you could kindly consider the following.

If the hearing of the Petition can be adjourned for a period of 7 days subject to the following:

a. A Personal Guarantee to be given in the amount of £25,000 in favour of your client – together with a list of my personal assets provided to you by my solicitor

b. A repayment schedule to be redrawn over a period of six months with a payment of £5000.00 drawn from my personal funds to be made before the adjourned hearing

I am also prepared to give a company undertaking not to sell market or dispose of any company assets without prior consent from your client pending the signing of the Personal Guarantee.'

The email address that appeared on this particular email also appeared on other emails sent to Ian Simpson & Co by Mr Mehta, which did include his name typed at the end of the email. There were two matters of relevance to consider: whether the email could be considered a sufficient note or memorandum, and if so, whether it was signed by the party charged, that is, or on behalf of Mr Mehta. The email was, relatively speaking, a relatively rare example of a document that is brought into the purview of s 4 of the Statute of Frauds 1677.[3] This is because s 4 now only applies to contracts of guarantee, and the content of this email offered a guarantee, in that Mr Mehta offered to personally cover debts owed by the company.[4] Section 4 reads:[5]

Noe action shall be brought ... whereby to charge the defendant upon any speciall promise to answere for the debt default or miscarriages of another person ... unless the agreement upon which such action shall be brought or some memorandum or note thereof shall be in writing and signed by the partie to be charged therewith or some other person thereunto by him lawfully authorized.

District Judge Harrison, in giving summary judgment, considered that the email did amount to a note or memorandum of guarantee, although he did not explicitly comment on whether the names in the email address could amount to a signature. Judge Pelling QC agreed with District Judge Harrison on this point, and also held the email to be a note or memorandum that brought it within s 4 of the statute. He commented on the purpose of the statute as follows:[6]

'The purpose of the statute of frauds is to protect people from being held liable on informal communications because they may be made without sufficient consideration or expressed ambiguously or because such a communication might be fraudulently alleged against the party to be charged. That being so, the logic underlying the authorities I have referred to would appear to be that where (as in this case) there is an offer in writing made by the party to be bound which contains the essential terms of what is offered *and* the party to be bound accepts that his offer has been accepted unconditionally, albeit orally, there is a sufficient note or memorandum to satisfy s 4.'

The second question to consider was whether the email had been signed. Solicitors for J Pereira Fernandes SA already had a number of emails from Mr Mehta in which he included his name typed at the bottom of the text. In this respect, the evidence of a number of communications from the same address demonstrated that they were authentic. In any event, Mr Mehta did not dispute the email was sent. In this respect, the evidence upon which a decision could be made was greater than the evidence that Prakash J dealt with in *SM Integrated Transware Ltd v Schenker Singapore (Pte) Ltd.*[7] However, in this instance, the learned judge took the view that the email address was similar to an automatically generated name and facsimile number of the sender of a facsimile transmission, a state of affairs considered in the New York case of *Parma Tile Mosaic & Marble Co., Inc. v Estate of Fred Short, d/b/a Sime Construction Co.*[8] Counsel for J Pereira Fernandes SA submitted that the intent to sign was not relevant, and mentioned *Elpis Maritime Co. Ltd. v Marti Chartering Co. Inc.*,[9] which had different facts to the case in point, and also emphasised the decision in *Evans v Hoare*,[10] where the name and address were relied upon to serve as a signature. However, the learned judge pointed out that Cave J made it clear, at 597, that the place of the signature was not relevant: 'Whether the name occurs in the body of the memorandum, or at the beginning, or at the end, if it is intended for a signature there is a memorandum of the agreement within the meaning of the statute.' Judge Pelling QC then went on to indicate that the name of the party to be bound must be intended for a signature, but the further comments made by Cave J after the text quoted by Judge Pelling QC, are of relevance: 'In the present case it is true that the name of the defendants occurs in the agreement; but it is suggested on behalf of the defendants that it was only put in to shew who the persons were to whom the letter was addressed. The answer is that there is the name, and it was inserted by the defendants' agent in a contract which was undoubtedly intended by the defendants to be binding on the plaintiff; and, therefore, the fact that it is only in the form of an address is immaterial.'[11] Cave J then discussed the facts and decision in *Schneider v Norris*,[12] and, in consideration of the facts of this case, said 'This shews that it is unimportant how the name came to be inserted in the document.'

The learned judge considered that this approach was supported by the decision in *Caton v Caton*,[13] where Richard Bewley Caton, aged 78 in 1852, a clergyman of the Church of England, proposed marriage to Mrs Harriet Henley, a widow of about 60 years of age. Both parties owned property, and Mr Emmet, a solicitor, was requested to draw up the settlement upon the basis of a draft written by the Reverend Caton. After the settlement was prepared, the Reverend Caton first suggested to Mrs Henley it was too long, and later suggested they could save expense by not executing the settlement at all. Mrs Henley agreed not to execute the settlement on his promise that he would strictly and faithfully carry out the terms of the memorandum, and leave certain property to her in his will. Despite the remonstrations of Mr Emmet that Mrs Henley ought to insist upon entering the settlement before marriage, Mrs Henley married the Reverend on 7 February 1853. The Reverend Caton took possession of Mrs Henley's property and paid her £80 a year. By his own reckoning, Mrs Henley's fortune was estimated at £14,904. At the time of their marriage, the Reverend showed Mrs Henley a will that appeared to be in conformity with the promise he made. It was duly executed. He died on 24 January 1864, when it then transpired that he had made a new will, without the knowledge of Mrs Caton, revoking all others, leaving her with less than she otherwise expected. Legal action was taken to attempt to have the marriage settlement drawn up in the hand of the Reverend Caton acknowledged as a binding marriage contract, the performance of which Mrs Caton sought to enforce. The agreement began with the introductory words 'in the event of a marriage between the under-named parties' and the initials of the Reverend Caton appeared four times with reference to particular instructions. The Vice-Chancellor, Stuart found for the appellant at first instance, a decision that was reversed on appeal by Cranworth LC. Upon further appeal to the House of Lords, the appeal was dismissed. The sole question was whether, where the Reverend's initials appeared on the document, they served to apply to the entire document. It was determined that the document was a mere draft of proposal for a settlement, and there was insufficient evidence to show the initials of the Reverend applied to the entire document. On the position of the initials, Lord Chelmsford LC said at 139:

'The cases on this point cited in the course of the argument establish that the mere circumstances of the name of a party being written by himself in the body of a memorandum of agreement will not of itself constitute a signature. It must be inserted in the writing in such a manner as to have the effect of "authenticating the instrument," or "so as to govern the whole instrument," to use the words of Sir *William Grant*, in the case of *Ogilvie v Foljambe* [(1817) 3 Mer 53; 36 ER 21], or in the language of Mr. Justice *Coleridge*, in *Lobb and Knight v Stanley* [(1844) 5 QB 574; 114 ER 1366], "so as to govern what follows." Now I cannot think that the occurrence of Mr. *Caton's* name in the manner in which it appears can possibly be taken to govern the entire memorandum, although the whole of it is in his handwriting.' (Italics in the original)

He continued at 139–140:

'The name of the party, and its application to the whole of the instrument, can alone satisfy the requisites of a signature. In the memorandum in question, Mr. *Caton's* name is incidentally introduced with reference to a particular purpose, or as matter of description, and as this mention of his name would clearly be insufficient in itself, it cannot have any new effect given to it by the introductory words of the memorandum.'

Lord Westbury said, at 143 that what is alleged to constitute the signature must:

' ... be so placed as to shew that it was intended to relate and refer to, and that in fact it does relate and refer to, every part of the instrument. ... it must govern every part of the instrument. It must shew that every part of the instrument emanates from the individual so signing, and that the signature was intended to have that effect. It follows, therefore, that if a signature be found in an instrument incidentally only, or having relation and reference only to a portion of the instrument, the signature cannot have legal effect and force which it must have in order to comply with the statute, and to give authenticity to the whole of the memorandum.'[14]

1   [2006] 1 WLR 1543; [2006] 2 All ER 891; [2006] 1 All ER (Comm) 885; [2006] All ER (D) 264 (Apr); [2006] IP & T 546; The Times 16 May 2006; [2006] EWHC 813 (Ch).
2   In the reports, it is said that Mr Mehta caused one of his members of staff to send the email. The email was sent on Tuesday 20 February 2005 at 20:30. It was subsequently confirmed in May 2006 to Ian Simpson & Co by the Insolvency Service in Manchester that no employee or salary records were recorded as being delivered up for Bedcare (UK) Limited.
3   For a history of the Statute, see W. S. Holdsworth A History of English Law Volume VI (Methuen & Co), 379–397; Holdsworth considered the Statute was out of date when he wrote this text, at 396: '... the prevailing feeling both in the legal and the commercial world is, and has for a long time been, that these clauses have outlived their usefulness, and are quite out of place amid the changed legal and commercial conditions of to-day.'
4   Halsbury's Statutes of England and Wales Volume 11 (4th edition 2000 Reissue), 221.
5   Halsbury's Statutes of England and Wales Volume 11 (4th edition 2000 Reissue), 220; Chronological Table of the Statutes Part 1 (HMSO).
6   [2006] 2 All ER 891 at 16.
7   [2005] 2 SLR 651, [2005] SGHC 58.
8   155 Misc.2d 950, 590 N.Y.S.2d 1019 (Supp. 1992), motion for summary judgment affirmed, 209 A.D.2d 495, 619 N.Y.S.2d 628 reversed 663 N.E.2d 633 (N.Y. 1996), 640 N.Y.S.2d 477 (Ct.App. 1996), 87 N.Y.2D 524.

9   [1992] 1 AC 21, HL.

10 [1892] 1 QB 593; (1892) 66 LTRep NS 345.

11 [1892] 1 QB 593 at 597–598.

12 (1814) 2 M & S 237; 105 ER 388.

13 (1867) LR 2 HL 127.

14 This case might be compared to the decision in the case decided by the Master of the Rolls, *De Biel v Thomson* 3 Beav. 469 and subsequently affirmed by the Lord Chancellor and reaffirmed upon further appeal, *Hammersley v De Biel, an infant, by Blake* [1845] 12 Clark & Finnelly 45; 8 ER 1312 where an extremely vague promise, the evidence of which was very tenuous, was upheld under the Statute of Frauds.

10.23   Earlier cases on the physical position of the signature also emphasizes the need to consider the intent behind the signature, as commented by the Lord Chief Baron in *Stokes v Moore*,[1] where the defendant prepared instructions for the renewal of a lease, written in his own hand and with his name appearing in the body of the draft. It was held, first, not to be a sufficient memorandum of agreement, and second, not considered signed by the defendant. The Lord Chief Baron discussed this at 222: 'The purport of the statute is manifest, to avoid all parol agreements, and that none should have effect, but those signed in the manner therein specified. It is argued that the name being inserted in any part of the writing is a sufficient signature. The meaning of the statute is, that it should amount to an *acknowledgment by the party* that it is his agreement, and if the name does not give such authenticity to the instrument, it does not amount to what the statute requires.' (Italics in the original) Eyre B also commented at 223:

> 'The signature is to have the effect of giving authenticity to the whole instrument, and if the name is inserted *so as to have that effect*, I do not think it signifies much, in what part of the instrument it is to be found: it is perhaps difficult, except in the case of a letter with a postscript, to find an instance where a name inserted in the middle of a writing can well have that effect; and there the name being generally found in a particular place by the common usage of mankind, it may very probably have the effect of a legal signature, and the extend to the whole; but I do not understand how a name inserted in the body of an instrument and *applicable to particular purposes*, can amount to such an authentication as is required by the statute ....' (Italics in the original)

In *Ogilvie v Foljambe*,[2] a letter written by the plaintiff relating to the sale of a lease situated in Grosvenor Place began 'Mr Ogilvie has the pleasure to acquaint Mr Foljambe ....' In this instance, the name was held by Sir William Grant, Master of the Rolls, to govern all that followed in the letter. His comments are noted at 62: 'Another question is, whether, taking the agreement to be sufficiently explicit in terms, it has the signature which is required by the statute. It is admitted that, provided the name be inserted in such manner as to have the effect of authenticating the instrument, the provision of the act is complied with, and it does not much signify in what part of the instrument the name is to be found.' In *Holmes v Mackrell*,[3] a promissory note written in the hand of the defendant with his name written on top, but not signed at the end, was held to be a sufficient signature for the document. One submission argued by S. Temple QC for the defendant was that the signature must be at the foot of the document, to which Crowder J responded, at 792 'Is it the less the signature of the party, because he writes his name at the top of it?' The learned counsel in turn responded to this question 'In the case of a will, it is true, the signature under Car. 2, c. 3, s.5, might be in any part of it: but, even there, it must have been made with the design of authenticating the instrument.' In his judgment at 796, Crowder J intimated why this issue was of some importance:

> 'In the case of a note written in the third person, the name at the commencement serves to authenticate the document just as well as a formal signature at the foot of it. If, then, the signature is sufficient, what does the defendant say here? In effect he says, – "I have given two promissory notes for 510*l.*, and I am now liable upon them." That is a plain and deliberate and unconditional acknowledgment of a debt, and it is clear from the case of *Tanner v Smart*, 6 B. & C. 603, 9 D. R. 549, and the authorities which have followed it, that, where there is an absolute and unconditional acknowledgment of an existing debt, a promise to pay is to be inferred. It seems to me that the acknowledgment here is one from which a promise to pay must necessarily be inferred.'

It appears that judges, when dealing with cases where a promise was made that affected an innocent party, and the person making the promise subsequently sought to avoid being held to their promise by arguing a technical point that the promise was not signed, thus making it unenforceable, were, generally, not willing to allow the person making the promise to succeed on such a technicality. Two of the most notable English cases, *Lobb and Knight v Stanley*[4] and *Tourret v Cripps*,[5] neither of which was cited or discussed in this case, illustrates that similar situations had arisen in the past, and lawyers and judges have previously been required to deal with similar factual situations as in *J Pereira Fernandes SA v Mehta*. In *Lobb*, Stanley, a certified bankrupt, gave a written promise signed by him after his bankruptcy. Three undated letters were produced, one of which read 'Mr Stanley begs to inform Mr Lobb ......' It was considered sufficient that he began the text with his name, and his name governed the promise that followed. In *Tourret v Cripps*,[6] Mr R L Cripps wrote in his own hand on a sheet of memorandum paper an offer to lease parts of 14 and 15 Mortimer Street, Cavendish Square. The memorandum was not signed by him, but contained, at its head, the words 'From Richd. L Cripps' and his address. Tourret, who took an action against Cripps for specific performance, accepted the offer. His printed name served as a signature and to hold him to the promise he made.

1   (1786) 1 Cox 219; 29 ER 1137.
2   (1817) 3 Mer 53; 36 ER 21.
3   (1858) 3 C.B. (N.S.) 789; 140 ER 953.
4   (1844) 5 QB 574; 114 ER 1366.
5   (1879) 48 L J Ch 567; 27 WR 706.
6   (1879) 48 L J Ch 567; 27 WR 706. These cases were reviewed by Buckley J in *Hucklesby v Hook* 82 LT 117.

10.24   The position of a name in a document has also exercised the judicial mind in the United States of America.[1] For instance, a warrant of attorney was held to be executed even when the defendants failed to sign a retail instalment contract on the reverse side, because a signature had been affixed to the face of the document,[2] and a number of cases have been taken under the Statute of Frauds.[3] The inclusion of a name in a document can serve two purposes: to establish that they have signed a document and as a means of identifying a party. This issue is illustrated in the 1916 case from Virginia of *Sutherland v Munsey*.[4] The facts are that Lafayette Sutherland and his wife Mary intended to sell their property in the county of Russell in Virginia to J. G. Muncy and H. Hardway of Russell & Wise Co. The buyers prepared an agreement for the sale and purchase of the real estate, continuing the name of the parties as follows: 'This agreement made and entered into this the 18 day of August, 1910, by and between Lafayette Sutherland, Virginia, and Mary G. Sutherland, his wife of the county of Russell and State of Virginia, parties of the first part, and J. G. Muncy and H. Hardway of Russell & Wise Co., Va. As parties of the second part.' The document was signed at the end by Mr and Mrs Sutherland by means of their respective marks. The buyers refused to complete, and Mr and Mrs Sutherland took action for specific performance. In an appeal from the Circuit Court, Russell County, it was held that the writing of the names at the beginning of the document were there for the purposes of identification, not as a signature. Harrison J provided the opinion of the court at 884:

'It is, we think, clear that the names of the appellees, in the connection in which we find them, were not designed as signatures, nor written there for the purpose of authenticating the instrument, but were written in that connection for an entirely different purpose – that of identification. The language is in the usual form of introduction to such an instrument, and the entire instrument, including the location of the names of all the parties, is in the usual form – the form that would have been used if the paper been drawn tentatively without the intention of signing it. It was necessary to identify the parties to this instrument, and the names of the appellees appear with the names of all the parties, in that portion of the instrument where the names of the parties are usually mentioned for the purpose of identification.'

However, Judge Pelling QC sought to distinguish the case of an email by making the point at 28 and 29 that, in his view, the issue was:

'However, that is not the issue in this case. Here the issue is whether the automatic insertion of a person's e mail address after the document has been transmitted by either the sending and/or receiving ISP constitutes a signature for the purposes of s 4.

29. In my judgment the inclusion of an email address in such circumstances is a clear example of the inclusion of a name which is incidental in the sense identified by Lord Westbury in the absence of evidence of a contrary intention. Its appearance divorced from the main body of the text of the message emphasises this to be so. Absent evidence to the contrary, in my view it is not possible to hold that the automatic insertion of an e mail address is, to use Cave J's language, "*intended for a signature*". To conclude that the automatic insertion of an email address in the circumstances I have described constituted a signature for the purposes of s 4 would I think undermine or potentially undermine what I understand to be the Act's purpose, would be contrary to the underlying principle to be derived from the cases to which I have referred and would have widespread and wholly unintended legal and commercial effects. In those circumstances, I conclude that the e mail referred to at [3] above did not bear a signature sufficient to satisfy the requirements of s 4.' (Italics in the original)

In this particular instance, the learned judge made observations about the technicalities of email in the absence of expert evidence, as did Lyberopoulos J, the learned President of the court in the Greek case 1327/2001 – Payment Order. The assumptions made by the learned judge with respect to email software and how it works led him to determine that the appearance of the email address was divorced from the main body of the message. He concluded, in the absence of any evidence to the contrary, that the email address could not, therefore, be intended as a signature. It is suggested, with respect, that this approach cannot be correct. If the members of the court took this approach in *Tourret v Cripps*,[5] the printed words 'From Richd. L Cripps' and his address, it could be argued, were not printed on the paper to indicate his assent to accepting an offer of a lease. The learned members of the court might have speculated as to the purpose of having stationery printed, and whether each time a letter or note is sent, whether the use of the note was sufficient evidence to demonstrate the intent to sign. In this instance, as in other cases, judges looked to the document for evidence to indicate intent, and the name printed on the top of the stationery was sufficient to hold the man to his promise.

The learned judge also did not consider the email as a complete document. The information contained in the From, To, Sent and Subject part of the email cannot be disconnected from the body. The information is neither separate when presented visually on a screen, nor when printed out on paper. In addition, the source code (usually hidden) is also an integral part of the email, and this set of metadata is of considerable evidential value, as argued by the applicant in the pleadings in the case of Tribunale Mondovì, 7 giugno 2004, n. 375 (decr.), *Giur. It. 2005, 1026.* Further, should the method used to cause an email address be attached to a particular email be of relevance, then other factors ought to be considered, including the very mechanism by which the application software brings together the disparate objects together to permit the user to view the email on screen, because each object will be in a different storage location on the computer.

A similar issue relating to email correspondence confronted Phelan J in the Canadian case of *Dursol-Fabrik Otto Durst GmbH & Co. c. Dursol North America Inc.*[6] in proceedings for contempt of court where the defendant and his company were the subject of a number of orders prohibiting the marketing and selling of goods. One of the issues to determine was whether the defendant, Robert Scott, used email correspondence to market and sell products. In his evidence, he claimed he was ignorant of both email addresses and how the signature that appeared at the end of emails worked. The evidence indicated he sent out emails that identified him in his corporate capacity, thereby acting as an electronic signature. In this case, the court heard appropriate technical evidence as well as the evidence from the defendant. The learned judge did not believe the defendant because his evidence was both contradictory and inconsistent. In reaching his decision, the learned judge made some interesting and highly pertinent remarks about the use of email and the practical aspects of using email that bear repeating, at 56:

> 'Even if one accepted Scott's explanation, which I do not, he was a business man who used computers constantly to transact business. He took no steps to deal with his address and signature. In today's world such ignorance, or, more importantly, the refusal to secure the technical assistance to deal with these types of matters, is not acceptable. Scott exhibited recklessness and a complete disregard for the obligations he had under this Court's Orders.'

The technical evidence demonstrated that, contrary to the defendant's assertions, he could see the default signature he set up, thus contradicting his claim that he was not aware his signature appeared at the end of the email. Further, it was also established that the defendant had a number of different email addresses, and had the option of using whichever address he chose when sending and responding to correspondence. The learned judge explicitly rejected the contention, at 71, that the defendant's claimed lack of knowledge of email addresses and signatures was a mitigating factor in disobeying a court order.

---

1   For further cases relating to individual States, see Richard A. Lord, A Treatise on the Law of Contracts, (West Group, 1999), Volume 10, Chapter 29, 29:35 note 30.

2   Illinois (1965): *The First National Bank of Elgin v Husted*, 205 N.E.2d 780 1965.

3   Federal (1828): *Barry v Coombe* 26 U.S. 640, 1 Pet. 640, 1828 WL 2995 (U.S.Dist.Col.), 7

L.Ed. 295 a statement of account written entirely by Robert Barry, with his name at the top of the statement, and signed by Griffith Coombe and the bottom of the statement, were held to be sufficient particulars of the property to be sold and signed by both parties.

California (1897): *California Canneries Company v Scatena*, 117 Cal. 447, 49 P. 462, 49 A.Jur. 380, 112 A.L.R. 937 the place of signature was irrelevant when agreeing to buy 150 tons of Fosters, Mary's Choice and Salways peaches at $20 per ton delivered for the purposes of canning.

Illinois: *McConnell v Brillhart*, 17 Ill. 354, 1856 WL 5329 (Ill.), 65 Am.Dec. 661, 7 peck (IL) 354.

Massachusetts (1896): *New England Dressed Meat & Wool Co., v Standard Worsted Co.*, 165 Mass. 328, 43 N.E. 112, 52 Am.St.Rep. 516.

4   119 Va. 791, 89 S.E. 882.

5   (1879) 48 L J Ch 567; 27 WR 706. These cases were reviewed by Buckley J in *Hucklesby v Hook* 82 LT 117.

6   2006 FC 1115.

10.25   One further point might be usefully considered, and that is the purpose of the email address, which is highly relevant. The address acts to ensure the communication reaches the person it is addressed to, otherwise, an email address, even if different by one letter, number or dot is unforgiving, and it will not reach its destination, unlike a letter sent by way of post, where a human being can extract information from the envelope and use their knowledge to effect delivery of an envelope incorrectly addressed. It is also suggested that the 'From' address is also used with the intent to identify the sender (it being the function of the 'Reply-to' address to indicate where, by default, a reply will be sent). If it follows that the 'From' line of an email acts to designate the sender, then the act of signature is the irrevocable despatch of the email. Additional technical evidence may be adduced to demonstrate a connection to the person that sent, or caused to be sent, a document in electronic format, taking into account all of the data associated with the document, including the metadata, client software, and any other technical information that may not be obvious on the face of the document as presented on the screen to a recipient without further exploration of the technical attributes of the software. In this respect, it is difficult to see how the email address can be considered to have merely appeared or is incidental: it is a crucial element of the document. This, it is suggested, also corresponds to the advice offered by the Law Commission:[1]

'3.37   We do not believe that there is any doubt that clicking on a website button to confirm an order demonstrates the intent to enter into that contract. That will satisfy the principal function of a signature: namely, demonstrating an authenticating intention. We suggest that the click can reasonably be regarded as the technological equivalent of a manuscript 'X' signature. In our view, clicking is therefore capable of satisfying a statutory signature requirement (in those rare cases in which such a requirement is imposed in the contract formation context).

3.38　It might be said that the click differs from other accepted forms of signature in that it does not produce a visible signature. However:

(1)　The general trend in English law is that the validity of a signature depends on its satisfying the function of a signature, not on its being a form of signature already recognised by the law.

(2)　In combination with the information which will be available as to the email address of the 'clicker', a click is capable of satisfying the second and third functions identified in paragraph 2.6. The combination could be regarded as analogous to signing by way of a stamp.

(3)　Some old authorities did suggest that a signature was required to be a 'mark' which would, by definition, be visible. We believe it is unlikely that the courts would regard such authorities as binding in modern conditions.

(4)　On most websites the purchaser's details will appear on screen (whether entered by the purchaser on that occasion, or automatically as a result of previous transactions). Sometimes this will involve the use of an individual password. The combination of the details, any password, and the click could be regarded as analogous to a manuscript signature or a typed signature.

(5)　The vendor's system may display or record the click in a visible form.

(6)　The click may generate writing; the record of the transaction in the vendor's system and any confirmatory response to the purchaser.

(7)　Even if a click is less secure than a manuscript signature, reliability is not essential to validity.

Conclusions on signatures

3.39　Digital signatures, scanned manuscript signatures, typing one's name (or initials) and clicking on a website button are, in our view, all methods of signature which are generally capable of satisfying a statutory signature requirement. We say that on the basis that it is function, rather than form, which is determinative of the validity of a signature.'

It is the action of clicking the 'send' icon, or causing an agent to click the 'send' icon, that is the act of authentication. This view accords with the comments offered in the Law Commission Report, where it is suggested that the clicking of an icon probably constitutes the technological equivalent of signing with mark, and is therefore a signature. Further, the action of clicking the 'send' icon tends to be the irrevocable dispatch of the communication (if the person is quick enough, they may, depending on the software, stop the computer from sending the email), and can be similar to, or the equivalent of, the act of writing a manuscript signature or affixing a stamp to a document. In this respect, the information contained in the email address serves the same function as the use of headed notepaper in *Tourret v Cripps*. Cripps took a sheet of headed notepaper and wrote a promise on the paper. In this instance, Mehta either himself or through an agent, caused an email to be written containing a promise. Instead of taking out a physical piece of notepaper and writing on it, he or his agent used a digital device, namely a computer. The information contained in the email address served the same purpose as the name and address on the notepaper used by Cripps. Conceptually, there is no difference between the two: the cases are merely separated by time. Prakash J gave her reasons for accepting the name in an email address based upon the same principle in *SM Integrated Transware Ltd v Schenker Singapore (Pte) Ltd*[2] at 92: 'There is no doubt that at the time he sent them out, he intended the recipients of the various messages to know that they had come from him. Despite that, he did not find it necessary to identify himself as the sender by appending his name at the end of any of the emails whether the messages were sent to his colleagues or to third parties like Mr Heng. I can only infer that his omission to type in his name was due to his knowledge that his name appeared at the head of every message next to his email address so clearly that there could be no doubt that he was intended to be identified as the sender of such message.'

There was a mention of the Electronic Communications Act 2000, but no consideration was given to the provisions of s 7,[3] or whether s 7 applied to the facts of this case. Arguably, an email address is brought within the ambit of the Act as a form of electronic signature. First, the question is whether the email address can be considered a signature for the purposes of the Act, and the provisions of s 7(2)(a) have to be considered. Section 7(2) provides:

'(2) For the purposes of this section an electronic signature is so much of anything in electronic form as:
  (a) is incorporated into or otherwise logically associated with any electronic communication or electronic data; and
  (b) purports to be so incorporated or associated for the purpose of being used in establishing the authenticity of the communication or data, the integrity of the communication or data, or both.'

As discussed above, an email will not arrive at its destination without a correct address, and if a person sending an email wishes the person receiving the email to reply, they must also use an accurate 'reply-to' email address, otherwise the recipient will not be able to respond. It is suggested above that there is a purpose for including a name or other form of description (such as the use of a title in lieu of a name) in the address of an email: to identify the sender. Also, technically, an email includes the various addresses in the email. Without an address, there would be no purpose in sending or receiving email correspondence. If the email address is not logically incorporated into the body of the text to be sent, the content will not be sent or received. To relate the email address to the provisions of s 7(2), it is necessary to consider the elements of an electronic signature.

(a) So much of anything in electronic form: This is such a wide-ranging provision that the address associated with an email must come with the term, just as the hidden metadata. Without the email address, the email could not be sent and received.

(b) Incorporation or logical association for the purpose of establishing authenticity or integrity. The thing in electronic form must be incorporated or logically associated with the communication or data for the purpose of being used to establish the authenticity or the integrity of the communication or data, or both. For the thing to be an electronic signature, it must be affixed to the data for a purpose: that is, to authenticate the communication or data or provide for the identity of the communication or data.

An email address clearly comes within the requirements of this provision: it is in electronic form, and the name included in the email address is included for the purpose of establishing the authenticity of the content. If the name were a nickname or pseudonym, rather than a proper name or part of a proper name, the same conclusion would apply, based on the previous decisions at common law. If it is accepted that the email address, or the name of the person in an email address can be considered an electronic signature, and can be admitted into evidence under the provisions of s 7(1).[4]

Finally, the Law Commission considered the nature of the evidence required to demonstrate the intent to authenticate. An objective test was proposed:

'3.29 Because signatures affect many areas of personal and commercial life, it is essential that the courts develop a straightforward approach. We believe this should be by way of a purely objective test: namely, would the conduct of the signatory indicate an authenticating intention to a reasonable person? This approach is consistent with the authorities, flexible and would, over time, produce the greatest certainty.'

With the utmost respect, it is suggested that this is test cannot be right, because an objective test would need to be based on an analysis of the surrounding circumstances, including the technology, and the average person using the technology probably varies widely in terms of their technical understanding and ability, partly because the technology changes so rapidly. It is suggested that a subjective test may be more appropriate.[5] This is the view taken by Flemming DJP in *Chisnall and Chisnall v Sturgeon and Sturgeon*,[6] where he held that the signing of a contract for the sale of an erf is achieved by a mark or marks with the function of making the document an act of the signer, and of signifying assent to the content of the document. He indicated at 645 F, that 'An enquiry concerning assent must, of course, not be into what the signatory subjectively planned but what his acts signify to the other party.'

This is what the English authorities have also held up to this point. A subjective test will allow a judge to both consider the surrounding circumstances and to consider what was in the mind of the sender at the moment they are deemed to sign. If the facts of *J Pereira Fernandes SA v Mehta* are considered in this light, the only conclusion can be reached is that the email in question was signed. The surrounding circumstances in this case, as in *SM Integrated Transware Ltd v Schenker Singapore (Pte) Ltd*, were as follows:

(a) The email was from Mr Mehta.

(b) Mr Mehta knew that his email address would appear in the email, which went to show that it came from him; it also enabled the recipient to respond; as a result, the email address was his unique mark.

(c) There was a course of correspondence between the parties by email.

(d) The email contained a promise made by Mr Mehta or under his authority.

(e) Mr Mehta admitted email was sent, which indicated that he adopted the content of the email.

In summary, it is suggested that the requirement for a signature is not dependent and should not be limited by technology, and this is borne out by the case law from the past. Lawyers and judges have been required to consider how new technologies effect the underlying legal principles. The decisions reached in the past remain relevant: the conclusion was, and remains, that any form of mark, whatever the technology used, can demonstrate intent, and this should be no different when considering electronic signatures. Taking this into account, and with respect, the decision by Judge Pelling QC cannot be right. In addition, the learned judge suggested, in reaching this decision, that to conclude otherwise would lead to 'widespread and wholly unintended legal and commercial effects.' In fact, this decision has led to the opposite: there is now a great deal of uncertainty, especially amongst lay people, who cannot be expected to understand that this decision only refers to s 4 of the Statute of Frauds, and only to guarantees. This decision in incompatible with the previous decisions on identical facts, albeit in applying the legal principles to different technologies, and sends a signal out that implies that a person may no longer be held to their promise for the lack of typing their name into the body of an email.[7]

1   Law Commission 'Electronic Commerce: Formal Requirements in Commercial Transactions Advice from the Law Commission'.

2   [2005] 2 SLR 651, [2005] SGHC 58.

3   The learned judge stated, at 30, that it was his understanding that the Electronic Communications Act 2000 was enacted to give effect to Directive 2000/31/EC on certain legal aspects of information society services, in particular electronic commerce, in the Internal Market (Directive on electronic commerce) (OJ L 187/1, 17.7.2000). This is not correct. The aim of the Act was to implement the provisions of Directive 1999/93/EC of the European Parliament and of the Council of 13 December 1999 on a Community framework for electronic signatures, OJ L 13, 19.01.2000, p. 12, as set out in Note 19 of the Explanatory Notes to the Act.

4 Judge Pelling QC expressed the view, at 30, that typing a name into the main body of an email can constitute an electronic signature, which must be right.
5 The subjective test is proposed by Mr Pépin Aslett, counsel for J Pereira Fernandes SA, Nicholas Bohm and the author.
6 1993 (2) SA 642 (W).
7 Clive Freedman and Jake Hardy, 'J Pereira Fernandes SA v Mehta: A 21st century email meets a 17th century statute,' Computer Law & Security Report, 2007, Volume 21 Number 1, 77–81 for a similar view.

GREECE

Civil Procedure Code

10.26 In the Greek case of 1327/2001 – Payment Order,[1] a Greek company entered an oral agreement with a Czech company situated in Prague, by which the Czech company agreed to provide lodging arrangements for groups of Greek tourists sent by the Greek company. The invoice of the Greek company was not paid on time. There was an exchange of emails between the companies, and the Czech company recognized the debt in an email dated 27 July 2000, sending a further email on 12 September 2000 in which it was made clear that the company intended to pay the invoice and reiterated the promises made in the earlier email. For the emails to be admissible in evidence, they had to come within the meaning of a 'private document' as defined in articles 443 and 444 of the Greek Civil Procedure Code:

> 'Article 443 Civil Procedure Code: Elements of private documents. A private document has conclusive power only when it has the manuscript signature of its editor or, instead of a signature, a mark that he (the editor) drew on the document and is verified by a notary or any other public authority, which confirms that the mark is placed instead of the signature and that the editor declared that he cannot sign.
>
> Article 444 Civil Procedure Code: Official books of merchants and other professionals. The definition of private documents also contains
>
> (1) the books that merchants and professionals are obliged to keep under commercial law or other statutes
> (2) the books that lawyers, notaries, doctors, pharmacists and nurses are obliged to keep under current statutes
> (3) photographic and cinematic representations, recordings and any other mechanical representation.'

The learned President of the Court, Lyberopoulos J identified a number of criteria that were specific to email that might lend email to being defined as a private document: first, the method by which a user authenticated themselves to an Internet Service Provider in the process of setting up an email account, leading to the conclusion that the account holder had access to the account; second, the use of a unique email address, and finally the form or layout of the content of the document. The learned judge concluded that the email address constituted proof of the identity of the sender, which meant an email could be considered a private document under the provisions of the Code. The comments of the learned judge, as translated, indicated his line of thinking:

> '... each user electronic address is unique, in that it is chosen by the sender himself, and has the characteristic of a manuscript signature, even though it does not have the traditional form of a signature. The above-mentioned are valid regardless of where the sender's electronic address appears in relation to the text that it accompanies when it appears on the screen of the computer, or its mechanical representation on paper; this follows because it is necessary to take into consideration that the authentication of the sender and the binding to his will of the content that is included in the electronic message....'[2]

The judge was also satisfied that the email was authentic and the evidence demonstrated that it was sent by the person whose name was in the email address, thus satisfying the provisions of article 445 of the Civil Procedure Code. With respect to the status of the email correspondence, it was held that the original copies of the communication were the files as stored in the hard disk of the computer, and the emails were capable of being printed on paper and ratified by an attorney at law. These conclusions do not answer all of the legal issues relating to this form of evidence, because it appears the learned judge made a number of assumptions about the veracity of the technology and how it works that cannot be reconciled with the reality, and in the absence of any expert evidence. The applicant applied to the court to order the defendant to pay the sums due by way of special proceedings of a payment order, which is subject to articles 623–634 of the Civil Procedure Code. The application can be made by a party to whom a debt is owed on the condition that the obligation of payment and the amount is proved. In this case, Lyberopoulos J held that the email address was a signature under the provisions of articles 443 and 444(3) of the Civil Procedure Code.

1   English translation by Michael G. Rachavelias, Case Translation – Greece, *Digital Evidence Journal*, 2006, Volume 3 Number 1, 57–60; Georgia Skouma, Case Note, *e-Signature Law Journal* (now the *Digital Evidence Journal*), 2004, Volume 1 Number 2, 95–98.
2   Michael G. Rachavelias, Case Translation – Greece, 58.

ISRAEL

Legal fees arrangement

10.27   In Israel, Hagai Brenner J determined, in a claim for legal fees in the case of *Atias v Salfan Ltd*,[1] that there was no basis for the defendant's claim that a legal fees agreement between her and the plaintiff was not signed. The plaintiff sent an email to the defendant in which he summarized their joint understanding of the legal fees. The defendant confirmed that understating in a reply message, and used an expression that literally translates to 'No problem'. A legal fees agreement is not required to be in writing (although recommended) and the email correspondence between the two parties was determined to be sufficient proof of the existence of the agreement. In the absence of any other information, such as whether the defendant also signed her name in the reply email, it may be inferred that Hagai Brenner J reached the decision based on the email address of the defendant.

1   Tel-Aviv Peace Court Civil Case 24210/06, (5 July 2006, unpublished decision).

ITALY

Legal proceedings

10.28   In Italy, in the case of Tribunale Mondovì, 7 giugno 2004, n. 375 (decr.), *Giur. It. 2005, 1026,* a lawyer sought payment of fees in the sum of €3,304.80 in respect of assistance provided to a client in criminal proceedings before the Mondovì Criminal Court. The defendant acknowledged the debt in an email dated 29 April 2004, and promised that payment would occur by no later than 1 May 2004. Having failed to make the payment, the lawyer took action to recover the debt. In his pleadings, the lawyer set out the arguments to show that the email was a document in writing and signed with an electronic signature. To demonstrate the email was a document, he prayed in aid the provisions of article 1(1)(b), of Presidential Decree 445/2000, that an electronic document is 'an electronic representation of legally relevant acts, facts or data,' and article 8, which provides for the validity of such a document, providing that 'the electronic document, whoever made it, the registration on electronic support and the transmission with electronic instruments, are valid and relevant for any legal effect, if they conform to the provisions of this Decree.' To demonstrate the email was signed with an electronic signature, the lawyer pointed to the address of the sender, which goes to show that the person who wrote the email must have inserted a username and a password. He then turned his attention to the provisions of article 10(2) of the Decree, which provides that 'The electronic document, signed with an electronic signature, satisfies the legal requirement of written form,' and then questioned whether the email was signed. Article 1(1)(cc) of the Decree specifies that an electronic signature is 'a set of data in an electronic form, which is attached or logically connected to other electronic data, used as a method of authentication.' The argument thus ran:

> 'To say that an email has been signed with an "electronic signature" (a "simple" one, as opposed to a "digital" signature, which is a particular type of qualified electronic signature, which guarantees a higher authenticity

and, consequently, is a certified private document under Article 1, first Paragraph, sub-section n and 10, Paragraph 3 of the Decree) it shall contain a set of data in electronic form which may be connected with other data used as a method of authentication (the law refers to an undersigning, but this is a [judicial fiction – better than – fictio iuris,] as electronic data cannot be signed: the same applies to digital signatures and other electronic signatures).'

The judge upheld the motion and issued a summary judgment, as requested. In issuing the summary judgment, it is implied that the judge accepted the email address as an electronic signature. The use of a password and username implied that the person that sent the email had authenticated themselves sufficiently accurately with the Internet Service Provider. This evidence emphasises a degree of authentication that serves to provide for the authenticity of the email, although it does not seem to have been questioned in this case.[1]

1   For a translation of the pleadings, see Gian Paolo Coppola, 'Case Note', *Digital Evidence Journal*, 2007, Volume 4 Number 1, 44–46.

SINGAPORE

Civil Law Act

10.29   In Singapore, whether the name in an email address could be an electronic signature was raised in the case of *SM Integrated Transware Ltd v Schenker Singapore (Pte) Ltd*.[1] In this instance, Prakash J determined that it was possible for an email address to be a form of electronic signature for the purposes of s 6(d) of the Civil Law Act (Cap 43, 1994 Rev Ed). In this case, SM Integrated entered into negotiations to provide warehousing space and logistics services to Schenker. Schenker intended to enter a contract with a third party to handle dangerous goods, which in turn meant Schenker needed more storage facilities than it actually had. SM Integrated and Schenker prepared a draft agreement by way of meetings and the exchange of email correspondence, the content of which included reference to the transaction and the terms of the draft agreement. The agreement was never signed. Schenker subsequently failed to enter a contract with the third party, and because it no longer required the additional storage space, it declined to sign the draft agreement. SM Integrated took an action for damages suffered as a result of the alleged repudiation of the proposed lease, claiming that a combination of the draft agreement and the correspondence by email relating to the terms of the agreement demonstrated that an agreement had been formed. Schenker took the view that there was no contract, because the negotiations failed to produce a final agreement, but even if a valid contract existed, it did not satisfy the requirements of the Electronic Transactions Act 1998 (Cap 88 of 1999), in that it was neither in writing nor signed.

The arguments put forward by Schenker were not accepted. It was held that all the essential terms had been agreed, which meant an agreement for the lease did exist, and that if any conditions precedent of relevance existed, they will have been satisfied by the repudiation of the lease by Schenker. In her reasons for judgment, Prakash J gave careful consideration to the issue of whether or not the correspondence by email that passed between the parties was capable of satisfying the statute of frauds requirements of the s 6(d) of the Civil Law Act (Cap 43, 1994 Rev Ed), which states:

'Contracts which must be evidenced in writing

6.   No action shall be brought against –
    (d)   any person upon any contract for the sale or other disposition of immovable property, or any interest in such property;

unless the promise or agreement upon which such action is brought, or some memorandum or note thereof, is in writing and signed by the party to be charged therewith or some other person lawfully authorised by him.'

Counsel for Schenker argued that the signature and writing requirements regarding this particular type of contract were not capable of being satisfied electronically because of the provisions of s 4(1)(d) of the Electronic Transactions Act 1998, which states that the Act does not apply to 'any contract for the sale or other disposition of immovable property, or any interest in such property.' This argument was rejected. It was held that the provisions of the Act required judges to construe its terms in accordance with the terms set out in section 3, particularly s 3(b):

'Purposes and construction

3.   This Act shall be construed consistently with what is commercially reasonable under the circumstances and to give effect to the following purposes:
    (a)   to facilitate electronic communications by means of reliable electronic records;
    (b)   to facilitate electronic commerce, eliminate barriers to electronic commerce resulting from uncertainties over writing and signature requirements, and to promote the development of the legal and business infrastructure necessary to implement secure electronic commerce;'

In reaching a decision on this matter, it was reasonable to consider the position at common law and by construing the provisions of s 6(d) Civil Law Act 1994, not by 'blindly relying on s 4(1)(d) of the ETA.'[2] It was also held that the communications exchanged by email were in writing.[3] Apart from the legal basis of the decision that the emails were in writing, Prakash J, at paragraph

81, took a realistic and sound approach by making it clear that, despite the claim that the emails did not constitute writing, the facts did not correspond to such a contention:

'81   In this case, the parties readily admitted that they had sent and received each other's email messages. No one argued or testified that the printed copies of the emails that appeared in the bundle of documents were not true copies of the emails that they had seen on-screen and responded to electronically. Neither Mr Tan nor Mr Luth objected to the contents of the printed copies of their respective email messages. In fact, they confirmed that they had sent out those various messages and attached the printouts as exhibits to their respective affidavits. Mr Tan did not resile from any of his emails. He did not deny receiving the email messages and attachments sent by Mr Tan and Ms Yong (in particular he did not deny receiving Ms Yong's email of 27 January 2003 and the draft LSA that was an attachment to that email). He specifically confirmed he had sent out his response in the email of 4 February 2003 and commented in court on the contents of that email.'

Arguments that email and other documents created in digital format do not constitute 'writing' are disingenuous. The law is often derided for not responding to the development of new technologies, yet the comments made by judges in the nineteenth century indicated they were perfectly willing and able to apply legal principles to new forms of technology. It is widely recognized that digital data is the mainstay of many businesses and government across the world, and to suggest that evidence from such sources is not admissible because it is not a 'writing' is bordering on the preposterous.

Mr Tan did not append his name at the bottom of the email, so the only evidence of a signature comprised the content of the heading: 'From "Tan Tiean Tye"<tian-tye.tan@schenker.com.' The name in the email address was considered a signature, and in reaching this conclusion, Prakash J referred to the Massachusetts case of *Shattuck v Klotzbach*,[4] and the seventh circuit case of *Cloud Corporation v Hasbro, Inc.*[5] In her judgment, Prakash J provided a clear exposition of the underlying principles that were established in the English and American courts in the nineteenth century:

'91   I am satisfied that the common law does not require handwritten signatures for the purpose of satisfying the signature requirements of s 6(d) of the CLA. A typewritten or printed form is sufficient. In my view, no real distinction can be drawn between a typewritten form and a signature that has been typed onto an email and forwarded with the email to the intended recipient of that message.

92   One minor difficulty in this case is that Mr Tan did not append his name at the bottom of any of his email messages. All his email messages, however, including the message dated 4 February 2003 and sent to Ms

Yong, had, near the start thereof, a line reading "From: "Tan Tian Tye" <tian-tye.tan @schenker.com>". Mr Tan confirmed in court that he had sent out those messages. There is no doubt that at the time he sent them out, he intended the recipients of the various messages to know that they had come from him. Despite that, he did not find it necessary to identify himself as the sender by appending his name at the end of any of the emails whether the messages were sent to his colleagues or to third parties like Mr Heng. I can only infer that his omission to type in his name was due to his knowledge that his name appeared at the head of every message next to his email address so clearly that there could be no doubt that he was intended to be identified as the sender of such message. Therefore, I hold that the signature requirement of s 6(d) is satisfied by the inscription of Mr Tan's name next to his email address at the top of the email of 4 February 2003.

93   I recognise that one person's email facility can, in some cases, be accessed by a third party who can then send out messages which purport to be authentic messages from the owner of that email address. If that happened, the owner of the address would be entitled to dispute the authenticity of the messages purportedly sent by him. That is not the case here. Further, such dispute would be as to the person who initiated the message and would not be decided on the basis of whether the message bore a signature.'

In the same year, Lai Kew Chai J referred to the decision of Judith Prakash J in the bankruptcy proceedings of *Wee Soon Kim Anthony v Lim Chor Pee*.[6] Although the learned judge did not have to consider the email correspondence in this case, having determined that the exchange did not form a valid agreement because there was no meeting of the minds, nevertheless he commented, at 39, that he considered the exchange of email correspondence was likely to satisfy the written record and signature requirements of s 111 of the Legal Profession Act (Cap 161, 2001 Rev Ed).

1   [2005] 2 SLR 651, [2005] SGHC 58.
2   [2005] 2 SLR 651, paragraph 76.
3   [2005] 2 SLR 651, paragraphs 77–85.
4   14 Mass. L. Rptr 360; 2001 WL 1839720 (Mass. Super.).
5   314 F.3d 289 (7th Cir. 2002).
6   [2005] 4 SLR 367, [2005] SGHC 159.

UNITED STATES OF AMERICA

Means of authentication

10.30   It was held in the United States of America in the federal eleventh circuit criminal case of *United States of America v Siddiqui*,[1] that an email was correctly authenticated under the requirements of Fed.R.Evid. 901(a), because a number of internal factors supported the authenticity of the email, including the email address: 'msiddiquo@jajuar1.usouthal.edu,' the use of a nickname of the sender, 'Mo,' written at the end of the email, and pertinent content.[2] With respect to the content of an email address, it was observed by Wilson DJ in footnote 4 in the case of *Poly USA, Inc. v Trex Company, Inc.*:[3]

> 'In its initial supporting brief, Poly claimed that when Beladakis signed the May 28, 2004, emailed document that it became binding on both parties because Trex "signed" the document with an electronic signature by sending it through a Trex email account. See 15 U.S.C. § 7006 ("The term 'electronic signature' means an electronic sound, symbol, or process, attached to or logically associated with a contract or other record and executed or adopted by a person with the intent to sign the record."). Poly did not pursue this argument at the hearing nor in its additional briefing. Nevertheless, the court finds the use of a Trex email account to send an email does not necessarily constitute an electronic signature under 15 U.S.C. § 7006 and, moreover, that Trex did not intend to electronically sign the emailed document by sending it from a Trex email account. Thus, the May 28 emailed document was not binding.'

In commenting upon the suggestion that an email address can demonstrate proof of intent, although rejecting that it could in this particular case, the learned judge made the pertinent observation that the use of the email address does not necessarily constitute an electronic signature where there is no intention to sign. This must be correct, and whether an email address is capable of constituting a form of electronic signature will depend on the facts of each case.

1   235 F.3d 1318 (11th Cir. 2000).
2   See also *International Casings Group, Inc. v Premium Standard Farms, Inc.*, 358 F.Supp.2d 863 (W.D.Mo. 2005), 2005 WL 486784; and New York: *Medical Self Care, Inc., v National Broadcasting Company, Inc.*, 2003 WL 1622181 (S.D.N.Y.) in a Memorandum Opinion, Swain J determined that an email containing the text 'ConAgra is OK' constituted written consent authorizing SelfCare to assign its remaining advertising time to ConAgra. It is not clear if the person sending the email typed their name at the bottom of the email. If not, the learned judge implied acceptance of the authenticity of the email from the email address alone.
3   W.D. Va. No. 5:05-CV-0031 (1 March 2006).

A manuscript signature that has been scanned

10.31   A variation of the biodynamic version of a manuscript signature is where a manuscript signature is scanned from the paper carrier and transformed into digital format. The files containing the representation of the signature can then be attached to a document. This version of a signature is used widely in commerce, especially when marketing materials are sent through the postal system and addressed to hundreds of thousands, if not millions, of addresses. It could be argued that when sending a document by facsimile transmission, that the recipient of the document has in their possession this version of the manuscript signature: the entire document is scanned and transmitted, together with the content. Arguably, this is the form of signature that was discussed in the case of *Re a debtor (No 2021 of 1995)*, *Ex p, Inland Revenue Commissioners v The debtor; Re a debtor (No 2022 of 1995)*, *Ex, Inland Revenue Commissioners v The debtor*[1] where a completed form of proxy was sent by facsimile transmission. Although the report does not clearly state the proxy form, as transmitted, contained the manuscript signature of the relevant official from the Commissioners of Inland Revenue, it can be inferred that a manuscript signature had been appended to the original form of proxy that was sent by facsimile transmission. Laddie J offered an opinion in relation to this point at 351f–g:

> 'For example, it is possible to instruct a printing machine to print a signature by electronic signal sent over a network or via a modem. Similarly, it is now possible with standard personal computer equipment and readily available popular word processing software to compose, say, a letter on a computer screen, incorporate within it the author's signature which has been scanned into the computer and is stored in electronic form, and to send the whole document including the signature by fax modem to a remote fax. The fax received at the remote station may well be the only hard copy of the document. It seems to me that such a document has been "signed" by the author.'

This observation must be correct. Providing the sending party intended the recipient to accept such a signature as a method of authentication and to act upon the content of the document transmitted, the method used to transmit the signature remains merely a means by which the document or message is communicated. The means of communication used should not affect the legal consequences that follow the delivery and subsequent receipt of the document.

1   [1996] 2 All ER 345, Ch D.

DENMARK – MORTGAGE REDEMPTION

10.32   In 2006, a registration judge in Denmark refused to cancel a mortgage because the signatures were not added by means of a manuscript signature. The Danish Western High Court upheld this decision in case U.2006.1341V. The facts were that a mortgage bank N delivered a mortgage for the purpose of cancellation. The scanned signatures of A and B were affixed to the cancellation endorsement. By a notice circulated to all judicial districts, N had authorised A and B to jointly endorse the mortgage by means of scanned manuscript signatures. The endorsements were added or attached to the original mortgage. The registration judge refused to cancel the mortgage because the signatures were not added by means of a manuscript signature in accordance with s 9(1) of the Danish Registration of Property Act. The Danish Western High Court upheld this decision, and took the view that under s 261(2) of the Danish Administration of Justice Act, the endorsement must be signed, and in accordance to established case law, pleadings must be available in their original form, and photocopies or facsimiles are therefore not sufficient. In addition, the registry took the view that, on grounds of due process, manuscript signatures are still required on documents to be registered (or cancelled), and that any change of this state of the law should, if necessary, be clarified by the legislature in the same way as the provisions on digital signatures.[1]

1   It is anticipated that a case report will be published in the Digital Evidence Journal in 2007.

GERMANY — 'WRITING'

10.33   In a case before the Federal Supreme Court (BGH–Bundesgerichtshof), file number XI ZB 40/06, NJW 2006, 3784 regarding Sec. 130 ZPO: (10.10.2006), it was held that scanned manuscript signature is not sufficient to be qualified as 'in writing' under s 130(6) ZPO if the signature is printed on a document and then sent by facsimile transmission. This ruling appears to prevent the admission into evidence of a document twice removed from the source. First, the signature is scanned and then printed on the document, then the document is sent on by means of facsimile transmission. As an item of evidence, such a document might be highly suspect in the absence of a clear acknowledgment by the person whose signature it is, that they were entirely responsible for the entire process or they authorized another person to produce the document and transmit it, and they adopted the content of the document as their own.

FRANCE — EMPLOYMENT

10.34   In France, the case of Cour de Cassation, soc., 17 mai 2006, 04-46706 also considered the legal effect of a scanned signature. In this instance, an employee of the Association of the La Réunion Marine Park was dismissed on 27 January 2002. A claim for unfair dismissal was issued. The only relevant issue for present purposes was that the dismissal letter had not been signed, but took the form of a letter bearing a signature that had been scanned. On 25 May 2004, the Court of Appeal of Saint-Denis de la Réunion held that a scanned manuscript signature did not constitute an electronic signature, as defined by article 1316 – 4 of the French Civil Code, but nevertheless considered that the dismissal letter had been validly signed. Upon appeal to the Cour de Cassation, the supreme French civil court, the employee argued that the Court of Appeal should have decided that the dismissal letter was not admissible, as the Court of Appeal had found the signature had been rendered into digital format earlier. On this point, the Cour de Cassation held that the fact that the signature had been put into digital format on the dismissal letter might affect the formal process of the dismissal procedure, but it did not in itself deprive the dismissal of substantive justifiable grounds. The Cour de Cassation appeared to leave open the question of whether or not the electronic signature did affect the dismissal procedure. In this instance, the Cour de Cassation, in fact, held that there were justifiable substantive grounds for the dismissal.

Biodynamic version of a manuscript signature

10.35   There are products available that permit a person to produce a biodynamic version of their manuscript signature. For instance, some delivery companies use hand held devices that require the recipient of an item of post or parcel to sign on a screen acknowledging receipt of the mail. Another method of obtaining a digital version of a manuscript signature is where a person can write their manuscript signature by using a special pen and pad. The signature is reproduced on the computer screen, and a series of measurements record the behaviour of the person as they perform the action. The measurements include the speed, rhythm, pattern, habit, stroke sequence and dynamics that are unique to the individual at the time they write their signature. The subsequent electronic file can then be attached to any document in electronic format to provide a measurement of a signature represented in graphic form on the screen. Whilst it appears that this concept might be usefully applied in the electronic environment, the drawbacks are as significant as for any other form of generating electronic signatures, including problems relating to the protection of personal data.[1]

1   See Ross Anderson Security Engineering, 13.8 for an indication about what can go wrong with biometric systems, and Jan Grijpink Biometrics and Privacy CLSR Vol 17 no 3 2001, 154–160.

A digital signature

10.36   The use of digital signatures (also, confusingly called electronic signatures in some jurisdictions, especially in Europe as a result of the language used in the EU Directive) has been taken up by a number of judicial systems, mainly in civil jurisdictions, to permit the submission of papers electronically to a court. What is of interest, is that the relying party, namely the court, are relying on one small item to persuade it that the sender is the person whom they claim to be: the password that enables the sender to cause a computer to affix the digital signature to the document. In reality, the reliance rests on the integrity of the password and the security in place to protect the password and private key. It is generally recognized that the password is an exceedingly weak mechanism, as indicated by P. C. van Oorschot and Julie Thorpe:[1]

> 'The ubiquitous use of textual passwords for user authentication has a well-known weakness: users tend to choose passwords with predictable characteristics, related to how easy they are to remember. This often means passwords which have "meaning" to the user. Unfortunately, many of these "higher probability" passwords fall into a tiny subset of the full password space. Although its boundaries vary depending on its exact definition and the probabilities involved, we refer to this smaller subset as the probable password space.

> Ideally, users would choose passwords equi-probably from a large subset of the overall password space, to increase the cost of a dictionary attack, ie, a brute-force guessing attack involving candidate guesses from a prioritized list of "likely passwords". If a password scheme's probability distribution is non-uniform, its entropy is reduced.'

Given the willingness of people to share their passwords to strangers,[2] or provide their password in return for a pen,[3] a bar of chocolate,[4] the chance to win tickets to the theatre,[5] or the opportunity to win chocolate Easter eggs,[6] it is to be wondered why the digital signature (which is, arguably, a flawed concept looking for a problem to solve) is considered to be so important by some legislators. The weaknesses are also explored by Petr Petr Švéda and Václav Matyáš Jr.[7] The authors illustrate, at paragraph 3, that when a person has a digital signature on their computer, the user or owner 'cannot be sure that no further signature processes will be executed in the background when using his private key,' and they make the point in paragraph 4, that 'It is very hard to build a system or an application that does not compromise its security. There are a lot of potential problems – eg, it can be misused, one of the components can fail, as well as the signing application, keys stored on hard disk or in memory are vulnerable' and they go on to indicate, at 4.1: 'At the time of writing, we know of no technology that can make a hardware device fully resistant to penetration by a skilled and determined attacker from a powerful organization. A lot of experts believe that absolute protection will remain unattainable. So the total cost of breaking a hardware device has to be much more than the value of stored and protected information.' It is noted elsewhere that the 'advanced electronic signature', a creature of the EU Directive on electronic signatures, is predicated on the use of smart cards, yet the authors of this paper are clear in their own mind that the evidence demonstrates how vulnerable smart cards are, at 4.2:[8]

> 'A smart card is a simple and inexpensive security module. It consists of multiple components combined with a single chip that uses external

power supply and clock. When a card is used as a personalized trusted device it generates a key pair locally, stores the private key locally, and only publishes the corresponding public key. The biggest problem with smart cards is that they lack a direct communication channel to the user. None of current available smart cards has a really trustworthy user interface. The user is completely dependent on potentially untrusted devices to get some information about his transactions. For example if the personal computer to which the smart card has been connected is compromised, it might ask the smart card to sign completely different message to that which the user sees.

Many successful attacks have occurred because smart cards were exposed to more sophisticated attackers than designers anticipated,[9] where design principles for tamper resistant smart cards are also discussed. The smart card without trustworthy user interface is a typical example of an architectural error. Many attacks are also possible due to protocol and application programming interface failures.'

The authenticity of documents sent electronically, whether as an attachment to an email, or in the form of an email or any other format of electronic communication, need only be questioned if it is obvious that the document is suspicious in some way. It is declaimed regularly that email, for instance, can easily be modified in transit, sent to the wrong address, or copied without the knowledge of the sender or receiver: it will not surprise the reader that such problems also occur to communications sent by other means. Whilst it is admitted that some or all of these attacks might have occurred to correspondence sent by way of email, it is very strange, given the billions of messages sent every day, that the courts are not overwhelmed by the sheer number of cases related, for instance, to the modification of email in transit. Digital signatures are supposed to resolve such 'problems', yet they are not used on any scale,[10] although the Italian certified email system is making an attempt to widen the scope of the use of digital signatures.[11] There seems to be an unquestioning reliance on the use of digital signatures that has no bearing on the risks associated with the use of the technology, and the probability that somebody would deliberately wish to spend time and effort in submitting false papers to a court of law, when there are more lucrative methods of stealing money. This reliance is also manifest in the assumption made that a digital signature proves the person whose signature it is, was the person that caused the computer to affix the signature to the document, as in the Portuguese case of (Evora) Ac. RE 13-12-2005 (R.982/2005), in which an email was sent with a digital signature attached. In this instance, it was determined that the digital signature served to authenticate the document, and guaranteed the identity of the sender as well as the integrity of the message. Whilst a digital signature is capable of identifying the sender, it cannot guarantee the sender caused the digital signature to be affixed to the message.

1   P. C. van Oorschot and Julie Thorpe 'On the Security of Graphical Password Schemes,' (Carleton University – School of Computer Science Technical Report TR-05-11, December 21, 2005), Introduction, available online at www.scs.carleton.ca/research/tech_reports/index.php?Abstract=2005/tr-05-11_0031.

2   'Workers give Passwords to Total Strangers in Scruples Survey,' Managing Information, 11 April 2002, online at www.managinginformation.com/news/content_show_full.php?id=469; Maxim Kelly, 'Chocolate the key to uncovering PC passwords,' The Register, 17 April 2007, online at www.theregister.co.uk/2007/04/17/chocolate_password_survey/.

3   Office Management, Issue 01.0603, 3, online at www.officemanagement.uk.com/tbpages/pdfs/OMM01_0603.pdf.

4   'Passwords revealed by sweet deal,' BBC News, 20 April 2004, available online at www.news.bbc.co.uk/1/hi/technology/3639679.stm.

5   'How to sell your self for a song,' BBC News, 24 March 2005, available online at www.news.bbc.co.uk/1/hi/technology/4378253.stm.

6   'Easter eggs bypass security,' OUT-LAW News, 18 April 2006, available online at www.out-law.com/page-6843.

7   Petr Petr Švéda and Václav Matyáš Jr., 'Digital Signatures and Electronic Documents: A Cautionary Tale Revisited' Upgrade, Volume V, issue no. 3, June 2004 available online at www.upgrade-cepis.org/issues/2004/3/upgrade-vol-V-3.html.

8   Klaus Schmeh in Cryptography and Public Key Infrastructure on the Internet (Wiley, 2001), has a different view, although acknowledges attacks are possible, 15.2.3.

9   A reference here to R. J. Anderson, Security Engineering: A Guide to Building Dependable Distributed Systems (John Wiley & Sons, 2001).

10 Simson L. Garfinkel, Jeffrey I. Schiller, Erik Nordlander, David Margrave, and Robert C. Miller, 'Views, Reactions and Impact of Digitally-Signed Mail in e-Commerce' (Financial Cryptography and Data Security Ninth International Conference, February 28–3 March 2005, Roseau, The Commonwealth of Dominica) available online at www.simson.net/ref/2004/fc2005_smime_submitted.pdf.

11 Roberta Falciai and Laura Liberati, 'The Italian certified email system,' Digital Evidence Journal 2006, Volume 3 Number 1, 48–52.

ADMINISTRATIVE PROCEEDINGS

The Netherlands

10.37 Judges are, naturally, required to implement the law enacted by politicians, and many decisions based on digital signatures illustrate the extreme lengths to which the politicians cause users to go to, in order to use what is a very useful form of communication: that of email. The case of LJN: AW6886, Rechtbank Maastricht, 05/860 WSFBSF K1,[1] illustrates the nature of this problem. The plaintiff, a student, applied for a student grant for students living away from home. The Informatie Beheer Groep (IGB), the Dutch institution responsible for the processing of the various grants, informed her that she would receive the higher grant from 1 March 2005. She was already in receipt of a grant for students living at home, which is lower than the amount received when living away from home. The plaintiff did not agree with this decision, having lived away from home since 1 January 2005 and had properly informed the IBG of this. She sent two emails to the IBG in which she explained her situation and set out her complaint, and objected to the decision of the IBG. The IBG rejected her notice of objection, and thereupon the plaintiff initiated legal action.

In reaching its decision, the court had to decide whether the email could be considered a proper notice of objection. Article 2:13 of the Dutch General Administrative Law Act allows for notices of objection to be sent electronically, providing the provisions of part 2.3 of the General Administrative Law Act are taken into account. Article 6.5 of the Act states that a notice of objection has to be signed. Article 2.16 of part 2.3 of the Act states that this can be electronically if the method of authentication is trustworthy enough, having regard to the nature and the content of the electronic message and the purpose for which it is being used. Article 2.16 also states that the requirements of art. 3:15a from the second paragraph up to and including the sixth paragraph of the Dutch Civil Code should be taken into account. This states:

'Civil Code Book 3, Title 1 General Provisions, Section 1A Electronic Patrimonial Transactions

Artikel 15a Boek 3 Burgerlijk Wetboek

1.   Een elektronische handtekening heeft dezelfde rechtsgevolgen als een handgeschreven handtekening, indien de methode die daarbij is gebruikt voor authentificatie voldoende betrouwbaar is, gelet op het doel waarvoor de elektronische gegevens werden gebruikt en op alle overige omstandigheden van het geval.

2.   Een in lid 1 bedoelde methode wordt vermoed voldoende betrouwbaar te zijn, indien een elektronische handtekening voldoet aan de volgende eisen:
     a.   zij is op unieke wijze aan de ondertekenaar verbonden;
     b.   zij maakt het mogelijk de ondertekenaar te identificeren;
     c.   zij komt tot stand met middelen die de ondertekenaar onder zijn uitsluitende controle kan houden; en
     d.   zij is op zodanige wijze aan het elektronisch bestand waarop zij betrekking heeft verbonden, dat elke wijziging achteraf van de gegevens kan worden opgespoord;
     e.   zij is gebaseerd op een gekwalificeerd certificaat als bedoeld in artikel 1.1, onderdeel ss, van de Telecommunicatiewet; en
     f.   zij is gegenereerd door een veilig middel voor het aanmaken van elektronische handtekeningen als bedoeld in artikel 1.1, onderdeel vv, van de Telecommunicatiewet.

3.   Een in lid 1 bedoelde methode kan niet als onvoldoende betrouwbaar worden aangemerkt op de enkele grond dat deze:
     –   niet is gebaseerd op een gekwalificeerd certificaat als bedoeld in artikel 1.1, onderdeel ss, van de Telecommunicatiewet;
     –   niet is gebaseerd op een door een certificatiedienstverlener

als bedoeld in artikel 18.16, eerste lid, Telecommunicatiewet afgegeven certificaat; of
- niet met een veilig middel voor het aanmaken van elektronische handtekeningen is aangemaakt als bedoeld in artikel 1.1, onderdeel vv, van de Telecommunicatiewet.

4. Onder elektronische handtekening wordt een handtekening verstaan die bestaat uit elektronische gegevens die zijn vastgehecht aan of logisch geassocieerd zijn met andere elektronische gegevens en die worden gebruikt als middel voor authentificatie.

5. Onder ondertekenaar wordt degene verstaan die een middel voor het aanmaken van elektronische handtekeningen als bedoeld in artikel 1.1, onderdeel uu, van de Telecommunicatiewet gebruikt.

6. Tussen partijen kan van lid 2 en 3 worden afgeweken.

Article 15a

1. An electronic signature shall have the same juridical effects as a handwritten signature, if the method employed for authentication is sufficiently reliable, having regard to the purpose for which the electronic data are used and to all other circumstances of the case.

2. A method referred to in paragraph 1 is presumed to be sufficiently reliable if an electronic signature meets the following requirements:
   a. it is uniquely linked to the signatory;
   b. it is capable of identifying the signatory;
   c. it is created using means that the signatory can maintain under his sole control; and
   d. it is linked to the electronic data to which it relates in such a manner that any subsequent change of the data is detectable;
   e. it is based on a qualified certificate referred to in article 1.1, subparagraph *ss* of the *Telecommunicatiewet* (Telecommunication Act); and
   f. it is generated by a secure means for the making of electronic signatures as referred to in article 1.1, subparagraph *vv* of the *Telecommunicatiewet*.

3 A method referred to in paragraph 1 shall not be considered insufficiently reliable solely on the ground that it is:
   - not based on a qualified certificate referred to in article 1.1, subparagraph *ss* of the *Telecommunicatiewet*;
   - not based on a certificate issued by a certification-service provider as referred to in article 18.16, paragraph 1 of the *Telecommunicatiewet*; or

> – not created by a secure signature-creation device as referred to in article 1.1, subparagraph *vv* of the *Telecommunicatiewet*.

4. An 'electronic signature' means a signature consisting of electronic data which are attached to or logically associated with other electronic data and which serve as a method of authentication.

5. 'Signatory' means the person who uses a means for the generation of electronic signatures as referred to in article 1.1, subparagraph *uu* of the *Telecommunicatiewet*.

6. Parties may between themselves agree to exclude the provisions of paragraphs 2 and 3.'

The email was sent by a hotmail account, which, it was held, does not meet the requirements of the legislation. Even though the IBG consider emails send by hotmail as a proper notice of objection, the court held that they do not have the freedom to do so, since the requirements of the law were disregarded.

1   Available online at www.zoeken.rechtspraak.nl/resultpage.aspx?snelzoeken=true&searchtype =kenmerken&vrije_tekst=AW6886.

SUBMISSION OF ELECTRONIC APPLICATIONS TO COURT

10.38 In some jurisdictions, such as many states in the United States of America, courts have accepted the submission of documents electronically for some time, whilst other jurisdictions are just beginning to make suitable arrangements. Once legislation was passed to enable the use of electronic signatures in some jurisdictions, various attempts were made to submit application and other responses to courts electronically, not always with success.[1] An interesting aspect of using digital signatures arises with respect to the monetary value of the certificates that accompany the signature. The Certification Authorities issue certificates linked to a monetary value to limit liability on the certificate. When submitting documents to a court, it would hardly seem necessary to link the digital signature to the monetary value placed on the certificate, because the content of the document is the item of value, and the court does not rely on the monetary value of the certificate to accept documents electronically. However, this issue arose in the German case of FG Münster 11 K 990/05 F (Electronically signed statement of claim – On the interpretation of the term 'monetary limitation') before the Finance Court of Münster in Westphalia on 23 March 2006. Counsel for the plaintiff filed a statement of claim together with other documents by way of an email with a qualified electronic signature in accordance with the German Signature Act (Signaturgesetz). The corresponding signature certificate contained a monetary limitation of €100. The court dismissed the case, because the procedural rules required the claim to be filed with a valid qualified electronic signature, and an electronic signature containing a monetary limitation was not a qualified electronic signature under the signature act that was capable of replacing a manuscript signature on a written statement of claim. The plaintiff argued that the monetary limitation corresponding to the certificate only applied to the conclusion of contracts and not to other declarations signed with the corresponding qualified electronic signature. However, it was held that the term 'monetary limitation' implies a mechanism designed to protect the user against any financial consequences, and not just the conclusion of contracts exceeding the amount for which the certificate was covered. As a result, and because the minimum legal court fees before the financial courts exceed €100, a qualified electronic signature limited to €100 could not be used to file a statement of claim by way of email.

This decision caused some consternation in Germany, as pointed out by Dr Martin Eßer:[2]

'This decision may not only cause confusion and uncertainty for lawyers using qualified electronic signatures with monetary limitations, but may also increase scepticism towards electronic signatures with the public. The opinion of the members of the Financial Court may not convince the members of the Appeal Court, because the court disregarded two persuasive and systematic arguments:

First, the purpose of the signature is to ensure the originator's identity and the integrity of the signed and submitted document. A monetary limitation is not necessary to put this characteristic of the signature into question. Even though the signature contains a monetary limitation, this does not have any effect on the integrity and authenticity, as both can still be verified by the recipient.

Secondly, the monetary limitation has to be legally qualified as a declaration of will of the originator. As such it has to be interpreted by the recipient – the court – like every other declaration of will. The court has to examine in good faith the objective intention of the originator pursuant to the general principles emanating from sections 133 and 157 of the German Civil Code (Bürgerliches Gesetzbuch – BGB). According to these principles, the court should have come to the conclusion that a monetary limitation only applies to financial transactions, and not to the transmission of a statement of claim to a court. The transmission of a statement of claim is not a financial transaction and the plaintiff's lawyer does not intend to conclude any contract with the court. Therefore any monetary limitation should not have been taken into consideration by the court.'

The Federal Finance Court (BFH – Bundesfinanzhof) subsequently heard the appeal to this decision,[3] and it was held that if such a signature contained a monetary restriction which restricts the kind of transactions it can be used for, the restriction does not impair the validity of the signature for the purposes of legal appeals.

Below are some examples where the legislation was sufficient to permit electronic filing into court.

1   Anna Nordén, Case note: Sweden Case no 2572-2573-2002, Swedish Supreme Administrative Court (*Sw: Regeringsrätten*), 18 December 2002, *e-Signature Law Journal* (now the *Digital Evidence Journal*), 2004, Volume 1 Number 1, 40; Philippe Bazin, Case Notes: *Élections municipales de la Commune d'Entre-Deux-Monts*, Case No 235784, Conseil d'Etat, 28 December 2001 and *Société Chalets Boisson v. M. X.*, Case No 00-46467, Cour de Cassation, chambre civile 2, 30 April 2003, *e-Signature Law Journal* (now the *Digital Evidence Journal*), 2005, Volume 1 Number 2, 93–94; Professor Carlos Alberto Rohrmann, Case Note – Brazil and 'Comments about the Brazilian Supreme Court electronic signature case law' *Digital Evidence Journal*, 2006, Volume 3 Number 1, 109–117.

2   Dr Martin Eßer, Case Note – Germany, *Digital Evidence Journal*, 2006, Volume 3 Number 2, 121–122.

3   File number XI R 22/06; BB 2007, 92 (leading record only, otherwise not published at the time of this revision).

LEGAL EFFECT OF ELECTRONIC DOCUMENTS

Brazil

10.39   In the Apelação Cívil (Civil Appeal) N. 2006.01.99.025080-7/GO of September 19, 2006, the Tribunal Regional Federal – 1a. Região (Federal Appeal Court of the 1st Region) decided that a tax collection lawsuit should not be dismissed because a digital signature was used to send documents electronically. The members of the court accepted that the digital signature was valid, following the Medida Provisoria 2200.

Hungary

10.40   In Hungary, the decision in case number BH2006/324, which is a libel case (press rectification lawsuit), held that documents in electronic format shall be considered as drawn up in writing and capable of generating legal effects only if they are furnished with an identifiable signature pursuant to the applicable legal provisions, that is with an advanced electronic signature. This finding was extended to contracts as well.

Colombia

10.41   During 2002, Mr Samper was subject to unsolicited bulk email sent for marketing purposes by a company owned by Mr Tapias, and after attempting, on several occasions, to have it stopped, he eventually took legal action against those responsible. The writ was served on the defendants by email. The proceedings were assigned to the Municipal Court of Rovira, Tolima.[1] The case of *Juan Carlos Samper Posada v Jaime Tapias, Hector Cediel* *and others*[2] is of interest for two principle reasons. First, the defendant argued that the court was not competent to hear the case because the court was located in Rovira, and the facts occurred in the city of Bogotá, and that the parties reside in Bogotá. The learned judge, Alexander Díaz García dealt with this objection swiftly:[3]

'The court however considered that the defendant has not understood that all behaviour based on information technology has a virtual component, and may not be uniquely limited to the material venue. The court expressed its surprise that a person somewhat familiar with the new technologies should argue that the venue may only be determined by the territorial element, taking into consideration the virtual element of information technologies.'

In reaching his decision on this point, the learned judge took the view that the characteristics of the new technology and the services offered are not limited to a physical and formal venue. In addition, s 95 of the Colombian Statute of the Administration of Justice (Law 270 of 1996) contemplated the use of the new technologies in the service of justice:

'Los juzgados, tribunales y corporaciones judiciales podrán utilizar cualesquier medios técnicos, electrónicos, informáticos y telemáticos para el cumplimiento de sus funciones. Los documentos emitidos por los citados medios, cualquiera que sea su soporte, gozarán de la validez y eficacia de un documento original siempre que quede garantizada su autenticidad, integridad y el cumplimiento de los requisitos exigidos por las leyes procesales. Los procesos que se tramitan con soporte informático garantizarán la identificación y el ejercicio de la función jurisdiccional por el órgano que la ejerce, así como la confidencialidad, privacidad, y seguridad de los datos de carácter personal que contengan en los términos que establezca la ley.

Judges, courts and other judicial corporations are allowed to use any technical, electronic, and telematic means in order to accomplish their duties. Every document issued by the mentioned means, whatever its support should be, will be considered as valid as an original document, as long as its authenticity, integrity and the fulfillment of procedural law's requirements are guaranteed. Every procedure handled with technical supports, will guarantee the identification and the authorities' jurisdictional duty, as the confidentiality, privacy and security of the personal data included, according to the terms set forth by the law.'

The further point was observed that documents issued by such methods are as valid and efficient as an original document as long as the originality, authenticity and integrity of the document are guaranteed, and the procedural requirements set forth by the applicable regulations are met. The learned judge concluded the matter by observing that 'The venue for Constitutional Judges comprises all the national territory and the applicable regulation does not exclude this court's venue in the cyberspace, taking into account the facts under discussion took place in cyberspace.'[4] The defendant also argued that the documents sent by the court required a digital signature. However, this was also dismissed, based on the provisions of s 6 of Law 527 of 1999 regarding the validity of an email, which provides:

> 'Artículo 6°. Escrito. Cuando cualquier norma requiera que la información conste por escrito, ese requisito quedará satisfecho con un mensaje de datos, si la información que éste contiene es accesible para su posterior consulta.
>
> Lo dispuesto en este artículo se aplicará tanto si el requisito establecido en cualquier norma constituye una obligación, como si las normas prevén consecuencias en el caso de que la información no conste por escrito.

> Article 6th. Written. Whenever any regulation requires the information to be in writing, such requirement will be satisfied by a data message; if the information such message contains is accessible for its later consultation.
>
> The provisions in this article will apply both, if the requirement established in any regulation constitutes an obligation, and if the regulations anticipate consequences in case the information is not in writing.'

Where the regulation requires that the information be sent in writing, an email will suffice, providing the email is available to the parties for further consultation. In this instance, the emails were available to both parties. Furthermore, it was observed that the law only requires the use of digital signatures in certain circumstances, and where a digital signature was not used, the law provided the requirements to assure the content of the message is original. It was held that the absence of a digital signature did not affect the correspondence sent by the court, and in any event, the court could not affix a digital signature to an email, because it did not have the facilities.

1   Rovira is a town in the region of Tolima, and the events took place in Bogotá.
2   Decisión 73-624-40-89-002-2003-053-00.
3   Valeria Frigeri and Manuel F. Quinche, Case Note, *e-Signature Law Journal* (now the *Digital Evidence Journal*), 2005, Volume 2 Number 1, 65–72; 66.
4   Valeria Frigeri and Manuel F. Quinche, Case Note, 67.

Czech Republic

10.42 In the Czech Republic, the Constitutional Court had cause to determine the validity of papers sent to the court electronically in case number IV. ÚS 319/05, issued on April 24, 2006. By way of introduction, an application to a civil court in the Czech Republic can be submitted in writing, orally in the form of a deposition, in electronic form, by way of telegraph or by facsimile transmission. Where an application is submitted by facsimile transmission or in electronic form, the application must be supplemented by presenting the original application within a fixed period of time, or an application must be completed in writing which has the same wording as the application previously submitted in the electronic form or facsimile transmission. An application which has not been supplemented in accordance with the Civil Procedure Code will not be taken into consideration by the court. In this case, the members of the court upheld the ability to use a digital signature in respect of section 11 of the Electronic Signatures Act for the purposes of the signing of applications sent to the courts. Section 11 provides, as amended:

'§ 11

(1) V oblasti orgánů veřejné moci je možné za účelem podpisu používat pouze zaručené elektronické podpisy a kvalifikované certifikáty vydávané akreditovanými poskytovateli certifikačních služeb (dále jen „uznávaný elektronický podpis"). To platí i pro výkon veřejné moci vůči fyzickým a právnickým osobám. Pokud je uznávaný elektronický podpis užíván v oblasti orgánů veřejné moci, musí kvalifikovaný certifikát obsahovat takové údaje, aby osoba byla jednoznačně identifikovatelná. Strukturu údajů, na základě kterých je možné osobu jednoznačně identifikovat, stanoví ministerstvo prováděcím právním předpisem.

(2) Písemnosti orgánů veřejné moci v elektronické podobě označené elektronickou značkou založenou na kvalifikovaném systémovém certifikátu vydaném akreditovaným poskytovatelem certifikačních služeb nebo podepsané uznávaným elektronickým podpisem mají stejné právní účinky jako veřejné listiny vydané těmito orgány.

(3) Orgán veřejné moci přijímá a odesílá datové zprávy podle odstavce 1 prostřednictvím elektronické podatelny.

Section 11

(1) For the purpose of signing in the sphere of public authorities, it shall be possible to use only advanced electronic signatures and qualified certificates issued by accredited certification service providers (hereinafter referred to as "recognised electronic signatures"). That shall apply also to the exercise of public authority on natural and legal persons. If a recognised electronic signature is used in the sphere of public authorities, the qualified certificate must contain such data as to make the person unequivocally identifiable. The structure of data on the basis of which it is possible to unequivocally identify a person shall be laid down by the Ministry in an implementing legal regulation.

(2) Documents of public authorities in electronic form marked by an electronic mark based on a qualified system certificate issued by an accredited provider of certification services or signed using a recognised electronic signature shall have the same legal effect as public deeds issued by those authorities.

(3) A public authority shall receive and send data messages under paragraph 1 using an electronic filing office. It means that any application may be submitted to the court, using an electronic form accompanied with an advanced electronic signature and qualified certificates issued by accredited certification service providers, regardless of whether the application relates to the criminal, civil or administrative procedure.'

The Constitutional Court, in considering the historical and systematic interpretation of the Civil Procedure Code, together with the comparative interpretation of other codes such as the Criminal Procedure Code and the Administrative Procedure Code, reached the conclusion that an application may be submitted to the court in electronic form without any original supplements if it is accompanied by a recognized electronic signature in accordance with section 11 of the Electronic Signatures Act, providing it is accompanied by an advanced electronic signature and qualified certificate issued by an accredited certification service provider. However, it also held valid that applications submitted in electronic form without such a signature must be supplemented by presenting the original of application within a fixed period of time. The decision made in this case was held to conform with the intended purpose of the legislative effort to make it easier to send applications to the court in electronic form, as they should have the same effect as applications in the written form on paper.

This decision was followed by a decision of the Supreme Court of the Czech Republic, case number 5 Tdo 1059/2006, issued on September 20, 2006, in which it was held that applications to the court relating to criminal procedure that are submitted in electronic form, cannot be taken into consideration unless provided with a recognized electronic signature in accordance with section 11 of the Electronic Signatures Act.

Estonia

10.43 In 2003, an appeal in the case of *AS Valga Külmutusvagunite Depoo (in bankruptcy)*[1] was head before the Administrative Chamber of Tallinn Circuit Court consisting of Lilianne Aasma, Ruth Virkus and Silvia Truman, regarding the ruling filed by *AS Valga Külmutusvagunite Depoo (in bankruptcy)*[2] against a Tallinn Administrative Court Ruling of March 17, 2003. The appellant submitted a response to the court by email on February 27, 2003. The email was signed with a digital signature, in compliance with clause 3(1) of the Digital Signatures Act (Digitaalallkirja seadus Vastu võetud 8. märtsil 2000. a. (RT I 2000, 26, 150)):

'Digitaalallkirjal on samad õiguslikud tagajärjed nagu omakäelisel allkirjal, kui seadusega ei ole neid tagajärgi piiratud ning on tõendatud allkirja vastavus käesoleva seaduse § 2 lõike 3 nõuetele.

A digital signature has the same legal consequences as a hand-written signature if these consequences are not restricted by law and if the compliance of the signature with the requirements of subsection 2(3) of this Act is proved.'

The court refused to acknowledge that the submission had been made, because it was not in the form required by the rules of procedure, and it required the appellant to submit a properly compiled and signed response on paper with a manuscript signature. This decision was the subject of the appeal. In reversing the lower court, the members of the Administrative Chamber of Tallinn Circuit Court considered the legal effect of a digital signature was the equivalent of a manuscript signature, as provided by clause 3(1) of the Digital Signatures Act, and there was no reason why the information sent by email could not be accepted. The Tallinn Administrative Court ruling of March 17, 2003 in administrative matter no 3-366/2002 was annulled, and the matter referred back to the court of first instance in order to continue the performance of the acts set out in article 33 of the Code of Administrative Court Procedure.[3]

1   Administrative matter no 2-3/466/03.
2   Administrative matter no 3-366/2002.
3   Viive Näslund, Case Report, *e-Signature Law Journal* (now the *Digital Evidence Journal*), 2004, Volume 1 Number 1, 35–39.

Germany

10.44   One case from Germany has already been mentioned above. There have been a number of cases in different jurisdictions in Germany relating to the filing of applications and appeals to court by email, and they have all concluded that the law requires the application to be submitted with a digital signature (also called a qualified electronic signature if using the language of the EU Directive). The cases cover a range of courts:

(a)   Federal Finance Court (BFH – Bundesfinanzhof), file number VII B 138/05; BFH/NV 2006, 104 regarding new Sec. 52a FGO: (14.09.2005). For an appeal to be submitted in due form it must contain a qualified electronic signature if submitted electronically, otherwise it is inadmissible. In this case the appeal was submitted by an ordinary, signed, email and was thus held to be inadmissible.

(b)   Higher Administrative Court Rheinland-Pfalz (OVG Rheinland-Pfalz – Oberverwaltungsgericht), file number 10 A 11741/05, NVwZ-RR 2006,

519 re new Sec. 55a VwGO: (21.04.2006). An electronically submitted document had no legal effect and is not suited to meet a procedural deadline if it is not provided with a qualified electronic signature. In this case, the deadline for appeal was not met for that reason.

(c) Higher Administrative Court Bavaria (Bayerischer VGH – Verwaltungsgerichtshof), unpublished, file number 12 ZB 05.2821 regarding old Sec. 86a VwGO: (08.11.2005) Old Sec. 86a VwGO also required a qualified electronic signature for an appeal submitted in electronic form to be admissible. In this case the appellant submitted an appeal by ordinary, signed, email which was not sufficient. The appeal did not qualify as 'in writing' under Sec. 152 VwGO. See also Higher Administrative Court Hesse (Hessischer VGH – Verwaltungsgerichtshof), file number 1 TG 1668/05, DÖV 2006, 438 regarding old Sec. 86a VwGO: (03.11.2005), reaching the same conclusion as the previous case.

(d) Administrative Court Sigmaringen (VG Sigmaringen – Verwaltungsgericht), VBlBW 2005, 154, file number 5 K 1313/05 regarding old Sec. 86a VwGO: (27.12.2004). If submitted in electronic form, an objection against an administrative decision must be provided with a qualified electronic signature to be admissible, otherwise it is not qualified as 'in writing' under Sec. 70 VwGO. In this case the objection sent by ordinary email was not sufficient.

The reasoning is demonstrated in the case of 10 A 11741/05, a decision of the Higher Administrative Court of Rhineland-Palatinate (OVG Rheinland-Pfalz) dated April 21, 2006, where a claim by a soldier in a dispute over service hours was not accepted by a lower administrative court. In this instance, the soldier filed an appeal through his lawyer to the Higher Administrative Court. The document setting out the grounds of appeal was sent as an attachment to an email without a qualified electronic signature, as defined by s 3(3) of SigG (*Signaturgesetz*, German Signature Act), and as required by the procedural rule of s 55(a)(1)(3) VWGO. The appeal was rejected, because the document sent to the court did not have a qualified electronic signature. The court indicated that the history of the legislative process demonstrated the need for a qualified electronic signature. Section 55a VwGO replaced the old Section 86a VwGO on April 1, 2005, and under the provisions of the amended section 86a VwGO, the use of a qualified electronic signature was not an imperative formality, but a procedural rule. However, the wording of the new section 55a VwGO meant the court had to conclude that the use of a qualified electronic signature is a mandatory formal requirement. The decisions reached by judges in Germany are startling, as any lawyer from a common law background will acknowledge, but the conclusions judges are required to reach because of the law also concerns many German lawyers.[1]

---

1   Dr Martin Eßer, Case Note – Germany, *Digital Evidence Journal*, 2007, Volume 4 Number 1, 49–50.

Switzerland

10.45 In the past, the Federal Court has decided that a complaint sent by facsimile transmission would not meet the required formality of writing set forth by law and was therefore not accepted (BGE 121 II 252; 112 Ia 173); it also reached the same conclusion in connection with complaints handed in by email (1P.254/2005 of August 30, 2005). These decisions may now be treated differently as a result of the provisions of art. 42(4) BGG (Bundesgerichtsgesetz; Federal Act on the Swiss Supreme Court of June 17, 2005, into force 1 January 2007). This article allows the electronic filing of briefs with the Swiss Supreme Court if a certified digital signature is used.

FORMATION OF CONTRACT

Argentina

10.46 The legislation in Argentina follows the functional equivalent concept, and the legislation itself is discussed in more detail elsewhere. Two cases have occurred that illustrate the way the law has been interpreted and applied. In the case of *Huberman Fernando Pablo c/Industrias Audiovisuales Argentinas SA s/ despido*,[1] it was decided that an email sent by an employee did not constitute an acceptable method of a resignation without the inclusion of a digital signature, and in *Cooperativa de Vivienda Crédito y Consumo Fiduciaria LTDA c/Becerra Leguizamón Hugo Ramón s/incidente de apelación*,[2] it was decided that an email without a digital signature attached is not recognized as a document signed by the parties under the terms of Law 25.506. The decisions in both cases reflect the fact that only digital signatures are recognized as an equivalent to a manuscript signature in the absence of an agreement between the parties that another form of electronic signature is acceptable.

1   (29884/02 S. 56885 – CNTRAB – SALA VI – Buenos Aires, 23 de febrero de 2004 (Published in www.elDial.com.ar Cite: elDial AA1E25).
2   CNCOM – SALA A 16645/2006 – Buenos Aires Junio 27 de 2006 (Published in www.elDial.com.ar Cite elDial – AA379B).

SIGNING HEALTH RECORDS

France

10.47 The practical problems of ensuring that when a digital signature is used, the person whose signature it is was the person that has used the signature is clearly highlighted in the case of Conseil d'Etat Fédération Nationale des Infirmiers, 26 mars 2004, 255265. Although the word 'digital signature' is not used in the outline of this case, it is highly probable that the signature referred to is a digital signature, because they are placed on cards, and the insertion to two cards simultaneously helps to ensure that the holder of the digital signature is the person who 'signs' with the signature. In this instance, the National Union of Nurses (the Fédération Nationale des Infirmiers) sought a ruling that guidelines (a circulaire) dated 26 January 2003 of the National Health Insurance Body (La Caisse Nationale d'Assurance Maladie) concerning the electronic transmission of healthcare forms by nurses and midwives for the reimbursement or payment of nursing services were null and void. Arguments were submitted concerning the extent of the power of the Caisse Nationale d'Assurance Maladie to issue the guidelines. In terms of an electronic signature, the practical problem at issue was that, according to the guidelines, the signature of the healthcare form affixed in an electronic form should occur by the simultaneous reading of the patient's individual electronic card and that of the health professional. It appears that the National Union of Nurses issued the challenge on the ground that it is not always possible for the two cards to be inserted at the same time, and therefore in practice, the signature would not comply with article R 161-43 of the Social Security Code. A subsequent decree was introduced on 28 April 2003, which permitted the reading of the individual electronic card and the medical professional card to take place at separate times. However, the decree was introduced subsequent to the guidelines and therefore this raised the question of the legality of the guidelines. The Conseil d'Etat declared the guidelines of 20 January 2003 null and void.

For a technical description of digital signatures, including related matters, see the separate chapter in this text.

Chapter 11

Parties and the risks

The number of possible parties linked to the generation of an electronic signature will differ, depending on the type of signature used. The number of links in the chain, and how secure those links are, will give rise to different levels and types of liability, although some of the parties may be considered to be too far removed from the creation of the signature to incur any liability, whether contractual or non-contractual.

Links in the chain

11.1 Consider some of the links in relation to the following examples.

A biodynamic version of a manuscript signature

11.2 A biodynamic version of a manuscript signature will probably be created using a proprietary pad that measures the various dynamics of the signature as it is written. Thus the reliability of the software, how secure it is, how it interacts with the software on the user's computer and what methods are used to provide for the security of the measurements are open to scrutiny. The person or organization using such technology will then have to consider the security of the biodynamic measurements, including how they are to be stored, how they are to be destroyed, who has access to the measurements and how they are used. Once the measurements are attached to a document or message, the next question is how to prevent the recipient from using the measurements without authority.

A scanned manuscript signature

11.3   A manuscript signature that has been scanned may represent less of a risk if an original document, by way of example, is sent by facsimile transmission. A number of people may have cause to handle both the original document and the paper printed out at the recipient's machine. The greatest risk is at the location where the original document is retained, because the technology available to scan original manuscript signatures is now readily available. Thus a third party may, if they obtain an original document, scan the manuscript signature and use it improperly. It must be emphasised that this risk is manifest for every document in existence that has an original manuscript signature affixed to it, but the potential for misuse is probably low in comparison to other methods of forgery used by criminals. Consider the practical use of a scanned signature one stage further, and assume an organization or individual uses such a signature when transmitting documents or messages electronically. In this case, the same risks apply to such a signature, which will be reduced to digital format, as arise for a biodynamic measurement of a manuscript signature as described above.

One further risk relating to this form of signature was the subject of research at the University of Derby in England. A study conducted by Nazia Mehrban and Dr Ian James Turner at the Faculty of Education, Health and Science looked at a number of manuscript signatures and scanned versions of the same signatures. They compared the two for some of the features that make a signature unique. It was found that there were up to ten differences between the two signatures. It was observed that many features that make manuscript signatures difficult to forge (stroke order, pooling of ink, stroke direction) are not present in the scanned version of a signature. This means that somebody intent on forging a signature can more easily copy from a scanned version of a signature and more easily pass the manuscript signature of another as their own if the only reference material available to the person relying on the signature is a scanned signature. It was also found that the type of pen used also appears to have an influence on the number of differences observed. Ballpoint pens proved to be the best, followed by fountain pens. Apparently roller ball pens were the worst.[1]

1   Dr Turner, Lecturer in Forensic Science and Biology, has confirmed with the author that a paper will be submitted to set out the findings of this research in full. At the time of writing it was anticipated that the reference might be as follows: Nazia Mehrban and Ian James Turner, 'A Comparison of the identifying features in Signatures and Digitally Scanned Signatures' *Journal of American Society of Questioned Document Examiners*, 2007.

A typed name

11.4   Typing a name on an electronic document represents the easiest way of authenticating a message, whilst also providing for the weakest evidence.

Clearly, anybody can type the name of another person or organization into an electronic document with the intention of causing the recipient to believe the message originates from a person or entity other than the person that originated the document or message. Such an action may intend to deceive or misrepresent some fact. Superficially, the evidential weight to be given to a name typed on to a document or message is less than the weight to be given to a biodynamic or scanned signature. However, it should be noted that whilst the name typed on to a document is the easiest to forge, biodynamic and scanned signatures are open to being misused equally as easily.

The 'I accept' icon

11.5 Clicking the 'I accept' icon placed on a website may, in theory, only affect two people: the seller and the buyer. It is highly unlikely that such security exists in the physical world, as the potential number of parties involved in the transaction can be quite high. Consider a simplified example. Alice offers to sell goods over the internet. Alice has paid Bob, a website designer to design and operate the website. Carol, an internet service provider, hosts the website. Carol provides a secure connection to the credit card provider on the page the 'I accept' icon is placed. It may be that each of these parties are interconnected as well, so that whenever the 'I accept' icon is clicked, each of the parties will be made aware that it was clicked, and they will also know at what time it was clicked. In the unlikely event this is the case, all the timing mechanisms on each of the systems will have to be synchronized to provide for a reasonable audit trail for evidential purposes. If the parties to this chain do not interconnect, which is the most likely scenario, a failure by just one of those in the chain to pass on the details of an order or acceptance of an order, could cause Alice to face an irate customer for failing to deliver. Consider the position from the point of view of a consumer. If a number of people in the household (bearing in mind that members of a household do not have to be family members) have access to the same computer, it will be perfectly possible for a member of that household to enter a contract in the name of another member by clicking on the 'I accept' icon and ordering in the name of another person in the household. The person ordering may be a visitor with a licence to enter the premises as a guest of a household member. The nature of any dispute that may occur could be restricted to members of the household, and never enter the public domain. However, there is a potential for a member of the household or a guest to be accused of theft or fraud when buying goods and services online without authority of the person whose name is used to authenticate the contract.

Digital signatures – closed systems

11.6 Conventional or symmetric cryptographic systems are probably at greater risk to challenges than any other form of electronic signature, because the relying party necessarily shares the shared secret key, and can use it to forge a message from the other party. These systems operate within a closed environment and usually between only two participants, or a limited number of fixed participants, such as some systems within the banking industry, although it should be noted that the Society for Worldwide Interbank Financial Telecommunications (SWIFT) implemented digital signatures with its own public key infrastructure in the early 1990s.[1]

1   Fred Piper, Simon Blake-Wilson and John Mitchell, *Digital Signatures Security & Controls* (Information Systems Audit and Control Foundation, 1999), comments by Erik Guldentops, CISA on behalf of SWIFT in the Forward, v.

Digital signatures – individual control of keys

11.7 Asymmetric cryptographic systems where an individual creates and controls their own public key poses a slightly lower risk to both the sending and relying party, because the parties do not share a secret that the recipient can use to forge the sender's messages. First, the sending party will be reliant on the technology provided by a third party to enable them to create a key pair. Then they will need to ensure they take appropriate security measures to prevent the private key from being misused. The recipient may have to undertake careful due diligence to ensure the public key is that of the person who claims it is their public key. Then, when they receive a document or message to which an electronic signature is attached, they will also have to satisfy themselves that the message came from the anticipated source, and that the signature has not been revoked for any reason. If asymmetric cryptographic systems, where an individual creates and controls their own public key, are used for commercial transactions between individuals or entities, both parties will have to consider the risks very carefully.

Participants in the public key infrastructure

11.8 A number of people or organizations that use the public key infrastructure are likely to find themselves liable in one way or another. Those most at risk are:
(a)   The sender of a signed message, where an individual or legal entity obtains an individual identity certificate in which their identity will be associated to the value of a public key, which in turn is linked to the value of a private key under their control.
(b)   The certification authority, which issues the individual identity certificate. It must be emphasized that there will probably be more than one certification authority involved in any one transaction.
(c)   The registration authority (where used by a certification authority), which undertakes to confirm the identity of an individual or legal entity.[1]

(d) A receiving party, where they:
 (i) receive an electronic communication that has been signed electronically, and
 (ii) act in reliance on a relevant individual identity certificate by using the public key affirmed in the certificate and associated with the identity of the sender, thus verifying that the communication was signed using the corresponding private key, which in turn implies that the communication originated from the sender.

1 A registration authority may perform more than this function: Carlisle Adams and Steve Lloyd *Understanding PKI Concepts, Standards, and Deployment Considerations* (Addison-Wesley, 2nd edn, 2003), 86–87.

Digital signatures – public key infrastructure

11.9 Applying a signature using public key cryptography can involve a number of parties. For instance, a key pair may be issued by one party and an individual identity certificate issued by another. Even where the same authority issues both, checking the identity of the person or organization that applied for a digital signature may be undertaken by yet another organization, a registration authority. Thereafter, the subscribing party retains the private key, whilst the public key is held in a public depositary by the certification authority. The subscribing party has the duty of securing the private key, whilst the recipient will probably be required to undertake a reasonable amount of due diligence to confirm whether the key has been revoked before relying upon it. Potential liability lies with the certification authority for not keeping the certificate revocation list up-to-date, with the registration authority for not checking the identity of a subscribing party properly, with the subscribing party for not securing their private key properly and with the recipient where they fail to undertake even a minimum amount of due diligence.

TYPES OF DIGITAL SIGNATURE

11.10 The plethora of certificates that are available may also cause problems. If a person or legal entity wants to use a certificate, they will need a separate certificate for every application and browser. For instance, the verification features in the Netscape Communicator Security Advisor will only determine whether a certificate is valid for S/MIME email. Sending and receiving parties must ensure they have compatible encryption and signing software, for example, PGP is not compatible with S/MIME, although some organizations are beginning to offer solutions that are independent of the software of both parties. An additional issue relates to the fact that certificates are packaged with wrappers. For example, PKCS #12 wrapping permits the user to move the certificate and corresponding private keys from one computer to another on floppy disks. Other certificates have different types of wrappers, and a further complication is that the industry standard X.509 certificate is available in two formats, including RSA and DSA variants.[1]

1   See Roedy Green, 'Certificates' for an interesting discussion about some of these issues, available from www.mindprod.com/jgloss/certificate.html.

Smart cards

11.11   A further set of risks can be identified with the use of smart cards, where a private key is included on the card to act as part of a digital signature mechanism. The number of parties that will bear a risk will vary, depending on how a key is added to the card. Thus, if the keys are added to the card during production, the producer may fail to ensure the copies of the keys are properly destroyed after being added to each individual card, or may have insufficient security in place to prevent keys being siphoned off before they are added to the card or are destroyed after being added to the card. The possibilities for organized crime are, potentially, enormous.

The number of parties to any given method of electronic signature will depend on a range of factors, most of which will probably involve a contractual arrangement of varying degrees of formality. Each contract will attempt to exclude responsibility for any warranties and exclude and limit liability. In the event that an electronic signature is disputed, the parties involved in a civil case may find that the cost of adducing evidence that has any value in a court will far outweigh the claim in damages. In a criminal case, those prosecuting and defending may have to take great care to ensure they understand the complexity of the relationship between the various parties, depending on the nature of the electronic signature used.

How liability can be incurred

11.12   The participants, especially in an open environment, can find themselves liable for a range of acts and omissions. This list is not meant to be exhaustive, but indicates the main areas where liability may arise when key pairs are used to sign electronic documents within a public key infrastructure.

(a)   The sending party may claim they did not authorize the creation of the signature in a particular instance. This might occur when a family member or fellow employee without authority uses the private key.

(b)   Alternatively, the sender's private key may have been compromised, permitting an unauthorised person to gain access to and use the key without authority.

(c)   The communication was sent with the electronic signature affixed, but the sender did not intend the communication to have any legal effect.

(d)   The communication was sent with the electronic signature affixed, but the sender was coerced into sending the communication with the electronic signature affixed against their will.

(e) The communication was sent with the electronic signature affixed, but the sender revoked the certifying certificate.

(f) The communication was sent with the electronic signature affixed, but when the sender realised they did not want to be bound by the promise, they revoked the certifying certificate immediately.

(g) A certificate may have been issued to an impostor, or it may incorrectly link the identity of one person or legal entity with a public key that has been allotted to another.

(h) Where a certification authority fails, upon request, to suspend or revoke a private key that has been compromised, or is dilatory in so doing.

(i) Where the private key of the certification authority is compromised, leading to the creation of fraudulent certificates.

(j) A breach in security occurs that leads to the possibility that information can be stolen.

(k) Where attribute certificates are incorrectly generated or allocated, or where a certificate is not issued or where there is a delay in issuing a certificate.

(l) Where access to the certificate repository or certificate revocation list of the certification authority is interrupted or compromised, thereby preventing a relying party being able to verify whether a certificate has been revoked.

(m) Where a certificate has been suspended or revoked incorrectly.

(n) Where the certificate authority publishes erroneous information.

(o) In the event a duplicate key is generated improperly.

The most likely dispute arising from the use of key pairs within a public key infrastructure will probably be to do with the actual transaction itself, rather than any problems relating to the failing of the certification authority. Where there is a dispute about a failure of the certification authority, the amount of liability the certification authority impose contractually will probably be far less than the value of the underlying transaction, although this will not prevent a challenge on the basis that the limit is unreasonable.

Types of loss

11.13 The following list is merely a number of examples that could occur, all of which will have both criminal and civil ramifications:

(a) Relying party Alice claims for loss flowing from having acted in the belief that she contracted with Bob when Alice did not, in fact, contract with Bob.

(b) Alice claims for her loss flowing from being held liable for entering a contract with Bob, when Alice did not enter the contract but the revocation of Alice's private key was published too late.

(c) Alice tries, unsuccessfully, to enter a contract with Bob, but fails to do so successfully because the certification authority's certificate failed correctly to embody Alice's public key.

The first two claims depend on whether liability attaches to a subscriber for signatures made by others. This is a critical question that underlies most of the other examples, but depends on the resolution of issues on which the industry and government participants in the debate remain somewhat silent.

Assumptions in public key infrastructure

11.14 The rationale behind the public key infrastructure is this: when a certification authority issues a certificate, it bases the issuance of the certificate on its Certificate Practice Statement and terms of trade. A contractual relationship is formed between the certification authority and the customer who buys the certificate.[1] Whilst the certificate purports to verify the identity of an individual person or legal entity, it is the merchant or person receiving the certificate that relies on the content of the certificate.[2] The logic is as follows:[3]

(a) The individual or entity provides the certification authority with sufficient evidence acceptable to the certification authority or registration authority to demonstrate that they are who they say they are. Depending on the level of the certificate obtained, this information could be merely name, address and the number of a driving licence. For certificates that will support high value transactions, the person or entity seeking a certificate may be required to provide more robust evidence, including physically appearing before a notary public.

(b) The certification authority provides the user with a certificate.

(c) The individual or entity is then given a keyholder's name.

(d) The keyholder is the person or entity that obtained the certificate.

(e) This is all the relying party needs to know.

There are a number of flaws with this logic. For instance, John Smith of York may wish to enter a contract with a company who is not aware of his identity. The company cannot distinguish, when it looks at the certificate, how many John Smiths live in York and whether this particular John Smith is the person identified with the certificate. Unless the certificate provides the company with a unique identifier identifying this particular John Smith (which they may or may not provide), and the company wishes to confirm John Smith's identity, it must consider other ways of doing so. If a certification authority were to undertake to positively identify a subscribing party, the information that might be needed to satisfy the recipient may be so extensive that few individuals or legal entities would consider subscribing for such a certificate.[4] In conclusion, a certification authority provides a very narrow promise when issuing a certifying certificate. It does not appear that certification authorities seek first to establish the identity of a person and then go on to verify that identity. It is crucial to understand that verification is not the same as identification.[5]

The certification authority generally does not share a secret with the person to whom they provide a certificate. Many certification authorities use the information collected by a credit bureau to identify the identity of the applicant. This means the identification process is based on the accuracy of the data collected by the credit bureau and the effectiveness of the credit bureau in keeping the information up to date. Another issue is whether the recipient of the electronic signature trusts the originator's certification authority.

1   IdenTrust provides a contractual framework that binds both the user and the recipient, see www.identrust.com.
2   Thomas J Smedinghoff, Certification Authority Liability Analysis (American Bankers Association, 1998) www.bakernet.com/ecommerce/CA-Liability-Analysis.doc for a discussion of the issues relating to the liability of certification authorities in the north American context.
3   Carl Ellison and Bruce Schneier, 'Ten Risks of PKI: What You're not Being Told about Public Key Infrastructure' *Computer Security Journal* Volume XVI Number 1, 2000 page 2, available online at www.schneier.com/paper-pki.pdf, see two responses to this article: Ben Laurie at www.apache-ssl.org/7.5things.txt and Aram Pérez available at homepage.mac.com/aram-perez/responsetenrisks.html; 'PKI Assessment Guidelines', C.4.2 'Attribution presumptions in digital signature statutes'.
4   For a useful discussion see Carl Ellison 'Improvements on Conventional PKI Wisdom' paper for the 1st Annual PKI Research Workshop – Proceedings, 165–175.
5   Jan Grijpink and Corien Prins, 'Digital anonymity on the internet' *The Computer Law and Security Report* November/December 2001 Volume 17 Issue 6 379–389, 381(a).

Potential risks associated with the use of digital signatures[1]

11.15   This section sets out some of the types of attack that can undermine the reliability of a digital signature. The discussion is elementary in nature, and no attempt is made to offer a comprehensive review of the risks. The underlying premise for the maintenance of confidence in the reliability of digital signatures is that the risks relating to the public key infrastructure should be fully understood by the people that are responsible for running the systems. In addition, lawyers must grasp the fundamental issues if they are to offer accurate and pertinent advice to clients in relation to problems that may arise over the use of digital signatures. Attacks can be categorized in various ways, and the discussion below aims to highlight a number of types of attack. The extent of the security measures in place, either on the computer or the system upon which the certifying certificate is located, is an important factor in evaluating the possibility that a system can be compromised. Clearly there is a balance to be struck between the cost of a certificate and the liability accepted by the issuing authority and other participating parties.

1   Fred Piper, Simon Blake-Wilson and John Mitchell, *Digital Signatures Security & Controls* (Information Systems Audit and Control Foundation, 1999), chapter 4; Niels Ferguson and Bruce Schneier *Practical Cryptography* (Wiley Publishing, 2003).

Weak links

11.16 Invariably an attacker will seek to take advantage of a system by manipulating the weakest link, in the same way that a burglar will go though an open window, rather than attempt to jemmy open a stoutly defended door. However, one problem with the security surrounding the use of a private key linked to a certificate is which link is considered to be the weakest. A weak link is not always apparent. A system designer may decide, in association with others, what the weak links are, but an attacker may well consider that one of the strongest aspects of the system is an easier point to attack for them, given their expertise and depth of knowledge. A list of potential risks follow:

(a) The make-up of passwords. If a password is easy to use, it will invariably be an easy target for an attacker to crack, given the availability of software that can launch a dictionary attack. Should a password be a random number that is difficult to remember and is subject to being altered each week, many users will invariably write the password down and retain it in a place that might be easy to find.

(b) Some types of attack will not be envisaged at the time the system is designed and implemented. Weaknesses will be exposed in the light of advances in research and new technology.

(c) The design of a system may be effective, but might be used in a way that was not envisaged. An example is Secure Electronic Transaction. This protocol permits a person to send their credit card number securely over the internet. Credit card numbers tend not to be stolen by intercepting them as the details pass over the internet. In most instances, a hacker obtains the credit card details by breaking into the database of a merchant. It is irrelevant whether a buyer gives their credit card number over the telephone, by post or over the internet. In each instance, the details of the credit card are entered into the merchant's database. Most databases are open to attack via a connection to the internet, and this is invariably the method by which information is obtained.

MISUSE OF COMPUTER POWER

11.17 It is also possible for a computer to be controlled to a degree that the holder is, unwittingly, contributing computer power as part of a collective effort to crack keys.

THE FRAUDULENT SUBSTITUTION OF A PUBLIC KEY FOR THAT OF A GENUINE USER

11.18 This is where an impostor substitutes his or her own public key for that of the genuine user. There is no attempt to recreate the certificate of the genuine user. The attacker can sign a document with a false public key that identifies the genuine user incorrectly.[1]

1   Fred Piper and Matt Robshaw, 'Cryptography – A Snapshot Of Where We Stand', *Informa-tion Security Bulletin*, June 2001, 21.

THEFT OF KEYS

11.19 Organizations must ensure there is sufficient protection from employees or directors using their position of power and influence in collusion with others to steal keys or encryption secrets. Other, indirect ways to get around the security provided by digital certificates is to wait for the subscriber to make an error; or where a thief puts a website up and directs the subscriber to the website, and then asks them to give the relevant passwords, and finally some hackers will simply crack the security system and replace crucial pieces of software with code in the browser or signing tools to enable them to use the certificate.

Failure of security

11.20 The extent of the security measures in place, either on the computer or the system upon which the certificate is located, is an important factor in evaluating the possibility that a system can be compromised. Clearly there is a balance to be struck between the cost of a certificate and the liability accepted by the issuing authority. Some of the potential areas for concern are set out below.

ATTACKS

11.21 Attacks can be described as direct or indirect, depending on how they are planned and executed. There are various well-known categories of direct attack, some of which are noted below:
(a) Passive attacks, where the attacker examines all the digital signatures produced by the user and then attempts to bring into being a message with a counterfeit signature. In this scenario the attacker seeks to reproduce the same digital signature that the user would use.
(b) Chosen signature attacks, where the attacker obtains the digital signatures on some messages passing through a system that they then decide to use to smooth the progress of a forged signature on other messages. In this scenario, the attacker attaches their own digital signature to the message, and their signature is accepted as genuine because it is verified with the wrong public key.
(c) Adaptively chosen digital signature attack, where the attacker decides which message they will sign because of the messages they have previously received.

Hacking into the computer

11.22 Other types of attack include hacking into the system that supports the certificate. A hacker can obtain access to the user's system and use the private key of the user. If a hacker is successful, the user may either not have taken sufficient steps to ensure they had adequate security in place to prevent such an attack, or they may have failed to properly implement the security measures that were in place to prevent such an attack. This is an example of forgery or misappropriation of identity: a legitimate certificate is used that purports to come from the user, but which is actually not authorised by the legitimate user.[1] Examples of simple security measures that can be easily attacked include the use of a password to enter the computer as discussed above or, if the key number is stored on a smart card, how resistant the card is to attack.[2]

1   One example of a virus and what it can do to a system is discussed by Raymond Perry, 'The BadTrans Virus and E-conveyancing', *Computers and Law*, December 2001/January 2002, Volume 12, Issue 5, 8–9.
2   Ross Anderson *Security Engineering: A Guide to Building Dependable Distributed Systems* (Wiley Computer Publishing, 2001), 290–296.

Danger from malicious software

11.23   The open nature of the internet means hackers could infect computers with a virus or Trojan horse that can be designed to steal private keys. The risks of hackers gaining entry to computers and networks increased with Digital Subscriber Link (DSL) and cable modem technologies. Without a DSL connection, the computer is assigned a dynamic address each time a person connects to the internet. Whilst connected on a DSL line, a computer may have either a permanent Internet Protocol (IP) address or a dynamic IP address, depending on the internet service provider, although a customer can request a static address. Where a computer has a persistent connection to the internet, the risk to attack and penetration by a third party is greater. As McCullagh and Caelli point out, by having a permanent IP address, a user is more vulnerable to attack by a hacker.[1]

1   Adrian McCullagh and William Caelli 'Non-Repudiation in the Digital Environment', 7 available online at www.firstmonday.org/issues/issue5_8/mccullagh/.

Side-channel attacks

11.24   A hacker can, by carefully measuring the amount of time it takes the system to perform the operations of a private key, obtain the fixed Diffie-Hellman exponents, factor RSA keys and break other cryptographic systems. Such an attack is possible because other variables relating to the performance of the hardware and software can be monitored by the hacker to exploit measurements in timing to find the entire key. Such an attack is computationally inexpensive against a vulnerable system.[1] A hacker can also exploit the variation in voltage consumed in order to derive information about the private key number.[2] For instance, some computational processes run so slowly that it is possible to see the mathematical functions performed by the software. Smart cards are also vulnerable to this type of attack. The card is plugged into a reader or encoder and the information contained on the memory is protected by secondary protection. Where the reader or encoder is powered by a battery that is running low in power, it is possible to obtain access to the memory by by-passing the security mechanism on the card.

1   Paul C Kocher, 'Timing Attacks on Implementations of Diffie-Hellman, RSA, DSS, and Other Systems', www.cryptography.com/resources/whitepapers/TimingAttacks.pdf.

2   Fred Piper and Matt Robshaw, 'Cryptography – A Snapshot Of Where We Stand', *Information Security Bulletin*, June 2001, 22; John Kelsey, Bruce Schneier, David Wagner and Chris Hall 'Side Channel Cryptanalysis of Product Ciphers', *Journal of Computer Security*, Volume 8, Number 2–3, 2000, 141–158 available online at www.schneier.com/paper-side-channel2.pdf.

Failure of the verification system

11.25   As discussed elsewhere, one of the problems with using a key pair is how to determine that the public key is authentic. This is where the concept of a trusted third party can be useful. A certification authority issues a certificate that purports to bind an entity to a public key. The significant issue for a certification authority is the establishment of reliability in its systems, such that subscribers to the service have sufficient confidence in the certification authority to justify the trust they place in the service. Some of the most significant risks that every certification authority faces are discussed below.

CERTIFICATION REVOCATION LISTS

11.26   Some certification authorities support certification revocation lists. This allows a person or business to check the revocation list to determine whether a certificate has been revoked or has expired. There may be many reasons for revoking a certificate, including:

(a)   The certificate revocation list should be digitally signed by the certificate authority using its root certificate to prevent a certificate revocation list from being forged.

(b)   The certificate revocation list is dated by the certification authority, which means that every certificate revocation list expires.

(c)   Every certificate revocation list has a higher sequence than the one issued previously, to prevent forgery.

(d)   The person wishing to check a particular certifying certificate must know where to find a suitably recent certificate revocation list.

(e)   The certificate revocation list must actually be obtained.

(f)   The contents of the certificate revocation list must be authenticated.

(g)   The person relying on a certifying certificate must actually use the certificate revocation list.

The most important point to bear in mind about a certificate revocation list is the information to be obtained is that the data was not modified and that the private key was used to affix the signature. The recipient does not know who affixed the signature, what the conditions were when the signature was affixed, whether the named keyholder had sole control over the corresponding private key or what security arrangements were in place to ensure the private key could only be used by the keyholder.

SUBVERTING THE 'ROOT' KEY

11.27 Certification authorities use root public keys.[1] Thus, if an attacker can add their own public key to the root key list, the attacker can issue its own certificates. These certificates will be treated exactly like legitimate certificates.

1 For an example, see the VeriSign Key Hierarchy, available at www.verisign.com/repository/hierarchy/.

OBTAINING ACCESS TO THE CERTIFICATION AUTHORITY'S PRIVATE KEY

11.28 Protecting the key pair of the certification authority is essential. The secret key of the certification authority is vulnerable to attack. If the private key is stolen, the thief can produce an unlimited number of ostensibly valid, but forged certificates.

CERTIFICATION AUTHORITY ERRONEOUSLY ISSUING CERTIFICATES TO SOMEBODY CLAIMING TO BE OTHER THAN THEY ARE

11.29 For the public key infrastructure to be trusted, a certification authority must ensure that the architecture and systems that support and issue certificates cannot be abused by somebody obtaining a certificate in the name of another person or entity.

Third party suppliers in the chain

11.30 As the example (discussed in detail in the chapter dealing with non-contractual disclaimers and negligence) of VeriSign issuing two certificates to somebody claiming to represent Microsoft Corporation in 2001 illustrates, there may be a number of weaknesses in the security chain that will affect the reliability of the certifying certificate, including the hardware, software, internet connectivity and time stamping functions – all of which are not within the control of the user or of trusted third parties.

Chapter 12

Contractual liability

12.1 The normal law of contract will apply to the formation of contracts with certification authorities, and the reader is referred to the standard textbooks for the principles, especially those matters that are not discussed in this text. The purpose of this chapter is to explore some of the more significant issues that will affect the parties to a digital signature within the context of the law of England and Wales. In particular, the relationship between the certification authority, subscribing party and verifying party; and the validity of the contract, including the contractual terms, between the certification authority and the subscribing party.

The recipient

12.2 A certification authority will enter a contract with a subscribing party, and will therefore be liable to that party for any breach of contract. However, the contract between the certification authority and the subscribing party is also a contract for the benefit of a third party, called in the industry a 'relying party'. The term 'relying party' is not an accurate description as used by certification authorities. If a recipient of a digital certificate could rely on it immediately they received it without any further action, then the use of the word 'relying' would accurately reflect their action. However, it is clear from the documents produced by certification authorities that they intend and may seek to require the recipient of a digital signature to undertake a degree of due diligence before relying on the certificate. It could be argued that where the certification authority successfully creates a contractual relationship with a recipient, they become a verifying party. This is because the recipient is obliged to undertake a number of checks on the certificate, amongst other acts of confirmation, before relying on it. However, if the certification authority has not succeeded in creating a contractual relationship with the recipient, it could be that they are indeed a relying party. In this text, the phrase 'verifying party' will be used to more accurately illustrate the nature of the obligations that certification authorities wish to impose on recipients of digital signatures.[1] Paradoxically, this is a contract between a subscriber and the certification authority for the benefit of a relying party that cannot be enforced by the party to whom the contract is directed.[2]

1 Brian Gladman, Carl Ellison and Nicholas Bohm 'Digital Signatures, Certificates and Electronic Commerce' version 1.1 revised 8 June 1999 available online at www.jya.com/bg/digsig.pdf.

2 Chris Reed *Internet Law: Text and Materials* (Cambridge University Press, 2004) paragraph 5.5 for a discussion on the liability of certification authorities at a high level of generality, covering a number of jurisdictions.

The offer

12.3 An offer indicates a willingness by one party to enter a binding contract as soon as the person to whom it is addressed accepts the offer. In the context of a digital signature operating within a public key infrastructure, the certification authorities intend a relying party to be bound, it seems, by a quasi-contract. At this early stage in the analysis, two questions arise: first, whether a certification authority has, as a matter of fact, offered a recipient the option of entering a contractual relationship. If there is no contract, the form of the relationship may be indeterminate. Second, if there is an offer, the next question is to whom the offer is addressed.

WHETHER THERE IS AN OFFER

12.4 An analysis of what constitutes an offer by a certification authority to a recipient can comprise two main attributes: the wording used by the certification authority to demonstrate whether they intend to enter into a legally binding contract, and the nature of the terms that comprise the document, if the document cannot, on the face of its title, be construed as an offer. First, consider the title given by certification authorities to the terms they wish to impose on recipients.

The title

12.5 A 'BT Trust Services Relying Third Party Charter'[1] has been prepared that BT require a recipient to read, understand and follow before they validate a digital certificate issued by BT. This document is not entitled an 'offer' nor a 'contract' and the words 'offer' and 'contract' are not used in the document. Amongst a number of requirements that the recipient is expected to undertake, the document refers to the BT Certification Practice Statement, in particular to paragraph 2.1.4.[2] A close reading of the relevant sections of the Certification Practice Statement fail to indicate the use of the word 'contract', although reference is made in the fifth paragraph to paragraph 2.1.4, with the comment that '… the Relying Third Party Charters state that assent of the terms is a condition of using or otherwise relying on Certificates.' This is the closest recognition there is in these two documents that there is a suggestion of a contractual relationship. However, it does not follow that BT do wish to enter a contract with a recipient. This point is illustrated by considering the content of the sentence following on from the sentence quoted above, which goes on to state 'Relying Parties that are also End Users agree to be bound by Relying Party terms under this section, disclaimers of warranty, and limitations of liability when they agree to the Charter(s).' This comment indicates that BT also intends to incorporate the Relying Party terms into the contract they have with subscribing parties.

On the face of these documents, BT appear to have taken great care not to create a contract that a recipient can enter, and thus rely upon if they fulfil their obligations. However, judges have never permitted a party to hide behind the form of an arrangement, if, upon close scrutiny, the substance of the matter is precisely that which one or both the parties seek to avoid. It is therefore useful to analyse the language used in this document more closely. In particular, the use of the word 'charter'. Three entries are listed in the Oxford English Dictionary for this word: two as a noun and one as a verb.[3] The second entry for noun is 'A repository for charters or deeds' and is not relevant to this discussion. The first entry for 'charter' as a noun provides the following entries that are relevant for this analysis:

'*lit.* A leaf of paper; a legal document or 'deed' written (usually) upon a single sheet of paper, parchment, or other material, by which grants, cessions, contracts, and other transactions are confirmed and ratified.

2. A written evidence, instrument, or contract executed between man and man: a.

b. applied *esp.* to the documents or deeds relating to conveyance of landed property.

c. *spec.* A document embodying the contract between owners and merchants for the hire of a ship and safe delivery of the cargo; more fully charter-party. Also, the contract thus made.

3. Privilege; immunity; publicly conceded right.'

The entry for 'charter' as a verb is:

'1. *trans.* To grant a charter to; to bestow or establish by charter.

2. To privilege, license.

3. To hire (a ship or aircraft) by charter-party. Hence *colloq.* To hire (a vehicle, etc.).'

The meaning of the word 'charter' is closely associated with written evidence of a contract between two parties. Although the word is used frequently in relation to shipping and aircraft, nevertheless it has a clearly defined meaning that implies the existence of a contract, which is evidenced in writing. The additional meanings 'Privilege; immunity; publicly conceded right' and 'To privilege, license' may offer a way out of the possible conclusion that a charter does mean a contractual relationship is offered by the certification authority. The examples set out in the entry 'Privilege; immunity; publicly conceded right' begin in 1565 and end with a quote from De Quincy, and the meaning of the word listed under this heading refer to the ability of an individual to speak up without let or hindrance, which the entry 'To privilege, license' also illustrates.

It is suggested that the ordinary meaning of 'charter' is synonymous with the use of the word 'contract', and in this instance, it can be construed that BT have prepared a contract that may be taken up by a relying party, which in turn may form a contract between them. The exclusion of the words 'offer' and 'contract' and the form of words chosen to describe this document cannot hide its function, which is a contract setting out the obligations and rights of both parties. The name and language used cannot hide the function, and the use of the word 'assent' suggests acceptance of an offer.

A comparison with the way in which other certification authorities approach their relationship with a recipient may also be persuasive evidence of the way this matter is dealt with in accordance to the standards of the industry. For instance, Cable & Wireless plc have a set of 'Relying Party Standard Terms and Conditions of Use'[4] the name of which implies that Cable & Wireless intend to enter an agreement with a recipient. Equifax deals with the matter in a slightly different way, by incorporating obligations on the recipient as part of the Certificate Practice Statement:[5]

'3.   Relying Party Obligations

Relying Parties must verify that the Equifax SecureMark Certificate is valid by examining the Certificate Revocation List before initiating a transaction involving such Equifax SecureMark Certificate.

Equifax and GeoTrust do not accept any responsibility whatsoever for reliance on an Equifax SecureMark Certificate that is on the Certificate Revocation List.'

VeriSign also has a Relying Party Agreement.[6] This document makes it explicit that the recipient is entering an agreement with VeriSign when it undertakes to use any of the protocols in relation to the verification of a certificate. It can be argued that the relationship between BT and VeriSign is

also relevant to this issue. This is because the BT Certification Practice Statement makes it clear that BT is part of a global public key infrastructure called
the VeriSign Trust Network. The Trust Network operates by means of sub-
domains, of which BT is one. Another member of this network is Thawte
Consulting (Pty) Ltd, whose Relying Party Agreement[7] has similar features
to the VeriSign Relying Party Agreement. Both Thawte and VeriSign clearly
intend the recipient to enter an agreement with them, and thus become a
verifying party, before using the protocols made available to undertake due
diligence. The network is governed by the VeriSign Trust Network Certificate Policies[8] and each sub-domain has a Certification Practice Statement
that controls the relationships between the certification authority, subscribing
party and verifying party. The Trust Network Certificate Policies requires all
'Primary Certification Authorities' to abide by the terms the requirements of
this document.[9] This includes the matters that must be covered, including the
Subscriber Agreement and the Relying Party Agreements.[10]

As a result of the forgoing discussion, two factors emerge that serve to suggest the relying party terms are meant to be enforceable against a third party,
and hence are contracts. First, many certification authorities have relying
party agreements or include references to relying parties in their certification
policies. This appears to be a norm for the industry. Second, in the particular
case of BT, it can be argued that the 'Charter' is a document that is meant
to be a contract. The basis for this conclusion rests with the nature of the
language used and the contractual obligations BT has as part of the VeriSign
Trust Network.

1   Issue 4 dated July 2004 available online at www.trustwise.com/repository/rpa/.
2   BT Certification Practice Statement version 3.04 last updated 18 December 2003 available
     online at www.trustwise.com/repository/CPS/cps.htm.
3   *Oxford English Dictionary*, (Electronic version), Second Edition, 1989 and Additions, 1993–
     7.
4   Available online at www.cwsecurity.net/rpa/.
5   Version 3.0 [Effective 30 June 2003] available online at www.equifaxsecure.co.uk/policies/
     cps.html Part II A 3.
6   Available online at www.digitalid.verisign.com/services/client/help/relying_party.htm.
7   Available online at www.thawte.com/en/guides/pdf/cpsrelyingparty.pdf.
8   Version 2.3 effective November 11, 2006 available online at www.verisign.com/repository/
     vtnCp.html.
9   Paragraph 1.3.1.
10   Paragraph 2.2.

The terms

12.6   The certification authority makes a promise about the accuracy of the
information contained in the certificate, in combination with the existence of
a link between the certificate and the public key that purports to identify the
entity named in the certificate. The language used by certification authorities
differs slightly. The following examples indicate the general flavour:

First, it is appropriate to consider the representations made in the marketing material produced by BT to identify the nature of the promise made. The BT website offers various explanatory documents to visitors, one of which is headed 'Trust Services from BT',[1] which includes an explanation of 'Digital certificate.' The answer provides the essence of the promise, slightly altered from that reported in the first edition of this text. It reads as follows:

'A digital certificate is the electronic counterpart to a passport, driving licence, or membership card. It is a credential, issued by a trusted authority that individuals or organisations can present electronically to prove their identity or their right to access information.

Digital certificates enable the holder to digitally sign and also encrypt documents online. When a trusted entity issues a digital certificate, it verifies that the owner is not claiming a false identity – just as a government issuing a passport officially vouches for the identity of the holder.'

VeriSign also provide similar marketing materials, and in a paper entitled 'Digital ID A Brief Overview'[2] the following analysis is made respecting a digital signature, or 'ID':

'A Digital ID, sometimes called a digital certificate, is a file on your computer that identifies who you are. Some software applications use this file to prove your identity to another person or computer. Here are two common examples:

- When you bank online, your bank must be sure that you are the correct person to get account information. Like a driver's license or passport, a Digital ID confirms your identity to the online bank.
- When you send important e-mail to someone, your e-mail application can use your Digital ID to "digitally" sign the e-mail message. A digital signature does two things: it lets the recipient know the e-mail is from you, and it tells them the e-mail was not tampered with from the time you sent it to the time they received it.

The comments in these examples are not accurate. First, a digital certificate is not the electronic counterpart to a passport, driving licence, or membership card. A passport is not a document that 'officially vouches for the identity of the holder': it is a travel document. A driving licence does not prove identity: it merely provides proof that the person whose name is on the document is permitted to drive certain categories of vehicles. A membership card is merely a document that grants the person named in the card certain privileges, in accordance with any rules that might be enforced by the organization issuing the card. A digital signature does not prove the identity of the sender, nor does it prove the person whose private key was used, was the actual person that caused the digital signature to be affixed to the email or to obtain access to the online bank account.

In the BT Trust Services Relying Third Party Charter, there is reference to the relying party '...validating a VeriSign Trust Network (VTN) digital certificate issued by BT (a "Certificate") ...' and submitting a query in search to '... verify a digital signature created with a Private Key corresponding to a Public Key contained in a Certificate ...' all of which is very vaguely phrased, but in the light of the nature of the difficulties inherent in the infrastructure that surrounds the use of a public key infrastructure, such a set of vague suggestions may also be helpful to a relying party. The BT Certification Practice Statement provides a warranty to end users and relying parties at paragraph 2.2.1.1 as follows:

'2.2.1.1 Certification Authority Warranties to End Users and Relying Parties

BT's Contracts and other Contracts shall include, a warranty to End Users that:

● There are no material misrepresentations of fact in the Certificate known to or originating from the entities approving the Certificate Application or issuing the Certificate,
● There are no errors in the information in the Certificate that were introduced by the entities approving the Certificate Application or issuing the Certificate as a result of a failure to exercise reasonable care in managing the Certificate Application or creating the Certificate,
● Their Certificates meet all material requirements of this CPS, and
● Revocation services and use of a repository conform to this CPS in all material aspects.

BT's Relying Third Party Charters contain a warranty to Relying Parties who reasonably rely on a Certificate that:

● All information in or incorporated by reference in such Certificate, except Non-verified End User Information, is accurate as defined in CPS §§ 3.1.8.1, 3.1.9,
● In the case of Certificates appearing in the BT repository, that the Certificate has been issued to the individual or organisation named in the Certificate as the End User, and that the End User has accepted the Certificate in accordance with CPS § 4.3, and
● The entities approving the Certificate Application and issuing the Certificate have complied with this CPS when issuing the Certificate.'

Cable & Wireless now refer specifically to reliance by a third party, but the only relevant text in the practice statement, with the exception of the caveats sprinkled throughout, are contained in clause 2.1.5, as follows:

'2.1.5.   Relying Party Obligations

Relying Parties may be required under a relevant CP to complete a relying party agreement that may contain defined duties, responsibilities or obligations or determine the trust in a certificate based on the CP (and consequently the CPS) under which the Certificate was issued.

Generally, Relying Parties fulfil their obligations under this CPS by:

1   Securely obtaining the Certificate of the CA they trust in the trust hierarchy, which may include verification of the CA's Certificate hash (thumbprint).

2   Exercising due diligence and reasonable judgement before deciding to rely on a certificate based service, as well as:
   (a)   Performing a Certificate Path Validation to a trusted point in the PKI hierarchy
   (b)   Obtaining, where appropriate, Certificate status using either a CRL or a validation service (as defined in a relevant CP)
   (c)   Only trusting and relying on a Certificate that has not expired, or been revoked or been suspended and if a proper chain of trust can be established.

3   Ensure they comply with any relevant laws and regulations which may impact their rights to use certain cryptographic instruments.'[3]

In summary, the first question is whether certification authorities make an offer to recipients. The discussion above helps to demonstrate that there is strong evidence to suggest that an offer is made to recipients of digital certificates. It can be argued that both the words used define the offer, and the terms themselves suggest certification authorities have made an offer, subject to obligations. The question that remains is whether the certification authorities can be bound by their words. It is a matter of determining whether the words used in the various documents and marketing materials are sufficient to induce a reasonable person to believe that the certification authority intends to be bound, even though the statements made by most certification authorities are ambiguous as to whether they will be bound.

1   Available online at www.btglobalservices.com/en/products/trustservices/freeguides/free_guide.html.
2   (A VeriSign White Paper, 2004), available online at www.verisign.com/stellent/groups/public/documents/guides/005326.pdf.
3   Cable & Wireless PKI Certification Practice Statement, Document number 1491-PD009-023, May 2002, available online at www2.cwsecurity.net/files/cps.pdf.

NATURE OF THE OFFER

12.7   The offer to verifying parties is not directed to a particular person, and a verifying party is not required to inform the certification authority that they intend to accept the offer by conforming to the obligations imposed by the relevant agreement. The nature of the offer is a unilateral offer in a similar fashion to *Carlill v Carbolic Smoke Ball Co*[1] that the verifying party accepts. Such an offer can be made to an individual, specified group of persons or to the world at large. It could be argued that such an offer is made to a specific group of persons, on the premise that certifying authorities anticipate only verifying parties with a connection to subscribing parties will rely on any obligations the certification authorities choose to commit themselves to. Although this may narrow the class of persons that are likely to take up the offer, nevertheless the breadth and number of such a class of persons will probably not be known to the certification authority. In addition, the public key of the subscribing party is placed in a public repository, thus suggesting that the offer, for all practical purposes, appears to be a unilateral offer to the entire world.

1   [1893] 1 QB 256; 57 JP 325; 62 LJQB 257; 4 R 176; 41 WR 210; 67 LT 837; 9 TLR 124, CA.

Accepting the offer

12.8   To accept the offer, the recipient is required to assent to the terms. One of the practical problems that a recipient may have is that they may have no knowledge of the relying party agreement or certificate practice statement. It is possible for their attention to be drawn to the agreement by way of a notice, usually included in the information linked to the certificate. An example will be considered below, where a sending party has signed an email with a digital signature from VeriSign, Inc. The email will usually bear a message that is similar to the one below:

'This message has been digitally signed by the sender.

Signed e-mail from others allows you to verify the authenticity of a message – that the message is from the supposed sender and that it has not been tampered with during transit. Signed mail messages are designated with the signed mail icon.

Any problems with a signed message will be described in a Security Warning which may follow this one. If there are problems, you should consider that the message was tampered with or was not from the supposed sender.'[1]

A security warning may follow, especially if the certificate is no longer valid. The warning may look like the example given below:

'Security Warning[2]

There are security problems with this message.

Please review the highlighted items listed below:[3]

Message has not been tampered with

You do trust the signing digital ID

The digital ID *is* expired

The sender and digital ID have the same e-mail address

The digital ID has not been revoked or revocation information for this certificate could not be determined.

There are no other problems with the digital ID'[4]

The recipient has the option of clicking on the certificate or the icon 'View digital ID' at the bottom of the security warning. If the recipient decides to find out more about the certificate by clicking on the relevant icon, a pop-up box will appear with some, all or more than the following attributes:[5] the box is headed 'Signing digital ID properties' and has four separate headings: General (this is the view the relying party will see immediately), Details, Certification Path and Trust.

1   This text is the content of the message revealed in the body of an email received by the author to which a digital signature was attached. It is not clear whether the software or the digital message itself has produced this text, but the author wishes to acknowledge use of this text, although it is not clear to whom the acknowledgment should be addressed. With apologies, but the example used in this second edition is the same as for the first edition, because the author has only had one email sent to him with a digital signature attached in nine years, even when corresponding with employees of organizations that sell digital signatures, despite the marketing materials of two providers that illustrate the dangers of sending email without a digital signature or in plain text: from BT: 'E-mail plays a major role in business communications, offering the competitive advantages of increased speed and reduced costs. Messages can be sent, quickly and cheaply, across the Internet and across the world, to customers, colleagues, suppliers and trading partners. But many of these messages contain commercially or personally sensitive details. And that's the problem.

E-mail is highly vulnerable to hackers. Messages can be read or tampered with, impersonated or waylaid, without either the sender or designated recipient any the wiser.

Maintaining a second type of non-Internet e-mail system especially for confidential messages is neither economical nor user-friendly. A far more efficient and cost-effective solution is a Digital Certificate, which acts as an automatic electronic passport.' (BT marketing comments available online at www.btglobalservices.com/en/products/trustservices/solutions/semail.html); from VeriSign: 'In the physical world, you protect your written correspondence by putting it in an envelope before posting. In the online world, sending an email message is like sending a postcard: it is easy to intercept and read as it travels across the Internet. Instead of risking disclosure of your private emails, safeguard them with a VeriSign Digital ID.

Installed in your Web browser or email software, a Digital ID serves as an electronic substitute for sealed envelopes and handwritten signatures, enabling you to:
● Digitally sign email messages to assure recipients that the email really was sent by you.
● Encrypt email contents and attachments, protecting them from being read by online intruders. Only your intended recipient can decrypt them.'
(VeriSign marketing comments available online at www.verisign.com/products-services/security-services/pki/pki-application/email-digital-id/index.html)

2   These words are usually published in a red font.
3   A tick or a cross will be used against each of the items listed, indicating whether the relying party should carefully consider the item or items highlighted that cause concern. The items highlighted may also be published in a red font.
4   This text is the content of the security warning revealed in the body of an email received by the author to which a digital signature was attached. It is not clear whether the software or the digital message itself has produced this text, but the author wishes to acknowledge use of this text, although it is not clear to whom the acknowledgment should be addressed.
5   For the purposes of this example, a certificate issued by VeriSign, Inc will be used.

GENERAL

12.9   The general view provides details of the status of the certificate, for instance, whether it has expired or the status of its validity. It will also set out the following information: to whom it has been issued; the entity that has issued the certificate; the period of validity of the certificate. A further box within this view is named 'Issuer Statement'. If the recipient clicks on this icon, a new box pops up headed 'Disclaimer'. In this particular example, there is a substantial amount of room for text in this box, but the only text added to the box reads: 'VeriSign's CPS incorp. By reference liab. ltd (c) 97 VeriSign'. The recipient has two more icons at the base of this pop-up box. One is named 'Close' and the other 'More Info'. If the icon 'More Info' is clicked, the software links, or attempts to link, to the internet and takes the recipient to a web page at www.verisign.com/CPS,[1] which in turn is linked to the Certification Practice Statement.

1   Providing, of course, the link is available and no intervening acts prevent the link from being effected.

DETAILS

12.10   By clicking on the 'Details' icon, the recipient is presented with a separate page that has the following information contained within a frame, which the viewer must scroll down in order to view all of the information: version; serial number; signature algorithm; issuer; valid from; valid to; subject (can be the full email address); public key; basic constraints; certificate policies; Netscape cert type; CRL distribution points; thumbprint algorithm; thumbprint. The viewer can click on a number of these attributes. By clicking on 'Certificate Policies', a box in the bottom half of the page highlights the relevant text, which includes a policy identifier number and goes on to state 'Policy Qualifier Id = CPS' and 'Qualifier: https://www.verisign.com/CPS.' This is a further reference to the VeriSign Certification Practice Statement. The recipient can also click on to 'CRL Distribution Points', and the text in the box in the bottom half of the page then changes to read: 'CRL Distribution Point. Distribution Point Name: Full Name: URL=http://www.crl.verisign.com/class1.crl.' This is a reference to the certification revocation list.[1]

1   When the author clicked on this particular hyperlink on 7 August 2003, the web page could not be found. The viewer was then directed by the software to open the cri.verisign.com page and then look for the relevant link. This particular page revealed 59 links. At a loss as to which link was the correct one, two files were opened and subsequently downloaded: 'Class1Individual.crl' and 'Class1GW.crl'. Only one of these files had a list of certificates that has been revoked, and the serial number of the invalid certificate attached to the email received by the author was not present. Clearly the author either did not find the appropriate certificate revocation list, or the certificate had yet to be revoked by VeriSign, some weeks after the certificate expired.

CERTIFICATION PATH

12.11   The icon named 'Certification Path' has a number of certificates in the form of a tree, beginning with the root certificate and ending with the particular certificate attached to the document. By clicking on the top-level certificate, a pop-up box appears, headed 'Signing digital ID properties'. The viewer is permitted to view this certificate, and upon clicking on the certificate, a further pop-up box appears which provides details of the authority it was issued by and the entity to which it was issued. At the highest level, the party issuing the certificate may also be the party to whom the certificate has been issued. The dates of validity are also provided, such as valid from 29 January 1996 to 2 August 2028. It is also possible to click on to the second level certificate. Again, a pop-up box appears with similar information provided to the higher-level certificate. In this example the period of validity is from 12 May 1998 to 13 May 2008. The recipient can also click on an icon named 'Issuer Statement', and the software then links or attempts to link to the internet and takes the recipient to a web page at www.verisign.com/repository/RPA, which is where the Relying Party Agreement is located.

TRUST

12.12   The fourth icon on the main menu, 'Trust' also brings a separate page to the attention of the viewer. The nature of this content will vary as between certification authorities. A statement may be made as to the value of the certificate, such as 'Certificate trusted for E-mail Encryption and Authentication.'

There is a similarity between the digital ID files produced by certification authorities. The layout and content is standard across the industry, based as they are on the X.509 certificate. Nevertheless the content can differ, and a comparison with the Cable & Wireless Issuing CA_p7.p7c Digital ID File, will demonstrate a nuance of difference between the methods adopted by the certification authorities to bring the relying party terms to the notice of the user. When exploring the first, 'General' open page, the recipient can click on the icon with the words 'Issuer Statement'. A pop-up box appears, headed 'Disclaimer', the contents of which reads: 'Reliance on this certificate by any party assumes acceptance of the standard terms and conditions of use and the Certification Practice Statement which can be found at the Cable & Wireless WebSite.' A further icon with the name 'More Info' will, if clicked, request the software to link or attempt to link to the internet to take the viewer to a web page at www.cwsecurity.net. Under the heading 'Certificate Policies' if the relying party clicks on to the 'key usage' icon, the following text is revealed to indicate how the certificate can be used: 'Digital Signature, Non-Repudiation, Key Encipherment, Data Encipherment, Key Agreement, Certificate Signing, Off-line CRL Signing, CRL Signing (fe).' Finally, the 'Certification Path' page has three tiers of certificates in the form of a tree. By clicking on the second tier certificate, the viewer is offered the opportunity to click on a further icon named 'Issuer Statement', and the software will then seek to connect the user to the internet, in particular to a web page at www.us-hosting.baltimore.com/CPS/OmniRoot.html.

Effectiveness of notice

12.13   The party relying on the terms must do what is reasonably sufficient to give the other party notice of the conditions. This is particularly important when considering the limitation and exclusion of liability, and provisions excluding liability for negligence.[1] There is no English authority on this point in relation to what constitutes notice on the world wide web, but the case of *Specht v Netscape Communications Corporation and America Online, Inc.*[2] illustrates how the principles may be applied in England and Wales. In this instance, Netscape provided a free 'plug-in' software program called SmartDownload to enhance the functioning of the Netscape browser program. A dispute arose with a number of people that downloaded the software, because it was claimed that the software sent personal information to the software provider when the software was used to obtain access to the internet. To resolve the dispute, Netscape sought to rely on a clause in the licence agreement to refer the matter to an arbitrator. Notice of the licence was provided on the same web page as the download icon, but the visitor had to scroll down the page to find the notice. Had they done so, they would have found a hypertext link that, if they clicked on the icon, would have taken them to a web page entitled 'License & Support Agreements.' The judgment of the Southern District of New York was appealed before McLaughlin, Leval and Sotomayor CJJ. The judgment of the appeal court was given by Sotomayor CJ. It was held that the notice of the licence was not adequate, and a reference to such terms on a part of the screen that could not been viewed was not sufficient to put a potential user of the free software on enquiry or as constructive notice of the terms. Whilst this decision took into account the fact that the software was provided at no cost, nevertheless the notice of the terms was not considered sufficient, as observed by Sotomayor CJ at 35(a):

'After reviewing the California common law and other relevant legal authority, we conclude that under the circumstances here, plaintiffs' downloading of SmartDownload did not constitute acceptance of defendants' license terms. Reasonably conspicuous notice of the existence of contract terms and unambiguous manifestation of assent to those terms by consumers are essential if electronic bargaining is to have integrity and credibility. We hold that a reasonably prudent offeree in plaintiffs' position would not have known or learned, prior to acting on the invitation to download, of the reference to SmartDownload's license terms hidden below the 'Download' button on the next screen.'

As outlined in the previous section, if the recipient takes the time and trouble to look at the information contained in the certificate in detail, they will become aware that there are references to a number of websites that may be of relevance. The effectiveness of such a notice will, it is argued, depend on whether a court considers the steps taken by the certification authority are sufficient to alert the recipient that they are expected to agree to the terms set out in a relying party agreement, and whether the conduct of the recipient is sufficient to demonstrate their acceptance of the terms set out in a relying party agreement.

In the example used above, the certification authority has sought to alert the recipient to the Relying Party Agreement, Certification Practice Statement and Certificate Revocation List. A reference was also made to the limitation of liability by the short phrase 'VeriSign's CPS incorp. By reference liab. Ltd'. Bearing in mind the amount of information that can be included in a certificate of this nature, it may be determined that by any objective measure, very little attempt has been made to make a statement of reasonable length and explanation in plain English as to precisely what the certification authority expects of the recipient. There is no clear statement to the effect that the recipient cannot rely on the certificate until they have carried out the due diligence set out in the relying party agreement. The reference to the incorporation of the certification practice statement by reference is hardly a model of clarity, especially given the amount of space available on the relevant page to offer a more appropriate and informative explanation. The most pertinent point is the failure to offer an adequate explanation, given the way in which certification authorities seek to ensure a recipient is deemed to accept the terms of a relying party agreement and thereby become a verifying party.

Recipients of digital certificates are urged by certifying authorities to read the terms of the relying party agreement before they undertake any action to verify the certificate or rely upon the representations made in the certificate. However, failing that, a number of certification authorities attempt to ensure the recipient is bound by the terms of the agreement by deeming that they accept the terms of the agreement when they carry out any act of validation or reliance, even where they do not read the terms of the agreement.

The notice of the various documents that the recipient is required to consult before undertaking any due diligence before relying on the certificate appears to be relatively opaque. Also, the apparent failure to provide adequate notice is compounded by deeming the recipient to be aware of, and to accept, the relying party agreement as soon as they undertake any action likely to be considered an act that leads to the verification of the status of a certificate. The examples set out below help to demonstrate this point.

1   *Olley v Marlborough Court Limited* [1949] 1 KB 532, CA; [1949] 1 All ER 127; *Hollier v Rambler Motors (AMC) Limited* [1972] 1 All ER 399.
2   306 F.3d 17 (2nd Cir. 2002).

BT

12.14   The BT Trust Services Relying Third Party Charter requires the recipient to read the Charter before validating a digital certificate or obtaining access to the certificate revocation list or any other information. However, the recipient is deemed to have accepted the Charter even if they have not read it, and BT further relies on the assumption that the recipient has made themselves aware of the Charter if a query is submitted:

'You will be deemed to have accepted this Charter by validating or relying upon a Certificate or the information embedded in a Certificate, or by accessing or using the Repository, even if you have not read the Charter. You demonstrate your knowledge and acceptance of the Charter by submitting a query to search for, or to verify the revocation status of a Certificate or by otherwise relying on or using any information or services provided by BT's Repository or the BT Trust Services website. If you do not accept the Charter, do not submit a query and do not download, access or use any BT CRL. Customers of BT Trust Services are reminded that their reliance on or use of Certificates is governed by the Conditions for BT Trust Services.'[1]

1   BT Trust Services Relying Third Party Charter Issue 4 (July 2004) paragraph 2 available online at www.trustwise.com/repository/rpa/.

CABLE & WIRELESS

12.15   The introduction to the Cable & Wireless Relying Party Standard Terms and Conditions of Use is wholly in capital letters and bold text, and informs the recipient that 'These terms and conditions of use become binding on you and you become a relying party (as defined below) when you attempt to validate a Cable & Wireless digital certificate or otherwise access, use or reply upon a Cable & Wireless digital certificate or certificate revocation list.'[1]

1   Introductory paragraph available online at www.cwsecurity.net/rpa/.

VERISIGN

12.16 The introductory paragraph, typed in capital letters of the VeriSign Relying Party Agreement[1] requires the recipient to read the agreement before validating a digital certificate, or obtain access to the database of certificate revocations and other information. The first clause goes on to determine the moment the agreement becomes effective: 'This Relying Party Agreement becomes effective when you submit a query to search for a certificate, or to verify a digital signature created with a private key corresponding to a public key contained in a certificate, or when you otherwise use or rely upon any information or services provided by VeriSign's Repository or website.'[2] The terms of the Thawte Relying Party Agreement, although longer and more comprehensive than the VeriSign document, are sufficiently similar to the VeriSign agreement to not merit any further treatment.[3]

1   VeriSign Public Certification Services, Relying Party Agreement available online at www.digitalid.verisign.com/services/client/help/relying_party.htm; this agreement differs from another VeriSign Relying Party Agreement available online at www.verisign.com/repository/rpa.html.
2   The following web address is then provided where the relying party can obtain access to relying party agreements: www.verisign.com/repository/rpa/index.html.
3   Available online at www.thawte.com/en/guides/pdf/cpsrelyingparty.pdf.

EQUIFAX

12.17 There does not appear to be a specific agreement for recipients with respect to certificates offered by Equifax Secure, although the following is included on the website: 'Obligations of Relying Parties: A relying party may justifiably rely upon a certificate only after confirming that the certificate has not been revoked or expired by using the URL listed in the Certificate Distribution Point contained within the subscriber's certificate and determining that such certificate provides adequate assurances for its intended use.[1] The Certificate Practice Statement covers the matter as follows: '3. Relying Party Obligations Relying Parties must verify that the Equifax SecureMark Certificate is valid by examining the Certificate Revocation List before initiating a transaction involving such Equifax SecureMark Certificate.'[2]

1   Available online at www.equifaxsecure.co.uk/policies/spds.html#Obligations%20of%20Relying%20Parties.
2   Certificate Practice Statement Version 3.0 (Effective 30 June 2003) available online at www.equifaxsecure.co.uk/policies/cps.html#iia. The text does not appear correctly when using Safari or Firefox.

NETRUST

12.18 Netrust of Singapore operates on a similar basis to that of IdenTrust. A relying party is required to be a subscriber: '1.3.5.2 A Relying Party must also be a Subscriber in the Netrust PCS to be able to enjoy any of the benefits, including the indemnities provided by Netrust (if any), of the Netrust PCS as set out in the CPS or applicable CP' hence the issue of whether there is a contract between the certification authority and the relying party is not relevant.[1]

For a recipient to be in a position to accept an offer, they must be aware of both the existence of the agreement and its terms. There must be an unqualified expression of assent. Thus it is debatable whether the steps taken to bring the relying party agreement to the notice of a recipient can be described as effective. Further, the assumption that a recipient is bound by the relying party terms (including the terms set out in the certification practice statement) if they undertake any act of verification or reliance without reading the terms, appears not to conform with the requirement that they must assent effectively to the terms on offer. It appears that certification authorities seek to bind a recipient by a mixture of notice (the effectiveness of which is to be doubted) and acceptance by conduct. Whilst it is possible to accept an offer by conduct, acceptance is not effective unless it is clear that the verifying party acted with the intention of accepting the offer. Where a certification party relies on the act of a recipient, it is doubtful whether they can be said to have accepted the offer. Indeed, the relying party agreements are phrased in such a way that any act of reliance or attempt to verify the authenticity of a certificate carried out by the recipient will immediately bind them to the agreement, even though they have not had sight of, or read the document. It seems that a recipient is in a similar position to the buyer in *Jayaar Impex Ltd v Toaken Group Ltd*,[2] where the parties entered an oral agreement for the purchase and sale of Nigerian gum arabic grade 1. It was held that the act of the buyer in taking delivery of the gum arabic did not amount to acceptance of a set of written terms that the seller sought to impose between the time the contract was formed and the performance of delivery. Where it is debatable that notice of the relying party agreement has been given, the certification authority will seek to rely on the deemed acceptance of the recipient. However, it cannot be said the act of a recipient, when they obtain access to a certification revocation list to verify a certificate, for instance, is the unqualified acceptance and assent to the terms of such an agreement.

1   Certificate Practice Statement (Version 2.0.4) August 2002 see also paragraph 2.1.5; the Netrust website is available at www.netrust.com.sg.
2   [1996] 2 Lloyd's Rep 437.

Communication of acceptance

12.19   As a general rule, acceptance must be communicated to the entity making the offer. However, the certification authority can waive the requirement that a verifying party must communicate acceptance of the offer. The classic example is the acceptance of an offer by conduct, especially where a contract is unilateral and the conduct is in the form of a positive act, which could describe the actions of a verifying party where they systematically check the provenance of a certificate. The moment of acceptance could be construed as the time when the recipient completes the steps to confirm the validity of the certificate.

Certainty of terms

12.20 The central thrust of a set of terms should be to make the obligations and benefits clear to both parties. If the terms are too vague, they cannot give rise to a binding contract. Judges will consider various factors when assessing the terms of an agreement, including custom and trade usage, reasonableness, the duty to resolve uncertainty and meaningless and self-contradictory terms, will consider various factors. Consideration of the terms imposed by certification authorities may yield a helpful analysis of precisely what a verifying party is required to do, what mechanisms they have to use to achieve what is required of them, whether they are able to carry out all the obligations set out in a relying party agreement and whether the time and effort it takes to realise all of the requirements may mean the verifying party is better off by contacting the sending party by email, postal letter or telephone to authenticate the message or document sent with a digital signature.

DEFINED OBLIGATIONS

12.21 The BT Trust Services Relying Third Party Charter[1] is a useful starting point. The following terms apply to a recipient in accordance with the terms of this Charter. The terms can be divided between wide-ranging requirements relating to the interpretation of knowledge and what appear to be well-defined obligations. Those obligations that appear to be well defined are as follows:

(a) The recipient is required to use the repository in accordance with the provisions laid down in the certification practice statement.

(b) The provisions set out in the certification practice statement govern any act of reliance by the recipient on the content of a certificate.

(c) The specific procedures set out in paragraph 2.1.4 of the certification practice statement must be followed.[2]

The BT Certification Practice Statement, which acts as a mutually supporting crutch to the Charter, sets out additional terms in paragraph 2.1.4, as follows:

(a) The verifying party is required to check the status of a certificate on which they wish to rely, as well as all the certificates in the chain in accordance with the requirements set out in paragraphs 4.4.10 and 4.4.12, both of which refer to the need to check the certificate revocation list.

(b)   The verifying party is required to assent to the terms as a condition of using or otherwise relying on certificates: 'Finally, the Relying Third Party Charters state that assent to the terms is a condition of using or otherwise relying on Certificates. Relying Parties that are also End Users agree to be bound by Relying Party terms under this section, disclaimers of warranty, and limitations of liability when they agree to the Charter(s),' although there do not appear to be any instructions as to how they can notify BT of their acceptance.

1   BT Trust Services Relying Third Party Charter Issue 4 (July 2004) available online at www.trustwise.com/repository/rpa/.
2   BT have indicated that if a recipient relies on a certificate without first complying with the procedures set out in paragraph 2.1.4 of the certification practice statement, any reliance by them on or use of the certificate will be '... considered unreasonable and in derogation of your duty of care under the Common Law of England and Wales.'

INTERPRETATION OF KNOWLEDGE TERMS

12.22   The terms of the charter require the verifying party to undertake the following obligations:[1]
(a)   The requirement to make an informed decision.
(b)   Acknowledgements that the verifying party:
    (i)   Has sufficient access to information.
    (ii)   Is responsible for deciding whether they should rely on a certificate or information embedded in it.
    (iii) Understands that a private key can be stolen or another form of compromise can occur that means the theft will not be detected, resulting in a stolen or compromised key being used to forge a digital signature to a document.

The BT Certification Practice Statement sets out further terms, as follows:[2]
(a)   BT does not accept responsibility for assessing the appropriateness of the use of a certificate,[3] but the verifying party is required to make a number of independent assessments:
    (i)   Independently assess the appropriateness of the use of a certificate for any given purpose.
    (ii)   Determine that the certificate will, in fact, be used for an appropriate purpose.
(b)   The verifying party is also required to use appropriate hardware and software:
    (i)   This particular obligation bears quoting in more detail, if only to demonstrate the vagueness of the proposition: '... the appropriate software and/or hardware to perform digital signature verification or other cryptographic operations they wish to perform.'
    (ii)   The mechanism includes '... identifying a Certificate Chain and verifying the digital signatures on all Certificates in the Certificate Chain.'

(iii) Further, a verifying party is not permitted to rely on a certificate unless the particular verification procedures set out in (ii) above are successful, although it is not clear what BT mean by 'procedure' – whether it means a particular course of action or a set of instructions to perform the task of verification.

(c) Where the verifying party undertakes all the checks set out in the various terms, and those checks are successful, the recipient will be entitled to rely on the certificate, and thereby become a verifying party, provided that reliance upon the certificate is reasonable under the circumstances.

BT is not the only certification authority that seeks to enforce terms of this nature. A brief summary of a number of other certification authorities illustrate similar patterns:

(a) Cable & Wireless set out a number of obligations that a relying party must perform in paragraph 2.1.5.[4]

(b) In its Relying Party Agreement,[5] VeriSign uses an almost identical mix of obligations between relatively defined terms and the interpretation clauses that are set out in the BT Charter. Of interest is a contradiction between two terms in this particular agreement that seem to acknowledge the true value of some types of certificate. Clause 1.4.1.1 describes the value and uses to which a Class 1 certificate can be put, including their use for digital signatures, amongst other examples. However, the provisions of clause 1.4.2 'Prohibited Certificate Uses' takes away from the verifying party any semblance of value in a digital signature of this class: 'Class 1 Certificates shall not be used as proof of identity or a support of non repudiation of identity or authority.' This example serves to illustrate the nature of the promise that accompanies a digital signature – certainly a class 1 certificate issued by VeriSign.

(c) The only obligation that Equifax appears to require of a recipient is the need to verify the certificate is valid by perusing the certificate revocation list before relying on the certificate.

From a practical point of view, if a subscribing party uses a digital signature to authenticate their identity when sending correspondence by email, the question a recipient has to ask is: for what reason? Even if they take the time to undertake the long list of due diligence as set out by BT, VeriSign and other certification authorities, and retain the evidence in a format that could withstand forensic analysis in court, the recipient will have to justify why they used a particular type of software or hardware and explain why they made the decisions they did against a standard that could be subjective or objective, depending on the policy decisions determined by a court.

There is a range of risks that will affect the reasonableness or otherwise of the terms set out by the certification authorities in the relying party agreements. Whilst these are discussed elsewhere, such risks include, but are not limited to, poor key management, failure by the subscribing party to look after their key properly, the software used by the verifying party being unable to obtain access to the relevant certification revocation list and a failure in the links on the various websites. Suffice to say the vagueness of many of the terms may lead a court to reach the conclusion that such agreements are too wide-ranging and vague to be enforceable.

1   Paragraph 2.1.4.
2   Paragraph 2.1.4.
3   A challenge is possible when considering the content of Table 2 – Certificate Properties Affecting Trust and paragraph 1.3.4 Applicability.
4   Cable & Wireless PKI Certification Practice Statement, Document number 1491-PD009-023, May 2002, available online at //www2.cwsecurity.net/files/cps.pdf.
5   Available online at www.digitalid.verisign.com/services/client/help/relying_party.htm.

CONTINGENT CONDITIONS PRECEDENT

12.23 Relying party agreements are agreements that are subject to the verifying party performing a number of conditions before the certification authority will accept any obligations for the service they provide. Even if the meaning of such wide ranging phrases as 'informed decision', 'assess the appropriateness of the use' and 'sufficient access to information' was obvious to both parties, it is debatable whether the verifying party could prove they undertook all the necessary care to fulfil the requirements imposed by the certification authorities. It is not clear what standard is required of the verifying party when undertaking due diligence and reasonable enquiry. What might be 'reasonable' may be dependent upon the expertise of the verifying party, bearing in mind the nature of the internet and the complex nature of software as it interacts with operating systems. For instance, where a consumer is persuaded to have a digital certificate on their home computer, it is to be expected that their knowledge of the issues will be rudimentary at best, unless they are computer-literate. By comparison, a corporation with a dedicated IT department can be expected to be familiar with the risks associated with relying on a digital certificate and act accordingly. Thus there is a rationale for taking a subjective approach to the standard of due diligence expected of a verifying party, depending on their expertise and knowledge.

Implied terms

12.24 It is for a judge to decide whether terms should be implied, and whether terms are implied will depend on a range of general considerations that are set out in the relevant textbooks. It is well established that a term will be implied to give efficacy to the contract.[1] If a term is to be implied between a certification authority and a verifying party, it will be crucial to understand the precise nature of the promise made by a certification authority.

1   *The Moorcock* (1889) 14 PD 64.

THE NATURE OF THE PROMISE

12.25 A subscribing party enters a contract with a trusted third party, usually called a certification authority. In essence, the contract is for a key pair (a private key retained by the subscribing party and a public key retained and made public by the certification authority) and an individual identity certificate.[1] It is possible for the certification authority to provide both the key pair and the certificate, or the certificate only. The purpose of the individual identity certificate is to act as a link between the use of the private key by the subscribing party and the public key held by the certification authority. The role of the certification authority is to verify the association between the private key and the identity of the subscriber, even if the express terms do not articulate this obligation in quite the same way. In consequence, a verifying party will look to the certification authority to confirm the association between the private key and the identity of the subscriber.

The question for a court will be the precise nature of the term to be implied, if a term is to implied.

At one end of the continuum the following promise by the certification authority could be implied:

> 'If the certificate attached to the key verifies the link with the identity of the subscribing party that sent you the digital signature, then I accept liability for the link between the subscriber and the key unless I have previously given you notice that the key has been revoked.'

This is an absolute promise that no certification authority can make within the public key infrastructure, although such a promise might be required and appropriate as between organizations such as banks in a closed system, for instance.

One intermediate position could be described thus:

> 'If the certificate attached to the key verifies the link with the identity of the subscribing party that sent you the digital signature, then I accept liability for the link between the subscriber and the key where I have acted with reasonable care and skill to ensure that you have the ability to determine with speed and accurately whether the key has been revoked.'

This position is relatively close to the express terms offered by certification authorities, except that certification authorities rarely articulate that they will act with reasonable care and skill, and require the verifying party to comply with stringent procedures before any liability is accepted.

Another intermediate position may involve a duty of care to keep the key secret, whilst ensuring there is an accurate and speedy method for the verifying party to check it has not been revoked. This may be a more appropriate term to effect between the subscribing party and the certification authority, although it is a term that is included in the relevant agreement with the subscribing party. A further alternative would be to imply this particular term as between the subscribing party and the recipient. The critical issue for such an implied term is who is to prove the breach of duty.

At the other end of the continuum, the subscribing party may be taken to say:

'If this key verifies my signature by providing a link to my identity in the certificate, then I accept the digital signature is binding on me if it was effected by me or with my authority. If I deny that I attached the signature to the document, it will be for you to prove that it was affixed by me or with my authority.'

In this instance, the recipient may well wonder why the subscribing party went to the expense of using a digital signature to begin with, because such a promise holds very little of value.

Finally, there is a term implied by s 13 of the Supply of Goods and Services Act 1982 (as amended) that the certification authority will carry out the service with reasonable care and skill. This term can be excluded, and certification authorities take full advantage of the ability so to do. Of interest will be the standard to be applied to certification authorities: whether it is the standard of a professional person or that of an artisan. Finally, it may be construed that the special relationship that exists between the certification authority and the verifying party may demonstrate that the certification authority impliedly warrants that the service it offers will be reasonably fit for the purpose for which it required, namely to verify the link between the subscriber and the key used to affix a digital signature to a document or message. Such an implied warranty may be justified as a matter of public policy.

1   Other types of certificate include accreditation certificates and authorization and permission certificates.

Consideration

12.26   A contract is not, generally, enforceable unless it is supported by the passing of consideration between the parties. The certification authority may give something of value to the verifying party by making a promise. In the case of BT, the value on offer to the verifying party is set out in the BT Relying Party Charter:

'BT will comply with the assurance level for information contained in a Certificate as specified in the description of each class of Certificate in section 1.1 of the CPS. In particular, BT represents that all information contained in a Certificate, except non-verified customer information, has been validated in accordance with the procedures in the CPS.'[1]

In return, the verifying party relies on the accuracy of the information in reliance upon the promise, having given consideration by undertaking the due diligence required by the Charter. Consideration for the promise and reliance upon the promise could move from the benefit of relying on the certificate.

One further possibility is to postulate that there is a benefit to the certification authority, in that certification authorities want customers to accept the service they offer. Should they offer verifying parties a sufficiently efficient and easy service, they will increase the take-up of digital signatures. Conceptually, this is similar to the concept of bank cheque guarantee cards.

However, the reality of the complexity, and therefore the risks, inherent in the public key infrastructure may be such that unilateral contracts of this nature will be impossible to enforce because the vagueness of their terms is such that a verifying party cannot comply with the obligations. As a result, the reality of the consideration provided by the verifying party may be another factor that will defeat the attempts at enforcing a relying party agreement unilaterally.

1   BT Trust Services Relying Third Party Charter Issue 4 (July 2004) available online at www. trustwise.com/repository/rpa/.

REALITY OF CONSIDERATION

12.27   To be effective, the consideration that passes does not have to be adequate, but it must be capable of being estimated by reference to a value. For instance, if it is impossible for the verifying party to perform the terms of a relying party agreement fully, it is probably correct to accept that such a contract is impossible to perform. The terms laid down by the certification authority may be considered to be illusory, because they cannot be performed to the standard required, and any consideration given by the verifying party by undertaking due diligence, for instance, is based on a misunderstanding of the impossibility of conforming to the terms with sufficient rigour, although the standard of due diligence will have to be decided by a court. As a result, and in combination with the weaknesses proposed in the previous discussion, this may prove fatal to the imposition of unilateral relying party agreements on a verifying party.

Privity of contract

12.28   It will be a matter of law whether a contract exists between the certification authorities and verifying parties. The principle in English law is that a contract will only generate rights and obligations between the parties to the contract. The discussion above demonstrates that certification authorities seek to impose fairly substantial burdens on a verifying party in exchange for what may be considered a very narrow promise. In the absence of a contract between the two parties, the doctrine of privity of contract will prevent exemption clauses being applied to protect certification authorities from claims by verifying parties.

Of interest is the scenario where a person relies on a certificate without verifying it, and they are misled by an error in the certificate that leads them to suffer a loss, and they can show that verification would have been successful if they had undertaken it (in that the certificate was genuine and had not been revoked). Arguably, a claim should not fail merely because they omitted a step that neither would nor should have affected their conduct.

STATUTE LAW

12.29   However, with the passing of the Contracts (Rights of Third Parties) Act 1999,[1] this position may have altered the balance in favour of the verifying party. In essence, the Act allows third parties to enforce contracts made for their benefit. The right is set out in s 1(1):

'Subject to the provisions of this Act, a person who is not a party to a contract (a "third party") may in his own right enforce a term of the contract if:

(a)   the contract expressly provides that he may, or
(b)   subject to subsection (2), the terms purports to confer a benefit on him.'

The provision of s 1(1)(a) is clear. The contract may expressly provide that the verifying party may enforce a term of a contract. However, in many cases, this right is expressly excluded, as it has been in clause 5.12 of the terms and conditions for the BT ID Certificate between BT and a subscribing party:[2]

'5.12   Notwithstanding any other provision in this Contract, a person who is not a party to this Contract has no right under the Contracts (Rights of Third Parties) Act 1999 to rely upon or enforce any term of this Contract. Nothing in this Contract shall affect any right or remedy of a third party which exists or is available other than as a result of the aforementioned Act.'

The other certification authorities mentioned in this text do not appear to have included such a restriction in their terms or certification practice statements.[3] Where a contract excludes the ability of a verifying party to rely on a contract between the subscribing party and the certification authority, the next step is to examine whether a verifying party can take advantage of the terms of the contract under the provisions of s 1(1)(b). This section is subject to the provisions of s 1(2), which provides that 'Subsection (1)(b) does not apply if on a proper construction of the contract it appears that the parties did not intend the term to be enforceable by the third party.' Bearing in mind the existence of the BT Relying Party Charter and other third party agreements provided by other certification authorities, it may be possible to construe such agreements, together with the promises or warranties offered to third parties, as intending a verifying party to have the benefit of the contract between the subscribing party and the certification authority, despite any attempt to expressly exclude the right. However, even if this was the case, the verifying party '... must be expressly identified in the contract by name, as a member of a class or as answering a particular description ...'[4] It could be argued that a verifying party is expressly identified as a third party that will benefit from the provision of the service. Although verifying parties will not be identified by name, they clearly belong to a class that is recognized by both the certification authority and the subscribing party, both directly and by implication.[5]

1   The Act received the Royal Assent on 11 November 1999 and applied to all contracts made on or after 11 May 2000, unless the parties to a contract decided to apply the terms of the Act to contracts made after the Royal Assent was given: s 10(2) and (3).
2   ID Certificate End User Contract Issue 1 (12 September 2002), available online at www. trustwise.com/repository/PDF/enduser_idcertsv4.PDF.
3   See Thomas Roe 'Contractual Intention under Section 1(1)(b) and 1(2) of the Contracts (Rights of Third Parties) Act 1999' 63 MLR 887 at 891–893 for a discussion about the relevancy or otherwise where no provision has been made for third party rights.
4   Section 1(3).
5   Thomas Roe 'Contractual Intention under Section 1(1)(b) and 1(2) of the Contracts (Rights of Third Parties) Act 1999' for a discussion of the burden of proof and matters to be taken into account when construing the contract for the purposes of section 1(2).

Validity of the contract

PRE-OFFER INFORMATION

12.30   There are four elements that must be in place under English common law for a contract to be legally binding: offer, acceptance, consideration and the intention to enter a legally binding relationship. Additional pre-contract formalities have now been introduced in the European Union for contracts entered over the internet. Businesses are now obliged to provide a certain amount of information under the terms of the Distance Selling Directive[1] and the Directive on Electronic Commerce,[2] together with the Consumer Protection (Contracts Concluded By Means of Distance Communication) Regulations 2000 (SI 2000 No 2334) and the Electronic Commerce (EC Directive) Regulations 2002, that transpose into English law most of the provisions of these Directives.[3] These provisions only apply within the European Union. Whilst the provisions of the Distance Selling Directive apply only to consumers, the Directive on Electronic Commerce applies to both businesses, unless they have agreed otherwise, and consumers. Consideration is given to the issues raised by the Directives and Regulations, for two reasons. First, a number of vendors offer to sell key pairs for the purpose of electronic signatures by way of the internet.

Second, bearing in mind that the nature of the service is to provide a key pair to enable a user to sign a document in electronic format under the terms of the Electronic Communications Act 2000, it is apposite that such services will predominantly be available by way of the internet.

1   Directive 97/7/EC of the European Parliament and of the Council of 20 May 1997 on the protection of consumers in respect of distance contracts, OJ L 144, 04/06/1997 p. 0019–0027.
2   Directive 2000/31/EC of the European Parliament and of the Council of 8 June 2000 on certain legal aspects of information society services, in particular electronic commerce, in the Internal Market OJ L 178, 17.7.2000, p. 1; Communication from the Commission to the Council, the European Parliament and the European Economic and Social Committee on the implementation of Directive 1997/7/EC of the European Parliament and of the Council of 20 May 1997 on the Protection of Consumers in respect of Distance Contracts (COM/2006/0514 final).
3   Consumer Protection (Contracts Concluded By Means of Distance Communication) Regulations 2000 SI 2000/2334, which came into force on 31 October 2000 (Reg 1(1)) and amended by the Consumer Protection (Distance Selling)(Amendment) Regulations 2005 (SI 2005 No 689) in force 6 April 2005; Directive 2000/31/EC of the European Parliament and of the Council of 8 June 2000 on certain legal aspects of information society services, in particular electronic commerce, in the Internal Market ('Directive on electronic commerce') OJ L178, 17 July 2000 p. 1; The Electronic Commerce (EC Directive) Regulations 2002 SI 2002/2013, which came into force on 21 August 2002, with the exception of regulation 16, which came into force on 23 October 2002 (Reg 1(2)).

DISTANCE SELLING DIRECTIVE

12.31   Where goods and services are sold by mail order, over the telephone, by facsimile transmission or over the internet, the process is undertaken at a distance from the consumer.[1] Until recently, there was little legislation in place to cover this type of transaction, with the exception of the Consumer Protection (Cancellation of Contracts Concluded away from Business Premises) (Amendment) Regulations 1987 SI 1987/2117,[2] otherwise known as the Doorstep Selling Regulations, and the Mail Order Transactions (Information) Order 1976, which was revoked by the new Regulations.[3] Definitions of a consumer, a supplier and a distance contract are provided in regulation 3(1), as follows:
(a)   a consumer is 'any natural person who, in contracts to which these Regulations apply, is acting for purposes which are outside his business;'
(b)   a supplier means 'any person who, in contracts to which these Regulations apply, is acting in his commercial or professional capacity'
(c)   a distance contract means 'any contract concerning goods or services concluded between a supplier and a consumer under an organised distance sales or service provision scheme run by the supplier who, for the purpose of the contract, makes exclusive use of one or more means of distance communication up to and including the moment at which the contract is concluded.'

In setting out the relevant regulations, it will be assumed that the certification authority is supplying a service, as opposed to goods.

1 Schedule 1 to the Consumer Protection (Contracts Concluded By Means of Distance Communication) Regulations 2000 SI 2000/2334 provides a list of examples of distance contracts.
2 Amended by the Consumer Protection (Cancellation of Contracts Concluded away from Business Premises) (Amendment) Regulations 1998 SI 1998/3050.
3 SI 1976/1812, revoked by regulation 2.

Information required prior to the conclusion of the contract

12.32 The provisions of regulation 7 require the supplier, 'in good time' and before the conclusion of the contract, to provide the consumer with the following information:

'(i) the identity of the supplier and, where the contract requires payment in advance, the supplier's address;
(ii) a description of the main characteristics of the goods or services;
(iii) the price of the goods or services including all taxes;
(iv) delivery costs where appropriate;
(v) the arrangements for payment, delivery or performance;
(vi) the existence of a right of cancellation except in the cases referred to in regulation 13;
(vii) the cost of using the means of distance communication where it is calculated other than at the basic rate;
(viii) the period for which the offer or the price remains valid; and
(ix) where appropriate, the minimum duration of the contract, in the case of contracts for the supply of goods or services to be performed permanently or recurrently;'

In addition, in the unlikely event the service ordered by the consumer is not available, the supplier must provide a substitute service of equivalent quality and price.[1] Regulation 7(3) requires the commercial purpose to be made clear, and 7(2) requires the supplier to provide the information 'in a clear and comprehensible manner appropriate to the means of distance communication used, with due regard in particular to the principles of good faith in commercial transactions and the principles governing the protection of those who are unable to give their consent such as minors.' Most of the requirements of the Regulations seem to be obvious, and most businesses will incorporate all, if not more than, the minimum amount of information required.

1 Regulation 7(1)(b).

Written and additional information

12.33 The supplier is required, by regulation 8(2), to provide the consumer with information that must be in writing, or in another durable medium that is available and accessible to the consumer. It must also be provided before the contract is concluded or in good time, but in the case of the provision of a service, during the performance of the contract. The information relevant to the sale of a service includes:

(a) the information set out in Regulation 7(1)(a);
(b) the geographical address of the place of business of the supplier to which the consumer may address any complaints;
(c) information about any after-sales services and guarantees; and
(d) the conditions for exercising any contractual right to cancel the contract, where the contract is of an unspecified duration or a duration exceeding one year.
(e) prior to the conclusion of a contract for the supply of services, the supplier shall inform the consumer in writing or in another durable medium which is available and accessible to the consumer that, unless the parties agree otherwise, he will not be able to cancel the contract under regulation 10 once the performance of the services has begun with his agreement.

Cancellation of the contract

12.34 A consumer has the right to cancel a contract under the provisions of regulation 10. Where a consumer serves a notice of cancellation, the contract shall be treated as if it had not been made.[1] A notice cancelling the contract must be in writing or in another durable medium that is available and accessible to the supplier. It does not matter how the notice is expressed, providing it indicates the consumer's intention to cancel the contract.[2] The consumer can deliver the notice of cancellation by hand to the supplier; send it by post, or facsimile transmission, or by electronic mail.[3] By the terms of regulation 12, the cancellation period for contracts for the supply of services begins with the day on which the contract is concluded and ends as provided in paragraphs (2) to (4), as follows:[4]

'(2) Where the supplier complies with regulation 8, the cancellation period ends on the expiry of the period of seven working days beginning with the day after the day on which the consumer receives the goods.

(3) Where a supplier who has not complied with regulation 8 provides to the consumer the information referred to in regulation 8(2), and does so in writing or in another durable medium available and accessible to the consumer, within the period of three months beginning with the day after the day on which the consumer receives the goods, the cancellation period ends on the expiry of the period of seven working days beginning with the day after the day on which the consumer receives the information.

(3A) Where the performance of the contract has begun with the consumer's agreement before the expiry of the period of seven working days beginning with the day after the day on which the contract was concluded and the supplier has not complied with regulation 8 on or before the day on which performance began, but provides to the consumer the information referred to in regulation 8(2) in good time during the performance of the contract, the cancellation period ends:

    (a) on the expiry of the period of seven working days beginning with the day after the day on which the consumer receives the information; or

    (b) if the performance of the contract is completed before the expiry of the period referred to in sub-paragraph (a), on the day when the performance of the contract is completed.

(4) Where none of paragraphs (2) to (3A) applies, the cancellation period ends on the expiry of the period of three months and seven working days beginning with the day after the day on which the consumer receives the goods.'

The consumer does not always have the right to cancel. In the case of a service, the right of a consumer to cancel the contract will not be available, unless the parties agree otherwise, if the supplier has complied with regulation 8(3) and the supplier has begun to perform the contract with the consumer's agreement before the end of the cancellation period that applies under regulation 12.[5]

1   Regulation 10(2).
2   Regulation 10(3).
3   Regulation 10(4).
4   As amended by the Consumer Protection (Distance Selling)(Amendment) Regulations 2005 (SI 2005 No 689).
5   Regulation 13(1)(a).

Breaching the Regulations

12.35 The practical effect of the provisions of the Consumer Protection (Contracts Concluded By Means of Distance Communication) Regulations in relation to the issuing of key pairs is only too clear. Failing to comply with the requirements will mean a consumer has extended rights to cancel the contract. It is possible for a consumer to obtain a key pair and use them for up to three months before demanding the contract be cancelled and for the price of the contract to be refunded. Also, both the Director General of Fair Trading and the Trading Standards Departments are required to consider any complaint about a breach of the Regulations. Should it be determined that a breach has occurred, both organizations have the power to apply to a court for an injunction or to apply for a Stop Now Order against the supplier.[1]

1   The Stop Now Orders (EC Directive) Regulations 2001 SI 2001/1422 came into force on
    1 June 2001 (Reg 1(2)) and apply to a number of laws and regulations, which are set out in
    regulation 2(3).

Directive on Electronic Commerce

INFORMATION SOCIETY SERVICES

12.36   Article 2(b) of the Directive defines a service provider as 'any natural
or legal person providing an information society service', and Article 2(c)
defines information society services as 'services within the meaning of Article
1(2) of Directive 98/34/EC as amended by Directive 98/48/EC', which in
turn is summarised in Recital 17 as (in part) 'any service normally provided
for remuneration, at a distance, by means of electronic equipment for the
processing (including digital compression) and storage of data, and at the
individual request of a recipient of a service.' The Department of Trade and
Industry have issued a set of guidance notes that accompany the Regulations.
The concept of information society services 'covers a wide range of economic
activities that take place online, including selling goods and services online'[1]
and the provision of public and private keys for the purpose of creating an
electronic signature could fall within the definition of goods or a service.

1   A Guide for Business to The Electronic Commerce (EC Directive) Regulations 2002 (SI
    2002/2013) (DTI, 31 July 2002), paragraph 2.14.

WHETHER KEY PAIRS ARE GOODS OR SERVICES

12.37   There is no clear definition of whether something sold over the
world wide web in digital format is goods or a service.[1] This can be important,
because the Supply of Goods and Services Act 1982 imposes less rigorous
standards on the service provider than if the items sold are goods, and it
affects the terms that are implied into the contract and the standard of quality
with which the product will have to comply. The leading case in England and
Wales is *St Albans City and District Council v International Computers Ltd.*[2] In
this instance, St Albans City and District Council entered into a contract with
International Computers Ltd (ICL) for the supply of a computer system to be
used in administering the collection of the community charge. An error in the
software meant that the charges set by the Council were incorrect. During the
course of the installation of the computer, an employee of ICL took a disk to
the Council's premises. The disk contained the program. He then transferred
the program into the computer and retained the disk. Thus the Council did
not have a physical item in their possession that contained the software. One
of the questions Sir Iain Glidewell LJ addressed in his judgment was whether
the program was an item of goods or the provision of a service. He said, at
493a-b:

'In both the Sale of Goods Act 1979, s 61, and the Supply of Goods and Services Act 1982, s 18, the definition of goods includes 'all personal chattels other than things in action and money'. Clearly, a disk is within this definition. Equally clearly, a program, of itself, is not.'

Clearly there is a distinction between a physical item, such as a disk, and a steam of data in the form of a computer program. Thus if a key pair produced an electronic signature partly by means of a smart card interacting with the terminal on a computer, one of the keys forming the pair would be contained on a physical format. A useful analysis of the relationship between software and goods was discussed by Lord Penrose in *Beta Computers (Europe) Limited v Adobe Systems (Europe) Limited*[3] regarding a contract for the supply of standard software stored on a physical medium. The crucial point made by Lord Penrose, is to ensure the role of the physical carrier does not dominate the characteristic of the product.[4] The present position, as pointed out by Sir Iain Glidewell LJ above, is that a software program is not goods. With respect, this must be right. Consider the analysis of the private key contained on a smart card one stage further with these comments in mind. It is possible to infer that immediately a key is stored on a physical medium, it becomes goods. However, as pointed out by Lord Penrose, such a conclusion is conceptually unsustainable, because it leads to a distortion of the actualité.[5] If a key becomes goods when it is stored on a physical medium such as a smart card, the result is to subordinate one component of a complex service or product to a different set of legal provisions from the other components of the service or product. Such a result would lead to anomalies in the terms to be implied if an electronic signature (especially digital signatures issued with a public key infrastructure) were to be subject to different implied terms, depending on whether the key was stored on a physical carrier such as a smart card or stored in a computer. To take this discussion one stage further, a subscribing party may, depending on the nature of the service they have paid for, receive key pairs that have been pre-generated through the postal service. These key pairs will invariably be stored on a smart card or token. Alternatively, even where a private key is sent to the subscribing party by electronic means, the certification authority not only urges the subscriber to back up their certificate and private key, but also encourages them to do so on a physical medium such as a floppy disk.[6] This action by a subscribing party may then cause further arguments that centre on whether the subscribing party can claim additional legal protection because they stored the electronic data on a physical item as the result of advice from the certification authority.

It has been suggested that there are two reasons for considering the supply of digital media as goods rather than services.[7] The first consideration relates to the attributes that digital data shares with tangible goods, such as the movement, distribution and storage of data. Clearly, a key can be moved by being sent to the subscriber. The second argument, which has less force in relation to key pairs, is that digital data does not create unique contractual relationships, and they do not depend upon the exercise of skill or labour. The provision of key pairs will depend on an individual relationship between the provider and the subscriber, and the formation of the key pair will require skill on behalf of the provider or subscriber. One further suggestion is that the service provider is providing a combination of service and goods, a hybrid, in which the service element is predominate.[8]

One resolution of this issue in relation to key pairs may lie in the comments by Sir Iain Glidewell LJ respecting the term to be implied to the contract in the St Albans case, in that it should have been '… reasonably capable of achieving the purpose specified in the 'Statement of User Requirements' in ch 5 of St Alban's invitation to tender, and that as a result of the defect in release 2020 ICL were in breach of that implied term.'[9] Service providers providing key pairs in a public key infrastructure have a range of documents that relate directly to any contract that a subscriber enters. They also have a variety of statements in their literature, especially on websites, that make assertions about the quality of the key pairs and the infrastructure they create. As a result, it may be possible to use these documents and statements to reach a similar level of legal certainty as to the implied terms, whether a key pair is classed as a service or goods. It is also to be noted that the World Trade Organization initiated a work programme on electronic commerce in 1998, and part of the remit was to examine and report on the classification of services and goods by the respective Councils.[10] It appears that no clear agreement has been reached for items that can be a physical item as well as service, if delivered by electronic means.

To conclude this discussion, the reader's attention is drawn to the comments made by Lord Penrose in the Beta case:

> 'It would have a somewhat odd result that the dominant characteristic of the complex product, in terms of value or of the significant interests of the parties, would be subordinated to the medium by which it was transmitted to the user in analysing the true nature and effect of the contract.'[11]

This does not preclude, as further pointed out by Lord Penrose, a claim based on the nature of the goods if the physical medium was defective, or the components that form part of the storage medium are faulty, or the data stored on the medium had been corrupted at or before the item was supplied to the subscribing party. However, the crucial distinction to make is the character of the transaction, not the subject-matter. For instance, where a subscriber is supplied with a key pair over the internet, they receive a service; where they buy a smartcard preloaded with a key pair, that is a supply of goods. In the case of St Albans City Council, there was a contract for work and materials, in the course of which they were supplied with some goods and some services. Some of the software with which they were supplied may have taken the form of a supply of goods, though some clearly did not. It is a mistake to think that the 'information content' of some goods makes them somehow different from 'ordinary' goods. The same information could take the form of a computer program, and perhaps be supplied by way of a service. The fact that different rules of law may apply, depending on whether goods or services have been supplied in a particular case, arises from policy errors in the formulation of statute law, which should not be allowed to distort the underlying classification of the facts by courts trying to avoid anomalies.[12]

1   Sacha Wunsch-Vincent, *The WTO, the Internet and Trade in Digital products: EU-US Perspectives*, (Hart Publishing, 2006).
2   [1996] 4 All ER 481 CA Civil Division.
3   [1996] FSR 367; [1996] CLC 832; [1996] SLT 604; [1997] Info TLR 73; [1996] Masons CLR 16, OH.
4   [1996] FSR 367 at 376.
5   [1996] FSR 367 at 376.
6   For an example of the advice given by BT see 'Frequently Asked Questions for ID Certificates', available online at www.trustwise.com/repository/idcertsfaq.htm.
7   Michael Chissick and Alistair Kelman *Electronic Commerce Law and Practice* (3rd edn, Sweet & Maxwell, 2002) paragraph 3.09.
8   A. Michael Froomkin 'The Essential Role of Trusted Third Parties in Electronic Commerce' 75 Oregon L Rev 49 (1996) and also available online at www.osaka.law.miami.edu/~froomkin/articles/trusted.htm.
9   [1996] 4 All ER 481 CA Civil Division at 494f.
10 Sacha Wunsch-Vincent, *The WTO, the Internet and Trade in Digital products: EU-US Perspectives*, (Hart Publishing, 2006).
11 [1996] FSR 367 at 376.
12 The author is indebted to Nicholas Bohm for the extension of this analysis.

ESTABLISHMENT OF PROVIDER

12.38   It does not follow that a provider is established where the website and server is geographically located. The meaning of a service provider is deliberately wide in scope, to take into account the complex arrangements made by companies when operating from different locations across the world. Regulation 2(1) defines a service provider thus:

'"established service provider" means a service provider who is a national of a member State or a company or firm as mentioned in Article 48 of the Treaty and who effectively pursues an economic activity by virtue of which he is a service provider using a fixed establishment in a member State for an indefinite period, but the presence and use of the technical means and technologies required to provide the information society service do not, in themselves, constitute an establishment of the provider; in cases where it cannot be determined from which of a number of places of establishment a given service is provided, that service is to be regarded as provided from the place of establishment where the provider has the centre of his activities relating to that service; references to a service provider being established or to the establishment of a service provider shall be construed accordingly;'

The physical location of the server is not relevant to where a service provider is established. If it is not clear where a provider is established, the definition provides for the following tests: First, consider whether the economic activity is being carried on from a fixed establishment. Second, decide whether the use of the fixed establishment is for an indefinite period. Evidence that a company employs people to work in a building that it either leases or owns will be helpful in determining the establishment in a fairly simple case. However, in more complex instances, it may not be clear where a company is established, because their physical operation may be situated in a jurisdiction outside the European Union, accept credit card payments in England and deliver goods from local distribution centres in each jurisdiction. The complexity of such arrangements were understood when the Directive on Electronic Commerce was passed, and Recital 19 illustrates how the matter should be approached:

> 'The place at which a service provider is established should be determined in conformity with the case-law of the Court of Justice according to which the concept of establishment involves the actual pursuit of an economic activity through a fixed establishment for an indefinite period; this requirement is also fulfilled where a company is constituted for a given period; the place of establishment of a company providing services via an Internet website is not the place at which the technology supporting its website is located or the place at which its website is accessible but the place where it pursues its economic activity; in cases where a provider has several places of establishment it is important to determine from which place of establishment the service concerned is provided; in cases where it is difficult to determine from which of several places of establishment a given service is provided, this is the place where the provider has the centre of his activities relating to this particular service.'

Unfortunately this recital illustrates that it may not be clear to the company where the centre of activity is established, although the Department for Trade and Industry have offered the following advice in their Guide, at paragraph 2.12: 'Where it is difficult to determine from which of several places of establishment a given service is provided, it is the place where the service provider has the centre of its activities relating to that particular service.' Where a company is not sure of the position, the relevant enforcement authority may be in a position to help determine this issue.

GENERAL INFORMATION TO BE PROVIDED BY A PERSON PROVIDING AN INFORMATION SOCIETY SERVICE

12.39 Where the service provider is established in the European Union, they are obliged to provide the following information to the customer:

(a)   the name of the service provider;
(b)   the geographic address at which the service provider is established;
(c)   the details of the service provider, including his electronic mail address, which makes it possible to contact him rapidly and communicate with him in a direct and effective manner;
(d)   where the service provider is registered in a trade or similar register available to the public, details of the register in which the service provider is entered and his registration number, or equivalent means of identification in that register;
(e)   where the provision of the service is subject to an authorisation scheme, the particulars of the relevant supervisory authority;[1]

The information set out above must be made, in accordance with regulation 6(1), '… available to the recipient of the service and any relevant enforcement authority, in a form and manner which is easily, directly and permanently accessible.' Failure to provide the information in the manner required lends the provider liable to an action for damages for breach of statutory duty.[2] It is crucial to note the need to ensure the information is made available easily and permanently. Thus the information must be available to the visitor after they have left the website.

1   The Electronic Commerce (EC Directive) Regulations 2002 SI 2002/2013, regulations 6(1)(a)–(g) and 6(2).
2   The Electronic Commerce (EC Directive) Regulations 2002 SI 2002/2013, regulation 13.

INFORMATION TO BE PROVIDED WHERE CONTRACTS ARE CONCLUDED BY ELECTRONIC MEANS

12.40   The Electronic Commerce (EC Directive) Regulations set out, in regulation 9, the information that a service provider must provide, before a consumer places an order. Parties that are not consumers may agree to waive these provisions. The following information must be provided 'in a clear, comprehensible and unambiguous manner':
(a)   the different technical steps to follow to conclude the contract;
(b)   whether or not the concluded contract will be filed by the service provider and whether it will be accessible;
(c)   the technical means for identifying and correcting input errors prior to the placing of the order; and
(d)   the languages offered for the conclusion of the contract.[1]

The requirement of regulation 9(1)(a) may incorporate a list of steps the buyer must take before they enter the contract. These provisions are straightforward, as are the provisions of regulation 9(1)(c), which requires the service provider to allow the buyer to identify when they have made an error and to correct the error. Also, the requirement relating to language, as set out in regulation 9(1)(d), merely requires the service provider to indicate which languages they offer. There is no obligation to provide information in a particular language. The provisions of regulation 9(1)(b) are more complex. There are two options in determining how to deal with these provisions. The first is to permit the buyer to have a part order available on the website until they decide, at some future date, to complete the order. By offering this option, the service provider must ensure that the yet to be completed order is linked at all times to the terms and conditions of sale that are current at the time the buyer finally decides to finish their purchase and enter the contract. The second option is not to offer this facility at all.

Regulation 9(3) also provides that where terms and conditions apply to the contract, 'the service provider shall make them available to him in a way that allows him to store and reproduce them.' This will apply to providers of individual identity certificates. All providers of such certificates will have a set of terms by which the contract will be governed. In the case of Chamber SimplySign, for instance, they are set out in a Subscriber Agreement, version 1.01 dated 20 February 2004.[2] However, this is not the only document that governs the contract. Clause 1 makes it clear that the Certificate Policy governs the contract as well.

The importance of complying with the requirements of the Electronic Commerce (EC Directive) Regulations lies in the remedies a consumer may exercise. The service provider's liability is set out in regulation 13. In the case of regulations 6 and 9(1), the service provider is liable for damages for breach of statutory duty. Where the service provider fails to allow a consumer to identify and correct errors before entering the contract, regulation 15 permits the consumer to rescind the contract, unless a court orders otherwise on the application of the service provider. Finally, regulation 14 gives the person entering a contract the right to seek an order to require the service provider to comply with the requirement set out in regulation 9(3).

It is not difficult to provide the information required by both Directives. Certificate authorities are advised to ensure the information is freely available and obvious. In the case of a website, there are two mechanisms that can be used to bring this information to the attention of the viewer. It can be displayed as a reference statement without a hyperlink, perhaps on the front page, although the sheer volume of information that must be provided may not make this an attractive option. A second option is to provide the information on a dedicated page, with a standard hyperlink. The crucial point about using a hyperlink is to ensure the link is readily available at all times, and is, perhaps more importantly, brought to the attention of the potential customer at or before the point of sale. Bearing in mind people viewing websites do not necessarily go into a website through the front page, it is important to ensure the hyperlink, if used, is easy to notice.

1   Regulations 9(1)(a)-(d), 9(2) and 9(3).
2   See www.simplysign.co.uk/terms.html.

Terms and representations

12.41 Representations made before the contract is created can be incorporated into the agreement. Such representations are often made orally before the contract is formed, although an exchange of emails or the content of a web page are all open to being construed as statements that are capable of being incorporated into the contract. Such statements may be interpreted as being express terms of the contract, even though they do not form part of the documentation that applies specifically to a particular product or service. If the buyer is influenced to purchase a key pair because of statements made on a website or in any other material that is, objectively, untrue, it is possible for the certification authority to face an action under the provisions of the Misrepresentation Act 1967. This is particularly important, given the range of documents that some certification authorities maintain on their websites.

Exemption clauses

12.42 Standard form terms and conditions of trade are used widely, and many contracts are governed by such trading terms imposed by one party on the other. The primary object of a set of trading terms is to allocate the risks between the parties. For the seller, the aim is to minimise their obligations and liabilities. The purpose is to anticipate what difficulties, if any, that might arise when the contract is performed and to set out the consequences when there is a failure of performance. This may mean the seller will seek to limit or avoid liability, or both limit and avoid liability where they are in breach of the contract, and to limit or avoid liability for the consequences of any act of negligence. However, it is often the case that such terms are not negotiable as between parties of unequal strength, and the terms that govern the contract tend to be imposed by the economically dominant seller. As a result, the law steps in to mitigate the worst excesses of such terms.

There are various approaches that can be used to exclude or modify liability. Service providers selling key pairs invariably incorporate a combination of these approaches in the terms that accompany the various commercial products and services they offer. Broadly, the types of exemption clauses that are used can be categorised as follows:

(a) Clauses that limit or reduce a liability, such as drafting negative terms to exclude or modify liability by excluding duties that would normally arise, or by excluding the circumstances that would otherwise allow a term to be implied, such as making the buyer rely on their skill and judgement in deciding to buy.

(b) Clauses that exclude or restrict liability, such as restricting a liability in damages or drafting terms that remove the right of a party to rescind the contract.

(c) Clauses that seek to exclude or restrict the party in default to compensate the other party fully. This can be achieved by limiting the amount of damages that can be claimed or by providing procedural restrictions, such as requiring a claim to be made in a particular way (such as in writing, or directed to a particular person); imposing a time limit on initiating proceedings (this might be enforceable if it can be proved that such a clause was necessary and the period stipulated is not unreasonable) or the imposition of arbitration proceedings before taking legal action, although these clauses are subject to statutory regulations when dealing with consumers.

Judicial control

12.43 Two forms of control exist, the common law and the provision of legislation. Statutory controls supplement, but do not replace the common law. Even where terms are controlled by statute, they are subject to control by the judges, because judges decide what is fair and reasonable. Both these terms, 'fair and reasonable,' are used in the Unfair Contract Terms Act 1977 and the Unfair Terms in Consumer Contracts Regulations 1999[1]. Where contracts have been negotiated between parties or by trade organisations, the judges will rarely have any objections to contract terms. This is mainly because such contracts might well have been negotiated between parties of equal or near equal strength, and do not involve consumers. Different criteria apply for standard contract terms. In general terms, judges seek to identify the intention of the parties as expressed in the contract. To help achieve this, judges will consider all the words used in the contract, taking into account the circumstances in which the contract was concluded.

1   SI 1999/2083; at the time of writing, a new Bill, the Unfair Contract terms Bill, was being considered by the legislature; Unfair Terms in Contracts Report on a reference under section 3(1)(e) of the Law Commissions Act 1965 (The Law Commission and the Scottish Law Commission, February 2005) (LAW COM No 292) (SCOT LAW COM No 199).

RULES OF CONSTRUCTION

12.44 As judges have been required to make decisions between disputing parties, so they have developed rules of construction. The provisions of the Unfair Contract Terms Act 1977 and Unfair Terms in Consumer Contracts Regulations 1999 will apply to the types of clause discussed below. Of particular importance, is the ability of the Director General of Fair Trading to require clauses that appear to the Director to be unfair, to be re-drafted. Attention should be given to the Bulletin produced by the Director General when such clauses are drafted. The Bulletin has been published since May 1996, and now includes a considerable body of examples where terms were considered unfair and how they were rewritten. Of particular relevance is the Unfair Contract Terms Guidance issued by the Office of Fair Trading. This comprises a number of guides to what the Office of Fair Trading believes to be fair and unfair terms in consumer contracts. The most important rules are discussed below, and examples of such clauses are taken from the terms and conditions for a BT ID Certificate.[1]

1   www.trustwise.com/repository/CPS/cps.htm.

Exemption clauses

12.45   To be effective, an exemption clause must be expressed in clear language that is free from ambiguity. The purpose of the clause must be clear. In the case of clauses 5.7 and 5.8 of the terms and conditions for a BT ID Certificate, BT make it clear to a subscribing party that BT prevents anybody other than the subscriber from using the certificate. The purpose is not made clear, but can be inferred from the nature of the contract:

'5.7   Your Certificate is provided solely for your own use and must not be passed on to anyone else to access the Scheme.

5.8   You are solely responsible for any transactions of any kind entered into between you and the Scheme, or any third party accessing or acting in reliance on the Service. BT will not be a party to or in anyway responsible for any transaction between you, the Scheme or any third party.'

Precise provision for loss

12.46   The actual words used in the clause must be clearly directed to the precise occurrence or loss that has taken place for the party relying on the clause to take advantage of the term. Clauses 5.2 and 5.3 of the terms and conditions for the BT ID Certificate, demonstrate the precise loss and what action BT will take to remedy the problem if it occurs.

'5.2   You are responsible for the security and proper use of all PINs, Private Keys and passwords used in connection with your Certificate, and for protecting them from Compromise.

If you:

(a)   attempt to modify a PIN, a Private Key or a Public Key; or
(b)   forget or lose your PIN or password, and also your Private Key;

BT will be unable to repair or replace your Certificate. In these circumstances, you must contact the Helpdesk to revoke your Certificate after which this Contract will terminate. Before BT will revoke your Certificate, you must satisfy such security checks as BT may operate.'

Widely drafted terms

12.47   Clauses must come within the meaning and scope of the purpose of the contract. Terms that are so widely drafted that by imposing them would defeat the purpose of the contract cannot be effective. The terms imposed upon verifying parties by certification authorities are exposed to challenge under this head, as discussed above.

Doubtful meaning

12.48 Where there is a doubt in the meaning of a clause, the meaning of the clause will be construed in the interests of the party against whom the term is being enforced and contrary to the interests of the party who drafted it. Whichever party relies on the terms of such a clause has the burden of demonstrating that the terms of the clause apply in the circumstances of the particular case.[1]

1   The 'contra proferentem' rule.

Liability for negligence

12.49 Liability for negligence can only be excluded where the words that are used specifically point towards the intention of the parties that negligence would be excluded in the context of the contract. In the case of the terms and conditions for the BT ID Certificate, the following clauses are in place between BT and the subscribing party:

'9   LIMITATION OF LIABILITY

9.1   BT accepts unlimited liability for death or personal injury resulting from its negligence and paragraphs 9.2 and 9.3 do not apply to such liability.

9.2   BT is not liable to you, either in contract, tort (including negligence) or otherwise for direct or indirect loss of profits, business or anticipated savings, nor for any indirect or consequential loss or damage or for any destruction of data.

9.3   BT's liability to you either in contract, tort (including negligence) or otherwise in relation to this Contract is limited to 125% of the value of the amounts paid by you to BT in relation to your Certificate, for any single incident or series of related incidents, during this Contract.

9.4   The liability limits set out in paragraph 10.3 govern all of your uses of the Service, including without limitation your reliance on Certificates issued to third parties.'

Indemnity clauses

12.50 Indemnity clauses are clauses in which one party requires the other to indemnify them against their liability in negligence to third parties. The

BT Trust Services Certification Practice Statement includes the following indemnity clauses that apply to the subscriber, who will have entered a contract with BT, but also to a verifying party, that may not have a contract with BT.

'2.3.1   Indemnification by End Users and Relying Parties

2.3.1.1   Indemnification by End Users

To the extent permitted by applicable law, BT's Contracts require, and other Contracts shall require, End Users to indemnify BT and any non-BT CAs or RAs for:

- Falsehood or misrepresentation of fact by the End User on the End User's Certificate Application,
- Failure by the End User to disclose a material fact on the Certificate Application, if the misrepresentation or omission was made negligently or with intent to deceive any party,
- The End User's failure to protect the End User's private key, to use a Trustworthy System, or to otherwise take the precautions necessary to prevent the compromise, loss, disclosure, modification, or unauthorised use of the End User's private key, or
- The End User's use of a name (including without limitation within a common name, domain name, or e-mail address) that infringes upon the Intellectual Property Rights of a third party.

2.3.1.2   Indemnification by Relying Parties

To the extent permitted by applicable law, BT's Contracts and Relying Third Party Charters require, and other Contracts shall require, Relying Parties to indemnify BT and any non-BT CAs or RAs for:

- The Relying Party's failure to perform the obligations of a Relying Party,
- The Relying Party's reliance on a Certificate that is not reasonable under the circumstances, or
- The Relying Party's failure to check the status of such Certificate to determine if the Certificate is expired or revoked.'

It is to be wondered how these events give rise to a loss or liability suffered or incurred by the indemnified parties.

Such terms will be subject to the test of reasonableness under section 4(1) of the Unfair Contract Terms Act 1977, which provides:

'(1)   A person dealing as a consumer cannot by reference to any contract term be made to indemnify another person (whether a party to the contract or not) in respect of liability that may be incurred by the other for negligence or breach of contract, except in so far as the contract term satisfies the requirements of reasonableness.

(2)   This section applies whether the liability in question:
    (a)   is directly that of the person to be indemnified or is incurred by him vicariously;
    (b)   is to the person dealing as consumer to someone else.'

Apparently there has yet to be a case on the reasonableness of indemnity clauses in consumer contracts.[1] Some of the provisions of the indemnity terms produced by BT above may appear reasonable as against the subscribing party. However, it is open to debate whether all of the sub-clauses that refer to the subscribing party and any of the clauses that apply to the verifying party can be considered reasonable, taking into account the inherent complexity of the infrastructure that accompanies the use of digital signatures, especially when BT recognises the dangers, by warning recipients that a subscribing party may lose control of their private keys without realising it:

'Customers of BT Trust Services are obliged to inform BT if their Private Keys are compromised, and on receipt of such a notice BT will revoke the compromised Certificate and post notice of the revocation in the Certificate Status List. However, you acknowledge the possibility of theft or other form of compromise of a Private Key corresponding to a Public Key contained in a Certificate which may not be detected, and of the possibility of use of a stolen or compromised key to forge a digital signature to a document.'[2]

1   Richard Lawson, *Exclusion Clauses and Unfair Contract Terms* (Sweet & Maxwell, 8th edn, 2005), 9.09.
2   BT Trust Services Relying Third Party Charter Issue 4 (July 2004) available online at www.trustwise.com/repository/rpa/.

Control by statute

12.51   Two of the most important statutes that affect the reliance that can be placed on exclusion and limitation of liability clauses are the Unfair Contract Terms Act 1977 and the Unfair Terms in Consumer Contract Regulations 1999.[1] The Regulations supplement the 1977 Act and impose a general test of fairness to any standard term in a contract between a supplier of goods and service and a consumer.

The Unfair Contract Terms Act 1977 applies to all contracts between businesses and consumers. It also applies to contracts between businesses where one of the parties enters the contract on the standard terms of the other party. However, it does not apply to contracts of insurance, contracts relating to land, intellectual property or the formation and dissolution of companies.[2] The Act also does not apply to contracts for the supply of goods where:
(a)   the goods in question are, at the time of the conclusion of the contract, in the course of carriage, or will be carried, from the territory of one State to the territory of another; or

(b) the acts constituting the offer and acceptance have been done in the territories of different States; or

(c) the contract provides for the goods to be delivered to the territory of a State other than within whose territory those acts were done.[3]

This clause may become of some significance in the case of key pairs, especially when a service provider is situated in a jurisdiction other than within the United Kingdom. It is debatable whether an agreement for the provision of a key pair or a certificate comes within the definition of goods, unless a private key is supplied that is stored on a carrier. Bearing in mind judges have used the guidelines set out in Schedule 2 of the Act to cover terms selling goods and services, the interpretation of this particular provision may have far-reaching consequences if digital signatures are subject to litigation. If interpreted literally, the provision is clearly restricted to goods and not services.

The Act is concerned with terms that exclude or limit business liability for losses caused by negligence or breach of duty of care,[4] for breach of the implied terms relating to the goods in contracts for the sale or supply of goods[5] or for other statutory breaches.[6] Those contracts that are affected by the Act are where one party deals with the other as a consumer, or where one party deals on the other's written standards terms of business.[7]

1   SI 1999/2083.
2   Schedule 1, s 1.
3   Section 26(4).
4   Sections 1(3)(a) and 2(1).
5   Sections 6 and 7.
6   Section 6.
7   Section 3(1).

TEST OF REASONABLENESS

12.52 If exclusion clauses or indemnity clauses[1] are drafted into a set of trading terms, to be effective they must satisfy the test of reasonableness. The test is set out in s 11(1). The requirement of reasonableness is '… that the term shall have been a fair and reasonable one to be included having regard to the circumstances which were, or ought reasonably to have been, known to or in the contemplation of the parties when the contract was made.' Whether a clause is reasonable, therefore, depends on the circumstances known and foreseeable at the time the contract was made. The burden of proof is upon the person that relies on the clause to show it is reasonable.[2] Furthermore, where the service provider seeks to limit liability to a set amount of money, the judges are to determine the reasonableness of the limitation by having regard to the resources available to provide for the liability and how far it was possible to obtain insurance cover for the risk.[3]

Schedule 2 contains a number of guidelines for the application of the reasonableness test.[4] These guidelines are not exhaustive, but they are used by judges for assessing the fairness or otherwise of contract terms:

(a)   the strength of the bargaining positions of the parties relative to each other, taking into account (among other things) alternative means by which the customer's requirements could have been met;

(b)   whether the customer received an inducement to agree to the term, or in accepting it had an opportunity of entering into a similar contract with other persons, but without having to accept a similar term;

(c)   whether the customer knew or ought to reasonably to have known of the existence and extent of the term (having regard, among other things, to any custom of the trade and any previous course of dealing between the parties);

(d)   where the term excludes or restricts any relevant liability if some condition is not complied with, whether it was reasonable at the time of the contract to expect that compliance with that condition would be practicable;

(e)   whether the goods were manufactured, processed or adapted to the special order of the customer.

1   Section 4.
2   Sections 11(5) and 24(4).
3   Section 11(4).
4   These guidelines expressly apply to contracts for the sale or goods and hire-purchase (s 6) and other contracts for the supply of goods (s 7). However, judges have held that they can be applied in most instances.

Control by regulation

12.53   The Unfair Terms in Consumer Contracts Regulations 1994 (SI 1994/3159) implemented the Council Directive on unfair terms in consumer contracts.[1] They, in turn, were revoked and replaced by the Unfair Terms in Consumer Contracts Regulations 1999 (SI 1999/2083),[2] which more closely followed the provisions of the Directive. The scope of the Regulations creates a separate regime from that of the Unfair Contract Terms Act 1977, although in the event a clause is disputed, its validity will be considered against both the Regulations and the Act.

1   Council Directive 93/13/EEC of 5 April 1993 on unfair terms in consumer contracts OJ L 95, 21.04.1993 p. 29.
2   In force from 1 October 1999.

SCOPE OF THE REGULATIONS

12.54   The Regulations apply to any unfair term in a contract that has not been individually negotiated, and has been concluded between a seller or supplier and a consumer.[1] Contractual terms that reflect mandatory or statutory provisions are, however, excluded from the provisions of the Regulations.[2] If a term is unfair, it is not binding on the consumer.[3] As with the 1977 Act, the Regulations cannot be evaded by making the contract subject to the law of a state other than a constituent part of the United Kingdom.[4]

1   Regulations 5(1) and 4(1).
2   Regulation 4(2).
3   Regulation 8(1).
4   Regulation 9.

THE MAIN PROVISIONS

12.55   There are two requirements imposed by the Regulations.

Written contracts

12.56   The seller or supplier are required to express written terms in 'plain, intelligible language'.[1] Where there is doubt about the meaning of a written term, the interpretation that favours the consumer will apply, with the exception of proceedings brought under Regulation 12.[2]

1   Regulation 7(1).
2   Regulation 7(2).

Fairness

12.57   All terms, whether written or oral, require to be fair when they have not been individually negotiated.[1] A contract term that has not been individually negotiated is considered to be unfair if the effect of the term causes a significant imbalance in the rights and obligations arising between the parties under the contract, to the detriment of the consumer.[2] If a term has been individually negotiated, the seller or supplier has the burden of proving it was negotiated. Schedule 2 to the Regulations provides an indicative and non-exhaustive list of the types of terms that may be considered unfair.

An unfair term will be assessed in accordance with the provisions of regulation 6(1):

'... taking into account the nature of the goods or services for which the contract was concluded and by referring, at the time of conclusion of the contract, to all the circumstances attending the conclusion of the contact and to all the other terms of the contract or of another contract on which it is dependent.'

The assessment of fairness will not relate to the definition of the main subject matter of the contract or to the adequacy of the price providing they are written in plain language.[3] There is a difficulty with this provision when considering the explanation of the main subject matter prepared by certification authorities. For instance, the BT Certification Practice Statement provides a warranty to the verifying party at paragraph 2.2.1.1, but it may not be entirely clear precisely what the promise is. A verifying party merely wants to rely on the digital certificate that accompanies a subscribing party's public key when the key is used to verify a signature on a message or document. The Director General of Fair Trading made the following observation in relation to this point:

'In our view, it would be difficult to claim that any term was a core term unless it was central to how consumers perceived the bargain. A supplier would surely find it hard to sustain the argument that a contract's main subject matter was defined by a term which a consumer has been given no real chance to see and read before signing – in other words if that term has not been properly drawn to the consumer's attention. We regularly see terms which are claimed to be 'core terms' but which are given no prominence and are indeed rather coyly tucked away in the small print.'[4]

In the narrow survey of those certification authorities mentioned in this text, it is not always easy to determine precisely what the definition of the main subject matter of the contract is – especially for the verifying party. To consider the example of VeriSign, there is a reference to the promise made to a verifying party, but first the verifying party has to find the VeriSign Relying Party Agreement,[5] then the document must be carefully scanned to find the relevant promise, located in clause 9:

'9. VeriSign Warranties. VeriSign warrants to Relying Parties who reasonably rely on a Certificate (i) that all information in or incorporated by reference in the Certificate, except for Nonverified Subscriber Information, is accurate; (ii) that Certificates appearing in the Repository have been issued to the individual or organization named in the Certificate as the Subscriber, and the Subscriber has accepted the Certificate by downloading it from a website or via an email message sent to the Subscriber containing the Certificate; and (iii) the entities that approved the Certificate Application and issued the Certificate have substantially complied with the VeriSign CPS when issuing the Certificate.'

Where a term is not written in plain language and there is doubt about the meaning of a written term, the term will be construed in the meaning most favourable to the consumer.[6]

---

1   Regulation 5(1).
2   Regulation 5.
3   Regulation 6(2).
4   Office of Fair Trading *Unfair Contract Terms Bulletin* Issue No 2 September 1996 page 13.
5   VeriSign Relying Party Agreement available online at www.verisign.com/repository/rpa. html; this agreement differs from another VeriSign Public Certification Services, Relying Party Agreement available online at www.digitalid.verisign.com/services/client/help/rely-ing_party.htm.
6   Regulation 7(2).

COMPLAINTS RELATING TO UNFAIR TERMS

Director General of Fair Trading

12.58 The Director General of Fair Trading has a duty to consider any complaint that any contract terms drawn up for general use is unfair, except where the complaint appears to the Director to be frivolous or vexatious.[1] The Director may apply for an injunction against any person that appears to the Director to be using an unfair term for general use in contracts concluded with consumers, and has the power to obtain documents and information from any person to help with the consideration of a complaint.[2] The Director is also required to publish decisions relating to unfair terms, including court judgments, injunctions, undertakings, voluntary withdrawals and amendments of any terms.[3]

1 Regulation 10(1).
2 Regulations 12(1) and 13(3).
3 Regulation 15.

Qualifying bodies

12.59 The Regulations provide for a number qualifying bodies to consider a complaint that a contract term is unfair. The list of qualifying bodies is set out Schedule 1, and when a qualifying body informs the Director General of Fair Trading that they have agreed to consider a complaint, they are then under a duty so to do.[1] Qualifying bodies have similar powers to that of the Director, such as obtaining information and applying for injunctions.[2]

1 Regulation 11(1).
2 Regulations 13(5) and 12(3).

Chapter 13

Non-contractual disclaimers and negligence

13.1 The effectiveness of a digital signature issued within a public key infrastructure lends itself to challenge because of the number of links in the infrastructure. The range of possibilities in which liability may occur is discussed more fully in relation to contractual liability. However, where no contract exists, the party at most risk is a relying party, where a certification authority has not verified the information contained in a certificate properly, or where a certificate has been revoked for some reason, but the certification authority has not advertised the revocation.

A subscribing party will also be at risk where they inform the certification authority that their private key, for example, has been compromised, and the certification authority fails to post the revocation on the certificate revocation list in a timely manner. In such a circumstance, the subscribing party will probably have a contractual relationship with the certification authority that will govern the relationship, but in the event such an incident occurs, the standard of care expected of the certification authority will be considered.

If a recipient makes a claim against the certification authority because the purported signer denies they are liable, the requirements of the tort of negligence must be addressed in determining whether a certification authority will be liable to a recipient in the absence of a contractual relationship:

(a) The existence in law of a duty of care owed by the certification authority. This calls into question the degree of reasonable conduct that a certification authority must adhere to, regardless of any other cause of harm that may occur.

(b) Whether the duty of care was breached. In this instance, it is a question of whether the certification authority failed to conduct itself to the standard set by the law.

(c) To what extent the certification authority will be held liable for the harm caused, taking into account other causes of the harm suffered. This relates to the legal causation, or degree of remoteness.

(d) The particular type of damage to the particular claimant was foreseeable and not too remote.

The question in any claim of negligence is whether the defending party owed a duty of care to the claimant. A certification authority provides a mixture of services and information. An example of a service would be the generation of a key pair, although it is possible for a certification authority or a trusted key generation agency to perform this service. The certification authority will be responsible for providing information, including the identification of a person named in an individual identity certificate, and the information contained in the certificate repository and the certification revocation list. Where a certification authority is negligent in generating a key pair for instance, a claim in contract may well be more appropriate than a claim in negligence, although the pleadings may well include a claim in negligence in the alternative. If a certification authority generates the key pair, the opportunities for negligence include keeping a copy of the private key and releasing it without authority, generating a non-functioning pair, or generating a cryptographically weak pair, so that the private key is deducible from the public key with less computational effort than ought to be the case for the length of the keys. The risks to recipients will not always be the same as they are to subscribing parties.

Statutory liability

EU Directive on electronic signatures[1]

13.2 The European Union have provided for a statutory liability in accordance with the provisions of article 6, by which certification-service-providers can be found negligent for the information contained in a certificate issued as a qualified certificate. The definition of a certification-service-provider covers 'an entity or a legal or natural person who issues certificates or provides other services related to electronic signatures;'[2] and therefore appears to include registration authorities as well as certification authorities. The liability is restricted to qualified certificates, and article 6(1)(a) refers to the accuracy of the information, as set out below:

'Article 6   Liability

1.   As a minimum, Member States shall ensure that by issuing a certificate as a qualified certificate to the public or by guaranteeing such a certificate to the public a certification-service-provider is liable for damage caused to any entity or legal or natural person who reasonably relies on that certificate:

(a)   as regards the accuracy at the time of issuance of all information contained in the qualified certificate and as regards the fact that the certificate contains all the details prescribed for a qualified certificate;

(b)   for assurance that at the time of the issuance of the certificate, the signatory identified in the qualified certificate held the signature-creation data corresponding to the signature verification data given or identified in the certificate;

(c)   for assurance that the signature-creation data and the signature-verification data can be used in a complementary manner in cases where the certification-service-provider generates them both;

unless the certification-service-provider proves that he has not acted negligently.'

The liability is imposed for the accuracy and quantity of the information contained in the certificate where a recipient reasonably relies on the certificate. What is meant by reasonable reliance is discussed below, and will include the information made available to the recipient as well as any investigation into the ability of a recipient to find relevant information that may cause them to become a verifying party. Where a claim for negligence is made, the certification-service-provider is required to prove that it has not acted negligently. The directive also permits certification-service-providers to set financial limits on the use of qualified certificates:

'3.   Member States shall ensure that a certification-service-provider may indicate in a qualified certificate limitations on the use of that certificate provided that the limitations are recognisable to third parties. The certification-service-provider shall not be liable for damage arising from use of a qualified certificate which exceeds the limitations placed on it.

4.   Member States shall ensure that a certification-service-provider may indicate in the qualified certificate a limit on the value of transactions for which the certificate can be used, provided that the limit is recognisable to third parties. The certification-service-provider shall not be liable for damage resulting from this maximum limit being exceeded.'[3]

The limit that a certification-service-provider may impose on the use of qualified certificates is subject to being 'recognisable to third parties,' although article 6(5) provides that these provisions are without prejudice to the Directive on unfair terms in consumer contracts.[4] The phrase 'recognisable to third parties' introduces a subjective element to the level of the limitation imposed by a certification-service-provider, although this requirement may be satisfied if the certificate includes the limit of liability accepted for any given certificate. Defining what is an acceptable limit will depend on a variety of factors, including the use to which such a qualified certificate is expected to be put, whether the limit was realistic and if the certification-service-provider set the limit in the light of dealing with the risk on terms that are commercially viable. The liability in negligence under the directive only extends to qualified certificates. There is no statutory liability for certificates for electronic signatures in other formats. This means it remains questionable whether a notional duty can be applied to certification authorities for other types of electronic signature.

1   Directive 1999/93/EC of the European Parliament and of the Council of 13 December 1999 on a Community framework for electronic signatures, OJ L 13, 19.01.2000, p. 12.
2   Article 2(1)(11).
3   Article 6(3) and 6(4).
4   Council Directive 93/13/EEC of 5 April 1993 on unfair terms in consumer contracts OJ L 95, 21.4.1993, pp. 29–34.

United Kingdom

13.3   Article 6 of the Directive concerning the liability of certification-service-providers is implemented by regulation 4 of the Electronic Signatures Regulations 2002.[1] The text of article 6 has been retained almost without change in the Regulations.

1   SI 2002/318.

RELIANCE ON A QUALIFIED CERTIFICATE

13.4   Regulation 4(1) applies where a certification-service-provider issues a certificate as a qualified certificate[1] or provides a guarantee, as follows:

'(1)   Where:

(a)   a certification-service-provider either:
    (i)   issues a certificate as a qualified certificate to the public, or
    (ii)   guarantees a qualified certificate to the public.'

The first point to note is the reference to 'the public.' This term may have been deliberately used in article 6 of the Directive to incorporate as wide an audience as possible. If judges construe this term widely, the effect will be that any person or legal entity taking advantage of a qualified certificate will benefit under the terms of these Regulations. Whilst it may be obvious that the subscribing party will benefit under regulation 4(1)(a)(i), it is not clear who will benefit in relation to a guarantee, unless a guarantee is construed as a warranty contained in the relevant terms or certification practice statement. If the meaning of 'guarantee' does cover such warranties, then it is possible that a receiving party may also benefit from the provisions of these Regulations.

Subsection (1)(b) sets out the matters upon which the member of the public can rely:

'(b) a person reasonably relies on that certificate for any of the following matters:

(i) the accuracy of any of the information contained in the qualified certificate at the time of issue,

(ii) the inclusion in the qualified certificate of all the details referred to in Schedule 1,

(iii) the holding by the signatory identified in the qualified certificate at the time of its issue of the signature-creation data[2] corresponding to the signature-verification data[3] given or identified in the certificate, or

(iv) the ability of the signature-creation data and the signature-verification data to be used in a complementary manner in cases where the certification-service-provider generates them both.'

First, the person must reasonably rely on the certificate or any of the matters set out in subsections (i) to (iv). The test of reasonableness is discussed below, and those parties that will come within the scope of the protection afforded by regulation 4 will be the signing party, and possibly the receiving party. It will be for a court to decide whether a receiving party, to take advantage of the protection, must undertake reasonable due diligence in relation to a qualified certificate. Bearing in mind the degree of reliability that such a certificate is required to have under the terms of the Directive, this is a debatable point.

Consider the matters in more detail:

(a) The accuracy of the information contained in the qualified certificate at the time of issue. This is a very narrow requirement that focuses on a particular time in space. This requirement, and the protection it affords, can only apply to a subscribing party if the term of this subsection is construed strictly. It will be for the certification-service-provider to ensure the information included in the qualified certificate is verified to a high standard, although the liability is restricted to the time of issue, which means if the information alters after the qualified certificate has been issued and during the lifetime of the certificate, it will be for the subscribing party to inform the certification-service-provider of the change in circumstances. This matter is dealt with in the contract between the parties in any event.

(b) The inclusion in the qualified certificate of all the details referred to in Schedule 1.[4] The list set out in the schedule can be described as that which is required of an X.509 certificate in any event, and it is the recipient that will probably be the principle beneficiary of the duty under this subsection.

(c) The third matter refers to the link between the subscribing party and the public and private keys that are identified in the qualified certificate at the time of its issue. Both the subscribing party and the recipient may benefit from the protection of this subsection, but this obligation is also limited in time and space to the time of issue. Thus whilst the certification authority is required to certify that the subscriber has the private key, it is not required to certify that the subscriber is the only party who has access to it – indeed, nor would the certification authority be in a position to know this, even at the time the certificate is given, and certainly not at a later time. Where it is impossible to give such an assurance, the recipient has very little useful assurance that a verified signature is that of the person named in the certificate. In which case, it is to be wondered what the point of the qualified certificate actually is.

(d)   The fourth requirement is for the certification-service-provider to ensure that where it generates the public and private keys for the subscribing party, it does so in a way that enables the data to be used appropriately. This duty will certainly be of benefit to the subscribing party, who will also be subject to any contractual provisions imposed by the certification-service-provider.

1   Regulation 2 provides that a qualified certificate is a certificate that (a) meets the requirements in Schedule 1 to the Regulations, which is taken from Annex I of the Directive, and (b) is provided by a certification-service-provider who fulfils the requirements set out in Schedule 2, which is taken from Annex II of the Directive.

2   Regulation 2 defines 'signature-creation data' as 'unique data (including, but not limited to, codes or private cryptographic keys) which are used by the signatory to create an electronic signature.'

3   Regulation 2 defines 'signature-verification data' as 'data (including, but not limited to, codes or public cryptographic keys) which are used for the purpose of verifying an electronic signature.'

4   The list of requirements set out in Schedule 1 are set out in Chapter 4, and are not replicated here.

BURDEN OF PROOF

13.5   For a person to have grounds for a claim, the certification-service-provider must owe them a duty and they will have to suffer a loss as a result of such reliance.[1] A certification-service-provider will be liable in damages in respect of any extent of the loss where they:

'(i)   had a duty of care existed between him and the person referred to in sub-paragraph (b) above, and

(ii)   had the certification-service-provider been negligent,

then that certification-service-provider shall be so liable to the same extent notwithstanding that there is no proof that the certification-service-provider was negligent unless the certification-service-provider proves that he was not negligent.'[2]

It is of interest to note that the extent of the loss by a claimant seems to be 'any extent,' which suggests that the claim is for all losses that flow from the failure of the certification-service-provider to undertake its duties with due care – unless the limit imposed on the qualified certificate by the certification-service-provider acts as a limiting factor to any claim. The certification-service-provider is subject to proving they were not negligent if a claim is made under the terms of this duty. One question that will exercise a court in determining whether the certification-service-provider is not negligent, is the standard of care that should apply to the certification-service-provider. The certification-service-provider will seek to adduce a range of evidence to discharge the burden, but there are a number of helpful documents that will act to steer the court towards the standards laid down by the industry. VeriSign Inc., have issued a 'VeriSign Trust Network European Directive Supplemental Policies' document, and version 1.1 became effective on 30 September 2005.[3] This document sets out the usual duties and obligations to be found in a certificate practice statement, and also sets out the various issues that should be addressed when issuing a qualified certificate, including identification and authentication; operational requirements; physical, procedural and personnel security controls; technical security controls; certificate and certificate revocation list profile and other matters relating to administration. This document makes reference to a technical specification issued by the European Telecommunications Standards Institute (ETSI), 'Qualified Certificate Profile.'[4] Interestingly, this later version of the document omits reference to another ETSI document, 'Policy Requirements for certification authorities issuing qualified certificates,'[5] which was mentioned in the earlier version. If a certification-service-provider follows the standards set out by the Institute, it is probable a court will consider the standard as a guide in the process of the certification-service-provider discharging their burden. Of interest are the comments in Annex A to 'Policy Requirements for certification authorities issuing qualified certificates,' in relation to the liability of a certification-service-provider. First, in respect to the potential liability faced by a certification-service-provider, the observation is made respecting the extent of the possible liability, which may be wide:

> '... liability limits is on a transaction basis, and the CA may not be able to control the number of transactions for which it becomes liable, the CA may not have control over its overall liability.'[6]

Second, an assumption has been made by those drafting this document: that is, a recipient of a qualified certificate is assumed to have the duty to undertake reasonable care to carry out the checks required by a certification-service-provider:

> '...where a CA negligently fails to issue a timely revocation list, but the relying party fails to check whether the revocation list exists, the legal cause of any loss suffered by the relying party probably is not the CA's negligence, but the relying party's failure to check. Had the relying party checked, it would have noticed that the revocation list was out of date and acted accordingly'[7]

Whilst this commentary is carefully worded to refer to the probability that a failure by a recipient to check a certificate revocation list may not be the fault of a certification-service-provider, nevertheless is makes an assumption that there is a duty upon the recipient so to do. Regulations 4(3) and (4) provide for an identical duty of care and burden of proof as regulations 4(1) and (2) in relation to a person that relies on a qualified certificate, namely the recipient. Although regulation 4(3)(b) refers to a person reasonably relying on a qualified certificate, there is no suggestion that the recipient is required to undertake due diligence and become a verifying party. There is, at present, no legal rule that a relying party must authenticate the signature of a sending party, with the exception of the presumptions that have been imposed by various statutory instruments.

1   Regulation 4(1)(c).
2   Regulation 4(1)(d).
3   Available online at www.verisign.com/repository/edsp/index.html.
4   ETSI TS 101 862 v1.3.1 (2004–03).
5   ETSI TS 101 456 v1.2.2 (2002–04).
6   Policy requirements for certification authorities issuing qualified certificates ETSI TS 101 456 v1.2.2 (2002–04) Annex A 'Potential liability in the use of electronic signatures' (I)(A).
7   Policy requirements for certification authorities issuing qualified certificates ETSI TS 101 456 v1.2.2 (2002–04) Annex A 'Potential liability in the use of electronic signatures' (I)(A).

Negligent statement

13.6   The tort of negligence occurs once damage has occurred, which leads to the conclusion that the duty is not to cause damage carelessly. However, where a loss stems from the information contained with an individual identity certificate, or a failure to notify the revocation of a certificate, the claim will be economic in nature, rather than a physical loss or damage to person or property. As a result, a more restrictive approach is taken to negligent statements. The principles have been established by a range of cases deriving from *Hedley Byrne & Co Ltd v Heller & Partners Ltd*,[1] the latest of which, *Caparo Industries plc v Dickman*,[2] set out the approaches to be taken into account in determining whether a notional duty of care is to be imposed, bearing in mind the European Union has only provided for a limited statutory duty of negligence in relation to information contained in a qualified certificate.

1   [1964] AC 465; [1963] 3 WLR 101; [1963] 2 All ER 575; [1963] 1 Lloyd's Rep 485; 107 Sol Jo 454, HL.
2   [1990] 2 AC 605; [1990] 1 All ER 568; [1990] 2 WLR 358; [1990] BCLC 273; [1990] BCC 164; 134 Sol J 494; [1990] 12 LS Gaz R 42; [1990] NLJR 248, HL.

The threefold test

13.7 The two issues of proximity and fairness are the significant considerations relating to this test. The courts will consider the proximity between the parties, which is created as a result of the relationship; the causal proximity fashioned by the link between the conduct and any injury and the nature of any responsibility the defendant undertook towards the claimant. In reaching a decision, the judges will be influenced by consideration of policy in balancing the private interests of the parties against the interests of the legal system. In this respect, the courts will also consider what is fair and reasonable, and whether it is in the interests of justice to impose a notional duty on the defendant. This balancing act requires the judges to consider whether the interests of the claimant can be satisfactorily protected if no duty were to be imposed.

Assumption of responsibility

13.8 Whether the defendant is responsible to the claimant depends on an objective test, as stated by Lord Goff[1] and augmented by Lord Steyn:

> 'The touchstone of liability is not the state of mind of the defendant. An objective test means that the primary focus must be on things said or done by the defendant or on his behalf in his dealings with the plaintiff. Obviously, the impact of what the defendant says or does must be judged in the light of the relevant contextual scene. Subject to this qualification, the primary focus must be on exchanges ... which cross the line between the defendant and the plaintiff.'[2]

The requirement is for the defendant to take responsibility for performing the task, but not for legal liability towards the claimant. By taking responsibility for the task, the defendant creates the special relationship between the parties. There is also the question of whether a claimant can be said to rely on a statement. First, it must be established that the claimant relied on the statement to establish the cause of the negligent act. Second, the claimant must be shown to have reasonably relied on the statement made by the defendant: it is this reliance that helps to establish the special relationship. An additional concept is the introduction of the claimant's vulnerability to harm, which takes into account the control by the defendant of any rights enjoyed by the claimant,[3] although this factor will probably be regarded as one of the factors that should be taken into account when applying the threefold test.[4]

1   *Henderson v Merrett Syndicates Ltd* [1995] 2 AC 145 at 181.
2   *Williams v Natural Life Foods Ltd* [1998] 1 WLR 830 at 835.
3   *Perre v Apand Pty Ltd* (1999) ALR 606.
4   Anthony M Dugdale and Michael A Jones, general editors, *Clerk & Lindsell on Torts* (Sweet & Maxwell, 19th edn, 2006) 8-87 to 8-107.

The combined approach

13.9 This approach demonstrates that the different ways of analysing the notional duty are mutually supportive. Considerations of assumption of responsibility and reliance remain relevant, and the court is also able to consider the fairness and justice of the notional duty in the context of the situation. The common points have been summarised by Neill LJ in *James McNaughton Paper Group Ltd v Hicks Anderson & Co*[1] in which he identified six matters to be considered:

(a) The purpose for which the statement was made.

(b) The purpose for which the statement was communicated.

(c) The relationship between the adviser, the advisee and any relevant third party.

(d) The size of any class to which the advisee belongs.

(e) The state of knowledge of the adviser.

(f) Reliance by the advisee.[2]

1 [1991] 2 QB 113 at 125.

2 See also the comments by Lord Bingham at 639 in Reeman v Department of Transport [1997] PNLR 618. The following analysis will follow the more detailed discussion in Anthony M Dugdale and Michael A Jones, general editors, *Clerk & Lindsell on Torts*, 8-87 to 8-107.

THE PURPOSE FOR WHICH THE STATEMENT WAS MADE AND COMMUNICATED

13.10 An individual identity certificate issued by a certification authority purports to identify a natural or legal person and indicates that the entity is in possession of a private key corresponding to the public key contained in the certificate. The information contained in the individual identity certificate will probably include some, all or part of the following information, depending on the type of certificate used:[1]

(a) The version of the certificate.

(b) The serial number of the certificate.

(c) The subscriber's name, place and date of birth, whether the subscriber is a natural person; if a legal entity, the name of the company.

(d) The subscriber's legal domicile and virtual domicile (this can be the email address).

(e) The date the certificate was issued and the date of expiry.

(f) The name of the authority that issued the certificate.

(g) The public key and algorithm identification of the subscribing party.

(h) Algorithm identification and digital signature.

(i) The limit of value that can be attributed to the use of the certificate.

Given the nature of the information contained in the certificate, it can be argued that the purpose of the information and the service provided, that is to authenticate an entity, is such that the certification authority assumes responsibility to those who rely on the certificate. As for the certificate revocation list, there are a number of reasons why certificates will cease to be valid. One example is where the private key has been compromised, which means the relying party cannot be certain that the public key is to be trusted to link the identity of the private key to the person named in the certificate; another reason is related to the life of a certificate, because the validity of a certificate will usually be limited by time. The purpose of the certificate revocation list is to alert the user community and to inform them that they can no longer rely on a particular certificate linked to a specific public key for a particular identity. Thus it is possible to conceive that a certification authority will have two notional duties: to undertake sufficient checks to ensure the information is correct and to ensure the certificate revocation list is up to date.

1   'Legal and Regulatory Issues for the European Trusted Services Infrastructure – ETS' Final Report by ISTEV, Chapter 2 paragraph 2.5; Carlisle Adams and Steve Lloyd Understanding PKI Concepts, Standards, and Deployment Considerations, 72–73 for the structure of an X.509v3 certificate.

RELATIONSHIP BETWEEN THE PARTIES

13.11   Under this head, three issues should be addressed:

(a)   The nature of the relationship between dependence and independence for the information contained in the certificate or the certificate revocation list.

(b)   The contractual matrix may well be relevant to help to determine the nature of the relationship between dependence and independence.

(c)   Finally, the scope of the contract between the parties is a possible factor a court will take into account in determining this issue.

Classes of certificate

13.12   Certification authorities issue different classes of certificate. For instance, BT issued three types of certificate in the past.[1] The BT Certification Practice Statement (Version 3.04, effective date 18 December 2003) describes the types of certificate at 1.1.1:

'Class 1 Certificates offer the lowest level of assurances within BT's Subdomain. They are individual Certificates, whose validation procedures are based on assurances that the End User's distinguished name is unique and unambiguous within the CA's Subdomain and that a certain e-mail address is associated with a public key. They are appropriate for digital signatures, encryption, and access control for non-commercial or low-value transactions where proof of identity is unnecessary.

Class 2 Certificates offer a medium level of assurances in comparison with the other two Classes. Again, they are individual Certificates. In addition to the Class 1 validation procedures, Class 2 validation procedures add procedures based on a comparison of information submitted by the Certificate applicant against information in business records or databases or the database of a BT-approved identity proofing service. They can be used for digital signatures, encryption, and access control, including as proof of identity in medium-value transactions.

Class 3 Certificates provide the highest level of assurances within BT's Subdomain. Class 3 Certificates are issued to organisations and Administrators for CAs and RAs. Class 3 organisational Certificates are issued to devices to provide authentication; message, software, and content integrity; and confidentiality encryption. Class 3 organisational Certificates provide assurances of the identity of the End User based on a confirmation that the End User organisation does in fact exist, that the organisation has authorised the Certificate Application, and that the person submitting the Certificate Application on behalf of the End User was authorised to do so. Class 3 organisational Certificates for servers (Secure Server IDs and Global Server IDs) also provide assurances that the End User is entitled to use the domain name listed in the Certificate Application.'

Class 1 certificates were issued to individuals. The identity of the subscribing party was not checked for this class of certificate, although a search would be conducted of the name and e-mail address for the purpose of ensuring the distinguished name is unique and unambiguous within the certification authority's domain. In such cases, the value of the certificate will be very low. These certificates are described in Table 2 to the BT Certification Practice Statement as 'Modestly enhancing the security of e-mail through confidentiality encryption, digital signatures, and web-based access control, where proof of identity is unnecessary. Applications requiring a low level of assurances in comparison with the other Classes, such as non-commercial web browsing and e-mail.'

1   BT now only offers Class 2 certificates and Test Class 1 certificates within its Subdomain of the VTN, although it continues to support Class 3 certificates ordered up to 26 September 2003.

Contractual terms

13.13　However, an important issue for a recipient will be how easy it is for them to discover whether the certification authority has taken any measures to confirm the information provided by the subscribing party. Where higher-grade classes of certificate are issued, a certification authority will take additional measures to confirm the accuracy of the information provided by the subscribing party. By way of an example, the BT ID Certificate for individuals is governed by a set of terms.[1] Section 1 of the terms provide a number of definitions:

(a) the certificate is defined as 'a digital record issued and digitally signed by BT in accordance with the authentication requirements of the Service';

(b) the service is defined as 'the certification authority services provided by BT in managing Certificate authentication, generation and life cycle support of your Certificate, in accordance with the Scheme and BT CPS';

(c) BT CPS 'means the BT Certificate Practice Statement, which describes the practices and procedures used by BT to operate it's certificate management Service';

(d) Scheme 'means the Government Gateway scheme for e-Government services in the UK'

(e) Contract 'means these conditions and the Enrolment Form.'

By this means, BT seeks to incorporate the terms and conditions, the Government Gateway scheme and the BT Certificate Practice Statement into the contract with the subscribing party. There is no BT Certificate Practice Statement, but there is a BT Certification Practice Statement.[2] The BT Certification Practice Statement (BT CPS) is based upon the VeriSign Certificate Practices Statement,[3] although the only VeriSign document of a similar nature is entitled VeriSign Certification Practice Statement (VeriSign CPS).[4] It will be assumed that the inconsistency between the actual titles of these documents and the references made in the BT documents are merely typographical errors. The BT Certification Practice Statement indicates that BT is part of a global public key infrastructure called the VeriSign Trust Network (Network). VeriSign and each affiliate have authority over a portion of this Network, called a sub-domain. The BT Certification Practice Statement describes the practices that BT uses for the following matters:

(a) securely managing the core infrastructure that supports the Network, and

(b) issuing, managing, revoking, and renewing Network certificates.[5]

Other documents that govern the contract are set out later in the BT Certification Practice Statement. They comprise a number of supplementary documents that relate to security and operational issues, which in turn supplement the BT Certification Practice Statement and VeriSign Certification Practice Statement by setting out more detailed requirements. They are:

'Ancillary security and operational documents that supplement the CP and CPS by providing more detailed requirements, such as:

- The VeriSign Security Policy, which sets forth security principles governing the VTN infrastructure, and the BT Security Policy which sets out the security principles within the BT Sub domain.

- The Security and Audit Requirements Guide, which describes detailed requirements for BT concerning personnel, physical, telecommunications, logical, and cryptographic key management security.

- The Enterprise Security Guide, which describes detailed requirements for Managed public key infrastructure Customers and Gateway Customers concerning personnel, physical, telecommunications, logical, and cryptographic key management security.
- Key Ceremony Reference Guide, which presents detailed key management operational requirements.'[6]

Of the documents set out above, three are not made available to the public, namely VeriSign and BT Security Policies, Security and Audit Requirements Guide and Key Ceremony Reference Guide. These documents are not available publicly to '... preserve the security ...' of the Network.[7] A number of additional contracts are also imposed on users of their services by BT: 'Ancillary Contracts imposed by BT. These Contracts would bind Customers, End Users, and Relying Parties of BT. Among other things, the Contracts flow down VTN Standards to these VTN Participants and, in some cases, state specific practices for how they must meet VTN Standards.'[8] A list of documents is provided in the BT Certification Practice Statement, although it is not intended to be exhaustive.[9]

It can be seen that there are a number of documents that affect the contract between a certification authority and a subscribing party. It is not always obvious where they can be found, and the subscriber will not be given copies of some of the documents that affect the security of the infrastructure within which the key pair will be used. It may be possible to tease out the complexity of the dependence or otherwise of the parties by reference to all of the documents that are relevant to the service, but the problem will be that few subscribing or recipients will be aware of all the relevant terms. Alternatively, it may be possible to establish a notional duty on the basis of those documents that are most obviously available, depending on how 'most obviously available' is construed by a court.

1   www.trustwise.com/repository/PDF/enduser_idcertsv4.PDF.
2   www.trustwise.com/repository/CPS/cps.htm.
3   BT Certification Practice Statement, 1.
4   www.verisign.com/repository/CPS/.
5   BT Certification Practice Statement, 1.
6   BT Certification Practice Statement, 2–3.
7   BT Certification Practice Statement, 3.
8   BT Certification Practice Statement p 3.
9   BT Certification Practice Statement Table 1 Availability of Practices Documents, 3.

Accuracy of the information

13.14   A notional duty to ensure the information contained in the certificate is accurate seems to have a sound basis from the point of view of the terms upon which BT accepts an application from a subscribing party. Although the subscribing party is bound by the warranties as to the accuracy of the information they provide, nevertheless BT undertakes an exercise to conclusively validate the information provided, despite the warranties demanded of the subscribing party. If BT validates the information, the next question is whether other certification authorities also undertake to check the information provided by a subscribing party. The following certification authorities based in the United Kingdom offer certificates:

(a) Equifax Secure Limited provides a range of certificates that are intended to be used by business, government departments, universities and special interest groups.[1] The Equifax Subscriber Agreement requires the subscribing party to offer the usual warranty as to the accuracy of the information they provide,[2] and in turn provides a warranty that 'the Certificate accurately records information provided to Equifax by the Subscriber'[3] and that 'it will take all reasonably practicable measures to verify the accuracy of such information.'[4] There are two linked Statements,[5] although it is not clear which document forms part of the contract with the subscriber, although it can be assumed that both documents probably form part of the contract terms. In any event, both documents offer a limited warranty that the information contained in the certificate '... accurately reflects the information provided ...' and Equifax has '... taken reasonable steps to verify that the information within the Certificate is accurate.'[6]

(b) SimplySign and Trustis provides digital certificates under the name of Chamber SimplySign by the British Chambers of Commerce.[7] The service offered is only for businesses, and there is a Subscriber Agreement (v1.01 20 February 2004). This document provides a summary of the terms and conditions that apply to the contract, and refers the reader to the Certificate Policy set out in the form of a PKI Disclosure Statement. The subscribing party warrants the accuracy of the information they provide under the terms of clause 5. SimplySign offer a strong warranty by clause 2 of the PKI Disclosure Statement, which states 'Certificates provided by this service, deemed Level-2 Class, are supported by the use of strong cryptography and highly robust Registration mechanisms and thus support a level of trust and security comparable with the highest level of Certificate available from many public schemes.' Clause 6 also offers a somewhat more limited warranty, which appears to be somewhat at odds with the earlier statement: 'By signing a Certificate containing a Policy identifier which indicates the use of this Policy, the Issuing Authority certifies to all who reasonably rely on the information contained in the Certificate, that the information in the Certificate has been checked according to the procedures laid down in this Policy.'

Finally, because the use of digital signatures purports to authenticate entities in a connected environment that spans the globe, the terms upon which

other certificate authorities accept applications will be persuasive in determining what dependence, if any, there is in the relationship between certification authority and users and whether a duty should be imposed, together with
the extent of the duty. The examples noted below refer to three certification
authorities from jurisdictions other than the United Kingdom.

(a) VeriSign, Inc is a company established in the state of California in the
United States of America. One of the services it offers is a Client ID
Certification Service, which is controlled by a Client ID Subscriber
Agreement. The Subscriber Agreement mentions the VeriSign
Certification Practice Statement (Version 3.3, 15 November 2006).[8]
For the purposes of this discussion, it is only necessary to discuss the
Class 1 certificate. The information provided by a subscribing party in
relation to Class 2 and 3 certificates is subject to closer scrutiny. The
Class 1 certificate has the lowest level of assurance, and they are issued
to individual subscribers only. The authentication procedure adopted by
VeriSign is, in accordance with clause 1(i): 'Class 1 Certificates. Class 1
Certificates offer the lowest level of assurances within the VTN. The
Certificates are issued to individual Subscribers only, and authentication
procedures are based on assurances that the Subscriber's distinguished
name is unique and unambiguous within the domain of a particular
issuer of Certificates (a 'Certification Authority') and that a certain
e-mail address is associated with a public key. Class 1 Certificates are
appropriate for digital signatures, encryption, and access control for
non-commercial or low-value transactions where proof of identity is
unnecessary.' The subscribing party is required to warrant the accuracy
of the information provided to VeriSign,[9] whilst VeriSign warrants, in
clause 6.1(a), that 'there are no errors introduced by VeriSign in your
Certificate information as a result of VeriSign's failure to use reasonable
care in creating the Certificate.' The terms of this warranty are governed
by paragraph 9.6.1 of the Certificate Practice Statement, in which
VeriSign warrants that 'There are no errors in the information in the
Certificate that were introduced by the entities approving the Certificate
Application or issuing the Certificate as a result of a failure to exercise
reasonable care in managing the Certificate Application or creating
the Certificate.' The subscribing party is also required by the terms of
paragraph 9.6.3 of the Certificate Practice Statement to warrant that 'All
information supplied by the Subscriber and contained in the Certificate
is true.'

(b) Thawte Consulting (Pty) Limited is a company established in South
Africa, and is also based in Delaware, United States of America.[10] This
certification authority provides a Personal E-mail Certificate, which
is issued to a user at no cost. Two documents comprise the agreement
with the subscribing party, the Terms and Conditions of Thawte
Personal Certificates and the Certification Practice Statement,[11] which

is incorporated by reference in the Terms and Conditions. Before issuing a certificate, Thawte require the user to agree to the Terms and Conditions. The terms and conditions appear in a small pop-up box, and are in turn incorporated in a smaller box that the user must scroll down before accepting. It is possible to cut and paste these terms, but a less sophisticated user will probably not have the knowledge to do this. Upon accepting the terms, the user is then taken through a series of separate pages, asking for a variety of information. The Terms and Conditions indicate the nature of the information that might be required: national identification number, passport number, driver licence number or tax number, depending on your nationality; full name and date of birth; employer's name, size and address (if employed); home address and contact details; preferred currency. Thawte do not offer, in the Terms and Conditions, any warranties regarding the accuracy of the verification procedure, nor do they require the subscribing party to provide a warranty, although the process of providing the information is equated to a contract of good faith, because the subscribing party is warned that if they proceed with the enrolment process, they are expected to do so in good faith: 'If you proceed with your enrolment, you must do so in good faith. If you submit false information or mis-use the system or any data in any manner, you will be subject to personal claims and your employer may also be subject to claims if it is proven that your employer was cognizant of your actions. You shall also be responsible for reimbursing Thawte if Thawte incurs any liability from your breach of this agreement.' In comparison, the Certification Practice Statement requires the subscribing party to warrant that 'All information supplied by the Subscriber and contained in the Certificate is true',[12] although the certification authority provide two warranties. First, 'There are no material misrepresentations of fact in the Certificate known to or originating from the entities approving the Certificate Application or issuing the Certificate' and 'There are no errors in the information in the Certificate that were introduced by the entities approving the Certificate Application or issuing the Certificate as a result of a failure to exercise reasonable care in managing the Certificate Application or creating the Certificate.'[13]

(c)   Netrust Pte Limited is a certification authority licensed by the Controller of Certification Authorities for Singapore.[14] Netrust offer a range of certificates to individuals and businesses, each of which has a cap on liability. The terms for each type of certificate are contained in a Certificate Policy, which comprises up to four pages, and incorporates the Certificate Practice Statement.[15] Every Certificate Policy includes the following description in the introductory first paragraph: 'When Netrust issues a certificate, it is making a statement that the certificate is associated with the person or equipment uniquely named within the certificate.' In comparison, the disclaimer paragraph (which is also identical in each Certificate Policy) does not warrant that any certificate supplied or provided by Netrust will be error-free, and there is a wide-ranging general exclusion applied to quality, merchantability, or suitability or fitness for any particular purpose. Compare these statements with the process of identification. For instance, there are two types of disk-based certificates, the Gold Individual (Disk) and the Silver Individual (Disk). To subscribe to the Gold Individual (Disk), the subscriber is required to register in person before the certification authority under the provisions of the registration requirements set out in clause 3(A) of the Certificate Policy. This clause refers to the more detailed procedure set out in clause 4.1 of the Certification Practice Statement, which also sets out the documents the certification authority will require to see before issuing a certificate. Alternatively, when applying for a Silver Individual (Disk), the registration process will be conducted by way of the internet or e-mail. The Certificate Practice Statement also sets out the obligations imposed upon the subscribing party in clause 2.1.4.1, one of which includes the requirement that 'All statements or information provided by the Subscriber in the Certificate application forms must be complete, accurate, true and correct in all respects and could be verified by Netrust or the ORA'.[16] The Certificate Practice Statement sets out the methods of registration and identification in part three. The identity of a legal entity will be authenticated under the provisions of clause 3.1.8. The process includes the provision of appropriate documentation to the certificate authority, and the verification of the identity of the entity by the certification authority. It also includes verifying the authority of the individual acting on behalf of the organization. The rules governing the authentication of the identity of an individual are set out in clause 3.1.9, and will differ in accordance with the class of certificate. Where validation takes place by way of e-mail, 'identification and authentication of the individual will be done by checking and verifying that the e-mail address of the subscriber does in fact exist.'[17]

Where a subscribing party applies for a certificate, every certification authority requires the subscribing party to provide accurate information. In the examples used above, the certification authorities tend, with exceptions, to disclaim liability for the accuracy of the information contained in a certificate, yet every certification authority validates some or all of the information provided by a subscribing party to differing degrees. Equally, each certification authority, in advertising the range of certificates available, emphasises the limited value of certificates they issue at the lower end of the scale. Thus the VeriSign Class 1 certificates provide '... the lowest level of assurances ...' and are claimed to only be appropriate for commercial transaction of low value;'[18] in comparison, the free certificate issued by Thawte does not indicate a degree of value to the certificate.

Certification authorities operate within a paradox. They insist that a subscribing party provides them with accurate information, which they then authenticate by various means. The method by which the information is verified is usually made explicit. Once the information is included in a certificate, a certification authority may not warrant that the information is accurate. One of the questions that need to be considered is the use to which the information is put. Each certification authority explains the use to which a certificate can be put in slightly different language, but the reason for obtaining a certificate for a public key, is to make the subscribing party's digital signature on a message or document more readily accepted by the intended recipient. When used, a digital signature is intended to authenticate the sender. If the certification authority will not warrant the accuracy of the information contained in the certificate, then a recipient cannot trust the certificate, which leads to the conclusion that no value attaches to individual identity certificates issued within a public key infrastructure.

1   www.geotrust.com/resources/cps/pdfs/Equifax_SecureMark_SA.pdf.
2   Clause 4.1.
3   Clause 6.1.1.
4   Clause 6.1.2.
5   Service Policy Disclosure Statement, V.03-06-30.01, available online at www.equifaxsecure.co.uk/policies/spds.html – this document refers the viewer to the Certificate Practice Statement Version 3.0 (Effective 30 June 2003), available online at www.equifaxsecure.co.uk/policies/cps.html.
6   Certificate Practice Statement Version 3.0 (Effective 30 June 2003), Part II General Provisions Section B.
7   www.simplysign.co.uk/.
8   The Subscriber Agreement is available online at www.verisign.com/repository/subscriber/SUBAGR.html and the Certification Practice Statement is available online at www.verisign.com/repository/CPS//.
9   Clause 6.2.
10   www.thawte.com.
11   Terms of Use for Thawte Personal Certification and Web of Trust Services v. 2.0 (06-05) available online at www.thawte.com/secure-email/personal-email-certificates/index.html#; Certification Practice Statement (Version 3.3, 12 December 2006) available online at www.thawte.com/cps/.
12   Clause 2.2.3.1.
13   Clause 2.2.1.1.
14   The web address for Netrust is www.netrust.com.sg and the website for the Infocomm Development Authority of Singapore is www.ida.gov.sg.
15   Version 2.0.4 dated August 2002.
16   ORA means Organization Registration Authority.
17   Clause 3.1.9.2.
18   Client ID Subscriber Agreement clause 1(i).

Failure of verification

13.15   The importance of verifying the identity of the person or legal entity is partly illustrated by the failure of VeriSign to make adequate checks on the identity of a subscribing party in January 2001. On 29 and 30 January 2001, VeriSign Inc. issued two Class 3 Software Publisher certificates incorrectly to a person falsely claiming to represent Microsoft. The certificates were issued to 'Microsoft Corporation'. The error was discovered whilst undertaking the second stage of a routine fraud screening exercise in mid-March. A notice in the form of a Security Alert was immediately issued, alerting users to the risk, and set out the terms of the problem:

> 'The risk associated with these certificates is that the fraudulent party could produce digitally signed code and appear to be Microsoft Corporation. In this scenario, it is possible that the fraudulent party could create a destructive program or ActiveX control, then sign it using either certificate and host it on a Web site or distribute it to other Web sites.'[1]

VeriSign notified Microsoft of the error, posted a public notice and revoked the certificates on its certificate revocation list. This matter did not end with the posting of the public notice on the certificate revocation list, however.[2] The person wishing to obtain access to the certificate revocation list must have the correct uniform resource locator (URL). The URL is the address from which the certificate revocation list can be downloaded. There are two technical issues that affect the ability to download a suitably-recent certificate revocation list:

(a)   How the certification authority tells you where to obtain the relevant certificate revocation list.

(b)   Whether your computer carries out the functions you require.

There are many different ways to obtain a certificate revocation list, and because there is no standard within the industry, no one method is mandatory.[3] Regardless of the method used, the significant issues for every relying party, which they may not be aware of, are as follows:

(a)   The certificate revocation list should be digitally signed by the certificate authority using its root certificate to prevent a certificate revocation list from being forged.

(b)   The certificate revocation list is dated by the certification authority, which means that every certificate revocation list expires.

(c)   Every certificate revocation list has a higher sequence than the one issued previously, to prevent forgery.

(d)   The person wishing to check a particular certificate must know where to find a suitably-recent certificate revocation list.

(e)   The certificate revocation list must actually be able to be obtained by a relying party.

(f)   The contents of the certificate revocation list must be authenticated.

Any duty that is to be imposed on a certification authority should take into account the complexity of these issues. If Guerin was correct, and Microsoft did design the software to take a user to the address where the certificate revocation list existed only if the address was provided by the certification authority with the certificate, then establishing the responsibility for passing this knowledge on to a relying party will be a necessary perquisite to any possible defence by a certification authority. Apparently, VeriSign did not issue Class 3 Software Publisher certificates with an address for the certificate revocation list. This appears to mean that, at the time of the incident, the user of the relevant Microsoft software was not able to retrieve the certificate revocation list of a given certifying certificate issued by VeriSign. At the time of this incident, Guerin reached the conclusion that Microsoft did not have software that had a working revocation infrastructure.[4] Microsoft did not agree with this analysis, and published a rebuttal that is no longer available,[5] to which although Guerin rebutted the points raised by Microsoft in his article. However, the position seems to be clearer as a result of information archived on the internet, and the report located on U. S. Department of Energy Computer Incident Advisory Capability website, referring to 'L-062: Erroneous Verisign-Issued Digital Certificates for Microsoft' the following text is included from, it appears, Microsoft:[6]

> 'VeriSign has revoked the certificates, and they are listed in VeriSign's current Certificate Revocation List (CRL). However, because VeriSign's code-signing certificates do not specify a CRL Distribution Point (CDP), it is not possible for any browser's CRL-checking mechanism to download the VeriSign CRL and use it. Microsoft is developing an update that rectifies this problem. The update package includes a CRL containing the two certificates, and an installable revocation handler that consults the CRL on the local machine, rather than attempting to use the CDP mechanism. Versions of the update are being prepared for all Microsoft platforms released since 1995. However, because of the large number of platforms that must be tested, the patches are not available at this writing.'

If it is the case that a vendor of software such as Microsoft did not have a working revocation infrastructure in place in the past, then it could be argued that past certificates can hardly be said to be reliable. As a result, the evidential weight to be given to a certificate must be considered against these practical problems, otherwise the evidence may be so poor as to make the concept of a certificate irrelevant. A court should take such practical issues into account when deciding whether a duty of care should be imposed on a certification authority.

---

1   VeriSign Security Alert Fraud Detected in Authenticode Signing Certificates March 22, 2001, no longer available, but an 'Advisory' is available online at www.verisign.com/support/advisories/authenticodefraud.html; for the Microsoft Security Bulletin MS01-017, see www.microsoft.com/technet/security/bulletin/MS01-017.mspx; U. S. Department of Energy Computer Incident Advisory Capability, L-062: Erroneous Verisign-Issued Digital Certifi-

cates for Microsoft, at www.ciac.org/ciac/bulletins/l-062.shtml; Ferdinand Gomes, 'Security Alert: Fraudulent Digital Certificates' (SANS Institute, 2003), available online at www.sans. org/rr/whitepapers/certificates/679.php.

2   Gregory L Guerin, 'Microsoft, VeriSign, and Certification Revocation', at www.amug.org/ ~glguerin/opinion/revocation.html last viewed on 17 May 2001, but no longer available, 4.

3   Guerin, 5; Carlisle Adams and Steve Lloyd Understanding PKI Concepts, Standards, and Deployment Considerations, 107–126.

4   Guerin, 8–11.

5   www.microsoft.com/technet/security/verigisn.asp last viewed on 17 May 2001.

6   www.ciac.org/ciac/bulletins/l-062.shtml.

Nature of the certificate

13.16   The service offered by certification authorities is similar in nature to the facts in *Ministry of Housing and Local Government v Sharp*.[1] In this case, the defendant negligently issued a certificate on a piece of land. The statement omitted to specify the charge held by the claimant over the land. A buyer, in reliance upon the certificate, bought the land. As a result, the claimant's charge over the land was no longer enforceable. In this instance, a duty was imposed on the defendant because it issued a statement to a third party with a particular purpose. The purpose of the statement was to set out the charges held against the land, and in so doing, to protect a class of person within which the claimant fell. In this case, the purpose of the statement was to secure a class of person against loss. If it is considered that a certification authority should have a similar notional duty for the information contained in an individual identity certificate, the purpose of the statement must be carefully considered. As a result, there is a compelling argument to suggest that the certification authority creates a relationship of dependence. Such a relationship can be described as being between the certification authority and the subscribing party, and also between the certification authority and any recipient. It must be recalled that the purpose of the information contained in the certificate is to bind the identity of a subscriber to a key pair. The subscribing party intends to use the certificate to authenticate themselves, and a recipient is expected to rely on the content of the certificate as being accurate. Whether a recipient can depend on the content of a certificate without undertaking any due diligence will be a matter for subsequent discussion.

1   [1970] 2 QB 223.

KNOWLEDGE OF THE DEFENDANT

13.17   In respect of knowledge, a notional duty will depend upon two factors:

(a)   Whether the certification authority knew or ought to have known that the statement in the certificate and certificate revocation list will be relied upon by a particular class of person in connection with the use to which the certificate is put.

(b)   Whether the certification authority knew or ought to have known that a party will rely on the information contained in the certificate and certificate revocation list without obtaining independent advice.

Various relationships will exist between different parties to a certificate. The subscribing party will provide personal information to the certification authority or registration authority. The certification authority will verify the information provided by the subscribing party, although the extent of the verification procedures adopted by the certification authority will differ, according to the class of certificate issued and the policy adopted by the certification authority. A relying party will look to the certificate to provide accurate information that they can rely on. In the event a mistake is made as to the accuracy of the information contained in the certificate, it does not follow that the information at fault will be the information identifying the subscriber. It is possible for the content entered by the certification authority to be incorrect, and this information, if incorrect, can also cause third parties to rely on the certificate in error. Equally, if the certificate revocation list is not maintained and up to date, a recipient may well rely on a certificate to their detriment, only later to discover the particular certificate they relied upon had been revoked.

The scope of the contract and the contractual relationships may also be factors which could be taken into account when determining whether a duty should be imposed, because certification authorities take great care to emphasise the need to be careful when relying on the information contained in the certificate. The contractual documents will provide evidence as to the state of knowledge of the certification authority. Certification authorities enter a direct contractual relationship with the subscribing party within public key infrastructure, and also attempt to establish a contract with recipients without forming a contract in its strictest terms. There are two contractual mechanisms used by certification authorities to deal with reliance on the information contained in certificates and certificate revocation lists.

Assumption of knowledge

13.18   One thread that previously linked most certification authorities in their response to this issue was to assume a certain level of knowledge and understanding on any party that subscribes to, or relies upon, a certificate. This no longer appears to be the case in some instances, although BT retains this assumption:[1]

> 'You acknowledge that you have sufficient access to information to ensure that you can make an informed decision as to the extent to which you will choose to rely on or use a Certificate or the information embedded in it. You further acknowledge that you are responsible for deciding whether to rely on a Certificate or information embedded in it.'

1   BT Trust Services Relying Third Party Charter, Issue 4 (July 2004).

Obligations of recipients

13.19 All certification authorities attempt to impose obligations on recipients. By way of example, consider the terms set out by BT in its Certification Practice Statement.[1] The relevant paragraph is 2.1.4, entitled 'Relying Party Obligations'. This clause refers to the BT Relying Third Party Charters, the provisions of which elaborate upon the terms contained in the Certification Practice Statement.[2] The terms of this paragraph in the Certification Practice Statement requires a recipient, before they carry out an act that can be construed as an act of reliance, to '.... independently assess the appropriateness of the use of a Certificate for any given purpose and determine that the Certificate will, in fact, be used for an appropriate purpose.' The recipient is expected to identify all of the various certificates along the chain of certificates, must not rely on a certificate unless the verification procedure is successful, and is required to check the status of a certificate on which they wish to rely, as well as all the certificates in its certificate chain:[3]

> 'The Relying Third Party Charters further state that Relying Parties must utilise the appropriate software and/or hardware to perform digital signature verification or other cryptographic operations they wish to perform, as a condition of relying on Certificates in connection with each such operation. Such operations include identifying a Certificate Chain and verifying the digital signatures on all Certificates in the Certificate Chain. Under these Charters, Relying Parties must not rely on a Certificate unless these verification procedures are successful.
>
> The Relying Third Party Charters also requires Relying Parties to check the status of a Certificate on which they wish to rely, as well as all the Certificates in its Certificate Chain in accordance with CPS §§ 4.4.10, 4.4.12. If any of the Certificates in the Certificate Chain have been revoked, according to the Relying Third Party Charters, the Relying Party must not rely on the End User Certificate or other revoked Certificate in the Certificate Chain.'

Checking the chain of certificates may not only take time, but may be confusing, a drain on computing power and difficult if the software is not configured to link the recipient to the certificate revocation list.[4] The terms upon which the recipient is expected to base their reliance, even after checking the chain of certificates, remains circumscribed:

> 'The Relying Third Party Charters state that if all of the checks described above are successful, the Relying Party is entitled to rely on the Certificate, provided that reliance upon the Certificate is reasonable under the circumstances. If the circumstances indicate a need for additional assurances, the Relying Party must obtain such assurances for such reliance to be deemed reasonable.'[5]

An attempt has been made by BT to impose a duty of care on the recipient where they rely or use a certificate, including the information embedded in the certificate, without complying with the provisions of paragraph 2.1.4 in the Certification Practice Statement. The relevant text explains that failing to comply with the procedures will mean '... your reliance on or use of that Certificate or the information will be inconsistent with this Charter and will be considered unreasonable and in derogation of your duty of care under the Common Law of England and Wales.'[6] This resumé of the conditions that BT seeks to impose on relying parties seems to be no longer replicated amongst the other certification authorities discussed in this text.

Certification authorities clearly aim to circumscribe the right of a recipient to rely on the information contained in a certificate and the certificate revocation list. The class of person that might be considered to be a recipient may depend on the nature of the certificate. Where the purpose of a certificate is to identify employees in an organization within a closed system, for instance, the class of person will be clear to both the user and the recipient of a certificate. However, the wider use of a certificate linked to a key pair within an open public key infrastructure is to act as a form of signature by individuals and legal entities in the open communication system of the internet. The low take-up of this form of signature may be because of a range of factors, one of which may be that there is simply no market for digital signatures within a public key infrastructure, or perhaps it is because only people and legal entities with sufficient technical knowledge to understand how to use a digital signature are in a position to use such devices effectively. For this form of electronic signature to reach a wider audience, those using the infrastructure, whether they are subscribing parties or recipient, will need to know whether they will be required to consider taking independent advice before committing themselves to using digital certificates.

In deciding whether a notional duty should be imposed on a certification authority, the first issue is whether the certification authority knew a particular class of people would rely upon the statement made in the certificate. As commented upon by A. Michael Froomkin, in one sense the contractual framework constructed by certification authorities defines the tort, because anybody relying on the certificate '... can reasonably be expected to take the trouble to read the terms incorporated into the certificate.'[7] Thus the class of people that a certificate authority might reasonably be expected to rely upon a certificate could be those that take the time and trouble to:

(a)   Locate and obtain copies of all the relevant documents pertaining to the terms upon which they can rely on the information contained in the certificate.

(b)   Follow the procedures set out by the certification authority.

(c)   Retain sufficient evidence of a high probative value to prove they read the relevant terms and undertook the necessary exercise in due diligence.

It is probable that this class of person, also known as a verifying party if they undertake such actions, may be very narrowly defined, because the majority of users will not be aware of the complexity of the infrastructure or the risks associated with failing to be aware of checking components such as the certificate revocation list, to give just one example.

The second issue is whether the certification authority knew or ought to have known that a recipient will rely on the information contained in the certificate without obtaining independent advice. To continue the analysis in the contractual context, certification authorities attempt to educate both subscribing and recipients. For example, BT have produced a series of 'Frequently Asked Questions for ID Certificates'[8] and guidance for a subscribing party about protecting their private key.[9] The amount of information and advice provided in these papers, together with the links to other websites that are also included in the body of these documents, may constitute the provision of advice and guidance in the context of establishing the nature of the relationship between the certification authority, registration authority (if part of the chain), subscribing party and recipient. To what extent the recipient can be said to need to seek independent advice may depend on the value and importance to be attached to the additional educational materials that certification authorities provide on their websites.

1   Version 3.04 last updated 18 December 2003.
2   Issue 4 (July 2004) is the most recent version, available online at www.trustwise.com/repository/rpa/.
3   BT Certification Practice Statement, Version 3.04 last updated 18 December 2003, 2.1.4.
4   A. Michael Froomkin 'The Essential Role of Trusted Third Parties in Electronic Commerce' Part I paragraph C.
5   BT Certification Practice Statement, Version 3.04 last updated 18 December 2003, 2.1.4.
6   BT Trust Services Relying Third Party Charter Issue 4 (July 2004).
7   A. Michael Froomkin 'The Essential Role of Trusted Third Parties in Electronic Commerce' Part III A paragraph 2 b.
8   www.trustwise.com/repository/idcertsfaq.htm.
9   'Protect Your Digital Certificate; Protect Your Private Key' available online at www.trustwise.com/repository/Private_Key/PrivateKey_FAQ.html.

REASONABLE RELIANCE

13.20   Whether a duty is owed will depend on:
(a)   Whether the claimant is entitled to rely on the statement.
(b)   What independent advice, if any, there is available to the claimant.
(c)   The nature of any contractual safeguards.
(d)   The authority and skill of the certification authority.

It can be stated with some certainty that certification authorities are aware that third parties will rely upon the certificates they issue. In attempting to restrict liability, different types of certificate are offered, each with a different financial limit against which liability will be accepted. Certification authorities are aware of the use to which certificates are put, which is why it is important for a certification authority to ensure the parties relying on the certificate understand the degree of reliance they should place upon a certificate. The various certification practice statements take great care to make it clear to recipients about the steps they should take before relying on the information contained in a certificate.

In all probability, the recipient is entitled to rely on the information, but whether a duty will arise may depend on whether the reliance was in accordance with any express assumption of responsibility by the certification authority. This, in turn, may depend on the limitation of liability imposed on certain types of certificate and any warranties the certification authorities offer in their contractual terms. The limitation of liability may also depend on the class of certificate that a subscriber may decide to subscribe to, as well as any course of dealing and usage of trade that may have developed during the time digital signatures have been issued by certification authorities and used by subscribing parties. In this respect, it may be useful to note the guidance issued by the American Bar Association when determining the reasonableness of reliance:

'The following factors, among others, are significant in evaluating the reasonableness of a recipient's reliance upon a certificate, and upon digital signatures verifiable with reference to the public key listed in the certificate:

(1) facts which the relying party knows of which the relying party has notice, including all facts listed in the certificate or incorporated in it by reference,

(2) the value or importance of the digitally signed message, if known,

(3) the course of dealing between the relying person and subscriber and the available indicia of reliability or unreliability apart from the digital signature,

(4) usage of trade, particularly trade conducted by trustworthy systems or other computer-based means.'[1]

Trusting a certification authority to authenticate the identity of a subscribing party forms part of these criteria. The failure of VeriSign to notice a fraudulent application to a Class 3 certificate was serious. This certificate was issued under the terms of the Certification Practice Statement in force at the material time.[2] It is useful to provide the current general description of the certificates available as described by VeriSign, which does not differ greatly from the documents referred to in the previous edition of this text:[3]

'1.4.1   Appropriate Certificate Usages

1.4.1.1   Certificates Issued to Individuals

Individual Certificates are normally used by individuals to sign and encrypt e-mail and to authenticate to applications (client authentication).

While the most common usages for individual certificates are included in Table 1 below, an individual certificate may be used for other purposes, provided that a Relying Party is able to reasonably rely on that certificate and the usage is not otherwise prohibited by law, the VTN CP, the CPS under which the certificate has been issued and any agreements with Subscribers.

1.4.1.2   Certificates Issued to Organizations

Organizational Certificates are issued to organizations after authentication that the Organization legally exists and that other Organization attributes included in the certificate (excluding nonverified subscriber information) are authenticated e.g. ownership of an Internet or e-mail domain.

It is not the intent of this CPS to limit the types of usages for Organizational Certificates. While the most common usages are included in Table 2 below, an organizational certificate may be used for other purposes, provided that a Relying Party is able to reasonably rely on that certificate and the usage is not otherwise prohibited by law, by the VTN CP, by any CPS under which the certificate has been issued and any agreements with Subscribers.'

In Table 1 accompanying the text above, the assurance level given for a Class 3 certificate is described as 'High assurance Level' and can be used for signing, encryption and authentication. Table 7 at paragraph 3.2.3 sets out the criteria for authenticating the identity of an individual:

'Class 3   The authentication of Class 3 individual Certificates is based on the personal (physical) presence of the Certificate Applicant before an agent of the CA or RA, or before a notary public or other official with comparable authority within the Certificate Applicant's jurisdiction. The agent, notary or other official shall check the identity of the Certificate Applicant against a well-recognized form of government-issued photographic identification, such as a passport or driver's license and one other identification credential.'

The degree of authentication for this class of certificate is of a high level, as illustrated in Table 2, which indicates that Class 3 certificates are of a 'high assurance' level, and they can be used for code and content signing, secure SSL/TLS sessions and authentication. Paragraph 1.4.1.3 provides comments in relation to the level of assurance:

'1.4.1.3   Assurance levels

Low assurance certificates are certificates that should not be used for authentication purposes or to support Non-repudiation. The digital signature provides modest assurances that the e-mail originated from a sender with a certain e-mail address. The Certificate, however, provides no proof of the identity of the Subscriber. The encryption application enables a Relying Party to use the Subscriber's Certificate to encrypt messages to the Subscriber, although the sending Relying Party cannot be sure that the recipient is in fact the person named in the Certificate.

Medium assurance certificates are certificates that are suitable for securing some inter and intra-organizational, commercial, and personal e-mail requiring a medium level of assurances of the Subscriber identity, in relation to Class 1 and 3.

High assurance certificates are individual and organizational certificates Class 3 Certificates that provide a high level of assurance of the identity of the Subscriber in comparison with Class 1 and 2.

High assurance with extended validation certificates are Class 3 certificates issued by VeriSign in conformance with the Guidelines for Extended Validation Certificates.'

The references made above to the current position, taken from the Veri-Sign Certification Practice Statement do not differ greatly from the documents referred to in the previous edition of this text. When applying for a class 3 certificate, whether in the past or now, an individual was required to appear personally before a trusted entity such as a notary or local registration authority. The authentication of a business entity is described in paragraph 3.2.2:

'3.2.2   Authentication of Organization identity

Whenever a certificate contains an organization name, the identity of the organization and other enrollment information provided by Certificate Applicants (except for Nonverified Subscriber Information) is confirmed in accordance with the procedures set forth in VeriSign's documented Validation Procedures.

At a minimum VeriSign shall:

- Determine that the organization exists by using at least one third party identity proofing service or database, or alternatively, organizational documentation issued by or filed with the applicable government agency or competent authority that confirms the existence of the organization,
- Confirm by telephone, confirmatory postal mail, or comparable procedure to the Certificate Applicant certain information about the organization, that the organization has authorized the Certificate Application, and that the person submitting the Certificate Application on behalf of the Certificate Applicant is authorized to do so. When a certificate includes the name of an individual as an

authorized representative of the Organization, the employment of that individual and his/her authority to act on behalf of the Organization shall also be confirmed.

Where a domain name or e-mail address is included in the certificate VeriSign authenticates the Organization's right to use that domain name either as a fully qualified Domain name or an e-mail domain.'

The failure of this method of verification highlights the assertion made in the Cabinet Office Report 'Identity Fraud: A Study' (July 2002), that databases are not always clean – and relying on just one form of checking may be considered careless, as a result.[4]

1   Digital Signature Guidelines, August 1996 (Information Security Committee, Section of Science and Technology Information Security Committee, American Bar Association), 5.4.
2   Version 1.2 published on May 30, 1997 previously available online at www.verisign.com/repository/CPS.
3   VeriSign Certification Practice Statement (Version 3.3, 15 November 2006).
4   Paragraphs 3.3 and 3.13.

Foreseeability and remoteness

13.21   The foreseeability that a harm might occur is part of the test to decide whether a notional duty exists. The question is what the court, with the benefit of hindsight, decides is foreseeable, taking into account the evidence presented by the parties. This aspect of foreseeability permits judges to reach policy decisions with the aim of establishing or raising standards of behaviour. In the context of a certificate linked to a key pair or the accuracy of the certification revocation list, the question is how aware the certification authority was of the harm that might be caused if it was negligent in carrying out its duties. The evidence of such knowledge is readily available in the contractual documents created by the certification authorities, and the answer may lie in the attitude judges take in considering public policy.

FACTUAL DUTY

13.22   Should it be determined that certification authorities have a notional duty to ensure the information contained in an individual identity certificate and certification revocation list is accurate (in addition to the statutory duty imposed in relation to qualified certificates within the European Union), the next issue to consider is whether damage to the particular claimant was foreseeable. The principle is illustrated in the example of *Bourhill v Young*.[1] The defendant, driving a motorcycle, caused an accident that in turn led the plaintiff to suffer nervous shock as a result of witnessing the incident. The defendant owed the driver of the other vehicle a duty, but the duty did not extend to a third party. The potential claimant must establish that they belong to a class of victims that a certification authority would foresee might be injured by failing to provide accurate information.

In cases of economic loss where the claimant has relied on the statement made by the certification authority, the notional duty is restricted to persons who form a class for whom the statement was intended. The issue will be whether the claimant falls within this particular class, and it is possible to conceive that only those claimants that have carried out certain amount of due diligence, as recommended by the contractual documents produced by certification authorities, may fall within this class of injured party. If this is the case, then the numbers of people that fall within this class will, potentially, be very small. Should the courts limit claimants to the class of persons that come within the foreseeability test, the relevance of a digital signature may be questionable.

A claim for pure economic loss is normally recovered by an action in contract. Whether a contract exists between a certification authority and a claimant will depend upon whether the claimant is a subscribing party or a recipient. If the claimant is a recipient, most certification authorities have gone to great lengths to imply the existence of a contractual relationship with a recipient, although the elements of a legally binding contract are not all in place. One of the most difficult aspects of pure economic loss is the kind of loss that a certification authority can reasonably contemplate as a consequence of its breach of duty. The category of loss is construed narrowly, only permitting the normal loss of profits.[2] Whatever the scope of the duty is determined, will be central to the losses that could be claimed by the defendant. In the case of *Banque Bruxelles Lambert SA v Eagle Star Insurance Co*[3] Lord Hoffman decided that where there is a duty to take reasonable care to provide information upon which another will rely, the responsibility will be limited to the consequences of the information being wrong. Such losses could, potentially, be large if a recipient relies on the information contained in a certificate or on the accuracy of the certificate revocation list for the purpose of authenticating high-value transactions. However, to ensure the duty imposed is a fair one, the courts may well take into account the levels of liability attached to different types of certificate, and the representations made by certification authorities as to the suitability of certain levels of certificate in reaching a decision about the type of loss that can be levelled against certification authorities. As an example, the contents of Table 2 'Certificate Properties Affecting Trust,' in the BT Certification Practice Statement, illustrates the types of certificate available, the degree to which BT confirms the identity of the applicant and the uses to which each type of certificate can be put, as recommended by BT. Three types of certificate are set out against the criteria, comprising Class 1, issued to individuals; Class 2 also issued to individuals within the remit of certain types of service offering, and Class 3, issued to individuals and organizations for particular purposes, as contemplated by the certification authority. Bearing in mind the failure of VeriSign to authenticate the identity of an individual in 2001 when issuing high-value class 3 certificates, it can be argued that the degree of authentication should be considered to require a fairly high standard of behaviour from a certification authority for certificates deemed by them as high value.

In considering the test of remoteness, the most important issue to decide is the scope of the duty. In other words, what loss can a certification authority reasonably contemplate if it breached a duty of care. This will depend on the scope of the duty, and it is the scope of the duty that might have to be contemplated against the contractual restraints imposed by the certification authority, which in turn must be balanced against the apparent public policy of encouraging greater use of digital signatures, however unsuccessful.[4]

1   [1943] AC 92.
2   Victoria Laundry (Windsor) Ltd v Newman Industries Ltd [1949] 2 KB 528.
3   [1997] AC 191.
4   Jan Hvarre, 'Electronic signatures in Denmark: free for all citizens' *e-Signature Law Journal*, (now the *Digital Evidence Journal*) 2004, Volume 1 Number 1, 12–16.

Breach of duty

13.23   The test for a breach of duty of care is whether the conduct of the defendant falls below that of the standard required by law, and the standard is set as the reasonable and prudent man.[1] More accurately, given the nature of the relationship between the parties, the question is whether there should be a duty of care, given the circumstances. If it is considered reasonable that a duty exists between the parties, the next question is the standard of care, which relates to the conduct that is reasonable, given the particular factual circumstances. The courts do not set criteria to determine what constitutes the standard of the reasonable and prudent man, because the behaviour of human beings is so unpredictable. It would be foolish to restrict the ability of the judges to resolve disputes, given the infinite variety of problems that can occur from the same set of circumstances.

1   Thomas J. Smedinghoff, Certification Authority Liability Analysis (American Bankers Association, 1998) Chapter 4 for a discussion in the context of the United States of America.

REASONABLENESS

The objective standard

13.24   The nature of reasonableness is subject to criteria, which provides a guide to judges in reaching conclusions about the reasonableness of the actions of the defendant. Where a duty of care is owed, the actions of certification authority will be judged against the activity in which it is engaged. This is an objective assessment, rather than a subjective one. The relevance of policy is always implicit, even if not made explicit. The objectivity of the standard in the case of digital signatures within a public key infrastructure may well be based on the ability of a certification authority to provide insurance cover for the activities it engages in. In addition, it has been suggested that any special relationship between the parties will not have a bearing on the variability of the standard to be imposed,[1] although if the claimant is considered to have contributed to their misfortune by failing to take reasonable care in their own interests, a reduction in damages may be considered appropriate. In this instance, the factors to be weighed in the balance will include:

(a) The effectiveness of the verification procedures.

(b) The speed and accuracy when placing postings on the certificate revocation list, and the ease by which a person can find a relevant revocation list.

(c) The ability of a certification authority to obtain appropriate insurance cover.

(d) The extent to which they educate participants and persuade recipients that a certain amount of due diligence will be required before relying on the information contained in a certificate and the certification revocation list.

A certification authority will normally seek to ensure a subscribing party informs it immediately, by the fastest means possible, that a certificate should be revoked for some reason: where, for instance, it is suspected that a third party contractor has obtained a copy whilst undertaking routine maintenance of a system. For instance, the BT ID Certificate is governed by terms and conditions and the BT Certification Practice Statement. By clause 5.4 of the terms and conditions, the subscribing party is required to '... immediately tell BT if you believe that there has been or is likely to be a Compromise of your Certificate.' The End User Obligations set out in paragraph 2.1.3 of the Certification Practice Statement require the subscribing party to 'promptly' notify the entity that approved their application and request revocation of the certificate, and to notify any person that may be reasonably expected by them to rely on their certificate. How to request the revocation of a certificate is set out in paragraph 3.4:[2]

'Revocation Request

Prior to the revocation of a Certificate, BT verifies that the revocation has been requested by the Certificate's End User, the entity that approved the Certificate Application. Acceptable procedures for authenticating End User revocation requests include:

- Having the End User submit the End User's Challenge Phrase (or equivalent thereof) and revoking the Certificate automatically if it matches the Challenge Phrase (or equivalent thereof) on record,
- Receiving a message purporting to be from the End User that requests revocation and contains a digital signature verifiable with reference to the Certificate to be revoked, and

- Communication with the End User providing reasonable assurances in light of the Class of Certificate that the person or organisation requesting revocation is, in fact the End User. Depending on the circumstances, such communication may include one or more of the following: telephone, facsimile, e-mail, postal mail, or courier service.'

A subscribing party, when requesting BT to revoke a certificate, has the twin duty of informing BT and any recipient they anticipate will rely on their certificate. Whilst these duties appear reasonable, one problem remains: with the exception of a postal address and email address provided in paragraph 1.4 of the Certification Practice Statement, it is not immediately apparent how a subscribing party can communicate with BT in a hurry, a state of affairs that has not altered since the first edition of this text. Similar provisions are provided in the VeriSign Certification Practice Statement[3] and the Thawte Certification Practice Statement,[4] both of which include telephone and facsimile numbers in their contact details. Netrust of Singapore also requires a subscribing party to 'promptly' notify Netrust or the applicable sponsor of their request to revoke the certificate.[5] Any such request may be made in person, by telephone or facsimile transmission, and checks will be made to authenticate the identity of the subscribing party before action is taken.[6]

A comparison of the various certification practice statements illustrates that the majority of certification authorities emphasise the need for a subscribing party to inform them promptly if they suspect their key has been compromised. Whilst it is not always clear how the subscribing party is to get in touch with the certification authority from the information contained in the certificate practice statements, it is possible that such information may be provided to the subscribing party in a separate notice once their application has been accepted. If this is not the case, then the efficacy of the notification procedure might be validly subject to criticism. The entire rationale surrounding the use of digital signatures hinges on the accuracy of the information contained in the certificate and whether a relying party can trust the certificate revocation list. It seems realistic to suggest, therefore, that it is reasonable to anticipate that a judge will impose a notional duty to provide a fast and effective means to subscribing parties to notify the certification authority of a possible compromise of their private key. In addition, it may also be reasonable to impose a notional duty on subscribing parties to notify relying parties of the compromise of their private key. The duty will be to notify those relying parties that they can reasonably foresee relying on their certificate, which may possibly be defined as the user community they are actually aware of. It is the duty of the certification authority to inform the world at large of the revocation.

An additional source of guidance is the UNCITRAL Model Law on Electronic Signatures.[7] Articles 9 and 10 provide guidance with respect to the conduct expected of a certification authority and the degree of trustworthiness. Article 9 sets out the criteria expected of a certification authority that provides services to support electronic signatures that may be used with the intention of having a legal effect:

'Article 9.   Conduct of the certification service provider

1.   Where a certification service provider provides services to support an electronic signature that may be used for legal effect as a signature, that certification service provider shall:

(a)   Act in accordance with representations made by it with respect to its policies and practices;

(b)   Exercise reasonable care to ensure the accuracy and completeness of all material representations made by it that are relevant to the certificate throughout its life cycle or that are included in the certificate;

(c)   Provide reasonably accessible means that enable a relying party to ascertain from the certificate:

(i)   The identity of the certification service provider;

(ii)   That the signatory that is identified in the certificate had control of the signature creation data at the time when the certificate was issued;

(iii)   That signature creation data were valid at or before the time when the certificate was issued;

(d)   Provide reasonably accessible means that enable a relying party to ascertain, where relevant, from the certificate or otherwise:

(i)   The method used to identify the signatory;

(ii)   Any limitation on the purpose or value for which the signature creation data or the certificate may be used;

(iii)   That the signature creation data are valid and have not been compromised;

(iv)   Any limitation on the scope or extent of liability stipulated by the certification service provider;

(v)   Whether means exist for the signatory to give notice pursuant to article 8, paragraph 1 (b), of this Law;

(vi)   Whether a timely revocation service is offered;

(e)   Where services under subparagraph (d) (v) are offered, provide a means for a signatory to give notice pursuant to article 8, paragraph 1 (b), of this Law and, where services under subparagraph (d) (vi) are offered, ensure the availability of a timely revocation service;

(f)   Utilize trustworthy systems, procedures and human resources in performing its services.

2.   A certification service provider shall bear the legal consequences of its failure to satisfy the requirements of paragraph 1.'

Whilst the article articulates the standards to be expected of certification authorities, nevertheless of interest are the provisions included in this article that a recipient is required to undertake due diligence and thus become a verifying party. The information set out in article 9(1)(c) is possible to obtain from the certificate itself, although it is to be noted that the provisions of article 9(1)(c)(ii) could be read as 'exclusive control', implying a much more stringent obligation than imposed by the EU Directive on electronic signatures. However, the requirements set out in article 9(1)(d) may not all be contained within the certificate that is attached to the message or document. The other evidence to suggest the recipient is expected to undertake due diligence and thus become a verifying party is set out in article 9(1)(e), (f) and 2. The notes in the Guide to Enactment reinforce the assumption that a recipient is expected to undertake a certain number of checks before relying on the certificate and public key.[8] If it is determined by a court that a recipient, if they are to rely on a certificate from a sending party, is to verify information relating to the certificate, it will be for the court to determine the lengths to which a verifying party must go to demonstrate the actions they undertook were reasonable.

Article 10 considers the practical criteria that may affect the ability of a certification authority to carry out its duties:

'Article 10.   Trustworthiness

For the purposes of article 9, paragraph 1 (f), of this Law in determining whether, or to what extent, any systems, procedures and human resources utilized by a certification service provider are trustworthy, regard may be had to the following factors:

(a)   Financial and human resources, including existence of assets;
(b)   Quality of hardware and software systems;
(c)   Procedures for processing of certificates and applications for certificates and retention of records;
(d)   Availability of information to signatories identified in certificates and to potential relying parties;
(e)   Regularity and extent of audit by an independent body;
(f)   The existence of a declaration by the State, an accreditation body or the certification service provider regarding compliance with or existence of the foregoing; or
(g)   Any other relevant factor.'

The criteria listed in this article illustrate some of the technical problems any electronic signature may experience when used over the world wide web, and in particular when digital signatures within a public key infrastructure are used. Certainly sub paragraphs (b) to (g) may have a bearing on the ability of participants to undertake reasonable care in relying on a particular certificate. However, if the criteria set out in subparagraph (a) are to be considered with any seriousness by a court, an electronic signature (or certainly a digital signature that involved a certification authority) may be of very little value to either a subscribing party or a recipient. If a certification authority is permitted to cite their financial and human resources, including existence of assets (or lack of such resources) as a reason for not abiding by the relevant industry standards as a bare minimum, then the entire concept falls into disrepute. It can hardly be considered proper for a certification authority to rely on such an argument, although a subscribing party may well have a claim against the certification authority for misrepresenting its ability to provide trustworthy certificates if it falls short of the standard.

1   Anthony M. Dugdale and Michael A. Jones, general editors, Clerk & Lindsell on Torts, 8-124.
2   This text is replicated in paragraph 3.4 of the Thawte Certification Practice Statement (Version 3.3, November 2006) and paragraph 3.4 of the VeriSign Certification Practice Statement (Version 3.3, 15 November 2006).
3   Paragraph 4.9.
4   Paragraph 2.1.3.
5   Certificate Practice Statement (Version 2.0.4, August 2002) paragraph 2.1.4.1.
6   Clause 4.4 Revocation.
7   The Model Law on Electronic Signatures was adopted by the Commission at its 727th meeting on 5 July 2001.
8   Guide to Enactment, paragraphs 142 to 145.

The balance between cost and benefit

13.25   A breach of duty also involves a balance between assessing whether a particular benefit will reduce the probability of a harm occurring. That certification authorities have addressed this issue is manifest in the limits of liability they will accept against each class of certificate. For instance, BT limit liability in its Trust Services Relying Third Party Charter[1] to £25,000 for any one incident or a series of related incidents and up to £100,000 for all incidents in any period of 12 months; Cable & Wireless limits liability to £10,000;[2] Equifax sets a limit of US$1,000;[3] Netrust place a cap of S$1,000 on each of its certificates, except where a certificate is issued as a test, where no liability is accepted;[4] Thawte restrict liability with respect to High Assurance certificates to two times the purchase price of the certificate;[5] where Chamber SimplySign states, in paragraph 3 that:[6] 'Chamber SimplySign does not set reliance limits for Certificates it issues. Reliance limits may be set by applicable law or by agreement.' The text then refers the reader to the limitation of liability clause in which there has been a serious attempt at reducing liability, and in one of the paragraphs comprising clause 9 states 'The Issuing Authority excludes all liability of any kind in respect of any transaction into which an End-Entity may enter with any third party.' VeriSign place caps on liability for each class of certificate, Class 1 US$100, Class 2 US$5,000 and Class 3 US$100,000.[7] However, the commercial response to the assessment of risk will also be considered in the light of other factors, including the likelihood of harm and what measures should be taken to reduce that harm, taking into account the state of knowledge that a court may ascribe to a certification authority at the time the harm occurred. Other issues that will be considered include:

(a) The knowledge of the defendant.

(b) The degree of likelihood that any harm might happen.

(c) The severity of the harm and the extent of the consequences that may follow.

(d) The cost of taking precautions and whether the certification authority provided sufficient resources to demonstrate it took reasonable care.

1   Issue 4 (July 2004) available online at www.trustwise.com/repository/rpa/.
2   Relying Party Standard Terms and Conditions of Use, available online at www.cwsecurity. net/rpa/.
3   Certificate Practice Statement June 2001 Part II C.
4   See individual certificates, available online at www.netrust.com.sg.
5   Certification Practice Statement Version 2.0 dated March 31, 2002 paragraph 2.2.1.3.
6   PKI Disclosure Statement (v1.01 20 February 2004).
7   Certification Practice Statement (Version 3.3, 15 November 2006), paragraph 9.8.

Community values

13.26 There are two communities whose interests are considered under this heading: the common practice exercised within the certification authority community, and the considerations that attach to the community in its widest sense, which may include balancing legal policy and the concept of justice against the reasonable expectations that particular standards should be maintained by the certification authority community in the interests of the wider community.

Evidence of the common practice adopted by certification authorities will be considered in determining whether a notional duty exists. However, certification authorities cannot assume that by conforming to a common practice within the industry, that they have acted properly. It can be argued that a certification authority has acted carelessly if the practice itself leads to the taking of unreasonable risks, such as the example of Lloyds bank, where the bank followed the practice adopted by the industry, but the practice itself gave rise to unreasonable risks.[1] However, that is not to say that standards developed by professional bodies will be disregarded. Where a certification authority adheres to any codes that may exist, a court will consider such evidence, but it may not serve to exonerate the certification authority, depending on the circumstances.[2]

Standards set out in legislation will help to indicate the aim of policy makers in establishing community values. In addition, and bearing in mind the concept of what is meant by a signature, a court may well take into account the comments and decisions made by politicians during the process of shaping the relevant legislation, as well as the changes brought about by politicians in providing for the use of electronic signatures between the government and subjects. Such evidence may be pertinent in seeking to understand what the

politicians sought to establish in terms of a community value and how important the policy makers viewed the new legislation in the development of community values in relation to the medium of the world wide web.

In an early public consultation paper 'Licensing of Trusted Third Parties',[3]
the government represented that the proposals contained in this document
were intended to make a significant contribution to the government's strategy
in developing the information highway in the United Kingdom. In section II
'Government policy framework', attention was given to the role of leadership
that the government had to play in '… certain key areas',[4] one of which was to
improve efficiency in government and to provide for the effectiveness of the
services it provides to industry and the public.[5] A discussion of cryptography
comprised section IV of the consultation paper, in which it was made clear
that the uses to which cryptography can be put were considered an essential
tool. The attributes of digital signatures were made abundantly clear:

'33.   Public key cryptography offers the benefits of confidential
transmissions and digital signature in an open network environment in
which parties do not know one another in advance, and without the need
to share secret key information. The Government believes this is vital for
electronic commerce between trading partners who may, of course, not
know each other.

34.   For a public key system to work in the public domain, not only must
the public key be freely accessible, but also the user must have a reliable
way of verifying the authenticity of public keys. Such an infrastructure,
for managing and certifying public keys, can be based on a hierarchy or
network of certificate authorities or Trusted Third Parties. A TTP would be
a *trusted* source of information about the keyholder in the form of a 'public
key certificate'. The certificate could be used to verify certain information
exchanged over a network.' (Text underlined in the original)[6]

When discussing trusted third parties, the consultation paper suggested
that 'TTPs need to offer value with regard to integrity or confidentiality and
assurance of the services and information involved in the communications
between business applications'[7] and suggested that such organizations should
offer, as a commercial and business benefit, the ability to take legal responsibility for their actions.[8] A further document produced by the government
was 'e-commerce@its.best.uk', which can be considered of greater weight in
relation to this issue than many other publications of a similar nature.[9] The
report was written after the end of a study by the Performance and Innovation Unit of the Cabinet Office. To achieve the 'vision', three challenges were
enumerated, including that of trust.[10] Each of these barriers were discussed in
slightly more detail, and the authors of this report stated that '… business and
consumers must be able to use e-commerce systems without undue fear of
fraud and with the same, or a greater, degree of confidence than they associ-

ate with physical transactions.'[11] In discussing trust in more depth, five issues were identified, that of fraud, privacy, anxiety about content, doubts over legal liability and how to obtain redress.[12] Issues raised under the heading of fraud include questions such as 'Is the seller authentic?' and 'Is the buyer genuine'.[13] Figure 10.3 considered the issues in tabular form, and in relation to fraud for both consumer and business, 'PKI Standard' is recommended to authenticate both parties and to secure credit transfers. This recommendation is discussed in further detail, and it is clear that the opinion of the government is that public key infrastructure is the best suited for e-commerce.[14] It was recommended that the 'PKI Standard' should be used to authenticate the parties, with the additional comment offered that using PKI Standards will authenticate contracts and help resolve disputes. Indeed, the report goes so far as to make it abundantly clear that public key infrastructure is the answer to the issue of authentication, as far as the government is concerned:

> 'The use of PKI will address the problems posed under 'fraud' because it ... allows both the sender and recipient to be positively identified ... and ... assists in determining liability by ensuring that the parties to a contract can be confidentially identified'[15]

A further document prepared by InterForum also helps to illustrate the policy adopted by the government and the certification authority industry over electronic signatures. In the White Paper 'Electronic Signatures – Signing up to the Digital Economy', a foreword was written by Patricia Hewitt, MP and Minister for Small Business and E-Commerce. In this foreword, the usual reasons for the perception that people were not using the internet to buy and sell online was reiterated thus:

> 'Successive studies, some of which are cited in the PIU Report ("e-commerce@its.best.uk") ... show that both business and members of the public are put off embracing electronic business because of fears that their information will be compromised. We must – together – find a way of overcoming these fears.'[16]

The minister emphasised that 'The importance of electronic signatures cannot be underestimated,' and if used correctly '... can underpin the trust and confidence which is so important to the success of the information revolution', indicating that the government intended to help deal with the issue by introducing the Electronic Communications Bill to 'encourage the use and acceptance of electronic signatures.'[17] Comments within the text of the document illustrate the inconsistencies that surround the two principal concerns: that of providing for the authentication of an entity in an electronic context, and the ability of the technology to provide satisfactory solutions to the problem. First, the need for authentication is repeated, with the observation that 'The paper-based signature currently underpins global commerce. However, for electronic commerce to succeed, this must be replaced by a trusted digital alternative',[18] and comments later in the paper indicate the value of digital signatures, by which a trusted third party '... vouches for the certificate owner's identity' and certification authorities '... play a fundamental role in the PKI by acting as the repository of trust' acting as the '... guarantor or the validity of the digital certificate.'[19] However, the paper goes on to indicate the dichotomy between the assumptions made by the government and the reality. Despite the assertions that digital certificates provide a '... strong method to tie an electronic document to an individual or organisation ...'[20] the digital signature has a critical weakness:

> 'Electronic signatures do not, of themselves, prove that a signed document came from the claimed sender. It only shows that someone had access to the token or PC on which the digital certificate and signing process was stored ... The electronic signature is only as strong as the production, personalisation and distribution mechanism by which it is delivered to the end customer/user and subsequently stored and used. There the underpinning processes are fundamental to ensuring the security of transactions.'[21]

Taking into consideration the membership of the Interforum Council, which includes BT, Cable and Wireless, Entrust Technologies, IBM and the Royal Bank of Scotland, it can be safely assumed that certification authorities are fully aware of the technical difficulties that accompany the use of public key infrastructure.

The views of the government in this matter can be gathered from the provisions set out in the Statutory Instruments that have begun to be issued with the intention of providing for the use of electronic signatures. By way of example, Part 3 of the Income Tax (Electronic Communications) Regulations 2000[22] set out the evidential provisions that will apply to the sending of information to the Commissioners of the Inland Revenue and the making of payments in connection with the provisions in the Statutory Instrument. Information will be treated as having been delivered providing all the conditions imposed by these particular Regulations, any other applicable enactment and any specific general direction given by the Board.[23] Regulation 6 (as amended) applies to the proof of identity of a sender or recipient of information:

> 'If it is necessary to prove, for any purpose, the identity of:
>
> (a) the sender of any information delivered by means of electronic communications to an official computer system, or
> (b) the recipient of any information delivered by means of electronic communications from an official computer system,
>
> the sender or recipient (as the case may be) shall be presumed to be the person recorded as such on an official computer system unless the contrary is proved.'

The general provisions relating to this Statutory Instrument require a person communicating in electronic format with the Board to use 'an approved method for authenticating any information delivered by means of electronic communications.'[24] Intermediaries may be used for the purpose of authentication by the Board, whilst the Board reserves the right to require the user to use an intermediary for the same purpose.[25] This example illustrates that it is envisaged that intermediaries will be used to authenticate the identity of the sender and recipient of electronic messages between the Board and a user, and that there is a presumption that the message has been sent by the person recorded on the official computer system. Should either the sender or recipient challenge the use of an electronic message as not emanating from them, the process of proving a negative will be time-consuming and costly. Bearing in mind the complexity of the infrastructure and risks associated with the use of digital signatures, including the complexity of the contractual matrix that underpins the whole process, this example illustrates the government's intention to adopt the use of digital signature technology for the wider good of the community.

There is, perhaps, one further consideration that may affect the decision by a court to impose a notional duty on a certification authority because of the greater good of the community. That is provided by the evidence from within the certification authority industry, and is based on the global framework that exists between various certification authorities. To begin the odyssey, consider the Individual ID certificate available from BT. The terms and conditions provide that the governing law shall be that of England and Wales,[26] and the terms also refer to the further conditions of the Certification Practice Statement. The Certification Practice Statement explains that BT is part of the VeriSign Trust Network, which is a global infrastructure of certification authorities.[27] Consistent with the approach of the terms and conditions that BT immediately require the subscribing party to accept, the law of England and Wales also apply insofar as it affects BTs sub-domain within the VeriSign infrastructure.[28] However, should a contract incorporate the Certificate Practice Statement by reference, then it is possible for the contract to have different provisions that determine the governing law than the Certificate Practice Statement.

The service offered by Cable & Wireless plc is not available to consumers, and is directed towards organizations. Clause 3.4 of the End User Certificate Policy,[29] provides that the policy is subject to the exclusive jurisdiction of the English courts. To provide one further example, the case of Thawte Consulting (Pty) Limited further illustrates the global nature of the infrastructure that has begun to develop for certification authorities. The introduction to the Certification Practice Statement (paragraph 1) sets out the range of services offered by Thawte, including root certification authorities for other organizations. There is a reference to VeriSign, Inc at the beginning of the document, but it does not become apparent until clause 1.4 that VeriSign is the organization that administers the Thawte Certification Practice Statement. The provision setting out the governing law is set out in clause 2.4.1, by which the laws of the state of California, United States of America, will apply to the validity of this Certification Practice Statement. A similar clause to that between VeriSign and BT is also in place, where the governing law may be altered if a local agreement incorporates the Certification Practice Statement by reference, but the local agreement sets out a different governing law. Of interest is the rationale provided in this Certification Practice Statement for the governing law, at paragraph 2.4.1: 'This choice of law is made to ensure uniform procedures and interpretation for all Thawte PKI Participants, no matter where they are located,' a clause which may cause problems for subscribing and relying parties in the future.

1   *Lloyds Bank Limited v E B Savory and Company* [1933] AC 201 HL.
2   Anthony M. Dugdale and Michael A. Jones, general editors, *Clerk & Lindsell on Torts*, 8-145.
3   A Public Consultation Paper on Detailed Proposals for Legislation, March 1997 with a Foreword by Ian Taylor MP, Minister for Science & Technology (DTI) and also published in JILT on 30 June 1997, available online at www2.warwick.ac.uk/fac/soc/law/elj/jilt/1997_3/taylor/.
4   Paragraph 12.
5   Paragraph 12 (c).
6   Paragraphs 33 and 34.
7   Paragraph 39.
8   Paragraph 42.
9   Performance and Innovation Unit Report, September 1999.
10 Paragraph 1.10.
11 Paragraph 1.13.
12 Chapter 10, paragraph 10.1.
13 Box 10.6.
14 Paragraph 10.21.
15 Paragraph 10.22.
16 Page 1. The author is not convinced of these assumptions, and this is a view shared by Professor Ross Anderson, amongst others, who argues that the overwhelming majority of cryptographic support systems will be concerned with protecting intellectual property rights: Ross Anderson, 'The real applications of cryptography', www.cl.cam.ac.uk/~rja14/dtiresponse/node9.html. This view is also shared by Jane K. Winn, 'The emperor's new clothes: the shocking truth about digital signatures and internet commerce', www-personal. umich.edu/~lsiden/tutorials/signed-applet/ShockingTruth.html, 1, 3. For a different view, see Adrian McCullagh and William Caelli, 'Non-Repudiation in the Digital Environment', www.firstmonday.org/issues/issue5_8/mccullagh/ who state that: 'With the advent of new digital signature technology, face-to-face communications as a manner of doing business will, in the not too distant future, become the exception rather than the norm' at 1.
17 Page 1.
18 Page 3(a).
19 Page 8 (b).
20 Page 3(a).
21 Page 10(a).
22 SI 2000/945, amended by the Income Tax (Electronic Communications) (Miscellaneous Amendments) Regulations 2001 SI 2001/1081.
23 Regulation 5.
24 Regulation 3(4)(c).

25 Regulation 4.
26 Clause 12.6.
27 The VeriSign Key Hierarchy table illustrates the complexity of the certification infrastructure, available online at www.verisign.com/repository/index.html.
28 Certification Practice Statement paragraph 2.4.1.
29 Cable & Wireless End User Certificate Policy (1491-PD0105-012 June 2002, Release 1.2).

Damages

13.27   The general principle of compensation is to compensate the claimant
for the loss they suffered, pecuniary and non-pecuniary, as a result of the
breach of duty. Linked to the payment of damages, is the requirement that
the compensation that is claimed is not too far removed from the breach
of duty. Any claim for pure economic loss is subject to the narrow criteria
relating to the remoteness of the loss, as demonstrated in the case of *Victoria
Laundry (Windsor) Ltd v Newman Industries Ltd*[1] where it was decided that the
defendant was only liable for the normal loss of profits that flow from their
breach of duty.

   A defendant is required to mitigate their loss, and it is possible that a court
may reach the conclusion that a subscribing party or a relying party will have
to demonstrate that the action they took after the tort was reasonable in
the circumstances. For a subscribing party, it may be considered that they
will have to inform the user community within their reasonable contemplation that they revoked their certificate. In addition, it may also be necessary,
depending on the circumstances of the case, that they should provide evidence of the actions they undertook to inform the user community that the
certificate was revoked. Where a recipient becomes aware of, or suspects that
a certificate may have been revoked or is not to be trusted after undertaking
appropriate and reasonable due diligence, it may be considered appropriate
for them to contact both the subscribing party and the certification authority
to set out their concerns, in order to establish the degree of reliance, if any,
that can be attributed to a suspect certificate.

1   [1949] 2 KB 528.

The notional duty

13.28   If digital signatures are to be considered in the same light as manuscript
signatures, then it can be argued that in fairness, a person or legal entity that
purports to offer such a facility should be taken to have a duty to ensure the
information that forms the individual identity certificate is accurate, and the
certificate revocation list is up to date and readily available. Should certificate
authorities not be subject to such duties, the value of a digital signature within
the public key infrastructure will be so low as to bring the infrastructure into

disrepute. In such circumstances, the public pronouncements of politicians and the laws that have been passed across the world may well be void of any meaning. As a result, it is foreseeable that a failure to ensure the information contained in an individual identity certificate is accurate, or the certificate revocation list is not up to date, can cause potential harm to the types of relationship that electronic signatures are meant to establish and nurture. In short, politicians have determined that there is a requirement to enable individuals and legal entities to authenticate themselves by electronic means; laws have been passed to permit the use of electronic signatures and for their admission in evidence in a court of law; certification authorities from around the world have created networks of trust, the purpose of which is to make the use of digital signatures easy to use, and on a regional basis, the European Union has provided for liability based on negligence through the mechanism of statute. These are powerful arguments to impose a notional duty in relation to the information contained in a certificate and the accuracy of the certificate revocation list.

Chapter 14

Evidence

14.1 In the event an electronic signature becomes the subject of a dispute, the party relying on the signature may wish to prove that the other party, whether the sending party or the recipient, intended to be legally bound to the terms of any document to which the electronic signature was associated. The sending party whose electronic signature was used may challenge the assertion that they affixed or authorized the fixing of their electronic signature to the document in question.[1] The problems relating to the way electronic signatures are created and used will highlight the types of evidential issues that may arise in the future.[2]

In addition, it might be necessary to pay particular care to ensure the pleadings adequately reflect the claims to be made at trial. For instance, in the United States federal case of *EPCO Carbondioxide Products, Inc. v JP Morgan Chase Bank, NA*,[3] EPCO sued JP Morgan Chase for refusing to renew letters of credit. EPCO alleged, amongst other claims, that the bank had made a written offer to restructure the debt and extend a letter of credit by an exchange of email correspondence. Under the provisions of the applicable law, that of Louisiana, all actions based on a credit agreement are barred unless the agreement is, amongst other things, in writing and signed by both the creditor and the debtor. In this particular instance, an error in pleading meant the point could not be taken:

'The magistrate judge, in his report and recommendation, concluded that to bring a claim for breach of a credit agreement, EPCO was required to plead either "the existence of a written agreement 'that is signed by the creditor and the debtor,'" or that "(1) EPCO accepted the offer by email, and (2) Chase agreed to conduct business by electronic means."'[4]

The members of the Court of Appeals for the Fifth Circuit agreed that the combined effect of § 6:1222 (2005) of the Louisiana Credit Agreement

Statute and § 9:2601 (2005) of the Louisiana Uniform Electronic Transactions Act created a significant evidentiary burden for EPCO, at 469–470:

> 'Taken together, these two statutes create a significant evidentiary burden for EPCO. Because it brings an action on a credit agreement, EPCO must prove, as an element of its claim, that there was a written credit agreement signed by both parties. If EPCO asserts that it submitted its signature electronically, it must prove that the parties agreed to conduct transactions by electronic means.'

The summary judgment was reversed and the matter remanded for further proceedings.

The general conduct of litigation is governed by the rules of procedure. The parties and the court identify the material facts in dispute through the pleadings, and the parties seek to provide proof of the facts that are material in the case. The aim of this chapter is to provide a brief outline of the procedure, then to consider the practical issues such as burden and standard of proof, relevance, admissibility and weight, hearsay and expert evidence. The reader is referred to the standard textbooks on evidence for further analysis.

1   This occurred in Germany in the three cases of OLG Köln, 19 U 16/02; LG Konstanz, 2 O 141/01 A; AG Erfurt, 28 C 2354/01; Michael Knopp, Case Note, OLG Köln, 19 U 16/02; LG Konstanz, 2 O 141/01 A; AG Erfurt, 28 C 2354/01, *e-Signature Law Journal* (now the *Digital Evidence Journal*), Volume 2 Number 2, 2005, 119–120.

2   Of particular concern is the illicit inclusion of malicious software, such as a Trojan horse on a computer without the knowledge of the owner. Such programs can be used by a third party to take control of a computer remotely. An unauthorized third party can then attach an electronic signature to a document purporting to originate from the owner of the computer. This defence was used in *R v Schofield* (Reading Crown Court, April 2003) and *R v Green* (Exeter Crown Court, October 2003). See also *R v Caffrey* (Southwark Crown Court, October 2003) for an acquittal based on the same defence; Esther George, 'UK Computer Misuse Act – the Trojan virus defence Regina v Aaron Caffrey, Southwark Crown Court, 17 October 2003,' *Digital Investigation*, Volume 1 Number 2, June 2004, 89.

3   2005 WL 1630096 (W.D.La. 2005), reversed and remanded by 467 F.3d 466 (5th Cir. 2006).

4   467 F.3d 466 (5th Cir. 2006) at 469.

Procedure

Civil proceedings

BEFORE THE TRIAL

14.2   Should the parties to a dispute fail to resolve the matter between them, they will have to contemplate asking a judge to reach a decision, based on the evidence put before the court. The Civil Procedure Rules 1999 (CPR) provide for the rules governing civil procedure. As soon as legal proceedings begin or the parties are put on notice that legal proceedings are contemplated, both parties have a duty to preserve every document that is relevant to the claim. The obligation includes documents upon which they may rely, together with any documents that adversely affect their case. Should one or both of the parties be reluctant to deliver up documents, a judge can order disclosure before action begins[1] and also has the ability to order disclosure against persons or entities that are not parties to the litigation.[2]

A document in electronic format is admissible to the same extent as any other form of evidence.[3] Further, s 8 of the Civil Evidence Act 1995 provides for the admissibility of statements in documents, and s 9 refers to the admission of the document itself. Copies of an original document can be adduced in evidence, regardless of how many removes there are between the copy and the original, although the document must be authenticated:

'8   Proof of statements contained in documents

(1)   Where a statement contained in a document is admissible as evidence in civil proceedings, it may be proved:
(a)   by the production of that document, or
(b)   whether or not that document is still in existence, by the production of a copy of that document or of the material part of it,
authenticated in such manner as the court may approve.

(2)   It is immaterial for this purpose how many removes there are between a copy and the original.'

Section 13 of the Civil Evidence Act 1995 defines 'document' to mean 'anything in which information of any description is recorded' and this definition is also adopted in CPR Pt 31, r 4: '"Copy" in relation to a document, means anything onto which information recorded in the document has been copied, by whatever means and whether directly or indirectly.'

1   CPR Pt 31, r 16.
2   CPR Pt 31, r 17.
3   *Derby & Co Ltd v Weldon (No 9)* [1991] 1 WLR 652, Ch D per Vinelott J at 658A-B.

THE TRIAL

14.3   The types of evidence adduced at a trial include the oral testimony of a witness and the submission of documentary and real evidence. There is a provision for expert witnesses to give evidence, which is controlled by CPR Pt 35. Expert evidence cannot be given without permission from the court, and the expert's duty is to help the court, which overrides their obligation to the client. Where documents are shown to form part of the records of a business or public authority, they can be received in evidence without further proof.[1] For such documents to be received in evidence, a certificate must be produced which is signed by an officer of the business or authority to which the records belong.[2]

1 Section 9(1) of the Civil Evidence Act 1995.
2 Section 9(2) of the Civil Evidence Act 1995.

Proving the accuracy of the evidence

14.4 Authentication is the process of convincing the court that a document is what it purports to be, proving the origin of the officer's signature and that the document has not been altered, or, where alterations have occurred, proving the nature of the changes. Proof is achieved by adducing oral evidence, such as management and operational procedures; circumstantial evidence, including, but not limited to, demonstrating the consistency of records, and evidence covering the technology used to record actions and process information.[1]

1 Stephen Mason, general editor, *Electronic Evidence: Disclosure, Discovery & Admissibility*, (LexisNexis Butterworths, 2007), Chapter 4 Evidentiary foundations.

Assessing the weight of evidence

14.5 Where the officer's signature has been authenticated, the court must still determine its weight as evidence, also known as probative value. The reliance that will be placed on the evidence will depend on the degree of authentication. Careful attention to detail is necessary, covering such areas as internal management procedures and record keeping; what occurred, when it occurred, who was involved, together with the need to demonstrate the reliability of any date and time stamping used. The difficulties that litigants will face in the future over computer evidence, especially respecting electronic signatures, will not decrease. In his judgment in the case of *Derby & Co Ltd v Weldon (No 9)*, Vinelott J set out five major difficulties at 658F–659C:

> '(a) Even when the relevant material is online and capable of being shown on screen or printed out, some means will have to be found of screening out irrelevant or privileged material. The party seeking discovery cannot be allowed simply to seat himself at his opponent's computer console and be provided with all necessary access keys.
>
> (b) There may be material on the computer which is not accessible by current programmes but which can be retrieved by reprogramming. Prima facie the powers of the court would extend to requiring that the computer be reprogrammed so as to enable the relevant information to be retrieved. Otherwise an unscrupulous litigant would be able to escape discovery by maintaining his records in computerised form and altering current programmes when litigation was in prospect so that information previously retrievable could not be retrieved without reprogramming. Of course questions may then arise as to

who bears the cost of any necessary reprogramming and whether it can be done without affecting current programmes.

(c)   If, as will often be the case, the computer is in daily use, the question may arise – it arose acutely in the instance case – whether access can be arranged, in particular whether any necessary reprogramming can be done or whether information stored in the archival or history files can be retrieved, without unduly interrupting the necessary everyday use of the computer.

(d)   Safeguards may have to be embodied in order to ensure that tapes or diskettes which may have deteriorated in storage are not damaged by use and that the use of them does not damage the computer's reader. In the instant case, the condition of some diskettes was such that read once they would be unreadable or only partially readable a second time and the use of some old diskettes in fact caused damage to the computer's reader.

(e)   In some cases it may be possible for the database to be copied by transfer on to a diskette or tape or directly on to another computer. If that is done the material may be capable of being analysed in ways which were not originally contemplated. Provision may have to be made available to the other party in good time so that he is not taken by surprise at the trial. In the instant case agreement was recently reached for the provision of further experts' reports dealing with information gleaned from parts of the plaintiffs' computer database which was transferred to Cooper's computer.'

Criminal proceedings

BEFORE THE TRIAL

14.6   The process of investigating a criminal matter is primarily undertaken by the police, and the legal framework seeks to balance the need to examine the allegations against the prevention of abuse and the protection of the rights of the individual. The activities of the police are subject to the Police and Criminal Evidence Act 1984 and the Code of Practice issued by the Home Secretary under the provisions of the Act. Under the provisions of the Criminal Procedure and Investigations Act 1996, the prosecutor is under a duty to disclose material which has not previously been disclosed to the defence and which in the opinion of the prosecutor undermines the prosecution case against the accused. Where the defence gives a statement of defence, the prosecutor is then required to disclose to the accused any prosecution material which has not previously been disclosed and which might reasonably be expected to aid the defence of the accused as disclosed in their statement. The obligation of disclosure is a continuing one.[1]

1 Section 9(1) to (3) and s 7(1) and (2) of the Criminal Procedure and Investigations Act 1996.

THE TRIAL

Witnesses

14.7 Where a trial takes place on indictment, a witness is usually summoned to give evidence in accordance with the Criminal Procedures (Attendance of Witnesses) Act 1965.[1] Third parties can be called upon to give evidence where they retain relevant material, either physically or if contained on a computer. Oral evidence as to authenticity will always be necessary to be able to produce some founding testimony as to the source or identity of the evidence, otherwise it can be rejected.

1 As amended by s 66 of the Criminal Procedure and Investigations Act 1996.

Types of evidence

Direct evidence

14.8 Direct evidence is the proof of the actual existence of an item by its production. In the case of a fact, the testimony or a declaration of an individual that actually perceived the fact will be required. Thus a receiving party can tell the court what they did when they undertook due diligence to verify the certificate of the sending party in the case of a digital signature. Also, where a sending party claim they did not affix their private key to a document or message, this assertion will also be direct evidence. This will also be the same in the case of other types of electronic signature, such as the icon on a website with the acknowledgement 'I accept'. Given the lack of electronic evidence if a party to an electronic signature takes issue over whether they affixed a signature to a document or message, or whether a receiving party undertook to verify the certificate attached to a message, a great deal of the court's time may be taken up with assessing direct evidence of this kind.

Real evidence

14.9 Evidence from a computer can be real evidence, depending on the form it takes. This is because real evidence can take the form of material objects other than documents that are produced in court. There is a distinction between a document that is a record of a transaction and the document as a thing in its own right. For instance, a computer document may be a record to show the 'I accept' icon was clicked. Alternatively, it may be possible that the electronic document itself can be the subject of a charge of theft, for instance. Whenever such evidence is submitted, a person will have to give evidence of the way in which the computer logged and audited the evidence. Where a statement originates from the functions a computer undertakes, it is possible to use the statement to demonstrate the circumstances in which the statement was made, and thereby seek to prove the assertion of the facts in the statement. An example is that of *R v Governor of Brixton Prison ex parte Levin*.[1] Vladimir Levin, a Russian citizen, was charged before the Federal District Court for the Southern District of New York with the Federal offences of wire fraud and bank fraud amongst other offences. He was alleged to have used a computer terminal in St Petersburg to obtain access to the computerized fund transfer service of Citibank NA in Parsipanny, New Jersey, and fraudulently made 40 transfers of funds amounting to US$10.7 million which had been processed by the system, but which the clients of Citibank, who purported to have made the transfers, denied having authorized. The United States government sought the extradition of Mr Levin after he was apprehended at Stansted airport on 3 March 1995. An appeal reached the House of Lords, and counsel for Mr Levin submitted that computer printouts generated by the bank were inadmissible because they were hearsay. This submission was rejected by Lord Hoffman, who stated at 746 C–D:

> 'The printouts are tendered to prove the transfers of funds which they record. They do not assert that such transfers took place. They record the transfers themselves, created by the interaction between whoever purported to request the transfers and the computer program in Parsipanny. The evidential status of the printouts is no different from that of a photocopy of a forged cheque.'

1   *R v Governor of Brixton Prison, Ex p Levin; sub nom Levin (Application for a Writ of Habeas Corpus), Re* [1997] A.C. 741; [1997] 3 WLR 117; [1997] 3 All ER 289; [1998] 1 Cr App R 22; [1997] Crim.L.R. 891; (1997) 94(30) L.S.G. 28; (1997) 147 N.L.J. 1990; (1997) 141 S.J.L.B. 148; *The Times* June 21, 1997; *Independent* July 2, 1997, HL.

Primary and secondary evidence

14.10   The terms primary and secondary evidence mainly refer to the kinds of proof that can be offered about the content of the document. By definition, primary evidence is considered to be the best, such as the production of an original document, for instance. It follows that secondary evidence tends to be a replacement for the best evidence, such as the provision of a copy of a document. In the world of electronic evidence, the concept of primary evidence may be somewhat of a misnomer, given the ability of electronic data to replicate data in digital form precisely. In any event, the rule regarding best evidence is no longer relevant since the decision in the case of *Masquerade Music Ltd v Springsteen*.[1] As a result of the comments made by Parker LJ in his judgment, it will be for a court to decide on what weight is to be attached to secondary evidence. However, where a party could produce the primary evidence but seeks to adduce secondary evidence, Parker LJ expressed the view at 85 that '… it may be expected that (absent some special circumstances) the court will decline to admit the secondary evidence on the ground that it is worthless.' In summary, the admissibility of secondary evidence will depend on what weight, if any, a court attaches to such evidence. However, there are circumstances when secondary evidence of the contents of a computer may be of greater quality than that of primary evidence. It will depend on what must be proved. Secondary evidence may be relevant as an accurate record of the contents of the memory at a previous point in time. Although a printout will be considered to be inferior evidence as to the content of the original memory as it was at the material time, it will be better evidence than what purports to be the original content of the memory at a later time. This is because it is a relatively easy task to alter the purported original record held in the memory, whilst concealing any evidence that an alteration has been effected.

1   [2001] EWCA Civ 563; [2001] CPLR 369; [2001] EMLR 25.

Secondhand or hearsay

14.11   The hearsay rule seeks to exclude previous statements made by any person, whether they are a witness or not, if the purpose of adducing the statement is to assert the truth of the contents of the statement.[1] Whether evidence is hearsay will depend on why it is to be adduced in evidence. The Civil Evidence Act 1995, which came into force on 31 January 1997,[2] abolished the rules relating to computer evidence and relaxed the rules relating to the admission into evidence of hearsay, although there are a number of exceptions in respect of criminal proceedings.[3] Hearsay is now admissible, in accordance with the provisions of s 1:

'Admissibility of hearsay evidence

(a)   In civil proceedings evidence shall not be excluded on the grounds that it is hearsay.
(b)   In this Act:
  (i)   "hearsay" means a statement made otherwise than by a person while giving oral evidence in the proceedings which is tendered as evidence of the matters stated; and
  (ii)   references to hearsay include hearsay of whatever degree.'

This provision is subject to a number of safeguards. First, the party seeking to adduce hearsay evidence must give notice in accordance with the provisions of s 2. Section 3 provides that where a party adduces hearsay evidence of a statement made by a person and does not call that person as a witness, the other party, with permission from the judge, can cross-examine the witness on the statement as if the person had given evidence in chief on the statement.

Section 4 of the Act also provides guidance about the considerations that are relevant to weighing hearsay evidence, discussed below.

The hearsay rule is different for criminal proceedings, and will continue to remain so. The Criminal Justice Act 2003 repealed the provisions relating to hearsay in the Criminal Justice Act 1988, as well as abrogating most of the common law of hearsay. The changes and the implications for criminal proceedings are fully covered in the main texts on evidence.[4] It is not proposed to deal with hearsay evidence in criminal trials, but where criminal acts are perpetrated using electronic signatures, criminal practitioners will have to assess the types of evidence they wish to adduce very carefully.

1   Hodge M. Malek, general editor, *Phipson on Evidence* (Sweet & Maxwell, 16th edn 2005), 25-02.
2   By the Civil Evidence Act 1995 (Commencement No 1) Order 1996, SI 1996/3217 under the authority of s 16(2) of the Civil Evidence Act 1995.
3   Hodge M. Malek, general editor, *Phipson on Evidence*, Chapter 30.
4   Hodge M. Malek, general editor, *Phipson on Evidence*, Chapter 30; Colin Tapper, *Cross and Tapper on Evidence* (LexisNexis Butterworths, 10th edn, 2004), Chapter XIV.

THE EVIDENCE FORMING A DIGITAL SIGNATURE

14.12   The evidential questions that surround a digital signature may well exercise the minds of lawyers in the future. Consider first the evidence that forms a digital signature. As can be seen from the description below, some of the electronic documents will be considered hearsay evidence and may well require oral evidence to prepare the introduction of such evidence, whilst other documents will be considered to be real evidence.

A certificate is issued,[1] which is a signed data structure that binds a public key to an identity. This certificate will purport to bind the public key to the information contained in the certificate. Part of the information contained in the certificate will be provided by the subscribing party, which may or may not be verified by the certification authority, and the remaining information will be provided by the certification authority. The subscriber will have a pair of keys, private and public. The key pairs may be generated by the keying material available to the subscribing party in their computer, by a registration authority, by the certification authority or by a trusted third party key generation facility.[2]

1   The use of the word 'certificate' is shorthand for an individual identity certificate based upon a X.509 version 3 public-key certificate.
2   Individuals can create their own private and public key pairs, or they can ask key generating organizations to do it for them. The reader should be aware that the creation and certification processes are distinct. The reader should also be aware that the same issues discussed in this chapter will apply to keys not certified by a third party, with the added complication that the level of authenticity may be lower because proving who the public key belonged to might be more difficult for any person wishing to rely on the uncertified key. How the key pair is generated may also be problematic if there is evidence that the software used to generate key pairs has flaws, such as being liable to generate weak keys.

CHAIN OF EVIDENCE FORMING A DIGITAL SIGNATURE

14.13 The links in the chain of evidence that bind a signature in digital format may be complex. The example of the digital signature illustrates the complexity of the process and the number of participants. With a digital signature the following set of links may not be unusual:

(a) First link: A subscriber enters a contract with a trusted third party key generation facility to generate a key pair. This key pair must then be distributed safely: the private and public keys to the subscribing party, and the public key to the certification authority.

(b) Second link: The certification authority creates the certificate. The subscribing party's public key must be incorporated into the certificate. This is the act of binding the subject name (the subscribing party) with their public key. This certificate is then digitally signed with the private key of the certification authority that issues the certificate.

(c) Third link: Once the certificate has been generated, it must be distributed. The methods used include physical delivery, posting the certificate in a public repository database to permit recipients to obtain access to the certificate over the internet, and distribution by means of email.

When a subscribing party uses their digital signature, a certification authority requires the receiving party to undertake a certain amount of due diligence. Individual certification authorities attempt to impose a varying range of obligations on a recipient. Whether a recipient will be required in law to undertake an exercise in due diligence will have to wait until a court is called upon to adjudicate on a dispute relating to the use or misuse of a digital signature. For the purpose of this discussion, it will be useful to indicate what actions a recipient might be required to undertake if they were obliged to verify the certificate used by the sending party.

VERIFYING THE INTEGRITY OF A CERTIFICATE

14.14 A recipient can go through a list of checks to assure themselves that the certificate links the sending party to the document or message that was signed.

Verify the certificate path

14.15 To trust the certificate sent by Alice, Bob must check all of the certificates back to the root or foundation certificate. Only by checking back to the foundation certificate can Bob determine whether he can trust the public key in Alice's certificate in relation to the purpose for which he will use it. The certificate attached to the message or document and the corresponding public key can only be trusted if every certificate and their corresponding keys in the path from the foundation key to Alice's key can be trusted. There are two phases to this exercise:

(a) Constructing the path, which requires Bob to bring together all the relevant certificates to form a complete path. This process may be complicated and time-consuming, because there may be a number of certification authorities in the chain, all of which have cross-certified their respective certificates. The assumption is that Bob can retrieve all of the certificates he needs to scrutinize them and put the chain of certificates together in a logical sequence. Bob must also check the issuing certificate of each of the certification authorities in the chain against a certificate revocation list.[1]

(b) Validating the path, where Bob must decide whether the path between each certificate is valid. This involves undertaking the mathematical computation to verify each digital signature; checking the validity period of each certificate for date of expiry; making sure each certificate has not been revoked, by checking the relevant certification revocation list, and then considering other issues such as the policies that apply to the certificate, any restrictions on the use of the key and if there are any other constraints on the use of the certificate.[2]

1   Microsoft offer guidance on this point, but fail to illustrate the complexity of searching all of the certificates in a chain, and how to identify where the chain begins and ends 'How to tell if a digital signature is trustworthy' online at www.office.microsoft.com/en-us/help/ HA012308751033.aspx; to understand the complexity of the task, see SP 800-89 *Recommendation for Obtaining Assurances for Digital Signature Applications* (National Institute of Standards and Technology, March 2006), also M. H. M. Schellekens *Electronic Signatures Authentication Technology from a Legal Perspective* (T M C Asser Press, 2004), 30–32, Klaus Schmeh, *Cryptography and Public Key Infrastructure on the Internet* (Wiley, 2001), 19.3.1–19.3.2, and Don Davis, 'Compliance Defects in Public Key Cryptography' Proceedings 6th Usenix Security Symp, (San Jose, CA, 1996), 171–178, for a discussion of some of the defects of PKI, relevant now as they were in 1996, available online at www.world.std.com/~dtd/.

2   Carlisle Adams and Steve Lloyd *Understanding PKI Concepts, Standards, and Deployment Considerations* (Addison-Wesley, 2nd edn. 2002), 147–149.

Other validation requirements

14.16   Once Bob has checked and validated the certificates and certificate path, he must then consider the following checks:

(a) Establish the integrity of the certificate by ensuring the digital signature on the certificate is properly verified.

(b) The certificate validity period must be checked, to ensure it is valid at the date and the time Bob intends to rely on it.

(c) The certificate has not been revoked. There are various methods to implement a certificate revocation list, as defined by the International Telecommunication Union.[1] Suffice to indicate, there are a number of variations, including, but not limited to, certificate revocation lists (which is a signed data structure that contains a list of revoked certificates); certification authority revocation lists, used to revoke the public key certificates of certification authorities and online certificate status protocol, which is a protocol that permits Bob receive a response to his request for information.

(d) The certificate has been used by Alice in accordance with the constraints set out in the certificate, including the relevant agreements and certification policies.

As a result, when determining the nature of the evidence, it is necessary to ascertain the source of the information and the uses to which the relevant document is put. It is worth recalling the nature of the promise made to a receiving party when a sending party affixes a digital signature to a document or message:

'Bob receives a message digitally signed by Alice with Alice's digital signature certificate attached. Alice's public key is incorporated into the certificate. The certificate purports to bind Alice's name with her public key, and in turn the certificate purports to assure Bob that the message was signed using a key verifiable by a key certified in a certificate issued to Alice.'

The nature of this promise is well illustrated by the following comment from the Select Committee on Trade and Industry, Seventh Report, House of Commons Session 1998-99, paragraph 12: 'Written signatures are tightly associated with people and weakly associated with documents, whilst digital signatures are tightly bound to documents and weakly bound to individuals (or identities).' The crucial point to remember is that a digital signature does not, of itself, provide evidence that the sending party actually caused the digital signature to be affixed to the message or document. This proposition can, in most instances of an open communication systems, be relevant in respect of any form of electronic signature. Where a certification authority is involved within the framework of a public key infrastructure, all the certification authority can do is give evidence about how the certificate was formed, where the information was obtained, and if they verified the information, what methods were used to verify the information. Thus a certification authority can give evidence as to the formation of the certificate, but the certificate cannot be adduced as evidence of the truth of the facts stated within it.

In civil proceedings, the Judicial Studies Board indicate that a certificate may be hearsay evidence as to the identity of the public key, and if a party relies on such a certificate, they must meet the requirements relating to notice of this evidence in accordance with section 2 of the Civil Evidence Act 1995 and the provisions of CPR Pt 33.[2] Once the party relying on the public key provides the relevant notice and particulars, it will be for the other party to raise an objection as to the authenticity or otherwise of the certificate. A party to civil litigation is taken to admit, in accordance with CPR Pt 31, the authenticity of a document disclosed to them under Pt 32, r. 19(1) unless they serve notice that they wish the document to be proved at trial. As far as criminal proceedings are concerned, a judge will be required to consider whether a certificate is admissible under the terms of s 24 of the Criminal Justice Act 1988.

1   Annex B to the International Telecommunication Union ITU-T X.509 (03/2000) 'Series X: Data networks and open system communications directory, ITU-T Recommendation X.509', available online at www.itu.int/rec/T-REC-X.509-200003-I/en.

2   Judicial Studies Board 'Digital Signature Guidelines' July 2000 paragraph 42, available online at www.jsboard.co.uk/publications/digisigs/; Katie Quinn, 'Computer evidence in criminal proceedings: Farewell to the ill-fated s.69 of the Police and Criminal Evidence Act 1984', *The International Journal of Evidence & Proof*, Volume 5, Number 3, 174–187.

ASSERTIONS CAN DIFFER

14.17   Much will depend on whether the recipient is suing the certification authority, or the purported signer. This, in turn, depends on what statement the purported signing party makes about the signature. For instance, the statement might be, 'Yes, that was signed with my private key, but not by me or with my authority.' In which case, the certification authority is not involved, because there was nothing wrong with its certificate. However, it might be, 'That was signed with a key having nothing to do with me.' In this case, the claim is against the certification authority that certified the verification key. If the certification authority admits it signed the relevant certificate, then it is irrelevant if the recipient becomes a verifying party and takes action to undertake due diligence. The issue is whether it is liable for any errors. If the certification authority denies signing the certificate, then the issue may depend on which certification authority cross-signed the relevant certificate. It will be difficult for a certification authority to admit it is their certificate, but claim that it should not be trusted because the verifying party (if the recipient chooses to become a verifying party) followed the chain of certificates. It cannot be for a certification authority to determine whether a recipient should have trusted its signature or not.

The admissibility of the electronic signature

14.18   The Electronic Communications Act 2000 permits an electronic signature to perform a similar role to that of a manuscript signature. The definition of an electronic signature is provided in s 7(2):

'(2) For the purposes of this section an electronic signature is so much of anything in electronic form as:

(a)   is incorporated into or otherwise logically associated with any electronic communication or electronic data; and

(b) purports to be so incorporated or associated for the purpose of being used in establishing the authenticity of the communication or data, the integrity of the communication or data, or both.'

An electronic signature is admissible in evidence in relation to the authenticity or integrity of the communication (discussed fully in chapter 4), as provided for in s 7(1):

'7(1) In any legal proceedings:

(a) an electronic signature incorporated into or logically associated with a particular electronic communication or particular electronic data, and

(b) the certification by any person of such a signature,

shall each be admissible in evidence in relation to any question as to the authenticity of the communication or data or as to the integrity of the communication or data.'

In the context of the Act, the meaning of authenticity relates to the single issue of verifying the person or entity, as provided for in s 15(2):

'In this Act:

(a) references to the authenticity of any communication or data are references to any one or more of the following:
    (i)   whether the communication or data comes from a particular person or other source;
    (ii) whether it is accurately timed and dated;
    (iii) whether it is intended to have legal effect;
    and

(b) references to the integrity of any communication or data are references to whether there has been any tampering with or other modification of the communication or data.'

On the issue of the authenticity of a communication or data, the provisions of s 15(2)(a)(i) to (iii) will be taken into account when considering whether the communication or data can be considered authentic.

(a) The communication or data comes from a particular person or other source (presumably a legal entity). As discussed above, there is no nexus between the certificate and public key in a digital signature and the affixing of the digital signature to a document or communication by a sending party. Similarly, it does not follow that where a contract is entered over the internet for the supply of goods or services, that the person who clicked the 'I accept' icon is the same individual represented in the contract. Thus it appears that the parties to a dispute may have to grapple with the issue of who signed a document or message where the actual signing is in dispute.

(b)   Crucial in electronic evidence is an audit trail that helps to fix the creation and movement of electronic data in time and space. It does not follow that the communication or data will be accurately timed and dated, and evidence may well be required in relation to these issues.

(c)   Whether the signing of a communication or document is to have legal effect will be the subject of close examination, depending on the nature of the case. The extrinsic evidence surrounding the facts will have a bearing on any proceedings. For instance, a document may be signed after a lengthy period of negotiations between two parties. If the document is signed with an electronic signature, and the party signing the document refuses to acknowledge they intended their signature to have a legally binding effect, evidence of the process leading up to the signing may be pertinent as to their intention when affixing the electronic signature to the document.

The Act provides, in s 7(3) for any person to certify that the electronic signature is a valid means of establishing the authenticity and integrity of the communication or data or both:

'For the purposes of this section an electronic signature incorporated into or associated with a particular electronic communication or particular electronic data is certified by any person if that person (whether before or after the making of the communication) has made a statement confirming that:

(a)   the signature,

(b)   a means of producing, communicating or verifying the signature, or

(c)   a procedure applied to the signature,

is (either alone or in combination with other factors) a valid means of establishing the authenticity of the communication or data, the integrity of the communication or data, or both.'

It will be useful to examine the provisions of s 7(3) to illustrate the nature of the evidence that may be required to demonstrate the authenticity and integrity of an electronic signature. Where an electronic signature is incorporated into or associated with a document or communication, a statement can be made by a person (it does not have to be a trusted third party, and might be made by the purported signer) confirming that:

(a)   The signature is a valid means of establishing the authenticity or integrity of the communication or data, or both. On the face of this sub-clause, this appears to be perfectly straightforward. Providing the sending party ensures their private key and certificate are safe from misuse or theft, it may be possible to state that the electronic signature used, if a digital signature, is capable of establishing the authenticity or integrity of the communication or data, or both.

(b) The means of producing the electronic signature may be more problematic. If the sender has produced their own key pair, then it appears that the sender can make such a statement, although whether such a statement will be accepted by a recipient that relies on the signature is debatable, and perhaps depends on the prior existence of a relationship between sender and recipient. Where the key pair is produced by a trusted third party, the statement may be more convincing, but information about the creation, internal management and security processes affecting the use of the private key may be equally open to cross-examination in either case. As described above, the public key must be incorporated into the certificate, so the certification authority, in the event a digital signature is at issue, will also be required to proffer a statement with similar questions to be asked as set out for the entity producing a key pair.

(c) It is not quite clear what is meant by the means of communicating the signature, unless it refers to the actual method by which a digital or other type of signature is delivered to the subscribing party. If this is what is meant by 'communicating,' then the certification authority, if one is used, will provide the statement. Once again, the issues relating to security may be considered in detail under cross-examination.

(d) The problems relating to verification of the signature are complex, as described above, and it is difficult to know if there is any single person, other than the recipient of an electronic signature (particularly a digital signature), who can provide an adequate statement of the verification procedure.

(e) It is uncertain what is meant by the words 'a procedure applied to the signature,' unless it refers to the method by which a signature was created, or the procedure of using the public key to test the association between the private key and the signature.

There is a more detailed discussion of these provisions elsewhere in this text, and it is not proposed to rehearse the same matters here.

Assessment of evidence

Burden of proof

14.19 Where litigation is contemplated if an electronic signature is the subject of a dispute, both parties will have to be aware of the volumes and quality of evidence they may have to bring before the court to prove their case or disprove the case of the other party. The nature of electronic evidence will be discussed briefly at a later point in this chapter, but an introduction to the various duties that the parties will incur in the process of litigation may serve to remind them of the difficulties they face, should they decide a judge is the only person to effect an adequate resolution to the problem.

The persuasive burden describes a requirement of a rule of law that is imposed on a party to prove or refute a fact in issue. The fact must be proved or disproved to the required standard of proof. It is for the party who asserts the facts of their case to prove it. If the party asserting their case fails to discharge the burden, the decision must go against them. In criminal cases, the general rule is the burden is for the prosecution to prove the defendant's guilt beyond reasonable doubt. The general rule in both civil and criminal proceedings is that the party bearing the persuasive burden also bears the evidential burden. This is usually discharged by adducing evidence, which can also be obtained from witnesses for the other side in cross-examination.

ELECTRONIC SIGNATURES AND THE BURDEN OF PROOF

Non-repudiation

14.20 By way of an introduction, there is a term, 'non-repudiation', that has become part of the vocabulary of digital signatures. Non-repudiation does not mean the system for non-repudiation is perfect. When an engineer uses the term in an engineering sense, they should mean that there is a high (and specifiable) degree of probability that the protocol can demonstrate a document or message was sent or received by a particular computer. The logic then seeks to take one step further, from the engineering domain into the legal domain, by arguing that if the system can demonstrate a message or document was sent or received, then it should be for the recipient to demonstrate is was not sent or received by them. The technical purpose is to bind users to specific actions in such a way that if they deny taking the action, they either demonstrate an intention to deceive, or they have been negligent in failing to secure the use of their private key adequately.

In legal terms, the meaning of 'non-repudiation' is different to that used in the engineering sense. A manuscript signature can be repudiated for a number of reasons, including that the signature is a forgery, or that, whilst not a forgery, the signature was obtained as a result of unconscionable conduct by a party to a transaction, fraud instigated by a third party or undue influence exerted by a third party. It is important to ensure the technical meaning does not override the need to restrain the meaning within a legal context. Where engineers use the term, it should not be mistaken that they are using it in a legal context, despite their misunderstanding that the term, in their view, should have a legal meaning.

The term 'non-repudiation' in the engineering sense for technical purposes is a property, probably attained through cryptographic methods, which demonstrates the message was sent from a particular computer.[1] However, non-repudiation is of no benefit without a secure time stamping service to demonstrate that a particular event occurred at a given time and date, or that a specific item of data existed before a specific date. This technical meaning of the term has begun to be used in a legal sense by vendors of the public key infrastructure, which in turn has tended to confuse legislators.[2] It has been suggested that the technical response by the International Organisation for Standardisation[3] is either to deny the right of the individual to repudiate an electronic signature or shifts the burden of proof from the recipient to the alleged user.[4]

1   See paragraph 1.20 of 'Digital Signature Guidelines Legal Infrastructure for Certification Authorities and Secure Electronic Commerce' (Information Security Committee Electronic Commerce and Information technology division Section of Science and Technology, American Bar Association, 1996) available online at www.abanet.org/dch/committee.cfm?com=ST230002.
2   Bruce Schneier *Secrets & Lies Digital Security in a Networked World* (John Wiley & Sons, 2000), 235 and Adrian McCullagh and William Caelli, 'Non-Repudiation in the Digital Environment', 5, www.firstmonday.org/issues/issue5_8/mccullagh/.
3   ISO/IEC TR 14516:2002, Information technology – Security techniques – Guidelines for the use and management of Trusted Third Party services.
4   McCullagh and Caelli, 3–4.

REPUDIATING ELECTRONIC SIGNATURES

14.21   A fundamental issue with respect to electronic signatures is the connection between the mental state of the person who may wish to be bound by the affixing of the electronic signature to a communication or document, and the act of affixing the electronic signature to the electronic message or document. The following issues are pertinent when establishing a nexus between the electronic communication and the electronic signature:

(a)   Whether the genuine user intended to be bound by the contents of the electronic document.

(b)   If another person used the private key without authorization, how they obtained access to the key.

(c)   Who should bear responsibility for the unauthorized use.

The party challenging the admissibility of the electronic signature may be making either one or all of the following claims:

(a)   The security used by the sender was not sufficient to prevent a third party from gaining access to their computer or system and making improper use of their key.

(b)   The procedures and technical abilities (such as the means of producing, communicating or verifying the signature) of the trusted third party were at fault.

(c)   Another organization in the chain that links the sending of the certificate and its receipt by the relying party, other than the trusted third party, was at fault.

Whichever party has the burden of proof will be required to submit evidence in response to the provisions of s 15(2) of the Electronic Communications Act

2000, together with any other extrinsic evidence that may be necessary to support the evidential burden. There is no doubt that the technology can, to a high degree of probability, prove that an electronic signature was affixed to a communication, but it cannot prove who made the signature. Given the state of the technology, it may be reasonable to infer that the holder named in the certificate affixed the electronic signature to the communication. However, the inference is weaker where there is little or no security in place on the computer or system upon which the private key sits.[1]

1   Mark Sneddon, 'Legal liability and e-transactions', Commonwealth of Australia, 2000, paragraph 3.2 (b)(i), available online at www.unpan1.un.org/intradoc/groups/public/documents/ APCITY/UNPAN014676.pdf.

RELIABILITY OF CERTIFYING CERTIFICATES AND BURDEN OF PROOF

14.22   Regardless of the technical meaning of the term 'non-repudiation', there are a number of problems that affect the reliability of systems which are used to affix digital signatures to an electronic communication:

(a)   The confusing design on the screen, which can lead a user to activate the signing function without knowing the significance others attach to the signature.

(b)   The software application may be set to send a receipt, but the recipient may not know the original sender sent the receipt. This also raises the question as to whether the receipt is authentic.

(c)   A design flaw in the public key infrastructure.

(d)   The open nature of the internet, which means hackers could infect computers with malicious software that can be designed to steal private keys or relay the keystrokes of the user, thereby obtaining the passwords used to obtain access to a private key. The risks of hackers gaining entry to computers and networks increased with Digital Subscriber Link (DSL) and cable modem technologies. Without a DSL connection, the computer is assigned a dynamic address each time a person connects to the internet. Whilst connected on an DSL line, a computer may have either a permanent Internet Protocol (IP) address or a dynamic IP address, depending on the internet service provider (ISP), although a customer can request a static address. Where a computer has a persistent connection to the internet, the risk to attack and penetration by a third party is greater. With a permanent IP address, a user is more vulnerable to attack by a hacker.

The general rule with respect to signed documents is this: a person is normally bound by their signature to a document, even if they fail to read and understand the content.[1] Where a party relies on a signed document and wishes to enforce it against the signing party, the relying party must prove the signature is that of the signing party, or the document was authorized by the signing party. This is so where the signing party claims they did not sign the document, or if they did sign the document, that they did so under duress or because of the fraud of a third party. It is not for the signing party to prove that they did not authorize the document or sign it.

In the case of *Brown v National Westminster Bank Ltd*,[2] Mrs Brown's signature was forged on a number of cheques. Under s 24 of the Bills of Exchange Act 1882, where a signature is forged or it is signed by a person not authorized to sign the cheque, the signature is not effective and does not confer any rights on the person possessing the cheque. This is the position even if the cheque has been forged by the negligence of the customer. The bank has a range of duties, as noted by Roskill J at 196(b), particularly to exercise all reasonable care about the advice offered, but also to only do that which the customer agrees to. However, this does not mean that the customer is always right. A customer can be precluded from claiming against the bank. In this instance, the bank manager took what action he could to alert Mrs Brown to the possibility that a number of cheques drawn on her account were forged. When it was clear that Mrs Brown did not take any action, he alerted Mrs Brown's son to his suspicions. In an action against the bank, it was for the bank to prove it took sufficient action to demonstrate it had undertaken due care. The burden then fell on Mrs Brown to show the cheques were forged, which she failed to do.

A person has a defence where they have been misled into signing a document that is essentially different to that which they intended to sign, a state of affairs that has usually, but not always, been induced by a fraud perpetrated upon the party signing the document.[3] However, this does not mean that a person should fail to exercise care when they affix their signature to a document in the absence of a fundamental mistake as to the content of the document. This occurred in *Saunders v Anglia Building Society*,[4] where Mrs Gallie signed what she understood was a deed of gift of her house to her nephew, but it was, in fact, a deed of assignment to a third party. Mrs Gallie raised the defence that she thought the effect of the document was to give her house to her nephew, but in fact it assigned her rights to a fraudulent third party.[5] It was agreed by the members of the House of Lords that the identity of the person to whom the house was assigned did not make the deed totally different in character to the document Mrs Gallie intended to sign, and her defence failed. Lord Hodson offered the following observations, 1019E, respecting the use of a signature:

'Want of care on the part of the person who signs a document which he afterwards seeks to disown is relevant. The burden of proving non est factum is on the party disowning his signature; this includes proof that he or she took care. There is no burden on the opposite party to prove want of care. The word 'negligence' in this connection does not involve the proposition that want of care is irrelevant unless there can be found a specific duty to the opposite party to take care.'

In his judgment, Viscount Dilhorne agreed with the comments made by Lord Hodson, and commented, 1023(E):

'In every case the person who signs the document must exercise reasonable care, and what amounts to reasonable care will depend on the circumstances of the case and the nature of the document which it is thought is being signed. It is reasonable to expect that more care should be exercised if the document is thought to be of an important character than if it is not.'

1   *British Estate Investment Society Ltd v Jackson (H M Inspector of Taxes)* (1954–1958) 37 Tax Cas 79 Danckwerts J at 87: 'It seems to me that the presumption in law is that the document has been properly signed until the contrary has been shown by a person who desires to upset that conclusion.'
2   [1964] 2 Lloyd's Rep 187 QBD Commercial Court.
3   An example is where a party signed a blank hire-purchase proposal form, and the dealer inserted incorrect figures before sending it to the finance company: *United Dominions Trust Ltd v Western* [1976] QB 513.
4   *Saunders v Anglia Building Society* [1971] AC 1004; [1970] 3 WLR 1078; 114 SJ 885; [1970] 3 All ER 961.
5   Known as 'non est factum'.

SHIFTING THE ONUS OF PROOF – UNCITRAL

14.23   It has been suggested that the technical meaning of 'non-repudiation' has the effect of either shifting the onus of proof from the recipient of the alleged electronic signature, or denying the right of the user of the certifying certificate to repudiate the certificate.[1] Whilst it is clear that 'non-repudiation' has different meanings in the legal sense and the technical sense, there is a further difference between the two, as pointed out by the same authors. That is the technical meaning relates to events that have taken place after the signature has taken place, and has no relation to the actual mechanism of the affixing of the digital certificate.[2]

The development of the two sets of uniform rules prepared by UNCITRAL, the Model Law on Electronic Commerce and the Model Law on Electronic Signatures, have influenced the legislation relating to electronic signatures produced by states.[3] In particular, both Model laws provide for the duties of the participants when using electronic signatures.

1   McCullagh and Caelli, 4.
2   McCullagh and Caelli, 6.
3   The Model Law on Electronic Commerce was adopted by the Commission on 12 June 1996, following its 605th meeting, which in turn was adopted by the General Assembly in Resolution 51/162 at its *85th plenary meeting on 16 December 1996*, and includes an additional article 5 bis as adopted by the Commission at its 31st meeting in June 1998. The Model Law on Electronic Signatures was adopted by the Commission at its 727th meeting on 5 July 2001.

Model Law on Electronic Commerce

14.24 Of relevance are the provisions of article 13 to the Model Law. Note 83 to the Guide to Enactment indicates that article 13 originates in article 5 of the UNCITRAL Model Law on International Credit Transfers. This defines the obligations of the sender of a payment order. Bearing in mind such a transfer would normally be subject to a contractual agreement between the parties, setting out the technical procedures agreed between each party (and any other parties in the chain) for such a transfer, it seems improbable that such a provision should affect a public key infrastructure which uses the open network of the internet. However, the text of article 13 is of interest, because the Model Law on Electronic Signatures was developed on the premise that it could have been incorporated into an extended version of the Model Law on Electronic Commerce:[1]

'Article 13. Attribution of data messages

(1) A data message is that of the originator if it was sent by the originator itself.

(2) As between the originator and the addressee, a data message is deemed to be that of the originator if it was sent:
   (a) by a person who had the authority to act on behalf of the originator in respect of that data message; or
   (b) by an information system programmed by, or on behalf of, the originator to operate automatically.

(3) As between the originator and the addressee, an addressee is entitled to regard a data message as being that of the originator, and to act on that assumption, if:
   (a) in order to ascertain whether the data message was that of the originator, the addressee properly applied a procedure previously agreed to by the originator for that purpose; or
   (b) the data message as received by the addressee resulted from the actions of a person whose relationship with the originator or with any agent of the originator enabled that person to gain access to a method used by the originator to identify data messages as its own.

(4) Paragraph (3) does not apply:
   (a) as of the time when the addressee has both received notice from the originator that the data message is not that of the originator, and had reasonable time to act accordingly; or
   (b) in a case within paragraph (3)(b), at any time when the addressee knew or should have known, had it exercised reasonable care or used any agreed procedure, that the data message was not that of the originator.

(5) Where a data message is that of the originator or is deemed to be that of the originator, or the addressee is entitled to act on that assumption, then, as between the originator and the addressee, the addressee is entitled to regard the data message as received as being what the originator intended to send, and to act on that assumption. The addressee is not so entitled when it knew or should have known, had it exercised reasonable care or used any agreed procedure, that the transmission resulted in any error in the data message as received.

(6) The addressee is entitled to regard each data message received as a separate data message and to act on that assumption, except to the extent that it duplicates another data message and the addressee knew or should have known, had it exercised reasonable care or used any agreed procedure, that the data message was a duplicate.'

It is pertinent to note the points made in the notes to Enactment in relation to the provisions of article 13. Guidance note 83 states that it is not the purpose of article 13 to assign responsibility between the parties, rather the purpose of the Article is to deal '... with attribution of data messages by establishing a presumption that under certain circumstances a data message would be considered as a message of the originator, and goes on to qualify that presumption in case the addressee knew or ought to have known that the data message was not that of the originator.' Earlier drafts of article 13 included, according to Guidance note 92, an additional paragraph, '... expressing the principle that the attribution of authorship of a data message to the originator should not interfere with the legal consequences of that message, which should be determined by other applicable rules of national law.' Whilst the article as presently drafted does not expressly make this point, nevertheless it seems clear from the provisions of article 13(1) that the onus of proof alters between the parties. The logic can be described as follows:

(a) If a user chooses to publish a verification key, it is assumed that when it is used, it will have been used by the user. It is presumed that the user, once they have a digital signature, will ensure that only they or a person authorized to use the signature will use it.

(b) Where a recipient wishes to rely upon the digital signature, provided they carry out adequate procedures to demonstrate the authenticity of the certifying certificate under article 13 (3)(b) and (5)[2] (i.e. undertake the verifying procedures set out for a digital signature), the recipient, thereupon becoming a verifying party, is permitted to assume the digital signature is that of the sender. In this instance, the recipient is under a duty to carry out such procedures. Whilst it cannot be said that there is a complete reversal of the burden of proof in the actions taken by the verifying party, by undertaking such actions, the verifying party may be taken to have accepted there is a direct link between the certificate (if a digital signature is used) and the sender. It can be argued that the verifying party will be deemed to have satisfied themselves that they could rely on the relationship between the certificate and the affixing of the signature to the message, above and beyond the promise made by the certification authority, that can only promise that the message was signed using a certificate issued to the user.

(c) Should the sender dispute they sent the message with the electronic signature attached, it should be for the sender to demonstrate that they did not send the message, but this proposition is to be doubted if the recipient becomes a verifying party, having undertaken due diligence.

1   Guide to Enactment, paragraph 65.
2   The provisions of Article 13(3)(a) will not apply unless the originating party agreed with the receiving party in advance what, if any, procedure the recipient should undertake before relying on the signature.

Model Law on Electronic Signatures

14.25   Further guidance is also available from the Model Law on Electronic Signatures. The Model Law does not deal in detail about the issues of liability that may affect the participants of an electronic signature, but it does consider the relationship between signatory and the certification authority by outlining the expected conduct that each should undertake in their respective roles.[1] The provisions of article 8 refer to the conduct of the signatory, as follows:

'Conduct of the signatory

1.   Where signature creation data can be used to create a signature that has legal effect, each signatory shall:

(a)   Exercise reasonable care to avoid unauthorized use of its signature creation data;

(b)   Without undue delay, utilize means made available by the certification service provider pursuant to article 9 of this Law, or otherwise use reasonable efforts, to notify any person that may reasonably be expected by the signatory to rely on or to provide services in support of the electronic signature if:

(i)   The signatory knows that the signature creation data have been compromised; or

(ii)   The circumstances known to the signatory give rise to a substantial risk that the signature creation data may have been compromised;

(c)   Where a certificate is used to support the electronic signature, exercise reasonable care to ensure the accuracy and completeness of all material representations made by the signatory that are relevant to the certificate throughout its lifecycle or that are to be included in the certificate.

2.   A signatory shall bear the legal consequences of its failure to satisfy the requirements of paragraph 1.'

There is a clear requirement that where a party decides to use an electronic signature, especially when in digital format using the public key infrastructure, they are expected to take reasonable care to protect the signature creation data and prevent unauthorized use of the signature creation data. The aim in drafting the provisions of articles 8, 9 and 11 is to provide a minimal 'code of conduct' for the parties involved with the use of an electronic signature.[2] Subparagraphs (a) and (c) apply to all forms of electronic signature, whilst subparagraph (c) only applies to digital certificates supported by a certificate. The use of the word 'reasonable' in this article illustrates the need for individual states to define what will be considered reasonable in the light of a dispute occurring. The provisions of paragraph 2 clearly leave it to a national court to determine what, if any, legal consequences will follow where a signing party fails to take care under the provisions of paragraph 1(a) or fails to inform receiving parties where their signature creation device has been used without authority or compromised.

A similar duty is held to be necessary for the relying party as set out in article 11:

'Conduct of the relying party

A relying party shall bear the legal consequences of its failure:

(a)   To take reasonable steps to verify the reliability of an electronic signature; or

(b)   Where an electronic signature is supported by a certificate, to take reasonable steps:
   (i)   To verify the validity, suspension or revocation of the certificate; and
   (ii)   To observe any limitation with respect to the certificate.'

Interestingly, article 2(f) of the Model Law does not distinguish between a recipient that relies on an electronic signature and a recipient that undertakes to verify the authenticity of an electronic signature. The meaning of a relying party is 'a person that may act on the basis of a certificate or an electronic signature.' Thus a relying party may decide to act on the basis of an electronic signature, but is not required to undertake any verification procedures. Note 148 in the Guide to Enactment identifies and separates two issues: whether the electronic signature is valid, and whether it is reasonable for a recipient to rely on an electronic signature that does not reach the standard set out in article 6. The note makes it clear that the intention is for the recipient to bear in mind whether and to what extent they should rely on the signature. The validity of the signature should not depend on the conduct of the relying party, although it is debatable whether certification authorities, in drafting their terms of trade and certification practice statements, have fully grasped this point. A close look at the provisions of article 6 will help to illuminate the underlying foundations relating to the validity of an electronic signature:

'Compliance with a requirement for a signature

1. Where the law requires a signature of a person, that requirement is met in relation to a data message if an electronic signature is used that is as reliable as was appropriate for the purpose for which the data message was generated or communicated, in the light of all the circumstances, including any relevant agreement.

2. Paragraph 1 applies whether the requirement referred to therein is in the form of an obligation or whether the law simply provides consequences for the absence of a signature.

3. An electronic signature is considered to be reliable for the purpose of satisfying the requirement referred to in paragraph 1 if:

(a) The signature creation data are, within the context in which they are used, linked to the signatory and to no other person;

(b) The signature creation data were, at the time of signing, under the control of the signatory and of no other person;

(c) Any alteration to the electronic signature, made after the time of signing, is detectable; and

(d) Where a purpose of the legal requirement for a signature is to provide assurance as to the integrity of the information to which it relates, any alteration made to that information after the time of signing is detectable.

4. Paragraph 3 does not limit the ability of any person:

(a) To establish in any other way, for the purpose of satisfying the requirement referred to in paragraph 1, the reliability of an electronic signature; or

(b) To adduce evidence of the non-reliability of an electronic signature.

5. The provisions of this article do not apply to the following: [...].'

The provisions of this article are considered core to the Model Law, and build upon article 7 of the Model Law on Electronic Commerce. The intention is to offer guidance as to how the test of reliability in paragraph 1(b) of article 7 can be satisfied.[3] Article 7 of the Model Law on Electronic Commerce reads as follows:

'Article 7. Signature

(1) Where the law requires a signature of a person, that requirement is met in relation to a data message if:

(a) a method is used to identify that person and to indicate that person's approval of the information contained in the data message; and

(b) that method is as reliable as was appropriate for the purpose for which the data message was generated or communicated, in the light of all the circumstances, including any relevant agreement.

(2) Paragraph (1) applies whether the requirement therein is in the form of an obligation or whether the law simply provides consequences for the absence of a signature.

(3) The provisions of this article do not apply to the following: [...]'

The intention behind the drafting of article 6 is to establish criteria that would apply to the technical form of an electronic signature that would establish certain legal effects. Legal effects would follow from electronic signature techniques that were recognized as reliable, and there would be no legal effect where an electronic signature technique was of lesser reliability than a reliable technique.[4] The provision of article 7 paragraph 1(a) of the Model Law on Electronic Commerce will produce a legal effect, no matter what form the electronic signature takes. However, it follows that what will constitute a reliable method of signature in the light of the circumstances will depend on what the trier of a fact will determine after the signature was used – perhaps months, if not years after its use. As a result, the intention behind the drafting article 6(3) in the Model Law on Electronic Signatures is to create a benefit in favour of particular types of techniques for affixing electronic signatures to a document or message. Thus the intention is to provide for the legal effect of, primarily, a digital signature, although it is left to the individual state to establish the legal effects and whether a presumption should apply.[5] The aim of article 6 is to provide for a presumption that the signatory, when they affix their electronic signature to a document or message, is presumed to have approved the linking of their identity with the data contained in the document or message.[6] *It is not a presumption that the person who has signed the data is in fact the signatory.*[7] Legal effects will only flow from the affixing of the signature if the nature of the document or message and surrounding circumstances indicate such an inference should be so drawn.[8]

The third party to a digital signature is the certification authority. The Model Law, in article 9, sets out the type of conduct expected of a certification authority.

'Conduct of the certification service provider

1. Where a certification service provider provides services to support an electronic signature that may be used for legal effect as a signature, that certification service provider shall:

(a) Act in accordance with representations made by it with respect to its policies and practices;

    (b)   Exercise reasonable care to ensure the accuracy and completeness of all material representations made by it that are relevant to the certificate throughout its lifecycle or that are included in the certificate;

    (c)   Provide reasonably accessible means that enable a relying party to ascertain from the certificate:

        (i)   The identity of the certification service provider;

        (ii)   That the signatory that is identified in the certificate had control of the signature creation data at the time when the certificate was issued;

        (iii)   That signature creation data were valid at or before the time when the certificate was issued;

    (d)   Provide reasonably accessible means that enable a relying party to ascertain, where relevant, from the certificate or otherwise:

        (i)   The method used to identify the signatory;

        (ii)   Any limitation on the purpose or value for which the signature creation data or the certificate may be used;

        (iii)   That the signature creation data are valid and have not been compromised;

        (iv)   Any limitation on the scope or extent of liability stipulated by the certification service provider;

        (v)   Whether means exist for the signatory to give notice pursuant to article 8, paragraph 1 (b), of this Law;

        (vi)   Whether a timely revocation service is offered;

    (e)   Where services under subparagraph (d) (v) are offered, provide a means for a signatory to give notice pursuant to article 8, paragraph 1 (b), of this Law and, where services under subparagraph (d) (vi) are offered, ensure the availability of a timely revocation service;

    (f)   Utilize trustworthy systems, procedures and human resources in performing its services.

2.   A certification service provider shall bear the legal consequences of its failure to satisfy the requirements of paragraph 1.'

A certification authority is expected to undertake its obligations as described in its own terms and policies. Paragraph 1(c) sets out what is considered to be one of the essential contents of the Model Law, and in relation to digital signatures, it is necessary to be able to associate the signatory with the public key as well as with the private key.[9] Note 146 of the Guide to Enactment indicates it was originally considered necessary to address the issues of liability, but it has now been left to individual states to determine. However, the note does include a number of factors that it is suggested would be useful to take into account when assessing the liability of a certification authority:

'(a) the cost of obtaining the certificate;

(b)   the nature of the information being certified;

(c)   the existence and extent of any limitation on the purpose for which the certificate may be used;

(d)   the existence of any statement limiting the scope or extent of the liability of the certification service provider; and

(e)   any contributory conduct by the relying party.'

It is to be noted that although the British government claims the provisions of the Electronic Communications Act 2000 are consistent with the various international enactments, it is doubtful that this is the case.[10]

1   Guide to Enactment, paragraph 77 also states that the issues relating to liability are left to applicable law.
2   Guide to Enactment, paragraph 137.
3   Guide to Enactment, paragraph 115.
4   Guide to Enactment, paragraph 118.
5   Guide to Enactment, paragraph 119.
6   This encompasses the use of corporate signature creation data, where several employees share the same method of creating a corporate signature. As a signature is created, so the data must be capable of identifying the particular individual that created the signature data. Guide to Enactment, paragraph 121.
7   This point is made in paragraph 78 to the Guide to Enactment, although the observation is made that 'At best, the digital signature provides assurance that it is attributable to the signatory.'
8   Guide to Enactment, paragraph, 120.
9   Guide to Enactment, paragraph 143.
10   Explanatory Note 19 reads: 'This Act is consistent with, and seeks to implement, certain provisions of the EU Electronic Signatures Directive (1999/93/EC), which was adopted on 13 December 1999 (OJ L 13/12, 19.1.2000). The Directive is intended to facilitate the use of electronic signatures and to contribute to their legal recognition throughout the European Union. Further details can be found on the EU website at: www.europa.eu.int/eur-lex/en/lif/dat/1999/en_399L0093.html. The Act is also compatible with the Cryptography Guidelines, published by the Organisation for Economic Co-operation and Development (OECD) on 19 March 97 (available on the OECD website at: www.oecd.org/subject/e_commerce), and the United Nations Commission on International Trade Law (UNCITRAL) Model Law on Electronic Commerce (available on the UN website at www.un.or.at/uncitral/english/texts/electcom/ml-ec.htm). Finally, the Act is also consistent, in scope and purpose, with the draft Uniform Rules on Electronic Signatures and Certification Authorities, which are currently under development in UNCITRAL.'

THE ONUS OF PROOF — ENGLAND AND WALES — COMMON LAW

14.26   In the light of the guidance provided by the UNCITRAL Model Laws, it seems self evident that there is need to consider how to allocate liability for an electronic signature between the participating parties. A person has total control over the use of their manuscript signature, and the legal rules that apply to manuscript signatures reflect this physical reality. However, once the accepted format of the signature changes, so it may be considered appropriate, depending on the nature of the transaction, for the legal rules that apply to the new format of signature to reflect the different range of risks associated with the new manifestation of signature. Consider the example of Charles Goodman, the solicitor who used a rubber stamp to sign a letter that accompanied his bill of costs.[1] Although the control of the rubber stamp was not the subject of judicial comment, Evershed MR noted at 554, that Mr Goodman '... kept the stamp locked up in his own room so as to be available only for his own use.' Although neither Mr Goodman's actions nor the comment by Evershed MR make an explicit point about taking reasonable care of the rubber stamp, nevertheless the implication that the rubber stamp should be kept safe is very clear. It is clear that Mr Goodman took reasonable care to ensure only he had access to the rubber stamp, and the observation by Evershed MR implied that this made the use of the rubber stamp acceptable as a method of authenticating documents. If Evershed MR had considered the matter further, that he might have reached the conclusion that there is a reasonable expectation in circumstances where a person decides to use a rubber stamp as a form of signature, that they can be expected, as a rule of law, to provide for the security of the use of the signature, and to take appropriate steps to guard against its use by unauthorized persons, as discussed in the dissenting opinion of Williams J in *Robb v The Pennsylvania Company for Insurance on Lives and Granting Annuities*,[2] discussed below. The matter of the security of a rubber stamp was also mentioned briefly in *British Estate Investment Society Ltd v Jackson (H M Inspector of Taxes)*[3] where an Additional Commissioner regularly used a rubber stamp to sign significant volumes of documents. In his judgment, Danckwerts J mentioned the measures taken in the office to provide for the safety and unauthorized use of the rubber stamp.[4] Once again, there is no explicit mention of the need for a signing party to provide for the security of the rubber stamp, and to protect it against misuse. However, the action of the signing party in providing for the security of the rubber stamp suggests that, even without a rule of law requiring them to take steps to secure the rubber stamp, they took such precautions because the nature of the instrument thus created permits others to use a recognized means of identifying and authenticating a document. If this train of thought is accepted, a number of points can be made in support of the requirements required by the UNCITRAL Model Laws and the contractual obligations that certification authorities seek to impose on subscribing parties and receiving parties, as follows:

(a) The evidence from Charles Goodman in *Goodman v J Eban Limited* and of the Additional Commissioner in *British Estate Investment Society Ltd v Jackson (H M Inspector of Taxes)* demonstrates that when the signing party acquired a rubber stamp as a means of affixing their signature to a document, they took appropriate precautions to safeguard it from misuse and theft.

(b) The comments by Evershed MR[5] and Danckwerts J,[6] imply that the authorized use of the rubber stamp rested on the care with which the signing party took of the item, and because the security of the rubber stamp was assured, the signature affixed to the document by the rubber stamp was authentic and therefore valid.

(c) In the event the recipient doubted the authenticity of the signature, they can undertake their own form of due diligence to verify the authenticity and validity of the signature. This point was made by Romer LJ at 564 in *Goodman v J Eban Limited* where he pointed out that 'If in fact his clients entertained any doubt as to the authenticity of the letter, nothing could be easier than to ask him, by telephone or letter, to confirm it.' Whilst the point made by Romer LJ is an explicit instruction as to what action the recipient could take, the comment was not necessarily meant to form a legal rule.

Although none of the comments made by the judges in these two cases are sufficient to form a rule of law in relation to such matters, nevertheless they recognized that where technology is used to provide a substitute to so physical an act as the affixing of a manuscript signature to a document, new considerations relating to the presumptions that should apply to signatures must be considered.

On the face of the decision of Waller J in *Standard Bank London Limited v Bank of Tokyo Limited*,[7] it appears that this train of thought may have already been adopted in England and Wales. In this case, the Bank of Tokyo in Kuala Lumpur arranged for three tested telexes to be sent to Standard, containing a secret code confirming and authenticating the authorized signatory of three letters of credit with a total face value of US$19.8m, and confirming that the Bank of Tokyo accepted all responsibilities and liabilities under those letters of credit. Evidence was adduced to indicate that banks not only used this system with confidence, but also used it to avoid arguments about authority. In this instance, the tested telexes were sent fraudulently.

The main thrust of the Bank of Tokyo's case was this: because they could establish that a fraudster must have been working in their tested telex department, Standard could only rely upon the apparent authority of the tested telexes. As a result, it argued that there was a lower test to establish the lack of apparent authority. Waller J disagreed with this argument at 502C, because the issue was not reliance on apparent authority:

'Standard rely first on a general representation by BOT that if a telex comes by tested telex that telex will be duly authorized by BOT (that representation on any view is authorised);

second they rely on the use of the tested telex mechanism itself as representing that the telex is authorized as the previous representation stated that it would be; and

thirdly they rely on the statement in the telex as being the authorised statement of BOT.'

The Bank of Tokyo was found liable for negligent misrepresentation because the tested telexes could not have been sent without negligence on the bank's part. Whether Standard had a duty to inquire into the authenticity of the tested telexes depended, in the view of Waller J, on the circumstances of each and every case.[8] Tested telexes contain codes or tests, which are secret between the sender and the recipient. This allows the recipient to accept without question that the telex was sent by and with the authority of the sender. The tested telexes in this instance were sent through other banks, because the Bank of Tokyo in Kuala Lumpur did not have a means of directly authenticating telexes between itself and Standard. By sending tested telexes, banks intend the receiving bank to act on the content without further instructions. This means the receiving bank requires the sending bank to:

(a) Confirm the person signing the document is an authorized signatory.

(b) Verify the signatory is authorized to sign the particular document.

(c) Provide sufficient evidence to satisfy the recipient that the sending bank authorized the sending of the telex.

Superficially, there is a similarity between the circumstances of this case and the public key infrastructure, where the authentication process has to go through so many channels. However, there is a distinction between a tested telex produced in a bank and the public key infrastructure. The authority of a telex is reliant upon internal systems within the bank.[9] No third party is involved in identifying the sender of the telex or authenticating the codes or text sent. In addition, the tested telex is sent through other banks over secure lines of communication. Conversely, the public key infrastructure operates over the internet, which was designed to be open and is, therefore, insecure. The link between the identity and authentication of a user of an electronic signature is not as cohesive as between such trusted parties as banks. There are significantly more links, which neither party has control over, in the chain between the sending party and receiving party of an electronic signature. As a result, it can be argued that there is a distinction between what can be termed a 'secure or closed communication system' and an 'open communications system'. Clearly the burden of proving that an electronic signature was used without authority must be borne by either the user or the relying party. In this instance, Waller J took the view that the sender was in full control of the environment in which the tested telex was sent, and decided that the burden should fall on the sender.

In the context of an open insecure network, however, different criteria might, based upon the protection of the consumer, be applied by the courts. Private individuals are being encouraged to use inherently insecure personal computers for digital signature at the request of parties that intend to rely on such signatures, such as governments and commercial entities. There are two points to note: first, it will be interesting to know if the government carries out the duties of a verifying party each time a subject communicates with a department electronically. Second, it will be for a court to determine what burdens are to be imposed on those who use a private key for the purposes of a digital signature.

1   *Goodman v J Eban Limited* [1954] 1 QB 550; [1954] 1 All ER 763; [1954] 2 WLR 581, CA.
2   40 W.N.C. 129, 3 Pa.Super. 254, 1897 WL 3989 (Pa.Super. 1897) *affirmed by* 186 Pa. 456, 40 A. 969, for dissenting opinion, see 186 Pa. 456, 41 A. 49.
3   (1954–1958) 37 Tax Cas 79; [1956] TR 397; 35 ATC 413; 50 R & IT 33.
4   (1954–1958) 37 Tax Cas 79 at 87.
5   *Goodman v J Eban Limited* [1954] 1 QB 550 at 554.
6   *British Estate Investment Society Ltd v Jackson (H M Inspector of Taxes)* (1954–1958) 37 Tax Cas 79 at 87.
7   [1995] CLC 496; [1996] 1 CTLR T-17.
8   [1995] CLC 496 at 501H.
9   A message using an authentication code sent through the SWIFT (Society for Worldwide Interbank Financial Telecommunication) system has the legal effect of binding the sender bank according to its contents: *Industrial & Commercial Bank Ltd v Banco Ambrosiano Veneto SpA* [2003] 1 SLR 221.

The recipient's procedural and due diligence burden

14.27 Whether it is for the user, when using an electronic signature, to bear such a burden, is debatable. For instance, the type of technology used, both its purpose and methodology, may have a bearing on this issue.[1] If it is accepted that the recipient is required to establish whether they could rely on the certificate in all the circumstances, they may be required to provide any or all of the evidence discussed above in relation to verifying the integrity of a certificate, depending on the nature of the challenge. Providing the recipient has carried out all the relevant checks required, it is possible to argue that it has discharged what can be described as a procedural and due diligence burden and has become a verifying party.[2]

1   Graham J H Smith *Internet Law and Regulation* (3rd edn, Sweet & Maxwell, 2002), 10–081.
2   Articles 6(1) and (2) of Directive 1999/93/EC of the European Parliament and of the Council of 13 December 1999 on a Community framework for electronic signatures, OJ L 13, 19.01.2000, p. 12 provide that where a certification authority issues a qualified certificate or guarantees such a certificate, the certification authority will be liable to the relying party unless it can prove it did not act negligently.

Sending party: the burden of proof of security and integrity

14.28 Once the verifying party, if it is required so to do, has satisfied a judge that it has discharged the procedural and due diligence burden, the user will need to address the issue of the security and integrity of their computer or system, amongst other topics of relevance in the circumstances. This can be described as the burden of proof of security and integrity, which comprises both a persuasive burden (or burden of proof on the pleadings) and the evidential burden of adducing evidence. It is useful to compare identical problems that have exercised the minds of people in the past, and what mechanisms were put in place to provide for the integrity of the method of proving intent.

In the case of the impression of a seal, the use of a seal became so common by the fourteenth century, that consideration had to be given to provide for additional evidence, other than the impression of a seal was affixed to the document, that the seal impression was not a forgery or added without authority. First, the crown might have a number of seals for different purposes: a signet for the secretary; a privy seal, which was in between the secretary and the Chancellor; the great seal, controlled by the Chancellor to authenticate the most formal of acts, and a finger ring, later called a privy signet for the personal affairs of the monarch.[1] Second, care was taken to destroy seal matrices in a public ceremony, as occurred when Edward III ascended the throne and had the great seal used by his father and grandfather broken into tiny pieces in his presence.[2] The physical object of the impression of a seal was undermined, just as any other form of authentication. The seal itself might be forged, or the seal of a dead person used, as in the case of Hannibal when he forged letters in the name of the dead Roman consul Marcellus after removing the signet ring from his body.[3] For instance, it was an offence to forge the royal seal: by the Statute of Edward III, counterfeiting the great and privy seals were treasonable offences, and one man who forged the seal of Henry II was only saved from being hanged by the king's mercy.[4] At common law it was a felony and regarded as a capital offence, and there are three medieval cases of this nature. A person could challenge a document where the seal was not right, or the right seal was attached to the wrong document. As seals became more common, the other issue was the degree of forgery for ordinary seals. There is evidence that illustrates people took their seal very seriously. In 1190, for instance, Adam son of Peter de Birkin broke his seal and replaced it. He went to the length of repeating a grant he had previously made to the abbey of Rievaulx.[5] There then developed a means of countersigning the main seal with the use of a secret seal as a counter-seal to one of the great seals. The great seal would be in the possession and under the control of the officer of state, and the secret seal in the possession of the owner, thus providing a double check to the authenticity of the document, because the second seal may be imprinted on to the great seal, providing two seal impressions on the same seal. The concerns for the security of the seal were sometimes carried to what seems like extraordinary lengths, but were probably routine. In 1214 the chapter seal of Salisbury cathedral was in the care of two cannons, but by 1353 it was kept in a chest with three locks, and was only used in the presence of all three cannons who held the keys. By the Statute of Acton Burnell in 1283, debts could be registered before the mayor, who issued a recognisance with a special seal supplied by the Crown. However, in 1285, the Statute of Merchants amended the previous statute, and ordered that the seal must be contained in two parts, the larger to be retained by the mayor, and the smaller to be retained by the clerk – indicating, according to one scholar, that there had been a scandal of some sort.[6] In the late thirteenth century, the seal of the corporation of Winchester was placed in a box with three locks, and the keys retained by two counsellors and one ordinary person, and this box in turn was itself kept in a chest with two keys, held by one counsellor and one other.[7]

Conceptually, there is little difference between the seal matrix and a rubber stamp, as is the nature of the security that ought to be considered to prevent the unauthorized use of the stamp. The 1897 Pennsylvania case of *Robb v The Pennsylvania Company for Insurance on Lives and Granting Annuities*[8] is highly instructive, pre-dating the use of electronic signatures in any form by one hundred years, yet the difference in time does not diminish the issues, even if they were articulated with different concepts and language by the judges at the time. In this case, money had been paid out on two cheques signed with the facsimile signature of the bank depositor by means of a rubber stamp. Neither cheque was authorized by Mr Robb. In 1893, Mr Robb, as the president of a commercial corporation, had occasion to send out a large number of invitations to a banquet. To save himself the trouble of signing each invitation, he had a rubber stamp made with a facsimile of his signature. After retiring, he rented a private office, and with the rent came the services of an office boy of about sixteen years of age. He employed the boy on various errands, including sending him to the bank to draw money on cheques. It can be inferred from the report that he used the rubber stamp to sign cheques. He kept the rubber stamp in a compartment inside a fireproof safe. He locked the compartment and put the key to the compartment in a drawer in the safe, behind some papers, and covered it up. He then locked the drawer, and placed the key into an unlocked drawer in the safe. He then locked the safe, and put the key in a little box, which he put in a wooden drawer or box, and this was kept on top of another safe. The plaintiff surmised that the office boy had watched his moves at some time in the past. The majority of the judges found that Mr Robb was not negligent in the use of the rubber stamp. The basis of their decision centred on whether he was negligent in failing to exercise care in preventing the rubber stamp from falling into the wrong hands. Rice PJ rejected the proposition that Mr Robb was bound to keep the stamp in a place that prevented any person from obtaining it without authority. However, no attempt was made by the majority judges to explain how the bank was in a position to challenge the signature, given that the signature was identical each time the rubber stamp was used, with the exception that the impression will vary in quality depending on the amount of ink used and the pressure applied to the stamp as the signature is affixed to the cheque. Whilst it was held that the bank was liable for the cheques, Williams J wrote a strong dissenting judgment that raises the modern issues with somewhat different language. His entire opinion is printed in the law report on page 49. The major part of his opinion, with which Sterrett CJ concurred, raises important issues that are relevant to digital signatures in particular:

'It is conceded that Mr Robb caused the stamp to be made with which this check was executed. He says he only intended to use it for a particular purpose, but it is perfectly apparent that he intended his signature produced by this stamp should be recognized as his by his friends and acquaintances who should receive it, as it certainly would be. The signatures made by it as they are presented to us in the paper books, when placed by the side of admittedly genuine signatures, are indistinguishable from them. Now, this stamp belonged to him, was made under his direction, and for his use. It was intended for the rapid production of his signature. It was in his possession. He was bound to take care of it as safely as of his own signature made by himself with his own hand. He was bound to do this at his peril. There is no question of reasonable or sufficient care in this case. As with the signed check, so with this stamp signature. When he put it in his safe, and left the key where it was possible for any one to get it, and so gain admission to the safe, he exposed himself to the loss that might follow, and that loss is his. He seeks in this action to put his own proper loss upon the bank that paid the checks, by alleging that the checks were forged. But they were not forged. The signature was his. He prepared it. All that can be said is that he did not affix it to the checks. But he had prepared it so that any one could affix it to a check or any other paper, and when so affixed it was absolutely impossible to tell that it had not been done by him. There would be some justification for his claim upon the bank if he had advised the banker that he had prepared such a signature that might by a possibility be clandestinely gotten from his possession, and given him an impression made by it, and pointed out, if he could have done so, how it might be distinguished from his signature as made by a pen; but he did nothing of the kind. If the bank is not protected by his signature made by means of his own private stamp, if it is bound at its peril to know and discriminate between his signature made with his pen and that made with his private stamp, then he has, by the use of the stamp, very greatly increased the responsibility and peril of the bank without so much as giving it notice or affording the slightest intimation of the necessity for additional vigilance in scrutinizing checks purporting to bear his signature. Upon every rule of commercial law, and upon every consideration of equity and good conscience, the judgment entered in the court below in this case should be reversed, and judgment should be entered here in favour of the defendant.'

The learned judge listed a number of issues that he considered to be of relevance: Mr Robb had the stamp made voluntarily; he intended the reproduction on the stamp to signify his signature; although the stamp was originally made for one purpose, he subsequently decided to use it to authorize cheques;

he failed to notify the bank that he was using a mechanical reproduction of his manuscript signature, because if the bank was made aware of this practice, it might have refused to honour such cheques, or if it accepted them, the bank might have taken additional care to ensure the signature was affixed by him with the intention of signing it; finally, he failed to take care of it, having, in the view of the minority judge, a duty to take care of it. Although the members of the jury and the majority of the appellate court reached the conclusion that the bank was liable because he had used sufficient due care to prevent its unlawful use by others. There is a difference of degree between securing a physical object such as a rubber stamp and a digital signature, but in the event of a dispute, it follows that it is the holder of the certificate and private key who is in the best position to prove either that the security in place was inadequate, which implies it would be possible for an unauthorized third party (internal or external) to use the private key improperly, or that the security in place was such that the certificate and private key could not be used improperly. The user will be in control of the following (this list is not exhaustive):

(a) The hardware and the software of the computer or system upon which the private key sits.

(b) The security in place in relation to the computer or system, the use of the system by employees and the control of any tokens used to store the private key.

(c) The ability of the user to revoke their private key promptly after finding out that their system or private key was compromised.

If the user wishes to argue their security was so poor that an unauthorized third party could have gained access to the system to send an electronic communication with an electronic signature attached without authority, the user will undoubtedly be admitting breach of contract with the vendor from whom they obtained the certifying certificate.[9] They may also be admitting they were negligent.

1   Dr Patricia M. Barnes and L. C. Hector, *A Guide to Seals in the Public Record Office*, (Her Majesty's Stationery Office, 2nd edn, 1968), 8; Pierre Chaplais, *English Diplomatic Practice in the Middle Ages*, (Hambledon and London, 2003), 97–98.

2   P. D. A. Harvey and Andrew McGuinness, *A guide to British medieval seals* (University of Toronto Press, 1996), 34.

3   Pierre Chaplais, *English Diplomatic Practice in the Middle Ages*, 6.

4   P. D. A. Harvey and Andrew McGuinness, *A guide to British medieval seals*, 33, 98–99.

5   Dr Patricia M. Barnes and L. C. Hector, *A Guide to Seals in the Public Record Office*, 29–30.

6   T. F. T. Plucknett, *Legislation of Edward I* (Oxford, 1949), 140, quoted in P. D. A. Harvey and Andrew McGuinness, *A guide to British medieval seals*, 111.

7   P. D. A. Harvey and Andrew McGuinness, *A guide to British medieval seals*, 58–62; 98–99.

8   40 W.N.C. 129, 3 Pa.Super. 254, 1897 WL 3989 (Pa.Super. 1897) affirmed by186 Pa. 456, 40 A. 969, for dissenting opinion, see 186 Pa. 456, 41 A. 49.

9   By way of example, the subscribing party provides a number of warranties in paragraph 2.2.3.1 of the BT Certification Practice Statement (Version 3.04, 18 December 2003), including 'No

unauthorised person has ever has access to the End User's private key.' It should be noted that no personal computer connected at any time to the internet can be regarded as secure enough to prevent access by an unauthorized third party, a point well understood by substantial commercial undertakings with adequate resources, because the problems of maintaining effective security with generally available technology are insoluble.

The persuasive and evidential burden of demonstrating weaknesses in the infrastructure

14.29 Once a communication leaves the user's computer or system, they relinquish control of the document or message. If the user can demonstrate the effectiveness of the security and integrity of their computer or system, the next link is the network over which the communication passes and the public key infrastructure that supports such items as digital signatures. In this instance, evidence may be required from a number of organizations in the chain (discussed in more detail below), including:

(a) The registration authority and the effectiveness of the registration procedure.

(b) The methods of management the certification authority uses to control its infrastructure.

(c) The effectiveness or otherwise of any third party supplier whose product or service is included in the chain.

If the recipient can demonstrate the due diligence they carried out was reasonable in the circumstances, and the user can demonstrate, to the required standard, the security and integrity of their computer or system, the question then becomes: which party to the proceedings has the persuasive and evidential burden of demonstrating any weaknesses in the infrastructure? Whichever party bears this burden, it will be an expensive process, bearing in mind the number of organizations that make up the chain. In a dispute, the burden of proof will inevitably be on the party that asserts the problem lies with third parties in the chain. It seems that all the recipient needs to do is to demonstrate procedural and due diligence. Thereafter, it is for the sender to either demonstrate lack of security, or the fault occurred as the result of failure by third parties in the chain, unlike the burden in proving a manuscript signature. This will inevitably mean that the sender will have to make this assertion in the pleadings, which will determine the persuasive burden (and invariably the evidential burden) will lie with the sending party.

SHIFTING THE ONUS OF PROOF — ENGLAND AND WALES — ELECTRONIC COMMUNICATIONS ACT 2000

14.30 By section 8(1) of the Electronic Communications Act 2000, Parliament has given the appropriate Minister the authority to modify the provisions of:

'(a)   any enactment or subordinate legislation, or

(b)   any scheme, licence, authorisation or approval issued, granted or given by or under any enactment or subordinate legislation

in such manner as he may think fit for the purpose of authorising or facilitating the use of electronic communications or electronic storage (instead of other forms of communication or storage) for any purpose mentioned in subsection (2).'

Whilst the power to modify legislation may be considered to be helpful in changing the law relating to the use of electronic signatures,[1] nevertheless the Act allows for the burden of proof to be shifted, if so desired by a minister. The relevant section is 8(4)(g), which reads as follows:

'(4)   Without prejudice to the generality of subsection (1), the power to make an order under this section shall include power to make an order containing any of the following provisions—

...

(g)   provision, in relation to cases in which the use of electronic communications or electronic storage is so authorized, for the determination of any of the matters mentioned in subsection (5), or as to the manner in which they may be proved in legal proceedings;'

The other relevant provision is s 8(5)(d). Section 8(5) provides:

'(5)   The matters referred to in subsection (4)(g) are:

(a)   whether a thing has been done using an electronic communication or electronic storage;

(b)   the time at which, or date on which, a thing done using any such communication or storage was done;

(c)   the place where a thing done using such communication or storage was done;

(d)   the person by whom such a thing was done; and

(e)   the contents, authenticity or integrity of any electronic data.'

In combination, s 8(4)(g) and (5)(d) gives scope to a Minister to determine where the burden of proof will lie in any particular order issued under the Act.[2] By way of example is the Social Security (Electronic Communications) (Child Benefit) Order 2002.[3] These Regulations amend a variety of Regulations relating to the provision and payment of child benefit,[4] by which article 3 inserts a new regulation 4C, authorizing the use of electronic communication to make a claim for, and to provide any certificate, notice, information or evidence connected with a claim for child benefit, although making such a claim by way of electronic communications is subject to the provisions set out in Schedule 9C. The use of electronic communications setting out the formalities that are provided for, to take into account the characteristics of

communications sent electronically. A person may use an electronic communication providing the Secretary of State gives permission to do so,[5] and other
conditions to be fulfilled are set out in the clauses that follow the permitting
clause:

'(4) The second condition is that the person uses an approved method
of:
(a) authenticating the identity of the sender of the communication;
(b) electronic communication;
(c) authenticating any claim, certificate, notice, information or
evidence delivered by means of an electronic communication;
and
(d) subject to sub-paragraph (7), submitting to the Secretary of
State any claim, certificate, notice, information or evidence.

(5) The third condition is that any claim, certificate, notice, information
or evidence sent by means of an electronic communication is in a
form approved for the purpose of this Schedule.

(6) The fourth condition is that the person maintains such records in
written or electronic form as may be specified in a direction given
by the Secretary of State.

(7) Where the person uses any method other than the method approved
by the Secretary of State, of submitting any claim, certificate, notice,
information or evidence, that claim, certificate, notice, information
or evidence shall be treated as not having been submitted.'

The amended material includes matters relating to evidential provisions
relating to the delivery of information by means of electronic communications, proof of identity, proof of delivery and proof of content of information.
The provisions for proof of identity are set out s 5:

'5. If it is necessary to prove, for the purpose of any legal proceedings,
the identity of:

(a) the sender of any claim, certificate, notice, information or evidence
delivered by means of an electronic communication to an official
computer system; or
(b) the recipient of any such claim, certificate, notice, information or
evidence delivered by means of an electronic communication from
an official computer system,

the sender or recipient, as the case may be, shall be presumed to be the
person recorded as such on that official computer system.'

Whilst the provisions of subparagraphs (a) and (b) appear not to be contro-
versial, the provision in subparagraph (c), providing for the presumption of

the identification of the sending party, is an example of the burden imposed upon those who elect to send a return by electronic means. The message is very clear: that a person who decides to take advantage of the ability to correspond with the Commissioners of Customs and Excise (now HM Revenue and Customs) by electronic communications, will have to pay particular care to the control of their private keys.

In particular, they will need to ensure that their computer or the system upon which the electronic signature and private key sits, is properly protected from the risks set out elsewhere. People using electronic signatures will have to determine what steps are reasonable to protect their private keys.

1   See Law Commission, 'Electronic Commerce: Formal Requirements in Commercial Transactions', December 2001, for a discussion on the issues relating to the formal requirements relating to commercial matters in England and Wales in respect of manuscript signatures, available online at www.lawcom.gov.uk/docs/e-commerce.pdf.

2   Nicholas Bohm, Ian Brown and Brian Gladman, 'Electronic Commerce: Who Carries the Risk of Fraud?', 2000 (3) *Journal of Information, Law and Technology (JILT)*, www2.warwick.ac.uk/fac/soc/law/elj/jilt/2000_3/bohm/ pointed this out at page 27 before the Bill was enacted.

3   SI 2002/1789.

4   Social Security (Notification of Change of Circumstances) Regulations 2001 SI 2001/3252; Child Benefit (General) Regulations 1976 SI 1976/956; Social Security (Guardian's Allowance) Regulations 1975 SI 1975/515 and the Social Security (Claims and Payments) Regulations 1987 SI 1987/1968.

5   Schedule 9C s 2(3).

Canada – Uniform Electronic Evidence Act

14.31   It is instructive to note how other jurisdictions have treated the issue of the burden of proof, and as a postscript to the discussion set out above, it may be of interest to note that the primary focus of the Uniform Electronic Evidence Act in Canada is to replace the concept of an original document with the proof of the reliability of a system instead of the reliability of an individual record, and using standards to demonstrate the reliability of a system. The relevance for electronic signatures lies in the provision relating to authentication in s 3:

'Authentication

3.   The person seeking to introduce an electronic record [in any legal proceeding] has the burden of proving its authenticity by evidence capable of supporting a finding that the electronic record is what the person claims it to be.'

As the comment to this section explains, this clause is intended to codify the common law on authentication.

Burden of proof – the Jitsuin

14.32 Since the eighth century, a similar system of authentication to that of the electronic signature has existed in the physical world, by which a signing party deposits an imprint of their mark with a trusted third party, and relying parties can rest assured that when the mark is used, they can rely on the authentication of the person by the mark. This is the Jitsuin of Japan. Inkan or hanko (name seals) are used very widely in Japan for a range of transactions, and some people may have up to five name seals. The purpose of a name seal is to confirm a person's intention to enter a transaction and to act as a form of identification. Two kinds of name seal are in common use in Japan, the Jitsuin (official or legal seal) and mitomein (personal seals). Any type of name seal can serve as a mitomein, but a Jitsuin must be registered. The use of a name seal in Japan is so much part of everyday life that foreigners, although they are permitted in some situations to use a manuscript signature instead of a name seal, are advised to obtain a name seal if they are going to remain in the country for any length of time.

MITOMEIN

14.33 This type of seal is used for everyday use, and is more commonly used to deposit or withdraw money at a bank; open bank accounts; buy a vehicle; register a marriage notice; register with the utility services or acknowledge the receipt of special mail or deliveries.

THE JITSUIN

14.34 Jitsuin are used instead of manuscript signatures to execute important documents. For instance, the Jitsuin Certificate is required as an attachment to the document of application for the transfer of registration in the real property registry at the Legal Affairs Bureau. The importance attached to the Jitsuin Certificate under Japanese Law is such that the transfer of the registration is essential for the perfection of the transfer of title of a real property. The Jitsuin is endowed with a legal presumption that is founded partly on the common understanding that a name seal either cannot be forged, or is difficult to forge, and partly on a very long history of use.

Registering a Jitsuin

14.35

(a) Jitsuin are required to conform to specific criteria: the name on the seal must conform to the registered name; the seal must have a border surrounding the name (and the border must not be missing or chipped); machine-made, mass-produced seals are not acceptable; the seal must be made of a material that cannot be altered easily, and the diameter must be greater than 8mm square but smaller than 25mm square.

(b)   Only the owner of a seal or a representative can apply to register a Jitsuin, and the applicant has to be over the age of 15 years.

(c)   A Jitsuin must be registered at the offices of the local government, whether village, town or city.

(d)   Upon applying for a Jitsuin Certificate, some local offices will send the applicant a letter of verification for the purpose of identifying the person applying. Alternatively, the usual range of documents will be required to be produced when the applicant attends the office. The registration takes place when the applicant attends the office with their seal, during which their identity is checked. Where a representative registers the seal, they will be required to provide a Letter of Attorney or a Letter of Advice Giving Right of Representation, which must be signed and sealed by the owner of the seal.

(e)   After registering the seal, the applicant is given an inkan card (it is now usual to give a card rather than a seal register or Jitsuin Certificate).

The Jitsuin Certificate

14.36   The Certificate includes the following information: an impression of the registered seal; the name of the seal holder; the date of birth of the seal holder; the gender of the seal holder; the address of the seal holder. The registration of the Jitsuin is tied to a particular geographical locality, so if the seal holder moves to another part of Japan or leaves Japan for good, the seal registration becomes null and void, and a new registration process must be undertaken at the new location. Where a Jitsuin is lost, the process is to attend the office that issues the Jitsuin Certificate and initiate the procedure to delete the registration. There is no procedure to notify relying parties that the Jitsuin has been stolen or lost.

Legal presumption of the Jitsuin Certificate

14.37   A Jitsuin Certificate proves the seal holder has adopted the impression of the seal that is recorded in the Certificate. The Civil Procedure Law provides for a legal presumption relating to the authenticity of a private document, as follows: 'A private document shall be presumed to be authentically executed if it bears the signature or seal of the principal or his representative.'[1] It appears that this presumption is rebuttable. This discussion is restricted to private documents, and does not include government documents.[2] For this presumption to operate, the party bearing the burden of proof is required to prove that the registered owner of the seal intended to affix an impression of their seal on the document. This intention may itself be presumed, if the relying party proves that the seal impressed on the document and the impression of the adopted seal held by the owner is the same. However, the relying party must also prove that the signing party has in fact adopted the seal. This fact is proved by using the Jitsuin Certificate, because the Jitsuin Certificate bears the adopted seal and the name of the signing party, thus it is easy for the relying party to prove that the signing party adopted the seal.[3] Once it is established that the signing party intended to affix an impression of their seal by operation of this presumption, the presumption under the Civil Procedure Law takes effect, and the document in question is presumed to be authentically executed.

This explanation demonstrates there are two levels of presumption, a process known as the 'Two Phase Presumption'. It involves the following steps:

(a) If the impression of the seal and the adopted seal held by the signing party are the same, then it is presumed that:

(b) The signing party intended to affix the seal impression, which in turn creates the presumption that:

(c) The document bearing the seal impression was authentically executed.

It is to be noted that there is no statutory requirement of due diligence in order to utilize this presumption.

1   Civil Procedure Law (Law No 109 of 1998) Article 228(4).
2   Civil Procedure Law (Law No 109 of 1998) Article 228 and 228(2) and (3).
3   This chain of presumption is reinforced by the provisions of Civil Procedure Law (Law No 109 of 1998) Article 229, which states: 'The authenticity of execution of documents may also be proved by a comparison of specimen of handwriting or seal impression'.

Rebutting the presumption

14.38   The signing party can rebut these presumptions. However, it is difficult to effectively prove that the document was not authentically executed, which is tantamount to trying to prove a negative. Of recent, this presumption has been found to pose problems in an age when it is very easy to forge name seals with the availability of advanced technology. This problem has reached national importance following a series of thefts from deposit accounts held in banks using forged or stolen seals. The problem is partly explained by Matsushita Shuli:[1]

'Door-picking artist quietly breaks and enters victim's house and nicks bank account passbook. The passbook, especially old ones, usually carries the seal image on the first page. The joker scans this image and prints it on the withdrawal slip with color printer. The bank teller accepts this slip and passbook as authentic, and victim's account will be emptied. Sometimes, the scanned digital image goes to hanko carving machine, too.

The real cause of trouble: It's the stamped image of one's hanko that is stored in the databases of government offices, banks and other public institutions. Not the particulars of physical hanko itself! And any image can be flawlessly reproduced in this era of digital processing. QED.'

1   Obtaining information about this problem is difficult. A budget committee at Congress was arranged to discuss 'The problem of seal impression' on 27 February 2003, by Mr Toshimasa Yamada of the Democratic Party and Mr Hideo Usui of the Liberal Democratic Party: links to this item no longer appear to be live. The Japanese Bankers Association (www.zengin-kyo.or.jp/en/index.html) does not address this problem specifically, but a glance through the archive will reveal figures for lost cheque books and banking books, and the losses sustained, which implies that thieves steal such items, together with the seal, and then steal money from the bank account. Slightly more information can be gleaned from an article by Matsushita Shuli, 'A futile effort to prop up hopeless Hanko system?' CNET Asia, 14 August 2006, online at www.asia.cnet.com/reviews/blog/mobileojisan/0,39050793,39390184,00.htm.

Expert evidence

14.39   Whether a dispute is the subject of a civil or a criminal trial, one or both parties will invariably be required to obtain the opinion of expert witnesses. The opinion of experts is admissible in evidence, and in civil proceedings such evidence is governed by Part 35 of the CPR. The Overriding Objective on Pt 1 will apply to such evidence. In criminal proceedings, the duties of expert witnesses are those laid down by common law, although they are not very different to the duties of an expert in civil proceedings.

Burden of proof – electronic signatures – a summary

14.40   The Jitsuin and the Jitsuin Certificate have been a very effective method of providing for the authenticity and intention of a person when entering into a legally binding agreement. A trusted third party undertakes to certify the nexus between the applicant and the Jitsuin. The presumption worked well in a society where the accurate copying of name seals was difficult for the would-be fraudster. However, with the advent of modern means of duplication, a tension has begun to be manifest between the assurance that an individual can prove their identity and thereby authenticate a document with the use of a Jitsuin Certificate in combination with a Jitsuin, and the failure to require the relying party to take steps to authenticate the identity of the person who claims the name seal is their adopted Jitsuin. To recap, the Jitsuin Certificate proves the seal holder has adopted the impression of the seal that is recorded in the Certificate. In modern Japan, the failure to balance the presumption that accompanies the use of a Jitsuin, with an accompanying duty to take steps to require the person using the name seal to provide the certificate of authenticity, has meant ordinary consumers suffer the loss. This is an example where advances in technology have caused problems in a system of authentication that has worked well over an extended period of time in Japanese history. Whilst a change to the law will not follow immediately, when a change does occur, a cultural shift will also have to take place, in which the relying party will have to take reasonable steps to verifying the signing party.

In the context of electronic signatures, and digital signatures in particular, there is a clear lesson to be understood. In the physical world where the signature-creation device is difficult to replicate accurately, a tri-part method of providing assurance can be very effective. The owner of the seal provides evidence of their identity to satisfy a nominated authority sufficiently for the authority to create a certificate to link the seal to the owner. The authority retains the evidence of the link, and the relying party can rest assured that the person with the seal, if authenticated with a certificate, is who they say they are. The flaw in this model in an age when a name seal is easy to duplicate, is to fail to impose a duty on the relying party to undertake sufficient due diligence to satisfy themselves that the holder of the seal is the person whose name seal is registered.

The use of a rubber stamp as a form of signature has similar properties to the name seal, but without the properties of the Jitsuin. In the cases of *Goodman v J Eban Limited*[1] and *British Estate Investment Society Ltd v Jackson (H M Inspector of Taxes)*[2] the respective recipients of the stamped documents did not question the authenticity of the stamped signature, but sought to challenge the format of the signature. Of interest was the underlying assumptions that were not fully articulated, that the owner of such a stamp is expected to keep it secure and prevent any unauthorized use and if the recipient was in any doubts as to the authenticity of the document signed with a rubber stamp, they could always take steps to verify the integrity of the document. Whilst these observations were made in passing and did not lay down a rule of law, nevertheless they represent underlying assumptions about the risks to be attached to the use of a means of providing authentication to a document, which may not always be under the control of the owner, at least in cases where the means in question are adopted for the convenience and advantage of the user, rather than the recipient.

The risks for the participants when using electronic signatures is, to a certain extent, similar to that of the Jitsuin and rubber stamp, depending on the type of electronic signature used. In the context of the digital signature, the trusted third party has taken the opportunity, in the absence of legislative requirements and by way of contract, to allocate the risks and responsibilities. Any subscribing party or receiving party that relies on such technology is either fully aware of the limitations associated with the use of a digital signature, or they have no concept of the issues, and uses a digital signature in ignorance of the risks they may face if their reliance were to be tested. Statute provides that where a trusted third party with a contractual relationship with its customer (a bank) debits the account of a customer with payment of a cheque the customer did not sign, the bank has no authority to take the money and therefore must credit the account with the amount charged.[3] This rule was not invented by politicians, but codified the decisions of judges. The allocation of risk with the Jitsuin is under threat because of the ease by which a name seal can be forged. When a customer uses an automatic teller machine that dispenses cash, the customer is not protected by the same law that protects their cheque book.

It was the judges during the nineteenth century that created the protection for those customers that affixed their manuscript signature to a cheque. All politicians did was to eventually codify the rule developed by judges.[4] It will be for judges to determine the allocation of risk and where the burden will fall in respect of electronic signatures. Whilst it will be important to take into account the suggestion made by Romer LJ in *Goodman v J Eban Limited*[5] where he suggested the recipient of a document stamped with a rubber stamp can take action to authenticate the document, the action and effort required to check that the writer of a letter intended to affix their signature by means of a rubber stamp is far less than the magnitude of the task facing a recipient of, in particular, a digital signature. The terms and content of the certification practice policies of the certification authorities demonstrate the complexity of the task faced by a recipient if they are expected to verify a digital signature.

1   [1954] 1 QB 550; [1954] 1 All ER 763; [1954] 2 WLR 581, CA.
2   (1954–1958) 37 Tax Cas 79; [1956] TR 397; 35 ATC 413; 50 R & IT 33.
3   Bills of Exchange Act 1882, s 24.
4   Nicholas Bohm, Ian Brown and Brian Gladman, 'Electronic Commerce: Who Carries the Risk of Fraud?' paragraph 2.
5   [1954] 1 QB 550 at 564.

Presumptions

14.41   The aim of a presumption is to reduce the need prove every item of evidence adduced in court, or to reduce the need for evidence in relation to some issues.

IRREBUTTABLE PRESUMPTIONS

14.42   Some presumptions are considered irrebuttable. Where an irrebuttable presumption operates, once a party has proved or have had one fact admitted, another fact will be presumed, and the other party cannot call evidence to the contrary.

REBUTTABLE PRESUMPTIONS

14.43   With a rebuttable presumption, after the proof of admission of the presumption is admitted into evidence, the court can presume another fact as a result. However, the other party then has the persuasive or evidential burden to disprove the presumed fact. One presumption that may apply to computers is the presumption that a machine is presumed to be in working order.[1] In the context of digital evidence, however, it is pertinent to be aware of the imperfections inherent in the way computers function, and how digital evidence is prone to alteration. Evidence derived from a computer must be admissible, authentic, accurate and complete in the same way as any other form of evidence. However, computers are also very volatile, in that a document, record or log can be altered very easily without leaving an obvious trace. Bearing in mind that much of the evidence accumulated about the use of an electronic signature will be by way of a computer or series of computers, all of which will be connected to the internet, the problems of relying on evidence generated by computers increase.[2]

1   Approved in *Castle v Cross* [1984] 1 WLR 1372, DC.
2   Peter Sommer 'Downloads, Logs and Captures: Evidence from Cyberspace,' [2002] CTLR 33–42; Stephen Mason, general editor, *Electronic Evidence: Disclosure, Discovery & Admissibility*, Chapter 2 The characteristics of electronic evidence.

Evidential weight

14.44 It will be evident from the above discussion that trusted third parties will need to guarantee that they can audit the evidential trail in relation to the use and control of the certificates they issue. In this respect, both the trusted third parties offering certificates and individuals challenging the admissibility of communications associated with electronic signatures will need to be able to demonstrate the integrity of their respective systems (or lack of integrity), as the case may be. The evidential weight to be given to evidence relating to electronic signatures is predicated on the degree of control exercised over the controlled and secure environment of all the parties in the chain. It follows that it will be for a judge to decide what weight, if any, is to be placed on the integrity of the infrastructure in the event of a dispute.

Cross-examination

14.45 Where computer evidence is submitted, it will always be possible for either party to the proceedings to challenge that evidence. This will be carried out by way of cross-examination. Where a party provides hearsay evidence without calling a witness, the other party is entitled to require the production of a witness to be cross-examined, in accordance with s 3 of the Civil Evidence Act 1995:

'3   Power to call witness for cross-examination on hearsay statement

Rules of court may provide that where a party to civil proceedings adduces hearsay evidence of a statement made by a person and does not call that person as a witness, any other party to the proceedings may, with the leave of the court, call that person as a witness and cross-examine him on the statement as if he had been called by the first-mentioned party and as if the hearsay statement were his evidence in chief.'

Should the party adducing the statement fail to produce a witness to be cross-examined, their position can be undermined in accordance with the provision of s 5(2) of the Civil Evidence Act 1995:

'(2)   Where in civil proceedings hearsay is adduced and the maker of the original statement, or of any statement relied upon to prove another statement, is not called as a witness:

(a)   evidence which if he had been so called would be admissible for the purpose of attacking or supporting his credibility as a witness is admissible for that purpose in the proceedings; and

(b)   evidence tending to prove that, whether before or after he made the statement, he made any other statement inconsistent with it is admissible for the purpose of showing that he had contradicted himself.

Provided that evidence may not be given of any matter of which, if he had been called as a witness and had denied that matter in cross-examination, evidence could not have been adduced by the cross-examining party.'

The provisions of this clause prevent evidence being adduced in the proceedings, the effect of which would be to provide a denial that could be final if the witness was called. In criminal proceedings, a statement may be excluded in accordance with ss 23 and 24 of the Criminal Justice Act 1988. Where a witness is not called upon, the provisions of Schedule 2 will apply.

Weight

14.46   Section 4 of the Civil Evidence Act 1995 sets out a number of guidelines which deal with the issues that should be considered when determining the weight of hearsay:

'(1)   In estimating the weight (if any) to be given to hearsay evidence in civil proceedings the court shall have regard to any circumstances from which any inference can reasonably be drawn as to the reliability or otherwise of the evidence.

(2)   Regard may be had, in particular, to the following:

(a)   whether it would have been reasonable and practicable for the party by whom the evidence was adduced to have produced the maker of the original statement as a witness;

(b)   whether the original statement was made contemporaneously with the occurrence or existence of the matters stated;

(c)   whether the evidence involves multiple hearsay;

(d) whether any person involved had any motive to conceal or misrepresent matters;

(e) whether the original statement was an edited account, or was made in collaboration with another or for a particular purpose;

(f) whether the circumstances in which the evidence is adduced as hearsay are such as to suggest an attempt to prevent proper evaluation of its weight.'

It is a matter for the judge to decide whether hearsay evidence is to be given any weight at all, and if so, how the evidence will be evaluated. In criminal proceedings, the provisions of the Criminal Justice Act 2003 provides for the assessment of hearsay statements.[1]

1 Hodge M. Malek, general editor, *Phipson on Evidence*, Chapter 30.

Direction

14.47 A judge in criminal proceedings will invariably direct the members of the jury to the weight they should give to the evidence adduced during the trial. With respect to civil cases, a judge will, in all probability, assess the weight of the evidence, although the conclusions reached may not be made explicit in the judgment.

Jurisdiction

14.48 If the core issue in a dispute centres on the use of an electronic signature, the matter will, in all probability, require careful consideration of the issues relating to the forum in which the dispute is heard, the law that will apply in resolving the dispute and how a judgment given in one jurisdiction may or may not be enforceable, directly or indirectly, in another. This text only considers the law in England and Wales, and these topics deserve a book to themselves, and the reader is, accordingly, referred to the relevant textbooks on the subject.

Chapter 15

Digital signatures

15.1 Cryptography is the method of hiding the contents of a message, used from ancient times to the present.[1] Encryption (or enciphering) is the process by which a plaintext (or cleartext) message is disguised sufficiently to hide the substance of the content. As well as ordinary text, a plaintext message can be a stream of binary digits, a text file, a bitmap, a recording of sound in digital format, audio images of a video or film and any other information formed into digital bits. When a message has been encrypted, it is known as ciphertext or a cryptogram. The opposite procedure, that of turning the ciphertext back into plaintext, is called decryption (or deciphering).[2] In essence, contemporary cryptographic systems change one set of symbols that have meaning (binary data) into a second set of symbols that has no meaning, by means of a mathematical process. Cryptography is usually required to undertake a number of functions, the most important of which is authenticity, rather than secrecy:

(a) To ensure the *authenticity* of the information. When sending or receiving information or placing an order, both parties need to know the origin of the message. The aim is to corroborate the identity of the entity (the identity of a person cannot be corroborated, because a person is not part of the communications process – the process only involves computers).

(b) To demonstrate the *integrity* of the message, because it is important to know if the content of the message has been tampered with.

(c) To provide an assurance, to the extent that is technically possible, that demonstrates an entity has been honest about the actions it has undertaken. The purpose is to bind users to specific actions in such a way that if they deny taking the action, they either demonstrate an intention to deceive, or they have been negligent in failing to secure the use of their private key adequately. This is called non-repudiation in the security industry. There are different types of non-repudiation: non-repudiation of origin, which prevents the entity that sent the message or document from denying that they sent it, and non-repudiation of receipt, where an entity cannot deny having not received a message or document. Other types of non-repudiation include non-repudiation of creation, non-repudiation of delivery and non-repudiation of approval.[3] This is a dangerous term, and one that lawyers should take particular care in understanding. It does not mean the system for non-repudiation is perfect, although some technical authors continue to assert that digital signatures are better than they actually are.[4] An engineer will mean that there is a high degree of probability that the protocol can demonstrate a document or message was sent or received. A leap in logic then occurs, and it will then be asserted that if the system can demonstrate a message or document was sent or received, then it is for the other party to demonstrate that it was not sent or received by them. Should such issues be raised in the event of a dispute, whoever bears the burden of proof and what presumptions, if any, apply, will partly depend on the claims made by each party.

(d) To provide for the *confidentiality* of a document.

In the electronic environment, cryptography is used as a substitute for a manuscript signature, described as a digital signature. To understand how a document can be signed electronically, it is necessary to be aware of how cryptography works.

1 David Khan *The Codebreakers, The Comprehensive History of Secret Communication from Ancient Times to the Internet* (Simon & Schuster, 1997); Simon Singh *The Code Book: The Secret History of Codes and Code-breaking* (Fourth Estate, 2000); Ross Anderson Security Engineering, 114 for further references.
2 Encipher and decipher are terms used in the ISO 7498-2 standard.
3 Carlisle Adams and Steve Lloyd *Understanding PKI Concepts, Standards, and Deployment Considerations* (Addison-Wesley, 2nd edn 2002), 51.
4 Klaus Schmeh *Cryptography and Public Key Infrastructure on the Internet*, 16.1.1 'The purpose of a digital signature is to ensure non-repudiation. This means that Alice cannot contest her completed signature in retrospect. When all is said and done, a digital signature is an excellent way of meeting this requirement.'

Algorithms and keys

15.2 The plaintext of a message is encrypted and decrypted by the use of a cryptographic algorithm (also called a cipher). There tend to be two related functions, one for encryption and another for decryption. In most instances, the secrecy of the algorithm will not matter, because modern cryptography uses a key. However, it is possible to have a restricted algorithm, so called because the security of the algorithm is based on ensuring the way it works is kept a secret. There are drawbacks to the use of restricted algorithms. If a user leaves the group or should the secret be revealed for any reason, then the algorithm must be changed. Further, there is no quality control or standardization, which means the algorithms can be easy to break. By using a key, a strong algorithm does not need to be secret and can be used by millions of users. As a result, there is no need to constantly develop new algorithms. A key can comprise a number of values. This range of values is called a keyspace. A key can be used to encrypt and decrypt a message, or there can be two separate keys, one to encrypt a message and another for decrypting the message. To complete the picture, a cryptosystem comprises an algorithm, all possible messages, all possible cryptograms and all possible keys.

Control of the key

15.3 To decrypt the ciphertext, the recipient needs to know both the decryption algorithm and the decryption key. Bearing in mind it is best to use a well-known algorithm, the way a key is controlled, managed and distributed becomes crucial. This is why the principle laid down by Auguste Kerckhoffs von Niuewenhof remains a fundamental rule of cryptanalysis: the security of a cryptosystem must depend on keeping the key secret.[1] This issue is discussed more fully when considering the weaknesses relating to cryptosystems.

1   A. Kerckhoffs. 'La Cryptographie Militaire.' *Journal des Sciences Militaires* January 9, 1883, 5–38 (reference provided by Ross Anderson *Security Engineering*) although this principle applied to a time when all systems were symmetric.

Disguising the message

15.4 There are two types of mathematical families that permit the message to be disguised: symmetric cryptographic systems and asymmetric cryptographic systems.

CONVENTIONAL OR SYMMETRIC CRYPTOGRAPHIC SYSTEMS

15.5 As the name infers, the encryption key can be computed from the decryption key and decryption key can be computed from the encryption key. In practice, these two keys are often identical when used in symmetric systems. As a result, the symmetric system is also referred to as secret-key algorithms, single-key algorithms, one-key algorithms or shared key ciphers. Two people can use the same system to send and receive encrypted messages to each other. Both the sender and the receiver must agree on the key before they can communicate. This system can have very long keys, which means a message can be very secure. The effectiveness of this system depends on the key, and is suitable for closed user groups where there is a strong element of mutual trust between the users, such as banks, the military, and intelligence agencies. However, a disadvantage is that the key must be kept secure and secret. Two people must have the key to communicate. If encrypted messages are to pass between large numbers of people, a large number of keys will have to be distributed. The security of the system will depend on those people with access to the keys to ensure they are kept secure and secret. Also, from the point of view of managing the keys, it is important for pairs of users to have different keys to reduce the risks of compromise when large numbers of people share a key. Some symmetric algorithms work on the plaintext, one digit at a time. These are called stream ciphers. Others work in groups of digits on the plaintext. The groups of digits are called blocks, and the algorithms called block algorithms or block ciphers. How an algorithm and the cipher work is important, because of their strengths and weaknesses. If an algorithm or cipher is easy to attack, then an application should not use it, and if losses occur because of the failure of either, then a successful legal action may be possible because it could be argued that the system was designed negligently.

Sending a message that has been encrypted only provides for the security of the content. It does not attribute the message to the source from which the message was sent. It is possible for an interceptor to intercept the message and send a substitute message in place of the original message. If a forger sends the message, the recipient will not be aware that the sender of the message has used the key improperly. Authentication seeks to corroborate the integrity of the message and authenticity of the sender. There are two types of authentication.

(a)   One-way authentication is where one party is authenticated to another party, such as a person using an automatic teller machine when they wish to withdraw cash or make a deposit. The user identifies themselves by using their personal identity number, and the card is authenticated cryptographically.

(b)   Two-way authentication, where both parties to a message seek to verify the attribution of data that purports to identify each other or the message or both, such as virtual private networks.

The process of authentication also uses a secret key. This is called the message authentication code or data authentication code. This mechanism can provide authentication without the need for secrecy. In symmetric cryptographic systems, the aim is for the originator and the legitimate recipient to be the only two entities that can create or check the message authentication code. This is an example of how the message authentication code can work:[1]

(a)   Alice sends a message in plaintext to Bob. Put simply, the computer that Alice uses encrypts the message by using a block algorithm or cipher. All of the ciphertext blocks are then discarded with the exception of the last block. The last block is the message authentication code. (Note: If Alice wants to provide for both the integrity and the privacy of the message, the message can also be encrypted again.)

(b) Bob receives the message. His computer computes what the message authentication code should have been. If Eve intercepted and altered the message, Bob will realise this, because the incorrect plaintext is re-encrypted, producing a non-conforming message authentication code. If the plaintext has been altered, the ciphertext blocks will be different, especially the last ciphertext block. If the plaintext has not been altered, the re-encrypted plaintext will not have changed, and Bob can be sure that Alice has sent the plaintext message.

However, this does not prevent Eve from listening in to Alice when she sends the message to Bob. Eve can then record every message, together with the message authentication code. Alternatively, she can delete the message sent by Alice, repeat old messages or change the order in which the messages are sent. Thus the message authentication code needs to include a scheme by which each message is numbered sequentially.

1   Alice, Bob, Carol, Dave and interloper Eve are used widely in cryptology. See 'The Alice and Bob After Dinner Speech' given at the Zürich Seminar, April 1984 by John Gordon by invitation of Professor John Massey available online at www.conceptlabs.co.uk/alicebob.html.

ASYMMETRIC CRYPTOGRAPHIC SYSTEMS (PUBLIC KEY)[1]

15.6   Using a symmetric cryptographic system with large numbers of users is difficult. Keys cannot be distributed over the open communications network, so they have to be distributed in other ways. Also, as a member leaves the group, so all the other members have to redistribute new keys. Thus, assuming a separate key is used for each pair in a group, and if there are 10 members of the group, 45 different keys will be required. The development of the asymmetric cryptographic system, or public key, helps to resolve this problem. With this system, keys only have one purpose: one key to encrypt and one key to decrypt. Given a large enough key, the decryption key cannot be calculated from the encryption key within a useful length of time (perhaps several centuries). The algorithms used in the system are commonly called 'public key' because the encryption key is usually made public. Anybody can use the encryption key to encrypt a plaintext message, but only the person with the decryption key that corresponds to the encryption key can decrypt the message. The encryption key is called the public key, and the decryption key is called the private key or secret key. The system can work in two ways.

1   The concept of public key cryptography was invented twice during the twentieth century. First, by James H. Ellis, Clifford Cocks, and Malcolm Williamson at British Intelligence GCHQ, whose work remained classified until December 1997. Second, two researchers at Stanford University, Whitfield Diffie and Martin Hellman, proposed the concept in 1976. Development of the principles can also be attributed to R. C. Merkle and to R. L. Rivest, A. Shamir and L. A. Adleman.

An individual creates and controls their own public key

15.7   The user generates a pair of keys using a trapdoor one-way function, containing the mathematical equivalent of a secret trapdoor. For the purposes of understanding the concept, this algorithm is easy to compute in one direction and difficult to compute in the opposite direction, unless you know the secret.[1]

Sending a message using public key cryptography
(a)   Alice and Bob decide to exchange messages that are encrypted.
(b)   Alice generates her own public and private keys using the software on her computer. Although she keeps the private key secret, she gives Bob her public key.
(c)   Bob writes his message and encrypts it using Alice's public key. He sends it to Alice.
(d)   Alice decrypts Bob's message using her private key.

This method of encrypting and decrypting messages means the private keys do not have to be distributed securely. In addition, it is possible for Alice to place her public key in a public database. The protocol then looks like this:
(a)   Bob goes to the database and obtains Alice's public key.
(b)   Bob writes Alice a message and uses her public key to encrypt the message. He then sends it to her.
(c)   Alice decrypts the message using her private key upon receipt.

There are problems in relation to the methods by which an individual creates and controls their own keys. An interceptor may intend to disrupt Alice's life by interrupting her ability to receive and send encrypted messages. It is possible for an interceptor to intercept, modify, delete and substitute a false message between the parties. Such a denial of service cannot be solved by the use of cryptography. This is how such an attack can work:
(a)   Alice sends her public key to Bob. Eve intercepts this key. She then sends her own key to Bob.
(b)   Bob sends his public key to Alice. Again, Eve intercepts this key and sends her own key to Alice.
(c)   When Alice sends a message to Bob, she encrypts it using what she thinks is Bob's public key. Eve intercepts this message and decrypts it with her private key. Having carried out whatever action she intends with the message, she then re-encrypts it with Bob's public key and sends it on to Bob.
(d)   The same process occurs when Bob sends a message to Alice.

---

1   It has yet to be proven that a mathematical function can have a one-way function, see Fred Piper, Simon Blake-Wilson and John Mitchell, *Digital Signatures Security & Controls* (Information Systems Audit and Control Foundation, 1999), 16.

Authenticating a signature using public key cryptography

15.8 The underlying rationale of public key cryptography is that a message can be attributed to a particular entity. First, Alice can use a key generation algorithm to generate a key pair: a private signing key and the public signature verification key, or she can use her existing key pair. She then publishes her public key on a database. Thereafter the example continues:

(a) Alice writes a message and wants to send it to Bob with her signature in electronic format. Her computer computes a signature from her private key and the message content.

(b) Alice then sends her message and the signature to Bob. The signature may be, but does not need to be, separate from the message. The signature operates in the same way as a message authentication code.

(c) Upon receipt of the message, Bob uses Alice's public key to verify that the corresponding private key signed the message.

However, given this scenario, Bob cannot be sure that the public key in the database is that of Alice. This does not resolve the issue of identifying the sender of the message. A person could generate their own public and private keys, post the public key on a database and claim it belongs to Alice. Bob might think he is sending messages to Alice, but in fact his message is posted to the interceptor. In addition, the interceptor could use their own private key to send messages to Bob, which he would assume came from Alice. There is further a problem with this method of adding a signature to a message, which in turn is inherent in any system that uses cryptography in the electronic environment to create a signature. The signature is not computed by Alice, but by her computer. Thus there is no direct evidence to show Alice appended the signature to the message.

Public key infrastructure

15.9 The concept of the public key infrastructure tries to resolve the problem by linking a public key to a named individual or legal entity.[1] The notion behind a public key infrastructure is to have organizations called trusted intermediaries, trusted third parties, trust service providers or certification authorities, that act to certify the connection between a person and their public key. In theory, the trusted third party guarantees the authenticity of the public key by issuing an individual identity certificate, which binds a name string to a public key. This in turn seeks to create a link between the provision of a key and the identity of the natural person or legal entity to which the key has been issued. It should be emphasised that users, when using a public key infrastructure, should aim to continue to generate their own key pairs. Where a third party generates the key pair on behalf of a user, the degree of security exercised over the key pair is reduced.

The certification authority issues an individual identity certificate, which has the following characteristics. It:

(a) Identifies the certification authority.

(b) Identifies the subscriber.

(c) Contains the subscriber's public key.

(d) Is signed with the Certification Authority's private key.

The individual identity certificate may also contain other information, such as the level of inquiry carried out before issuing the certificate. To acquire such a certificate, Alice will provide the certification authority with a copy of her public key and proof of her identity. The degree of proof of identity will differ, depending on the level of liability Alice wants to cover. When Alice sends a message to Bob, she also sends him a copy of her certificate. Alternatively, when she publishes her verification key, she publishes the certificate. Bob's computer will decrypt the message according to the key he has been given. It will then be for Bob in most circumstances, to undertake is own due diligence by checking the certificate revocation list to ensure the public key has not been revoked or has expired.

1 Ross Anderson *Security Engineering*, 401 notes there is some confusion between 'public (key infrastructure)' and '(public key) infrastructure'. He defines the first as an open system where the infrastructure can be used by any new application that is subsequently developed. He calls this open public key infrastructure. New applications cannot be used in the second, which he calls a closed public key infrastructure.

Difficulties with public key infrastructure

15.10 The advantage to the relying party of using the 'standard model' public key infrastructure digital signature is not that the signature provides greater security, but arises from persuading the subscribing party that because it is more secure, the user must take responsibility for every use of the private key, by whomsoever made. It must be emphasised, however, that the greater security of the mechanism does not, in fact, offer the subscribing party any protection against attacks, such as the theft of the key or the corruption of a terminal such that it signs something other than what is presented on the screen. The implied suggestion is that the system has a non-repudiation property, and it is this property that justifies the imposition of a non-repudiation term on the subscribing party. This cannot be right, because if the system genuinely possessed a non-repudiation property, it would not be necessary to impose such a term. Given that public key infrastructure digital signatures do not possess such a property, the acceptance of such a term invariably involves an acceptance of risk by the user. However, the nature and extent of the risk is not made clear, and it is highly improbable that ordinary users will have the knowledge, skills and resources to manage such a risk.[1]

1 Nicholas Bohm, Watch what you sign! *Digital Evidence Journal* 2006 Volume 1 Number 2, 43–47 for an analysis of the risks.

Authenticating the sender

15.11   There are various methods of obtaining sufficient evidence to demonstrate, with a degree of probability, that an electronic signature came from the person it purports to have been sent by. The aim is to gather sufficient evidence to be assured that the person sending the signature is the person they claim. Attempts are made, using various mechanisms, to obtain information from a combination of the following:

(a)   Proof by knowledge: what the person knows.
(b)   Proof by possession: what the person owns.
(c)   Proof by characteristics: what the person is.

When combined, the techniques relating to authentication can provide a higher level of authentication than a single method. In many instances, the method by which a person seeks to authenticate themselves is by a combination of hardware and software. A software component can retrieve and verify passwords. A token, such as a smart card, can be placed in a slot on a computer. Identification can be achieved by using a biometric measurement.

The ideal attributes of a signature in electronic format

15.12   Whether a signature is in manuscript form or electronic format, the purpose for the signature will not alter. However, when a signature is in electronic format, more considerations will apply to the signature. Whilst it is abundantly clear that a manuscript signature can be forged, or can be transferred from one piece of paper to another,[1] or that documents can be altered after they have been signed, digital signatures can help to resist attacks of these kinds. The attributes below set out the requirements of a digital signature:

(a)   The signature must be authentic. In this respect the method ought, ideally, to provide for the authentication of the origin of the data and the integrity of the message.

(b)   There ought to be a technical method in place that prevents the person appending the signature to the document from claiming later that they did not sign it. This is virtually impossible to achieve in the electronic environment. Care must be taken to distinguish between the degree of probability that a system can be designed to prevent a person from making such a claim, and any suggestion of a presumption that purports to bind the user to a signature that is verified.

(c)   The signature should not be capable of being forged, in that the private key is secure.

(d)   Where a signature is added to a message that comprises a legal act, the signature and its link to the relevant document should remain verifiable for as long as it is of legal importance.

(e)   The signature cannot be reused.

(f)   The document that has been signed cannot be altered without rendering the signature unverifiable.[2]

In the digital environment, it is considered technically possible to achieve all of these attributes – in theory, but it must be emphasised that the connection between the human and the machine cannot be bridged, and the technology is fallible.[3] Practical problems, which are discussed elsewhere, continue to exist with the implementation of a digital signature. However, the essential functions set out above can, largely, be met by the application of cryptography to the formation of a digital signature. As with manuscript signatures, there are always risks attached to the use of any form of electronic signature, and the user, whether a sending party or a relying party, should make themselves aware of the risks before using any form of electronic signature for high value transactions.

There is one further meaning that an electronic signature cannot, without education and training, provide. This is the addition of what was termed 'social meaning', or what can also be described as the 'significance of the act'. A ceremony is attached to the signing of a document, and when a person affixes their manuscript signature to a document, the importance of the act is reinforced by the physical nature of the act, because 'People intuitively understand that they are legally responsible for the documents to which they attach their autographs.[4] The function of attaching an electronic signature to a document or message is not understood in the same way as the use of manuscript signatures, partly because the signature can be applied to the document without any action by the individual to whom the signature is attributed, or without their knowledge.

1   For examples where the cutting and pasting of manuscript signatures have been upheld in the United States of America, see:

Iowa: *Ferguson v Stilwill*, 224 N.W.2d 11, (Iowa 1974) the signature of the Illinios Secretary of State, cut from an instrument and attached to a certificate of conviction, was sufficient in the absence of evidence to show the act of pasting was not authorized.

Maine (1841): *Richardson v Bachelder*, 19 Me. 82, 1841 WL 932 (Me.), 1 App. 82 where an attorney affixed the signature of the magistrate, which was physically on a slip of paper, to the writ, the writ was held to be properly issued, the magistrate having recognized and adopted it.

2   Jos Dumortier, Patrick Van Eecke and Ilse Anné *The Legal Aspects of Digital Signatures* (Interdisciplinary centre for Law & Information Technology, Katholieke Universiteit Leuven, 1998), Report I Part III B, 59; Bruce Schneier *Applied Cryptography* para 2.6.

3   Adam L. Young and Moti Yung, *Malicious Cryptography Exposing Cryptovirology*, (Wiley Publishing, 2004).

4   Jos Dumortier, Patrick Van Eecke and Ilse Anné *The Legal Aspects of Digital Signatures*, 77.

Methods of authentication

Authentication using secret codes

15.13 Secret codes or passwords have been used for some time, especially in banking. The code usually consists of a combination of digits or characters or both. The principle is based on ensuring the code is unique and only known to the user and the issuer. There is a shared secret between the two parties. The user identifies themselves by using the code, and the issuer, if the code is correct, assumes the person entering a transaction is the person to whom the code is assigned. Secret codes tend to be most appropriate when used in a closed community, as opposed to the open structure of the internet, because a secret code cannot guarantee the identity of the person using the code. However, it should be noted that the evidence of a shared secret will only be sufficient to satisfy the relying party that an authorized user used the code. Evidence of the procedures and systems used by the relying party will not be sufficient to prove to a third party, such as a court, that it was the user and not the relying party that added the code. It is posited that a secret code cannot be considered strictly as a signature, because the use of the code tends only to be used for the single characteristic of authenticating the user,[1] but two courts have decided otherwise, with respect, correctly, given the facts.[2] However, secret codes can be used as additional tools in a protocol, such as the generation of a key. The aim in generating a key is to be as unpredictable as possible, and one method of initiating the generation process is to use a secret key, such as a password. Another way of generating a key would be to use a pseudo-random number generator.

1   Ross Anderson *Security Engineering*, para 9.4 for a study of the problems relating to automatic teller machines; Jos Dumortier, Patrick Van Eecke and Ilse Anné *The Legal Aspects of Digital Signatures*, 60–63.
2   *Standard Bank London Ltd v Bank of Tokyo Ltd* [1995] CLC 496; [1996] 1 C.T.L.R. T-17 and *Industrial & Commercial Bank Ltd v Banco Ambrosiano Veneto SpA* [2003] 1 SLR 221.

Authentication using biometric measurements

15.14 This is the method by which it is possible to authenticate an individual through the measurement of physical characteristics. Whilst a biometric measurement has the ability to identify a person because it has reduced to digital format a unique characteristic of that individual, it cannot be a secret. Human characteristics comprise a number of attributes, some of which lend themselves to being measured:

(a) Appearance, such as height, weight, colour of skin, hair and eyes, visible physical markings, gender, facial hair, wearing of spectacles.
(b) Social behavioural traits, including voice recognition, style of speech, visible handicaps.

(c) Natural physiography, such as iris patterns, retinal scan, fingerprint or thumbprint verification, capillary patterns in earlobes, two or three dimensional facial recognition, veincheck and hand geometry, DNA patterns.

(d) Bio-dynamics, such as signature verification and the dynamics when using the keys on a keyboard.[1]

The use of biometrics has been hampered by the lack of processing power, amongst other factors. Until recently, neither the technology nor the infrastructure was in place to allow biometric measurements to be used on a wide scale, although there are an increasing number of products available on the market. There are significant difficulties with the use of biometric measurements, including the range of tolerances to reduce false negatives and increase false positives, or vice versa. The manufacturer of the device usually sets the tolerances, and a great many devices do not work.[2] The most prominent biometric system presently used to authenticate an individual is the recognition of their fingerprints, although voice recognition and facial recognition systems are in the process of being developed and implemented across the world, despite the problems that accompany their implementation. To offer an outline of some of the issues, if a face recognition system is installed, the purpose of the installation is crucial. If it is to help recognise terrorists in airports, as the International Civil Aviation Organization probably intends it to be, then biometric measurements need to be obtained of those terrorists that the authorities wish to identify. Unless a photograph exists of the person, then one must call into question the expense of installing such a system. A further problem relates to the accuracy of the software. In the unlikely event that the software is accurate to ninety per cent, one in ten people will be identified incorrectly as a terrorist. Multiply that false positive rate by the millions that travel through airports the world over each year, and it will be easy to imagine the chaos that will inevitably ensue, as well as the potential for legal action initiated by innocent travellers. A high false positive rate will also encourage those using the system to unofficially revise standing procedures for dealing with those instances where a person is positively identified, thus leading to the possibility of making mistakes.

1   Ross Anderson *Security Engineering* Chapter 13.
2   Ross Anderson *Security Engineering* Chapter 13.

FINGERPRINTS

15.15   Most fingerprint systems use optical or capacitive sensors for capturing the details of a fingerprint, such as branching and end points of the ridges. An optical sensor detects differences in reflection, whilst capacitive sensors detect differences in capacitance. Other systems use thermal sensors and ultrasound sensors. The process can be described thus: the image if the fingerprint is captured, features are then extracted from the image, and they are stored as templates on a database. Some systems encrypt templates and only manage the compressed images. Although widely used, there are problems associated with fingerprint scanners. The system can be attacked in a number of ways:

(a) The person being forced to press their finger against a scanner by a criminal.

(b) An impostor can use their own fingerprint and challenge the false rejection rate and false acceptance rate. Fingerprints tend to be categorized as 'loops', 'whorls' and 'arches', amongst other descriptions. If the attacker knows the category of the registered fingerprint and has a pattern similar to that of the registered one, there is a possibility that the scanner may not reject the false fingerprint.

(c) A person may have their finger severed, so a criminal can use the severed finger to defeat the scanning device.[1] This can be avoided where a device also gauges the temperature of the finger.

(d) The use of an artificial clone of the original fingerprint, where a fingerprint is copied by making a mould of the registered fingerprint, which is cheap to replicate and seems to be effective against many fingerprint devices.[2]

(e) Other attacks will work, depending on the nature of the fingerprint system. So, making a noise, flashing a light against the scanner; or heating up, cooling down, changing the humidity, hitting or causing the scanner to vibrate are all techniques that can cause the scanner to stop working within the tolerances to the environment.

Regardless of how easy it may be to defeat fingerprint reading systems, they seem to be most effective when used as a deterrence factor, especially in reducing false claims by people on state benefits.[3]

In summary, it is possible to use a measurement of a biometric characteristic to authenticate an individual, but such a measurement can only be used effectively in a closed system. There are too many problems associated with the use of biometric measurements in an open system. For instance, where a document is authenticated using a biometric measurement, the person relying on the measurement to authenticate the document will need to check the data against a database of biometric measurements. Unless there was such a depository in an open user community, the relying party will not be able to verify the source of the biometric measurement. Further, where human characteristics are reduced to numerical form by a biometric system, the system becomes susceptible to being deceived by the 'replay' of the relevant numerical information, even without the presence of the individual, unless the system as a whole can successfully be made secure against such an attack. Securing a database of biometric measurements is difficult to achieve in practice in distributed systems. A significant disadvantage of biometric measurements is the ease by which the measurement can be replicated by third parties for ulterior motives. Thus if biometric measurements are to be used, they can only be used effectively if they can prove two things: first, that the measurement actually was taken from the identified person at the time the measurement was taken, and second, that the measurement matches the data stored in the database.

1   Citibank have announced that it will set up a network of biometric ATMs in India. It is intended that thumbprints will be scanned to enable a customer to obtain access to their account. The report of this initiative does not indicate how the bank is going to deal with customer who have their thumbs cut off by thieves: Joe Leahy, 'Citigroup gives Indian poor a hand with thumbprint ATMs,' *Financial Times*, Saturday December 2/Sunday December 3, 2006, 15. See the example of Mr Kumaran, who had the tip of his index finger chopped off because the security system installed in his S-Class Mercedes Benz utilized the measurements of both the index fingers and thumbs of the owner. The immobiliser system caused the engine in the vehicle to cut out after a few minutes unless the owner pressed their finger or thumb on to the sensor. See a report at 'His finger for his car,' 31 March 2005, *New Straits Times*, archived at Persatuan Insurans Am Malaysia (General Insurance Association of Malaysia), *Insurance News*, available online at www.piam.org.my/news/insnews/ins_news.asp.

2   Tsutomu Matsumoto, Hiroyuki Matsumoto, Koji Yamada and Satoshi Hoshino *Impact of Artificial "Gummy" Fingers on Fingerprint Systems* paper prepared for Proceedings of SPIE Vol 4677 Optical Security and Counterfeit Deterrence Techniques IV Thursday-Friday 24-25 January 2002 available online at www.cryptome.org/gummy.htm.

3   Ross Anderson *Security Engineering*, 270.

Types of infrastructure for asymmetric cryptographic systems

15.16   There are, in broad terms, two types of infrastructure that provide for the signing of electronic documents by means of a digital signature: Pretty Good Privacy (PGP) software,[1] and public key cryptography. The discussion in this chapter will focus on the issues relating to the provision of key pairs that are provided and maintained by commercial organizations. However, it is to be noted that key pairs generated and used by individuals using PGP will also be subject to many of the issues discussed in this chapter. For this reason, a brief introduction to PGP is provided before discussing the issues relating to liability.

1   The International PGP home page is located at www.pgpi.org.

Pretty Good Privacy

15.17   This is a data encryption system developed by Philip Zimmerman in 1991. The PGP software includes packet formats that export a PGP key to a file and send it by email or on disk. There are two significant differences between PGP certificates and those used in public key infrastructure. The first is predicated on the method by which an identity can be established, or the model of trust used to ascertain an identity. It does not follow that the only means of establishing an identity is by way of a trusted third party.[1] By using PGP, the user joins a web of trust by acting as a certification authority and by having their own public keys certified by others. Carlisle Adams and

Steve Lloyd have described how it works, although it should be noted that the description is also an example of a non-hierarchical use of certificates:[2]

> '... Alice later receives a certificate purportedly belonging to Bob, she will see that this certificate is signed by David, whom she does not know, but that David's certificate is signed by Catherine, whom she does know and trust (for example, Catherine may have a certificate signed by Alice herself). Alice may then decide to trust Bob's key (by trusting the chain of keys from Catherine to David to Bob), or she may decide to reject Bob's key (judging that the "unknown" Bob is too many links away from the "known" Catherine).'

From this description, it becomes obvious why such a system is not appropriate for corporate, government or financial environments, although it might usefully be noted that the business model of the web of trust is similar to the usual model from the financial environment, where trust is based on introductions and references, and not on a hierarchical structure. The system also relies on users that are technically competent, and there is no control over how the trust model is set up, governed and controlled. In PGP, a key fingerprint (which is also found in X.509 certificates) supports public keys, which is a one-way hash of the public key. Various mechanisms are used to distribute public keys, one of which is a series of key servers. However, anybody can put a key on to such a server, connected to an email address, and it is not always clear when a public key has been revoked.[3]

The second difference between PGP and the public key infrastructure is the format of the certificate that each supports. The PGP certificate is different to the X.509v3 public-key certificates used by the public key infrastructure, although this situation is changing. Apparently version 6.5 of Open-PGP is now capable of supporting X.509 certificates. This does not, however, resolve the incompatibility between users of OpenPGP and S/MIME. As a result, there are barriers to interoperability, such as the incompatibility of the protocols, as well as the foundations used for the security of public key infrastructure security devices.[4] It remains to be seen whether vendors of public key infrastructure will offer products that support both.

1 Fred Piper and Sean Murphy *Cryptography: A Very Short Introduction* (Oxford University Press, 2002), 104–106; Carl M. Ellison 'Establishing Identity Without Certification Authorities' a paper presented at the 6th USENIX Security Symposium in San Jose July 22-25 1996 available at www.usenix.org/publications/library/proceedings/sec96/ellison.html.

2 Carlisle Adams and Steve Lloyd *Understanding PKI Concepts, Standards, and Deployment Considerations* (Addison-Wesley, 2nd edn 2002), 142.

3 Ross Anderson Security Engineering: *A Guide to Building Dependable Distributed Systems* (Wiley Computer Publishing, 2001), 440–441.

4 Carlisle Adams and Steve Lloyd *Understanding PKI Concepts, Standards, and Deployment Considerations*, 80; IETF RFC 4212/RFC4212 'Alternative Certificate Formats for the Public-Key Infrastructure Using X.509 (PKIX) Certificate Management Protocols' for further up-to-date information.

Types of public key infrastructure

15.18 In broad terms, there are two types of public key infrastructure structure. The type of structure will affect the nature and extent of the legal liability that participants are exposed to. This in turn will determine how participants manage their legal liability. The two categories are:

(a) A closed environment, where there is only one domain for all communications. This domain can be located in a single place for a single enterprise, or comprise a collection of enterprises, each of which operate under the same set of technical and operational procedures. One example may be a multinational company that operates in several jurisdictions and maintains an intra-company domain across the world. Another example may be a group of end users (both sending and receiving parties) that enter a network with one or more certification authorities by which liability is allocated according to agreed contractual terms between the parties. One vendor that operates in this way is IdenTrust.[1]

(b) An open environment, where a sender enters into an agreement with a certification authority to provide a certificate for a verification key, and where the relying parties are not known by either the sending party or certification authority in advance. The role of trusted third parties, also called certification authorities, is to provide certificates that link the identity of the owner to the public key. These bodies can be public or private, licensed or unlicensed. Whether a certification authority is in the hands of a public or private body, and whether is it licensed or unlicensed, it must be trustworthy.

1   The IdenTrust website is located at www.identrus.com.

Management of the key and certificate

15.19 The foundation of the public key infrastructure rests on asymmetric cryptography, with a public and private key pair. The public key is usually distributed in the form of a certificate, whilst the private key is a separate item with its own distinct structure that should be protected from being disclosed to unauthorized third parties when it is transported, used and stored. Once a person subscribes to a digital signature, a range of issues must be addressed that are referred to as lifecycle management, amongst other terms. Regardless of the name given to the process, procedures and processes must be in place to create the certificate and key pair, verify the identity of the applicant, distribute the certificate and cancel the certificate at the end of its period of validity or before, should it be compromised. The quality of software, design of the network and management of the security system all affect the way the keys and certificate are managed and stored. This is important, because a digital signature is not computed by the user, but by a computer. A computer will carry out the task on the instructions of a user, but a computer is not in a position to identify whether the instructions come from a legitimate user or the signals from unauthorized malicious software that has successfully embedded itself in the computer.

Identifying an applicant

15.20 It should be recalled that an individual could generate their own public and private key pair, using software on their computer. The individual then provides the certification authority with evidence of their identity. The type of evidence and degree of proof will depend on the nature of the type of certifying certificate required. In any event, the identity of the person or entity must be bound to the public key. When confirming the identity of a person or legal entity, a certification authority will be expected to comply with the requirements from a recognized body such as the European Telecommunications Standards Institute. The Institute have prepared what is termed a 'baseline' for policy requirements for certification authorities. Their paper 'Electronic Signatures and Infrastructures (ESI); Policy requirements for certification authorities issuing public key certificates'[1] sets out the scope on page 6, which provides the following:

'The present document specifies policy requirements relating to Certification Authorities (CAs) issuing public key certificates. It defines policy requirements on the operation and management practices of certification authorities issuing certificates such that subscribers, subjects certified by the CA and relying parties may have confidence in the applicability of the certificate in support of cryptographic mechanisms.

The policy requirements are defined in terms of three reference certificates policies and a framework from which CAs can produce a certificate policy targeted at a particular service.'

Services providers are required to make an explicit choice between these alternatives: 'Service Providers adopting the present document as a framework for their own particular certificate policy need to make an explicit choice between these three alternatives and state clearly in their certificate policy which alternative they have adopted.'

It also requires the certification authority to undertake a number of tasks, depending on the level of quality the certification authority adopts in relation to its certification policy, in particular to reliably identify the person or entity applying for a certifying certificate, as provided in paragraph 7.3.1:

'The CA shall ensure that evidence of subscriber's and subject's identification and accuracy of their names and associated data are either properly examined as part of the defined service or, where applicable, concluded through examination of attestations from appropriate and authorized sources, and that subscriber certificate requests are accurate, authorized and complete according to the collected evidence or attestation.'

As this summary indicates, the implication is that the certification authority, or the registration authority where such work is subcontracted out, should meet the applicant face-to-face, *where applicable*, and gather sufficient evidence supporting their identity. This is a time-consuming and expensive task if the link between the identity of the person or legal entity is to be of any probative value.[2] Where a certificate authority does not meet each applicant personally, the value of a certificate will be in proportion to the extent of authentication undertaken by the certificate authority.

---

1   ETSI TS 102 042 V1.2.4 (2007-03) and Schedule 2(d) to the Electronic Signature Regulations 2002 SI 2002/318 in relation to the issuance of qualified certificates. ETSI is not the only body offering standards. Various initiatives have been established at national, regional and international levels, including the International Chamber of Commerce www.iccwbo. org/; Internet Law and Policy Forum www.ilpf.org; the Internet Engineering Task Force www.ietf.org; the World Wide Web Consortium www.w3.org and the American Bar Association www.abanet.org. See also 'Guide on the Use of Electronic Signatures – Part 1: Legal and Technical Aspects' CEN Workshop Agreement CWA 14365-1 (March 2004) and 'Guide on the Use of Electronic Signatures – Part 2: Profile for Software Signature Creation Devices' CWA 14365-2 (March 2004) from the European Committee for Standardization. For an overview, see Fred Piper, Simon Blake-Wilson and John Mitchell Digital Signatures Security & Controls (Information Systems Audit and Control Foundation, 1999) Chapter 5 and Carlisle Adams and Steve Lloyd *Understanding PKI Concepts, Standards, and Deployment Considerations*, Part II.

2   It is to be presumed (this is a rebuttable presumption) that now the present government of the United Kingdom have brought in the Identity Cards Act 2006 (previously and euphemistically called 'entitlement' cards), that it will ensure sufficient sums of money (provided by those subjects that pay tax) will be allocated to ensure that the identity of each individual required to have such a card in their possession is guaranteed beyond reasonable doubt. Failure so to do will cause the concept of an 'identity' card to fall into disrepute, and the money will have been better spent on following the example of the French Republic and renovating the neglected railway infrastructure built by our Victorian forebears.

THE QUALITY OF THE EVIDENCE

15.21   Matters relating to the quality of evidence provided by the applicant must also be considered, as set out at paragraph 7.3.1 (d):

'The Service Provider shall collect either direct evidence, or an attestation from an appropriate and authorized source, of the identity (e.g. name) and, if applicable, any specific attributes of subjects to whom a certificate is issued. Submitted evidence may be in the form of either paper or electronic documentation. Verification of the subject's identity shall be by appropriate means and in accordance with national law.'

A number of general requirements apply to matters of identification, although the certificate authority does not have to follow the advice (paragraph 7.3.1 (e)):

'If the subject is a physical person evidence of the subject's identity (e.g. name) shall be checked against a physical person either directly or indirectly using means which provides equivalent assurance to physical presence (An example of evidence checked indirectly against a physical person is documentation presented for registration which was acquired as the result of an application requiring physical presence). Evidence for verifying other entities shall involve procedures which provide the same degree of assurance.'

A person

15.22   Where the applicant is a person, the policy provides for the following requirements that must be addressed by the certification authority (paragraph 7.3.1 (f)):

'If the subject is a physical person, evidence shall be provided of:

i.   full name (including surname and given names);
ii.   date and place of birth, reference to a nationally recognized identity document, or other attributes which may be used to, as far as possible, distinguish the person from others with the same name.'

Where a person is linked to an organization, such as an officer or employee, for instance, the policy sets out the requirements that are to be followed (paragraph 7.3.1 (g)):

'If the subject is a physical person who is identified in association with a legal person, or organizational entity (e.g. the subscriber), evidence shall be provided of:

i.   full name (including surname and given names) of the subject;
ii.   date and place of birth, reference to a nationally recognized identity document, or other attributes of the subscriber which may be used to, as far as possible, distinguish the person from others with the same name;
iii.   full name and legal status of the associated legal person or other organizational entity (e.g. the subscriber)
iv.   any relevant existing registration information (e.g. company registration) of the associated legal person or other organizational entity;
v.   evidence that the subject is associated with the legal person or other organizational entity.'

A legal entity

15.23 Where the applicant is a legal entity, the following further requirements are set out in the policy (paragraph 7.3.1 (h)):

'If the subject is an organizational entity, evidence shall be provided of:

i. full name of the organizational entity;
ii. reference to a nationally recognized registration, or other attributes which may be used to, as far as possible, distinguish the organizational entity from others with the same name.'

Given that Companies House does not undertake any material verification of companies, it is debatable whether there is a convincing way in which anyone can prove, or fail to prove, that they are an officer of a company. This issue is of particular importance, given the ease of misappropriating the trading name of a company registered with Companies House. This is how it works: a fraudster obtains copies of documents publicly available from Companies House with examples of the signatures of the officer of the company. They then obtain the necessary forms, and change the registered address and names of directors of the company. The next step is to begin buying goods and services on credit in the name of the company that has been hijacked. The swindle becomes apparent when the companies that have supplied the goods or services want paying. Another variation is for the thieves to open a bank account or apply for a credit card in the name of the company. Yet another twist is the use of such devices by criminals to launder money through a seemingly legitimate business. It should be noted that the responsibility for the accuracy of the information held by Companies House is on the directors and the company secretary, not the Registrar of Companies.[1]

1   'Identity theft at Companies House' *Computer Law & Security Report* Volume 18 number 5 September/October 2002, 370. Companies House has now introduced a service with the aim of preventing this occurring in the future. There are three levels of service offered: WebFiling, an online filing service; PROtected Online Filing, where Companies House will only accept forms relating to changes of address and directors' details electronically; the Monitor service, that enables the user to monitor documents filed into Companies House, covering the user's documents, as well as those of competitors and business collaborators.

The certificate

15.24 When the certification authority has verified the identity of the individual or entity to their satisfaction, they will issue a certificate. This is a computer record that affirms the connection of a public key to an identified person or corporate entity. The European Telecommunications Standards Institute have set out, at paragraph 7.3.3, the information that the certificate will include:

'(a) the certificates shall include:

    i.   identification of the certification-service-provider and the country in which it is established;

    ii.   the name of the subject, or a pseudonym which shall be identified as such;

    iii. provision for a specific attribute of the signatory to be included if relevant, depending on the purpose for which the certificate is intended;

    iv. the public key which corresponds to the private key under the control of the subject;

    v.   an indication of the beginning and end of the period of validity of the certificate;

    vi. the serial number of the certificate;

    vii. the electronic signature of the certification authority issuing it;

    viii. limitations on the scope of use of the certificate, if applicable; and

    ix. limits on the value of transactions for which the certificate can be used, if applicable.'[1]

It does not follow that a certification authority will undertake this task. There are a number of reasons for this. First, the cost of developing a suitable administrative infrastructure with the relevant expertise will be expensive. It may not, therefore, be possible to justify the cost. Second, there are a number of organizations that already have the relevant expertise, such as banks and credit reference agencies. Whilst the database these organizations use may be imperfect, as is the case with most databases,[2] nevertheless it makes sound economic sense not to replicate a service that already exists. Thus an added layer of contact will be introduced where a certification authority issues a certificate. First, the registration authority will take steps to verify the identity of the entity seeking a certificate. Upon confirmation of identity by the registration authority, the certification authority will then issue a certificate. Thus an additional layer of complexity is added to the mix surrounding the link between the person or entity seeking a certificate and the subsequent granting of the certificate. The next point to ponder is the entity that generates the registration authority's key. Whoever generates the registration authority's key will also be involved in the contractual web. In all probability, a contractual relationship will exist between the certification authority and the registration authority, and the contract will provide for the liability and warranties between each entity. Where liability will fall in the event of a dispute may depend on the particular circumstances of the case.

1   Carlisle Adams and Steve Lloyd *Understanding PKI Concepts, Standards, and Deployment Considerations* Chapter 6.

2   Cabinet Office 'Identity Fraud: A study' July 2002, 3.29–3.44.

The generation of the key pair belonging to the subscribing party

15.25 It is good practice for the subscribing party to generate their own key pair. Where the subscribing party generates a key pair, there is, theoretically, less of a risk of the private key being compromised. However, many subscribing parties will not have the software to generate their own key pair. This means a third party will be requested to generate a key pair on their behalf. There are two aspects to this that demonstrate a level of vulnerability that may be undesirable. The party generating the key pair will have to be trusted not to compromise the key, and the key pair will be vulnerable to attack or compromise when transported to the user.[1]

---

1   Carlisle Adams and Steve Lloyd *Understanding PKI Concepts, Standards, and Deployment Considerations*, 92–94; Fred Piper and Sean Murphy *Cryptography: A Very Short Introduction*, 109–110.

Validating the public key

15.26 Either the certification authority or the registration authority should carry out checks that the public key is actually that of the applicant, that is the applicant has the corresponding private key. The check is simple: it needs to be determined whether the subscriber can make a signature that can be verified by the public key. If carried out, such a check can protect both the subscribing party and the authority that undertakes the task, because it can ensure the subscribing party has submitted the correct key and the authority can demonstrate it undertook care to investigate and verify for itself that the public key was that of the applicant, thus making sure it did not certify an incorrect or invalid key.

Distributing the certificate

15.27 Once the certification authority has created a certificate, it is important for both the authority and the subscribing party to ensure the content of the certificate is accurate and relates to the correct entity. The certificate is usually sent electronically, which can present a number of problems:

(a)   Where the subscribing party signs to acknowledge receipt of the certificate, they will not necessarily agree its content. Where a certificate as been created by an impostor, evidence of receipt will be just that: evidence that the certificate was received. In an ideal world, the subscribing party should be required to indicate they received and accept the content of the certificate by using another certified signing key.

(b)   Before the certificate is issued, the certificate authority must decide whether to wait until it has received acceptance from the subscribing party by which the subscribing party acknowledges receipt of the certificate before it is delivered, or to issue the certificate and ask for a receipt. If the subscribing party does not send a receipt to the certification authority, then the certificate may have to be revoked immediately.[1]

It becomes clear that certification authorities must produce security policies that deal with some, if not all, of these issues. They should be made publicly available, and may well be incorporated into any contract that is formed between the certification authority and the subscribing party. Two types of document are often created: a certificate policy and a certificate practice statement. The names of these documents will differ between authorities, as will the division between them of their subject matter. Further, audit trails are crucial to check that the methods and procedures that control the process function correctly. Such audit trails must be secure and, ideally, be capable of being verified by an independent third party.[2]

1   Fred Piper, Simon Blake-Wilson and John Mitchell *Digital Signatures Security & Controls*, 36–37.
2   Fred Piper, Simon Blake-Wilson and John Mitchell *Digital Signatures Security & Controls*, 36–37; Carlisle Adams and Steve Lloyd *Understanding PKI Concepts, Standards, and Deployment Considerations*, 96.

Distributing certification authority keys

15.28 Individuals or entities wishing to use the public keys of different organizations or individuals may well have to visit each certificate authority to obtain the relevant public key. To help reduce the effort that is required to do this, certificate authorities may cross-certify the public keys of other certification authorities. There are two types of cross-certification:

(a) Where two certification authorities are part of the same domain. For instance, there are two levels within a given certification authority – the higher level may certify the lower level. This is called intradomain cross-certification.

(b) Where certification authorities are different entities, the process is called interdomain cross-certification.

Cross-certification can occur in two ways. One certification authority can cross-certify another unilaterally. Alternatively, two certification authorities can undertake a mutual cross-certification exercise. A cross-certificate can be issued to a certification authority, or a certification authority can issue it. The process of cross-certification is where a certificate authority gives copies of its keys to another certification authority. This is achieved either by handing over the key or by issuing special 'authority certificates', the purpose of which is to bind each certificate authority to its public key.

A further mechanism is to have a hierarchy of certification authorities, where higher-level authorities certify low-level authorities. In this case, the prospective user needs to verify the highest level certificate first, usually called a root certification authority, then to check the trail and validity of every authority certificate that lead to the certificate the user wants to trust or use.[1] On a final note, when a person buys a computer with software already installed, there are a number of certificates already installed in their browsers. As a result, the user, without realising it, trusts whoever supplied the computer to include appropriate authorities' certificates. The certificates can be deleted, and new ones added, if the user knows how. If the user does not update their browser, the certificates will eventually expire and produce sometimes rather obscure error messages when signatures are verified.

1   Carlisle Adams and Steve Lloyd *Understanding PKI Concepts, Standards, and Deployment Considerations*, 132–145 for a detailed discussion; Fred Piper, Simon Blake-Wilson and John Mitchell *Digital Signatures Security & Controls*, 37–38.

Revocation of a certificate

15.29   The certificate is used to bind the name of a person or entity with their public key. However, there may be many reasons for revoking a certificate before the expiry date, including, but not limited to:

(a)   The user is aware that the private key corresponding to the certificate has been lost or compromised.

(b)   The certificate holder asks for the certificate to be revoked.

(c)   The certification authority revokes a certificate where the holder breaches a term of the agreement.

(d)   Where the certificate was issued in error.

There are a range of technical solutions to providing public knowledge of certificates that have been revoked, but the most well known is the certificate revocation list.[1] A certification revocation list is a signed data structure that contains a list of those certificates that have been revoked. Where a list exists, there are a number of important issues that must be addressed:

(a)   The difference in time between the command to revoke the certificate and the last time the certificate was used.

(b)   The reliability of the revocation procedure, in other words, whether it can be relied upon to provide a definitive answer that can be trusted.

(c)   The number of revocation commands that the revocation system can handle at any one time.[2]

If a certification authority does not have a revocation list, the person seeking to determine whether to rely on a certificate needs to know how they can establish whether a key has been revoked or compromised. The European Telecommunications Standards Institute paper 'Electronic Signatures and Infrastructures (ESI); Policy requirements for certification authorities issuing public key certificates' referred to above, provides guidance to certification authorities respecting certificate revocation and suspension at paragraph 7.3.6. The provisions include the following:

(a)　The request is to be processed on receipt.

(b)　The request must be authenticated and checked to be from an authorized source.

(c)　The status of the certificate may be set to 'suspended' whilst the revocation is being confirmed.

(d)　Depending on the level of services offered, a certificate revocation list shall be published at least every 72 hours or 24 hours. However, where a certificate revocation list is used as the only means of providing revocation status information, every list is required to state a time for the next scheduled issue, although a new list may be published before the stated time of the next issue.

(e)　The certification authority must sign a certificate revocation list or an authority designated to undertake this task.

(f)　A certification authority is required to provide the revocation status of certificates as specified in their certification practice statement.

It will be noted that the verifying party is also required to determine:

(a)　Whether the certification revocation list is on a secure server.

(b)　Check the public key of the certification revocation list, which should refer to a higher-level certificate revocation list server, because the certification revocation list server cannot testify to the validity of its own public key.

Where a certification authority suffers a failure in their system, it is required to use its best endeavours to rectify the problem, as provided for in paragraph 7.3.6 (i): 'Upon system failure, service or other factors which are not under the control of the CA, the CA shall make best endeavours to ensure that this information service is not unavailable for longer than a maximum period of time as denoted in the certification practice statement.' It is also a conditional requirement of the Institute's policy that where the certification authority issues certificates to the public, 'Revocation status information shall be publicly and internationally available' (paragraph 7.3.6 (k)).

1　Carlisle Adams and Steve Lloyd *Understanding PKI Concepts, Standards, and Deployment Considerations*, 107–126.

2　Niels Ferguson and Bruce Schneier, *Practical Cryptography* (Wiley Publishing, 2003), 333.

Expiry of keys

15.30　Certificates have a fixed period of validity, in the same way that a royal seal matrix had, and they expire in due course. One technical question relates to how the life of the key is computed. Ellison and Schneier contend that the key has a 'theft lifetime' as a function of the vulnerability of the sub-system that stores the key. Other factors that also should be taken into account include the threat of physical and network exposure to attacks and how attractive the key is to an attacker.[1] In any event, there are three options available when a certificate expires:

(a) No action is taken.

(b) The certificate is renewed and the same public key is placed into a new certificate with a new period of validity.

(c) A new pair of public and private keys are generated and a new certificate is generated to provide for a certificate update.[2]

1 Carl Ellison and Bruce Schneier 'Ten Risks of PKI: What You're not Being Told about Public Key Infrastructure' *Computer Security Journal* Volume XVI Number 1 2000, 6 available in electronic format online at www.schneier.com/paper-pki.pdf.

2 Carlisle Adams and Steve Lloyd, *Understanding PKI Concepts, Standards, and Deployment Considerations*, 101–102.

THE DUTIES OF A USER

15.31 There are a number of points that people or organizations that use private keys should be aware of:

Management of private keys

15.32 The user must manage their private keys effectively and take measures that are appropriate to prevent the unauthorized use of the keys, and to protect them securely against any other form of attack, such as theft or misuse by a third party that gains access to the system by way of malicious software or other method.

Storage of private keys after expiry

15.33 When deciding whether to use private keys, their use should be carefully monitored, because different types of algorithm are used for different purposes. Thus consideration must be given to the possibility that a private key may be the subject of a s 49 notice under the Regulation of Investigatory Powers Act 2000, and the safe storage of keys that have expired.

Disposal of equipment with private keys

15.34 Particular care should be taken when disposing of the hardware that contains the private keys. The EU Directive on waste electrical and electronic equipment,[1] which had to be brought into force into member states by 13 August 2004,[2] requires all electrical and electronic equipment to be reused, recycled and subject to any other form of recovery to reduce the disposal of waste. With the exception of equipment that is used in connection with the protection of the essential interests of the security of member states,[3] the Directive applies to all IT and telecommunications equipment, including centralized data processing, mainframes, minicomputers, printer units, personal computing, personal computers, laptop computers, notebook computers, notepad computers, user terminals and systems and 'any other products and equipment for the collection, storage, processing, presentation or communication of information by electronic means.'[4] Producers are required to provide for the treatment of electrical and electronic equipment using the best available recovery and recycling treatments.[5]

1   Directive 2002/96/EC of the European Parliament and of the Council of 27 January 2003 on waste electrical and electronic equipment OJ L 37 13.3.2003, p. 24. In the United Kingdom, the Directive was implemented by The Waste Electrical and Electronic Equipment Regulations 2006 (SI 2006 No. 3289), the Regulations entered into force on 2 January 2007 (Regulation 1(2)); Regulations 15 to 17 and Schedule 4 entered into force on 1 April 2007 (Regulation 1(3)); Regulations 31 to 36 and 40 entered into force on 1 July 2007 (Regulation 1(4)).
2   Article 17(1).
3   Article 2(3).
4   Article 2(1), Annex 1A and IB.
5   Article 6(1).

Internal management

15.35 The internal management of a certification authority, which the individual user may not be familiar with, can affect the trust to be placed in the certificates issued. Such issues include, but are not limited to:
(a) The level and extent of the checks made on employees.
(b) How to verify the identity of the employees that control the keys.
(c) Policies on how keys are stored.
(d) What mechanisms are in place to verify that the relevant policies are followed.
(e) Whether the internal management of the certificate system is properly carried out.
(f) The level and extent of any insurance cover may also have a bearing on the suitability of different types of certificate issued.

The European Telecommunications Standards Institute provides a detailed list of administrative and management procedures at paragraph 7.4 that a certificate authority is required to apply, which must be adequate and relate to recognized standards.

Barriers to the use of the public key infrastructure

15.36 There are a variety of problems that affect those vendors that purvey digital signature services. For an industry in its infancy, perhaps this is to be expected. However, given the extent to which government and non-governmental agencies attempt to reach universal standards of various kinds, it does seem somewhat bizarre that some of the problems even exist. For instance:

(a) There is no standard in the industry relating to the provision of a directory service. A number of models exist and competing standards are in the process of being considered, as well as the development of proprietary solutions.

(b) Vendors do not implement some functions, and when they are implemented, they may be implemented in a different manner to another vendor. This leads to problems with interoperability between the systems of different vendors.

(c) The performance of the repository service where the certificate revocation list is held may be a problem. At present there are a limited number of vendors that operate a public key infrastructure, and the numbers of people using those that are available are in the minority. Whether the systems in place are capable of expanding with greater use in the future is open to debate.

(d) The number of people that have any knowledge of public key cryptography is small, although expanding. The numbers of personnel required are not limited to administrative personnel, but include people in senior positions that can develop the relevant policy documents, such as certification practice statements and interdomain interoperability agreements. The public key infrastructure strategy must also be considered and documented.[1]

1 Carlisle Adams and Steve Lloyd, *Understanding PKI Concepts, Standards, and Deployment Considerations* Chapter 25.

What a public key infrastructure can and cannot do

15.37 Depending on how it is used, a public key infrastructure has its uses. However, it is very important to be clear about what a digital signature can and cannot do.

What no form of electronic signature is capable of doing

15.38 A digital signature can provide for the authenticity of information. It binds key pairs with names. The recipient of a message or document with which a digital signature is associated can confirm the binding of the verification key with the name of the person whose private key has been used. But the recipient cannot determine whether the sending party authorized the use of the digital signature: this is also true of any other form of electronic signature.

THE WEAKEST LINK

15.39 Although an emphasis has been made in this text upon the reliance placed upon the activities of certification authorities and other participants in the public key infrastructure (registration authorities, directory services listing public keys, certification revocation list services – to name but a few), comparatively little discussion has been given to the weakest link in the chain of a digital signature. If Bob wants Alice to use a digital signature to authenticate her messages, he has got to persuade Alice that it is essential that when he receives a message or document from her, he can be completely assured, whether he decides to become a verifying party or not, that it was Alice, and only Alice, that caused the digital signature to be affixed to the document or message. He therefore has to persuade Alice that she must take such good care of her private key that she can accept the risk of being held responsible for unauthorised use of it by others. If Alice asks, not without reason, 'What's in it for me?' there seems to be no answer. Whether Bob decides to undertake the sometimes gargantuan task of carrying out the verification procedure or not, if he cannot satisfy himself that Alice kept her private key absolutely safe, he cannot be sure that Alice affixed the digital signature to the message. So he will try to insist that Alice carries the blame anyway.

THE BURDEN OF MANAGING THE PRIVATE KEY

15.40 The user of a digital signature is expected to keep their private key secure. Failure to do so will mean a mischievous member of staff or a malicious third party can append a digital signature to a document or message for nefarious purposes. The management of the private key acts to underpin the efficacy of a digital signature. Some of the issues that a recipient must give consideration to include those set out below.

By-passing passwords

15.41 Depending on the nature of the application software on any given computer or system, where a user has set their security setting to 'High' they will have to enter their password every time they wish to enter their private key to affix a digital signature to a document or message. Where their security setting is set to the default, 'Low', the messages will be automatically signed without any further intervention by the user. Given this scenario, any person with access to a computer or device containing an electronic signature in a powered-up state will be able to send messages or documents with an electronic signature affixed.

Another alternative is for the user to retain their private key in memory during the login session. A user must either enter their password every time they wish to use their private key to affix a digital signature to a document or message, or they retain their private key in memory during the login session. If a user keeps the private key in memory, it exposes the key to being stolen. Examples include leaving the computer unattended, thus permitting a third party to take sufficient action to steal the key. Alternately, if the private key is on a laptop computer and the laptop computer is stolen, it may be possible for the thief to obtain access to the private key. Further, malicious software has been developed to steal passwords and private keys. Finally, even if the private key is stored on an encrypted smart card, it must be used with a computer to sign a message or document, and the computer may have been maliciously programmed to sign a document or message other than the one the user intends to sign.[1]

---

1 Dr Adam L. Young and Dr Moti Yung, *Malicious Cryptography Exposing Cryptovirology* (Wiley Publishing, 2004) for further examples of how the technology can be used for malicious purposes.

Quality of passwords

15.42 There are a number of issues surrounding the question of passwords, and they are well documented. The important point to bear in mind, is that the entire edifice of the public key infrastructure and the security of the private key rests, to a very large extent, on the quality of the password used to protect it. Most of us prefer to use passwords that are easy to remember, which in turn makes a password easy to guess and vulnerable to attack. If the user does not have an effective control over the quality of the passwords used, the system will be vulnerable to an offline guessing attack.[1]

If a recipient of a digital signature intends to rely on the purported authority of the signature, they have a range of options:

(a) To rely on the signature without taking any affirmative action. The courts, on the basis that a recipient cannot, without going to extraordinary lengths, ensure the signature was authorized and is genuine, may accept this reliance. However, if a court were to consider this option as a possibility, it is conceivable that judges will take into account the arrangements between the sender and recipient before reaching a conclusive judgment. For instance, if a recipient relied on a digital signature attached to a high-value contract, a court may well consider it is appropriate in the circumstances that a recipient takes reasonable steps to authenticate and verify the digital signature, and to ensure the sending party duly authorized it.

(b) To rely on the signature after undertaking steps to verify and authenticate the certificate, thus becoming a verifying party. Should a dispute occur, one of the questions a court will probably address is to what extent were the actions taken by the verifying party adequate in the circumstances of the case, including their state of knowledge at the time.

(c) Ignore the digital signature and require the sending party to confirm their intentions by an alternative method, or to confirm, using another medium (such as letter, facsimile transmission or telephone), that the communication was sent by them.

As a result of the foregoing discussion, it becomes clear that public key cryptography is more suitable for server-to-server security, rather then for use on a desktop.

1   Don Davis, 'Compliance Defects in Public-Key Cryptography' a paper written for the Proceedings of the 6th Usenix Security Symposium (San Jose, CA, 1996) paragraphs 3.4 and 3.5 available online from www.world.std.com/~dtd/; Heiko Roßnagel and Jan Zibuschka, 'Integrating qualified electronic signatures with password legacy systems', *Digital Evidence Journal*, 2007, Volume 4 Number 1, 5–11.

What a digital signature can do

15.43   The other uses to which cryptography can be put within a public key infrastructure include demonstrating the integrity of the message and providing for the confidentiality of a document.

The reader should take heed of a final thought that many people pushing the value of digital signatures should keep clearly within their sights: using digital signatures within a public key infrastructure will not act to correct human behaviour.[1]

1   Don Davis, 'Compliance Defects in Public-Key Cryptography' paragraph 1; Carlisle Adams and Steve Lloyd, *Understanding PKI Concepts, Standards, and Deployment Considerations* Chapter 14 for a useful and more detailed discussion.

Control of algorithms

15.44   The use of encryption software to provide for the integrity and confidentiality of electronic data, and as a means of authenticating entities has meant that many states have revisited the controls that were imposed by the NATO countries on the movement of such technology since 1949. Some states continue to impose stricter export controls than others on such technology, whilst others will not permit the importation of these types of technology.[1] With the increasing use of cryptography technologies and the ease of which such technologies can be distributed around the globe, most states have accepted the need to liberalise the export regime. The discussion that follows focuses on the control of encryption internationally and regionally (covering the European Union), but does not address the position in individual nation states.

1   The OECD ICCP Working Party produced a report in February 1999 'Inventory of Controls on Cryptography Technologies' (DSTI/ICCP/REG (98) 4/FINAL). This report does not appear to be available in electronic format. However, see the informal survey 'An International Survey of Encryption Policy' by the Electronic Privacy Information Center,

Washington, DC (although it is not clear if this is kept up to date) available online at www2.epic.org/reports/crypto2000/overview.html; country reports are available online at www2.epic.org/reports/crypto2000/.

A dual-use item

15.45 Cryptography is designated as dual-use goods, that is goods that can be used for both a military and for a civil purpose, and is therefore subject to export and import controls. The following is a brief description of the history of the controls and an outline of the present position.

The Co-ordinating Committee for Multilateral Export Controls

15.46 The North Atlantic Treaty Organization established the Co-ordinating Committee for Multilateral Export Controls (COCOM) in 1949, which existed to control the export of strategic products and technical data from members of the committee to proscribed countries. The original participating states were the USA, UK, France, Italy, Belgium, the Netherlands and Luxembourg. The committee maintained, amongst others, the International Industrial List and the International Munitions List. Cryptography was controlled by the committee. At a High Level Meeting of the representatives of the 17 participating states on 16 November 1993, it was agreed to terminate COCOM and establish a temporary New Forum before establishing a new multilateral agreement. Former cooperating countries to COCOM were invited to join the New Forum. COCOM was disbanded on 16 November 1993 and subsequently dissolved on 31 March 1994.

The Wassenaar Arrangement

15.47 When COCOM was disbanded, the participating members continued to follow the guidelines whilst a new arrangement was agreed. The agreement to establish the Wassenaar Arrangement On Export Controls for Conventional Arms and Dual-Use Goods and Technologies was reached at a High Level Meeting held on 19 December 1995, with the inaugural Plenary Meeting being held between 2 and 3 April 1996 in Vienna, where the secretariat is established. This is the first global ministerial arrangement on export controls, and it received final approval of the 33 co-founding countries in July 1996. It began operating in September 1996.[1]

---

1   The participating states are Argentina, Australia, Austria, Belgium, Bulgaria, Canada, Croatia, Czech Republic, Denmark, Estonia, Finland, France, Germany, Greece, Hungary, Ireland, Italy, Japan, Latvia, Lithuania, Luxembourg, Malta, Netherlands, New Zealand, Norway, Poland, Portugal, Republic of Korea, Romania, Russian Federation, Slovakia, South Africa, Spain, Sweden, Switzerland, Turkey, Ukraine, United Kingdom and United States of America.

LEGAL STATUS OF THE WASSENAAR ARRANGEMENT

15.48 The Arrangement has been described as a 'legally non-binding agreement', because it is not an international treaty, and it has not been ratified in participating states.[1] Perhaps it is better described as a non-binding agreement that is intended to influence the way a participating state controls the import and export of goods defined in the Agreement.

1   Simo-Pekka Parviainen *Cryptographic Software Export Controls in the EU* (Postgraduate thesis for the University of Helsinki, Faculty of Law, Department of Public Law, July 2000) para 3.2.

PURPOSE AND SCOPE

15.49 The aim of the Wassenaar Arrangement is to contribute to regional and international security and stability. It is intended to achieve this by encouraging participating states to be open about how they deal with export controls. In addition, the emphasis is to prevent the build-up of arms and dual-use goods that may reduce stability in any given region, by requiring participating states to take responsibility for the transfer of conventional arms and dual-use goods and technologies. Whether an item can be exported or imported remains the responsibility of each participating state. As a result, the national laws, policies and regulations will continue to apply to dual-use goods.

The purposes and scope of the Agreement were set out in the 'Initial Elements', as adopted by a Plenary session between 11 and 12 July 1996, as subsequently amended. The scope of the Agreement is, in brief:

(a)   The aim is to contribute to regional and international security and stability, by promoting transparency and greater responsibility in the transfer of conventional arms and dual-use goods and technologies.

(b)   It complements and reinforces the existing control regimes for weapons of mass destruction and their delivery systems.

(c)   It is intended to enhance co-operation to prevent armaments and sensitive dual-use items being acquired by a state for military use where a situation or the behaviour of a state is, or becomes, a cause for serious concern.

(d)   It is also intended to prevent the acquisition of conventional arms and dual-use goods and technologies by terrorist groups and organisations, as well as by individual terrorists.

THE CONTROL OF ENCRYPTION PRODUCTS

15.50 The control of encryption products is governed by the List of Dual-Use Goods and Technologies and Munitions List, Category 5 Part 2 Information Security.[1] There are exceptions to items controlled by the List. They are set out in Category 5 Part 2 and comprise the following:

1   The most recent changes to this list can be found on the Wassenaar website.

Note 2 relating to Category 5 Part 2

15.51   There is no control over products when accompanying a user for the personal use of the user.

Note 3, the Cryptography Note

15.52   Items in categories 5.A.2 (Systems, equipment and components) and 5.D.2 (Software) are excluded where items meet all of the following criteria (note (e) indicates that the secretariat will provide details of items that are accessible to the appropriate authority in the exporter's country to determine whether the conditions described in paragraphs a–c, set out below, have been complied with):
(a)   Generally available to the public by being sold, without restriction, from stock at retail selling points by means of any of the following:
    1   Over-the-counter transactions;
    2   Mail order transactions;
    3   Electronic transactions; or
    4   Telephone call transactions;
(b)   The cryptographic functionality cannot easily be changed by the user;
(c)   Designed for installation by the user without further substantial support by the supplier.

5.A.2 Systems, equipment and components, item 5.A.2.a.1

15.53   This section refers to systems, equipment and components that are designed or modified to use cryptography, employing digital techniques that perform any cryptographic function other than authentication or digital signature, and includes, in 5.A.2.a.1:
(a)   An symmetric algorithm using a key length of more than 56 bits; or
(b)   An asymmetric algorithm where the security of the algorithm is based on any of the following:
    1   Factorisation of integers in excess of 512 bits (e.g. RSA);
    2   Computation of discrete logarithms in a multiplicative group of a finite field of size greater than 512 bits (e.g. Diffie-Hellman over Z/pZ); or
    3   Discrete logarithms in a group other than mentioned in 5.A.2.a.1.b.2 in excess of 112 bits (e.g. Diffie-Hellman over an elliptic curve).

Section 5.A.2 does not control the following:
(a)   Personalised smart cards:
    1   Where the cryptographic capability is restricted for use in equipment or systems that are excluded from control under entries set out in the Note to 5.A.2; or

2 For general public-use applications where the cryptographic capability cannot easily be changed by a user and it is specially designed and limited to allow protection of personal data stored within the card.

(b) Receiving equipment for radio broadcasts, pay television or similar functions related to provision of services to consumers.

(c) Equipment where cryptographic capability is not accessible to a user and which is specially designed and limited to allow for the execution of copy-protected software; access to copy-protected contents and stored on read-only media, or information stored in encrypted form on media (e.g. in connection with the protection of intellectual property rights) when the media is offered for sale in identical sets to the public; or copying control if copyright protected audio and video data.

(d) Cryptographic equipment specially designed and limited for banking or money transactions, including the collection and settlement of fares or credit functions.

(e) Portable or mobile radiotelephones for civil use that are not capable of end-to-end encryption.

(f) Cordless telephone equipment not capable of end-to-end encryption where the maximum effective range of cordless operation that is not boosted is less than 400 metres according to the manufacturer's specifications.

The technical notes in Category 5 Part 2 offer the following comments:

'1. Authentication and digital signature functions include their associated key management function.

2. Authentication includes all aspects of access control where there is no encryption of files or text except as directly related to the protection of passwords, Personal Identification Numbers (PINs) or similar data to prevent unauthorised access.

3. Cryptography does not include 'fixed' data compression or coding techniques.'

All other types of device and software must have an export licence. The Arrangement does not define what export regime a participating state should implement, but the controls must be 'fully effective'.[1] A short paper 'Best practices for effective enforcement' was agreed at the Plenary on 1 December 2000.[2] This paper sets out a list of best practices, covering preventative enforcement, investigations, the provision of effective penalties, international cooperation and the exchange of information.

The General Technology Note (NF (95) CA WP 1) refers to the transfer of technology for production or development, and provides:[3]

'Governments agree that the transfer of "technology" according to the General Technology Note, for "production" or "development" of items on this list shall be treated with vigilance in accordance with national policies and the aims of this regime.'

A further General Technology Note (WG2 GTN TWG/WP1 Revised 2) also makes it clear that: 'It is understood that Member Governments are expected to exercise controls on intangible "technology" as far as the scope of their legislation will allow.' Participating states are required to implement the terms of the Arrangement according to their national policies. As a result, the USA in particular has been subject to criticism, because of its past attempts to restrict the export of algorithms to those supporting keys no longer than 56 bits. The principal argument against the restriction of exporting cryptographic algorithms is based on the argument that cryptography is mainly used for protection, and is therefore defensive in its application, rather than offensive. In any event, controls remain, although the 'General Software Note' on page 3 of the Dual-Use List indicates that the Lists do not control software which is either:

'1. Generally available to the public by being:
    a. Sold from stock at retail selling points without restriction, by means of:
        1   Over-the-counter transactions;
        2   Mail order transactions;
        3   Electronic transactions; or
        4   Telephone call transactions; and
    b. Designed for installation by the user without further substantial support by the supplier; or
2. In the public domain.'

The phrase 'in the public domain' means, when it applies to technology and software (as defined) '... which has been made available without restrictions upon its further dissemination (copyright restrictions do not remove 'technology' and 'software' from being 'in the public domain."[4]

1   The Wassenaar Arrangement, Initial Elements, Appendix 4 fourth bullet point.
2   Available online at www.wassenaar.org/publicdocuments/2000_effectiveenforcement.html.
3   The Wassenaar Arrangement, List of Dual-Use Goods and Technologies and Munitions List, Statements of understanding and validity notes, (WA-LIST (06) 1, 06-12-2006), 200.
4   The definition is provided in Annex I to Council Regulation (EC) No 1334/2000 of 22 June 2000 setting up a Community regime for the control of exports of dual-use items and technology OJ L 159, 30.6.2000, p. 1–215. For those interested in the issues, see Bert-Jaap Koops *The Crypto Controversy A Key Conflict in the Information Society* (Kluwer Law International, 1999); Crypto Law Survey; Greg Taylor *Wassenaar – The Cryptic Enigma* Internet Law Bulletin 2 1999 available online from www.efa.org.au/Issues/Crypto/enigma.html; Dr Brian Gladman, *Wassenaar Controls, Cyber-Crime and Information Terrorism: A Report by Cyber-Rights & Cyber Liberties (UK)* available online at www.cyber-rights.org/crypto/wassenaar.htm; Electronic Frontiers Australia *The Walsh Report* available online at www.efa.org.au/Issues/Crypto/Walsh/.

Organisation for Economic Co-operation and Development (OECD)

15.54 The OECD discussed and drafted various sets of policy guidelines relating to the issues surrounding the use of cryptography during the last decade of the twentieth century. A 'Recommendation of the Council Concerning Guidelines for Cryptography Policy' was subsequently passed on 27 March 1997. The Guidelines for Cryptography Policy are not binding on members and are not part of international law. The guidelines provide for six principles, which are declared to be '... interdependent and should be implemented as a whole so as to balance the various interests at stake' and are set out in Part V:[1]

(a) Trust in cryptographic methods: this guideline maintains the need to provide that cryptographic methods are trustworthy to generate confidence in their use.

(b) Choice of cryptographic methods: users should be permitted to determine methods of cryptography that meets their needs, and government controls should be no more than essential in undertaking the responsibilities of government.

(c) Market driven development of cryptographic methods: the aim should be for competition to ensure the market in cryptographic methods continues to be open and competitive.

(d) Standards for cryptographic methods: internationally recognised standards making bodies should be involved with establishing standards, and governments, business and other experts should be included in this process.

(e) Protection of privacy and personal data: safeguards relating to privacy, including the provision of confidentiality of data and communications and the protection of the identity of individuals should be in place.

(f) Lawful access: when deciding upon what access government agencies should have in relation to cryptographic products, governments should weigh the benefits as well as the risks of misuse, additional expense of any supporting infrastructure and the prospects of technical failure, amongst other issues. It is suggested that a distinction should be made between keys that are used to protect confidentiality and keys used for other purposes.

(g) Liability: the liability of those providing cryptographic services should be made clear, and users should also be made fully aware of their liability where keys are misused.

(h) International co-operation: policies should be co-ordinated to promote the broad international acceptance of cryptology.

Given the vague nature of these guidelines, together with the lack of any ability to enforce the contents, they can best be described as of interest and of some help in developing a framework policy where none exists.

---

1 Guidelines for Cryptography Policy, Organisation for Economic Co-operation and Development, Part IV.

European Union

15.55 In 1998 the Commission began a review of the export controls that were originally established in 1994.[1] The Commission's Report indicated that the previous rules had not succeeded in persuading member states to establish a common system of controls, and the export licences of member states were not being recognised across the European Union.[2] As a result of this Report and the proposal for a new Council Regulation,[3] the regime was subsequently revised. The regulation of export of dual-use goods in the European Union is now governed by Council Regulation (EC) No 1334/2000 of 22 June 2000 setting up a Community regime for the control of exports of dual-use items and technology,[4] as amended.[5] The Regulations deal with the requirements and procedures for the licensing of transfers of goods, software and technology to destinations outside the European Union and between member states. Two decisions of the European Court of Justice in 1995 have confirmed the legal basis of the regulations under the provisions of Article 133 of the EC Treaty.[6] The right of member states to remain in control of matters relating to national security are acknowledged in recitals 6 and 12:

'(6) The responsibility for deciding an application for export authorisations lies with national authorities. National provisions and decisions affecting exports of dual-use items must be taken in the framework of the common commercial policy, and in particular Council Regulation (EEC) No 2603/69 of 20 December 1969 establishing common rules for exports.

(12) Pursuant to and within the limits of article 30 of the Treaty and pending a greater degree of harmonisation, Member States will retain the right to carry out controls on transfers of certain dual-use items within the European Community in order to safeguard public policy or public security. Where these controls are linked to the effectiveness of controls on exports from the Community, they will be periodically reviewed by the Council.'

1   The original regulation is Regulation (EC) No 3381/94 setting up a Community regime for the control of exports of dual-use goods and technology OJ L 367 12.12.1994, p. 1.
2   Report to the European Parliament and the Council on the application of Regulation (EC) 3381/94 setting up a Community system of export controls regarding dual-use goods, COM (1998) 258 final, May 1998.
3   Proposal for a Council Regulation (EC) setting up a Community regime for the control of exports of dual-use goods and technology 98/C 399/01 of 21 December 1998.
4   OJ L 159 30.6.2000 p. 1. Regulation (EC) No 3381/94 was repealed by Article 23, although the relevant provisions of this Regulation continue to apply for exports made before the entry into force of the new Regulation.
5   Council Regulation (EC) No 2889/2000 of 22 December 2000 OJ L 336 30.12.2000, p. 14; Council Regulation (EC) No 458/2001 of 6 March 2001 OJ L 65 7.3.2001, p. 19; Council Regulation (EC) No 2432/2001 of 20 November 2001 OJ L 338 20.11.2001, p. 1; Council Regulation (EC) No 880/2002 of 27 May 2002 OJ L 139 295.2002, p. 7 and Council Regula-

tion (EC) No 149/2003 of 27 January 2003 OJ L 3 5.2.2003, p. 1. Corrections have been made by Corrigendum, OJ L 176, 15.7.2000, p. 52 (1334/2000); Corrigendum, OJ L 10, 21.1.2002, p. 82 (2432/2001) and Corrigendum, OJ L 52, 27.2.2003, p. 11 (149/2003). The most recent version of the control lists are in Council Regulation (EC) No 394/2006 of 27 February 2004 amending and updating Regulation (EC) No 1334/2000 setting up a Community regime for the control of exports of dual-use items and technology OJ L 74 13.3.2006, p. 1.

6   Case C-70/94 *Fritz Werner Industrie-Ausrüstungen GmbH v Federal Republic of Germany* (ECR 1995 p I-3189); Case C-83/94 *Leifter, Krauskpof and Holzer* (ECR 1995 p I-3231).

PRINCIPLES

15.56   The principles that form the basis of the Regulations are also set out in the recitals. They include:

(a)   The effective control of dual-use items when they are exported from the Community (Recital 1).

(b)   An effective common system of export controls on dual-use items to provide for the international responsibilities and commitments (Recital 2).

(c)   A common system of control and harmonisation for the enforcement and monitoring to provide for the establishment of free movement of dual-use goods within the community (Recital 3).

(d)   The provision of common lists of dual-use items (Recital 5).

(e)   The control of the transmission of software and technology by means of electronic media, facsimile transmission or telephone (Recital 8).

There is a general requirement for member states to liaise with the Commission and to take appropriate measures to establish direct cooperation and exchange of information between competent authorities. In particular, the aim is to reduce the risk of disparity when applying export controls, such that it may lead to trading difficulties between member states.[1] Those dual-use items that are subject to export controls are set out in Annex I to the Regulation. In addition, the Regulation follows the Wassenaar Arrangement, and Category 5 Part 2 to Annex I of the Regulation covers information security.

1   Chapter III Article 9(2).

EXPORT

15.57   The Regulation defines 'export' in Article 2(b) as follows:

'(1)   an export procedure within Article 161 of the Community Customs Code;

(ii)   a re-export within Article 182 of that Code, and

(iii)   transmission of software or technology by electronic media, fax or telephone to a destination outside the Community; this applies to oral transmission of technology by telephone only where the technology is contained in a document the relevant part of which is read out over the telephone, or is described over the telephone in such a way as to achieve substantially the same result.'

Matters dealing with the authorization of exports are governed by Chapter III, Articles 6 to 10. A general export authorization is to be granted by the competent authorities of the member state where the exporter is established. Subject to the restrictions specified in Article 6(3), the authorization may be individual, global or general in nature.[1] It is valid throughout the Community, although if it is thought appropriate, the authorization may be subject to requirements and conditions, such as an obligation to provide an end-use statement.

Where exports require to be authorized, the competent authority will be responsible for issuing one of three types of authorization: individual, global or general.[2] For exports that do not need to be authorized, an exporter can use an open authorization called a 'Community General Export Authorisation No EU001'[3] which permits the export of all dual-use items specified in any entry in Annex I, with the exception of those listed in Annex II Part 2. This export authorisation is valid throughout the Community and to the countries listed in Annex II Part 3.

Export of dual-use items listed in Annex I require authorization in accordance with Article 3(1), although if an item is not listed in Annex I, a member state may still require an export to be authorized if it comes within the provisions of Articles 4 or 5. The Regulation does not apply where services are supplied or natural persons transmit technology across borders,[4] or where dual-use items pass through the territory of the Community.[5] A member state may prohibit or require authorization for the export of a dual-use item not listed in Annex I where it is in the interests of public security or relevant to human rights.[6]

When deciding whether to grant an export authorization, member states are required to take into account all relevant considerations, including:

(a)   the obligations and commitments they have each accepted as a member of the relevant international non-proliferation regimes and export control arrangements, or by ratification of relevant international treaties;

(b)   their obligations under sanctions imposed by a common position or a joint action adopted by the Council or by a decision of the OSCE or by a binding resolution of the Security Council of the United Nations;

(c)   considerations of national foreign and security policy, including those covered by the European Union Code of Conduct on arms exports;

(d)   considerations about intended end-use and the risk of diversion.[7]

Authority is granted by Article 9(2) for a member state to refuse to grant an authorization, or to annul, suspend, modify or revoke an export authorization, which they have already granted. Where an export authorization is annulled, suspended, modified or revoked, the member state is required to inform the competent authorities of the other member states and the Commission.

1 Article 10(1) requires individual and global authorizations to be issued in accordance with the Model forms provided in Annex IIIa, and Article 10(3) requires general export authorizations granted under Article 6(2) to be published in accordance with national laws and practices, and to be issued in accordance with the indications set out in Annex IIIb.

2 Chapter III Article 6(2).

3 Chapter III Article 6(1) and Annex II.

4 Chapter II Article 3(3).

5 Chapter II Article 3(4).

6 Chapter II Article 5(1).

7 Chapter III Article 8(a–d).

Chapter 16

Data protection

16.1 Electronic signatures come in various forms, and to illustrate a simple but disturbing way in which documents are used, one can look to the activities of some local councils in England. When a person wishes to request planning permission, they are required to submit a planning application, and their manuscript signature is affixed to the document. The documents that accompany a planning application are open to the public to view. However, of recent, some local authorities have taken to scanning the applications and publishing the application into pdf format before uploading the entire document on to a website, thus exposing the personal details of the individual to being viewed by the entire world. This action enables would-be thieves to obtain a perfect specimen of a manuscript signature that could be used for nefarious purposes in the future. This is just one of the problems that affect electronic signatures and the application of the principles of data protection, although it is recognized that a scanned signature in itself will not constitute personal data. This state of affairs in England illustrates one aspect of the problem of the networked era: rules put into place to provide for openness in pre-digital times are not always appropriate in the post-digital age. In this instance, the application of a rule requiring openness at a time when paper was paramount has been uncritically transposed into the digital age without thought to the wider repercussions.

The legal framework

Organisation for Economic Co-operation and Development

16.2 In the international context, the Organisation for Economic Co-operation and Development developed a set of guidelines, part of which included the need to consider the issues relating to the protection of personal data.[1] Principle 5 'Protection of privacy and personal data' sets out the expectation:

'The fundamental rights of individuals to privacy, including secrecy of communications and protection of personal data, should be respected in national cryptography policies and in the implementation and use of cryptographic methods.'

In discussing the issues relating to privacy, the guidelines expressly note the difference between cryptographic keys used for confidentiality and those used for authentication. Any user that intends to use a private key for the purposes of authentication must be made aware of the difference and undertake to ensure only the relevant algorithms are used for the purpose of generating a private key. Failure so to do may enable malicious individuals to use the private key not only to impersonate an individual, but also to send incriminating material electronically that can be associated with the innocent holder of the private key.[2]

1 1997 OECD Cryptography Guidelines: Recommendation of the Council dated 27 March 1997 available at www.oecd.org. See also *OECD Guidelines on the Protection of Privacy and Transborder Flows of Personal Data* (OECD, 2002) and Recommendation of the OECD Council concerning guidelines for consumer protection in the context of electronic commerce.

2 1997 OECD Cryptography Guidelines Part III Special issues for consideration with cryptography policy. See also OECD Ministerial Conference 'A borderless world: realising the potential of global electronic commerce' Action plan for electronic commerce, 7–9 October 1998 Ottawa Canada (SG/EC(98)9/REV5).

Data Protection Act 1998

16.3 The Data Protection Act 1998 was passed to enable the government to comply with its obligations under the European Union Directive.[1] The legislation applies to all personal data processed wholly or partly by automatic means, and to manual data in filing systems structured by reference to individuals. The rights of the individual are derived from the eight principles set out in Schedule 1, Part 1 of the Act, providing for personal data:

(a) To be processed fairly and lawfully.

(b) To be obtained for one or more specified purposes, and is not to be further processed in any manner incompatible with the purpose or purposes.

(c) To be adequate, relevant and not excessive in relation to the purpose or purposes for which they are processed.

(d) Must be accurate and, where necessary, kept up to date.

(e) Shall not be kept for longer than is necessary for the purpose or purposes.

(f) Processed in accordance with the rights of the data subject.

(g)   Appropriate technical and organizational measures shall be taken against unauthorized or unlawful processing of personal data and against accidental loss or destruction of personal data.

(h)   Not transferred to a country or territory outside the European Economic Area unless the recipient country has an adequate level of protection for the rights and freedoms of data subjects in relation to the processing of personal data.

The general principles of the Act will apply to the personal information related to a private key and certificate in the same way as any other form of personal data. The difference between say, personal data contained in the marketing files of a business and the personal data contained in a certificate, is that the person whose personal data is contained in the certificate expects the data to be shared with those they send a message or document to with a certificate affixed. By comparison, the data subject does not expect, unless they have given their explicit consent, the business to share their personal data with other organizations across the globe.

1   95/46/EC of the European Parliament and of the Council of 24 October 1995 on the protection of individuals with regard to processing of personal data and on the free movement of such data, OJ L 281, 23.11.1995 p. 31.

Guidelines

PKI Assessment Guidelines

16.4   The current draft of the PKI Assessment Guidelines[1] considers some of the issues, in particular it assumes that many end users, both consumers and businesses, will not be knowledgeable about the technology that underpins public key cryptography. Additionally, it is also thought that it cannot be presumed that '… all or even most certificate owners and users regularly read and understand the complex and often lengthy legal documents that usually govern the contractual relationships amongst the various parties in a PKI.'[2] Thus the guidelines emphasise the need of assessors to take particular note of the method by which a certification authority or registration authority incorporates the use of information practices into the contract with a subscribing party, and how personal data is to be used where a recipient decides to become a verifying party. It is suggested that participants within the public key infrastructure (certification authorities, registration authorities and the repository) should take reasonable steps to make subscribing parties aware of the links within the infrastructure and how their personal data is used.[3]

1   PKI Assessment Guidelines v0.30 June 2001 (Information Security Committee, Electronic Commerce Division, Section of Science and Technology Information Security Committee American Bar Association) C.5.
2   PKI Assessment Guidelines C.5.
3   C.5.1.1.

CARAT Guidelines

16.5 The National Automated Clearing House Association developed a set of guidelines for constructing policies for the use of public key certificates, consideration of which was given to the issue of confidentiality.[1] The guidance offered is that a certificate policy should provide that information in certificates is not confidential. The guide distinguishes between the types of privacy that should be considered in relation to electronic transactions:

(a) Data privacy, which refers to the privacy and accuracy of the data that a subscribing party knows is being collected.

(b) Transactional privacy, which refers to the privacy and accuracy of transactional data the subscribing party may not be aware of that is being collected. It does not follow that transactional data will be collected as it is generated. The point is, that where such data is collected, the subscribing party has the same right to privacy even where they are not aware that the data is being collected.[2]

The advice offered is to follow the OECD guidelines, as well as follow the laws in a prevailing jurisdiction. The issue of jurisdiction, which is not discussed in this text, was also an issue discussed by the PKI Assessment Guidelines.

1   Guidelines for Constructing Policies Governing the Use of Identity-Based Public Key Certificates (National Automated Clearing House Association, The Internet Council, Certification Authority Rating and Trust (CARAT) Task Force, January 2000) available online from www.internetcouncil.nacha.org/docs/CARAT_Final_011400.doc.

2   Part E paragraph 2.8, 2.

Australia

16.6 In Australia, the Officer of the Federal Privacy Commissioner has prepared a document, 'Privacy and Public Key Infrastructure: Guidelines for Agencies using PKI to communicate or transact with individuals.'[1] The document sets out the risks, both actual and potential. The first is whether the amount of information gathered is relevant to the level of certificate being issued or requested at the registration stage, contained in Public Key Certificates (which are also normally publicly available, in that it is conceivable that the transactions carried out by an individual may be tracked), and included in Public Key Directories and Certificate Revocation Lists, which in turn may enable the directories to be scanned for information and downloaded with a view of using the data in ways that interfere with the privacy of individuals. The comment offered on page 19 is: 'The issue to consider, from a privacy perspective, is whether PKI applications require the publication of a public key directory. If publication is considered necessary then a privacy protective option is to allow individual clients to opt out of having their public keys listed in the directory. This is similar to the way telephone subscribers may opt out of having their phone number published in the phone directory.' Another issue concerns logs and ephemeral data which are stored by servers hosting public key directories, Certificate Revocation Lists and other PKI transactions and maintained by CAs and agencies: such logs will normally retain details of when a certificate was viewed and what online transactions the individual entered into. It is a legitimate expectation that a relevant organization may maintain records of such activities; nevertheless, the logs could be used to monitor transactions and compile profiles of individuals using such services.

The Federal Privacy Commissioner offers nine guidelines, each of which includes a commentary. They are:

'Guideline 1 – Agency Client Choice on the Use of PKI Applications

Agencies should allow their clients to choose whether to use PKI for a particular transaction and to offer them alternative means of service delivery. The alternative need not always be an online alternative. In providing this choice agencies should advise their clients of the privacy risks and advantages associated with their use of PKI and alternative methods for that transaction.

Guideline 2 – Awareness and Education

Agencies and their contracted PKI service providers should co-operate closely to ensure that their clients are fully informed of the proper use of PKI and of the risks and responsibilities associated with the use of PKI, including the secure management of private keys.

Guideline 3 – Privacy Impact Assessments (PIAs)

Agencies should undertake a Privacy Impact Assessment before implementing a new PKI system or significantly revising or extending an existing PKI system.

Guideline 4 – Evidence of Identity

When developing PKI applications or contracting with PKI services providers, agencies should ensure that only minimum Evidence of Identity that is necessary for, or directly related to, the process is collected.

In addition, where a client wishes to obtain more than one certificate then the client should be given a range of options including:

- consenting to use a Gatekeeper certificate of equal or higher value to apply for a new certificate;
- consenting to the re-use of Evidence of Identity documentation previously provided by the client;
- or providing documentation on registration for an additional certificate.

Guideline 5 – Aggregation of Personal Information

In the course of PKI transactions with clients, agencies and their contracted PKI service providers should ensure that no detailed history of client transactions is created or used by the agency or contracted PKI service provider, except to the extent that this is required for system maintenance or evidentiary purposes.

Agencies and contracted PKI service providers should not use PKI transactions to collect personal information that is not necessary, or directly related to, the PKI business transaction.

Guideline 6 – Single or Multiple Certificates

Agencies should allow clients to use more than one certificate, where these are fit for the purpose of the relevant application. Agencies should also recognise certificates they have not issued where these certificates are fit for the purpose of the relevant application.

Guideline 7 – Subscriber Generation of Keys

Where an agency issues certificates or contracts for their issue, the agency should allow its clients the option of generating their own keys, provided that the agency is satisfied that subscriber key generation can be implemented securely.

Guideline 8 – Public Key Directories

Agency clients should be allowed to opt out of including their public keys in a public key directory (PKD) where the PKD is published.

Guideline 9 – Pseudonymity and Anonymity

Agencies should provide their clients with anonymous and pseudonymous options for transacting with them, to the extent that this is not inconsistent with the objectives and operation of the relevant online application.'

The European Union have not passed any specific legislation concerning the protection of data of the Public Key Infrastructure, but arguably, the provisions of Council Decision 92/242/EEC of 31 March 1992 in the field of security of information systems,[2] Directive 95/46/EC of the European Parliament and of the Council of 24 October 1995 on the protection of individuals with regard to processing of personal data and on the free movement of such data,[3] and Directive 2002/58/EC of the European Parliament and of the Council of 12 July 2002 concerning the processing of personal data and the protection of privacy in the electronic communications sector[4] go some way towards covering the personal data contained within a Public Key Infrastructure, whether implicitly or explicitly.

1   Currently available online at www.privacy.gov.au/government/guidelines/index.html#a.
2   OJ L 123, 8.5.1992, p. 19.
3   OJ L 281, 23.11.1995, p. 31.
4   OJ L 201, 31.7.2002, p. 37.

Practical issues[1]

Generating the private key

16.7   The most secure private key is that which is generated within the total control of the person that intends to use it. Thus a key pair can be generated from a personal computer, but the exposure to attack depends not on where they were generated, but on where the keys are stored, and personal computers are very weak from this point of view, especially when connected to a network. The existence of the clipper chip, the keystroke Trojan horse known as Magic Lantern and ECHELON, with its capacity to intercept communications across the globe, means there is a probability that national intelligence agencies across the world will have sufficient information to break any private key generated in a personal computer.[2] If a trusted third party generated the key pair for a person, then the user would have to be assured that the private key would only be available to them. In addition, further assurances would have to be made by the key generator respecting the security process, because it is very easy for a person to use the private key to impersonate the legitimate owner to the detriment of the actual owner.

1   The author is indebted to the early work of Graham Greenleaf and Roger Clarke 'Privacy Implications of Digital Signatures' Joint address, IBC Conference on Digital Signatures, Sydney, 12 March 1997 available online at www.anu.edu.au/people/Roger.Clarke/DV/DigSig.html, whose structure is followed in this section; see also M. H. M. Schellekens *Electronic Signatures Authentication Technology from a Legal Perspective* (TMC Asser Press, 2004) Chapter 5.
2   It is assumed that the reader is aware of these and other types of national and international arrangements to intercept communications by state security agencies. Even if the reader is not aware of these initiatives, in the normal course of events it is to be expected that a state will avail itself of such a facility as a matter of course. Websites that will introduce the reader to some of these types of interception device can be found at www.epic.org and www.statewatch.org. If the reader is in doubt that such initiatives exist, they may consider consulting the report by the European Parliament. The European Parliament set up a Temporary committee on the ECHELON interception system. The Minutes of 05/09/2001 – Provisional Edition 'European Parliament resolution on the existence of a global system for the interception of private and commercial communications (ECHELON interception system) (2001/2098(INI))' A5-0264/2001. The full report of 194 pages is entitled 'Report on the existence of a global system for the interception of private and commercial communications (ECHELON interception system) (2001/2098(INI))' FINAL A5-0264/2001 PAR1 PE 305.391.

Storage of the private key

16.8 Where an individual decides to take advantage of the ability to have and use a digital signature, the next issue they must consider is how the private key is stored, backed up and how the copies are stored. Any breach of security will increase the risks associated with the private key being used by a malicious person or organization to the detriment of the owner of the private key, should the security of the private key be so poor as to make it relatively easy to obtain for illicit purposes. The owner carries a significant risk when obtaining a digital signature, especially the impersonation of their identity by unauthorized individuals or organizations.

This warning does not only apply to individuals who have a private key, but to those organizations that require that each of their employees have a private key to authenticate themselves either within the organization or for external purposes. The same provisions respecting the protection of personal data apply.

Revocation of private keys

16.9 The act of revoking a private key will require the person with the private key to identify themselves to the certification authority. The authentication of the user will invariably be intrusive, but necessary if the key is to be revoked effectively and in a timely manner.

Data required for the certificate

16.10 Clearly either the certification authority or registration authority will require the intended subscriber to provide them with sufficient personal data to identify themselves to obtain and use a digital signature. Either or both organizations will be required to deal with the data in a manner appropriate to the jurisdiction within which the subscribing party is situated.

Contractual provisions in place

16.11 All certification practice statements include provisions relating to confidentiality and privacy. For instance, the BT Certification Practice Statement[1] sets out its contractual terms relating to confidentiality and privacy in paragraph 2.8. The reader is informed that BT has implemented a privacy policy, and the website is given.[2] In addition, the subscribing party is informed of the types of record that are maintained as confidential and private at paragraph 2.8.1:

'CA application records, whether approved or disapproved,

Certificate Application records (subject to CPS § 2.8.2),

Private keys held by Client Managed PKI Customers using Managed PKI Key Manager and information needed to recover such private keys,

Transactional records (both full records and the audit trail of transactions),

VTN audit trail records created or retained by VeriSign, BT, or a Customer,

BT audit reports created by BT or their respective auditors (whether internal or public),

Contingency planning and disaster recovery plans, and

Security measures controlling the operations of BT hardware and software and the administration of Certificate services and designated enrolment services.'

In addition, the certification practice statement provides for information that is not considered confidential or private, as outlined in paragraph 2.8.2:

'BT Subdomain Participants acknowledge that Certificates, Certificate revocation and other status information, BT's repository, and information contained within them are not considered Confidential/Private Information. Information not expressly deemed Confidential/Private Information under CPS § 2.8.1 shall be considered neither confidential nor private. This section is subject to applicable privacy laws.'

Further, BT reserves the right to release information of a private nature in response to search warrants and similar judicial notices in both criminal and civil proceedings.[3] To reinforce the need for BT to send data outside the European Economic Area, the contractual terms issued by BT provide for confidentiality in paragraph 7:

'7 CONFIDENTIALITY

7.1   You and BT will keep in confidence any written or oral information of a confidential nature obtained under this Contract. Without the written consent of the other, you and BT will not disclose that information to any person, other than (where applicable) employees of your organisation, or in the case of BT, the employees of a BT Group Company who need to know the information.

7.2   You acknowledge that in order to provide the Service, BT or its agents must examine, evaluate, and otherwise process your Customer Data, and that BT may choose or be required to send your Customer

Data outside the European Economic Area for processing. You grant BT permission to process or permit others (wherever located) to process your Customer Data in a manner BT considers reasonably necessary for the provision of the Service.

7.3   This paragraph 7 will not apply to any information:

(a)   which has been published other than through a breach of this Contract;
(b)   lawfully in the possession of the recipient before the disclosure under this Contract took place;
(c)   obtained from a third party who is free to disclose it;
(d)   which is independently developed; and
(e)   which a party is requested to disclose and if it did not could be required by law to do so.

7.4   This paragraph 7 will remain in effect for 5 years after the termination of this Contract.'[4]

This set of trading terms applies to an individual applying for an identity certificate approved for use with the government gateway, yet the drafting of this clause appears to be more appropriate as between organizations, rather than between an individual consumer and BT.

VeriSign Inc has an almost identical set of provisions in its certification practice statement, as does the Thawte certification practice statement. Equifax Secure offers similar protection using less words, but includes the right to use subscriber information on an aggregate basis:

'H.   Confidentiality Policy

1.   Individual Subscriber Information

Information regarding Subscribers that is submitted on applications for Certificates will be kept confidential by ESI and ESI shall not release such information without the prior consent of the Subscriber. Notwithstanding the foregoing, ESI may make such information available to courts, law enforcement agencies or other third parties upon receipt of a court order or subpoena or upon the advice of ESI's legal counsel. The foregoing confidentiality obligation shall not apply, however, to information appearing on Certificates, or to information regarding Subscribers that is already in the possession of or separately acquired by ESI.

2.   Aggregate Subscriber Information

Notwithstanding the previous Section, ESI may disclose Subscriber information on an aggregate basis, and the Subscriber hereby grants to ESI a license to do so, including the right to modify the aggregated Subscriber information and to permit third parties to perform such functions on its behalf. ESI shall not disclose to any third party any personally identifiable information about any Subscriber that ESI obtains in its performance of services hereunder.'[5]

The Chamber SimplySign Digital Certification Services provide the following text to the Subscriber Agreement in paragraph 6:[6]

'6. I acknowledge that certain information provided by me at the time of enrolment will be embedded in a digital certificate, and may be published in a directory of certificates and revocation information where required for the purpose of operating the digital certification services. I consent to the disclosure of this information for these purposes and understand that I have the right to correct any information about me. Further information on my rights in this respect is to be found in the Privacy Charter.'

As indicated, this text is expanded in the Privacy Charter,[7] where a number of promises are made, including those set out in paragraph 2:

'2.   Your Rights
- data held on you is accurately recorded as supplied
- data held on you is processed legally, fairly, securely and only for the purpose(s) for which it was originally collected
- you are made aware of the purposes to which your data are put and with whom it is shared
- you are able to see a copy of data held on yourself (whether originally supplied by you or by a third party) but not including PINs, passwords or passphrases and possibly certain other information that might create a security risk
- you are entitled to object to:
    - the processing to which your data is subjected, and
    - any additional marketing uses to which your data is put.
- if your data is sent to 'Third Countries' (ie outside the EU) then agreements are in place which ensure that the level of protection is not diminished.'

The document provides further indications as to how personal data will be dealt with by Chamber SimplySign Digital Certification Services.

Cable & Wireless include similar provisions to those set out above in relation to confidentiality of subscriber information, with the additional notes that the information that is made public is explicitly noted, in paragraph 2.6.2.1:

'Certificate information published in the C&W Directory Services is not confidential and is considered to be public knowledge, including:

1   Certificate status;
2   The date and time of Certificate suspension or revocation;

3   The period for which Certificate suspension applies;
User ID (End Users);
Email Addresses;
IP Addresses (where required for operational reasons).'[8]

This is a useful and welcome addition to a certification practice statement, because the nature of the information that must be made public is made clear to a potential subscriber.

The brief discussion set out above illustrates the nature of the personal data that is used to provide a digital signature, together with an indication of the organizations that might be called upon to deal with such data. Where an individual decides to have a digital signature, they would be wise to delve deeper into the security arrangements offered by the certification authority before considering using a certificate. As for digital certificates issued by organizations to employees, it will be for the organization to provide for the protection of the personal data, and employees would be wise to familiarize themselves with what security arrangements are in place before they agree to having such a signature, because failure to deal with the security of the personal data effectively could cause problems to the individual in years to come if their identity is misappropriated.

1   Version 3.04 last updated 18 December 2003.
2   In this version of the certification practice statement, the website is given as www.btignite. com/uk/products/trustservices/inform/privacy_policy.html. It is claimed that this policy is 'in compliance with CP § 2.8', but in reality is only a standard website privacy policy. A further series of questions and answers can be found at www.btglobalservices.com/business/ global/en/other/site_info/priv_policy.html. A visit to this web page is of interest. One question posed is 'How do BT Global Services protect data about me when it is transferred out of Europe?' The answer is less than reassuring: 'Countries in the European Economic Area (EEA) are required to have a similar standard of protection of personal data. This is not always the case outside that area. We do sometimes transfer data outside the EEA and before doing so take steps to ensure that there is adequate protection, as required by the Data Protection Act.' Thus the treatment of personal data outside the EEA is subject to the unknown criteria by which BT Global Services enforce the data protection principles.
3   Paragraphs 2.8.4 and 2.8.5.
4   ID Certificate End User Contract Issue 1 (12 September 2002).
5   www.equifaxsecure.co.uk/policies/cps2001.html#iih%22.
6   (v1.01 20 February 2004).
7   (v1.01 20 February 2004).
8   Cable & Wireless Certification Practice Statement (Document No 1491-PD0096-032 May 2002).

Table of international statutes

Alderney

Electronic Transactions (Alderney) Law, 2001[1]

1   Other than section 20, into force on 26 March, 2002 by the Electronic Transactions (Alderney) Law 2001 (Commencement) Ordinance, 2002.

Anguilla

Electronic Transactions Act 2006[1]

1   Published in the Gazette 29 September 2006.

Argentina

Ley De Firma Digital Nº 25.506[1]

1   Enacted on 12 November 2001, approved on 14 November 2001, published in the Official Bulletin on 14 December 2001 and promulgated on 11 December 2001. Regulations relating to certification authorities were issued in 2007: Decisión Administrativa 6/2007 Establécese el marco normativo de firma digital aplicable al otorgamiento y revocación de las licencias a los certificadores que así lo soliciten. Bs. As., 7/2/2007. VISTO la Ley Nº 25.506, los Decretos Nros. 2628 del 19 de diciembre de 2002, 624 del 21 de agosto de 2003, 1028 del 6 de noviembre de 2003; 409 del 2 de mayo de 2005 y 724 del 8 de junio de 2006. Published in the Official Bulletin (Boletin Oficial) 12 de febrero de 2007, Año CXV Número 31.093, p 1.

Australia

Commonwealth

Electronic Transactions Act 1999 (Cth)[1]

1   Royal Assent on 10 December 1999, date of commencement 15 March 2000 (Gazette No 10, 15 March 2000, p 549).

Australian Capital Territory

Electronic Transactions Act 2001 (ACT)[1]

1   Royal Assent 15 February 2001 (Gazette No 26, 28 June 2001, p 716); ss 1 and 2 in force 8 March 2001; sections 3–15 in force 1 July 2001 (Gazette No 26, 28 June 2001, p 716).

New South Wales

Electronic Transactions Act 2000 (NSW)[1]

1   Royal Assent 3 May 2000, in force from 7 December 2001 (Gazette No 188, 7 December 2001, p 9581).

Northern Territory

Electronic Transactions (Northern Territory) Act 2000 (NT)[1]

1   Royal Assent 14 December 2000, in force 13 June 2001 (Gazette No 23, 13 June 2001, p 3).

Queensland

Electronic Transactions (Queensland) Act 2001 (Qld)[1]

1   Royal Assent on 7 June 2001, ss 1–2 commenced on date of assent, remaining provisions commenced on 1 November 2002 (Gazette No 48, 1 November 2002, p 759 by SL 2002 No 286).

South Australia

Electronic Transactions Act 2000 (SA)[1]

1   Royal Assent on 7 December 2000, in operation on 1 November 2002 (Gazette No 96, 29 August 2002, p 3212).

Tasmania

Electronic Transactions Act 2000 (Tas)[1]

1   Royal Assent 13 December 2000 (Gazette No 20190, 23 May 2002, p 624 by SR 2001, No 47).

Victoria

Electronic Transactions (Victoria) Act 2000 (Vic)[1]

1   Royal Assent 16 May 2000 and into force on 1 September 2000, s 2 (Gazette No 20, 18 May 2000, p 967).

Western Australia

Electronic Transactions Act 2003 (WA)[1]

1   Royal Assent 24 March 2003, in force 2 May 2003 (s 2 and Gazette No 66, 2 May 2003, p 1491).

Austria

Signaturgesetz – SigG, BGBl. I Nr. 190/1999[1]

1   In force on 1 January 2000, and amended by GOG, BGBl. I No. 164/2005. Signaturverordnung – SigV, BGBl. II Nr. 30/2000, relates to technical matters amongst other things, in force on 3 February 2000, and amended by SigV, BGBl. II No. 527/2004.

Azarbaijan

Electronic Signatures and Electronic Documents 2004[1]

1   Last reading on 9 March 2004 in the Mejlis (Parliament) and signed by the president on the same day. The president issued a decree implementing the law on 26 May 2004, the day it came into force.

Bahrain

Legislative Decree No 28 of 2002

Bahamas

The Electronic Communications and Transactions Act 2003[1]

1   Number 4 of 2003 in the Gazette. Date of Assent 11 April 2003. In force in June 2003.

Barbados

Electronic Transactions Act, 2001–2

Belarus

Law on Electronic Documents No. 357-Z of January 10, 2000[1]

1   First published in the official newspaper Звязда (Zwiazda) of 18 January 2000 and entered into force on the day of its official publication. On 21 January 2000, it was also published in the National Register of Legal Acts of the Republic of Belarus (Natsyonalnyi rejestr pravovych aktow Respubliki Belarus), 2000, No. 7, 2/132. The Law has been altered twice by the Law of the Republic of Belarus No. 137-Z of June 29, 2006 (National Register of Legal Acts of the Republic of Belarus, 2006, No. 107, 2/1235); and by the Law of the Republic of Belarus No. 162-Z of July 20, 2006 (National Register of Legal Acts of the Republic of Belarus, 2006, No. 122, 2/1259).

Belgium

9 Juli 2001 Wet houdende vaststelling van bepaalde regels in verband met het juridisch kader voor elektronische handtekeningen en certificatiediensten[1]

Koninklijk besluit van 6 december 2002 houdende organisatie van de controle en de accreditatie van de certificatiedienstverleners die gekwalificeerde certificaten afleveren (Belgisch Staatsblad, 17 januari 2003)[2]

1 Publicatie: 29-09-2001 Inwerkingtreding : 09-10-2001 Dossiernummer : 2001-07-09/43.

2 French: Arrêté royal du 6 décembre 2002 organisant le contrôle et l'accréditation des prestataires de service de certification qui délivrent des certificats qualifiés (Moniteur Belge, 17 janvier 2003); English: Royal Decree of 6 December 2002 organising the supervision and accreditation of certification services providers issuing qualified certificates (Belgian State Gazette, 17 January 2003).

Bermuda

The Electronic Transactions Act 1999[1]

1 Royal Assent 5 August 1999, in force on 4 October 1999.

Bhutan

Bhutan Information, Communications & Media Act 2006

Brazil

Medida Provisória N° 2.200-2, de 24 de Agosto de 2001 Institui a Infra-Estrutura de Chaves Públicas Brasileira – ICP-Brasil, e dá outras providências[1]

1 Provides for the legal validity of electronic documents and electronic signatures. Medidas Provisorias (MP) are normally Presidential Bills which need to be sanctioned by Parliament after 30 days of publication. If they have not been sanctioned, they cease to be enforced after this period. If sanctioned, they become law. This specific MP has become law through Constitutional Amendment no. 32 of 2001, which determined that all MP not yet sanctioned by Congress by September 2001 but which were still in force at that time, were converted into law.

Brunei Darussalam

Electronic Transactions Order, 2000[1]

1 Published in the Gazette on 16 December 2000 and came into force, with the exception of Part X concerning the regulation of Certification Authorities, on 1 May 2001 by a notification published in the Gazette on 2 June 2001.

Bulgaria

Electronic Document and Electronic Signature Act 2001[1]

1 Promulgated, SG 34/2001.

Canada

Federal

Personal Information Protection and Electronic Documents Act, S.C. 2000, c. 5[1]

1 Part 2, Electronic Documents, proclaimed in force 1 May 2000. Regulations: Secure Electronic Signature Regulations, S.O.R./2005-30; Barbara McIssac QC and Howard R. Fohr, 'Legal update, Canada: PIPEDA's Secure Electronic Signature Regulations have been published,' *e-Signature Law Journal* (now the *Digital Evidence Journal*), 2005, Volume 2 Number 2, 109–110. Other relevant legislation may be found in consumer protection and evidence legislation for each jurisdiction. The Northwest Territories and Nunavut have not enacted any applicable legislation. Note also the Uniform Law Conference of Canada: Uniform Electronic Commerce Act and Uniform Electronic Evidence Act.

Alberta

Electronic Transactions Act 2001, S.A. 2001, C. E-5.5[1]

1 In force on Proclamation, 1 April 2003. Regulations: Electronic Transactions Act Designation Regulation, Alta. Reg. 35/2003 and Electronic Transactions Act General Regulation, Alta. Reg. 34/2003.

British Colombia

Electronic Transactions Act, S.B.C. 2001, c. 10[1]

1 In force on 19 April 2001 by BC Regulation 122/01.

Manitoba

Electronic Commerce and Information Act, C.C.S.M. 2000, C. E55[1]

1 Parts 1, 3–5, and 7 proclaimed in force 23 October 2000; Part 6 proclaimed in force 19 March 2001; Part 2 not yet proclaimed in force. Regulations: Common Business Identifiers Regulation, Man. Reg. 176/2002.

New Brunswick

Electronic Transactions Act, S.N.B. 2001, c. E-5.5[1]

Regulation 2002-24 filed 28 March 2002, by virtue of s 19 of the Electronic Transactions Act 2001, excluding certain Acts from the application of the provisions of the Electronic Transactions Act 2001

1 Royal Assent 1 June 2001, proclaimed and in force on 31 March 2002.

Newfoundland and Labrador

Electronic Commerce Act, S.N.L. 2001, c.E-5.2[1]

1 Royal Assent and in force on 13 December 2001.

Nova Scotia

Electronic Commerce Act, S.N.S. 2000, c. 26[1]

1 Royal Assent and in force on 30 November 2000.

Ontario

Electronic Commerce Act, S.O. 2000, c. 17[1]

1 In force on date of Royal Assent, 16 October 2000. See also Electronic Registration Act (Ministry of Consumer and Business Services Statutes), 1991, S.O. 1991, c. 44 and Designation of Acts, O. Reg. 759/93, applying only to those acts administered by the Ministry.

Prince Edward Island

Electronic Commerce Act, , R.S.P.E.I. 1988, c. E-4.1[1]

Electronic Evidence Act, R.S.P.E.I. 1988, c. E-4.3[2]

1 Royal Assent and in force on 15 May 2001.
2 Royal Assent and in force on 15 May 2001.

Quebec

An Act to establish a legal framework for information technology, R.S.Q. c. C-1.1[1]

1 Royal Assent and in force on 1 November 2001.

Saskatchewan

The Electronic Information and Documents Act, S.S. 2000, c. E-7.22[1]
The Electronic Information and Documents Regulations Chapter E-7.22 Reg 1[2]

1 Proclaimed in force, 1 November 2000. Regulations: Electronic Information and Documents Regulations, R.R.S. c. E-7.22 Reg. 1.
2 In force on 23 November 2003.

Yukon

Electronic Commerce Act, R.S.Y. 2002, c. 66[1]

Electronic Evidence Act, R.S.Y. 2002, c. 67[2]

1 Proclaimed in force, 27 March 2001.
2 Proclaimed in force, 27 March 2001.

Chile

Ley Sobre Documentos Electronicos, Firma Electronica y Servicios de Certificación de Dicha Firma No 19.799, 25 de marzo 2002[1]

Ley de bases sobre contratos administrativos de suministro y de prestación de servicios N° 19.886 11 de julio de 2003[2]

1   In force from the publication in the Official Gazette, April 12, 2002.
2   Chapter IV provides for the purchases in the public sector by electronic means. In force from the publication in the Official Gazette, July 30, 2003.

China

Electronic Signatures Law of the People's Republic of China of 2004[1]

1   Adopted at the 11th Meeting of the Standing Committee of the Tenth National People's Congress on August 28, 2004.

Colombia

Ley Por No 527 de agosto 18 de 1999 medio de la cual se define y reglamenta el acceso y uso de los mensajes de datos, del comercio electrónico y de las firmas digitales, y se establecen las entidades de certificación y se dictan otras disposiciones[1]
Ley 588 de julio 5 de 2000 Por medio de la cual se reglamenta el ejercicio de la actividad notarial[2]

1   The rules relating to certification entities were defined in more detail by Decreto 1747 de 2000 (September 11) se reglamenta parcialmente la ley 527 en lo relacionado con las entidades de certificación, los certificados y firmas digitales. Technical Standards relating to digital signatures were set forth by way of Resolución 26930 de 2000 de la Superintendencia de Industria y Comercio definiendo los estándares para la autorización y funcionamiento de entidades certificadoras y auditores.
2   Diario Oficial No. 44.071, de 6 de julio de 2000 provides for rules pertaining to the activities of public notaries.

Costa Rica

Ley número 8454, de Certificados, Firmas Digitales y Documentos Electrónicos[1]

1   Published in La Gaceta 197 on 13 October 2005. Regulations – Reglamento a la Ley de Certificados, Firmas Digitales y Documentos Electrónicos, Decreto Ejecutivo número 33018-MICIT. – were published in La Gaceta on 21 April 2006.

Croatia

Zákon o elektronickém podpisu[1]

1   The Electronic Signature Act, published in the Official Gazette Narodne Novine No. 10 in 2002 and came into force prior to 1 April 2002.

Cyprus

Law on the Legal Framework for Electronic Signatures and Associated Matters of 2004, Law No. 188(I)/2004[1]

1 The Act entered into force on the date of its publication in the Official Gazette of the Republic of Cyprus, 30 April 2004.

Czech Republic

Zákon č. 227/2000 Sb., o elektronickém podpisu a o změně některých dalších zákonů (zákon o elektronickém podpisu)[1]

1 Act No. 227/2000 Coll., on Electronic Signatures and the amendment to certain other acts (Electronic Signatures Act). Passed on June 29, 2000 and in force on 1 October 2000. The Act was amended by Act No. 440/2004 Coll., which came into force and effect on 26 July 26 2004. The main amendments included the addition of the 'qualified time stamp', which makes it possible to prove the existence of a digital document at a certain moment in time and before a given moment in time; the ability to use 'electronic marks' that utilize digital signature technology in the same way as advanced electronic signatures, but for a larger number of data messages; the use of electronic filing by public authorities is also covered, and the amendments also lay down the operational rules for electronic public deeds, which have the same legal effect as the public deeds issued by the public authorities.

Denmark

Lov om elektroniske signaturer Nr. 417[1]

1 Dated 31 May 2000.

Dominican Republic

Ley de Comercio Electrónico, Documentos y Firmas Digitales No. 126-02[1]

1 Dated 4 September 2002, published in the Official Gazette No.10172 of 29 September 2002. This law is complemented by the Ruling of Enforcement, Decree No. 335-03, issued by the Executive Branch on 8 April 2003.

Dubai

Law of Electronic Transactions and Commerce No. 2/2002

Ecuador

Ley de Comercio Electrónico, Firmas y Mensajes de Datos, Ley No. 67[1]

1 Registro Official (RO) **Sup 557** de 17 de Abril del **2002.**

Egypt

Law No 15/2004 on E-signature and Establishment of the Information Technology Industry Development Authority[1]

1 Adopted by Parliament on 17 April 2004. In 2005, the Minister of Telecommunication & Information issued an Executive Regulation under the law by Ministerial decree no. 109 on May 15, 2005, providing the legal and technical details relating to the enforcement of the law.

Estonia

Digitaalallkirja seadus Vastu võetud 8. märtsil 2000. a. (RT I 2000, 26, 150) jõustunud 15. detsembril 2000[1]

Tsiviilseadustiku üldosa seadus Vastu võetud 27. märtsil 2002. a (RT I 2002, 35, 216) jõustunud 1. juulil 2002[2]

1 Digital Signature Act, passed by Parliament on 8 March 2000 and entered into force on 15 December 2000 as published in the State Gazette (Riigi Teataja I 2000, 26, 150). The Act has been amended, and the current version of the Act entered into force on January 8, 2004.
2 This is a new General Part of the Civil Code Act, passed on 27 March 2002 and entered into force 1 July 2002 as published in the State Gazette (Riigi Teataja I 2002, 35, 216).

European Union

Directive 1999/93/EC of the European Parliament and of the Council of 13 December 1999 on a Community framework for electronic signatures[1]

1 OJ L 13, 19.01.2000, p.12.

Finland

Laki sähköisistä allekirjoituksista 24.1.2003/14[1]

1 Act on Electronic Signatures 24.1.2003/2003, passed 24 January 2003 and entered into force on 1 February 2003.

France

Loi No 2000-230 du 13 mars 2000 portant adaptation du droit de la preuve aux technologies de l'information et relative á la signature électronique[1]

Décret no 2001-272 du mars 30, 2001 pris pour l'application de l'article 1316-4 du code civil relatif à la signature électronique

Décret no 2002-535 du avril 18, 2002 relatif à l'évaluation et à la certification de la sécurité offerte parles produits et les systèmes des technologies de l'information[2]

Arrêté ministériel du mai 31, 2002 relatif à la reconnaissance de la qualification des prestataires de certification électronique et à l'accréditation des organismes chargés de l'évaluation[3]

1   This law amends article 1316 of the Code Civil to provide for electronic signatures; article 1317(2), that provides for an act of authentication to be made by electronic means, provided it is prepared and a record maintained in accordance with the relevant decree of the Conseil d'Etat and article 1326, which is formulated in such manner as to allow for unilateral commitments to be made electronically.

2   This decree provides for the accreditation scheme for certification service providers.

3   This Arrêté compliments the provisions of Décret no 2002-535 du avril 18, 2002.

Germany

Gesetz über Rahmenbedingungen für elektronische Signaturen (Signaturgesetz – SigG) vom 16.5.2001 (BGBl. I S. 876)[1]
VwVfG Verwaltungsverfahrensgesetz [I B 25][2]
BGB Bürgerliches Gesetzbuch (BGB)[3]
ZPO Zivilprozessordnung[4]

1   The German Signature Law and the Ordinance on Electronic Signatures have been amended by the Signaturänderungsgesetz (BGBl. Teil I v. 10.1.2005, p. 2–3), which entered into force on 11 January 2005. This eases the requirements for certification-service-providers and contains clarifying modifications.

2   Section 3(a) of this law implements SigG in German administrative law. This implements the digital signature and the infrastructure for certification authorities.

3   Section 126(a) implements the provisions of SigG into German civil law and gives digital signatures parity of treatment to the manuscript form; s 127 Abs 3 provides for types of electronic signature other than digital signatures to have the same standing as provided under SigG. It should be noted that sections 623 (cancellation of a contract of employment), 630 (employer's obligation to deliver certificates of employment), 766 (guarantees/bonds), 780 (promise to perform an act in which the obligation is created solely by the promise itself), 781 (acknowledgement of debt) of the BGB and Section 4 of the Consumer Loan Act (*Verbraucherkreditgesetz – VerbrKrG*) provide that in these specific instances, an electronic signature is not possible or invalid, which slightly mitigates the importance of section 126a BGB. These exceptions concern sections of the BGB that the legislator considered must remain as manuscript signatures.

4   Section 292(a) implements SigG in the German Code of Civil Procedure. This provides for the presumption that digital signatures conforming to the requirements set out in SigG are acceptable, subject to a challenge that the digital signature was misused without the authority of the subscribing party. On 1 April 2005 the Justizkommunikationsgesetz entered into force (BGBl. Teil I of 29.3.2005, p. 837-858). The law contains modifications of form requirements in respect of the German procedural code (ZPO). After previous amendments have been made to the German contract and procedural law as well as of the administrative law, it completes the adjustment of legal requirements for the use of electronic documents by establishing rules for the use of electronic documents in court procedure. At the same time, the evidence rule in the former § 292 a ZPO is replaced by the new § 371 a ZPO which provides for the analogical application of the rules on documentary evidence to electronic documents. Further rules concern the transformation of electronic documents to paper and vice versa, and the access to electronic records. Of the sections not explicitly mentioned, sections 130b, 298, and 298a ZPO, provide for entire case files in electronic form to be submitted (subject to separate laws of the Länder, some of which have been already been passed for single pilot projects).

Gibraltar

Electronic Commerce Act 2001[1]

1   Passed by the House of Assembly on 5 March 2001 and given assent on 8 March 2001, but this was subsequently changed to 14 March 2001 by Legal Notice 19/01. Brought into force on 22 March 2001 by Legal Notice 13/01. The citation has been altered pursuant to the commencement of the new Gibraltar Constitution in 2007. All Gibraltar statutes, previously known as Ordinances, have, since the commencement of the new Constitution on 2 January 2007, now been renamed as Acts.

Greece

Presidential Decree 150/2001[1]

1   Passed on 13 June 2001 and in force from the date published in the Gazette (Government Gazette, Issue A', No. 125/25.06.2001).

Guernsey

The Electronic Transactions (Guernsey) Law 2000[1]

1   Sections 1 to 9 came into force on 1 March 2001 by the Electronic Transactions (Guernsey) Law, 2000 (Commencement) Ordinance, 2001. Sections 15 to 18 came into force on 1 December 2000 by the Electronic Transactions (Guernsey) Law, 2000 (Commencement) (No 2) Ordinance, 2000. Sections 10 to 14, 19, and 21 to 24 came into force on the 1 October 2000 by the Electronic Transactions (Guernsey) Law, 2000 (Commencement) Ordinance, 2000. The provisions of sections 1 to 5 and 8 of the Electronic Transactions (Guernsey) Law 2000 do not apply to a number of transactions set out in the Electronic Transactions (Exemptions) Order, 2001 (SI No 13 of 2001).

Hong Kong

Electronic Transactions Ordinance 2000[1]
Electronic Transactions (Amendment) Ordinance 2004[2]

1   Section 32 and Part VII came into force on 18 February 2000 under the authority of the Electronic Transactions Ordinance (1 of 2000) (Commencement) Notice 2000 (L.N. 7 of 2000) dated 10 January 2000; sections 3, 5, 6, 7, 8 and 10 and Part IV and Part V (in relation to the matters referred to in Schedule 1) of and Schedules 1 and 2 to the Ordinance were brought into operation on 7 April 2000 by the Electronic Transactions Ordinance (1 of 2000) (Commencement) (No 2) Notice 2000 (L.N. 60 of 2000); Schedule 2 to the Electronic Transactions Ordinance was amended by the Electronic Transactions Ordinance (Amendment of Schedule 2) Order 2000 (L.N. 59 of 2000), adding 28 statutory bodies which exercise quasi-judicial functions to the Schedule. The law was amended by the Electronic Transactions (Amendment) ordinance 2004, Order number 14, into force on 30 June 2004. Note that Schedule 2 has been amended seven times, by L.N. 59 of 2000, L.N. 5 of 2002 s 407; L.N. 7 of 2004 s 55; L.N. 18 of 2004 s 69; L.N. 20 of 2004 s 59; L.N. 19 of 2005 s 7 and L.N. 23 of 2005 s 28.

2   This Ordinance amends the Electronic Transactions Ordinance 2000; Order number 14 of 2004, in force on 30 June 2004.

Hungary

2001. évi XXXV. Törvény az elektronikus aláírásról[1]

2   Digital Signature Act 2001. Passed by Parliament in May 2001, in force on 1 September 2001. The Act was amended by Act LV of 2004, and took effect on 19 July 2004.

Iceland

Lög nr. 28/2001 um rafrænar umdirskriftir[1]

2   Act No 28/2001 on electronic signatures, in force on16 May 2001, immediately it was passed by article 24.

India

Information Technology Act 2000[1]

1   In force on 17 October 2002 (s 1(3) and Vide G.S.R. 788 (E)), 17 October 2000.

Iran

Electronic Commerce Act 2004

Ireland

Electronic Commerce Act 2000

Isle of Man

Electronic Transactions Act 2000[1]

1   Supplemented by the Electronic Transactions (General) Regulations 2000.

Israel

Electronic Signature Law, 5761 – 2001[1]

1   Passed by the Knesset on 25 March 2001 and brought into force six months from the date of publication (s 27) on 4 October 2001. The Israeli Securities Law has also been amended to allow electronic certificates to be used: Securities Law (Amendment no. 22) (Electronic Report) 5763-2002; Securities Regulations (Signature Certificatory) 5763-2003 and Securities Regulations (Electronic Signature and Report) 5763-2003.

Italy

Legge 25 marzo 1997, n.59 *Delega al Governo per il conferimento di funzioni e compiti alle regioni ed enti locali, per la riforma della Pubblica Amministrazione e per la semplificazione amministrativa*[1]

Decreto del Presidente della Repubblica 28 dicembre 2000, n. 445 *Testo unico delle disposizioni legislative e regolamentari in materia di documentazione amministrativa*[2]

Decreto del Presidente della Repubblica 7 aprile 2003 n. 137 *Regolamento recante disposizioni di coordinamento in materia di firme elettroniche a norma dell'articolo 13 del decreto legislativo 23 gennaio 2002, n. 10*[3]

Decreto del Presidente del Consiglio dei Ministri 13 gennaio 2004 *Regole tecniche per la formazione, la trasmissione, la conservazione, la duplicazione, la riproduzione e la validazione, anche temporale, dei documenti informatici*[4]

Decreto Legislativo 7 marzo 2005, n. 82 *Codice dell'amministrazione digitale*[5]

Decreto legislativo 4 aprile 2006, n. 159 *Disposizioni integrative e correttive al decreto legislativo 7 marzo 2005, n. 82, recante codice dell'amministrazione digitale*[6]

1 (Suppl. ordinario n. 56/L, alla Gazz. Uff. n. 63, del 17 marzo) delegates powers to the Council of Ministers to provide rules and regulations to reform public administration and simplify procedures.

2 (Suppl. Ordinario alla Gazz. Uff. n. 42 del 20 febbraio 2001) This decree repealed Decreto del Presidente della Repubblica 10 novembre 1997, n. 513 (Gazz. Uff. n. 60 del 13 marzo 1998), which elaborated Law No 15/1997 and implemented the Italian electronic signature legislation.

3 (in Gazz. Uff., 17 giugno, n. 138).

4 (in Gazz. Uff., 27 aprile, n. 98).

5 (in Suppl Ord.n. 93 alla Gazz. Uff.,16 maggio, n. 112).

6 (in Suppl. ordinario n. 105 alla Gazz. Uff., 29 aprile, n. 99).

Japan

Law Concerning Electronic Signatures and Certification Services (Law No.102 of 2000)[1]

1 The date of the Law is 24 May 2000. The date of implementation was 1 April 2001. See also Cabinet Order for the enforcement of the Electronic Signature and Certification Services Act (2000).

Jersey

Electronic Communications (Jersey) Law, 2000[1]

1 Sanctioned by Order of Her Majesty in Council on 11 October 2000, into force on 1 January 2001 by the Electronic Communications (Jersey) Law 2000 (Appointed day) Act 2000. The Electronic Communications (Jersey) Order 2000 was passed to establish a framework for the progressive implementation of Part 3 of the Law.

Jordan

Electronic Transaction Law No. 85 of 2001[1]

1 Passed on 31 December 2001, enforceable after three months from the date of publication.

Korea

Electronic Signature Act (2005)

Latvia

Elektronisko dokumentu likums[1]

1   Adopted on 31 October 2002 and came into force as of 1 January 2003 (Publicēts Vēstnesis 169 20.11.2002).

Liechtenstein

Electronic Signature Act 2003[1]

1   The Electronic Signature Act (Gesetz vom 18. September 2003 über elektronische Signaturen; Signatur gesetz) was published in Lichtensteinisches Landesgesetzblatt on 11 November 2003. An ordinance laying out certain provisions in more detail has been issued: Verordnung vom 1. Juni 2004 über elektronische Signaturen (Signaturverordnung; SigV), published in Liechtensteinisches Landesgesetzblatt Nr. 130/2004 on 8 June 2004.

Lithuania

Elektroninio parašo įstatymas 2000 m. liepos 11 d. Nr. VII-1822, pakeistas 2002 m. birželio 6 d.[1]

1   The Law on Electronic Signature, passed on 11 July 2000, No. VIII-1822, as amended on 6 June 2002.

Luxembourg

Loi du 14 août 2000 relative au commerce électronique modifiant le code civil, le nouveau code de procédure civile, le code de commerce, le code pénal et transposant la directive 1999/93 du 13 décembre 1999 relative à un cadre communautaire pour les signatures électroniques, la directive 2000/31/CE du 8 juin 2000 relative à certains aspects juridiques des services de la société de l'information, certaines dispositions de la directive 97/7/CEE du 20 mai 1997 concernant la vente à distance des biens et des services autres que les services financiers[1]

1   Law of 14 August 2000 on electronic commerce modifying the Civil code, the New Code of civil procedure, the Commercial code, the Criminal code and transposing Directive 1999/93/EC of the European Parliament and the Council of 13 December 1999 on a Community framework for electronic signatures, Directive 2000/31/EC of the European Parliament and the Council of 8 June 2000 on certain legal aspects of information society services, in particular electronic commerce, in the Internal Market (Directive on electronic commerce) and certain provisions of Directive 97/7/EC of the European Parliament and the Council of 20 May 1997 on the protection of consumers in respect of distance contracts. This Law has been amended three times since it entered into force, although the amendments do not affect the

provisions relating to electronic signatures. Two Grand-Ducal Decrees have been adopted. Grand-Ducal Decree on electronic signatures, electronic payments and the creation of the Electronic Commerce Committee, adopted on 1 June 2001, and, Grand-Ducal Decree of 21 December 2004, which provides for rules on the notification of the service providers providing qualified certificates, setting up an accreditation system of service providers of certification, creating an Electronic Signature Committee and determining the accreditation procedure of external auditors.

Malaysia

Digital Signature Act 1997[1]

1   Amended by the Digital Signature (Amendment) Act 2001. The amendment is solely to transfer the role of the Controller of Certification Authorities to the Malaysian Communications and Multimedia Commission (MCMC). The MCMC is now empowered to exercise, discharge and perform the duties, powers and functions conferred on it under the Digital Signature Act 1997. The Electronic Commerce Act 2006 came into force in Malaysia on 19 October 2006, which provides for legal recognition of electronic messages used in commercial transactions, the use of electronic messages to fulfil legal requirements and to enable, as well as facilitate, commercial transactions by electronic means.

Malta

Electronic Commerce Act 2002[1]

1   The Minister for Transport and Communications designated 10 May 2002 as the date when the Act entered force (Legal Notice 109 of 2002) and under the provisions of Legal Notice 110 of 2002, the Malta Communications Authority was nominated as the Competent Authority for the purposes of the Act.

Mauritius

Electronic Transactions Act 2000[1]

1   Parts I to V, VII to IX, XI, XIII and section 41 of the Electronic Transactions Act 2000 were brought into force on 1 August 2001 by Presidential Proclamation No. 7 of 2001, 16 July 2001.

Mexico

The Commercial Code (Articles 80 and 89–114) and Civil Code (Articles 1803, 1805, 1811 and 1834) have been amended to provide for electronic transactions[1]

1   Published in the Official Gazette 29 May 2000 and entered into force on June 7, 2000. Amendments were made to the Federal Civil Code, Federal Commercial Code, Federal Civil Procedures Code and the Federal Consumer Protection Law. Further amendments to articles 89–114 were published in the Diario Oficial de la Fedracion (Official Mexican Gazette) on August 29, 2003, and these amendments will be in force in 90 days from the date of publication.

Mongolia

Draft Law on Information Technology[1]

1   Available online at www.open-government.mn/english/draftnew/ict.html.

Myanmar

Electronic Transactions Law (The State Peace and Development Council Law No. 5/2004)[1]

1   The 12th Waxing of Kason 1366 M.E. (30th April, 2004).

Nepal

The Electronic Transactions Ordinance, 2005[1]

1   No. 32 of the year 2061 B.S. [2005 A.D.], Nepal Gazette, Volume 54, Kathmandu, Extraordinary Issue 60, March 18, 2005 (2061/11/28 B.S.) in force immediately it was published in the Gazette, s 1(2).

Netherlands

Wet van 8 mei 2003 tot aanpassing van Boek 3 en Boek 6 van het Burgerlijk Wetboek, de Telecommunicatiewet en de Wet op de Economische Delicten inzake elektronische handtekeningen ter uitvoering van richtlijn nr. 1999/93/EG van het Europees Parlement en de Raad van de Europese Unie van 13 december 1999 betreffende een gemeenschappelijk kader voor elektronische handtekeningen (PbEG L 13) (Wet elektronische handtekeningen), Staatsblad 2003, 199[1]

1   Act of May 8, 2003 for the amendment of Book 3 and Book 6 of the Dutch Civil Code, the Telecommunications Act and Act on Economic Offences for implementation of the Directive no. 1999/93/EC of the European Parliament and of the council of December 13, 1999 on a community framework for electronic signatures (OJ L 13) (Electronic Signatures Act), Bulletin of Acts and Decrees 2003, 199. Since the Act has also been implemented in the Dutch Civil Code, it is necessary to refer to the relevant articles in the Telecommunications Act and the Act on Economic offences, when assessing the effect of an electronic signature. At the time this edition was updated, two resolutions have been adopted in December 2006 regarding the 'Besluit elektronische handtekeningen' and the 'Regeling elektronische handtekening'. These resolutions had not yet entered into force at the time of writing, and will not do so until certain articles of another Act, (Veegwet EZ 2005) will enter into force. The enforcement date depends on Royal Decrees, which have to be passed.

Netherlands Antilles

Landsverordening overeenkomsten langs elektronische weg (P.B. 2000, 186)[1]

1   State Ordinance Agreements By Electrical Means 2000.

New Zealand

Electronic Transactions Act 2002[1]

1   By s 2, two administrative provisions (ss 14(3) and 36) of the Act came in to force the day after the date of assent, 17 October 2002. The balance of the Act came into force as from 21 November 2003 pursuant to clause 2 of the Electronic Transactions Act Commencement Order (SR 2003/289). On the same day, 21 November 2003, the Electronic Transactions Regulations 2003 (SR 2003/288) came into force.

Norway

Lov om elektronisk signatur (esignaturloven) av 15. juni 2001 nr. 81[1]

1   In force on 1 July 2001. The name was changed on 17 June 2005, and a new §16a was introduced. This article enables the department to set requirements for the establishment of voluntary certification systems. These changes were brought into force on 1 July 2005.

Pakistan

Electronic Transactions Ordinance, 2002

Panama

Ley No 43 de 31 de julio de 2001 Que define y regula los documentos y firmas electrónicas y las entidades de certificación en el comercio electrónico, y el intercambio de documentos electrónicos[1]

1   Promulgated in the Official Gazette No. 24, 359 of August 3, 2001. The Code of Commerce Law No. 2 (August 22, 1916 Official Gazette No. 2,404 of August 22, 1916) Article 71 (on commercial accounting) and Article 210 (on commercial contracts) were amended by Articles 7 and 31 of Executive Decree No. 5 of 1997 – in respect of Article 71, see Resolution No. 201-909 of July 24, 1996 of the Revenue Directorate General, and Executive Decree No. 26 of February 1, 1996; Law No. 11 (January 22, 1998, Official Gazette No. 23,468 of January 27, 1998) amended by Executive Decree No. 57 (May 19, 1999, Official Gazette No. 23,468 of January 27, 1998) by which the technological storage of documents is regulated and other provisions are adopted; Executive Decree No. 34 April 6, 1998 Official Gazette No. 23,520 of April 13, 1998 establishing rules for submitting Accounting Records and Financial Statements.

Peru

Ley No 27269 Ley de Firmas y Certificados Digitales[1]

1   Approved by Congress on 26 May 2000 and implemented (reglamentada) by Supreme Decree No. 019-2002-JUS of 17 May 2002, published in the Official Gazette of 18 May 2002. Articulo 4 and Articulo 7 were later amended by Supreme Decree No. 024-2002-JUS of 11 July 2002, published in the Official Gazette of 12 July 2002. Articulo 11 was subsequently amended by Ley Que Modifica el Artículo 11 de la Ley No 27310, approved by Congress on 15 July 2000. See also Resolución Comisión de Reglamentos Técnicos Y Comercialse No

0103-2003-CRT-INDECOPI of 23 October 2003 (the Commission of Technical and Commercial Implementing Rules) makes reference to article 33 of the Implementing Regulations as appeared in Supreme Decree No. 019-2002-JUS of 17 May 2002. These new regulations are related to the accreditation of entities that are authorized to certify or verify digital signatures.

Philippines

Electronic Commerce Act of 2000, Republic Act No 8792

Poland

Ustawa z dnia 18 września 2001 r. o podpisie elektronicznym[1]

1   (Dz.U. z 2001, Nr 130, poz. 1450) (Law of 2001.09.18 on electronic signature (Journal of Laws 2001, No. 130, item 1450)) entered into force 16 August 2002. The Act on electronic signature of 18 September, 2001 (O.J. 2001/130/1450) has been altered six times (O.J. refers to 'Dziennik Urzedowy', the name of the official journal where law is published in Poland): O.J. 2002/153/1271 – article 83 of this act altered the article 33(2) of the Act on electronic signature; O.J. 2003/124/1152 – article 158 of this act altered article 10(5) of the Act on electronic signature; O.J. 2003/217/2125 – article 6 of this act altered article 24(2)(4), and altered article 26(1)(2), and abrogated article 75 of the Act on electronic signature; O.J. 2004/96/959 – article 68 of this act added a reference to the title of the Act about the implementation of directive 1999/93/WE of 13 December, 1999, and also added article (4)(5)(a); O.J. 2005/64/565 – article 45 of this act altered article 14(2) and article 58(3); O.J. 2006/145/1050 – article 2 of this act altered article 58(2).

Portugal

Decreto-lei no. 290-D/99, de 2 de Agosto[1]
Decreto-lei no. 375/99, de 18 de Setembro[2]
Decreto-lei no. 146/2000, de 18 de Julho[3]
Decreto-lei no. 234/2000, de 25 de Setembro[4]
Decreto-lei no. 62/2003, de 3 de Abril[5]

1   Seen and approved in the Council of Ministers on 22 July 1999. Enacted on 29 July 1999. Approved on 29 July 1999 by the President of the Republic. Published in Diário da República no. 178 (Series I-A) 1999-08-02, 4990(2). Entered into force the day after it was published. Decreto-Lei n.° 165/204, amends article 29 in Decreto-Lei n.° 290-D/99 of 2 august.; Decreto-Lei n.° 62/2003 amends Decreto-Lein.°290-D/99 of 2 august, and Decreto-Lei n.° 116-A/2006, creates an Electronic Certification system for the state infrastructure.
2   This law provides for the electronic transmission of invoices or equivalent documents, and for such documents to be the equivalent to the original invoices or equivalent documents issued on paper, provided that a digital signature is appended to it under the terms of Decree-Law nr. 290-D/99, de 2 de Agosto.
3   This law provides for the creation of the Instituto das Tecnologias de Informação na Justiça as accrediting authority of the digital signature providers (article 18-3-i.). The law was published 2000-07-18 and entered in force the day after it was published in Diário da República.

4   This law requires the consultative body Conselho Técnico de Credenciação (Accreditation Technical Committee) to support the Instituto das Tecnologias da Informação na Justiça (ITIJ – Institute of Information Technologies in Justice) in its role as the accreditation authority, with responsibilities for the accreditation and inspection of certifying entities. Published on 2000-09-25 and entered in force 5 days after it was published in Diário da República.

5   This decree-law amends articles 1-9, 11-22, 24-33, 37-39 of Decreto-Lei no. 290-D/99 de 2 de Agosto to bring the legal regime into line with the EU Directive for electronic signatures. This law provides for three types of electronic signature: electronic signature, advanced electronic signature and qualified electronic signature. Published in Diário da Republica no. 79 (Series I-A), 2003-04-03, 2170 and entered into force the day after it was published.

Puerto Rico

Ley de Firmas Electrónicas de Puerto Rico, Ley número 359 de Septiembre 16, 2004"; 3 L.P.R.A. § 8701, et seq.[1]

1   The new Act was approved in 2004: Puerto Rico Electronic Signature Act, Law No. 359 of September 16, 2004, 3 L.P.R.A. § 8701, et seq. (Codified version of the law in Laws of Puerto Rico Annotated (L.P.R.A.), Title 3, Chapter 98; Effective September 16, 2004). The old Act is no longer in effect: Capitulo 41A Firmas Digitales Agosto 7, 1998, Num. 188 3 L.P.R.A. § 1031 (2003) – The Digital Signatures Law of Puerto Rico, Law 188 of August 7, 1998, as amended, 3 L.P.R.A. §1031, et seq. This was the codified version of the old law, codified in the Laws of Puerto Rico Annotated, Title 3, Chapter 41A. Passed by the Puerto Rico Legislature and signed by the Governor. Effective on August 7, 1998.

Romania

Lege nr. 455 din 18 iulie 2001 privind semnătura electronică[1]

1   Publicat în Monitorul Oficial, Partea I nr. 429 din 31 iulie 2001. Relevant secondary legislation includes: Methodological and Technical Norms, adopted on 13 December 2001 and published in the Official Monitor no 847/28 December 2001; Law on time-stamping no. 451/2004 and published in the Official Monitor no 1021/5 November 2004; Law on electronic notary activities – 589/2004 – published in the Official Monitor no 1227, 20 December 2004 (this law in turn has secondary legislation: Minister of IT&C Order No. 221/16 June 2005).

Russia

Federal Law No. 1-FZ on Electronic Digital Signature[1]
Federal Law No. 149-FZ Information, Information Matters and Protection of Information[2]

1   Published on January 12, 2002. Article 160 Written Form of Deals of the Federal Law No. 51-FZ (first published on 5 December 1994; the latest changes and additions made on 29 December 2006) has been amended, and provides for the use of electronic signatures in contract. The third paragraph of Article 75 of Federal Law No. 95-FZ (Arbitral Code) (first published on 24 July 2002 with changes and additions made on 28 July 2004, 2 November 2004, 31 March 2005 and 27 December 2005) provides that documents, received by means of facsimile, electronic or any other communication, as well as documents signed by digital

signature are considered acceptable as written documents in cases and in the course envisaged by the Russian Legislation.

2 Published on July 27, 2006. The third paragraph of Article 11 of this law provides that an electronic message signed by a digital signature or other means analogous to handwritten signature is declared as an electronic document equivalent to a document signed with the handwritten signature, provided that there is no request that this document shall be in a hard copy.

Sark

Electronic Transactions (Sark) Law, 2001

Saudi Arabia

Regulation for Electronic Signatures in Law[1]

1 The Saudi Government through the Ministry of Councils issued this regulation in mandate on 26 March 2007.

Singapore

Electronic Transactions Act 1998 (Cap 88 of 1999)[1]

1 Passed by the Singapore Parliament on 29 June 1998, received the Presidential assent on 3 July 1998 and brought into force on 10 July 1998 under S 369/98, and as amended by the Electronic Transactions (Amendment) Act 2004 (No 54 of 2004), which was passed by Parliament on 16 November 2004 and assented to by the President on 29 November 2004.

Slovak Republic

Zakon c. 215/2002 Z.z.o elektronickom podpise a o zmene a doplneni niektorych zakonov[1]

1 Electronic Signature Law, as amended, adopted on 15 March 2002 and in force from 1 May 2002, with some provisions effective as of 1 September 2002, as subsequently amended by Act No. 679/2004 Z.z., Act No. 25/2006 Z.z. and Act No. 275/2006 Z.z.

Slovenia

Zakon o elektronskem poslovanju in elektronskem podpisu (uradno prečiščeno besedilo), Uradni list Republike Slovenije št. 98/2004[1]

Zakon o elektronskem poslovanju na trgu, Uradni list Republike Slovenije št. 61/2006[2]

1 Electronic Commerce and Electronic Signature Act (Official consolidated text), published in Official Gazette of the Republic of Slovenia, Nr. 98/2004, on September 9, 2004, and in force since September 24, 2004. This consolidated Act replaces Zakon o elektronskem poslovanju un elektronskem podpisu (Uradni list Republike Slovenije, št. 57-2615/2000) – Published in

the Official Gazette of the Republic of Slovenia (Uradni list Republike Slovenije) on June 23, 2000 and in force since 22 August 2000 (Electronic Commerce and Electronic Signature Act (Official Gazette of the Republic of Slovenia, Nr. 57 –2615/2000)).

2   Electronic Commerce Market Act, published in Official Gazette of the Republic of Slovenia, Nr. 61/2006, on June 13, 2006, and in force since June 28, 2006.

South Africa

Electronic Communications and Transactions Act 2002[1]

1   Into force on 30 August 2002 Government Gazette, 30 August 2002 No 23809, 2.

South Korea

Electronic Signature Act 1999· 2· 5 Act No. 5792[1]
Framework on Electronic Commerce[2]

1   Amended by 2001·1·16 Act No 6360 and 2001·12·31 Act No 6585.
2   Amended by 2002·1·19 Act No 6614.

Spain

Ley 59/2003, de 19 de diciembre, de firma electrónica[1]

1   Boletín Oficial del Estado (Official State Gazette) of 20 December 2003, No. 304. This law acts to strengthen the existing legal framework by incorporating modifications to and repealing the Real Decreto-Ley 14/1999, de 17 de septiembre, sobre firma electrónica.

Sri Lanka

Information and Communication Technology Act, No 27 of 2003[1]

1   This is an enabling Act that provides for the establishment of a National Committee on Information and Communications Technology in Sri Lanka.

Sweden

Lag (2000:832) om kvalificerade elektroniska signaturer[1]

1   Qualified Electronic Signatures Act (SFS 2000:832) was issued on November 2, 2000 and became effective on January 1, 2001.

Switzerland

Bundesgesetz vom 24. März 2000 über den Gerichtsstand in Zivilsachen (GestG)
Bundesgesetz vom 19. Dezember 2003 über Zertifizierungsdienste im Bereich der elektronischen Signatur (ZertEs)[1]

Verordnung vom 3. Dezember 2004 über Zertifizierungsdienste im Bereich der elektronischen Signatur (VZertEs)

1 The Zertifizierungsdiensteverordnung, ZertDV vom 12. April 2000 (Stand am 23. May 2000) is a Federal Decree, not a law, and the ZertES replaces the ZertDV. The Federal Act on Certification Services Concerning the Electronic Signature (ZertEs) came into force on January 1, 2005. It replaces ZertDV, which was annulled when the ZertEs was brought into force (cf. Art. 14 VZertEs). The ZertDV was designed as an experimental decree only and limited in time. It was aimed at supporting a broad offer of secure services in connection with electronic certification, favouring the use and the legal recognition of digital signatures and enabling the international recognition of the provider of certification services. The ZertDV did not achieve the aim. As a consequence, the Swiss government elaborated the new ZertEs. It contains provisions about the security infrastructure, which corresponds, in the main, to that set out in ZertDV, as well as the necessary rules regarding substantive recognition, registration law and liability. The ZertEs is complemented by a Federal Decree (VZertEs) and a Decree from the OFCOM (Federal Office of Communication) with further regulations. The latter contains a reference to an Appendix, which refers to other (mainly international) rules. Generally speaking, a digital signature in conformity with the ZertEs is equivalent to a manuscript signature for the purposes of statutory formal regulations (cf. Art. 14 (2) of the Swiss Code of Obligations [OR] and Art. 59a OR). On January 1, 2007 the BGG ('Bundesgerichtsgesetz'; Federal Act of the Swiss Supreme Court of June 17, 2005) came into force. By Art. 42 (4) electronic filing of briefs is possible with the Swiss Supreme Court if a certified digital signature is used. However, it should be noted that the electronic filing process as provided by the new Act is still quite complicated.

Taiwan

Electronic Signatures Law 2001[1]

1 The Law was promulgated on 14 November 2001 under Presidential Order No. Hua-Tsun g-I-Yi-9000223510, and became effective on 1 April 2002 under Executive Yuan Order No. Yuan-Yi-Jing-0910080314.

Thailand

Electronic Transactions Act B.E. 2544 (2001)[1]

1 Government Gazette, Decree Issue, Volume 118, Part 112 Kor., 4 December 2001, in force on 3 April 2002, 120 days after publication.

Tunisia

Loi n° 2000-83 du 9 août 2000 relative aux échanges et au commerce électroniques, JORT n° 64 du 11août 2000 p.1887[1]

1 The Electronic Transactions and Electronic Commercial Law, passed on 9 August 2001. Corresponding amendments have been made to the Penal Code on 2 August 1999 (Loi n° 99-89 du 02 août 1999 modifiant et complétant certaines dispositions du code pénal, JORT n° 63 du 06 août 1999, p. 1283), the Civil Code on 13 June 2000 (Loi n° 2000-57 du 13 juin 2000 modifiant et complétant certains articles du code des obligations et des contrats, JORT n° 48 du 16 juin 2000, p. 1456-1457) and the Commercial Code on 20 June 2000.

Turkey

Eleltronik Imza Kanunu Kanun No 5070[1]

1 Published in the Official Gazette on 23 January 2004 and entered into force on 22 July 2004. Regulation Elektronik İmza Kanunun Uygulanmasına İlişkin Usul ve Esaslar Hakkında Yönetmelik (Regulation regarding the Procedures and Principles on the Implementation of the Electronic Signature Law) published in the Official Gazette dated January 6, 2005, number 25692) aims to regulate the legal and technical aspects of digital signatures and their implementation in practice. Communiqué Elektronik İmza ile İlgili Süreçlere ve Teknik Kriterlere İlişkin Tebliğ (Processes and Technical Criteria relating to Electronic Signatures) published in the Official Gazette dated January 6, 2005, number 25692) aims to determine the procedures and technical criteria that need to be fulfilled with respect to digital signatures.

Turks and Caicos Islands

Electronic Transactions Ordinance 2000[1]

1 In force on 31 August 2001 by Legal Notice 42 of 2001 in Gazette Volume 152 Number 41.

Ukraine

On the electronic digital signature No. 852-IV of May 22, 2003[1]
On Electronic Documents and Electronic Document Circulation No. 851-IV of May 22, 2003[2]

1 Adopted by the Verkhovna Rada of Ukraine on May 23, 2003 first published in Uryadovyi Kurier (Governmental Courier) Newspaper No. 119 on July 2, 2003 and in force from January 1, 2004.
2 Both laws are complementary to each other and form the legal framework for transactions involving electronic signatures.

United Arab Emirates

Federal Law 1/2006 Concerning Electronic Transactions and Commerce Law[1]

1 Federal Law No. 36 of 2006 amends the law of Proof in Civil and Commercial Transactions (promulgated by Federal Law No 10 of 1992) and also reviews Federal Law No. 1 of 2006.

United Kingdom[1]

Electronic Communications Act 2003

1 Compromises three separate jurisdictions: England and Wales, Scotland and Northern Ireland. The Act received the Royal Assent on 25 May 2000, and extends to Northern Ireland by s 16(5). Sections 7, 11 and 12 came into force on 25 July 2000 in accordance with the provisions of the Electronic Communications Act 2000 (Commencement No 1) Order 2000 (SI 2000 No 1798).

United States of America

Federal

Electronic Signatures in Global and National Commerce Act (E-SIGN), 15 U.S.C. §§ 7001–7003[1]

1 E-SIGN will govern many, but not all, transactions in which electronic or digital signatures are used. It pre-empts state laws to the extent that if there is any conflict between the federal and state law, unless (1) the state has enacted the Uniform Electronic Transactions Act or (2) the state has adopted law which is congruent with E-SIGN. The Uniform Electronic Transactions Act is not itself law, except as adopted by individual states. At the time of writing, at least 43 states have adopted UETA.

State

ALABAMA

Alabama Uniform Electronic Transactions Code, Ala. Rev. Code Ann. §§ 8-1A-1 to 8-1A-20

ALASKA

Electronic Records and Signatures Act, Al. Stat. §§ 09.25.510

ARIZONA

Uniform Electronic Transactions Act, Ariz. Rev. Stat. Ann. §§ 44-7001 to 44-7051

ARKANSAS

Uniform Electronic Transactions Act, Ark. Code Ann. §§ 25-31-101 to 25-32-121

CALIFORNIA

Uniform Electronic Transactions Act, Cal. Civ. Code § 1624.5, §§ 1633.1 to 1633.17

COLORADO

Government Electronic Transactions Act, Colo. Rev. Stat. Ann. §§ 24-71-101 to 71.3-121

CONNECTICUT

Connecticut Uniform Electronic Transactions Act, Conn. Gen. Stat. Ann. §§ 1-266 to 1-286

KENTUCKY

Uniform Electronic Transactions Act, Ky. Rev. Stat. Ann. §§ 369.101 to 369.120

LOUISIANA

Uniform Electronic Transactions Act, La. Rev. Stat. Ann. §§ 9:2601 to 9:2620

MAINE

Uniform Electronic Transactions Act, Me. Rev. Stat. Ann. Tit. 10, §§ 9401 to 9507

MARYLAND

Uniform Electronic Transactions Act, Md. Code Ann., Com. Law II §§ 21-101 to 21-120

MASSACHUSETTS

Uniform Electronic Transactions Act, ALM GL ch. 110G, § 1 to § 18

MICHIGAN

Uniform Electronic Transactions Act, Mich. Comp. Laws Ann. §§ 450.831 to 450.849

MINNESOTA

Uniform Electronic Transactions Act , Minn. Stat. Ann. §§ 325L.01 to 325L.19

MISSISSIPPI

Mississippi Electronic Transactions Act, Miss. Code Ann. §§ 75-12-1 to 75-12-39

MISSOURI

Uniform Electronic Transactions Act, Mo. Rev. Stat. Ann. 432.200 to 432.295

MONTANA

Uniform Electronic Transactions Act, Mont. Code Ann. §§ 30-18-101 to 30-18-118

OREGON

Uniform Electronic Transactions Act, Or. Rev. Stat. §§ 84.001 to 84.064

PENNSYLVANIA

Uniform Electronic Transactions Act, Pa. Stat. Ann. Tit. 73, §§ 2260.101 to 2260.903

RHODE ISLAND

Uniform Electronic Transactions Act, R.I. Code R. §§ 42-127.1-1 to 42-127.1-20

SOUTH CAROLINA

Electronic Commerce Act, S.C. Code Ann. §§ 26-5-10 to 26-6-190

SOUTH DAKOTA

Uniform Electronic Transactions Act, S.D. Codified Laws §§ 53-12-1 to 53-12-05

TENNESSEE

Uniform Electronic Transactions Act, Tenn. Code Ann. §§ 47-10-101 to 47-10-123

TEXAS

Uniform Electronic Transactions Act, Texas Bus. & Com. Code Ann. §§ 43-001 to 43-021

UTAH

Uniform Electronic Transactions Act, Utah Code Ann. §§ 46-4-101 to 46-4-503[1]

1 The Utah Digital Signature Act, Utah Code §§ 46-3-101, was repealed by the Repeal of Utah Digital Signature Act S.B. 20. The governor signed the Act on 10 March 2006.

VERMONT

Vermont Electronic Transactions Act, Vt. Stat. Ann. 9 §§ 270to 290

VIRGIN ISLANDS

Uniform Electronic Transactions Act, Virgin Islands Code, §§ 101 to 120

VIRGINIA

Uniform Electronic Transactions Act, Va. Code Ann. §§ 59.1-479 to 59.1-497

WASHINGTON

Electronic Authentication Act, Rev. Code of Wash. Ann. §§ 19.34.010 to 19.34.903

WEST VIRGINIA

West Virginia Electronic Transactions Act, W.V. Code §§ 39A-1-1 to 39A-1-17; 39A-2-1 to 39A-2-12

WISCONSIN

Wisconsin Electronic Transactions Act, Wis. Stat. Ann. §§ 137.01, 137.04 to 137.06

WYOMING

Uniform Electronic Transactions Act, Wyo. Stat. Ann. §§ 40-21-101 to 40-21-119

United Arab Emirates

Federal Law Number 1 of 2006 regarding Electronic Transactions and Commerce

Uruguay

Ley No 16.002[1]
Ley No 16.736[2]
Ley No 17.243[3]

1   Published in the Official Gazette on 13 dic/988 – No 22764, articles 129 and 130 provide for the acceptance of documents sent electronically, taking into account the fact that the original document came into existence electronically.

2   Published in the Official Gazette on 12 jan/996 – N° 24457, articles 694 to 697 provide for electronic signatures to be used in matters relating to the government. Regulated by Decree N° 65/998.

3   Published in the Official Gazette on 6 jul/000 – No 25554, articles 24 and 25 refer to the State Computer Information System. Regulated by Decree No 382/003.

Vanuatu

Electronic Transactions Act No 24 of 2000[1]

1   *Assent 12 September 2000. Commencement: 6 November 2000.*

Venezuela

Decreto con Fuerza de Ley No.1.204 Sobre Mensajes de Datos y Firmas Electrónicas[1]

1   Official Gazette No 37.148 of 28 February 2001 Decreto N° 1.204 10 February 2001.

Vietnam

Law on E-Transactions (No. 51/2005/QH11)[1]

1   Passed on 29 November 2005 by the XIth National Assembly of the Socialist Republic of Vietnam during its 8th session. Under the provisions of article 53, the law entered into force on 1 March 2006. The Government of Vietnam issued Decree 57/2006/ND-CP of the Government dated 9 June 2006 (Decree 57) implementing the Law on E-Transactions in respect of e-commerce, which entered into force on 7 July 2006.

Orders made under the Electronic Communications Act 2000

2000

Commencement orders

Electronic Communications Act 2000 (Commencement No. 1) Order 2000,
  SI 2000 No. 1798 (C. 46) Article 2 Part 1

Section 4 amended

Regulation of Investigatory Powers Act 2000, section 82, Schedule 4(10)

Section 8 enabling

The Local Government and Housing Act 1989 (Electronic Communications)
  (England) Order 2000, SI 2000 No. 3056
The Companies Act 1985 (Electronic Communications) Order 2000, SI 2000
  No. 3373

Section 9 enabling

The Companies Act 1985 (Electronic Communications) Order 2000, SI 2000
  No. 3373

Section 16 enabling

Electronic Communications Act 2000 (Commencement No. 1) Order 2000,
  SI 2000 No. 1798 (C. 46)

2001

Section 8 enabling

The Local Government and Housing Act 1989 (Electronic Communications) (Wales) Order 2001, SI 2001 No. 605 (W. 28)

The Unsolicited Goods and Services Act 1971 (Electronic Communications) Order 2001, SI 2001 No. 2778

The National Health Service (Charges for Drugs and Appliances) (Electronic Communications) Order 2001, SI 2001 No. 2887

The National Health Service (Pharmaceutical Services) and (Misuse of Drugs) (Electronic Communications) Order 2001, SI 2001 No. 2888

The Prescription Only Medicines (Human Use) (Electronic Communications) Order 2001, SI 2001 No. 2889

The National Health Service (General Medical Services) (Electronic Communications) Order 2001, SI 2001 No. 2890

The Housing (Right to Acquire) (Electronic Communications) (England) Order 2001, SI 2001 No. 3257

The Public Records Act 1958 (Admissibility of Electronic Copies of Public Records) Order 2001, SI 2001 No. 4058

Section 9 enabling

The Unsolicited Goods and Services Act 1971 (Electronic Communications) Order 2001, SI 2001 No. 2778

The National Health Service (Charges for Drugs and Appliances) (Electronic Communications) Order 2001, SI 2001 No. 2887

The National Health Service (Pharmaceutical Services) and (Misuse of Drugs) (Electronic Communications) Order 2001, SI 2001 No. 2888

The Prescription Only Medicines (Human Use) (Electronic Communications) Order 2001, SI 2001 No. 2889

The National Health Service (General Medical Services) (Electronic Communications) Order 2001, SI 2001 No. 2890

The Public Records Act 1958 (Admissibility of Electronic Copies of Public Records) Order 2001, SI 2001 No. 4058

Section 10 enabling

The Local Government and Housing Act 1989 (Electronic Communications) (Wales) Order 2001, SI 2001 No. 605 (W. 28)

2002

Applied

The Environmental Impact Assessment (Uncultivated Land and Semi-Natural Areas) (Wales) Regulations 2002, Welsh SI 2002 No. 2127 (W. 214) Regulation 2

The Beet Seed (England) Regulations 2002, SI 2002 No. 3171 Regulation 2

The Cereal Seed (England) Regulations 2002, SI 2002 No. 3173 Regulation 2

The Police Act 1997 (Criminal Records) (Scotland) Regulations 2002, Scottish SI 2002 No. 143 Regulation 9

The Home Zones (Scotland) (No. 2) Regulations 2002, Scottish SI 2002 No. 292 Regulation 2

The Housing (Scotland) Act 2001 (Registered Social Landlords) Order 2002, Scottish SI 2002 No. 411 Regulation 2

Referred to

The Environmental Impact Assessment (Uncultivated Land and Semi-Natural Areas) (Scotland) Regulations 2002, Scottish SI 2002 No. 6 Regulation 2

The Plant Health (Phytophthora ramorum) (Scotland) Order 2002, Scottish SI 2002 No. 223 Article 2

The TSE (Scotland) Regulations 2002, Scottish SI 2002 No. 255 Regulation 3

Section 7 applied

Land Registration Act 2002, s 91

Section 8 applied

Tax Credits Act 2002, s 54

Section 8 referred to

Tax Credits Act 2002, s 54

Section 8 enabling

The Social Security (Electronic Communications) (Child Benefit) Order 2002, SI 2002 No. 1789

Section 9 applied

The Social Security (Electronic Communications) (Child Benefit) Order 2002, SI 2002 No. 1789

Section 9 enabling

The Social Security (Electronic Communications) (Child Benefit) Order 2002, SI 2002 No. 1789

2003

Applied

The Animal By-Products (Scotland) Regulations 2003, Scottish SI 2003 No. 411 Regulation 2

The Access to the Countryside (Dedication of Land) (England) Regulations 2003, SI 2003 No. 2004 Regulation 5

Referred to

Criminal Justice (Scotland) Act 2003 asp 7, section 82

The Nitrate Vulnerable Zones (Grants) (Scotland) Scheme 2003, Scottish SI 2003 No. 52 Article 2

The Less Favoured Area Support Scheme (Scotland) Regulations 2003, Scottish SI 2003 No. 129 Regulation 2

The Anti-Pollution Works (Scotland) Regulations 2003, Scottish SI 2003 No. 168 Regulation 2

The Pet Travel Scheme (Scotland) Order 2003, Scottish SI 2003 No. 229 Regulation 2

The Urban Waste Water Treatment (Scotland) Amendment Regulations 2003, Scottish SI 2003 No. 273 Regulation 1

The Road User Charging (Consultation and Publication) (Scotland) Regulations 2003, Scottish SI 2003 No. 292 Regulation 2

The Registration of Establishments Keeping Laying Hens (Scotland) Regulations 2003, Scottish SI 2003 No. 576 Regulation 2

The Plant Protection Products (Scotland) Regulations 2003, Scottish SI 2003 No. 579 Regulation 2

The Support and Assistance of Young People Leaving Care (Scotland) Regulations 2003, Scottish SI 2003 No. 608 Regulation 2

Section 7 applied

The Access to the Countryside (Dedication of Land) (England) Regulations 2003, SI 2003 No. 2004 Regulation 5

Section 8 applied

Criminal Justice (Scotland) Act 2003 asp 7, section 82

The Child Benefit and Guardian's Allowance (Administration) Regulations 2003, SI 2003 No. 492 Sch 2 para 1

Section 8 referred to

Criminal Justice (Scotland) Act 2003 asp 7, section 82

Section 8 enabling

The Building Societies Act 1986 (Electronic Communications) Order 2003, SI 2003 No. 404

The Patents Act 1977 (Electronic Communications) Order 2003, SI 2003 No. 512

The Town and Country Planning (Electronic Communications) (England) Order 2003, SI 2003 No. 956

The Council Tax and Non-Domestic Rating (Electronic Communications) (England) Order 2003, SI 2003 No. 2604

The Social Security (Electronic Communications) (Carer's Allowance) Order 2003, SI 2003 No. 2800

The Council Tax and Non-Domestic Rating (Electronic Communications) (England) (No. 2) Order 2003, SI 2003 No. 3052

Section 9 applied

Criminal Justice (Scotland) Act 2003 asp 7, section 82

Section 9 enabling

The Building Societies Act 1986 (Electronic Communications) Order 2003, SI 2003 No. 404

The Patents Act 1977 (Electronic Communications) Order 2003, SI 2003 No. 512

The Town and Country Planning (Electronic Communications) (England) Order 2003, SI 2003 No. 956

The Social Security (Electronic Communications) (Carer's Allowance) Order 2003, SI 2003 No. 2800

Section 11 repealed

Communications Act 2003, Sch 19

Section 12 repealed

Communications Act 2003, Sch 19

Section 15 amended

Communications Act 2003, Sch 17 para 158

2004

Referred to

The Less Favoured Area Support Scheme (Scotland) Regulations 2004, Scottish SI 2004 No. 70 Regulation 2

The Potatoes Originating in Egypt (Scotland) Regulations 2004, Scottish SI 2004 No. 111 Regulation 2

The Beef Carcase (Classification) (Scotland) Regulations 2004, Scottish SI 2004 No. 280 Regulation 12

The Avian Influenza (Survey Powers) (Scotland) Regulations 2004, Scottish SI 2004 No. 453 Regulation 5

The Plant Health (Phytophthora ramorum) (Scotland) Order 2004, Scottish SI 2004 No. 488 Article 2

Section 8 enabling

The Education Act 1996 (Electronic Communications) Order 2004, SI 2004 No. 2521

The Town and Country Planning (Electronic Communications) (Wales) (No. 1) Order 2004, Welsh SI 2004 No. 3156 (W. 273)

The Town and Country Planning (Electronic Communications) (Wales) (No. 2) Order 2004, Welsh SI 2004 No. 3157 (W. 274)

The Consumer Credit Act 1974 (Electronic Communications) Order 2004, SI 2004 No. 3236

The Town and Country Planning (Electronic Communications) (Scotland) Order 2004, Scottish SI 2004 No. 332

Section 9 applied

The Town and Country Planning (Electronic Communications) (Scotland) Order 2004, Scottish SI 2004 No. 332

Section 9 enabling

The Education Act 1996 (Electronic Communications) Order 2004, SI 2004 No. 2521

The Town and Country Planning (Electronic Communications) (Wales) (No. 1) Order 2004, Welsh SI 2004 No. 3156 (W. 273)

The Town and Country Planning (Electronic Communications) (Wales) (No. 2) Order 2004, Welsh SI 2004 No. 3157 (W. 274)

The Consumer Credit Act 1974 (Electronic Communications) Order 2004, SI 2004 No. 3236

The Town and Country Planning (Electronic Communications) (Scotland) Order 2004, Scottish SI 2004 No. 332

Section 10 enabling

The Town and Country Planning (Electronic Communications) (Wales) (No. 1) Order 2004, Welsh SI 2004 No. 3156 (W. 273)

The Town and Country Planning (Electronic Communications) (Wales) (No. 2) Order 2004, Welsh SI 2004 No. 3157 (W. 274)

2005

Referred to

The Salmonella in Laying Flocks (Survey Powers) (England) Regulations 2005, SI 2005 No. 359 Regulation 7

The Water Services etc. (Scotland) Act 2005 (Consequential Provisions and Modifications) Order 2005, SI 2005 No. 3172 Article 2

The Potatoes Originating in the Netherlands (Notification) (Scotland) Order 2005, Scottish SI 2005 No. 73 Article 2

The Plant Health (Import Inspection Fees) (Scotland) Regulations 2005, Scottish SI 2005 No. 216 Regulation 2

The Fodder Plant Seed (Scotland) Regulations 2005, Scottish SI 2005 No. 329 Regulation 26

The Tuberculosis (Scotland) Order 2005, Scottish SI 2005 No. 434

The Reporting of Prices of Milk Products (Scotland) Regulations 2005, Scottish SI 2005 No. 484

The Salmonella in Broiler Flocks (Sampling Powers) (Scotland) Regulations 2005, Scottish SI 2005 No. 496 Regulation 5

Section 7 applied

The Registration of Civil Partnerships (Prescription of Forms, Publicisation and Errors) (Scotland) Regulations 2005, Scottish SI 2005 No. 458 Regulation 3

The Registration of Independent Schools (Scotland) Regulations 2005, Scottish SI 2005 No. 571 Regulation 1

Section 8 enabling

The Social Security (Electronic Communications) (Miscellaneous Benefits) Order 2005, SI 2005 No. 3321

Section 9 enabling

The Social Security (Electronic Communications) (Miscellaneous Benefits) Order 2005, SI 2005 No. 3321

Section 15 applied

The Registration of Civil Partnerships (Prescription of Forms, Publicisation and Errors) (Scotland) Regulations 2005, Scottish SI 2005 No. 458 Regulation 3

Section 15 referred to

The Land Management Contracts (Menu Scheme) (Scotland) Regulations 2005, Scottish SI 2005 No. 225 Regulation 2

The Less Favoured Area Support Scheme (Scotland) Regulations 2005, Scottish SI 2005 No. 569 Regulation 2

2006

Applied

The Police Act 1997 (Criminal Records) (Scotland) Regulations 2006, Scottish SI 2006 No. 96, Regulation 16

The Avian Influenza (Slaughter and Vaccination) (Scotland) Regulations 2006 Scottish SI 2006 No. 337, Regulation 3

Referred to

The Older Cattle (Disposal) (Scotland) Regulations 2006, Scottish SI 2006 No. 4, Regulation 3

The Private Water Supplies (Scotland) Regulations 2006, Scottish SI 2006 No. 209, Regulation 2

The Water Services and Sewerage Services Licences (Scotland) Order 2006, Scottish SI 2006 No. 464, Article 1

The Transmissible Spongiform Encephalopathies (Scotland) Regulations 2006, Scottish SI 2006 No. 530, Regulation 2

The Environmental Impact Assessment (Agriculture) (Scotland) Regulations 2006, Scottish SI 2006 No. 582, Regulation 2

Section 7 applied

The Registration of Independent Schools (Scotland) Regulations 2006, Scottish SI 2006 No. 324, Regulation 2

Section 8 applied

The Automated Registration of Title to Land (Electronic Communications) (Scotland) Order 2006, Scottish SI 2006 No. 491

Section 8 enabling

The Non-Domestic Rating and Council Tax (Electronic Communications) (England) Order 2006, SI 2006 No. 237

The Registered Designs Act 1949 and Patents Act 1977 (Electronic Communications) Order 2006, SI 2006 No. 1229

The Transport Security (Electronic Communications) Order 2006, SI 2006 No. 2190

The Registration of Births and Deaths (Electronic Communications and Electronic Storage) Order 2006, SI 2006 No. 2809

The Housing Benefit and Council Tax Benefit (Electronic Communications) Order 2006, SI 2006 No. 2968

The Council Tax (Electronic Communications) (Scotland) Order 2006, Scottish SI 2006 No. 67

The Non-Domestic Rating (Electronic Communications) (Scotland) Order 2006, Scottish SI 2006 No. 201

The Electronic Communications (Scotland) Order 2006, Scottish SI 2006 No. 367

The Automated Registration of Title to Land (Electronic Communications) (Scotland) Order 2006, Scottish SI 2006 No. 491

Section 9 applied

The Council Tax (Electronic Communications) (Scotland) Order 2006, Scottish SI 2006 No. 67

The Non-Domestic Rating (Electronic Communications) (Scotland) Order 2006, Scottish SI 2006 No. 201

The Electronic Communications (Scotland) Order 2006, Scottish SI 2006 No. 367

The Automated Registration of Title to Land (Electronic Communications) (Scotland) Order 2006, Scottish SI 2006 No. 491

Section 9 enabling

The Registered Designs Act 1949 and Patents Act 1977 (Electronic Communications) Order 2006, SI 2006 No. 1229

The Transport Security (Electronic Communications) Order 2006, SI 2006 No. 2190

The Registration of Births and Deaths (Electronic Communications and Electronic Storage) Order 2006, SI 2006 No. 2809

The Housing Benefit and Council Tax Benefit (Electronic Communications) Order 2006, SI 2006 No. 2968

The Council Tax (Electronic Communications) (Scotland) Order 2006, Scottish SI 2006 No. 67

The Non-Domestic Rating (Electronic Communications) (Scotland) Order 2006, Scottish SI 2006 No. 201

The Electronic Communications (Scotland) Order 2006, Scottish SI 2006 No. 367

The Automated Registration of Title to Land (Electronic Communications) (Scotland) Order 2006, Scottish SI 2006 No. 491

Section 15 applied

Police, Public Order and Criminal Justice (Scotland) Act 2006 asp 10, sections 91, 95 and 97

Section 15 referred to

The Common Agricultural Policy (Wine) (Scotland) Amendment Regulations 2006, Scottish SI 2006 No. 311, Regulation 18

The Conservation of Salmon (Collection of Statistics) (Scotland) Regulations 2006, Scottish SI 2006 No. 572, Regulation 3

Standards

The plethora of standards on offer, which are agreed technical specifications to provide for interoperability between equipment and processes, appear to be limitless. An attempt has been made to list as many of the relevant standards in this appendix that apply to electronic signatures as possible, albeit the vast majority refer to the digital signature and the supporting infrastructure. No critical analysis is offered, but it is conceivable that, in the event of a dispute, the party bearing the burden of proof may have recourse to apply their mind to the relevant standards and to determine whether the standards were complied with, and if not, why not.

Whether a standard prevails will depend on the ease by which they can be implemented, or whether a commercial organization has adopted its own methodology, thereby side-stepping a standard that might already exist or is being developed. As pointed out by Klaus Schmeh in *Cryptography and Public Key Infrastructure on the Internet* (Wiley, 2001), at paragraph 10.2, 'A successful standard becomes a bible: anyone who wants to sell his or her product must observe it to the letter. A standard that does not prevail is not worth the paper on which it is printed.' Or, put another way, not worth the digital space within which it is stored and not printed. Standards also have an expiry date and seem, generally, to be constantly in draft form.

Formal Standardization Organizations

International Standardization Organization (ISO)
International Electrotechnical Commission (IEC) (www.iec.ch)
International Telecommunications Union (ITU) Standardization Section
United Nations Economic Commission for Europe (UN-ECE)
    (www.unece.org)

Note the provisions of the 'Memorandum of Understanding between the International Electrotechnical Commission, the International Organization for Standardization, the International Telecommunications Union and the United Nations Economic Commission for Europe concerning standardization in the field of electronic business' (24 March 2000), which carve out the areas of work for each organization.

International Standardization Organization

www.iso.org

ISO/IEC 14888-1:1998 Information technology – Security techniques – Digital signatures with appendix – Part 1: General (JTC 1/SC 27; ISO Standards; ICS: 35.040; Current stage 90.92; 2004-07-01)

ISO/IEC 15946-2:2002 Information technology – Security techniques – Cryptographic techniques based on elliptic curves – Part 2: Digital signatures (JTC 1/SC 27; ISO Standards; ICS: 35.040; Current stage 90.93; 2005-07-13)

ISO/IEC 14888-3:2006 Information technology – Security techniques – Digital signatures with appendix – Part 3: Discrete logarithm-based mechanisms (JTC 1/SC 27; ISO Standards; ICS: 35.040; Current stage 60.60; 2006-11-13)

ISO/IEC 15946-4:2004 Information technology – Security techniques – Cryptographic techniques based on elliptic curves – Part 4: Digital signatures giving message recovery (JTC 1/SC 27; ISO Standards; ICS: 35.040; Current stage 60.60; 2004-09-28)

ISO/IEC 15945:2002 Information technology – Security techniques – Specification of TTP services to support the application of digital signatures (JTC 1/SC 27; ISO Standards; ICS: 35.040; Current stage 90.20; 2007-01-15)

ISO/IEC 9594-8:1998 Information technology – Open Systems Interconnection – The Directory: Authentication framework (JTC 1/SC 6; ISO Standards; ICS: 35.100.70; Current stage: 90.93; 2003-10-23)

ISO/IEC 9594-8:2001 Information technology – Open Systems Interconnection – The Directory: Public-key and attribute certificate frameworks (JTC 1/SC 6; ISO Standards ICS: 35.100.70; Current stage: 90.92; 2004-11-11)

International Telecommunications Union (ITU) Standardization Section

www.itu.int

X.509: Information technology – Open Systems Interconnection – The Directory: Public-key and attribute certificate frameworks (Approved in 2005-08) (03/00) and (08/05)

X.842: Information technology – Security techniques – Guidelines for the use and management of trusted third party services (Approved in 2000-10) (10/00)

X.843: Information technology – Security techniques – Specification of TTP services to support the application of digital signatures (Approved in 2000-10) (10/00)

Formal European Standardization Organizations

European Telecommunications Standardization Institute (ETSI)
Comité Européen de Normalisation (CEN)
Comité Européen de Normalisation en Electrotechnique (CENELEC)

European Telecommunications Standards Institute

www.etsi.org
For further information, see 'Terms of Reference for Specialist Task Force STF 288 (PA1) TC ESI on International Harmonisation of ETSI Electronic Signature Standards', v 0.2.1 28 February 2005

TR 102 038 Ver. 1.1.1 (2002-04) TC Security – Electronic Signatures and Infrastructures (ESI); XML format for signature policies

TR 102 041 Ver. 1.1.1 (2002-02) Signature Policies Report

TR 102 044 Ver. 1.1.1 (DTR/ESI-000005) (2002-12-02) Electronic Signatures and Infrastructures (ESI); Requirements for role and attribute certificates

TR 102 045 Ver. 1.1.1 (DTR/ESI-000006) (2003-03-31) Electronic Signatures and Infrastructures (ESI); Signature policy for extended business model

TR 102 046 Ver. 1.1.1 (DTR/ESI-000007) (2003-02-20) Electronic Signatures and Infrastructures (ESI); Maintenance of ETSI standards from EESSI phase 2 and 3

TR 102 047 Ver. 1.1.1 (DTR/ESI-000008) (2004-02-24) International Harmonization of Electronic Signature Formats (ESI)

TR 102 040 Ver. 1.2.1 (RTR/ESI-000009) (2004-02-24) International Harmonization of Policy Requirements for CAs issuing Certificates (ESI)

TS 102 231 Ver. 1.1.1 (DTS/ESI-000010) (2003-10-06) Electronic Signatures and Infrastructures (ESI); Provision of harmonized Trust Service Provider status information

TS 102 158 Ver. 1.1.1 (DTS/ESI-000012) (2003-10-09) Electronic Signatures and Infrastructures (ESI); Policy requirements for Certification Service Providers issuing attribute certificates usable with Qualified certificates

TS 101 733 Ver. 1.4.0 (RTS/ESI-000013) (2002-09-12) Electronic Signatures and Infrastructures (ESI); Electronic Signature Formats

TS 102 023 Ver. 1.2.1 (RTS/ESI-000014) (2003-01-14) Electronic Signatures and Infrastructures (ESI); Policy requirements for time-stamping authorities Revised use of terminology (e.g. TSU TSA) to align with other International activities

TR 102 153 Ver. 1.1.1 (DTR/ESI-000015) (2003-02-19) Electronic Signatures and Infrastructures (ESI); Pre-study on certificate profiles

SR 002 176 Ver. 1.1.1 (DSR/ESI-000016) (2003-03-28) Electronic Signatures and Infrastructures (ESI); Algorithms and Parameters for Secure Electronic Signatures

TS 101 733 Ver. 1.5.1 (RTS/ESI-000017) (2003-12-15) Electronic Signatures and Infrastructures (ESI); Electronic Signature Formats

TS 102 280 Ver. 1.1.1 (DTS/ESI-000018) (2004-03-29) X.509 V.3 Certificate Profile for Certificates Issued to Natural Persons (ESI)

TR 102 046 Ver. 1.2.1 (RTR/ESI-000020) (2004-06-04) Electronic Signatures and Infrastructures (ESI); Maintenance of ETSI standards from EESSI phase 2 and 3

TR 102 272 Ver. 1.1.1 (DTR/ESI-000022) (2003-12-15) Electronic Signatures and Infrastructures (ESI); ASN.1 format for signature policies

TR 102 437 Ver. 1.1.1 (DTR/ESI-000023) (2006-10-03) Electronic Signatures and Infrastructures (ESI); Guidance on TS 101 456 (Policy Requirements for certification authorities issuing qualified certificates)

TS 101 456 Ver. 1.3.1 (RTS/ESI-000025) (2005-05-18) Electronic Signatures and Infrastructures (ESI); Policy requirements for certification authorities issuing qualified certificates

TS 102 042 Ver. 1.2.1 (RTS/ESI-000026) (2005-05-11) Electronic Signatures and Infrastructures (ESI); Policy requirements for certification authorities issuing public key certificates

TR 102 040 Ver. 1.3.1 (RTR/ESI-000027) (2005-03-17) Electronic Signatures and Infrastructures (ESI); International Harmonization of Policy Requirements for CAs issuing Certificates

TR 102 047 Ver. 1.2.1 (RTR/ESI-000028) (2005-03-17) International Harmonization of Electronic Signature Formats

TR 102 317 Ver. 1.1.1 (DTR/ESI-000029) (2004-06-04) Electronic Signatures and Infrastructures (ESI); Process and tool for maintenance of ETSI deliverables

TS 101 903 Ver. 1.2.2 (RTS/ESI-000031) (2004-04-02) XML Advanced Electronic Signatures (XAdES) (ESI)

TS 101 862 Ver. 1.3.2 (RTS/ESI-000032) (2004-06-02) Qualified Certificate profile (ESI)

TR 102 458 Ver. 1.1.1 (DTR/ESI-000033) (2006-04-20) Electronic Signatures and Infrastructures (ESI); Mapping Comparison Matrix between the US Federal Bridge CA Certificate Policy and the European Qualified Certificate Policy (TS 101 456)

TS 101 903 Ver. 1.3.2 (RTS/ESI-000034) (2006-03-07) XML Advanced Electronic Signatures (XAdES) (ESI)

TS 102 231 Ver. 2.1.1 (RTS/ESI-000038) (2006-03-10) Electronic Signatures and Infrastructures (ESI); Provision of harmonized Trust-service status information

TS 102 176-1 Ver. 1.2.1 (RTS/ESI-000039-1) (2005-07-12) Electronic Signatures and Infrastructures (ESI); Algorithms and Parameters for Secure Electronic Signatures; Part 1: Hash functions and asymmetric algorithms

TS 102 176-2 Ver. 1.2.1 (RTS/ESI-000039-2) (2005-07-12) Electronic Signatures and Infrastructures (ESI); Algorithms and Parameters for Secure Electronic Signatures; Part 2: Secure channel protocols and algorithms for signature creation devices

TS 101 733 Ver. 1.6.3 (RTS/ESI-000040) (2005-09-26) Electronic Signatures and Infrastructures (ESI); CMS Advanced Electronic Signatures (CAdES)

TS 102 904 Ver. 1.1.1 (DTS/ESI-000041) (2007-02-16) Electronic Signatures and Infrastructures; Profiles of XML Advanced Electronic Signatures based on TS 101 903 (XAdES) (ESI)

TS 102 734 Ver. 1.1.1 (DTS/ESI-000042) (2007-02-16) Electronic Signatures and Infrastructures; Profiles of CMS Advanced Electronic Signatures based on TS 101 733 (CAdES) (ESI)

TS 102 042 Ver. 1.2.2 (RTS/ESI-000043) (2005-06-14) Electronic Signatures and Infrastructures (ESI); Policy requirements for certification authorities issuing public key certificates

TR 102 438 Ver. 1.1.1 (DTR/ESI-000044) (2006-03-06) Electronic Signatures and Infrastructures (ESI); Application of Electronic Signature Standards in Europe

TS 101 862 Ver. 1.3.3 (RTS/ESI-000045) (2006-01-06) Qualified Certificate profile (ESI)

TR 102 572 Ver. 0.0.11 (DTR/ESI-000046) Best practices Framework to implement the Policy requirements for issuance and Storage of Digital Accounting Documents (SODA) (ESI) [Drafting Stage Current Status: Start of pre-processing (2007-02-28) Next Status: End of pre-processing (2007-03-30)]

TS 102 573 Ver. 0.0.4 (DTS/ESI-000047) Policy requirements for issuance and Storage of Digital Accounting Documents (SODA) (ESI) [Drafting Stage Current Status: Start of pre-processing (2007-03-05) Next Status: End of pre-processing (2007-04-03)]

TS 101 733 Ver. 1.7.3 (RTS/ESI-000048) (2007-01-11) Electronic Signatures and Infrastructures (ESI); CMS Advanced Electronic Signatures (CAdES)

TS 101 861 Ver. 1.3.1 (RTS/ESI-000049) (2006-01-27) Time-stamping profile (ESI)

TS 101 456 Ver. 1.4.1 (RTS/ESI-000050) (2006-02-02) Electronic Signatures and Infrastructures (ESI); Policy requirements for certification authorities issuing qualified certificates

TR (DTR/ESI-000051) Existing registered e-mail mechanisms in European Union Member States (ESI) [Drafting Stage Current Status: Start of work (2006-11-30) Next Status: Table of Contents and Scope (2007-01-30)]

TS (DTS/ESI-000052) Formats of Electronic Signatures for registered emails (ESI) [Drafting Stage Current Status: TB adoption of WI (2006-07-13) Next Status: Start of work (2007-07-13)]

TS (DTS/ESI-000053) Policies of TSPs applying signatures on registered emails (ESI) [Drafting Stage Current Status: TB adoption of WI (2006-07-13) Next Status: Start of work (2007-07-30)]

TS 102 176-1 Ver. 1.3.1 (RTS/ESI-000054-1) Electronic Signatures and Infrastructures (ESI); Algorithms and Parameters for Secure Electronic Signatures; Part 1: Hash functions and asymmetric algorithms [Drafting Stage Current Status: Creation of WI by WG/TB (2006-06-28) Next Status: TB adoption of WI (2006-09-01)]

TS 102 176-2 Ver. 1.3.1 (RTS/ESI-000054-2) Electronic Signatures and Infrastructures (ESI); Algorithms and Parameters for Secure Electronic Signatures; Part 2: Secure channel protocols and algorithms for signature creation devices [Drafting Stage Current Status: Creation of WI by WG/TB (2006-06-28) Next Status: TB adoption of WI (2006-09-01)]

TS 102 042 Ver. 1.2.3 (RTS/ESI-000055) (2006-12-08) Electronic Signatures and Infrastructures (ESI); Policy requirements for certification authorities issuing public key certificates

TS 101 456 Ver. 1.4.2 (RTS/ESI-000056) (2006-12-14) Electronic Signatures and Infrastructures (ESI); Policy requirements for certification authorities issuing qualified certificates

TS 102 042 Ver. 1.2.4 (RTS/ESI-000057) (2007-03-02) Electronic Signatures and Infrastructures (ESI); Policy requirements for certification authorities issuing public key certificates

Comité Européen de Normalisation

www.cen.eu

CWA 14167-1 Security Requirements for Trustworthy Systems Managing Certificates for Electronic Signatures – Part 1: System Security Requirements

CWA 14167-2 Security Requirements for Trustworthy Systems Managing Certificates for Electronic Signatures – Part 2: Cryptographic Module for CSP signing operations with backup – Protection profile (CMCSOB-PP)

CWA 14167-3 Security Requirements for Trustworthy Systems Managing Certificates for Electronic Signatures – Part 3: Cryptographic module for CSP key generation services – Protection profile (CMCKG-PP)

CWA 14167-4 Security Requirements for Trustworthy Systems Managing Certificates for Electronic Signatures – Part 4: Cryptographic module for CSP signing operations – Protection profile – CMCSO P"

CWA 14168:2001 Secure Signature-Creation Devices "EAL 4"

CWA 14169 Secure Signature-creation devices "EAL 4+"

CWA 14170 Security requirements for signature creation applications

CWA 14171 General guidelines for electronic signature verification

CWA 14172-1 EESSI Conformity Assessment Guidance – Part 1: General introduction

CWA 14172-2 EESSI Conformity Assessment Guidance – Part 2: Certification Authority services and processes

CWA 14172-3 EESSI Conformity Assessment Guidance – Part 3: Trustworthy systems managing certificates for electronic signatures

CWA 14172-4 EESSI Conformity Assessment Guidance – Part 4: Signature-creation applications and general guidelines for electronic signature verification

CWA 14172-5 EESSI Conformity Assessment Guidance – Part 5: Secure signature-creation devices

CWA 14172-6 EESSI Conformity Assessment Guidance – Part 6: Signature-creation device supporting signatures other than qualified

CWA 14172-7 EESSI Conformity Assessment Guidance – Part 7: Cryptographic modules used by Certification Service Providers for signing operations and key generation services

CWA 14172-8 EESSI Conformity Assessment Guidance – Part 8: Time-stamping Authority services and processes

CWA 14355 Guidelines for the implementation of Secure Signature-Creation Devices

CWA 14365-1 Guide on the Use of Electronic Signatures – Part 1: Legal and Technical Aspects

CWA 14365-2 Guide on the Use of Electronic Signatures – Part 2: Protection Profile for Software Signature Creation Devices

CWA 14890-1 Application Interface for smart cards used as Secure Signature Creation Devices – Part 1: Basic requirements

CWA 14890-2 Application Interface for smart cards used as Secure Signature Creation Devices – Part 2: Additional Services

Comité Européen de Normalisation en Electrotechnique

www.cenelec.org
M/279 Electronic signatures (accepted (99 BT) work in progress at CEN) – does not appear to be available to the public

Asia-Pacific Economic Cooperation

www.apec.org
Guidelines for schemes to issue certificates capable of being used in cross jurisdiction ecommerce (Security Task Group, APEC Telecommunications and Information Working Group, December 2004)

Australia

MP 75-1996 Strategies for the implementation of a Public Key Authentication Framework (PKAF) in Australia (5 November 1996)

Canada

Government of Canada PKI

For a list of relevant standards and further information provided online, go to www.tbs-sct.gc.ca/pki-icp/gocpki/gocpki_e.asp

GoC PKI Certificate and Key Management Interface Specification (Government of Canada Public Key Infrastructure (GoC PKI) V 1.0 March 2000

United States of America

National Institute of Standards and Technology Computer Security Division

http://csrc.nist.gov/pki/index.html

FIPS PUB 140-1, Security Requirements for Cryptographic Modules (11 January 1994)

FIPS PUB 140-1 Implementation Guidance for PIPS 140-1 and the Cryptographic Module Validation Program (10 January 2002)

186-2 Digital Signature Standard (DSS) (January 27, 2000)

186-3 Digital Signature Standard (DSS) (March 13, 2006: Draft Federal Information Processing Standard (FIPS))

196 Entity Authentication Using Public Key Cryptography (1997 February 18)

197 Advanced Encryption Standard (AES) (2001 November 26)

198 The Keyed-Hash Message Authentication Code (HMAC) (2002 March)

800-15 Minimum Interoperability Specification for PKI Components (MISPC), Version 1 (September 1997)

800-20 Modes of Operation Validation System for the Triple Data Encryption Algorithm (TMOVS): Requirements and Procedures (October 1999 original release date) (Revised April 2000)

800-25 Federal Agency Use of Public Key Technology for Digital Signatures and Authentication (October 2000)

800-38A Recommendation for Block Cipher Modes of Operation – Methods and Techniques (December 2001)

800-38B Recommendation for Block Cipher Modes of Operation: The CMAC Mode for Authentication (May 2005)

800-38C Recommendation for Block Cipher Modes of Operation: the CCM Mode for Authentication and Confidentiality (May 2004)

800-38D: Recommendation for Block Cipher Modes of Operation: Galois/ Counter Mode (GCM) for Confidentiality and Authentication (April 20, 2006: Draft Special Publication)

800-56A Recommendation for Pair-Wise Key Establishment Schemes Using Discrete Logarithm Cryptography (March 2006) (updated March 9, 2007)

800-57 Recommendation for Key Management (August 2005) Part 1 (updated March 9, 2007), Part 2

800-63 Electronic Authentication Guideline: Recommendations of the National Institute of Standards and Technology (April 2006 Version 1.0.2 (publication updated) (original release date June 2004) (see Appendix B for Errata Sheet)

800-67 Recommendation for the Triple Data Encryption Algorithm (TDEA) Block Cipher (May 2004)

800-78 Cryptographic Algorithms and Key Sizes for Personal Identity Verification (April 2005)

800-78-1, Cryptographic Standards and Key Sizes for Personal Identity Verification (July 3, 2006: Draft Special Publication)

800-89 Recommendation for Obtaining Assurances for Digital Signature Applications (March 2006)

800-90 Recommendation for Random Number Generation Using Deterministic Random Bit Generators (June 2006) (updated March 13, 2007)

Banking

European Committee for Banking Standards

www.ecbs.org

TR401 V1 Secure Banking Over the Internet (March 1997)

TR406 V4 Guidelines on Algorithms Usage and Key Management (September 2005)

TR409 V1 The Use of Audit Trails in Security Systems: Guidelines for European Banks (November 2001)

TR410 V1 Secure Card Payments on the Internet (November 2002)

TR410 V1 Secure Card Payments on the Internet – Addendum (March 2003)

TR411 V2 Security Guidelines for e-Banking: Application of Basel Risk Management Principle (August 2004)

TR601 V1 European Electronic Banking Standards Framework (EEBSF) (August 2001)

EBS602 V1.1 Electronic Payment Initiator (ePI) (July 2003)

TR603 V1 Business and Functional Requirements for Mobile Payments (February 2003)

TR604 V1 Interoperability of Bank Trust Services (July 2003)

SIG605 V1.1 Electronic Payment Initiator (ePI) (December 2003)
IG606 V1 Implementation Guidelines for Mobile Payments (March 2005)
TR607 V1 Country Specific Texts for the Electronic Payment Initiator (ePI)
(July 2003)

The main Internet Standardization Organizations

Institute of Electrical and Electronics Engineers (IEEE)
Internet Engineering Task Force (IETF)
Object Management Group (OMG)
The Open Group (TOG)
Open Mobile Alliance (OMA)
Organization for the Advancement of Structured Information Standards
(OASIS)
Unicode
Web3D Consortium (Web3D)
World Wide Web Consortium (W3C)

Institute of Electrical and Electronics Engineers

www.ieee.org
IEEE P1363.1: Standard Specifications for Public-Key Cryptographic Techniques Based on Hard Problems over Lattices (Version D9, 9 January 2007)
IEEE 1363-2000: Standard Specifications For Public Key Cryptography
IEEE 1363a-2004: Standard Specifications For Public Key Cryptography-Amendment 1: Additional Techniques
IEEE P1363: Standard Specifications For Public Key Cryptography
(expired in 2005)
IEEE P1363.1: Public-Key Cryptographic Techniques Based on Hard Problems over Lattices (Draft)
IEEE P1363.2: Password-Based Public-Key Cryptography (Draft)
IEEE P1363.3: Identity-Based Public Key Cryptography

The Internet Engineering Task Force

www.ietf.org
RFC 2527 Internet X.509 Public Key Infrastructure Certificate Policy and
Certification Practices Framework (Network Working Group) (March 1999)
RFC 3741 Exclusive XML Canonicalization, Version 1.0 (IETF Working Group: XML Digital Signatures)

RFC 3653 XML-Signature XPath Filter 2.0 (IETF Working Group: XML Digital Signatures)

Organization for the Advancement of Structured Information Standards

www.oasis-open.org

Digital Signature Service Core Protocols, Elements, and Bindings Version 1.0 (Committee Specification, 13 February 2007)

German Signature Law Profile of the OASIS Digital Signature Service Version 1.0 (Committee Specification, 13 February 2007)

Advanced Electronic Signature Profiles of the OASIS Digital Signature Service Version 1.0 (Committee Specification, 13 February 2007)

Asynchronous Processing Abstract Profile of the OASIS Digital Signature Services Version 1.0 (Committee Specification, 13 February 2007)

J2ME Code-Signing Profile of the OASIS Digital Signature Services (Committee Specification, 13 February 2007)

Abstract Code-Signing Profile of the OASIS Digital Signature Services (Committee Specification, 13 February 2007)

Electronic PostMark (EPM) Profile of the OASIS Digital Signature Service Version 1.0 (Committee Specification, 13 February 2007)

Entity Seal Profile of the OASIS Digital Signature Service (Committee Specification, 13 February 2007)

Signature Gateway Profile of the OASIS Digital Signature Service v1.0 (Committee Specification, 13 February 2007)

XML Timestamping Profile of the OASIS Digital Signature Services Version 1.0 (Committee Specification, 13 February 2007)

Commercial organizations

EMC^2

The Public-Key Cryptography Standards are specifications produced by RSA Laboratories

PKCS #1: RSA Cryptography Standard

PKCS #3: Diffie-Hellman Key Agreement Standard

PKCS #5: Password-Based Cryptography Standard

PKCS #6: Extended-Certificate Syntax Standard

PKCS #7: Cryptographic Message Syntax Standard

PKCS #8: Private-Key Information Syntax Standard

PKCS #9: Selected Attribute Types

PKCS #10: Certification Request Syntax Standard

PKCS #11: Cryptographic Token Interface Standard

PKCS #12: Personal Information Exchange Syntax Standard

PKCS #13: Elliptic Curve Cryptography Standard
PKCS #15: Cryptographic Token Information Format Standard
Note: PKCS #2 and PKCS #4 have been incorporated into PKCS #1

List of correspondents

I am grateful to the correspondents listed below for the time and trouble they have taken to ensure the list of statutes is accurate and up to date at the time of publication. On this occasion, because so much subordinate legislation has been passed in relation to electronic signatures, I decided to refrain from asking correspondents to update their subordinate legislation.

All of the correspondents listed below have answered questions and provided information to me during the course of long working days. Their help and co-operation has improved the content of this publication. Please note, where a website address is not given, it may be because the law firm in question is not permitted to have a website, in accordance with their professional code of conduct, although this is not the case in every instance.

Anguilla

Harry Wiggin, Consultant
Webster Dyrud Mitchell
Victoria House, PO Box 58, The Valley, Anguilla, British West Indies

www.websterdyrud.com

Argentina

Horacio Roberto Granero
Allende & Brea
Maipu 1300, 10 Piso (C10006ACT), Buenos Aires

www.allendebrea.com

Australia

Philip N Argy, Senior Partner, Intellectual Property & Technology Group
Mallesons Stephen Jaques
Level 60, Governor Phillip Tower, 1 Farrer Place, Sydney, New South Wales
2000

www.mallesons.com

Austria

Dr F. Schwank
Law Offices Dr F. Schwank
Stock Exchange Building, Wipplingerstrasse 34, A-1010 Vienna

www.schwank.com

Bahamas

W. Christopher Gouthro
Gouthro & Co.
Suite B, Second Floor, Regent Centre, Freeport

www.freeportgrandbahamalegal.com

Barbados

Z. Vanessa Kodilinye, Attorney-at-Law
Franklin House, Wildey Main Road, St. Michael BB14007

www.kodlaw.com

Belarus

Vasiliy Nesterovich
National Center of Legal Information of the Republic of Belarus
Berson st., 1a, 220701 Minsk

www.ncpi.gov.by

Belgium

Katia Bodard, Policy Manager ICC Belgium and Assistant Professor Vesalius
College (VECO), Brussels
Stuiversstraat 8 Rue des Sols, B-1000 Brussel/Bruxelles

www.iccwbo.be and www.vesalius.edu

Johan Vandendriessche
De Wolf & Partners
Bolwerksquare 1A Square du Bastion, 1050 Brussels

www.dewolf-law.be

Bermuda

Tonya Marshall, Barrister and Attorney
Conyers Dill & Pearman
Clarendon House, 2 Church Street, PO Box HM 666, Hamilton HM CX

www.cdp.bm

Bolivia

Eduardo R. Quintanilla B.
Quintanilla & Soria – Abogados
Calle Loayza N° 250, Edificio Castilla Piso 7, Casilla N° 3143, La Paz

www.qys-lawfirm-bo.com

Brazil

Marcelo Mansur Haddad and Paulo Octaviano Junqueira
Mattos Filho, Veiga Filho, Marrey Jr. e Quiroga Advogados
Alameda Joaquim Eugênio de Lima 447 – 014003-000 – São Paulo

www.mattosfilho.com.br

Brunei Darussalam

Y C Lee
Y C Lee & Lee, Advocates & Solicitors
Suites 507–511, 5th Floor, Kompleks Jalan Sultan, Jalan Sultan, Bandar Seri
   Begawan, BS8811

yclee@ycleelaw.com.bn

Bulgaria

George Dimitrov, Partner
Dimitrov, Petrov & Co
36 B Patriarh Evtimii Boulevard, Fl.4, Apt. 13, Sofia 1000

www.dpc.bg

Canada

Valerie C. Mann
Lawson Lundell LLP
1600 – 925 West Georgia Street, Vancouver, BC, V6C 3L2

www.lawsonlundell.com

Channel Islands

John Greenfield
Carey Olsen
7 New Street, St Peter Port, Guernsey, Channel Islands, GY1 4BZ

www.careyolsen.com

Chile

Jorge Quintanilla and Cristián Doren
FerradaNehme
Isidora Goyenechea 3477, piso 5, Las Condes, Santiago 7550071

www.fn.cl

China

Chen Jihong, Partner
Zhonglun W&D Law Firm
19/F, Golden Tower, No.1, Xibahe South Road, Chaoyang District, Beijing,
   100028

www.zhonglunwende.com

Colombia

Daniel Peña Valenzuela
Cavelier Abogados
Carrera 4 No. 72 – 35, Bogotá 8

www.cavelier.com

Costa Rica

Rodrigo Oreamuno B.
Facio & Cañas
5173-1000, San José

www.fayca.com

Croatia

Ranko Pelicaric, attorney at law
Law office Pelicaric
Mrazoviceva 8/I, Zagreb, Croatia

odv.pelicaric@inet.hr

Cyprus

Olga Georgiades, LLB, LLM, Advocate
Lellos P Demetriades Law Office
The Chanteclair House, 2 Sophoulis Street, 9th Floor, Nicosia 1096

www.ldlaw.com.cy

Czech Republic

Tomáš Pešek, attorney in law
Brzobohaty Broz & Honsa
Klimentska 1207/10, 110 00 Praha

www.bbh.cz

Denmark

Arne Møllin Ottosen, Advokat (H), LLM
KromannReumert
Sundkrogsgade 5, DK-2100 Købehhavn Ø

www.kromannreumert.com

Dominican Republic

Mary Fernández Rodríguez
Headrick Rizik Alvarez & Fernández
Avenida Gustavo Mejía Ricart corner of Abraham Lincoln Torre Piantini,
    Piso 6 Santo Domingo

www.hrafdom.com

Ecuador

Rodrigo Bermeo R.
Bermeo & Bermeo
World Trade Center, Torre B, Piso 12, Av. 12 de Octubre N 24-528 y Cordero,
    PO Box 17-12-881, Quito

www.bermeolaw.com

Egypt

Amr Z. A. Motaal
Abdel Motaal, Moharram & Heiza Law Firm
5 Al Zohour Street, Mostafa Mahmoud Square, Mohandessin – Giza, Postal
  Code 12311

www.ammh-lawfirm.com

El Salvador

Morena Zavaleta
Arias & Muñoz
F.A. Arias & Muñoz
85 Avenida Norte #825, Colonia Escalon, San Salvador

www.ariaslaw.com

Estonia

Viive Näslund, attorney-at-law
Advokaadibüroo Lepik & Luhaäär LAWIN
Dunkri Street 7, Tallinn 10123

www.lawin.ee

Finland

Kaisa Fahllund, Partner
Hannes Snellman
PO Box 333 (Eteläranta 8), FIN-00131 Helsinki

www.hannessnellman.com

France

Alistair McDonagh and Philip Jenkinson
SCP Triplet & Associés
75 boulevard Vauban, 59040 Lille Cedex, France

www.triplet.com

Germany

Dr Martin Eßer
Osborne Clarke
Innere Kanalstrasse 15, D – 50823 Cologne

www.osborneclarke.de

Gibraltar

Tim Garcia
Hassans
57/63 Line Wall Road, PO Box 199, Gibraltar

www.gibraltarlaw.com

Greece

Michael G. Rachavelias
Rachavelias & Partners Law Office
8, Meg. Alexandrou str, 41 222, Larissa

www.prlawyers.gr

Guatemala

José Augusto Toledo Cruz, Partner
Arias & Muñoz
Avenida La Reforma 7-62 Zona 9, Edificio Aristos Reforma, Oficina 1001 E,
   Guatemala City

www.ariaslaw.com

Honduras

Evangelina Lárdizabal, Partner
Arias & Muñoz
Colonia Palmira, Calle Colombia, Casa #2302, Tegucigalpa

www.ariaslaw.com

Hong Kong

Gabriela Kennedy, Partner
Lovells
23/F Cheung Kong Center, No 2 Queen's Road Central, Hong Kong

www.lovells.com

Hungary

Dr. András Szecskay
Szecskay Ügyvédi Iroda
H-1055 Budapest, Kossuth Tér, 16-17. III.

www.szecskay.com

Iceland

Hörður Felix Harðarson
Jonsson & Hall Law Firm
Sudurlandsbraut 4, IS 108 Reykjavik

www.law.is

India

Mr Tejas D. Karia, BSL, LLM (India), LLM (London School of Economics),
   Advocate (India), Solicitor (England & Wales), Principal Associate
Amarchand & Mangaldas and Suresh A Shroff & Co (Advocates &
   Solicitors)
Amarchand Towers, 216, Okhla Industrial Estate, Phase-III, New Delhi 110
   020

tejas.karia@amarchand.com

Indonesia

Achmad S.Kartohadiprodjo
Ali Budiardjo, Nugroho, Reksodiputro
Graha Niaga, 24th Floor, Jalan Jenderal Sudirman Kav. 58, Jakarta 12190

www.abnrlaw.com

Ireland

Paul Lambert
Merrion Legal
Suite 12 Butlers Court, 77 Sir John Rogersons Quay, Dublin 2

paul.lambert@merrionlegal.com

Israel

Haim Ravia, Advocate, Partner and Chair of the Internet, IT & Copyright
  Group
Pearl Cohen Zedek Latzer
5 Shenkar Street, PO Box 12704, Herzelia 46733

www.law.co.il and www.pczlaw.com

Italy

Avv. Luigi Martin
Infogiur Law Firm - Studio Legale e di Consulenza
Borgo Ronchini 3, 43100 Parma

www.infogiur.com

Japan

William R. Huss
Pillsbury Winthrop Shaw Pittman LLP
Fuerte Kojimachi Building, 5th Floor, 7-25, Kojimachi 1-chome, Chiyoda-
  ku, Tokyo 102-0083 Japan

www.pillsburylaw.com

Jordan

Yousef S. Khalilieh
Rajai K.W. Dajani & Associates Law Office
First Floor, Jordan Tower Building, 11 Aab (Culture) Street, Shmeissani, P O
  Box 5590, Amman 11183

www.dajanilaw.com

Latvia

Evita Gosa
Sorainen Law Offices
Kr. Valdemara iela 21, LV1010 Riga

www.sorainen.lv

Lebanon

Tania Zaroubi, CISA
Senior ICT Project Manager, Office of the Minister of State for Administrative Reform (OMSAR) Technical Cooperation Unit
STARCO Building, Georges Picot Street, Beirut

www.omsar.gov.lb

Liechtenstein

Dr. iur. Helene Rebholz LL.M.
Advokaturbuero Dr.Dr. Batliner & D. Gasser
Marktgass 21, Postfach 86, 9490 VADUZ, Fürstentum Liechtenstein

www.batlinergasser.com

Lithuania

Stasys Drazdauskas
Foigt and Partners/Regija Borenius
J.Jasinskio str. 16a, LT-01112 Vilnius, Lithuania

www.regija.lt

Luxembourg

Mario Di Stefano
Di Stefano & Sedlo
24 Avenue Marie-Thérèse, B P 2648, L – 1026

www.mds-legal.com

Malaysia

Deepak C. Pillai
Haryati Deepak
Suite 9B.03, Level 9B, Wisma E & C, No. 2 Lorong Dungun Kiri, Damansara Heights, 50490 Kuala Lumpur

www.hdlaw.com.my

Malta

Dr. Antonio Ghio B.A., LL.M. IT&T (Strathclyde), LL.D.
Fenech & Fenech Advocates
198 Old Bakery Street Valletta VLT 09, Malta

www.fenechlaw.com

Mauritius

Shakeel Mohamed
Mohamed Chambers
Suite 503–505, Sterling House, Lislet Geoffrey Street, Port Louis

smohamed@intnet.mu

Mexico

César Martínez Alemán
Barrera, Siqueiros Y Torres Landa
Pasco de los Tamarindos #150 PB, Bosques de las Lomas, México, D.F. 05120

www.bstl.com.mx

Netherlands

Reinout Rinzema
Stibbe
Strawinskylaan 2001, P O Box 75640, 1070 AP Amsterdam

www.stibbe.nl

Netherlands Antilles

Carine A.D. Jänsch
VanEps Kunneman VanDoorne
Julianaplein 22, PO Box 504, Curaçao

www.ekvandoorne.com

New Zealand

Laura O'Gorman, Partner
Buddle Findlay
The PricewaterhouseCoopers Tower, 188 Quay Street, PO Box 1433, Auckland

www.buddlefindlay.com

Nicaragua

Gloria María A. De Alvarado
Alvarado y Asociados
Colonial Los Robles VI Etapa, Costado Sur Monte de los Olivos 6 c arriba
   No. 75, PO Box 5983, Managua

www.alvaradoyasociados.com.ni

Norway

Svein Yngvar Willassen
Norwegian University od Science and Technology
OS Bragstads plass 2B
7491 TRONDHEIM

www.willassen.no

Oman

James Harbridge and Kamilia Busaidy
Trowers & Hamlins
Al Jawhara Building, Al Muntazah Street, Shatti Al Qurum, PO Box 2991,
   PC 112, Muscat

www.trowers.com

Pakistan

Shahid Jamil Khan
Rana, Khan & Gajana
Suite No 403, 4th (Executive) Floor, Sadiq Plaza, Mall Road, Lahore –
   54000

www.rkglawfirm.com

Panama

Fernando Noriega
Arosemena Noriega & Contreras
Edificio Interseco, 2nd floor, PO Box 0816-01560, Panama 5

www.anorco.com

Paraguay

Adriana M. Casati Allegretti
Vouga & Olmedo Abogados
Juan de Salazar 657 esq. Prof. Ramírez, Asunción

www.vouga-olmedo.com

Peru

José Barreda
Barreda Moller
Av. Angamos Oeste 1200, Lima 18

www.barredamoller.com

Philippines

JJ Disini (LLM) (Harvard Law School)
Disini & Disini Law Office, 304 UPAA Ang Bahay ng Alumni, Diliman,
    Quezon City 1100

www.disini.ph

Poland

Tomasz Kozlowski
KRPiA Gluchowski Jedlinski Rodziewicz Zwara & Partners
ul. Zielna 37, Warszawa ul. Armii Krajowej 116, Sopot

www.kancelaria-sopot.pl

Portugal

Siv Lindqvist de Sousa
Abreu & Associados - Sociedade de Advogados RL
Rua S. João de Brito, 605 E 4º Andar 4.1 - 4100-455, Porto

www.abreuadvogados.com

Puerto Rico

Pedro A. Barceló Lugo
William Estrella Law Offices PSC
150 Tetuan Street, Second Floor, PO Box 9023596, San Juan, P.R. 00902

www.welo.net

Qatar

Monita Barghachie
The Law Offices of Sultan M. Al-Abdulla
Advocates & Legal Consultants, P. O. Box 20464 , Doha

www.qatarlaw.com

Romania

Bogdan Manolea
Legile Internetului

www.legi-internet.ro

Russia

Vladimir Biriulin
Gorodissky & Partners Limited
129090, Moscow, Bolshaya Spasskaya street, 25 stroenie 3

www.gorodissky.ru

Saudi Arabia

Osama Al Sulaim and Yusuf Giansiracusa
Al Sulaim & Al Awaji International Law Firm
PO Box 22166, Riyadh 11495

yusuf@nournet.com.sa

Scotland

Euan F Duncan
McClure Naismith
292 St Vincent Street, Glasgow, G2 5TQ

www.McClureNaismith.com

Singapore

Bryan Tan
Keystone Law Corporation
9 Shenton Way, #06-01, Singapore 068813

www.keystonelawcorp.com

Slovak Republic

Tomáš Rybár
Čechová & Partners
Hurbanovo nam. 5, 811 03 Bratislava

www.cechova.sk

Slovenia

Domen Neffat
Odvetniška družba Colja, Rojs & Partnerji, o.p., d.n.o.
Tivolska cesta 48, 1000 Ljubljana

www.colja-rojs-partnerji.si

South Africa

Mark Hyslop, Director
Edward Nathan Sonnenbergs, Inc.
150 West Street, Sandton, Johannesburg

www.ens.co.za

South Korea

Kwang Hyun Ryoo, Partner, IT & Telecommunication Group
Bae, Kim & Lee
647–15, Yoksam, Gangnam, Seoul, 135-723

www.baekimlee.com

Spain

Eduardo Gómez de la Cruz
Gómez-Acebo & Pombo
Castellana 216, 28046 Madrid

www.gomezacebo-pombo.com

Sweden

Henrik Bengtsson
Advokatfirman Delphi & Co
PO Box 1432, SE-111 84 Stockholm

www.delphilaw.com

Switzerland

Dr. iur. Christoph Gasser, LL.M., and lic.iur. Stefanie Peters
Staiger, Schwald & Partner
Genferstrasse 24, Postfach 2012, CH-8027 Zürich

www.ssplaw.ch

Taiwan

Robert C. Lee and Katherine Lai
Yangming Partners
10F, No.89, Sungjen Rd., ShinYi District, Taipei, Taiwan

www.yangminglaw.com

Thailand

Noppramart Thammateeradaycho, Attorney
Tilleke & Gibbins International Limited
Tilleke & Gibbins Building, 64/1 Soi Tonson, Ploenchit, Bangkok 10330

www.tillekeandgibbins.com

Turkey

Hande Hamevi
Pekin & Pekin
10 Lamartine Caddesi, Taksim 34437, Istanbul

www.pekin-pekin.com.tr

Turks and Caicos Islands

Owen Foley
Misick & Stanbrook
Richmond House, P O Box 127, Leeward Highway, Providenciales, Turks
   and Caicos Islands, British West Indies

www.misickstanbrook.tc

Ukraine

Igor Svechkar, Senior Associate
Shevchenko Didkovskiy & Partners
2A Kostyantynivska Street, Kyiv, 04071

www.shevdid.com

United Arab Emirates

Hassan Arab, Partner and Head of Litigation Department
Al Tamimi and Company
P O Box 9275 Dubai

www.tamimi.com

United States of America

Thomas M. Dunlap
Dunlap, Grubb & Weaver, P.C.
1200 G Street, NW, Suite 800, Washington, D.C. 20005

www.dglegal.com

Uruguay

Diego Baldomir
Guyer & Regules
Pza. Independencia 811, 11100 Montevideo

www.guyer.com.uy

Venezuela

Ramon Andrade
Despacho de Abogados miembros de Macleod Dixon, S.C.
Centro San Ignacio, Torre Copérnico, Piso 8, Av. Blandín, La Castellana,
    Caracas 1060

www.macleoddixon.com

Vietnam

Nguyen Duy Linh, Senior Partner
VILAF – Hong Duc, lawyers
The Metropolitan, Suite 901 235 Dong Khoi Street, District 1 Ho Chi Minh
    City

www.vilaf.com

Resources

If you are not able to find relevant legislation under the name of the jurisdiction, then a possible starting point could be (apart from typing the name of the legislation into the Google search engine) one of the following websites:

Simone van der Hof hosts the Digital Signature Law Survey at https://dsls.rechten.uvt.nl/

Baker & McKenzie maintain a website with similar material to Simone at www.bmck.com

McBride Baker & Coles also have a useful website at www.mbc.com

Major portals

Australasian Legal Information Institute
www.austlii.edu.au/

British and Irish Legal Information Institute
www.bailii.org/

Canadian Legal Information Institute
www.canlii.org/

Hong Kong Legal Information Institute
www.hklii.org/

Pacific Islands Legal Information Institute
www.paclii.org/

World Legal Information Institute
www.worldlii.org/

The World Law Guide
www.lexadin.nl/wlg/

Argentina

Comisión Nacional de Valores has a good page with a list of legislation at www.cnv.gov.ar. Similar information is also available from the Firma Digital website at www.pki.gov.ar.

Australia

Australia seems to have led the world in providing legal information via the world wide web. There are a number of excellent websites available in Australia from which you will find legislation, including the National Library of Australia, available at www.nla.gov.au; the Australian Legal Information Institute at www.austlii.edu.au and SCALEplus, the legal information retrieval system owned by the Attorney-General's Department, which is an integral part of the Australian Law Online initiative at www.scaleplus.law.gov.au.

Austria

The most commonly used websites in Austria from which copies of the laws and regulations issued by the federal and provincial governments can be downloaded are: The legal information system of the Republic of Austria at www.ris.bka.gv.at, Österreichische Bundesgesetze at www.bgbl.at, Jusline at www.jusline.at and Aufsichtsstelle für elektronische Signaturen at www.signatur.rtr.at. Also try the A-Sit site at www.a-sit.at.

Bahamas

The Bahamian Government website has most but not all of the statute laws of the Bahamas, located at http:/laws.Bahamas.gov.bs/.

Barbados

The Supreme Court website, including the Magistrates' Court, is located at www.lawcourts.gov.bb/. This website includes a number of judgments available online.

Belarus

At present it is not easy to obtain legislation in electronic format, but the National Center of Legal Information of the Republic of Belarus is worth looking at occasionally: www.ncpi.gov.by. The Russian text of the Law is available at this location: www.pravo.by/webnpa/text.asp?RN=H10000357.

Belgium

The site of the official journal has a search engine at www.staatsblad.de.

Bermuda

Bermuda Laws Online is a helpful source of legislation, at www.bermudalaws.bm.

Brazil

The Ministérioda Ciência e Tecnologia includes a range of legislation on its website at www.mct.gov.br.

Brunei Darussalam

The Brunei Darussalam Information Technology Council has a copy of the legislation on the website at www.bit.gov.bn. See also the Attorney General's website at www.agc.gov.bn.

Bulgaria

The center for the study of democracy has a useful website at www.csd.bg; see also the Center for Law of the Information and Communication Technologies at www.clict.net.

Canada

Books and reports

Lisa K. Abe and Marie-Hélène Constantin, *Web Law: Agreements, Guidelines and Use Policies* (Markham, Ont.: LexisNexis Butterworths, 2005)

R.C. Campbell, ed. *Legal Issues in Electronic Commerce* 2d ed. (Concord, Ont.: Captus Press, 2002)

Department of Justice, Electronic Commerce Secretariat (1995) 'A Survey of the Legal Issues Relating to the Security of Electronic information', online at www.justice.gc.ca/en/ps/ec/summary.html

Michael Deturbide, *Consumer Protection Online* (Markham, Ont.: LexisNexis Butterworths, 2006)

Mark Fecenko and Anita Huntley, *E-commerce: Corporate-commercial Aspects* (Markham, Ont.: LexisNexis Butterworths, 2003)

Alan M. Gahtan, *Electronic Evidence* (Toronto: Carswell, 1999)

Michael Geist, *Internet Law in Canada* (3d ed. Concord, Ont.: Captus Press, 2002)

Sunny Handa, Claude Marseille and Martin Sheehan, *E-commerce Legislation and Materials in Canada 2005/2006* (Markham, Ont.: LexisNexis Butterworths, 2006)

Barry B. Sookman, *Computer, Internet and Electronic Commerce Law* (looseleaf) (Toronto: Thomson Carswell, 1989)

Barry B. Sookman, *Computer, Internet and Electronic Commerce Terms: Judicial, Legislative and Technical Definitions* (Toronto: Thomson Carswell, 2006)

George S. Takach, *Computer Law* (Toronto: Irwin Law, 2d ed., 2003)

Roger Tassé, *On-Line Consumer Protection: A Study on Regulatory Jurisdiction in Canada* (prepared for Industry Canada, Office of Consumer Affairs, 2001), online at www.ulcc.ca/en/cls/index.cfm?sec=4&sub=4n

Treasury Board of Canada Secretariat (2004) 'Policy for Public Key Infrastructure Management in the Government of Canada', online at www.tbs-sct.gc.ca/pubs_pol/ciopubs/PKI/pki1_e.asp#1a

Journals

Canadian Journal of Law & Technology (published approximately three times per year by CCH Canadian Ltd.), online at http://cjlt.dal.ca

Internet and E-commerce Law in Canada (monthly newsletter published by LexisNexis, available in print or by email), contact: ieclc@lexisnexis.ca

Online resources

Canadian Legal Information Institute (CanLII): central hub for free online access to Canadian case law and legislation: www.canlii.org

Industry Canada, Electronic Commerce Branch: consultation reports, studies, draft policies and legislation on electronic signature authentication, cryptography policy, consumer protection, the digital economy, etc: http://e-com.ic.gc.ca/epic/site/ecic-ceac.nsf/en/h_gv00021e.html

Information Technology Association of Canada (ITAC): website of industry advocacy organization: www.itac.ca

Uniform Law Conference of Canada: uniform (model) laws, commentaries, proceedings of conferences, background reports: www.ulcc.ca

The government Information site is located at www.nlc-bnc.ca

Department of Justice located at http://canada.justice.gc.ca.

Chile

A comprehensive list of laws is available on the website of Servico Nacional del Consumidor, located at www.sernac.cl/leyes/compendio/index.php and the Ministerio de Economia has a website with some information at www.entidadacreditadora.cl and a further website that may help is located at www.sii.cl.

China

The Ministry of Justice of the People's Republic of China has a website with information at www.legalinfo.gov.cn/english/englishindex.htm.

Colombia

The Superintendencia de Industria y Comercio has a range of materials on the website at www.sic.gov.co; see also the Ministerio de Comercio, Industria y Turismo at www.mincomercio.gov.co.

Costa Rica

The Centro de estudios Superiores de Derecho Publico includes materials on its website at www.pgr.co.cr and some information can also be obtained from www.costaricalaw.com. See also a general portal with a wide ranging list of websites at www.therealcostarica.com/government_costa_rica/government_websites.html.

Croatia

The website operated by Narodne Novine, the Official Gazette of Croatia, has legislation to download from www.nn.hr. See also the government website at www.vlada.hr, and the website operated by the Croatian Parliament (Hrvatski Sabor) at www.sabor.hr. Other websites of use include www.propisi.hr and www.poslovniforum.hr.

Cyprus

The Cyprus Government Gazette is located at www.cygazette.com, and there is a Cyprus Legal Portal at www.leginetcy.com/.

Czech Republic

The Ministry of the Interior of the Czech Republic at www.mvcr.cz has some information and legislation available in electronic format, and see Sagit Infornet at www.sagit.cz for copies of legislation as well. The full text of the laws of the Czech Republic and a number of cases decided in the Czech Republic can be found on the Salvia website, located at http://salvia.gurkol.net/. The website of The Chamber of Deputies of the Czech Republic is located here: www.psp.cz/ where information and current legislative procedures are available.

Denmark

The Ministeriet for Videnskab Teknologi og Udvikling (Ministry of Science Technology and Innovation) has the legislation in electronic format on its website at www.fsk.dk and at www.videnskabsministeriet.dk. The Forbruger-styrelsen also has legislation online at www.fs.dk.

Dominican Republic

The Instituto Dominicano de las Telecomunicaciones has some legislation on its website located at www.indotel.org.do.

Ecuador

The Corporación Ecuatoriana de Comercio Electrónico includes the law and regulation on its website at www.corpece.org.ec.

Estonia

The State Gazette is available at www.riigiteataja.ee.

European Union

The main portal to the European Union is through http://europa.int.eu. Although the search engine has been improved, it remains far from perfect. Obtaining a document through this website is not easy, although to be fair to those responsible for operating the website, they have a great deal of information to index.

Finland

The Oikeusministeriö (Ministry of Justice) in Finland has legislation on its website located at www.om.fi. Viestintävirasto (Finnish Communications Regulatory Authority) is in charge of supervision in compliance with the Act on Electronic Signatures, and the website is located at www.ficora.fi/en/. See also Finlex, which is a database for Finnish legislation and case law, located at www.finlex.fi/en/.

France

The website of the Minister of Justice has some information, at www.justice. gouv.fr. Some information will also be found at www.industrie.gouv.fr and www.legifrance.gouv.fr.

Germany

Some legislation can be obtained from the Übersicht site at www.iid.de, and the website operated by Bundesminsterium für Wirtschaft und Arbeit at www.bmwi.de has copies of legislation. The Minster of Justice website contains all major legislation at www.gesetze-im-internet.de/.

Gibraltar

The Laws of Gibraltar website has a list of laws to download at www.gibraltarlaws.gov.gi/ and the government website at www.gibraltar.gov.gi is more of a general portal.

Greece

Some information can be obtained from the National Telecommunications and Post Commission located at www.eett.gr.

Guatemala

Some websites offer a paid service, such as www.infile.com/leyes/index.php?id=142 and www.leyesdeguatemala.com and some are free, but are not a complete, such as www.unicef.org/guatemala/spanish/resources_2457.htm.

Guernsey

The e-business in Guernsey website at www.guernsey-on-line.com has some legislation, including the relevant law.

Hong Kong

Legislation can be found from the website entitled Information Technology at www.info.gov.hk.

Hungary

The communications Authority includes some information on its website located at www.hif.hu.

Iceland

Legislation can be found on the government website at http://raduneyti.is and on the website of the Althingi (Parliament) at www.althingi.is.

India

Legislation can be obtained from the India Code website at http://indiacode.nic.in.

Ireland

The Department of Enterprise Trade and Employment has some materials available at www.entemp.ie.

Israel

The Certification Authorities Registrar is on the Ministry of Justice website at www.justice.gov.il/MOJHeb/RashamGormimMashrim/ (English version at www.justice.gov.il/MOJEng/Certification+Authorities+Registrar/).

Italy

A great deal of legislation can be found on the Autortià per I'Informatica nells Pubblica Amministrazione website located at www.aipa.it. The Italia.gov.it website acts as a portal at www.italia.gov.it. See also the Italian justice site at www.giustizia.it and the website operated by Centro Nazionale per L'Informatica nella Pubblica Amministrazione at www.cnipa.gov.it.

Japan

The Ministry of Economy, Trade and Industry has some materials on its website at www.meti.go.jp.

Jersey

The Jersey Legal Information Board for legislation and much more is located at www.jerseylegalinfo.je.

Jordan

Legislation can be found on the REACH website run by the Jordan Computer Society at www.reach.jo. The National Information Technology Centre website is located at www.nic.gov.jo/.

Latvia

At the time of writing, this website: www.ttc.lv does not have the legislation relating to electronic signatures in translation, but the Latvian government issued a by-law in September 1998 to establish the Translation and Terminology Centre, and there is a distinct probability that the relevant law will be translated and made available on this website in due course.

Lithuania

The website of the Selmas of the Republic of Lithuania has some legislation on its website at www3.lrs.lt.

Luxemburg

The portail juridique is a portal to the government administration of the Grand-Duché de Luxembourg at www.etat.lu.

Malaysia

Legislation is available from the website of the Suruhanjaya Komunikasi den Multimedia Malaysia (Malaysian Communications and Multimedia Commission) located at http://mcmc.gov.my; see also Kementerian Tenaga, Komunikasi Dan Multimedia Malaysia (Ministry of Energy, Communications and Multimedia) at www.ktkm.gov.my, the Parliament of Malaysia website at www.parlimen.gov.my, the Suruhanjaya Komunikasi dan Multimedia Malaysia (Malaysian Communications and Multimedia Commission) at www.cmc.gov.my/the_law/legislation.asp, and Malaysian Cyber Laws at www.mycert.org.my/bill.html. For subscription only websites, see www.lawnet.com.my and www.cljlaw.com/.

Malta

The Ministry for Justice and Home Affairs provides legislation at www.mjha.gov.mt/justice/legalservices.html.

Mauritius

The National Computer Board has some legislation available at http://ncb.intnet.mu.

Mexico

The website run by the Congress of Deputies has a list of legislation available at www.cddhcu.gob.mx/leyinfo, whilst another legal site also offers legislation at http://legal.infosel.com.

Netherlands

The Officiële Publicaties website can be searched for copies of legislation at www.overheid.nl/op.

New Zealand

Legislation can be found from the Public Access to Legislation Project, located at www.legislation.govt.nz. It may also be possible to obtain legislation from the Parliamentary Council Office (Te Tari Tohutohu Papermata) at www.pco.parliament.govt.nz/. Some New Zealand case law can be found at www.austlii.edu.au/databases.html#nz.

Norway

The Lovdata site provides legislation at www.lovdata.no, also the University of Oslo has some legislation in translation at www.ub.uio.no/ujur/ilov. These two websites are linked.

Panama

Two websites have legislation available to download: fromSecretaria Nacional de Ciencia Technologia E Innovation at www.senacyt.gob.pa and Legal Infor Panamá at www.legalinfo-panama.com.

Paraguay

General information can be obtained from Asociación Paraguaya de Derecho Informático y Tecnológico (Paraguayan Association of Computer and Technological Law) at www.apadit.org.py.

Peru

The Congress of Peru website has a search facility at www.leyes.congresso.gob.pe.

Philippines

The Department of Transport and Communications has some material on its website at www.veranda.com.ph.

Portugal

The Information Society website Anacom has the legislation relating to electronic signatures and related regulations www.anacom.pt.

Romania

Two useful sites for the law in Romania are the Ministry of Communications and Information Technology at www.mcti.ro, and the Romanian Information Technology Initiative at www.legi-internet.ro.

Singapore

Singapore is well served with links to legislation, including www.ida.gov.sg and the website run by the Controller of Certification Authorities at www.cca.gov.sg, Infocomm Development Authority of Singapore at www.ec.gov.sg, and the certification authority Netrust at www.netrust.com.sg. The Attorney-General runs a site where all laws are available, at http://statutes.agc.gov.sg/.

Slovak Republic

Legislation is available from the National Security Authority located at www.nbusr.sk.

Slovenia

Legislation is available from the website of the National Assembly of the Republic of Slovenia at www.sigov.si. The e-government of the Republic of Slovenia has a number of links http://e-gov.gov.si, including the Government Centre for Informatics.

South Africa

Two sites are available to download copies of legislation: the government website at www.gov.za/acts and the Acts online site at www.acts.co.za.

South Korea

The Ministry of Legislation website is located at www.moleg.go.kr and the Ministry of Commerce and Industry may be of some help at www.mocie.go.kr. The Ministry of Government Legislation is located at www.klaw.go.kr/ and there is a commercial Internet Information Service (KLRI) located at http://elaw.klri.re.kr/indexE.jsp that provides an English translation service.

Spain

The Ministerio de la Presidencia has some links at www.boe.es and www.setsi.mcyt.es.

Sweden

The National Post and Telecom Agency at www.pts.se has some materials. See also the Ministry of Industry, Employment and Communications at www.naring.regeringen.se.

Switzerland

The website operated by the Federal Authorities of the Swiss Confederation has some materials at www.admin.ch.

Taiwan

The esign site run by the Institute for Information Industry has copies of the legislation in translation at www.esign.org.tw.

Thailand

Legislation is available on the Electronic Commerce Resource Center website Thailand's Export and Import Directory at http://thailandexim.com/law.html; see also Thailand PKI Forum at www.thailand-pkiforum.org; National Electronics and Computer Technology Center at http://ngi.nectec.or.th; Electronic

Transactions Commission at www.etcommission.go.th; The National Telecommunications Commission at www.ntc.or.th; The Council of State at
www.krisadika.go.th; The Supreme Court of Thailand at http://supremecourt.
or.th; The Central Intellectual Property and International Trade Court at
http://cipitc.or.th.

United Arab Emirates

Laws can be found on the Dubai courts website, located at www.djd.gov.ae/
and other jurisdictions are covered at www.mohamoon-uae.com/.

United Kingdom[1]

England and Wales

ENGLAND

Judgments

House of Lords Judgments
www.publications.parliament.uk/pa/ld/ldjudgmt.htm
www.worldlii.org/uk/cases/UKHL/

House of Lords Judicial Work
www.parliament.the-stationery-office.co.uk/pa/ld/ldjudinf.htm

Court of Appeal
www.bailii.org/databases.html

Court Service website
www.hmcourts-service.gov.uk/

1   Comprises three separate jurisdictions: England and Wales, Northern Ireland and Scotland.

Parliament

In essence, there are two types of legislation in the UK: an Act of Parliament
(known as a Bill until it becomes an Act of Parliament) and a Statutory Instrument. A Statutory Instrument derives its power from the provisions of an Act
of Parliament. For a Bill to become an Act of Parliament and therefore have
the force of law, it must be passed by the House of Commons, the House of
Lords and signed by the monarch.

An Act of Parliament is allocated two references. The first reference represents the number it is given, in chronological order, as the Royal Assent is

granted. This number is the number of the Act allocated as it is signed by the monarch during the current reginal year. The second reference is the year the Act was passed. Thus the Electronic Communications Act has two references: the year it was passed, 2000 and the number it was allocated in the reginal year (it is allocated as it is ready to sign), Chapter 7. To find an Act of Parliament on the hmso website, all you need is the year (if it dates from 1987) and the name or Chapter number.

The website run by the Office of Public Sector Information below provides links to legislation for all of the United Kingdom, including Northern Ireland, Scotland, Wales, chronological Tables of Local and Private Acts of Parliament, explanatory Notes to Public Acts (Every Act of Parliament has a set of Explanatory Notes published with the Act. Although these Notes do not have the force of law, they are helpful in understanding the rationale for particular sections within the Act. These notes cover the period from 1999), and Statutory Instruments and Draft Statutory Instruments.

United Kingdom Parliament
www.parliament.uk

Office of Public Sector Information
www.opsi.gov.uk/acts.htm

Official Documents
www.official-documents.gov.uk/

UKOP Online – Official Publications
www.ukop.co.uk/

The UK Statute Law Database (the official revised edition of the primary legislation of the United Kingdom)
www.statutelaw.gov.uk/

WALES

Statutory Instruments for the National Assembly for Wales
www.opsi.gov.uk/legislation/wales/w-stat.htm National Assembly for Wales

National Assembly for Wales
www.wales.gov.uk

Portals

Access to Law: Run by Active Lawyer and Inner Temple Library, this site covers general resources, legal subject areas in the UK, Commonwealth and other jurisdictions
www.accesstolaw.com/site/

British and Irish Legal Information Institute, covering England and Wales, Ireland, Northern Ireland, Scotland, and links to other collections around the world
www.bailii.org

eagle-i service, Institute of London, University of London: good gateway to the Institute of Advanced Legal Studies library catalogue and hyperlinks to numerous sources
http://ials.sas.ac.uk/links/eagle-i.htm

Intute: Law, Social Science Information Gateway
www.intute.ac.uk/socialsciences/law/

University of Kent at Canterbury: Excellent portal of the same quality as eagle-i service
http://library.kent.ac.uk/library/lawlinks/

United States of America

Federal

A good starting point for Federal law is located at www.thecre.com/fedlaw and another useful portal is available at www.findlaw.com, and there is a paper by Anneliese May, 'Comparison of Digital Signatures Legislation Information Policy and Technology Series' located online at www.ncsl.org/programs/lis/cip/DIGSIGN.HTM.

Uruguay

The Parlamento del Uruguay website has legislation to download from www.parlamento.gub.uy.

Venezuela

The government website is located at www.venezuela.gov.ve and the SiD website has some legislation at www.cpacf.org.ar. The Centro Nacional de Tecnologías de Informacíon (National Center for Information Technologies) is located at www.cnti.gob.ve with copies of legislation. The Superintendencia de Servicios de Certificación Electrónica (Electronic Certification Services Office) is located at www.suscerte.gob.ve with copies of relevant regulations pertaining to the digital signature infrastructure, and La Cámara la Economía Digital (Venezuelan Chamber of Electronic Commerce) is located at www.cavecom-e.org.ve.

Glossary

Algorithm

In mathematics, an algorithm is a process, or set of rules for solving a mathematical problem. Algorithms used in cryptology can be classified as polynomial time algorithms or exponential functions.

American Standard Code for Information Interchange (ASCII)

Letters, numbers and symbols are represented by either a binary or octal conversion table. The following examples demonstrate how this works.

Symbol	Octal	Binary
A	101	1 0 0 0 0 0 1
B	102	1 0 0 0 0 1 0
C	103	1 0 0 0 0 1 1
1	061	0 1 1 0 0 0 1
2	062	0 1 1 0 0 1 0
3	063	0 1 1 0 0 1 1
&	046	0 1 0 0 1 1 0
#	043	0 1 0 0 0 1 1

Asymmetric cryptography

A method of encryption where two different but related keys are used, one to encrypt a message and one to decrypt a message. Also known as public key cryptography.

Attribute certificates

An attribute certificate is issued by an Attribute Authority. It acts to bind a privilege or information relating to a permission to an identity in the form of a bit string that corresponds to an authentication mechanism.

Authentication

See separate entries for *data origin authentication* and *entity authentication*.

Binary digits

Computers operate using the binary system, in which the only digits used are 0 or 1, and a setting in a computer is either on or off, represented as 0 or 1.

Bit

A shortened version for a binary digit.

Block ciphers

Also, confusingly, called block algorithms. The plaintext is divided into blocks of set lengths and then combined with a key. The ciphertext is created block by block. Each bit in the encrypted block is dependent on every bit in the plaintext block and every bit in the key. For instance, in Data Encryption Standard (DES), which is used in banking, the plaintext is divided into blocks of 64 bits long. The Advanced Encryption Standard (AES), which is beginning to replace DES, has a block length of twice DES. Block ciphers can be used for confidentiality, authentication, to provide for the integrity of data or to generate the keys for stream ciphers.

Certificate

A block of data containing information relating to the public key of a user, signed by a certification authority.

Certificate repository

A certificate repository is a logically centralized database that stores public keys.

Certificate revocation list

A certificate revocation list (CRL) is a signed data structure that contains a list of certificates that have been revoked, for whatever reason. However, there are a number of other types of list. A CRL that contains end-entity information is called an End-entity Public-key Certificate Revocation List (EPRL). A CRL that only contains information about a certification authority is called a Certification Authority Revocation List (CARL), previously known as Authority Revocation Lists (ARLs).

Certification authority

See *Trusted Intermediary*.

Certification practice statement

A statement or document that sets out the processes and the methods followed by the certification authority.

Cipher

A method by which the meaning of what is written cannot be understood without knowing the key. To give one simple example, the sequence of the letters in the plaintext can be altered. The letters can be reversed: "Awake! For Morning in the Bowl of Night" would read thgiN fo lwoB eht ni gninroM rof !ekawA, or as it is normally written, in groups letters (in this example, groups of five), with only the text: thgiN folwo Behtn ignin roMro fekaw Amias, where the last four letters have been added to fill out the final group. Here the key is the procedure of reversing the letters.

Ciphertext

A message that has been encrypted.

Cleartext

A message which is not encrypted.

Cryptanalysis

The deciphering of cryptograms or ciphertext by someone other than the intended recipient of the message.

Cryptogram

A message that has been encrypted.

Cryptography

The practice of enciphering or encoding, using a method that is intelligible only to those possessing the key, usually by one of two methods, that of substitution or transposition. In the modern sense, it is the process of providing secure communications over insecure networks.

Data authentication code

See *message authentication code*.

Data origin authentication

This is concerned with verifying the origin of the data that is received.

Decryption

This is the process by which a decryption algorithm, when used with the appropriate decryption key, reproduces the plaintext from the ciphertext.

Digital signature

A digital signature is a signature that is specifically based on asymmetric cryptography, coupled with a one-way hash function, usually by way of a public key infrastructure.

Electronic signature

An electronic signature is a generic phrase referring to authentication of an entity. A signature can be manifest in different forms, and the term electronic signature is used to reflect methods other than the use of a public key infrastructure to sign a message or document.

Encryption

The process of encryption, of converting plaintext into ciphertext or into code.

Entity authentication

This refers to the process of verifying the identity of another person or legal entity.

False acceptance rate

This refers to the probability that a system analysing biometric measurements will incorrectly identify an individual that is not registered, or where the system does not reject an impostor. It is wise to require the manufacturer to establish the reasoning for the rates determined in the system.

False rejection rate

This refers to the probability that a system analysing biometric measurements does not identify a person that is registered.

Hash function

The cryptographic hash function is a one-way algorithm that can be used to produce a shortened version of a message. As a result, the condensed version of the message cannot be used to obtain the full message.

Individual identity certificate

An individual certificate issued by a trusted third party (such as a certification authority), which identifies a natural or legal person and indicates that the natural person or legal entity is in possession of a private key corresponding to the public key contained in the certificate.

Kerckhoffs principle

Auguste Kerckhoffs von Niuewenhof formulated a fundamental rule of cryptanalysis in "La Cryptographie Militaire" *Journal des Sciences Militaires* January 9, 1883, pp 5–38, that the security of a cryptosystem must depend on keeping the key secret.

Key (or cryptographic key)

Commonly a key is just a value, although it can comprise a set of instructions that set out how messages are to be encrypted and decrypted. Keys can be secret or public. Secret keys are only available for authorised personnel to have access to (until the keys are compromised, by cryptanalysis or intentionally), whilst public keys are published for anyone to see and use. A message encrypted with a public key remains secret until the secret key is used to decrypt it.

Key pair

To enable two parties to encrypt and decrypt messages, keys are generated to be used by the signing procedure and verifying procedure. Two keys are generated, comprising a signature key (also known as the secret key) and the verification key (also known as the public key). These are known as a key pair.

Message authentication code

This comprises a set of data, sent by the sender of a message that seeks to demonstrate either the message has not been altered in transit or confirms the identity of the person sending the message, or both. The message authentication code is added to the message using a key known only by the parties to the message.

Message digest

A message digest is the condensed version of a message that has been produced by applying a hashing algorithm to the original message. A person can use their private key to encrypt the hash to authenticate the message. The recipient can separate the message digest from the message and process it with the expected sender's public key, thus verifying the identity of the sender.

Metadata

The metadata refers to the data about data. It is a digest of the structure and subject matter of a resource.

Non-repudiation

This is a technical phrase that is used to claim that a system has been designed to prevent an entity from denying the occurrence of an action. Few if any such systems exist. The use of this phrase should not be confused with the burden of proof a party may bear in a dispute, nor the legal presumptions that will apply in any given situation. There are different types of non-repudiation. They include: non-repudiation of origin, with the aim of preventing the entity that sends a message or document from denying that they sent it; non-repudiation of receipt, where systems are in place to prevent an entity from denying have not received a message or document. Other types of non-repudiation include non-repudiation of creation, non-repudiation of delivery and non-repudiation of approval.

Plaintext

This is the message from which the ciphertext is prepared. Conversely, it is the message as revealed when the ciphertext is decrypted.

Protocol

A protocol is a sequence of steps designed to complete a task. For instance, some of the points included in a protocol will include the amount of information to be sent, how frequently the information is to be sent, how errors are dealt with and the parties involved in the particular transmission.

Public key cryptography (PKI)

A system that uses two different but related keys, a private key retained by the holder and a public key made available to anybody that wants to communicate with the holder of the private key in a secure manner.

Registration authority

A trusted third party that verifies the identity of an entity on behalf of a certification authority.

Relying party

When a recipient receives a digital certificate that is accompanied with a digital signature within the public key infrastructure, the recipient becomes a relying party where they rely, without taking any affirmative action, on the information contained in the certificate. Certification authorities seek to impose obligations on recipients by requiring them to undertake a range of checks before relying on the certificate by way of "Relying Party Agreements". See *verifying party*.

Stream ciphers

This is where a stream of binary digits are generated, and then combined with plaintext to produce a stream of ciphertext bits. An early stream cipher has been ascribed to Blaise de Vigenère, and Gilbert Vernam proposed the one time pad, where the key sequence is as long as the plaintext and nothing is repeated. The modern use is in a cipher where the plaintext is enciphered bit by bit. This is still used for high-level diplomatic and intelligence traffic.

Time stamp

The addition of the date and time to a message can help certify when a transaction took place. The message can be marked by both the sender and recipient, using their own clocks. Obviously, it is unlikely that both clocks will be synchronized, and either the sender or the recipient or both may falsify the time the message was sent and received. It is for this reason that a trusted intermediary may be used to validate the time at which the message was sent and received.

Trust Services Provider

See *Trusted Intermediary*.

Trusted Intermediary

An entity that undertakes to provide a causal link between an individual and their public key. Also called Trusted Third Party, Trust Services Provider or Certificate Authority.

Trusted Third Party (TTP)

See *Trusted Intermediary*.

Uniform resource locator

Abbreviated to URL, a uniform resource locator is the terminology used for an internet protocol (IP) address on the world wide web (www). Each page on the world wide web has a unique uniform resource locator, some of which may have a lot of extensions.

Verifying party

Upon receipt of a digital certificate that is accompanied with a digital signature, the recipient becomes a verifying party when they undertake the range of checks that certification authorities seek to impose before the recipient can rely on the certificate. The obligations laid down by certification authorities are set out in "Relying Party Agreements".

X.509 Certificates

There are a number of certificates available. The most widely used at present is the X.509 public-key certificate. The X.509 certificate is used to convey the value of a public key to a relying party. There are three versions of this certificate, and the third version was introduced in 1997 to correct the deficiencies in the previous versions. Other types of certificate include Simple Public Key Infrastructure certificates (SPKI) and Attributable certificates.

Index